Mary
K.
Downs
88'

Early Childhood Development

Early Childhood Development
Prenatal Through Age Eight

Sandra Anselmo

University of the Pacific

Merrill Publishing Company
A Bell & Howell Information Company
Columbus Toronto London Melbourne

Cover Photo: Tom McGuire

Published by Merrill Publishing Company
A Bell & Howell Information Company
Columbus, Ohio 43216

This book was set in Garamond.

Administrative Editor: Jeff Johnston
Production Editor: Rebecca Bobb
Art Coordinator: Mark Garrett
Cover Designer: Cathy Watterson
Text Designer: Rebecca Bobb

Library of Congress Catalog Card Number: 86-61864
International Standard Book Number: 0-675-20429-1
Printed in the United States of America
2 3 4 5 6 7 8 9—91 90 89 88 87

Photo Credits:
Dan Collins, pages 92 and 97.
Joanne Kash, page 357.
Blair Seitz, page 361.
All other photos by Sandra Anselmo.

Appreciation for photographs is expressed to all
individuals and to the following groups: San Joaquin
Local Health District, Offices of Dr. Eugene Lamazor
and Dr. Charles McCormick, Head Start of San
Joaquin County, Pulliam School, Rainbow School,
Little Mavericks School of Learning, Delta Day Care,
and Kinder-Care Learning Center.

The quotation on page 406 is from *The Second Self*
(pp. 29–30) by S. Turkle, 1984, New York: Simon &
Schuster. Copyright © 1984 by Sherry Turkle.
Reprinted by permission of Simon & Schuster, Inc.

The quotation on page 408 is from *Mindstorms* (p.
19) by Seymour Papert, 1980, New York: Basic Books.
Copyright © by Basic Books, Inc., Publishers. In
Great Britain, copyright © by The Harvester Press,
Ltd. Reprinted by permission of the publishers.

The quotation on page 414 is from White/Kaban/
Marmor/Shapiro, "The Development of Competence"
in *Experience and Environment: Major Influences
on the Development of the Young Child,* Volume 1,
edited by White & Watts, © 1973, p. 42. Reprinted by
permission of Prentice-Hall, Inc., Englewood Cliffs,
NJ.

For Christopher and David

Preface

Amy sucks on a pacifier and gazes intently at her father's face.

Justin persistently crawls to a group of older children who are building blocks in a pediatrician's waiting room.

Melissa walks across a crowded sandbox to settle next to a younger child with a bright array of toys.

Nikolas digs tunnels and builds roads near his friend, Robbie.

Shawna and Wilma use orange peel to cover their teeth and make monster noises for giggling younger children.

Jason sits next to his teacher and earnestly describes his reactions to the first spelling test.

Tom and Chico huddle apart from other children, making plans to build a fort.

These children and others enliven the pages of this book, which tells the story of development in the early childhood years. There has long been a need for a book with a comprehensive focus on the period extending from the prenatal months through eight years of age. This book shows the interrelationships in development over a span of years and builds a bridge between the first years of life and the initial part of elementary education.

Besides being devoted wholly to the formative early childhood years, this book has three other distinctive features. First, the study of strategies for observing children is combined with the study of theories and research about early childhood development. Readers take a process approach, learning to observe children's behaviors in natural settings and to record and summarize what they see. Throughout the book, exercises called *From Theory to Practice* encourage systematic application of skills in observation. A premise of this book is that people remember best what they discover themselves. Involvement with children through observation creates a meaningful context for the study of the theories and findings of others.

Second, early childhood development is presented within the context of our pluralistic society. The ecological approach shows how strongly cultural factors influence development. Research conducted in many cultural groups is integrated throughout the book in order to help readers understand the multitude and complexity of cultural variables. Topics include black English, cultural differences in parent-child interactions, and culture and school success. All readers must know that their own childhood experiences represent just one possibility found in a pluralistic society. By understanding the richness of cultural differences, readers are better able to interact with families from a variety of backgrounds.

Third, numerous vivid examples and illustrations help readers to understand early childhood development. Applications, often appearing in boxes, accompany all chapters and make the book particularly appropriate for readers who are in or plan to enter the helping professions and who want to learn to rear children more effectively. Applications include handling parent-child separations, encouraging philosophical thinking, stimulating creativity, and choosing day care.

ORGANIZATION OF THE BOOK

The first chapter gives an overview of major contemporary theories of early childhood development, and the second presents strategies for observing young children. After Chapter 2, the details of early childhood development are organized and presented chronologically. Part I (Chapters 3 and 4) discusses the events before and at birth. The focus then turns to the first year of life in Part II (Chapters 5,

6, and 7), ages one through three in Part III (Chapters 8, 9, and 10), and ages four through eight in Part IV (Chapters 11, 12, and 13). The book ends with a brief epilogue about middle childhood.

Because early childhood development is complex, Parts II, III, and IV are each divided into three chapters devoted to psychosocial, physical, and cognitive domains of development. *Psychosocial development* encompasses feelings, self-concept, and interactions within a broad social context; *physical development* deals with growth patterns, coordination, and body image; and *cognitive development* refers to thinking, problem solving, intelligence, and language. For clarity and specificity, the three domains are presented separately, but interrelationships are frequently noted.

ACKNOWLEDGMENTS

I would like to thank the reviewers of this book for their comments, criticisms, and suggestions on earlier drafts. These helpful reviewers include Sue Berger, University of Wisconsin at Milwaukee; Dianna Hiatt, Pepperdine University; Megan Goodwin, Central Michigan University; Mary Ware, Pennsylvania State University; Liz Christman Rothlein, University of Miami; Jeanne Morris, Illinois State University; June Vance, Edinboro University at Pennsylvania; and Donna Jarvenpa, San Diego State University. I also appreciate Bill Theimer's enthusiasm for the book in its formulation and the insights of Judy Van Hoorn on infant development.

Contents

1

Introduction and Theories of Early Childhood Development   1

What Is Early Childhood Development?   2

Why Study Early Childhood Development?   2
To Help to Rear Children, 3 □ *To Prepare for the Helping Professions, 3*

History of the Study of Early Childhood Development   4
Perceptions of Children in History, 4 □ *Beginning of Scientific Study of Children, 5*

Contemporary Theories in Early Childhood Development   8
Cognitive Theory, 8 □ *Behavioral Theory, 12* □ *Psychoanalytic Theory, 15* □ *Humanist Theory, 17* □ *Maturationist Theory, 20*

BOX 1.1   Nature and Nurture in Early Childhood   6

BOX 1.2   An Application of Piaget's Theory: Classification   11

BOX 1.3   An Application of Classical Conditioning: Lamaze Prepared Childbirth   14

BOX 1.4   An Application of Operant Conditioning: Behavior Modification   16

BOX 1.5   An Application of Social Learning Theory: Imitation   18

BOX 1.6   Applications of Erikson's Theory: Preserving Initiative   19

BOX 1.7   An Application of Humanist Theory: "I-Messages"   21

BOX 1.8   An Application of Maturationist Theory: Potty Training   22

2

Strategies for Observing Children   27

Observing Behaviors as They Occur   29
Narrative Observation, 30 □ *Vignettes, 32* □ *Child Diaries, 33*

Observing Predefined Behaviors   35
Checklists, 36 □ *Interviews, 39* □ *Time Sampling, 40* □ *Event Sampling, 42*

Summarizing Observations: Case Studies   46

Using Observation to Answer Questions   48

Unanswerable Questions and the Ethics of Science   48

BOX 2.1   Example of Narrative Observation   32

BOX 2.2   Examples of "Good" and "Bad" Vignettes   34

BOX 2.3   Example of Child Diary Entry 36

BOX 2.4   Example of Developmental Checklist: Infant Socialization   38

BOX 2.5   Example of Interview Using the *Methode Clinique*   40

BOX 2.6   Examples of Time Sampling 43

BOX 2.7   Example of Event Sampling Study   45

BOX 2.8   Example of Case Study Outline for Preschool Children   47

PART I
_____
BEFORE BIRTH, BIRTH,
AND THE EXPANDED FAMILY

3

Before Birth   53

Decision to Have a Child   54
Reasons to Have a Child, 54 □ High-Risk Pregnancies, 55

Chromosomes and Genes: Hereditary Basis of Life   58
Chromosomes and Genes, 58 □ Twins, 59 □ Gender, 59 □ Genotype and Phenotype, 60

The Causes of Congenital Malformations 61
Genetic Factors, 61 □ Environmental Factors, 62 □ Interaction of Factors, 67 □ Maternal-Fetal Blood Incompatibility, 68

Genetic Counseling   69

Reproductive Systems   72
Male Reproduction, 72 □ Female Reproduction, 73

Fertilization   73

Prenatal Development   75
Implantation Stage, 76 □ Embryonic Stage, 76 □ Fetal Stage, 78 □ Speculation about Maternal-Fetal Communication, 81

Prenatal Care of the Mother-to-Be   81
Medical Supervison, 81 □ Nutrition, 82 □ Cultural Differences in Prenatal Care, 83

Preparation for Parenthood   85

Training for Childbirth   87

BOX 3.1   Environmental Factors and Learning Disabilities   68

BOX 3.2   Genetic Counseling   69

BOX 3.3   Nutrition in Pregnancy   84

4

Birth and the Expanded Family   93

Birth   94
Stages of Labor, 94 □ "Normal" Delivery, 95 □ Caesarean Delivery, 96 □ Assessment of Newborns, 98

The Expanded Family   101
Cultural Factors in Parent-Infant Interaction, 101 □ Bonding, 102 □ Bonding with High-Risk Infants, 104 □ Special Needs of Fathers and Siblings, 106

BOX 4.1   Ethical Concerns   99

BOX 4.2   Parental Reactions to Newborns 102

BOX 4.3   The "Mystique" of Bonding 105

BOX 4.4   Helping Siblings Adjust to Newborns   108

PART II
THE FIRST YEAR OF LIFE

5
Psychosocial Development of Infants 115

A Sense of Basic Trust 116

Parent-Infant Rhythms 117
Rhythms with Fathers versus Mothers, 118 □ Rhythms in Various Cultures, 119

Attachment 121
Attachment Phase 1, 122 □ Attachment Phase 2, 123 □ Attachment Phase 3, 123 □ Attachment Phase 4, 123 □ Responses to Separation, 123 □ Effects of Attachment, 124 □ Negative Reactions to Strangers, 124 □ Cultural Differences in Attachment, 126

Infant Crying 127

Social Cognition 128
Origins of Social Understanding, 128 □ Perception of Emotions, 129

Temperament 129

Effects of Parental Employment 133

BOX 5.1 Strategies for Facilitating Development: Interpretation of Infant Cues 120

BOX 5.2 Strategies for Facilitating Development: Management of Separations 126

BOX 5.3 Strategies for Facilitating Development: Identification of and Responses to Patterns of Temperament 132

BOX 5.4 Strategies for Facilitating Development: Infant Day Care 134

6
Physical Development of Infants 139

Sensory Competence of Newborns 140
Vision, 140 □ Taste, 142 □ Smell, 142 □ Hearing, 143

Reflexes and Competence 143
Tonic Neck Reflex, 143 □ Rooting and Sucking Reflexes, 143 □ Burst-Pause Pattern, 144 □ Babkin Reflex, 144 □ Walking Reflex, 144 □ Placing, Babinski, and Grasping Reflexes, 144 □ Moro Reflex, 145 □ Protective Reactions, 145

Levels of Alertness 146
Sound Sleep, 146 □ REM Sleep, 147 □ Alertness, 147

Milestones of Physical Development 148
The First Three Months, 149 □ Three to Six Months, 150 □ Six to Nine Months, 150 □ Nine to Twelve Months, 152

Nutrition, Health, and Safety 154
Nutrition and Brain Growth, 154 □ Dental Health, 157 □ Immunization, 157 □ Handicaps, Prematurity, Illness, 160 □ Sudden Infant Death Syndrome, 161 □ Safety, 162 □ Abuse and Neglect, 163

BOX 6.1 Strategies for Facilitating Development: Infant Exercise 146

BOX 6.2 Strategies for Facilitating Development: Positive Discipline for Infants 151

BOX 6.3 Walking and Hopi Cradleboards 153

BOX 6.4 Strategies for Facilitating Development: Infant Vehicle Safety 164

BOX 6.5 Intervention Strategies when Parents Use Excessively Harsh Behavior 166

7

Cognitive Development of Infants   169

Interplay of Cognitive with Psychosocial and Physical Development   170
Cultural Goals for Infants, 170 □ Visual Attention, 171

Piaget's View of Cognition   172
Piaget's Substage 1: Birth to 1 Month, 172 □ Piaget's Substage 2: 1 to 4 Months, 173 □ Piaget's Substage 3: 4 to 8 Months, 175 □ Piaget's Substage 4: 8 to 12 Months, 176

Views That Differ from Piaget's   179
Imitation, 179 □ Understanding of Relationships, 179

Language Development   181
Newborn, 181 □ First Six Months, 181 □ Second Six Months, 183

Cultural Differences in Language Interactions with Infants   184

Early Intervention Programs   188

BOX 7.1   Strategies for Facilitating Development: Substage 2 Sensorimotor Activities   174

BOX 7.2   Strategies for Facilitating Development: Substage 3 Sensorimotor Activities   176

BOX 7.3   Strategies for Facilitating Development: Toys for Thinking   178

BOX 7.4   Strategies for Facilitating Development: Infant Assessment   186

PART II: FROM THEORY TO PRACTICE 191

PART III

ONE- TO THREE-YEAR-OLDS: ENERGY AND DETERMINATION MOBILIZED

8

One- to Three-Year-Olds: Psychosocial Development   195

Autonomy   196
Erikson's Concept of Autonomy, 197 □ Oppositional Behavior, 198 □ Effects of Temperament, 199 □ Transitional Objects, 203 □ Thumb Sucking, 203 □ Fears, 204

Influences of the Family Environment   206
Attachment and Separation, 206 □ Prosocial Behavior, 207 □ Awareness of Individual Differences, 208 □ Alternate Family Structures, 213 □ Abuse and Neglect, 214 □ Parent-Child Interaction Patterns, 215

Social Influences Outside the Family   218
Effects of Day Care, 218 □ Peer Relationships, 222 □ Effects of Television, 223

Cultural Differences   225

BOX 8.1   Strategies for Facilitating Development: Balancing Autonomy and Shame   199

BOX 8.2   Strategies for Facilitating Development: Dealing with Oppositional Behavior   201

BOX 8.3   Fears   205

BOX 8.4   Breaking Gender-Role Stereotypes   211

BOX 8.5   Race in Children's Literature   213

9

One- to Three-Year-Olds: Physical Development   231

Milestones of Physical Development   232
Large Muscle Skills, 232 □ Small Muscle Skills, 234 □ Drawing, 235 □ Perceptual-Motor Integration, 237 □ Maturation versus Experience in Physical Development, 240 □

Gender Differences, 241 □ *Cultural Differences, 242*

The Need for a Safe Environment   242
Preventing Injury in Automobiles, 243 □ *Preventing Poisoning, 244* □ *Preventing Burns, 246* □ *Preventing Drowning, 246*

The Need for a Healthy Environment   247
Relation of Health and Behavior, 248 □ *Relationship of Family Stress and Health, 249* □ *Physical Growth and Food Intake Patterns, 250* □ *Nutrition and Development, 253* □ *Maintaining Health, 254*

Forming a Positive Physical Image   256
Body Awareness, 256 □ *Toileting, 258* □ *Sex Education, 260*

BOX 9.1   Strategies for Facilitating Development: Perceptual-Motor Training   239

BOX 9.2   Dear Abby: Preventing Drowning   243

BOX 9.3   Strategies for Facilitating Development: Controlled Exploration   247

BOX 9.4   Strategies for Facilitating Development: Preventing "Bottle-Mouth" Cavities   256

Importance of Play   285
Definition of Play, 286 □ *Significance of Play, 287* □ *Cultural Influences, 288* □ *Pretense, 288*

Environments for Developing Cognition   293
Differences in Home Environments, 293 □ *Effects of Educational Intervention, 296*

BOX 10.1   Strategies for Facilitating Development: "Piagetian" Activities for Young Children   272

BOX 10.2   "Motherese" and "Fatherese"   278

BOX 10.3   Analyzing Child Diaries   280

BOX 10.4   Strategies for Facilitating Development: Language Screening   283

BOX 10.5   Strategies for Facilitating Development: Encouraging Pretense   292

PART III: FROM THEORY TO PRACTICE   300

10

One- to Three-Year-Olds: Cognitive Development   265

Piaget's Stages of Intellectual Development   266
Sensorimotor Substage Five, 266 □ *Sensorimotor Substage Six, 268* □ *Early Preoperational Thinking, 269* □ *Criticisms of Piaget's Theory, 273* □ *Applications of Piaget's Theory, 276*

Language Development   277
Receptive Language, 278 □ *First Words, 279* □ *Early Sentences, 281* □ *Vocabulary Expansion, 281* □ *Differences in Language Learning Environments, 284* □ *Cultural Differences: Black English, 284*

PART IV

EARLY SCHOOL YEARS (AGES FOUR THROUGH EIGHT): EXPLORING THE WORLD

11

Early School Years (Ages Four Through Eight): Psychosocial Development   309

Initiative and Industry   310
Erikson's Concept of Initiative, 310 □ *Erikson's Concept of Industry, 312* □ *Gender Differences, 313* □ *Corresponding Stage of Parenthood, 313*

Influences of the Family   314
Characteristics of Strong Families, 314 □
Parenting Styles and Prosocial Behavior, 316 □
Sibling Relationships, 316

Influences and Adjustments Outside the
Family   318
Peer Relationships, 319 □ *Effects of Television,
323* □ *Culture and School Adjustment, 326* □
Multicultural Understanding, 328

Childhood Stress   331
Differences in Coping Processes, 331 □
*Developmental Changes in Reactions to Stress,
333* □ *Protective Factors, 333* □ "Hurried"
Children, 335

Stability of Behavioral Characteristics Over
Time   336
Temperament, 336 □ *Aggression, 337*

BOX 11.1   Strategies for Facilitating
Development: Discipline Techniques that
Preserve Initiative   311

BOX 11.2   Mister Rogers' Philosophy
325

BOX 11.3   Strategies for Facilitating
Development: Guidelines for Using
Television Positively   326

BOX 11.4   Strategies for Facilitating
Development: Assessing Multicultural
Understanding   330

BOX 11.5   Stress in Childhood   332

BOX 11.6   A Child's View of Divorce
335

BOX 11.7   Strategies for Facilitating
Development: Children's Books Dealing
with Death   336

12

Early School Years (Ages Four Through Eight): Physical Development   343

Milestones of Physical Development   344
Large Muscle Skills, 344 □ *Small Muscle Skills,
346* □ *Drawing and Writing, 347* □

Perceptual-Motor Integration, 352 □ *Gender
Differences, 354*

Handicapping Conditions   355
Hearing Impairment, 355 □ *Visual
Impairment, 358* □ *Mental Retardation, 359* □
Emotional Disturbances, 359 □ *Specific
Learning Disabilities, 359* □ *Speech and
Language Impairment, 360* □ *Public Law
94–142, 360* □ *Handicaps and Cultural
Backgrounds, 361*

Forming a Positive Physical Image   363
Hyperactivity, 363 □ *Sexuality, 364* □
Attractiveness, 369

Forming Healthy Habits   371
Eating Habits, 371 □ *Health Care, 373* □
Fitness, 375 □ *Safety, 376*

BOX 12.1   Strategies for Facilitating
Development: Movement Exploration
352

BOX 12.2   Categories of Handicapped
Children: Public Law 94–142   356

BOX 12.3   Strategies for Facilitating
Development: Children's Books about
Handicaps   362

BOX 12.4   Strategies for Facilitating
Development: Prevention and Treatment
of Sexual Abuse   370

BOX 12.5   Strategies for Facilitating
Development: Teaching Safety Rules   376

13

Early School Years (Ages Four Through Eight): Cognitive Development   381

The Development of Logic   382
*Preoperational and Concrete Operational
Stages, 382* □ *Cross-Cultural Verifications of
Piaget's Theory, 391* □ *Other Ways of Using
Logic: Philosophical Thinking, 392*

Language Development   396

Linguistic Milestones, 396 □ *Language and Reading, 399* □ *Bilingualism, 400*

Continuing Role of Play   401
Creativity, 401 □ *Humor, 403* □ *Gender Differences in Play, 405* □ *Computers and Thinking, 406*

Effects of Early Education Programs   408
Programs for Low-Income Children, 409 □ *Programs for Advantaged Children, 412*

School Success   414
Social and Intellectual Competence, 414 □ *Motivation, 414* □ *Memory, 416*

Culture and School Success   417
Childrearing and Education, 417 □ *Cultural Variation in Language Use, 418* □ *Cognitive Style, 419*

BOX 13.1   Classification of Concept Representations   389

BOX 13.2   Strategies for Facilitating Development: Concrete Mathematics   391

BOX 13.3   Strategies for Facilitating Development: Advancing Children's Philosophical Thinking   395

BOX 13.4   Strategies for Facilitating Development: Nourishing Creativity   404

BOX 13.5   Strategies for Facilitating Development: Stimulating Intrinsic Motivation   416

PART IV:
FROM THEORY TO PRACTICE
422

EPILOGUE:
MIDDLE CHILDHOOD   ***425***

GLOSSARY OF KEY TERMS   ***427***

REFERENCES   ***439***

NAME INDEX   ***459***

SUBJECT INDEX   ***464***

ABOUT THE AUTHOR   ***480***

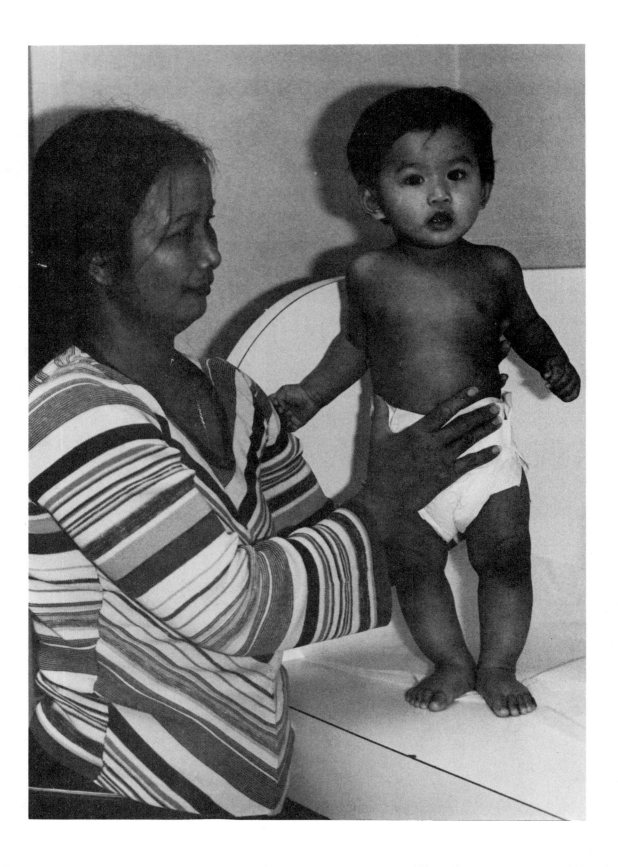

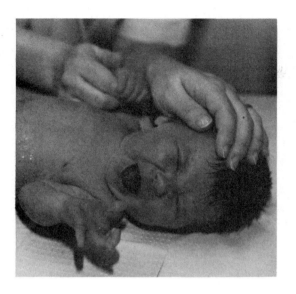

1

Introduction and Theories of Early Childhood Development

Key Ideas

What is Early Childhood Development?

Why Study Early Childhood Development?
To Help to Rear Children □ To Prepare for the Helping Professions

History of the Study of Early Childhood Development
Perceptions of Children in History □ Beginning of Scientific Study of Children

Contemporary Theories in Early Childhood Development
Cognitive Theory □ Behavioral Theory □ Psychoanalytic Theory □ Humanist Theory □ Maturationist Theory

Growing

At birth, I look and listen.
At one, I walk by myself.
At two, I learn to shout, "No!"
At three, I add, "I love you."
At four, I climb high and fast.
At five, I walk to "big school."
At six, I ride on two wheels.
At seven, I read real books.
At eight, I write you a poem.
    (Author unknown)

Many different theories attempt to explain the dramatic changes that take place between birth and eight years of age. This chapter gives an overview of major contemporary theories in early childhood development. Included are cognitive, behavioral, psychoanalytic, humanist, and maturationist theories. But first, early childhood development is defined, reasons for study are cited, and a brief history of the field is presented.

WHAT IS EARLY CHILDHOOD DEVELOPMENT?

This book defines **early childhood development** as the orderly psychosocial, physical, and cognitive changes that take place between the prenatal months and the early elementary-school years. Specifically, this book chronicles the developments in human beings from before birth through age eight. Early childhood development begins the continuous process of human development.

The boundaries for the study of early childhood development are somewhat arbitrary. The book begins with the events that occur even before birth. But where should it end? Naturally, eight-year-olds do not "graduate" from early childhood; nor do they realize that they are suddenly different. Instead, their development continues in much the same incremental fashion as before. Yet, since the age of eight usually marks a time of intellectual transition, it is designated as the end of early childhood. After the age of eight, most children begin to be able to think in rather different ways: their approach to solving problems becomes truly logical. The onset of a new type of logical thinking is as natural a marker for the end of early childhood as any other that might be chosen.

This book was written to help readers understand early childhood development within the context of a pluralistic, multicultural society. The following section presents some of the reasons for becoming knowledgeable about early childhood development.

WHY STUDY EARLY CHILDHOOD DEVELOPMENT?

An initial interest in early childhood development is likely to motivate readers to explore this book. There are many reasons to nurture that interest and to learn more about the early development of human beings. Two of these reasons are: to help with rearing children and to prepare for the helping professions.

To Help to Rear Children

Parents, parents-to-be, or others in close contact with young children want to be able to rear children in positive ways. But, they may not understand what behavior to expect in the early years and how they might influence it. The more people know about the development of young children, the more they can help special children achieve the full richness of their potential.

Parents want the best for their children, but many times parents cannot decide what to do in specific situations. Here is a sampling of puzzling situations that will be explained in this book:

Six-month-old Susan wakes up at night after beginning to sleep through. Her tired parents halfheartedly play with her because she seems to need comforting. The next night she wakes several times. What are Susan's needs and how should her parents help her?

Two-year-old Sammie shouts **NO** *even when he wants what is offered to him. How should his parents respond?*

Four-year-old Greg refuses to eat his fruit because he claims that his sister has more in her differently shaped bowl. Why does he perceive the situation in this way and what should his parents do?

Second-grade Laura announces that an older child touched her in uncomfortable ways. The more she is questioned, the more upset she becomes. What happened and what should her parents do?

The everyday interactions of parents and children could yield numerous examples of such puzzlers. The problem is not that parenting is inherently difficult, but that most parents are not completely prepared to take on the care of a relatively helpless infant and the young child who soon develops. Parents can be more relaxed and can enjoy their children's early years more fully if they learn what to expect and how to help.

To Prepare for the Helping Professions

Those who aspire to enter one of the **helping professions**—such as early childhood teaching, parent education, social work, nursing, music therapy, or recreation—have a need to understand early childhood development. The behavior of helping professionals is accepted by others as a model for interacting with young children. Professionals are asked about matters as diverse as thumb sucking, discipline, nutrition, suspected child abuse and neglect, speech problems, and bed wetting. Through their example, recommendations, and advice, they guide young children and their families. The responsibility is enormous. It is absolutely essential that all who enter the helping professions have a thorough knowledge of the development of young children.

Helping professionals must understand not only the patterns of early

Helping professionals need to understand early childhood development.

childhood development in their own cultural groups, but also those that are typical of other groups. In this book, research and examples illustrate the range of patterns of child rearing and development that exist in this multicultural society. By learning that any person's childhood experiences represent but one possibility within this range, helping professionals can become more sensitive in their interactions with families whose backgrounds are different from theirs.

HISTORY OF THE STUDY OF EARLY CHILDHOOD DEVELOPMENT

The scientific study of children is a recent event in human history. Only in the past two hundred years have children been recognized as different from adults and worthy of study in their own right. Before these recent centuries, life was harsh and the needs and expectations of society did not allow children to experience what is now called childhood. Children instead were thought to be miniature adults and were treated accordingly.

Perceptions of Children in History

The general difficulties encountered by people of all ages represent one reason why children in past centuries were less indulged than children today. Two more factors contributed to this situation: One was the teaching of churches that emphasized the inherent sinfulness of human beings. Parents were exhorted to "beat the devil" out of their children in order to ensure their salvation. The second factor was the parents' need to retain an emotional distance from children at a time when those children were likely to die in early childhood. Adulthood was frequently defined as beginning at twelve or thirteen years of age. Even so, parents who gave birth to a dozen children might have seen only two or three live to adulthood. Now the disease and malnutrition that resulted in so many deaths in early childhood have been largely eliminated, but in the last centuries the high mortality rate had an important influence on the treatment of children.

Until fairly recently, then, there was no time of childhood as currently defined. A human being from birth to about six years of age was considered to be an infant and was entrusted to the mother's care to be taught how to behave properly. By six or seven years, the person was apprenticed or otherwise put into gainful employment. Pictures of children in those days show them wearing cut-down versions of adult clothing and engaged in adult activities.

The interest in childhood as a unique phase of development had its roots in speculation about how adults acquire their ability to function. An English philosopher, John Locke (1632–1704), suggested that children are born neither inherently good nor bad but are the products of their environment. He hypothesized that children are born with a mind that is a **tabula rasa** (blank slate) upon which is written by experience all that the adult eventually knows and feels. Locke's ideas represented a radical departure from the doctrine of basic human sinfulness, but his writing was influential and began to be generally accepted.

In this intellectual climate, Jean Jacques Rousseau (1712–1778) wrote his famous book on education, *Emile.* In this book, Rousseau contended that the environment, not some original sinfulness, contaminates humans. Although his suggestions for child rearing received a great deal of criticism, Rousseau continued to write that children are essentially good and need to be provided with a supportive environment in which to develop.

The writings of Locke and Rousseau, in combination with the changes in society brought about by industrialization, altered the way children were perceived by society in Europe and North America. Industrialized society began to allow a time of childhood—an interlude before the necessity of assuming adult responsibilities. It is important to realize, though, that in most parts of the world industrialization came later than in Europe and North America, and the change in perception about childhood followed much later, too. In fact, there are still a few cultures that initiate children as young as five or six years of age into the work force of the community.

Specialists in early childhood development are interested in studying children in a wide variety of cultural contexts in an attempt to discover which aspects of development are universal and which are influenced by culture. This book reports the results of research done in other parts of the world as well as that conducted in the United States with members of various cultural groups.

Beginning of Scientific Study of Children

Johann Heinrich Pestalozzi (1746–1827), a Swiss citizen, is generally regarded as a pioneer in the modern scientific study of children. In 1774 he published a biography of his son, which was influential in calling attention to the process of development in the early years.

Over one hundred years later, Charles R. Darwin (1809–1882) built on the work of Pestalozzi in the biography of his own young son. Because Darwin was

BOX 1.1

NATURE AND NURTURE IN EARLY CHILDHOOD

The writing of Locke and Rousseau raised questions about how much of the children's development is a result of the nurturing that they receive both before and after birth and how much is a result of nature's processes. For years, with cyclic upswings and downturns, scientists have debated on both sides of the **nature** versus **nurture** (or heredity versus environment) issue.

In recent decades, almost all researchers have come to agree that nature and nurture interact with each other. However, the issue still surfaces from time to time, as was seen in the controversy sparked by Arthur Jensen (1969) who contended that there is a genetic basis for the lower average scores on standard intelligence (IQ) tests of black as compared with white and oriental Americans. The response of most scholars to Jensen's thesis was immediate and negative. Then and now, most experts disagree strongly with Jensen, citing as confounding factors the many environmental differences between blacks and other groups as well as the bias of traditional IQ tests toward information and patterns of thinking that are more familiar to whites and orientals than to blacks. Expert opinion holds that each child is born with a hereditary endowment that certainly has great influence; after conception, though, that person is influenced by diverse environmental factors.

After conception and the establishment of the hereditary destiny of an individual, any attempts at positive intervention must focus on aspects of the environment. The environment can be defined narrowly or broadly, and

a scientist, his biography was written in more precise behavioral terms than was usual at that time. Darwin even included the results of simple experiments—how his child reacted differently to forward and backward movement, for instance. The publication of Darwin's book made baby biographies popular, opened the door to a method of scientifically studying children, and set the stage for modern research in early childhood development.

The rapid expansion and improvement of scientific child study can be partially credited to the teaching, research, and vision of G. Stanley Hall (1846–1924). Hall, one of the first psychologists in the United States, was the teacher of such leaders in child development research as Arnold Gesell, a physician who was instrumental in charting the maturation of young children; John Dewey, an educator who led the movement, labelled progressive education, to provide a more democratic school environment; and Lewis Terman, a psychologist who invented the concept of intelligence quotient (IQ) after participating in the revision of the Binet tests of intelligence. In 1883 Hall wrote an influential book, *The Content of Children's Minds,* which represented a major step recently researchers have begun to ask new questions. Urie Bronfenbrenner (1979) has proposed an intricate and multilayered approach which he has labelled the **ecological environment**.

Bronfenbrenner believes that children are influenced at three different levels: immediate family and other intimate situations; more distant settings in which children are not direct participants, such as their parents' work places; and even further removed societal and cultural levels. To illustrate Bronfenbrenner's ideas about the complexity of the influences on children, it is possible to follow an infant, just learning to talk, across all three levels. At the innermost level, the infant will learn to talk most easily if adults believe that it is important and interesting to spend time in verbal interaction with youngsters. At the intermediate level, whether those adults have the time, energy, or inclination to talk with an infant depends on the demands, stresses, and supports coming from work and other settings outside of the home. And, at the outer level, external forces such as public policies relating to the availability and cost of good quality child care have a great deal to do with the degree of verbal stimulation that the infant receives during the hours when the parents are at work. At all three levels, there are consistencies within cultural groups and differences among them.

Bronfenbrenner provides the most complete and articulate formulation of an approach to studying the environments that affect children. In this book, the forces of heredity are explained and Bronfenbrenner's approach is then used to examine the complex influences of environment.

forward in the scientific study of children. Hall also began the first scientific journal in which research on child development could be published, *The Journal of Genetic Psychology*. And Hall was responsible for introducing Sigmund Freud to American psychologists by inviting him to Clark University for a series of lectures. Because of Hall's own activities and because of his role in training others, he is generally regarded as a leader in the scientific study of children in the United States.

Before contemporary theories are described, a definition of *theory* is in order. A **theory** is an organized system of hypotheses or statements, based on observations and evidence, that explains or predicts something. In early childhood development, theories have been formulated to explain and predict various aspects of children's behavior.

Some people have the notion that theories are not practical, but actually the saying that "nothing is as practical as a good theory" holds true. Theories allow observations to be organized into a coherent system. For example, Jean Piaget's theory of intellectual development helps adults to understand young children's perceptions about equality and inequality of quantity. The sections that follow describe Piaget's theory and other contemporary theories of early childhood development.

CONTEMPORARY THEORIES
IN EARLY CHILDHOOD DEVELOPMENT

This book takes an eclectic approach to the many interesting contemporary theories in early childhood development. **Eclectic** means that methods, ideas, and research findings are incorporated from the whole spectrum of contemporary theoretical positions: cognitive, behavioral, psychoanalytic, humanist, and maturationist. Early childhood development seems too complex to be satisfactorily explained by any one of these positions. The different theories sometimes offer divergent explanations for similar behavior patterns and sometimes focus on aspects of development that are not emphasized by other theories. In judicious combination, these contemporary theories explain and predict much of the behavior of young children. A general overview of these theories is presented in this section.

Cognitive Theory

An eight-year-old has learned a great deal since the day of her birth. **Learning,** defined as changes that occur in behavior as the result of experience, is of interest to parents, helping professionals, and others who deal with young children. And learning has been the subject of a considerable body of research by specialists in early childhood development. **Cognitive theory,** in contrast to other theories that are described, tends to place more emphasis on children's thought processes when they learn.

The theory of Jean Piaget (1896–1980) is the best-known and most highly developed of the cognitive theories. Piaget's theory has profoundly influenced early childhood development in this country; this influence may be somewhat surprising in light of the fact that Piaget's work was not widely available here until the 1960s. Perhaps one of the reasons for the speedy acceptance of Piaget's theory is that it rings true to anyone who has spent time with young children. It is clear that Piaget carefully observed young children, and his theory shows that there are distinctive patterns to their thought processes. For instance, Piaget wrote about Jacqueline's behavior at two years, seven months of age:

> Jacqueline seeing her sister Lucienne in a new bathing suit with a cap asked: *"What's the baby's name?"* Her mother replied that it was a bathing costume, but Jacqueline pointed to Lucienne herself and said, *"But what's the name of that?"* (indicating Lucienne's face) and repeated the question several times. As soon as Lucienne had her dress on again, Jacqueline exclaimed very seriously, *"It's Lucienne again"* as if her sister had changed her identity in changing her clothes. (Piaget, 1962, p. 224)

According to the theory of Jean Piaget, young children think in distinctive ways. For instance, they believe that a person can change identity by changing clothes.

Piaget explained many of these intriguing differences between the thinking of young children and that of adults, such as why children think that clothes can make people change or that the moon follows the car at night or that there is more milk in taller, thinner glasses than in shorter, wider glasses. Knowing about Piaget's theory changes the way we view young children and helps us understand them.

Piaget's observations of young children led him to propose that their thinking develops sequentially in four stages, three of which occur during the early childhood years. Table 1.1 briefly outlines the four stages: **sensorimotor**, **preoperational**, **concrete operational**, and **formal operational**. The first two are presented in considerable detail in Parts II, III, and IV of this book. In this section, Piaget's life and some general facets of his theory are described.

Jean Piaget was a precocious Swiss youth who published his first scientific article at the age of ten. The article featured his description of a rare bird, and the fact that he received his doctorate in the field of zoology at the age of twenty-two indicates that he continued his early interest throughout adolescence. He also read widely in philosophy and psychology during these years, and followed his formal education with work in psychoanalysis and with a

TABLE 1.1 *Piaget's Stages of Development*

Stage	Age
Sensorimotor	0–2 years
Children learn through their senses, beginning with reflexes, and through activity: touching, tasting, smelling, and manipulating materials.	
Preoperational	2–7 years
Children think with words and objects in an intuitive manner, with judgments based on perceptions rather than logic. Thinking is limited by the inability to deal with more than one variable at a time.	
Concrete operational	7 years–adolescence
Children think logically and expand knowledge. They use reasoning rather than perceptions to justify their judgments. Their thinking is still limited, however, to concrete, tangible objects and familiar events.	
Formal operational	adolescence
Young people think symbolically and hypothetically. Abstract thinking and concepts are now used.	

group engaged in refining Binet's intelligence tests. Piaget's theory reflects the influence of each of these early experiences.

Piaget came to believe that mental development might follow much the same kind of laws as physical development. His interest in biology, philosophy, and psychology directed him to study how children think, and he did so by means of a **methode clinique** or clinical interview, in which he asked questions in order to discover how children think and why they respond as they do.

As a biologist, Piaget recognized that children must organize their environment and must be able to adapt to changes in it if they are to survive. Piaget labelled these two biological principles as **schemata** (organized elements of thought), and the processes of **assimilation** and **accommodation** (the way humans process or adapt to new information). Assimilation is the attempt to make new information fit into existing schemata, while accommodation involves restructuring one's thinking by adding new information. The concepts of assimilation and accommodation can be illustrated by the feeding activities of a newborn male infant. Piaget believed that such an infant is born with a few reflexes such as sucking, grasping, and looking at objects, and that these reflexes soon develop into elementary schemata. The infant instinctively sucks his mother's breast and then at some later time is given a bottle. If the infant tries to suck the bottle in the same way he sucked his mother's breast, the infant would be attempting to make new information fit into the old schemata, or assimilating. When the infant finds that he cannot obtain milk in this manner,

**BOX
1.2**   **AN APPLICATION OF PIAGET'S THEORY:
CLASSIFICATION**

Five-year-old Dan likes to play with the button collection of his day care
provider, Sara. At first he seemed to concentrate his attention on the tactile
aspects of the buttons: he ran them through his fingers and felt individual
buttons. Soon, though, he noticed that Sara was making some kind of
arrangement with her buttons. She saw him watching her and asked, "Can
you tell how all of these buttons are alike?" Dan did not know, but Sara
showed him that all of the buttons in her arrangement were bigger than
most of the others. Other times when Dan asked to play with the buttons,
Sara arranged some of the buttons into groups by color or by number of
holes or by the material from which the button was made. It wasn't long
before Dan began making his own groups to "trick" Sara.

   The guided exploration of the buttons by Dan and Sara is helping
Dan to learn to classify. Classification is the ability to place objects into
consistent, logical groups. According to Piaget, classification is one of the
important schemata developed during the years between four and seven.
Piaget said that the ability to classify, like other types of learning, is gained
through many opportunities to handle and manipulate objects in the environment. Active, curious children develop classification and other logical
thinking skills gradually through their play. By interacting sensitively with
Dan and asking him thought-provoking questions, Sara has facilitated his
understanding of the process of classification.

*This child classifies buttons
according to color.*

he changes his way of sucking on the bottle, thus adding new information to the original schemata, or accommodating. All knowledge, according to Piaget, is the result of expanding our schemata from our original learnings based on reflexes. Children learn through a combination of maturation, social transmission, and the results of their own actions on the environment; schemata thus become increasingly complex. Children develop concepts such as *mother* by first assimilating all people as people, then gradually separating out the mother schemata, and finally accommodating to such concepts as mother, father, and others. Basically, then, assimilation refers to the attempt to make new information fit into previous experience; accommodation occurs when mental processing must change to include novel information, thus expanding mental organization.

Piaget said that children do not learn if they are intellectually satisfied at all times. The biological concept of homeostasis has its counterpart in Piaget's theory in what he called **equilibration**. Equilibration refers to the internal mental process of establishing equilibrium or balance in thinking. Young children can be quite happy (or at equilibrium) with some unique interpretations of experiences because they simply assimilate them into their existing schemata. To the adult way of thinking, these interpretations may be incorrect, but young children see no need to accommodate or change their thinking processes. As they grow older and have more experiences, however, they sense that something is not quite correct in their interpretations and feel the need for a new equilibrium reached through the assimilation-accommodation process. They gradually accommodate to new information by changing their schemata through the mental process of equilibration. The sense of disequilibrium or dissatisfaction with current explanations of events, then, leads to mental growth, according to Piaget's theory.

Behavioral Theory

Proponents of **behavioral theory** are not inclined to hypothesize about mental processes such as schemata, assimilation, and accommodation. Instead, they focus on the behaviors displayed by children when they are learning and afterwards. Another major difference between behavioral theorists and cognitive theorists such as Jean Piaget is the concept of stages of development. Behavioral theorists view development as being continuous, with no division into stages. To them, development occurs as children learn, and learning is a gradual, cumulative process. Learning is believed to lead to changes in observable behavior when the appropriate skills are learned.

The study of behavior has evolved over the years, and now there are three distinct types of behavioral theories: classical conditioning, operant conditioning, and social learning theory. Each of these behavioral theories is described separately.

Classical conditioning   Ivan P. Pavlov (1849–1936), a Nobel prize–winning Russian physiologist, discovered a process of learning called **classical conditioning**. Pavlov noted that when food is given to dogs, the dogs give an unlearned response, salivation. In a series of experiments, Pavlov found that, if he consistently rang a bell at the same time that he placed meat powder on dogs' tongues, eventually an association would be formed so that the bell alone would cause the dogs to salivate as if they were feeding. Pavlov called the ringing of the bell a **conditioned stimulus** and the response of salivation in the absence of food a **conditioned response**. He had succeeded in conditioning the dogs to salivate on the cue provided by the bell.

In this country, Pavlov's theory of classical conditioning was popularized by J. B. Watson (1878–1958). Watson believed that psychology would not assume status as a science unless it dealt with strictly observable behaviors. Watson applied Pavlov's theory to children, with his most famous subject being an eleven-month-old named Albert. Albert initially liked to play with white rats and would reach out if one were presented to him. Then Watson and his associates began striking a steel bar behind Albert just as the rat was presented. Albert was afraid of the noise and, after a few experiences with hearing the noise as he reached for the rat, Albert developed a fear of rats—even if no noise accompanied the presentation of a rat. Watson had conditioned the fear of rats in a child who previously had liked them. In fact, Albert's fear **generalized** to (or extended to include) other white furry animals, such as rabbits, and even to men with white beards. Unfortunately, there is no evidence that Watson tried to *extinguish* (or remove) this fear. Extinguishing Albert's conditioned response would have required repeated presentations of the rat without striking the steel bar. Gradually the response of fear would have disappeared.

Based on experiments like the one involving Albert, Watson asserted that children's behavior is totally determined by the events in their lives. In an article on child rearing, he declared:

> Give me a dozen healthy infants, well-formed and my own specified world to bring them up in and I'll guarantee to take any one of them at random and train him to become any type of specialist I might select—a doctor, lawyer, artist, merchant, chief, and yes, even into a beggerman and thief regardless of his talents, penchants, tendencies, abilities, vocations and race of his ancestors. (Watson, 1928, p. 104)

According to Watson and other believers in classical conditioning, heredity plays an insignificant part in development and experience is all-important.

Operant conditioning   B. F. Skinner, a psychologist at Harvard University, shared many of Watson's views and wrote a novel, *Walden Two* (1948), to illustrate the world that Watson was describing. However, Skinner thought that classical conditioning alone was not adequate to explain how children learn, and he formulated a model of another type of conditioning, **operant conditioning**. It was Skinner's belief, and the major premise of operant conditioning, that the consequences of children's behavior—in the form of reward or punishment—determine whether a behavior will recur. In operant conditioning, then, a child is put into a situation in which a desired response is likely to occur. When it does, the child is immediately **reinforced** or rewarded. For example, a young child who often shouts inappropriately indoors might receive verbal praise each

---

BOX 1.3   **AN APPLICATION OF CLASSICAL CONDITIONING: LAMAZE PREPARED CHILDBIRTH**

Marsha and Henry Morgan learned to apply the principles of classical conditioning in their Lamaze prepared childbirth classes. They began attending these classes during the last month of pregnancy. They were taught to raise Marsha's pain threshold during labor and delivery by using certain conditioned breathing patterns to block out the perception of pain.

Breathing patterns were conditioned during hours of practice by Marsha, with Henry as her coach. Marsha was conditioned to respond with the appropriate breathing patterns—deep chest breathing, accelerated panting, pant-blow breathing, or light panting—immediately when Henry gave the verbal signal. The various breathing patterns were each useful during specified parts of labor and delivery. However, Marsha was trained to respond *as conditioned* and was not supposed to think about how to breathe or to question Henry's commands. When Henry said "Pant," Marsha was conditioned to pant in the manner practiced.

Marsha and Henry felt an increased sense of control of and involvement in labor and delivery because of their Lamaze training. And they experienced an interesting application of classical conditioning principles.

---

time she uses her "inside voice." If the verbal praise is rewarding to her, she will increase the use of her inside voice. If no consequence is paired with shouting, that behavior will disappear.

Skinner (1974) and other proponents of operant conditioning make a strong distinction between reinforcement and punishment. They use reinforcement to increase the chances that desirable behavior will be repeated. They suggest avoiding the use of punishment, though, because it only suppresses undesirable behaviors temporarily and does not change patterns of behavior. The reason punishment has been found to be ineffective is that it does not teach children what behavior is expected. Children may have some idea of what the adult does *not* want and they often have negative feelings about the entire incident, but they do not necessarily know what the correct behavior should have been. Many behaviorists believe that, rather than punishing children, parents or other adults should help them to demonstrate correct behavior and reinforce correct behavior.

The theory of operant conditioning has provided specialists in early childhood development with a wealth of information about how children learn and with ways of analyzing and changing particular behaviors. Even though operant conditioning does not address children's internal mental functioning, operant conditioning makes important contributions to knowledge about children's behavior.

Social learning theory Social learning theorists consider themselves to be in the tradition of the classical and operant conditioning theorists, but they believe that neither classical nor operant conditioning is adequate to account for the rapidity and complexity of children's learning. **Social learning theory** proposes instead that children learn quickly by imitating certain behaviors that they observe. According to social learning theorists, children learn from observing and imitating people who are powerful and significant in their lives, and this imitated behavior can be learned without reinforcement or with only vicarious reinforcement (observing another person being praised). Albert Bandura (1977) and his associates at Stanford University have been in the forefront of articulating a theory of social learning that goes well beyond operant and classical conditioning. Their theory modifies some basic principles of conditioning, such as the necessity for reinforcement.

In his early research, Bandura and his associates (Bandura, Ross, & Ross, 1963) showed how children can learn aggressive behavior. He had one group of children observe an adult playing with toys, becoming frustrated, and beginning to hit a bobo doll while exclaiming, "Hit it. Pow." Another group of children observed an adult whose frustration was not followed by aggressive behavior. Bandura found that the group of children who observed the aggressive behavior demonstrated significantly more aggressive behavior in play than did the group of children who had not observed the aggression. This experiment and others that followed it led Bandura and other social learning theorists to the conclusion that children can learn without reinforcement.

Social learning theory helps with understanding aspects of children's behavior that cannot be explained in terms of conditioning. Since research on social learning is a relatively recent phenomenon, additional information is likely to be obtained about children's learning from further studies in this area.

Psychoanalytic Theory

Erik Erikson is the major contemporary proponent of psychoanalytic theory. Erikson, a Dane who spent his childhood in Germany, was a student of Freud's daughter, Anna. After receiving his license to practice psychoanalysis, Erikson came to the United States, where he was affiliated with Harvard and other institutions of higher learning. In addition to practicing child-psychoanalysis and teaching about it, he investigated child rearing practices on Sioux and Yurok Indian reservations, and studied World War II soldiers who suffered from what was then called "shell shock." Erikson built on the theory of Sigmund Freud (1856–1939), but Erikson's broad experiences with many types of people led him to see the limitations in Freud's emphasis on sexuality as the basis of our impulses and drives. Erikson elaborated on Freud's theory and modified it significantly by adding the component of social interaction. Erikson's version of psychoanalytic theory has been termed the **psychosocial theory** of development. Whereas Freud had built a theory around the development of the child within the family, Erikson's theory considers the child and family within their broader social context.

BOX 1.4   **AN APPLICATION OF OPERANT CONDITIONING: BEHAVIOR MODIFICATION**

Tia Garcia applied a type of operant conditioning, behavior modification, to teach her young son to react positively when placed in his car seat. Behavior modification is a way of using operant conditioning to change behavior. The steps in applying behavior modification are as follows: (1) Decide exactly what behavior you want a child to acquire; (2) Decide what reinforcers (rewards) will be meaningful to that child; (3) Shape the behavior—that is, divide progress toward the desired behavior into small steps that the child can successfully master and reinforce achievement of each step; and (4) Continue to reinforce success occasionally even after the behavior has been changed as planned.

At the time that Tia began her program of behavior modification, her one-year-old, Georgio, had not had much experience with riding in his car seat. Then Tia attended a workshop that convinced her that his safety required use of the car seat, but each time she tried to place him in it, Georgio cried, kicked his legs, and thrashed his arms. Tia realized that it was too much to expect that Georgio would suddenly become a model passenger when in his car seat. She decided that it would be necessary to shape his behavior. She knew that he responds well to praise and that he likes frozen yogurt and fruit juice.

Tia made a plan for Georgio that included taking him to the car frequently to put him in his car seat. Before he had a chance to object, she praised him warmly for sitting quietly in his seat and gave him a spoonful of frozen yogurt or a sip of fruit juice. When Georgio attained success at

Erikson proposed that there are eight stages of psychosocial adjustment during the human life span, as shown in Table 1.2. The first four of these stages are helpful for understanding early childhood development.

Erikson identified each stage by its contrasting elements—**trust versus mistrust, autonomy versus shame and doubt, initiative versus guilt,** and **industry versus inferiority.** Each pair of contrasting elements can be visualized as the two ends of a continuous line. According to Erikson, the desirable resolution of each stage falls toward the positive end of this imaginary line, with children ideally developing a sense of trust, autonomy, initiative, and industry. However, even those positive resolutions should be tempered and not absolute. For example, although toddlers need to develop a sense of autonomy or independence, two-year-olds with absolute autonomy would be a danger to themselves and a problem within and beyond the family. Their autonomy needs to be tempered by the sensations of shame and doubt that would follow if they neglected the rights and feelings of others.

sitting pleasantly in his car seat for a brief period, Tia gradually expanded the amount of good behavior necessary for him to be reinforced. Eventually, Georgio learned to be an uncomplaining passenger in his car seat on short and then longer car trips. Tia could now feel more assured of his safety, thanks to behavior modification, an application of operant conditioning.

Behavior modification can be used to teach young children to react positively in their car seats.

In Erikson's theory, the stages are sequential. It is necessary for children to resolve one stage positively in order to be successful with the next. The sequential stages show the time of ascendency of a certain pair of contrasting elements, but these same elements are also dealt with later in life. For instance, at ages four and five, initiative versus guilt is the most important psychosocial problem with which young children must deal. But throughout the life span, children and adults have many additional encounters with initiative and guilt.

Erikson's theory has implications for how children are treated at home, in day care centers, at school, and in other settings. His theory helps adults understand the psychosocial needs of young children.

Humanist Theory

The writings of the existential philosophers in the 1920s and 1930s introduced the **humanist** perspective as a way of looking at development. The existential

BOX 1.5   AN APPLICATION OF SOCIAL LEARNING THEORY: IMITATION

Jeff Reynolds, a preschool teacher, applies social learning theory every day at group time. When one of the four-year-olds in his group speaks out of turn, bothers another child, or restlessly moves around, he calls attention to someone in the group who is behaving appropriately. His verbalizations in these situations point out positive behaviors and include comments like the following: "I like the way Timmy is raising his hand," and "Good, Lisa is keeping her hands in her own lap," and "I'm glad that most of you are sitting in our circle." Mr. Reynolds finds that the children respond to his comments by imitating the children to whom he has called attention so that they will also be favorably noticed. Mr. Reynolds feels that he is very effective in managing young children's behavior by applying principles of social learning theory.

At group time, this teacher applies social learning theory. Children imitate each other in the positive behaviors that he notes.

philosophers believed that humans are creatures of choice—not passive with predetermined or programmed actions, but active in making choices about how they will live.

Two prominent humanists have influenced early childhood development: Carl Rogers and Abraham Maslow. Carl Rogers (1961) was a psychotherapist who had been trained as a psychoanalyst. In his practice of psychotherapy in the 1940s, he introduced a radical new approach based on the premise that humans are basically good, basically capable, and have within themselves the potential to develop optimally. Rogers proposed no theory of development as such, but he was very influential in affecting the lives of children through his

TABLE 1.2 *Erikson's Stages of Psychosocial Development*

Age	Stage	Strength Developed
0–1 year	Trust vs. mistrust	Hope
2–3 years	Autonomy vs. shame	Willpower
4–5 years	Initiative vs. guilt	Purpose
6–12 years	Industry vs. inferiority	Competence
Adolescence	Identity vs. role confusion	Fidelity
Young adulthood	Intimacy vs. isolation	Love
Middle age	Generativity vs. stagnation	Care
Old age	Ego integration vs. despair	Wisdom

BOX 1.6   **APPLICATIONS OF ERIKSON'S THEORY: PRESERVING INITIATIVE**

Allen found himself frequently at odds with his four-year-old daughter, Susan. In one particularly trying late-afternoon period, Allen was discouraged to hear himself repeatedly shouting at Susan to stop running through the house and teasing her younger brother. Allen decided to join a parenting class to see if he could discover other ways of handling the challenges that Susan was presenting.

In the parenting class, Allen learned about Erik Erikson's theory. He realized that his frequent shouting was probably making Susan feel guilty about her behavior but was not changing it. He wanted Susan to feel that she could take initiative successfully and asked his class instructor for suggestions of ways to redirect Susan's behavior and still preserve her sense of initiative.

In the case of Susan's running in the house, Allen learned to recognize the positives in her behavior and to redirect the negatives. He would say, "Oh, you are full of energy today! Let me see you run in place up to the count of 100!" Or, on nice days, "Let's take those running legs outside!" In the case of Susan's teasing of her younger brother, Allen learned to offer Susan controlled choices. He would say, "Susan, either you will give that toy back or I will take it from you and ask you to leave this part of the apartment for a few minutes." With controlled choices, Susan could exercise her initiative and still stay within boundaries that were comfortable for the rest of the family.

own writings and those of others who incorporated his views. Followers of Rogers have included Haim Ginott, author of *Between Parent and Child* (1965); Don Dinkmeyer and Gary D. McKay, authors of *Systematic Training for Effective Parenting* (STEP) (1976); and Thomas Gordon, author of *P.E.T.—Parent Effectiveness Training* (1975).

Abraham Maslow (1968, 1971), another important proponent of humanist theory, developed a hierarchy of human needs. According to Maslow, humans have certain needs, called **deprivation needs**, that must be met before they are free to develop their most creative characteristics. The deprivation needs include physiological needs (basic needs for maintenance of the body); safety needs (shelter, protection from danger); belongingness needs (love, affection); and esteem needs (self-esteem and esteem from others). Only after deprivation needs have been satisfied can people be motivated by **being needs**, or the pursuit of values such as truth, honesty, beauty, and goodness. At the highest level of Maslow's hierarchy, people can test themselves, expand their horizons, and become **self-actualized** or truly creative, productive members of society. Maslow's major contribution to early childhood development was his contention that children will choose to do things that promote their growth if their deprivation needs are met.

The humanists have made a significant contribution to the study of early childhood development. They have reacted strongly against the behaviorist position that humans are passively shaped by the environment. They have emphasized how much of behavior is determined by active choices.

Maturationist Theory

Maturationists emphasize the role of genetically determined growth patterns and deemphasize the role of environmental stimulation in early childhood development. They base their beliefs on the work of Charles Darwin (1809–1882) and Karl Pearson (1857–1936), who studied intellectual capacity and physical growth patterns. These men concluded that parents who are bright in intellect and tall generally have children who are bright and tall, and that parents who are dull in intellect and average in height tend to have children who are dull and average. G. Stanley Hall elaborated on the early studies and taught his students that development is determined primarily through a hereditary process of maturation. One of Hall's students, Arnold Gesell (1880–1961), and Gesell's colleagues at the Yale University School of Medicine have subsequently been leaders in articulating the maturationist approach to development.

To show the importance of maturation in development of specific skills, Gesell organized some experiments with twins. In one of these experiments, one of each pair of twins was given extensive practice in walking before the children would have been "ready" to walk, according to the norms established at Yale. The other of each pair of twins received no practice or training in walking. Gesell demonstrated in this experiment that, when the twins with no practice were "ready" to walk, they quickly equalled the skill in walking of the twins

**BOX
1.7** **AN APPLICATION OF HUMANIST THEORY:
"I-MESSAGES"**

Thomas Gordon (1975) teaches important principles of parent-child communication in his book *P.E.T.—Parent Effectiveness Training.* In the book, he encourages parents to focus their attention on the particular situation at hand, not on general personality characteristics of the child. Gordon would have parents banish from their verbal repertoire such comments as, "You're such a slob" and "I've never seen such a messy child." Instead, he suggests that parents use what he calls *I-messages.* I-messages tell the child how parents feel about behavior. For instance, the parent might say, "I feel upset when I see your brand new bedspread in a heap on the floor." According to Gordon, this type of communication allows children to view their parents as real people with their own valid needs and, within an atmosphere of mutual respect and understanding, children are motivated to change their behavior. Many parents have applied Gordon's humanist ideas with success.

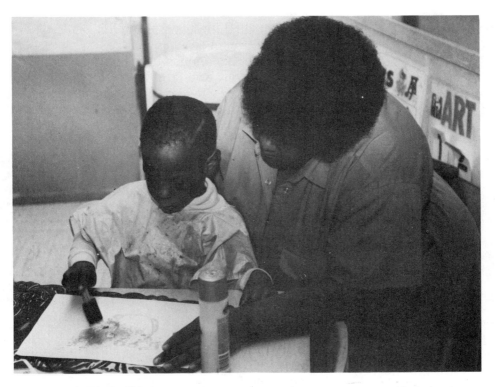

"I-messages" from adult to child communicate feelings about specific behaviors. In this case, the adult said, "I like the way you've made a design."

BOX
1.8

AN APPLICATION OF MATURATIONIST THEORY: POTTY TRAINING

Paul wants his son, Bob, to be successful in potty training, and one of Paul's considerations is Bob's level of maturation. Paul has decided not to introduce the idea of using the potty to Bob until Bob shows several of the following signs of readiness:

☐   Bob stays dry for several hours.
☐   Bob shows an awareness that he is about to or has just urinated.
☐   Bob understands simple instructions and directions.

By taking Bob's maturation into account before expecting Bob to urinate on the potty, Paul is helping his son to be successful.

who had practiced. Gesell cited this experiment and similar ones as evidence of the importance of maturation in development.

Gesell and his associates determined the ages at which different physical, mental, and behavioral functions mature in children. They recorded detailed information about height and weight; age of teething, crawling, walking, and grasping objects; rate of vocabulary growth; and patterns of social interaction. The **norms** or average ages of attainment discovered by Gesell were widely disseminated beginning in the 1920s, 1930s, and 1940s (Gesell & Ilg, 1949), and Gesell became an influential leader in the area of early childhood development. The data that he gathered were very thorough and complete and are still used today. Gesell's data are most appropriate when applied to white, middle-class children—the group Gesell studied—and are not necessarily appropriate for application to children with other ethnic and cultural backgrounds.

In the course of his research, Gesell enumerated some general principles of growth that remain important today. One of these principles is the **cephalo-caudal** principle, which states that growth proceeds generally from the head (cephalo) down toward the tail (caudal) area. Another is the **proximo-distal** principle, which states that the brain, nerves, and organs (located close or proximal to the body) develop earlier than the hands, feet, and other extremities (located at a distance or distal from the body).

The continuing influence of maturationists such as Gesell can be observed in strict age guidelines for school entrance and in casual remarks that characterize children by age—"terrible twos," "trusting threes," or "frustrating fours." Although research conducted in connection with other theories has shown that environmental factors are more important than Gesell believed, maturation must be considered in the study of early childhood development.

SUMMARY

1. Early childhood development describes the changes in human beings from the prenatal period through eight years of age.
2. The study of early childhood development can help in rearing children and in preparing for the helping professions.
3. The scientific study of children has taken place only in the past two hundred years.
4. Industrialization and the views expressed by John Locke and Jean Jacques Rousseau combined to allow a time of childhood to occur before adult responsibilities were assumed.
5. Pioneers in the scientific study of children included Pestalozzi, Darwin, and Hall.
6. Theories are organized systems of hypotheses, based on observations, that explain or predict behavior.
7. The study of early childhood development is influenced by cognitive theory, behavioral theory, psychoanalytic theory, humanist theory, and maturationist theory. These several theories of early childhood development can be viewed as complementary ways to understand how children change over time.
8. Jean Piaget has been the best-known proponent of cognitive learning theory. His theory explains development in terms of four stages: sensorimotor, preoperational, concrete operational, and formal operational thinking.
9. Behavioral learning theory has evolved from classical conditioning to operant conditioning to social learning theory.
10. In classical conditioning, Pavlov and others succeeded in linking a conditioned stimulus, such as ringing a bell, with a response, such as salivation.
11. In operant conditioning, Skinner and others put children in situations in which a desired response was likely to occur and then rewarded that response.
12. In social learning theory, Bandura and his associates showed how much children learn from observing and imitating, without the necessity of a reward.
13. Erik Erikson, the major proponent of psychoanalytic theory, explains development in terms of eight "ages" or stages, the first four of which take place in early childhood.
14. Humanists have emphasized the extent to which children's behavior is determined by active choices.
15. Maturationists, following in the footsteps of Gesell, emphasize the role of genetically determined growth patterns in shaping development.

KEY TERMS

early childhood development	learning	assimilation
helping professions	cognitive theory	accommodation
tabula rasa	sensorimotor	equilibration
nature versus nurture	preoperational	behavioral theory
ecological environment	concrete operational	classical conditioning
theory	formal operational	conditioned stimulus
eclectic	methode clinique	conditioned response
	schemata	generalized

extinguish

operant conditioning

reinforced

social learning theory

psychosocial theory

trust versus mistrust

autonomy versus shame and doubt

initiative versus guilt

industry versus inferiority

humanist

deprivation needs

being needs

self-actualized

maturationists

norms

cephalo-caudal

proximo-distal

FOR FURTHER READING

Cognitive Learning Theory

Piaget, J. & Inhelder, B. (1969). *The psychology of the child.* New York: Basic Books.

Behavioral Learning Theory

Bandura, A. (1977). *Social learning theory.* Englewood Cliffs, N.J.: Prentice-Hall.

Bijou, S. W., & Baer, D. M. (1961). *Child development.* (Vol. 1). Appleton-Century-Crofts.

Skinner, B. F. (1974). *About behaviorism.* New York: Knopf.

Skinner, B. F. (1948). *Walden two.* New York: Macmillan.

Psychoanalytic Theory

Erikson, E. H. (1963). *Childhood and society.* 2nd ed. New York: W. W. Norton.

Erikson, E. H. (1982). *The life cycle completed.* New York: W. W. Norton.

Humanist Theory

Maslow, A. H. (1970). *Motivation and personality.* (2nd ed.). New York: Harper & Row.

Rogers, C. R. (1961). *On becoming a person.* Boston: Houghton Mifflin.

Maturationist Theory

Ames, L. B., Gillespie, C., Haines, J., & Ilg, F. L. (1979). *The Gesell Institute's child from one to six.* New York: Harper & Row.

2

Strategies for Observing Children

Key Ideas

Observing Behaviors as They Occur
Narrative Observation □ *Vignettes* □ *Child Diaries*

Observing Predefined Behaviors
Checklists □ *Interviews* □ *Time Sampling* □ *Event Sampling*

Summarizing Observations: Case Studies

Using Observation to Answer Questions

Unanswerable Questions and the Ethics of Science

Two very different observations were conducted simultaneously by students of early childhood development.

Jeff The boy was really angry at being removed from the storytime. The teacher had to send him to another room.

Tom Carlos, age six, raised his hand when the teacher asked what might happen next in the story. He stood up and said loudly, "I know, I know!" The teacher called on Sarah, saying, "I like the way Sarah waited to be called on before speaking." Carlos jumped again to a standing position, shouted, "I raised my hand, too!" and continued talking so that Sarah's words were not understandable. The teacher asked Carlos to sit down quietly or leave the group. Carlos chose to leave the group with another teacher but returned silently within two minutes.

Jeff and Tom were both in the same room at the same time, but they did not "see" the same things in the classroom scene that they watched. Jeff, the first of the observers, is a beginner in the scientific study of young children. He generalized about the events that he watched and left out many details that would help us to understand Carlos' reactions. Tom, on the other hand, has received some instruction in observing children and included considerably more information about what was happening. These two observations illustrate the importance of knowledge, skill and practice in maximizing what is learned during time spent with young children.

Jeff and Tom were making narrative observations, one of the strategies for observing the behavior of young children as it occurs. Similar strategies include recording vignettes and keeping child diaries. A different type of strategy involves observing predefined behaviors. This second type of strategy is implemented by using checklists, interviews, time sampling, and event sampling. The findings from the various strategies of observation can be summarized in a case study of a particular child.

Observation is at the very core of most scientific endeavors. Biologists, physicists, chemists, astronomers, and other natural scientists observe and record phenomena, form hypotheses, and then devise experiments to test these hypotheses. So it is also in the study of early childhood development. By learning systematic strategies of observation, students become better able to understand children's behavior; gain insight into their psychosocial, physical, and cognitive development; and then generate hypotheses or ideas, answer specific questions, and plan appropriate activities.

In Chapter 1, it was pointed out that observation provided the foundation for the early scientific study of young children. However, the observation of children in natural settings fell out of favor with researchers during most of the twentieth century. Instead of observational methods, they used experimental methods that brought children into laboratories in attempts to control as many variables as possible and to isolate causes and effects of behavior. Much has been learned from experimental methods, but gradually specialists in early childhood development have also rediscovered observation as a method of child study.

Now, in this last part of the century, the pendulum has swung to an intermediate point between the early position of using only observational methods in child study and the more recent trend of rejecting naturalistic observation in favor of experimental methods. There are several reasons to explain the resurgence of interest in the observation of children in natural settings. First, scientists and nonscientists alike have been intrigued by the detailed, in-depth observations of animal behavior conducted by such persons as Jane Goodall. These observations have provided the foundation for many new hypotheses about animal behavior and have suggested hypotheses about human behavior as well. Second, the focus of early childhood development has shifted to the study of younger and younger children. Experimental methods that depended on the cooperation of children in laboratories have been found to be inappropriate to the study of newborns, infants, and toddlers. Third, and most important, a movement in the field of early childhood development has been calling for the ecological study of development. Bronfenbrenner (1979) and others have pointed out that many experimental studies are so controlled and so specific that they cannot adequately lead us to generalizations about the real environments in which children live. Bronfenbrenner and others recommend that children be studied in their natural contexts: the immediate family environment, intermediate environments that impinge on them, and the larger social and cultural structure. (See Box 1.1 in Chapter 1.)

This chapter presents strategies for observing the behavior of young children as it naturally occurs, observing predefined behaviors, and summarizing observations in case studies. Table 2.1 lists the eight strategies for observing young children that are described in this chapter. The premise of this chapter is that all students of early childhood development can and should become scientific in their observation technqiues. Learning *how* to observe young children while studying early childhood development enables the student to integrate theory and practice.

OBSERVING BEHAVIORS AS THEY OCCUR

Observing the ongoing behaviors of young children is more challenging than may at first seem to be the case. Most beginners need considerable help in learning to give objective, descriptive accounts rather than their own judgments, inferences, and conclusions about what they have seen. The following two observations illustrate "good" and "bad" descriptions.

> "Good:"   Beth leaned forward in her seat and fixed her eyes on the experiment. She remained nearly immobile in that position for the full five minutes of the teacher's explanation.
> "Bad:"   Beth seemed very attentive.

In the observation with "good" description, Beth's behavior is described in enough detail to make it possible to visualize her in the classroom environment. However, in the observation with "bad" description, an inference is drawn but no substantiating data are offered. Later, given only the observer's inference, it would not be possible to reconstruct what Beth did that led the observer to think that she was attentive.

TABLE 2.1   *Strategies for Observing Young Children*

Type of Strategy	Strategy	Use
Observing behaviors as they occur	Narrative observation	Record continuously for a period of time Show running account of all that happens
	Vignettes	Record from time to time Select incidents or behaviors that seem significant
	Child diaries	Record regularly, perhaps daily Note developmental changes
Observing predefined behaviors	Checklists	Record regularly or from time to time (depending on objectives) Check presence or absence of behaviors
	Interviews	Record responses to selected questions Explore the reasons for responses
	Time sampling	Record behavior taking place in short, uniform time intervals Examine frequency and duration of behaviors that occur often
	Event sampling	Record behaviors of a specified type Gather information about behaviors that occur infrequently
Summarizing observations	Case study	Summarize development of a particular child Provide a basis for conclusions, recommendations

SOURCE: Adapted from *Observational Strategies for Child Study* by D. M. Irwin and M. M. Bushnell, 1980, New York: Holt, Rinehart & Winston. Copyright 1980 by Holt, Rinehart & Winston. Adapted by permission.

This section provides guidelines for being descriptive, objective, and scientific in using narrative observations, vignettes, and child diaries. These strategies for observing young children enhance understanding of children and their natural environments.

Narrative Observation

Narrative observation is an effective strategy for studying young children. It gives an on-the-spot record of behavior at the time it occurs, including as much detail as possible. Narrative observation can be planned to take place at certain times of each day or week and can provide a rich source of information.

In order to conduct a narrative observation, an observer needs some time without direct responsibility for involvement with the child or children to be studied. Equipment can be modest—a notepad and a writing instrument—or,

*Narrative observation rec-
ords a child's behavior as it
occurs.*

audio tape can record quietly dictated observations, or video cameras can cap-
ture selected activity. Children will be interested in what an observer is doing,
and the most honest responses to their questions seem to be, "I'm writing down
some things I'm learning," and "I'm doing some work for my teacher." These
vague responses seem to satisfy young children and yet allow them to remain
uninhibited by the knowledge that an observer is intently watching what they
are doing.

The basic task in narrative observation is to record everything that happens
in a certain time period in a certain setting. The setting should be described,
along with some details of the activity that is taking place. Then the observer
records all activities, and a child's reactions to changes in routines, use of materials, and social interactions. Along the margin of the notes, the observer records the passage of time. Usually, noting one-minute intervals allows generalizations to be made later about the amount of time a child spent in various kinds
of activities.

The language used in narrative observations should be as colorful as the
child who is being observed. If that child moves across the room, observers
select verbs and adverbs that show how readily or reluctantly, how quickly or
slowly, how purposefully or absentmindedly, etc. Good narrative observers can

make children seem to "come alive" on the written page because of their choice of words.

It is important to know, however, that colorful language is very different from judgmental language. In narrative observations, the observer tries to avoid making judgments about how the child is feeling or what the child is thinking. Instead of saying, "She seemed unhappy," the narrative observer describes her actual behaviors: "Her eyes turned downward, she stopped talking in mid-sentence, and a tear rolled out of the corner of her eye." Using descriptive language means that the reader of a narrative observation can recreate the event rather than having to trust that the observer's judgments or conclusions were accurate.

A series of narrative observations of a specific child can provide important information about that child's development. Parents, helping professionals, and others can draw conclusions from narrative observations in order to understand the course of an individual child's development. Learning to make accurate narrative observations is an excellent first step in studying young children.

Vignettes

Vignettes of child activity are similar to but more limited than narrative observations. **Vignettes** are defined as accounts of particularly meaningful events in children's development. These events may show attainment of particular devel-

---

BOX 2.1   **EXAMPLE OF NARRATIVE OBSERVATION**

After lunch four-year-old Daniel and his mother were stretched out on the couch in cozy conversation.

12:32   Daniel said, "I'm going to grow up to be a daddy." His mother responded, "Yes, little boys grow up to be men and little girls grow up to be women."

12:33   Daniel stared at the ceiling. He alternately squinted and opened his eyes wide. He cleared his throat three times.

12:34   "Mom," continued Daniel finally, "It's sure going to be crowded in your bed when I'm grown up." His mother furrowed her brow and asked, "Why do you think so?" "Well," responded Daniel, stretching his arms and legs, "If I'm going to be a Daddy and if Bud (Daniel's brother) is going to be a daddy, there'll be three daddies all in your bed."

12:35   "Oh," said his mother, "I see what you mean. Well, probably we'll be able to work it out so we won't be crowded. Maybe you and Bud can keep sleeping in your own beds, even when you're all grown up." Daniel gazed again at the ceiling and said, "What's that?" His mother followed his gaze, stared also, and said, "A spider, I think. Shall we get it?"

opmental milestones or represent typical or interesting incidents. Selecting material for vignettes can help in recognizing salient aspects of children's behavior. By recording vignettes, the details of that behavior can be preserved for later analysis.

The events that form the basis for vignettes are unpredictable in their pattern of occurrence and can be recorded by adults who are participants with the children. For instance, the teacher who noted Sharon's developing awareness of individual differences was working on a puzzle with her.

> Sharon, a three-year-old, and I worked together on a puzzle for about twenty minutes. She carried on a conversation about the puzzle and where the different pieces should go. During this time, I observed that she was looking at my face rather intently. All of a sudden she asked, "What is that?" and pointed in the direction of my face. Having an idea of what she might be thinking about, I pointed to the freckles also on my hands and asked, "Do you mean these spots?" She looked at my hand and repeated, "What is that?" I told her simply, "They are freckles." She paused for a moment and then went back to working on the puzzle. (Anselmo, 1977)

Because vignettes are recorded only when events seem meaningful, adults can interact with children rather than having to sit apart from them with pens poised.

Vignettes have in common with narrative observations the necessity for describing the setting, time and activity; using exact words in recording conversations; including details of interactions with other people; and using descriptive, objective language. Once techniques of recording narrative observations are mastered, the same skills can be applied to recording vignettes. A collection of vignettes can provide insights about children that cannot be obtained in any other way.

Child Diaries

A **child diary** gives accounts of the day-to-day changes and milestones attained by a young child. Entries are made regularly, perhaps even daily, by someone who interacts frequently with the child. Usually, child diaries are kept by parents or close relatives who are excited by the process of early childhood development. Keeping such a diary requires discipline and commitment, but those who have succeeded report that they have become more alert to nuances of behavior and more sensitive to the needs of young children.

Child diaries provide detailed, permanent accounts of development. They preserve information about the timing and circumstances surrounding events such as the first shaky independent steps, the early sentences, and the solo ride on a bicycle without training wheels. Child diaries portray a wide range of a child's development, show continuity and change from month to month and year to year, and depict the child in settings that are comfortable and familiar. The written word can be supplemented with modern audio and video recordings.

Child diaries are useful to parents in answering questions that arise later. Diaries can serve as useful adjuncts to parents' memories, especially when the

BOX 2.2   **EXAMPLES OF "GOOD" AND "BAD" VIGNETTES**

Example 1:
Vignette Using Judgmental Language

Sally wouldn't give Marion a block, (so) Marion pushed Sally (as hard as she could), shouting, "You dummy!" Sally was (very surprised.)

Example 2:
Vignette Using Descriptive, Nonjudgmental Language

Marion, age 3, and Sally, age 5, were together in the block corner. The two girls alternated placing blocks on a tower until they had used all the blocks but one—located near Sally. Sally began balancing the last block in a vertical position at the top of the tower. Marion turned to Sally and said, "Me. Give it to me." Sally did not respond verbally but pointed to the vertical block, now at the top of the tower.

Marion stood up, pulled back her shoulders, and pushed Sally against the tower, saying, "You dummy!" in a loud voice. Sally's eyes widened and her mouth opened as she silently looked from Marion to the toppled tower.

Commentary on Vignettes 1 and 2

The first vignette gives the conclusions or judgments of the observer but few details about what happened before and after the pushing episode. Certain words are circled to show their inappropriateness in vignettes. The word *so* implies a cause and effect relationship that may or may not be accurate; *as hard as she could* is a judgment about which the observer is unlikely to have evidence; and *very surprised* is another conclusion that would be better expressed in terms of behavior.

Note that vignette 2, besides avoiding the words that are circled, gives much more information about Marion's and Sally's responses to frustrated desires. Such a vignette, used by the day care teacher, could provide the basis for an interesting discussion during a parent-teacher conference.

passage of time may have caused them to exaggerate the precociousness of a first child and worry about the development of a second or third child. Or, if parents are concerned that a child is showing too much or too little of some behavior, they can refer to past diary entries to determine whether their perception is accurate and whether a pattern exists. And, most excitingly, child diaries reveal the uniqueness of each child. Diary entries not only give a record of the regularities of development, but they also highlight the individual preferences and desires of children.

Child diaries, kept over the years by the parent of these boys, reveal the continuities of development and the uniqueness of each child.

Child diaries have been shown to have two main disadvantages. First, entries in child diaries, especially if made by proud parents, are subject to many types of bias and may be unreliable. And, second, being in the necessary close contact with a child over a long period is an inefficient research strategy for the nonparent. Even so, in the past several decades, researchers in the area of early language have made important discoveries by keeping detailed diaries of the language development of their own children. And in the 1920s and 1930s, Jean Piaget, by carefully recording observations of his own children, worked out a theory of development which could then be tested by observing other children in other settings. It is now clear that child diaries, even with their disadvantages, hold potential as a strategy for the study of young children.

OBSERVING PREDEFINED BEHAVIORS

Observing behaviors as they occur provides important information about the development of young children. But sometimes adding more specificity and structure to observations is more efficient. This section presents four strategies for observing predefined behaviors: using checklists, interviews, time sampling, and event sampling.

BOX 2.3   **EXAMPLE OF CHILD DIARY ENTRY**

Jenny (two years, three months) is now able to discuss novel experiences with someone who was not present at the time. For instance, a full day after she and I were at the lake and saw a dead fish, she volunteered to her father, "Dead fish. Don't touch. Dirty." And, upon returning from the grocery store, she similarly told him, "Tiny baby," referring to the newborn she had just seen.

She is very observant in noting subtleties. We were outside and I was throwing a ball, which she would fetch. She would say, "Get it!" as she ran after it and "Got it!" after she had it in hand.

Jenny continues to make jokes by making statements that she knows are contrary to fact. Today she said, "Mommy . . . boy," and then laughed and laughed.

She's becoming very skillful in classifying vehicles. She not only uses the gross categories of car, truck, cycle, and bike but uses modifiers of size such as little truck or big car. She also knows some other types of categories—cement truck, bulldozer, ice cream truck. Her very favorite right now is the garbage truck.

She seems to have the language ability to meet almost all of her daily needs. She can deliver messages from one adult to the other. Before dinner I told her to ask Daddy to wash his hands, please. She rode her little bike to her dad and said, "Ready, hands." When the two of them came into the kitchen together, she exclaimed, "Clean hands!" and pointed at them.

All of these strategies require that terms be defined precisely. For instance, aggressive behavior can be defined as being limited to such physical actions as hitting, scratching, pushing, or pulling another individual. Or, the definition can be expanded to include verbal behavior such as screaming, threatening, or calling names. In either case, the behaviors specified in the definition must be those that can be directly observed, leaving little subjective judgment to the observer. The more clearly terms are defined, the more information can be gained from the strategies for observing predefined behaviors.

Checklists

A **checklist** is a list of behaviors that have been deemed important to note or observe. In the hands of skilled veterans, checklists provide an efficient means of ascertaining the presence or absence of certain behaviors. For instance, a parent or teacher might use a checklist to find out whether a preschooler can count to ten and line up objects in one-to-one correspondence. In the hands of beginners in the study of early childhood development, checklists give insights into behaviors that are appropriate for children of certain ages. Without a checklist to give structure, it is difficult for beginners to know what is typical and what is atypical.

Experienced parents and professionals can make their own checklists. First, they decide what they want to find out. Then they phrase their objectives in terms of behaviors that can be observed as present or absent. Finally, they check off the behaviors.

The following brief checklist was devised by parents whose children participate in a play group together. The purpose of the checklist is to determine whether children can recognize, name, and match colors.

Child points to appropriate one-inch cube when asked, "Show me the _____ one."

_____red
_____blue
_____yellow
_____green

Child names color when shown a one-inch cube.

_____red
_____blue
_____yellow
_____green

Child matches color when given a one-inch cube of specified color and a box of cubes of four colors.

_____red
_____blue
_____yellow
_____green

Such a checklist has many advantages. Parents can be systematic in establishing whether each child can recognize, name, and match any or all four of the target

A checklist can be used to observe social responses of young children.

colors. The procedure is quick and efficient, giving a great deal of information in a short period of time. And, if desired, the accomplishments on the checklist can be dated to provide a permanent record of when these colors were first recognized, named, and matched.

Beginners in the study of early childhood development will probably want to use some of the excellent checklists developed by professionals in the field. These checklists give beginners a sense of the wide range of normal development at a given age level.

Checklists serve important functions: they tell whether certain behaviors

---

BOX 2.4   EXAMPLE OF DEVELOPMENTAL CHECKLIST: INFANT SOCIALIZATION

Age Level	Behavior	Date Achieved
Newborn	Stops crying or quiets when picked up and held.	
1 mo.	Eyes follow moving object or person. Quiets to face or voice.	
2 mo.	Regards persons alertly. Excites, smiles, moves arms and legs, vocalizes. Smiles at others besides mother. Responds differentially to people.	
3 mo.	Looks at face and eyes of person talking to him or her. Crying decreases dramatically.	
4 mo.	Laughs aloud in social play; wails if play is interrupted Vocalizes, smiles, and reaches for familiar persons more than strangers.	
6 mo.	Expresses protest (resists adult who tries to take toy.) Discriminates strangers.	
7 mo.	Smiles, pats, vocalizes to mirror image.	
9 mo.	Responds to name with head turn, eye contact, and smile.	
10 mo.	Responds to a verbal request, usually in regard to games.	
11 mo.	Repeats performance laughed at. Begins to establish the meaning of *NO*.	
12 mo.	Gives a toy to adult upon request.	

From *The Early Learning Accomplishment Profile for Developmentally Young Children, Birth to 36 Months* (pp. 86–89) by M. E. Glover, J. L. Preminger, and A. R. Sanford, 1978, Winston-Salem, NC: Kaplan Press. Copyright 1978 Early LAP. Reprinted by permission.

are present or absent, and they provide a permanent record of when the many "firsts" of early childhood were achieved. However, it is important to be aware that, for all their advantages, checklists do not describe *how* the behavior occurred, nor do they tell about frequency or duration of the behavior.

Interviews

Interviews, or one-to-one verbal interactions between adults and young children, begin to be appropriate when children learn to express themselves comfortably in response to questions. A great deal of information can be gained by directly asking young children about their ideas and beliefs.

Interviews may be planned in many ways. One approach is modeled after the *methode clinique,* which was used by Jean Piaget to learn about the thinking processes of young children. As he gained experiences in working with young children, Piaget began to build his interviews around the use of concrete objects that would stimulate young children to think. He and the children manipulated the objects and discussed the children's responses to his questions.

In the *methode clinique* the interview has a predetermined structure. That structure is tied to the manipulations being carried out with the objects that the interviewer introduces to the child. For instance, in trying to ascertain a young child's understanding of number concepts, the interviewer might move red and black checkers in and out of direct visual one-to-one correspondence, repeatedly asking whether there are more red, more black, or the same number, and why. (See Box 2.5 for the complete description of such an interview.) Although the interview is structured, the interviewer has the flexibility to probe into the reasons for the child's responses. The purpose of the *methode clinique* is to find out as much as possible about children's thinking.

To gain the maximum amount of information from an interview, keep in mind several general considerations. First, rapport with the child should be established before beginning the interview. Rapport can be established by talking with the child about favorite television programs or about family and school activities. Second, the interview should be conducted in a quiet place where there are unlikely to be disturbances. And, third, all of the child's responses should be accepted with interest, even if they seem incorrect from an adult perspective. The child should be assured that there are no right or wrong answers to the questions that will be asked; the purpose of the interview is to find out how children think and why. Explanations can be probed, if necessary, by saying that another child responded in the opposite way and asking about the reasons for this different response. Carefully conducted interviews with young children uncover interesting differences between their thinking processes and those of older children and adults.

When children are too young to be able to respond to questions, useful information can be gained by interviewing their parents. Many of the same considerations described above are relevant in these adult interviews.

**BOX
2.5**

EXAMPLE OF INTERVIEW
USING THE *METHODE CLINIQUE*

After learning about Jean Piaget's theory, Max Stein was eager to find out about his five-year-old daughter's understanding of number concepts. To do so, he lined up eight red checkers and eight black checkers on the table. The checkers were placed in direct visual one-to-one correspondence, as shown below.

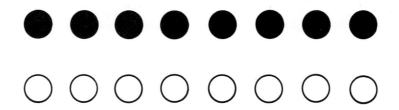

He began the interview by asking Allison, "Are there more checkers here (pointing to the red checkers) or more checkers here (pointing to the black checkers) or the same amount in both lines?" Allison looked carefully at the lines of checkers, counted them, and replied, "There are the same."

Max said, "Now watch what I am going to do," and moved the red checkers so that the distances between the checkers were increased, as shown below.

Time Sampling

Time sampling is a strategy for observation that documents the frequency (and sometimes the duration) of certain behaviors. The behaviors that are observed are treated as "samples" or examples of usual behaviors, and predictions are made from the sample about the overall pattern of behavior. Time sampling does not yield a picture of the whole child, but instead gives detailed information about specific behaviors of individuals or groups of children.

In time sampling, behavior is recorded at certain times rather than continuously. Depending on the behavior, the observations might be made for fifteen minutes in the morning and again for fifteen minutes in the afternoon, or for one-half hour in the middle of the day. Within this schedule, a child might be observed for the whole time or for a certain unit of time, perhaps one minute, and all instances of specific behaviors would be recorded. Time sampling is useful for answering questions such as the following: How often does four-year-old Chris suck his fingers? What percentage of the time is eight-year-old Megan out of her desk chair? How often and for how long does one-year-old Sean cry?

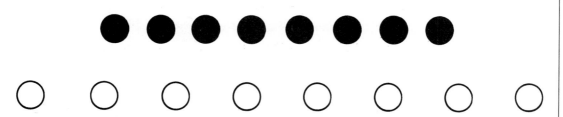

Again he asked Allison, "Are there more here (pointing to the red checkers), or more here (pointing to the black checkers), or the same in both?" Allison looked at the two rows of checkers and answered, "There are more here (pointing to the red row)."

Max asked, "Why do you think so, Allison?" Allison shrugged and said, "You can see. It's so-o-o long."

Max did several other manipulations of the checkers and questioned Allison about each. In all cases, Allison's responses were based on how the checkers looked rather than on logical thinking about consistent characteristics of number. Before conducting this interview, Max had believed that Allison understood number in the same way he did because she could count so well. Yet in the interview, Max could see that counting did not help Allison to respond logically to the task: one line of eight could seem to be more than the other line of eight, if the checkers were rearranged. The interview helped Max to understand his daughter's thinking process better and to have more appropriate expectations of her.

Time sampling should be used only when behaviors occur frequently—at least once in a fifteen-minute period. Behaviors that occur relatively infrequently, like expressions of sympathy, are not easily studied by using time sampling. (Event sampling, to be described next, would be a more appropriate strategy for studying infrequent behaviors.)

Before a time sampling study begins, the purposes of the study must be decided, behaviors defined, and recording forms organized. A good illustration of this preparation is one of the best-known of the early studies using time sampling. Mildred B. Parten (1932–33) wanted to study differences in social participation in relationship to the age of the child. She first defined categories of social participation so that any social participation would be included in a category but none would be included in more than one category. The following is an example of her operational definition for *parallel activity*—one of six categories of social participation:

Parallel activity   The child plays independently, but the activity he chooses naturally brings him among other children. He plays with toys that are like those which

A time sampling study can determine how often and for how long infants cry.

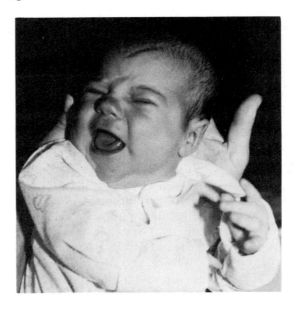

the children around him are using but he plays with the toy as he sees fit, and does not try to influence or modify the activity of the children near him. He plays *beside* rather than *with* the other children. There is no attempt to control the coming or going of children in the group.

After defining six categories of social participation, Parten memorized the definitions and their placement on her recording form so that she could record quickly and easily. And, before she could begin observing, she had to decide who she would observe and for how long. She decided to observe two- to five-year-old children during their free play time (one hour each day) over a nine-month period. She observed each child in the group for one minute, according to a random ordering of names. By using time sampling, Parten was able to draw some interesting conclusions about children's play.

In time sampling studies using several observers, everyone must be consistently in agreement in their recording. In all such studies, it is important to know that each observer is recording the same behavior in the same way every time that behavior occurs. A training period using videotapes can give observers practice in recording and can provide a needed check on consistency (called **reliability** in the jargon of early childhood development).

Time sampling yields important data on children's behavior. These data can provide the foundation for making parenting, teaching, or other decisions, or for seeking professional referrals.

Event Sampling

Event sampling provides a way to study behaviors that occur too infrequently for time sampling to be used. In event sampling, the observer begins to record when a predefined event or type of behavior occurs. Event sampling is more efficient than narrative observation, more systematic than recording vignettes or

BOX 2.6

EXAMPLES OF TIME SAMPLING

Andrea Barnes wanted to find out how often her two-year-old bit her siblings or parents. She devised a time sampling study and recorded the following results.

Name of child: Betty   Age: 2,2
Dates of observation: 2/10–2/14
Times of observation: 10:30–11:00

Days	Tallies	Total
1	||	2
2	|||	3
3	|	1
4	||||	4
5	⧻	5

Average per day: 3 biting episodes per day for the five days

Megan Smith had the sense that her four-year-old son was sucking his thumb more rather than less over time. She devised the following form for a time sampling study:

Name of child: Rob   Age: 4,6
Description of behavior: sucking thumb
Dates of observation: 7/20–7/24
Times of observation: 9–9:30 and 3:30–4

Days	Time (from) (to)	Minutes
1		
2		
3		
4		
5		

Average: ____ minutes per day

child diary entries, and more descriptive of the natural context than time sampling.

In event sampling, the observer waits for an occurrence of an event that has previously been carefully defined. Each time the event occurs, the observer gathers information corresponding to categories that have been delineated on a recording form. When a sufficient number of events has been recorded, the

Event sampling can be used to study the incidence of pretending.

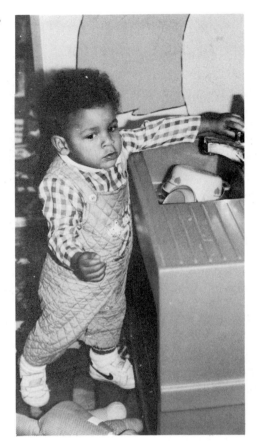

data are analyzed to determine the frequency, context, and outcomes of that type of behavior.

An illustration of event sampling is provided by a classic study of children's quarrels (Dawe, 1934). Helen C. Dawe was working in a preschool and had made arrangements with other staff members to free her from responsibility for dealing with quarrels among children. Over a period of time, she noted the following information about quarrels that took place during free play time: duration, gender and age of participants, location, cause, and resolution. At the end of four months she had collected enough information to make some interesting generalizations about quarrels among preschool children.

The length of time needed for event sampling is not easy to specify in advance, and this ambiguity is a disadvantage of using this strategy. Event sampling is probably most useful to parents, teachers, or other helping professionals who are routinely in contact with children. For these people, event sampling allows the systematic collection of data, which can then be used to make decisions about children's behavior.

Any observable behavior can be studied using event sampling. Even very infrequent behavior, such as expressions of sympathy or patriotism, can be stud-

BOX 2.7   **EXAMPLE OF EVENT SAMPLING STUDY**

Marge Kent and her aide, Ken Rico, had the feeling that the children in their kindergarten class had become unusually demanding of adult attention. They wondered if the children's demands were as frequent as they seemed and if the adults were being responsive. They designed an event sampling study to investigate the outcomes of children's bids for attention. They enlisted the help of parents who could come into the classroom to watch for these events and record the following outcomes:

Categories for Scoring Column G

IA (Immediate Attention): Adult focuses on child within 2 seconds of attention bid.
DA (Delayed Attention): Adult focuses on child within 5 seconds of attention bid, but with a delay of at least 2 seconds.
I (Ignores Bid): Adult does not respond to attention bid.

Categories for Scoring Column H

+A (Positive Affect): The adult's affect (the emotional tone of his or her response) is positive.
−A (Negative Affect): The adult's affect is negative.

They devised the following form for recording information about the outcomes of children's bids for attention.

A Event	B Child	C Gender	D Age	E Attention Bid(s)	F Duration	G Outcome Behaviors	H Affect	Comments
1.								
2.								
3.								
4.								
5.								

Adapted from OBSERVATIONAL STRATEGIES FOR CHILD STUDY by D. Michelle Irwin and M. Margaret Bushnell. Copyright © 1980 by Holt, Rinehart and Winston. Reprinted by permission of CBS College Publishing.

ied if the behavior is carefully defined. And the type of paper-and-pencil work done by Dawe can be greatly simplified by modern technological advances. Sound or videotape recording makes noting behaviors relatively easy, and allows later analysis of behaviors that are fleeting or subtle.

SUMMARIZING OBSERVATIONS: CASE STUDIES

A **case study** is a report that summarizes many observations of a given child. The observations themselves provide an important link between theory and practice in early childhood development. Further learning is involved in the sometimes challenging process of summarizing and organizing a number of observations into a coherent study of a child.

Case studies are compiled from information gathered by means of all of the strategies introduced so far—narrative observations, vignettes, child-diary entries, checklists, interviews, time sampling, and event sampling. Writing a case study necessitates the pulling together of disparate bits of information on psychosocial, physical, and cognitive development. An example of an outline for a case study is given in Box 2.8. Because data come from more than one source, case studies give a more thorough description of development than does any single observational strategy.

The child whose development is summarized in a case study "comes to life" as an individual with unique strengths and needs. Insights gained from case studies help parents and professionals make decisions about children. Case studies, as used by educators and other helping professionals, are recognized as valuable tools for enhancing understanding of young children.

Consistent with Bronfenbrenner's (1979) views of environmental influences on children, case studies seek to portray children in as many different environments and situations as possible. Data can be obtained from many of the significant people in children's lives: parents, teachers, doctors, and other specialists. The influences on children are complex, and the more that is learned about these influences, the deeper the understanding of young children.

When writing case studies for class projects, the author should protect the child's privacy by substituting a fictitious name for the child's own. When case studies are written in educational settings, the child's rights are further protected by the Family Educational Rights and Privacy Act, passed by the United States Congress in 1974. This act gives parents and students the right to inspect school records and to challenge any material that they feel is inaccurate. It also requires written permission before information from a student's school file can be released to others. Because of the privacy act, access to some information in children's files may be denied, and what is written in case studies may be made available to children's parents. Accurate recording of behaviors and conversations, rather than opinions or interpretations, will result in case studies that give parents no grounds for challenge.

BOX 2.8 **EXAMPLE OF CASE STUDY OUTLINE FOR PRESCHOOL CHILDREN**

Name of child: _____   Report date: _____

Age of child: _____   Reporter: _____

Date of preschool entrance: _____

A   General description of child
B   Relationship of child to self
   1   Personal task accomplishment (dressing, toileting, washing, caring for personal property)
   2   Speaking capacity (articulation, structure, usage)
   3   Moving capacity (control of basic movement; patterning of walk, run, jump, balancing, hop, gallop, skip)
   4   Pattern of affective expression (moods, responses to frustration)
   5   Situational responses (making choices, solving problems, persistence)
C   Relationship of child to adults
   1   Adults as supporters of self-control
   2   Adults as resources for assistance
D   Relationship of child to other children
   1   General interactions (quality, quantity)
   2   Situationally specific interactions (conflict resolution, turn taking, sharing)
E   Relationship of child to groups
   1   Basic responsibilities (care of and respect for materials, observation of space boundaries)
   2   Participation in group activities (story, music, movement, trips, snack)
   3   Conduct during transitions
F   Relationship of child to objects and ideas
   1   Objects manipulated as body extensions (tricycle, balls, pencils, scissors)
   2   Objects shaped or formed (clay, finger paint)
   3   Objects used for construction (blocks, building games, woodworking, pasting, gluing, puzzles)
   4   Drawing and painting
   5   Language activity (attending, observing, writing symbols, reading, concept usage)
   6   Concept development (causation, seriation, number, space, time, classification, measurement)

Adapted from *The Challenge of Day Care* by S. A. Provence, A. Naylor, and J. Patterson, 1977, New Haven: Yale University Press. Copyright 1977 by Yale University Press. Adapted by permission.

USING OBSERVATION TO ANSWER QUESTIONS

Using the observation strategies described in this chapter can help us answer many questions about the behavior and development of young children. The boxes have given some examples of the range of situations in which these strategies are appropriate. Further examples are found in the *From Theory to Practice* sections at the ends of Parts II, III, and IV of this book. These sections give guidance in applying each observation strategy to answer questions about young children of a particular age range. Making observations extends one's learning beyond the printed page into memorable life situations, facilitates an understanding of early childhood development, and provides a basis for becoming a confident and competent parent or helping professional.

UNANSWERABLE QUESTIONS AND THE ETHICS OF SCIENCE

Some questions about young children cannot be answered without violating the **ethics of science**. Making observations to collect data about such questions would sanction placing children in situations which would cause them bodily or psychological harm. A few of these unanswerable questions follow: How much pain can a one-year-old endure? How hard does a beating have to be in order to be called abusive? How does the social behavior of eight-year-old children change as a result of school failure?

In earlier years ethical concerns about research with children were not given as much attention as they now receive. As just one example, recall John Watson's experimental conditioning of fear of white rats in Albert, described in Chapter 1. Because of studies such as that one, Congress passed a law requiring that all institutions that receive federal funds for research involving human beings certify that no physical or psychological harm will come to participants. The Society for Research in Child Development has its own set of standards, which delineates the rights of children and the responsibilities of researchers and journal editors. These standards assert that children's rights supersede those of researchers, and require informed consent of children's parents or guardians before any research can be undertaken.

All students of early childhood development have the responsibility to see that the children who are observed are in no way harmed. The privacy of children and their parents must be respected by reporting results so that the subjects are not recognizable. Ethical observers work to protect the rights of children and their families. Taking the time to consider important ethical issues is a small price to pay for the excitement of making discoveries about how children develop.

SUMMARY

1   Learning systematic strategies of observation enables us to understand children's behavior and gain insight into their psychosocial, physical, and cognitive development.

2 Strategies for observing the ongoing behavior of young children—narrative observation, vignettes, and child diaries—use objective, descriptive language.

3 Narrative observation involves writing down everything that happens in a certain period in a certain setting.

4 Vignettes are accounts of particularly meaningful events in children's development.

5 Child diary entries are made regularly by parents or others in close contact with a child; they give accounts of day-to-day changes and milestones.

6 Specific predefined behaviors can be observed efficiently by using checklists, interviews, time sampling, and event sampling.

7 Checklists are lists of behaviors. They can be used for systematically observing whether the listed behaviors are present or absent in a given child.

8 Interviews give opportunities for one-to-one verbal interaction with children to find out about their thinking processes.

9 Time sampling documents the frequency and possibly the duration of certain behaviors.

10 Event sampling records details of specific types of behaviors.

11 Case studies are reports that summarize many observations of a given child.

12 All of these strategies of observation answer questions about the behavior and development of young children.

13 Ethical observers must safeguard the rights and privacy of young children at all times.

KEY TERMS

narrative observation	interviews	case study
vignettes	time sampling	ethics of science
child diary	reliability	
checklist	event sampling	

FOR FURTHER READING

Strategies of Observational Research

Almy, M., & Genishi, C. (1979). *Ways of studying children* (rev. ed.). New York: Teachers College Press.

Bentzen, W. (1985). *Seeing young children: A guide to observing and recording behavior.* Albany, NY: Delmar.

Cartwright, C. A., & Cartwright, G. P. (1984). *Developing observation skills* (second ed.). New York: McGraw-Hill.

Irwin, D. M., & Bushnell, M. M. (1980). *Observational strategies for child study.* New York: Holt, Rinehart and Winston.

Strategies of Experimental Research

Vasta, R. (1979). *Studying children: An introduction to research methods.* San Francisco: W. H. Freeman.

I

Before Birth, Birth, and the Expanded Family

Mary Johnson has just been informed by her doctor that her pregnancy test is positive. She came to the doctor thinking that she had the flu and is therefore surprised to learn that she is in the ninth week of pregnancy, counting from the time of fertilization. Amazingly, the beginnings of all essential external and internal structures are present in the fetus. Although no one could look at her and know that she is pregnant, many of the most important prenatal developments have already taken place.

Mary Johnson is experiencing a complex set of sometimes conflicting emotions. Many expectant parents are excited about the new life they have created. But often, as with Mary, their excitement is tinged by worry, fear, uncertainty or similar emotions. Some of the worry, fear, and uncertainty can be assuaged by accurate, understandable information about what they are now experiencing and what lies ahead. In this part of the book information is provided about a wide spectrum of events that precede, accompany, and immediately follow the birth of an infant.

Part I is divided into two chapters. The first, Chapter 3, deals with the months before birth—the parental decision-making processes, and the genetic input and physiological developments that lead to an infant's birth. The second, Chapter 4, explains the birth process itself and explores issues raised by the addition of an infant to a family.

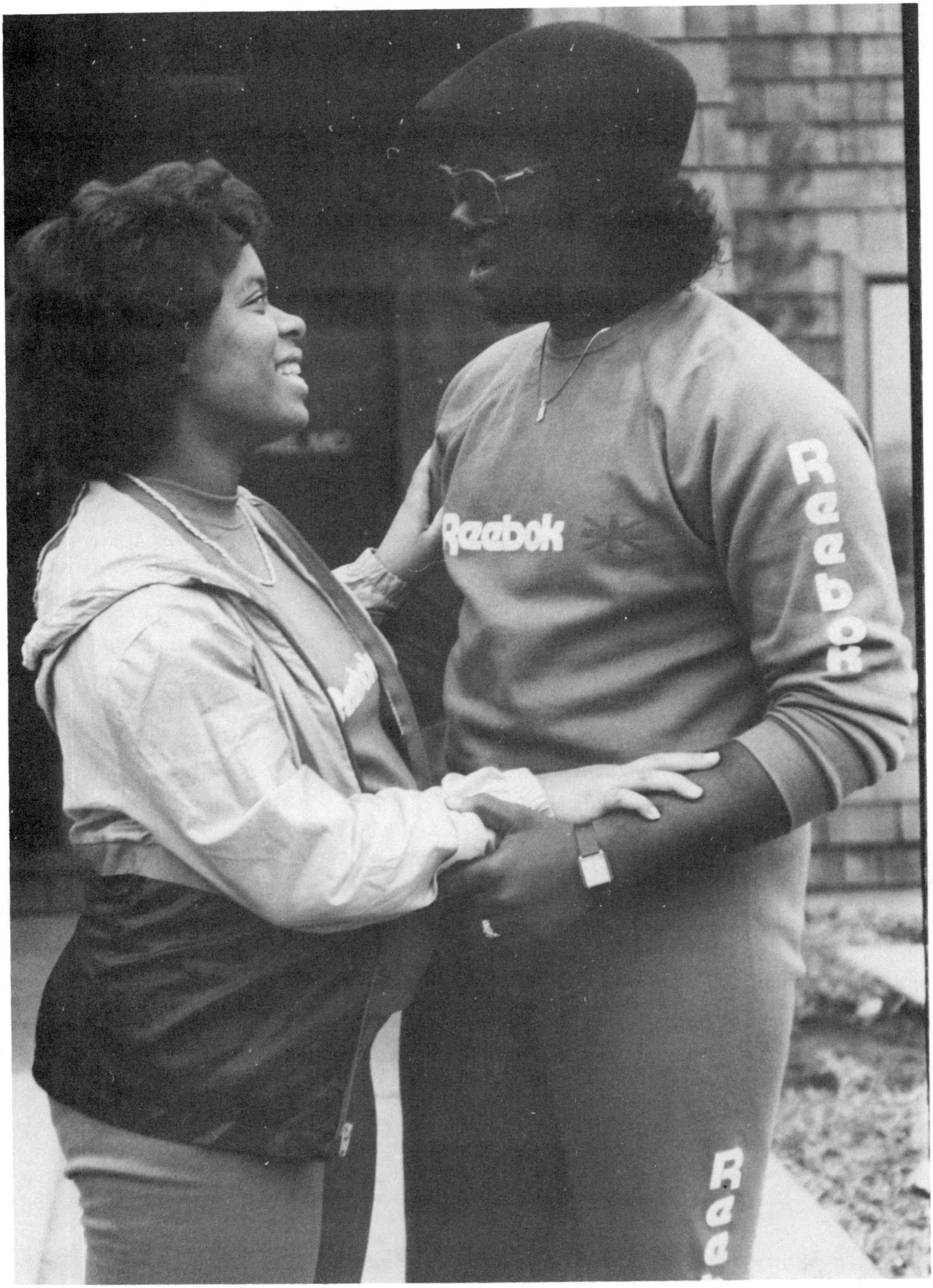
Reebok
Reebok

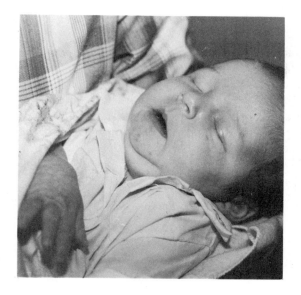

3

Before Birth

The author expresses gratitude to Dr. Alice S. Hunter, biologist, who provided advice and resources for the preparation of this chapter.

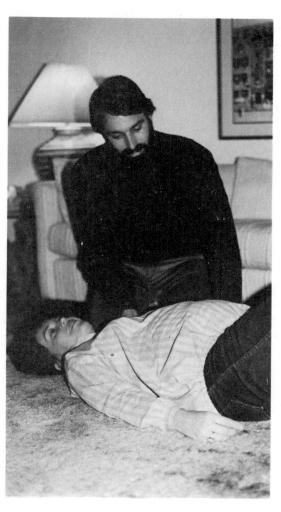

Key Ideas

Decision to Have a Child
Reasons to Have a Child □ High-Risk Pregnancies

Chromosomes and Genes: Hereditary Basis of Life
Chromosomes and Genes □ Twins □ Gender □ Genotype and Phenotype

Causes of Congenital Malformations
Genetic Factors □ Environmental Factors □ Interaction of Factors □ Maternal-Fetal Blood Incompatibility

Genetic Counseling

Reproductive Systems
Male Reproduction □ Female Reproduction

Fertilization

Prenatal Development
Implantation Stage □ Embryonic Stage □ Fetal Stage □ Speculation about Maternal-Fetal Communication

Prenatal Care of the Mother-to-Be
Medical Supervision □ Nutrition □ Cultural Differences in Prenatal Care

Preparation for Parenthood

Training for Childbirth

Each year seems to bring with it new discoveries and more complete understanding about the importance of developments that occur before an infant's birth. Significant topics include chromosomes and genes—the hereditary basis of life—and congenital malformations, genetic counseling, fertilization, prenatal development, and prenatal care. The chapter begins and ends with discussions of some of the psychological factors that influence first the decision to have a child and then the prospective parents' readiness to take on new roles.

DECISION TO HAVE A CHILD

Readers of a regional newspaper spontaneously responded with nearly two hundred letters to an essay about not having children. Most readers wrote that they would want to have children, if given the opportunity to live their lives again. These satisfied parents wrote about joy, satisfaction, and fulfillment. However, some parents indicated that they would *not* choose to have children, if the decision were being made now. These dissatisfied parents cited unrelenting responsibility, financial hardships, time commitment, lack of privacy, stress, and various sacrifices. Some parents stayed on the fence and said that they would have children again but under other circumstances, such as when they were older or more settled, after more education had been completed, when involved in a more stable relationship, and so on (*San Jose Mercury News,* 1982). Such a large volume of unsolicited mail in response to the essay about not having children gives testimony to the importance that people attribute to this decision.

In dealing with the decision to have a child, this section considers first the reasons for which parents have children. Then information is presented about risks to pregnancy that can be part of the decision-making process.

Reasons to Have a Child

For many people, having a child is an affirmative decision, based on thoughtful consideration. Natural and artificial methods of family planning now enable couples to limit the size of a family, space pregnancies, or remain childless. Social pressures to have a child soon after marriage are diminishing, and it is becoming more acceptable for couples to indicate their preference for a childless marriage. Within the context of these changing views and increased options, some affirmative reasons for having a child include the following:

□ I like being around children. I am interested in the things they do and would like to have a child with me all of the time.
□ I want to share my love with a child and also my ideas and values.
□ I want to share my life with a child and to invest myself in setting limits and giving guidance.
□ I want to care for a child, providing for health, safety, and security.

☐   I am willing to spend the next eighteen years (or more) being responsible for another human being.

Deciding to have a child involves making a major commitment. Ideally, both potential parents should explore the goals they have set for their lives, their attitudes toward children, and the stability of their relationship.

Sometimes having a child is the result of a conscious decision, but the decision is based on unrealistic expectations or a lack of understanding of what is involved in day-to-day life with children. Some people have a child because they want someone who will love them more than anyone else; these people are disillusioned when confronted with the reality of an infant whose many needs must be met. Some people have a child because they think that parenthood helps them to cross the line from childhood to adulthood; these people find their own growing-up process complicated by the unending responsibility for another life. Some people have a child to make their lives or their relationships happy; these people find that the many positives they anticipated are accompanied by a loss of flexibility, privacy, and freedom, all of which increase the stress on their already unsettled lives or relationships. People who have children primarily to meet their own unfulfilled needs are almost always disappointed. Parents do receive rewards of many kinds, but they should be prepared to give more than they get back. Giving people who really want to be parents are in the most positive position to meet the many challenges that parents face in raising children.

High-Risk Pregnancies

Not all pregnancies have the same likelihood of producing a healthy infant. High-risk pregnancies are those in which the mother or fetus has a significantly higher than average possibility of disability or death. This section focuses on two particular risks: low maternal age and parental characteristics that may lead to child abuse. Some of the genetic and medical risks are described elsewhere. Prospective parents should consider the risk factors for mother and child as part of the overall decision to have a child.

Some high-risk pregnancy factors are summarized in Figure 3.1. Of these factors, low maternal age is receiving considerable attention from heath care and other professionals. In fact, as this chapter was being written, a local paper gave front page coverage to the subject: "Teen-age Pregnancy: A National Epidemic" (Serrano, 1983). Calling teenage pregnancy an epidemic may seem dramatic until the data are examined:

> Every year more than a million American teenagers become pregnant. Ten percent of 15- to 19-year-olds become pregnant and another 30,000 pregnancies occur in mothers under age 15. (Dickman, 1981)
>
> Projections are that 40% of the current group of 14-year-olds will have at least one pregnancy before reaching age twenty and 20% will have one or more births. (Alan Guttmacher Institute, 1982)

These teenage pregnancies are risky for mother and infant (and have implications for father, grandparents, and society).

I. *Socio-Economic Factors*
   1. Low socio-economic occupation of father
   2. Inadequate financial support
   3. Poor housing
   4. Severe social problems (broken home, absent father, marital difficulties, etc.)
   5. Unmarried, particularly teenage
   6. Minority status (Black, Puerto Rican, Mexican, Indian)
   7. Nutritional deprivation in childhood, adolescence, or before pregnancy

II. *Demographic Factors*
   1. Maternal age under 16 or over 35 years
   2. Short stature (under 152 cms)
   3. Weight 20% above or below normal
   4. Heavy cigarette smoking
   5. Family history of severe inherited disorders
   6. Poor obstetric history
      a. history of infertility
      b. previous abortion
      c. a number of closely spaced pregnancies
      d. four or more previous pregnancies
      e. previous multiple pregnancy
      f. previous premature labor
      g. previous prolonged labor in each pregnancy
      h. previous ectopic pregnancy
      i. previous caesarean section
      j. previous mid-cavity forceps delivery
      k. previous low birth weight baby
      l. previous birth of infants four or more kg
      m. previous stillbirth or neonatal death
      n. previous baby with cerebral palsy or neurologic deficit
      o. previous baby with birth injury or malformations
      p. previous hydatidiform mole or choriocarcinoma
   7. Thrombophlebitis or embolism
   8. Heart disease
   9. Endocrine disorders (adrenal, pituitary)
   10. Metabolic disorders (hyperthyroidism)

FIGURE 3.1 *High-Risk Pregnancy Factors*
From "High Risk Pregnancies: Obstetrical and Perinatal Factors" (pp. 68–69) by R. A. Chez, E. J. Culligan, and M. B. Wingate, 1976, in *Prevention of Embryonic, Fetal, and Perinatal Disease,* edited by R. L. Brent and M. I. Harris, Bethesda, MD: National Institutes of Health.

The following statistics illustrate the risks involved in teenage pregnancies:

The mortality rate for mothers 14 years and younger is 60% higher than for women in their early twenties; for mothers between 15 and 19, it is 13% higher. (Dickman, 1981)

Infants born to teenage mothers are more likely to have birth defects that cause them to die before one year of age or to have life-long disabilities. (Nye and Lamberts, 1980)

11. Persistent albuminuria
12. Tuberculosis or other severe pulmonary disease (asthma)
13. Venereal and other infectious diseases
14. Iron deficiency anemia
15. Macrocytic anemia
16. Sickle cell anemia
17. Other hemoglobinopathies
18. Weight loss greater than 5 lbs.
19. Obesity
20. Malignancy
21. Surgery during pregnancy
22. Major congenital anomalies of the reproductive tract
23. Maternal mental retardation, major emotional disorders, severe epilepsy
24. Drug addiction or chronic alcoholism

III. *Maternal Medical Factors*
  1. Infrequent or no prenatal care
  2. Incompetent cervix
  3. Toxemia
  4. Hypertensive disorder of pregnancy
  5. Chronic renal disease, repeated urinary tract infection or repeated bacteriuria
  6. Diabetes mellitus and pre-diabetes

IV. *Fetal-Maternal Factors*
  1. Rh sensitization
  2. Other significant sensitization, e.g. Kell, ABO incompatibility
  3. Administration of certain drugs during fetal organogenesis
  4. Certain viral infections and protozoan diseases (e.g., rubella, herpes simplex, cytomegalovirus, toxoplasmosis)
  5. Exposure to extensive ionizing radiation
  6. Fetus too large or too small for period of gestation
  7. Intra-uterine growth retardation

V. *Placental and Membrane Factors*
  1. Vaginal bleeding
  2. Chronic retroplacental bleeding
  3. Circumvallate placenta
  4. Primary placental insufficiency
  5. Placenta praevia or abruptio placentae
  6. Premature rupture of membranes
  7. Polyhydramnios

Why is teenage pregnancy so risky? The four main problems are inadequate medical care, poor nutrition, biological immaturity of the teenage mother, and a complex combination of economic and social stress factors. Medical supervision can prevent danger to mother and fetus, but few pregnant teenagers seek out needed prenatal care in the first or even second trimesters; some do not obtain medical care until delivery. Good nutrition is vital during pregnancy, but nutrition is particularly a problem for low-income pregnant teenagers; current policy in many states restricts public assistance for nutritional needs until after an infant is born. Biological immaturity of the very young mother leads to increased danger of anemia and other associated problems among pregnant teenagers. And, a complex combination of economic and social stress factors results in a strong relationship between being born to a teenage mother and later developing such social problems as child abuse, delinquency, alcoholism, and drug abuse (Dickman, 1981).

Part of the reason that teenage pregnancy is receiving so much attention is that the accompanying risks could be almost entirely avoided by helping teenagers to postpone pregnancy while receiving education about appropriate prenatal care. Many concerned groups and individuals are working with teenagers to achieve these goals.

Another kind of risk is the possibility that parents and offspring will not form a good relationship. Ray Helfer (Klaus and Robertson, 1982) has identified five parental characteristics that are commonly found in cases of child abuse: neglect or abuse during the parent's own childhood; current absence of supportive personal relationships; poor marital relationship; low self-esteem; and parent-child role reversal (i.e., the parent sees the child as a source of emotional support). Prospective parents with these characteristics should be encouraged to seek counseling before having a child.

An informed decision to have a child includes consideration of the various risk factors associated with a particular pregnancy. Problems with a genetic basis also should be considered, but genetic disease cannot be satisfactorily understood until after an explanation of the hereditary basis of life.

CHROMOSOMES AND GENES: HEREDITARY BASIS OF LIFE

How each person develops depends on genetic information contributed by both parents at the time of fertilization. A whole range of characteristics, from hair color to structure of the heart, is programmed by one or more pairs of **genes** which are in turn contained in **chromosomes** at the very center (nucleus) of all the cells of our bodies.

Chromosomes and Genes

Normal individuals have forty-six chromosomes, arranged in twenty-three pairs. The main exceptions are the sperm and egg cells, which each contain twenty-three unpaired chromosomes. This reduction in the number of chromosomes takes place through the process of meiosis, which involves two cell divisions. In meiosis the two chromosomes in each of the twenty-three pairs are separated and distributed to different cells. After meiosis, each mature sperm or ovum contains one member of each pair of the chromosomes. Sperm and egg then fuse at conception to form a single cell with forty-six chromosomes, half from each parent. This process makes each new infant a unique individual with his or her own combination of traits from both parents.

Only since the 1960s have scientists begun to understand how genetic information is transmitted. An exciting account of the clues that researchers followed in trying to determine the structure of genes was written by Watson (1968). Years of research revealed that each chromsome contains thousands of genes. Genes, in turn, are composed of deoxyribonucleic acid (DNA). **DNA** is the substance through which biological information is transferred. Researchers found that the molecular structure of the chemical DNA is in the form of a coil or double helix. When the fertilized egg divides and subdivides, the two strands in the DNA double helix uncoil, and each of the strands takes with it the exact pattern of chemicals that it needs to reproduce itself.

Some human traits require the involvement of many pairs of genes, and some need only one pair. In all cases, DNA contains complicated information that allows formation of chains of protein that develop into tissue and organs, control other genes, and regulate body processes.

Twins

An infant's genetic endowment is like no one else's, unless that infant has an identical (**monozygotic**) twin. In the case of identical twins, the zygote formed by the union of sperm and egg splits, and the two identical halves begin to develop independently. These twins look alike and share identical inherited characteristics. But not all twins are identical. Fraternal (**dizygotic**) twins are twice as common as identical twins. Fraternal twins develop when two ova (rather than the usual one ovum) are released and are fertilized by different sperm. Fraternal twins do not share any more inherited characteristics than do any other two siblings. They can look very much alike, somewhat alike, or very different, and the same is true for other traits. Fraternal twins can be the same gender or not.

Gender

A person's **gender** is determined at the time of fertilization by the kind of sperm that fertilizes the ovum. Each ovum carries one X chromosome, but some sperm carry an X chromosome and some a Y. If the ovum is fertilized by an X-bearing sperm, a female (XX) will develop; if the ovum is fertilized by a Y-bearing sperm, a male (XY) will develop. Thus, it is the father's sperm that determines the gender of the child.

Some work recently has shown that various procedures can increase the probability of having a boy or a girl. For instance, Ronald Ericsson, a specialist

The nearly identical appearance of these twins confuses teachers and friends.

in reproductive physiology, has developed a gender preselection method which he has licensed to seventeen fertility centers around the world (Saltus, 1983). Ericsson claims an 80-percent success rate for his clients, who are usually parents of female children who want a boy-girl mix in their families. Ericsson's system works in the following manner: Just before the time that a woman's ovulation is expected, a sperm specimen from her partner is placed in a glass column. According to Ericsson, Y-bearing sperm swim slightly faster than X-bearing sperm and are first to reach some albumin, a protein in the glass column. The woman is then artificially inseminated with the sperm in the albumin, which Ericsson claims are about 80-percent Y-bearing.

Procedures such as Ericsson's arouse a high level of controversy. Among most parents, the good health of their expected infant is the most important specification, but many cultural groups within our country and abroad maintain a strong desire and preference for male children. Because of this "universal" preference for males, some specialists, such as John C. Fletcher at the National Institutes of Health, have argued that gender preselection is inherently sexist.

Even if prospective parents do not want to choose the gender of a child, they might like to select or avoid some other characteristic. The technology for doing so is not yet developed; but, if it ever is, it will be based on the distinction between genotype and phenotype.

Genotype and Phenotype

Children often wonder why their hair or eye color, body type, or some other characteristic differs from that of their parents or siblings. As described earlier, each infant is genetically unique because of the new chromosomal makeup resulting from the process of meiosis and fertilization. The **genotype** is the totality of a person's genetic heritage and includes all of the genes that are inherited from both parents. The genotype includes *recessive* genes, which are never expressed because they happen to be paired with dominant genes. The **phenotype**, on the other hand, is a description of a person's actual traits that result from interaction of genes with each other and environment.

Most complex human characteristics, such as intelligence, are **polygenic**, or caused by the interaction of many genes and not just a simple pair. Quantitative traits such as intelligence and size are also influenced by interaction with the environment, increasing variability. The best evidence for the effect of environment on the development of these traits comes from the study of identical twins. Twins with exactly the same genotype may differ considerably in phenotype, especially if developing in different surroundings.

The distinction between genotype and phenotype sometimes explains the appearance of certain traits and diseases. Hemophilia, a disease that interferes with blood clotting, is caused by a **recessive gene** that appears only on the X chromosome. If one of a woman's two X chromosomes carries the recessive gene for hemophilia, she will not be afflicted but will be a carrier of the disease. Sons receive only one X chromosome from their mother. Thus, if the son of a carrier receives an X chromosome that carries the recessive gene for hemophilia, that son will inherit a serious disease that leads to profuse bleeding even from slight wounds. Daughters of carriers cannot inherit the disease unless their father has the disease, but they may carry the disease as part of their genotype. It has been found that 120 traits, including color blindness, myopia, and juvenile muscular dystrophy, are also transmitted as part of the genotype through X chromosomes.

THE CAUSES OF CONGENITAL MALFORMATIONS

Congenital malformations are structural or anatomical abnormalities that are present when an infant is born. These malformations may be visible on the body, limbs, or head of an infant, or may be hidden within the infant's body. About twenty percent of deaths in the period just before and just after birth can be related to congenital malformations, and later they are the single greatest cause of severe illness and death in infancy and childhood (Moore, 1983).

It is usual to discuss the causes of congenital malformations in two separate categories: genetic factors and environmental factors. That convention will be followed, but then a third category will deal explicitly with malformations that are brought about by an interaction of factors, and a fourth category will discuss maternal-fetal blood incompatibility. The primary sources of information about congenital malformations are excellent books on embryology and heredity by Moore (1983) and Gardner (1983).

Genetic Factors

Genetic factors seem to predominate as causes of congenital malformations. About 1 in 200 newborns have abnormalities in either the number or structure of chromosomes.

Numerical abnormalities Numerical abnormalities of chromosomes usually take place as a result of errors in cell division. Ordinarily chromosomes exist in twenty-three pairs: twenty-two ordinary chromosomes plus two X chromosomes for females and one X and one Y chromosome for males. Most embryos lacking one or more chromosomes die. However, some embryos lacking a sex chromosome survive and show symptoms of Turner syndrome, including small size, webbed neck, and absence of sexual maturation.

In another, more frequent type of numerical abnormality, three chromosomes are in the place of the usual pair. The disorder, called *trisomy,* is caused when chromosomes do not separate and a sperm or egg cell has twenty-four rather than the usual twenty-three chromosomes. If that sperm or egg is involved in fertilization, there are forty-seven rather than forty-six chromosomes. The most common condition of this type is trisomy 21 or Down syndrome, in which a third chromosome number 21 is present. The incidence of Down syndome is 1 in 800 births. Symptoms include mental retardation, a characteristic facial structure, and congenital heart defects. Trisomies increase in frequency of occurrence with increases in maternal age. Down syndrome, for instance, is present in 1 in 2,000 births to mothers under twenty-five years of

This child has Down syndrome, a numerical abnormality of chromosomes recognizable by delayed development and a characteristic facial structure.

age, but 1 in 100 mothers over the age of forty (Figure 3.2). Trisomy of sex chromosomes leads to impaired sexual development and sterility. Once in awhile, infants are born with four or five sex chromosomes. They are usually mentally retarded and physically impaired.

Structural abnormalities Structural abnormalities of chromosomes, sometimes called Mendelian disorders, result from submicroscopic defects, usually in the DNA of one gene. Mendelian disorders are thought to take place by mutation, which occurs when DNA is not replicated accurately, causing permanent genetic changes that can be transmitted from parent to child. Mendelian disorders can remain unexpressed (hidden) for many generations, as is the case when only one chromosome carries the abnormality. Or they can be expressed and seen, as when both chromosomes of a pair carry the defective DNA. About two thousand Mendelian disorders have been identified. Examples include cystic fibrosis, Tay-Sachs disease, thalassemia, and sickle cell anemia. Individual Mendelian disorders are rare, but some ethnic groups have frequencies as high as 1 in 100 births.

Environmental Factors

For a long time scientists assumed that genetic factors were responsible for most congenital malformations, but now it is known that certain agents can

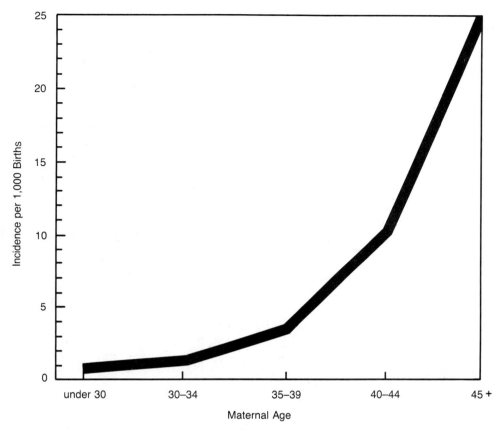

FIGURE 3.2 *Relationship Between Down Syndrome and Maternal Age*
From "Genetic Diseases" (p. 223) by Benirschke et al., 1976, in *Prevention of Embry-onic, Fetal, and Perinatal Disease,* edited by R. L. Brent and M. I. Harris, Bethesda, MD: National Institutes of Health.

cause malformations. The agents, called **teratogens**, include drugs, viruses, and other environmental factors that increase the incidence of congential malfor-mations. A new field of scientific study, teratology, has emerged in the past dec-ades. Teratology is the study of abnormal development and the causes of con-genital malformations.

One of the problems that complicates teratology is that the same agent can have varying effects, depending on when in pregnancy exposure is received. For instance, exposure to teratogens during the first two weeks may interfere with implantation or cause abortion of the embryo. Exposure to teratogens during the fifteenth through sixteenth days from fertilization can lead to conditions that alter the basic internal or external structure of the embryo. Each organ has a critical period of rapid cell division during which teratogens have the most damaging effect on development. (See Figure 3.3) Introduction of teratogens during the later fetal period does not usually alter basic structure, except of teeth, genitals, or the central nervous system, but can affect growth, intellectual development, and other important aspects of functioning.

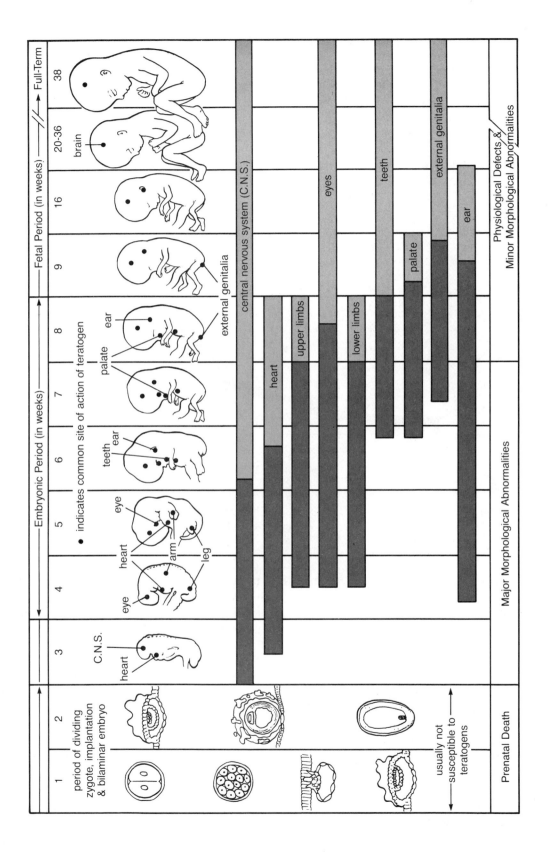

Some of the damage done by teratogens during the fetal period may not be apparent at birth or for years later. The situation with diethylstilbestrol (DES) illustrates the delayed effect that a teratogen can have. DES is a hormone that was given in the 1950s and 1960s to prevent miscarriage. At the time DES was thought to be harmless, but in the mid-1960s doctors began to discover cases of vaginal cancer in teenage girls. These unusual cases were eventually linked with the mothers' use of DES to prevent miscarriage of those pregnancies.

As this example shows, drugs prescribed during pregnancy can reach an unintended recipient, the developing embryo or fetus, and act as teratogens. The medical community once believed that the placenta insulated the fetus from any effects of drugs taken by the mother, but it is now understood that almost all drugs can cross the placenta to reach the fetus. Pregnant women who require medication for the maintenance of their own health should have specialized medical care in order to minimize the risks of congential malformations.

The case of the drug thalidomide alerted physicians to the need for special safeguards in prescriptions written for pregnant women. In 1960, West German doctors noted a particularly high incidence of births of infants with severely deformed limbs and other problems. Cases also were reported in other parts of Europe. Investigation revealed that the mothers of all afflicted infants had taken the drug thalidomide early in pregnancy.

In general, the teratogenic potential of prescribed drugs can be put into one of the following categories: (*a*) some are positively identified as teratogenic, such as thalidomide; (*b*) some have teratogenic potential under some conditions, such as aspirin during the first three months of pregnancy; and (*c*) some seem to have no negative effects.

Most experts in teratology recommend that drugs other than those absolutely necessary for the health and welfare of the pregnant woman and her fetus be avoided. However, studies of drug usage show that the average pregnant woman takes four different medications, many prescribed by her physician, and that only six percent of pregnant women take no drugs at all (Gray & Yaffe, 1983). In the cases of most of these over-the-counter and prescription drugs, there has not yet been adequate research showing the short- and long-range effects on pregnant women and their offspring.

Alcohol abuse, affecting one to two percent of women of child-bearing

FIGURE 3.3 (*opposite page*)   *Critical Periods in Human Prenatal Development*
Schematic illustration of the sensitive or critical periods of human development. Dark shading denotes highly sensitive periods; lighter shading indicates stages that are less sensitive to teratogens. Note that each organ or structure has a critical period during which its development may be deranged, and that physiological defects, functional disturbances, and minor morphological changes are likely to result from disturbances during the fetal period. Severe mental retardation may result from exposure of the developing human to high levels of radiation during the 8- to 16-week period. (From K. L. Moore: "Before We Are Born," 2nd ed., Philadelphia: W. B. Saunders Co., 1983, p. 111.)

age, has been shown to lead to intrauterine growth failure, joint abnormalities, congenital heart disease, and withdrawal symptoms in newborns. This set of symptoms is known as **fetal alcohol syndrome** (Figure 3.4). Even moderate alcohol consumption may have adverse effects, especially in the first trimester of pregnancy.

The infants of women addicted to heroine, methadone, and morphine are addicts at birth and experience difficult withdrawal symptoms, which can lead to death. The long-range effects of the use of LSD and marijuana before and/or

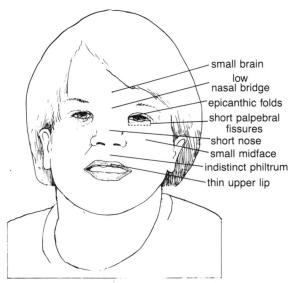

Facial features that are characteristic of FAS.

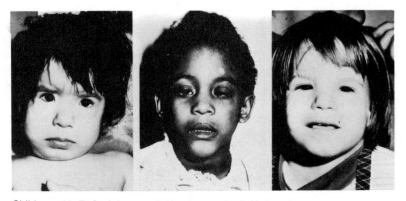

Children with FAS of three racial backgrounds: (left) American Indian, (center) black, and (right) white. All are mentally retarded.

FIGURE 3.4 *Facial Characteristics of Children with Fetal Alcohol Syndrome (FAS)*

From "Teratogenic Effects of Alcohol in Humans and Laboratory Animals" by A. P. Streissguth, S. Landesman-Dwyer, J. C. Martin, and D. W. Smith, 1980, *Science, 209,* p. 355. Copyright 1980 by the AAAS. Reprinted by permission.

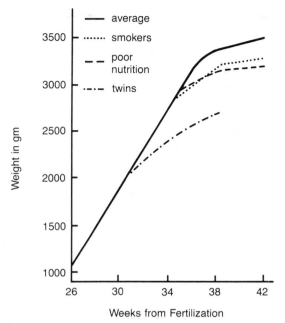

FIGURE 3.5 *The Effect of Maternal Smoking on Birth Weight*
Graph showing the rate of fetal growth during the last trimester. Average refers to babies born in the United States. After 36 weeks the growth rate deviates from the straight line. The decline, particularly after full term (38 weeks) probably reflects inadequate fetal nutrition caused by placental changes. Note the adverse effect on fetal weight created by mothers who smoke heavily or eat a poor-quality diet. (Adapted from Gruenwald, P.: Growth of the human fetus. I. Normal growth and its variation. *Amer. J. Obstet. Gynec.* 94:1112, 1966; from K. L. Moore: "Before We Are Born," 2nd ed., Philadelphia: W. B. Saunders Co., 1983, p. 77.)

during pregnancy have not been conclusively demonstrated, but our current knowledge leads to the hypothesis that there may be damage. Smoking during pregnancy results in infants with low birth weight (see Figure 3.5) and in an increased incidence of stillbirths.

Interaction of Factors

Some congenital malformations are not linked with specific defects in genes or chromosomes. Instead, they seem to result when two or more genetic factors interact. Individually, these genetic factors would be considered variants rather than defects, but in combination they cause problems. In other cases, malformations occur because of the relationship between genetic factors and environmental agents. Examples of congenital malformations arising from an interaction of factors include spina bifida (open spine) and anencephaly (absence of the brain), congenital heart disease, cleft lip and palate, club feet, and congenital dislocation of hips. Neither the genetic nor the environmental factors involved in these disorders have been conclusively identified.

BOX 3.1

PRENATAL ENVIRONMENTAL FACTORS AND LEARNING DISABILITIES

At an interdisciplinary meeting, researchers from several scientific fields discussed the influence of prenatal environmental influences, including smoking, drinking, drugs, and pollutants, on the incidence of learning disabilities in childhood. *Learning disabilities* is the term used to designate difficulties in listening, speaking, reading, writing, reasoning, or mathematics that are due to problems with the central nervous system. Only as recently as the past decades have researchers discovered that some children's learning difficulties do stem from these problems with the central nervous system. Millions of children with normal or above average intelligence have learning disabilities.

Although the educational system has made strides in diagnosing and teaching children with learning disabilities, the interdisciplinary group of researchers is seeking to discover what causes these difficulties and how they can be prevented. The consensus of the researchers (Brown, 1983) at this time is that there is a strong likelihood of a relationship between even moderate levels of exposure to certain prenatal environmental influences and later learning disabilities. They believe that there is no level of smoking, drinking, consumption of drugs, or exposure to pollutants which can be considered safe for the pregnant woman. The absence of profound retardation or noticeable physical defects does not preclude the presence of damage to the central nervous system that can cause later learning disabilities. Their recommendation is that women who are or may become pregnant abstain from smoking, drinking alcoholic beverages, use of prescription or over-the-counter drugs (except those absolutely necessary for health), and exposure to pollutants.

Maternal-Fetal Blood Incompatibility

Incompatibility of maternal and fetal blood cells can cause congenital malformations. The most serious malformations occur if the mother's red blood cells lack a component called the **Rh factor**—named after the rhesus monkeys in which it was discovered—and if the father's blood cells have this component. The mother is then said to be "Rh negative" and the father "Rh positive." Problems arise when the fetus of an Rh-negative mother inherits Rh-positive blood from the father. If blood from that fetus enters the mother's bloodstream, as often happens through the rupture of small blood vessels in the placenta, the mother's blood produces antibodies against the blood of the fetus. The production of antibodies typically does not affect the first fetus, but later fetuses can be killed or injured by these antibodies. Rh incompatibility is responsible for about five thousand stillbirths and twenty thousand congenital malformations each year (Gardner, 1983).

The Rh factor in blood cells is controlled by a dominant gene. The genetic structure cannot be altered, but there are two possible forms of treatment. The first involves replacing the blood supply of the fetus in the uterus before birth or at the time of delivery. The second form of treatment involves giving mothers a vaccine, Rhogam, designed to protect them from inflicting Rh disease on their fetuses. This vaccine must be given within days of the birth of the first Rh-positive infant. Both forms of treatment show promise in reducing the incidence of congenital malformations or death due to Rh incompatibility.

GENETIC COUNSELING

Helen and Frank (see Box 3.2) are typical of the individuals who seek genetic counseling. They have already given birth to a child with severe multiple handicaps and they are afraid to risk another pregnancy without having some idea about the likelihood of having a second child with similar problems. **Genetic counseling** as they experienced it had five main phases. First, the counselor gathered information about the family and then communicated the medical facts, including diagnosis, cause of the disorder, and management. Second, the

---

BOX 3.2

GENETIC COUNSELING

Helen and Frank have a two-year-old with multiple handicaps. Since birth, Sarah has been enrolled in a special program for high-risk infants. Helen and Frank attend parent meetings and try to carry out the goals of the program as they work with Sarah at home.

Helen and Frank would like to have another child, but they worry about whether they could cope with another child with such severe mental and physical handicaps. They thought that they alone would have to make the difficult decision about whether to risk another pregnancy until Helen's doctor suggested that they seek genetic counseling at a large medical center.

Their counselor determined that Sarah's handicap was genetically transmitted and estimated the risk in their case of having a second child with the same problems. With that specific information in mind, Helen and Frank decided to have a second child.

About four months into the pregnancy, Helen had some amniotic fluid removed and tested. Several weeks later, Helen and Frank were thrilled to learn that their expected second daughter did not share Sarah's handicaps. No one could promise them that the new baby would be healthy, but at least they could rule out the problem that they feared most.

counselor explained how heredity contributes to the disorder and to the risk of recurrence. Third, the counselor outlined alternatives for dealing with the risk of recurrence. Fourth, the counselor offered guidance and support in choosing a course of action that would be compatible with family values and beliefs. And, fifth, the counselor helped the parents adjust to their child's disorders and to the risk of recurrence. (Benirschke et al., 1976).

Genetic counseling can be supplemented with procedures such as **amniocentesis** (extraction and analysis of the amniotic fluid in the uterus), blood testing, and ultrasound (use of sonar waves to show specific physical outlines of the fetus). Amniocentesis is usually done after the sixteenth week of pregnancy. The amniotic fluid is obtained by inserting a needle through the abdominal wall into the woman's uterus (see Figure 3.6). The amniotic fluid contains fetal cells and can be used for genetic analysis. Amniocentesis is suggested only when a woman has a higher than normal chance of having a child with a defect, such

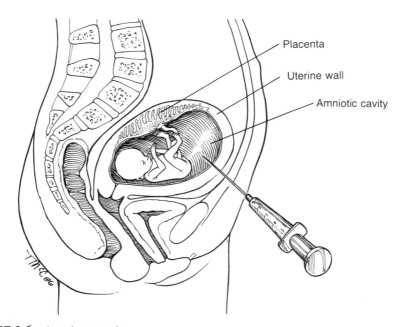

Placenta

Uterine wall

Amniotic cavity

FIGURE 3.6 *Amniocentesis*

A needle is inserted through the lower abdominal wall and the uterine wall into the amniotic cavity. A syringe is attached and amniotic fluid is withdrawn for diagnostic purposes (e.g., for cell cultures or protein studies). Amniocentesis is relatively devoid of risk, especially when combined with ultrasonography for placental localization. The risk of injuring the fetus with the needle is also minimized by using ultrasound. The technique is usually performed at 15 to 16 weeks of gestation. Prior to this stage of development, there is relatively little amniotic fluid, and the difficulties in obtaining it without endangering the mother or the fetus are consequently greater. There is an excessive amount of amniotic fluid (polyhydramnios) in the case illustrated in this figure. (From K. L. Moore: "Before We Are Born," 2nd ed., Philadelphia: W. B. Saunders Co., 1983, p. 78.)

as Down syndrome, that can be discovered in this way. Nearly one hundred chromosomal disorders can be detected prenatally by analyzing fetal cells. Spina bifida and anencephaly can also be diagnosed by testing the amniotic fluid for high levels of fetal proteins such as alpha fetoprotein (AFP). In addition, amniocentesis can give interesting incidental information—the gender of the fetus.

Amniocentesis must usually be postponed until about sixteen weeks after fertilization when there is sufficient amniotic fluid for a safe procedure. Several weeks are then required for analysis, which means that a pregnancy can be in its fifth month before results of analysis are available. Waiting until midpregnancy for this information can extract an emotional toll from the prospective parents.

Ultrasound tests can confirm some diagnoses and are also used to ascertain the presence of hydrocephalus, a buildup of fluid in the brain. Ultrasound is sound with frequencies above the range of human hearing and with shorter wavelengths than those of audible sound. Not only are ultrasound techniques useful in diagnosing some fetal problems, they are also used to chart fetal development and to determine fetal placement during other procedures, such as amniocentesis. Hospital ultrasonic equipment, placed on the abdomen over a pregnant woman's uterus, produces an image of the fetus. This image can be interpreted by trained physicians, most of whom believe that there are no side effects attributable to ultrasonic examinations.

Unfortunately, none of these procedures can guarantee the health of the fetus because there are a number of birth defects that cannot yet be detected before birth. But about 97 percent of the high-risk patients using these procedures find that their fetus is free of the suspected defect (March of Dimes, 1980).

Another supplement to genetic counseling involves testing for carriers of genetic defects. Testing for carriers is useful when there is a large proportion of carriers of the genetic trait in the population. Of course, there is no danger to the carrier; the problem arises when a child is born to two carriers of the same harmful trait or to a mother who has an X-linked defect. It has been found that simple blood tests can identify carriers of traits such as sickle cell or thalassemia. Regarding the sickle cell trait, 8 percent of American blacks are carriers of the defective sickle cell gene, and 1 in 600 black children has the resulting disease, sickle cell anemia. The disease causes fatigue, shortness of breath, pain, low resistance to infections, and clogging blood vessels in internal organs. Frequent blood transfusions can keep some patients alive but there is as yet no cure for sickle cell anemia. In the case of thalassemia, about 1 in 25 individuals of Italian or Greek ancestry are carriers, and 1 in 2,500 babies develops the most severe form of the disease. Infants with thalassemia seem normal at first but during the first year or two they develop frequent infections, enlarged liver and spleen, and brittleness of bones. Blood transfusions are necessary for life to continue and, again, there is no cure.

Screening programs have also been developed for carriers of some metabolic disorders, such as Tay-Sachs disease. Enzyme levels in blood or skin cells can be measured in order to identify carriers of Tay-Sachs and related diseases.

Tay-Sachs strikes Ashkenazi Jewish descendents, with about 1 in 30 being car-riers of the defect. There is no treatment or cure when an infant is born with Tay-Sachs. From about six months of age, the brain and nervous system stop functioning, leading to deterioration and death in early childhood.

Screening programs have also been developed for newborns. Phenylke-tonuria (PKU), a disease resulting in retardation, is transmitted by a recessive gene and occurs once in about 18,000 births. PKU cannot be detected prenatally but is treatable if a special diet is given from birth until five or more years of age. Nearly all states require routine screening of all newborns for PKU.

Screening programs and genetic counseling can involve participants in making some very difficult ethical decisions. If a man discovers that he is a car-rier of a genetic disease, what consequences does that information have for his plans to marry and to have children? Or, if the results of an amniocentesis indi-cate that a fetus has multiple handicaps because of a genetic defect, does the couple choose to continue or to terminate the pregnancy? Abortion has been legal in this country since a Supreme Court decision in 1973, but its legality does not ease the pain of deciding whether to terminate a pregnancy that is desired. The more advances that are made in medical science, the more difficult the options, choices, and challenges will be for those who are contemplating having a child and for those who have already conceived.

Even with partial knowledge of genetic disorders available today, Benirschke and others (1976) have said that if all pregnant women over 35 had amniocentesis and chose to abort fetuses with Down syndrome, the incidence of the disorder would be reduced by 57 percent; if all pregnant women over age 30 were screened and chose to abort, the incidence would be reduced by 73 percent. By the same token, expansions of screening and counseling programs could entirely prevent sickle cell anemia and Tay-Sachs disease. The Benirschke group is approaching its subject from the perspective of medical probabilities, but the decisions for each family involved in these statistics remain in the sphere of ethics and values. All of the questions and the answers that families agonize over have vital importance in the study of child development.

REPRODUCTIVE SYSTEMS

The continued existence of any species depends on having a way of producing new generations. Human reproduction involves the union of sex cells from males and from females. The successful union of these sex cells, **fertilization**, is described in the next section. As background for understanding fertilization and the prenatal development that follows, a brief overview of male and female reproduction is given.

Male Reproduction

Male and female sexual functioning is governed by the pituitary gland, which is located at the base of the brain and is itself controlled by the hypothalamus, another part of the brain. From the time of puberty, the pituitary gland stimulates males' testicular tissue to produce a consistent supply of sex hormones and therefore of sperm.

The temperature of the body is too high for sperm to be produced within it. For this reason, before birth the sex glands or testicles descend into the scrotum. Occasionally this movement does not take place and surgical intervention is necessary.

When a mature or maturing male is sexually excited, the erectile tissue fills with blood, the penis stiffens, and sperm move quickly to the upper part of the urethra through the spermatic cord. There the prostate adds substances that stimulate both the sperm and the uterus; the seminal vesicles contribute a substance containing sugar. At ejaculation, three to five cubic centimeters of seminal fluid are vigorously pumped through the urethra by the pelvic muscles. In that seminal fluid are several hundred million vigorously swimming sperm.

Each sperm has a head, which contains genetic material, and a tail, which propels it. Sperm swim together with all heads in the same direction. They are so small that billions could fit into a tablespoon. In a hospitable environment, such as is provided by a woman's body, sperm can live for several days.

At intercourse, sperm enter the uterus through a mucus plug in the cervix (or neck of the uterus). The texture of this mucus varies at different times of the menstrual cycle. When an ovum is about to enter the Fallopian tube, the mucus is clear, allowing sperm to pass easily from the vagina to the uterus.

Female Reproduction

In females, the pituitary gland acts on the ovaries in approximately four-week menstrual cycles that begin at puberty. A million egg cells are already in a female's ovaries at birth. About two weeks into the menstrual cycle, the pituitary gland secretes hormones that cause one of the follicles in the ovary to absorb liquid, expand, rupture, and release the ovum. Ovulation has thus occurred. The ovum is .005 inches in diameter, or only barely visible to the unaided eye. After ovulation, the follicle in which the ovum developed produces a hormone called progesterone to stop the ripening of other eggs and to prepare the uterine lining for the ovum. If fertilization does not occur, the uterine lining is shed during menstruation and the process starts all over again.

When the ovum is released by the rupturing follicle, it moves to the mouth of the Fallopian tube. Each Fallopian tube is about four or five inches long and receives ova from the adjacent ovary and also sometimes from the opposite ovary.

The ovum can be fertilized during a period of about twenty-four hours. If fertilization does not take place, the ovum disintegrates and is shed in the next menstruation, along with the uterine lining.

FERTILIZATION

Fertilization is the process of beginning a new life. It starts with contact between sperm and ovum and ends with intermingling of paternal and maternal

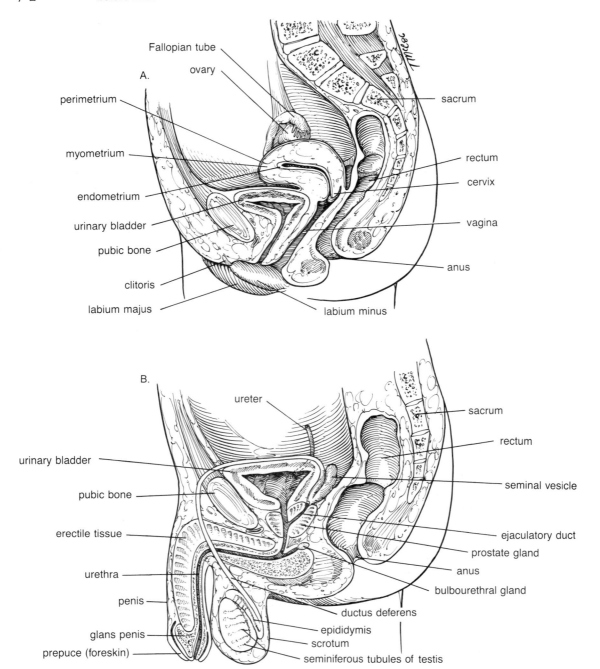

FIGURE 3.7 *Male and Female Reproductive Systems*
Schematic sagittal sections of the pelvic region showing the reproductive organs. *A,*
Female. *B,* Male. (From K. L. Moore: "Before We Are Born," 2nd ed., Philadelphia:
W. B. Saunders Co., 1983, p. 11.)

chromosomes. The result of the fusion between sperm and egg is called a **zygote**. This zygote is the first cell of a developing human being.

Besides creating a new life, fertilization performs three other significant functions. First, the union of sperm and egg, each carrying twenty-three chromosomes, restores the usual number of forty-six chromosomes in the zygote. Second, the process of fertilization insures variation among human characteristics. Half of the chromosomes coming to the zygote are from the mother and half from the father; the zygote consequently has a unique intermingling of characteristics. Third, the gender of the zygote is determined by the kind of sperm that fertilizes the ovum.

The zygote spends the early part of the first week after fertilization in the Fallopian tube on the way to the uterus. Signals from the ovary control muscles in the Fallopian tube as the fertilized ovum moves toward the uterus. During this time the Fallopian tube gives nourishment to the growing group of cells.

In the Fallopian tube, the zygote undergoes cell division. Before the entire cell divides, each chromosome is duplicated precisely. Then the two like chromosomes separate from each other and move into two new cells, called blastomeres. Other cell divisions follow rapidly in an orderly fashion, producing smaller and smaller blastomeres. The mechanism of duplication enables an infinite series of new cells to receive the same genetic material.

By the third day after fertilization, a ball of about sixteen blastomeres is formed. At about five or six days after fertilization, the conceptus reaches the uterus. At this time two different parts can be recognized: an inner cell mass which gradually differentiates into a human being, and outer cells which later become the **placenta** (the organ that permits the exchange of materials carried in the bloodstreams of the mother and the developing new life).

It has been estimated that from one-third to one-half of all zygotes do not survive even two weeks after fertilization. Termination of pregnancy before the new life can sustain itself outside the uterus is called **abortion**. Almost all abortions in the first several weeks occur spontaneously, even before women realize they are pregnant. Data from several studies indicate that chromosomal abnormalities cause about fifty percent of these spontaneous abortions (Moore, 1983).

In recent years, researchers have successfully fertilized human ova in laboratories. This laboratory fertilization is called **in vitro fertilization** (in contrast with **in vivo** or normal fertilization). After a ball of about sixteen blastomeres forms through cell division, the zygote is transferred from the laboratory to the mother's uterus. A number of healthy infants, sometimes called "test-tube babies," have been born to infertile women through this technique.

PRENATAL DEVELOPMENT

Prenatal development is divided into stages in various ways. Obstetricians and prospective parents often divide pregnancy into three equal periods or **trimesters**. More descriptive, however, is another type of division made by *embryologists,* scientists who study prenatal development. Embryologists refer to three stages that correspond to developments after fertilization. The first stage is implantation. In the first stage—implantation—the life that became possible at fertilization is called a *zygote* or *conceptus.* The second stage begins after implantation and extends through the first eight weeks following fertilization. During the second stage, the developing life is called an **embryo**. The third and final stage begins at nine weeks after fertilization and continues until birth. The human embryo is then called a **fetus**, which means "offspring" in Latin. The fetus in stage three has many recognizable human characteristics. In this book the convention of embryologists is followed, and prenatal development is divided into implantation, embryonic, and fetal stages.

Following the course of human prenatal development seems almost like taking a fantasy voyage. Generations of new parents feel awe, wonder, and respect when they view the newborn infant who developed from the union of sperm and ovum.

Implantation Stage

Implantation is the embedding of the zygote where it can be nourished and grow. The process of implantation is completed by the end of the second week after fertilization. At implantation the zygote is a sphere consisting of outer cells that will form a placenta to nourish growth, and inner cells that will develop into the human being.

The most common and healthiest sites for implantation are around the midportion of the uterus. Occasionally, though, implantation occurs near the entrance to the uterus from the vagina. In such a case—a condition called *placenta previa*—the placenta can grow to cover this entrance, and can cause serious bleeding during pregnancy. Placenta previa requires regular monitoring by physicians to minimize risks.

It is possible for implantation to occur outside the cavity of the uterus. Over ninety percent of these extrauterine implantations (called *ectopic* implantations) occur in the Fallopian tubes. Within eight or fewer weeks from fertilization, tubal pregnancies usually result in rupture of the Fallopian tube, hemorrhage, and death of the embryo. The rupture and hemorrhage endanger the mother's life and surgical removal of the ruptured tube is necessary.

Embryonic Stage

The embryonic stage begins after implantation and extends until the end of the eighth week after fertilization. During the embryonic stage, all the major organ systems begin to form, although their function is still minimal. Because the organs are developing, exposure of an embryo to teratogens can cause major congenital malformations.

Dramatic changes in appearance of the embryo occur during this stage. The embryo resembles a disc during the third week after fertilization. By the eighth week, though, the embryo has taken on a distinctively human appearance. Because of the importance of changes during this stage, we chronicle them week by week, beginning with the third week after fertilization.

Week 3   The third week after fertilization often coincides with the first missed menstrual period. Most pregnancy tests establish the presence of a hormone, human chorionic gonadotropin (HCG), which originates from the placenta. This hormone goes into the mother's blood to prevent menstruation, is excreted through the kidneys, and can be detected by testing the urine. Although cessation of menstruation may be the first sign of pregnancy, it does not necessarily follow that bleeding at the expected time of menstruation rules out pregnancy. There can be some bleeding from the area where the zygote is implanting.

The third week is important because some critical structures form. The basis is laid for the skull, the sternum, and the vertebral column; the central nervous system; and a primitive cardiovascular system. In fact, the circulation of blood is believed to begin by the end of the third week, making the cardiovascular system the first to function. In the third week, the embryonic disc changes from round to pear-shaped.

Week 4   By the fourth week the placenta is well enough developed to facilitate exchanges between embryo and mother. From maternal blood to embryo come water, nutrients, and hormones. Wastes pass from embryo to mother through the placenta. During week four, the umbilical cord begins to form.

Although the basis for organ development is laid in the first three weeks, it is only during the fourth week that major organs begin to be definitive in form. The nervous system, cardiovascular system, and renal system undergo rapid expansion. The first sensory organs appear—the precursors of the inner ears, the lenses of the eyes, and the tongue. Lung buds form and the esophagus and stomach are delineated.

The rapid development of internal organs affects the external structure of the embryo. During the fourth week, the embryo changes from a disc-shaped to a tubular structure. The head and neck regions are disproportionately large. Late in the fourth week arm and leg buds appear.

Week 5   At the start of the fifth week of development, the embryo measures 7mm—about the same diameter as most pencils. Even though the embryo is small, most of its organ systems are already present. Organ systems continue rapid growth in the fifth week; and new structures appear, such as the cerebrum, cerebellum, and spleen.

The most striking change during week five is the development of the face of the embryo. Expansion of the cerebral hemispheres creates a forehead, and lens pits and nasal pits are visible. By the end of the fifth week, the face seems recognizable as human.

There are other highlights of the fifth week. Limb buds show signs of hand or foot development. Spinal nerves, cranial nerves, and olfactory pits form. The esophagus elongates and the stomach rotates. The liver mass enlarges and the heart changes from an organ with two chambers to one with four. Internal and external genitalia form, but there is as yet no differentiation between males and females.

Week 6   As the sixth week begins, the embryo is about 14 mm long. The most important milestone of the sixth week of development is that the neuromuscular system is operational, although at a primitive level. Touching the skin of the embryo can evoke a movement response—the first step toward spontaneous movement in the next weeks.

In the sixth week, facial changes are again notable. The upper lip forms, the eyes move to face forward, the ears become defined and the nose now has a tip. The face appears quite human with these changes.

Changes also take place in the urogenital system. In week six, the internal genitalia become distinctly either ovaries or testes. The external genitalia, however, do not differentiate until later in development.

Weeks 7–8   The seventh and eighth weeks mark the last part of the embryonic stage of development. For the most part, the continuing development of organs is rather modest in comparison to that which took place earlier. A few external changes occur: the proportions of the limbs begin to approximate those found in adults, fingers and toes develop further, eyelids develop, and all body contours become more rounded. By the end of the seventh week, establishment of organs and organ systems is complete. The embryo is still small, measuring 23 mm at the start and 30 mm at the end of the week.

Sometime during the seventh or eighth week of development, the mother may note the absence of a second menstrual period. She may seek medical confirmation of pregnancy and begin to receive regular examinations. However, any teratogens inflict the most severe damage during the embryonic stage, before the mother may know that she is pregnant.

Fetal Stage

The word *fetus* derives from a Latin word meaning offspring. The start of the fetal stage is the point at which the new life has become recognizable as a human being. Week nine, counting from the time of fertilization, is usually considered to be the beginning of this stage. The fetal stage ends at birth, which usually occurs thirty-eight weeks after fertilization.

The fetal stage is characterized mainly by growth and differentiation of tissues and organs. Few new structures appear during the fetal stage, but there are dramatic changes in size and weight. Development in the fetal stage is described in units of four or five weeks.

Weeks 9–12   During the first four weeks of the fetal stage, the length of the fetus more than doubles. At the end of twelve weeks from fertilization, the arms have reached appropriate adult proportions. The legs, however, are less well developed and are still somewhat shorter than their final relative length. Growth of the head now slows in comparison with growth of other parts of the body (see Figure 3.8).

External genitalia of males and females seem similar at the start of the ninth week. However, by the twelfth week, mature genital form is apparent. The fetus begins to move during the ninth to twelfth weeks, but the mother cannot yet detect the movement.

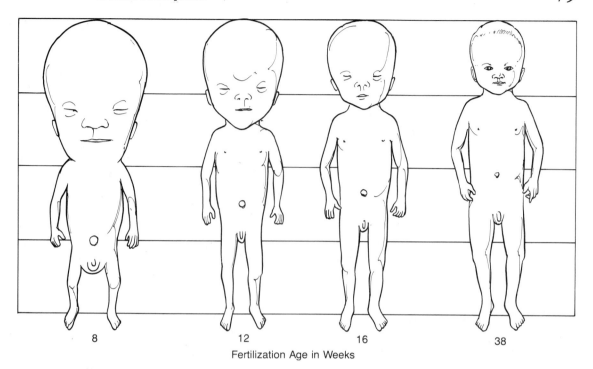

8   12   16   38

Fertilization Age in Weeks

FIGURE 3.8 *Changes in Body Proportions During Fetal Stage*
Diagram illustrating the changing proportions of the body during the fetal period. By 36 weeks the circumferences of the head and the abdomen are approximately equal. After this, the circumference of the abdomen may be greater. All stages are drawn to the same total height. (From K. L. Moore: "Before We Are Born," 2nd ed., Philadelphia: W. B. Saunders Co., 1983, p. 70.)

Weeks 13–16 During these weeks, the most dramatic changes are in size, as shown in Figure 3.9. By the sixteenth week, the lower limbs have lengthened, and the head, limbs, and body are closer to achieving the relative proportions of adulthood. If X rays are taken, the skeleton shows clearly.

Weeks 17–20 During these four weeks, fetal movements, called **quickening**, are often felt by the mother. Growth slows during these weeks, but fat forms and provides a source of heat production for infants in the period after birth.

The skin is covered with a greasy, cheeselike coating, *vernix caseosa,* which protects the skin of the fetus from the effects of amniotic fluid. By the twentieth week, the body of the fetus is covered with fine downy hair, called *lanugo,* which perhaps serves to hold the vernix on the skin. Hair also appears on the scalp and eyebrows.

Weeks 21–25 These five weeks are a time of substantial weight gain of the fetus. All organs are well developed, but fetuses born at this point are likely to die because their respiratory systems remain immature.

The Fetal Period

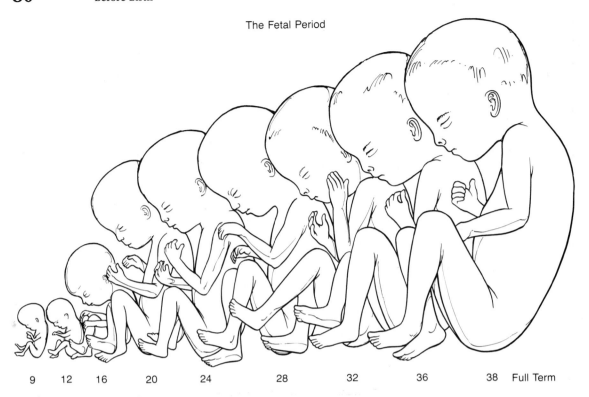

9   12   16   20   24   28   32   36   38   Full Term

FIGURE 3.9   *Changes in Size During Fetal Stage*
The embryonic period ends at the end of the eighth week; by this time, the beginnings of all essential structures are present. The fetal period, extending from the ninth week until birth, is characterized by growth and elaboration of structures. Sex is clearly distinguishable by 12 weeks. (From K. L. Moore: "Before We Are Born," 2nd ed., Philadelphia: W. B. Saunders Co., 1983, p. 5.)

It has long been known that fetuses at this stage are capable of learning. In a classic study (Spelt, 1948), a vibration was paired with a loud noise that made fetuses kick. After repeated exposures, the fetuses kicked when presented with the vibration but not the noise.

Weeks 26–29   The respiratory system gradually completes development, and the nervous system becomes capable of directing breathing movements and providing some control of body temperature. Thus, fetuses born prematurely after the twenty-sixth week can survive.

More fat forms under the skin, giving a smoother, rounder appearance. Often fetuses begin to assume an upside-down position as birth approaches. In males, the testes begin to descend.

Weeks 30–34   By the end of these weeks, the fetus's arms and legs often have filled out. At thirty weeks from fertilization, the fetus's pupils reflexively change in size when exposed to light.

Weeks 35–38 At thirty-five weeks from fertilization, fetuses have a firm grasp and spontaneously turn toward light. Growth slows, but most fetuses are already rounded by this time. The average size of a fetus at birth is seven pounds and nineteen and one-half inches. At the time of birth, both male and female fetuses have prominent chests and protruding breasts.

Birth is expected at about thirty-eight weeks after fertilization, and most infants are born within ten or fifteen days of this time. Second and later pregnancies last longer than first pregnancies; these infants are usually larger at birth than their older siblings.

Speculation about Maternal-Fetal Communication

In a controversial book about prenatal development, *The Secret Life of the Unborn Child* (Verny, 1981), the author presents the viewpoint that the fetus is a sensing, feeling being. He traces his interest in prenatal psychology to a stay with a friend who was seven months pregnant. He found her often sitting alone in the evening and singing a beautiful lullaby to her unborn baby. He became intrigued when his friend told him after her son's birth that this particular lullaby soothed her son, no matter how hard he might be crying. Verny has since come to believe that mothers and fetuses communicate and that a woman's actions, thoughts, and feelings can influence her unborn child.

Verny presents evidence that an expectant mother's emotional state influences her unborn child. Verny is not speaking of momentary emotions, such as distress or worry, but rather extreme emotions, such as the stress brought about by war, famine, or death of a spouse. Verny asserts that, in the grip of strong emotion, a pregnant woman's body chemistry is altered and so is the fetus's. According to Verny, intense and ongoing emotions can change an unborn child's normal biological rhythms. Verny even proposes that there may be certain times in development when the fetal brain and nervous system are most vulnerable to overflows of maternal neurohormones.

Many of Verny's ideas are speculative but they deserve some attention in a book of this type because, just as they have not been conclusively proved, they have not been disproved. Though knowledge of prenatal development has increased in the recent past, it is necessary to await further developments to authenticate or repudiate Verny's assertions.

PRENATAL CARE OF THE MOTHER-TO-BE

Appropriate prenatal care of the mother-to-be involves two key components: medical supervision and good nutrition. Both components are important to the healthy development of the fetus. Information about these components is presented and then cultural differences in prenatal care are described.

Medical Supervision

A woman should schedule an appointment with a doctor or medical clinic at the first signs of pregnancy. Usually absence of menstruation is the first clue, but other body changes sometimes also take place (for example, increased need for rest, tenderness of breasts, and nausea in the morning). All the embryonic growth taking place in the early weeks of pregnancy create changes in a pregnant woman's body at that time. The complexity and importance of this early embryonic growth also highlight the need for women in the childbearing years to take good care of their bodies—if not for themselves, for the embryo that may be developing.

At the first visit to a doctor or clinic, the pregnancy is confirmed by one of several tests. A complete medical history is taken, and some current information is recorded: weight, blood pressure, and general health. Blood tests determine if the woman is anemic, has syphilis, or can anticipate Rh blood incompatiblity. A pelvic examination adds additional information about the probable duration of the pregnancy.

Women with certain medical problems will require especially close supervision. Toxemia, heart disease, respiratory disease, renal disease, diabetes, and anemia are all examples of maternal conditions that are accompanied by risks to the woman and fetus. Monitoring of the woman's blood pressure and the fetus's growth can help prevent some complications and allows routine rather than later emergency action with regard to other problems.

Nutrition

While no medical authority has ever advised poor nutrition during pregnancy, the importance of good nutrition has been underscored as more is understood about fetal development. For many years, the fetus was viewed as a perfect parasite; it was assumed that if a woman were well nourished enough to become pregnant she would be able to supply the needs of her fetus. Evidence now shows that infants of malnourished mothers may be permanently handicapped.

Research indicates that undernutrition during pregnancy may cause permanent damage to the fetal central nervous system; in these cases, the person's lifelong capacity for intellectual functioning is reduced. It has been found that there are two major periods of brain growth by cell division: the division of nerve cells takes place between the tenth and twentieth weeks of prenatal development; and the growth of glial cells takes place from the twentieth week of prenatal development to four months after birth (Werner, 1979). If undernutrition takes place during periods of growth by cell division, the actual number of cells in the brain (and other parts of the body) may be reduced. Later behavioral problems can be related to malnourishment during pregnancy, and damage from malnutrition after birth is more likely if there was poor maternal nutrition before birth (Winick, 1976). The possible long-term effects of poor nutrition during pregnancy are sobering.

Many poorly nourished fetuses have been assumed to be premature. Because of this confusion, the use of the term *premature* is being discontinued in medical circles. Instead infants are called **preterm** if they are born early, and **small for date** if they are born at term but have not grown as would be expected. Poor maternal nutrition results in infants who are small for date and have low birth weight. Infant mortality and incidence of handicapping conditions are directly related to low birth weight.

Though weighing over eight pounds at birth, this infant was considered to be preterm because of the immaturity of his lungs.

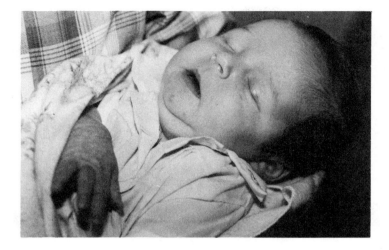

Fortunately, nutritional supplementation before and during pregnancy can be very effective in increasing birth weights and later functioning levels of individuals. Cross-cultural research has demonstrated that providing nutritional supplementation during pregnancy shows a high relationship to improved performance on psychological tests during the first three years of life (Werner, 1979).

Women are recommended to gain at least twenty-five pounds during pregnancy and more if there is a previous history of undernutrition. A balanced daily diet during pregnancy is similar to the distribution that is taught in general nutrition training: four servings of milk and milk products, four servings of protein foods, four servings of fruits and vegetables, and three servings of grain products. Seeing that all pregnant women have access to adequate nourishment should be a high national priority.

Cultural Differences in Prenatal Care

When does cultural background begin to influence the course of human development? The treatment of prenatal development has shown that various environmental forces, including the adequacy of nutrition, affect embryonic and fetal development. Cross-cultural studies are documenting these relationships and demonstrating others.

Many of the cultural differences in prenatal care are correlated with economic status. Some sources of prenatal medical care, such as public health department clinics and county hospitals, are operated mainly for the poor. Kenneth Keniston (1977) has asserted that black, Spanish-speaking, and other cultural and ethnic groups are usually the ones who use medical services that are underfunded or thought to be less desirable than alternatives.

The critical role of good nutrition in pregnancy has been discussed, but Americans do not have equal access to the resources needed for healthy prenatal nutrition. Myron Winick (1976) has made the following dramatic statement about the economic basis for differences in birth weights: "If birth weights

BOX 3.3   NUTRITION IN PREGNANCY

From *Recipe for Healthy Babies* by March of Dimes Birth Defects Foundation, 1983, White Plains, NY: March of Dimes. Copyright 1983 by March of Dimes Birth Defects Foundation. Reprinted by permission.

TABLE 3.1 *Comparative Infant Mortality Rates, by Race: 1950 to 1978.*

(Number of infant deaths per 1,000 live births)

Year	Total	White	Black and Other Races
1978	13.8	12.0	21.1
1970	20.0	17.8	30.9
1960	26.0	22.9	43.2
1950	29.2	26.8	44.5

Infants who are black or of other races other than white are more likely to die than are white infants.

From *Characteristics of American Children and Youth: 1980* by U.S. Bureau of the Census, 1982, Washington, DC: U.S. Government Printing Office.

are equal, poor babies survive as well as rich babies, black babies as well as white babies'' (p. 98). His underlying point, of course, is that birth weights are not equal and neither are survival rates (see Table 3.1, showing comparative infant mortality rates). The social costs of poor nutrition and low birth weight are great because those who survive have a higher than average incidence of various developmental problems. William Frankenburg (Brown, 1981) reports that half of the infants born into poverty circumstances will have problems in school.

Recommendations of the Carnegie Council on Children (Keniston, 1977) are for sweeping social, economic, and political change. The Council asserts that social scientists have been too apt to study the development of children in isolation from their social context. To enhance the prenatal and postnatal environments of children of all cultures, the Council urges establishment of an integrated network of family services that will assure proper health care for children before and after birth.

PREPARATION FOR PARENTHOOD

Pregnancy provides a time of transition for prospective parents as they anticipate new roles. Ellen Galinsky (1981) has used the theory of Erik Erikson as a framework for analysis of this transition. She believes that reactions during pregnancy can be divided into three stages, with each stage having its own unique tasks. In all three stages, parents-to-be are forming images to help them to prepare for the birth of a new child. These images are based on their own experiences as children and on their own and other people's experiences with children. As the pregnancy progresses, the prospective parents reject some images and elaborate on others.

According to Galinsky, the first stage takes place during the first three

*According to Galinsky's the-
ory, parents-to-be form images
to help them prepare for
childbirth.*

months of pregnancy. The task of this stage is acceptance of the pregnancy. This task is more immediate and compelling for women because of the daily changes in their bodies; men can delay dealing with this stage because the development of the pregnancy seems more distant from them. The second stage begins when fetal movement is felt. Movement of the fetus brings about a focus on the real-istic details surrounding childbirth, such as planning to take time off from work. Fantasies also intensify and the parents reassess their own upbringing. The main task of stage two is recognition of the developing child as an individual who is part of the parents but also separate. Stage three encompasses the last three months of pregnancy. Two conflicting feelings often coexist during this period: impatience to get on with the birth and dread of giving up the closeness and unity with the fetus. Many parents feel that they are experiencing one of the few inevitable events in their lives. The infant will come, whether they will it or not, ready or not. The key task of the last stage of pregnancy is to prepare for the physical separation from the fetus caused by the birth, and for their life with the infant after that. Fantasies become more complete, including impressions of hair and eye color and other characteristics.

Fantasies and feelings about pregnancy during this last trimester have been found to be related to the number of drugs given to women during labor.

Fear, depression, tension, and irritability during the last trimester seem to lead to increased discomfort during labor, and the medical staff usually respond to this discomfort by increasing medication. The result of increased medication during labor and delivery, in turn, has the well-documented effect of depressing the performance of infants on various tasks after birth. In fact, some studies have shown negative effects of drugs given in childbirth on infants up to seven months old (Yang, 1981). Helping families deal with problems and worries during pregnancy can help prevent a series of events that is likely to start off the parent-child relationship at a disadvantage.

Some prospective parents face more problems than is usual in dealing with the developmental tasks of pregnancy that Galinsky proposes. These families have major sources of stress caused by financial or marital problems, illness, isolation from family members, death, or perhaps the long-term effects of poverty or discrimination. Research has shown that the degree of parental involvement with the fetus during pregnancy can be used to predict later feelings toward the infant (Valentine, 1982). Given these research findings, it seems important for helping professionals to assist parents in dealing with sources of stress so that the pregnancy can fulfill its function as a time of preparation.

TRAINING FOR CHILDBIRTH

Expectations about parental roles in childbirth have seemed to move through a full circle in the past century. Before modern medications were available, like it or not, the key adult in dealing with labor and delivery was the mother, perhaps assisted by a physician, nurse, or midwife. Change took place when general anesthetics came into wide usage, and the mother's role began to be considered to be more passive: she was sedated and the physician and other hospital personnel were the principal adult participants in the delivery of the baby.

Many parents have felt dissatisfied with their forced passivity during childbirth, and these parents have been joined by health care personnel in founding the prepared childbirth movement. There are various approaches, two of the most prominent of which are the Lamaze and Leboyer methods.

The **Lamaze** (Karmel, 1959) **method** uses conditioning principles to teach the mother to handle pain and discomfort by breathing in certain patterns. The father-to-be or other companion has an important role as "coach" and provider of support. Mother-to-be and coach practice breathing techniques together during the last months of pregnancy. During childbirth, these breathing techniques allow the woman to control her pain. Proponents of the Lamaze approach are not opposed to the possibility of women's request for medication during delivery, but women with this preparation use less medication than do unprepared women. Other approaches to prepared childbirth are based on the Lamaze approach. Most are effective in bolstering the confidence of prospective parents and giving them a sense of control.

The **Leboyer** (1975) **method** focuses more on the circumstances of birth

The Lamaze method of prepared childbirth uses principles of classical conditioning to teach the mother-to-be to handle pain by breathing in certain patterns.

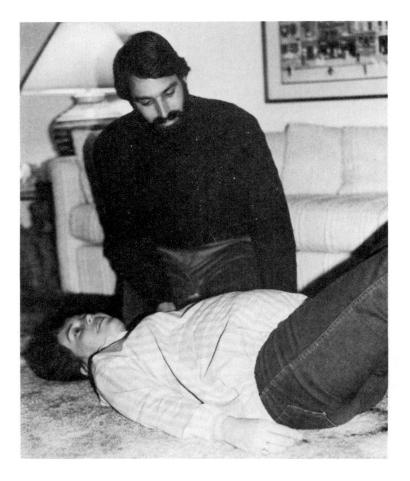

than on the preparation of parents-to-be. Leboyer has advocated delivering infants in dimly lit rooms, putting them immediately in soothing lukewarm water, and then placing them on the mothers' abdomens. His purpose is to ease the transition of the infant from the uterus into the world, presumably eliminating the shock of birth and aiding adjustment to life. Some physicians argue that Leboyer's method makes detecting distress difficult and leads to a higher risk of infection.

Many parents-to-be seek to make decisions about the location as well as the circumstances of birth. Some choose home birth, citing as advantages the naturalness of the surroundings and the possibility of increased control over events. However, the medical community is almost unanimous in its negative response to the idea of home births. The most important disadvantages of home birth involve danger to mother and child; sometimes no one can know in advance when either or both will suddenly be at risk and in need of the life supports that a hospital can offer. In partial compromise, many hospitals now offer "home birthing" rooms, which are furnished in a cozy manner but have the most advanced medical technology close at hand. In hospital birthing rooms, sometimes the entire family is present to assist in welcoming the infant.

SUMMARY

1   Having a child should be an affirmative decision, made after careful thought about timing and the responsibility involved.
2   Some pregnancies are associated with higher than average risks, and these risks should be evaluated as part of the decision to have a child.
3   A person's development is determined by genetic information contributed by both parents at the time of fertilization.
4   Monozygotic twins develop from the same zygote and have the same genetic heritage; dizygotic twins do not share any more inherited characteristics than any other siblings.
5   Gender is determined by the sperm that fertilizes the ovum.
6   Genotype is the totality of a person's genetic heritage; phenotype is a description of a person's actual traits.
7   Congenital malformations result from genetic factors, environmental factors, interaction of factors, and maternal-fetal blood incompatibility.
8   Genetic counseling can help prospective parents assess the risks of giving birth to infants with certain types of genetic problems.
9   Fertilization involves the intermingling of maternal and paternal chromosomes when ovum and sperm meet.
10 Prenatal development is divided into three stages: implantation, embryonic, and fetal.
11 Appropriate prenatal care includes regular medical supervision and good nutrition.
12 Prospective parents prepare for their new roles by forming images.
13 Parents make choices about their level of active participation in childbirth and the circumstances of the birth.

KEY TERMS

genes	congenital malformations	in vitro fertilization
chromosomes	teratogens	in vivo fertilization
DNA	fetal alcohol syndrome	trimesters
monozygotic	Rh factor	embryo
dizygotic	genetic counseling	fetus
gender	amniocentesis	implantation
genotype	ultrasound	quickening
phenotype	fertilization	preterm
polygenic	zygote	small for date
recessive gene	placenta	Lamaze method
	abortion	Leboyer method

FOR FURTHER READING

Prenatal Development

Contact the local chapter of the March of Dimes for pamphlets on prenatal development, genetic counseling, and ways to prevent birth defects.

Gardner, E. J. (1983). *Human heredity.* New York: John Wiley & Sons.

Moore, K. L. (1983). *Before we are born: Basic embryology and birth defects* (2nd ed.). Philadelphia: W. B. Saunders.

Nilsson, L., Ingelman-Sundberg, A., & Wirsen, C. (1981). *A child is born.* New York: Dell/Seymour Lawrence.

Preparation for Childbirth and Parenthood

Galinsky, E. (1981). *Between generations: The six stages of parenthood.* New York: Times Books.

Macfarlane, A. (1977). *The psychology of childbirth.* Cambridge, MA: Harvard University Press.

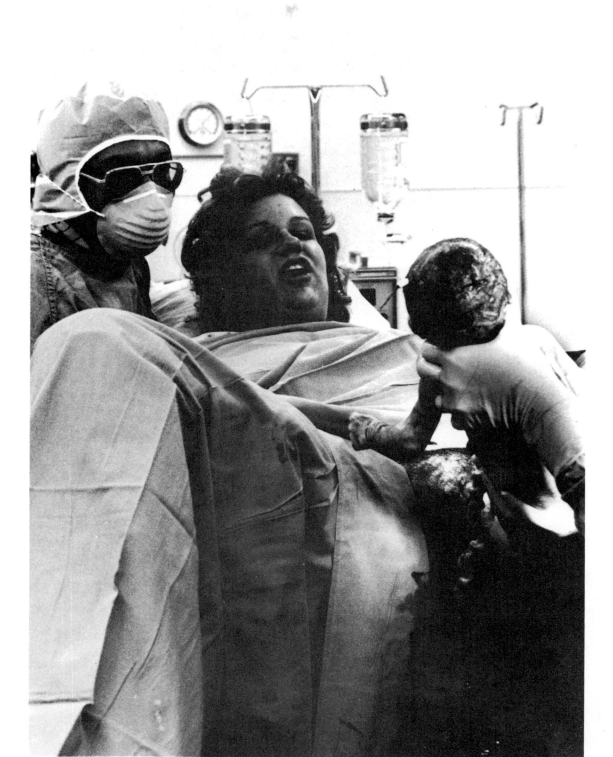

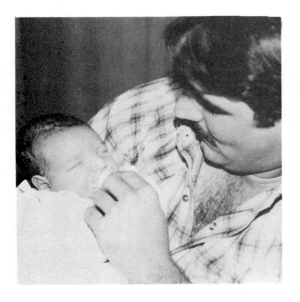

4

Birth and the Expanded Family

Key Ideas

Birth
Stages of Labor □ *"Normal" Delivery* □
Caesarean Delivery □ *Assessment of Newborns*

The Expanded Family
Cultural Factors in Parent-Infant Interaction
□ *Bonding* □ *Bonding with High-Risk Infants*
□ *Special Needs of Fathers and Siblings*

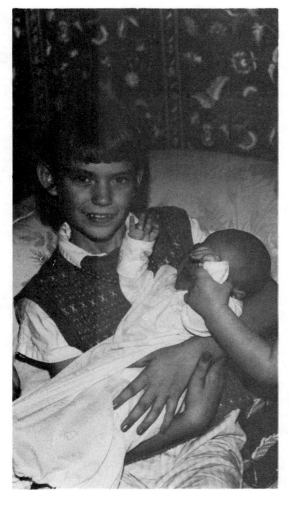

Birth renews the human species and often evokes in us a sense of hope and expectation. This chapter deals with the events surrounding birth and the adjustments families make following birth. The first half of the chapter describes the three stages of labor, the experiences of two families with childbirth, and the ways in which the well-being of newborns is assessed. The second half of the chapter deals with the processes by which newborns are incorporated into families.

BIRTH

Childbirth is the culmination of months of development during which a single cell becomes a complex human being. Researchers do not yet understand precisely how a hormonal signal begins contractions of the uterus and the birth process but, with this signal, the fetus starts its entry into the world.

Stages of Labor

The birth process or period of **labor** is often divided into three stages: (1) opening of the cervix, (2) delivery of the infant, and (3) delivery of the placenta. A description of these stages of labor follows.

Stage one   In the first stage of labor contractions of the uterus dilate or enlarge the **cervix**, the opening of the uterus, to a diameter of about ten centimeters. Within this stage, or occasionally before, membranes rupture to allow amniotic fluid to escape. The first stage of labor is the longest, lasting from fourteen to sixteen hours in a first childbirth.

Stage two   During the second stage of labor, the fetus emerges from the mother's body. Contractions of the uterus increase in frequency, forcing the fetus through the cervical canal and vagina. As the infant emerges from the mother's body, mucus is removed by suction from its nose and mouth.

Some profound changes in the circulatory system begin to take place when newborns first breathe air into their lungs. Vessels and structures that received oxygen through the umbilical cord during prenatal development are no longer needed, and are transformed in the days and weeks after birth. There is a gradual transition from a fetal to an adult pattern of circulation.

After delivery of the infant, the obstetrician clamps and cuts the umbilical cord. Nurses add drops to the infant's eyes to prevent infection, put on an indentification bracelet to match the mother's, and weigh and measure the infant. Generally the second stage of labor lasts several hours in a first birth

The position of the fetus can make a difference in the progress of labor during the second stage. Normally fetuses present themselves for delivery head first. Sometimes, however, delivery is complicated by the fact that the fetus is in another position. Physicians have found that some fetuses can be manually turned before delivery, some can be delivered with instruments even in their unorthodox positions, and some must be delivered surgically.

Stage three The third stage of labor is the time from delivery of the infant to delivery to the placenta. Contractions continue after the birth of the infant, and usually the placenta is expelled spontaneously within one-half hour from the end of the second stage of labor.

Although no description of childbirth can account for the actual variations that exist, it is helpful to consider two common patterns. In the first, Miwa and Paul delivered their daughter vaginally without much medication. In the second, Mary and Jose delivered their son by emergency Caesarean section.

"Normal" Delivery

Miwa and Paul went to the hospital immediately after they decided that she was in labor. Miwa had not been in a hospital in this country, and the hustle and bustle that confronted her made her want to turn around and walk out. Her next contraction made her clutch Paul's arm as he resolutely propelled her through the halls. In the maternity ward, it took some time for Paul to make himself understood to the nurse at the desk, who spoke only English. Finally, the doctor on duty examined Miwa and found that her cervix was just beginning to dilate. The doctor explained that Miwa and Paul would probably be more comfortable going through the early part of the first stage of labor in their own home. She advised them to return when the contractions were five minutes apart. Paul, however, had decided that he wanted only the best for Miwa and to him the best was to be found in the hospital.

As Miwa held Paul's arm, the situation was decided: her membranes broke, removing the plug of mucus that protects the fetus from infection. The doctor approved admission of Miwa to the hospital, and after the paperwork was completed, Paul joined her in a labor room.

Paul wanted to save Miwa and discomfort and anxiety, so he requested medication for her when Mrs. Gilroy, a nurse, came in. Mrs. Gilroy explained that it would be good for Miwa to go as long as possible without medication. Medications cross the placenta, enter infants' circulation, and depress their central nervous systems. Researchers have found that the effects of significant amounts of medication during labor show up on tests of infants' problem-solving behavior for as long as seven months after birth (Yang, 1981). Paul was torn between his desire to help Miwa and his concern for the infant. When he translated Mrs. Gilroy's explanation, Miwa seemed to gain a measure of control and asked Paul to find out what they should be doing.

Mrs. Gilroy gave Paul instructions about helping Miwa to use abdominal breathing and to focus on something in the labor room during contractions. Paul had originally thought that he would leave the handling of the delivery to the professionals, but he accepted his role as Miwa's support person. Mrs. Gilroy looked in regularly, as did the physician on duty. Mrs. Gilroy found Paul and Miwa to be eager recipients of her suggestions and wished that they had attended childbirth education classes offered by the hospital.

Miwa's labor lasted throughout the night. She discovered that her pains did not continue to grow more severe over time, even though they occurred more frequently. At one of the doctor's visits, Miwa cried in alarm that the fetus had stopped moving. The doctor assured her through Paul that it is normal for the fetus's movements to be greatly reduced during labor. The cushioning amniotic fluid is gone, and the contracting uterus is moving the fetus into positon.

Toward morning, Miwa's labor pains were close together and her cervix was fully dilated. Mrs. Gilroy's replacement, Ms. Garcia, prepared Miwa for the delivery room. There, the anesthesiologist explained to Paul the options for medication, which by this time would not reach the fetus before the impending delivery. They chose a cervical block, a local anesthetic, which was administered while Dr. Reynolds and Paul scrubbed up. Paul and Dr. Reynolds helped Miwa learn to pant when she first felt the urge to push the fetus out. Dr. Reynolds made a small incision in the perineum, called an episiotomy, and then had Paul tell Miwa to go ahead and push.

Miwa squeezed Paul's hands with great intensity, and with that contraction the infant's head appeared. Dr. Reynolds removed the mucus from the infant's nose and mouth, and with the next contraction the infant's body appeared. With another contraction Dr. Reynolds carefully assisted their daughter into the world. As Miwa and Paul watched, their daughter began to cry loudly and Dr. Reynolds cut the umbilical cord. With several more contractions, the placenta was expelled.

Dr. Reynolds handed their daughter to Miwa, who held her gently. Their daughter seemed to look right at Miwa and Paul, and they thought that she was beautiful.

Caesarean Delivery

Mary and Jose had taken Lamaze prepared childbirth classes during the last months of pregnancy and felt very strongly about going through childbirth without unnecessary medication. They had found an obstetrician who would apply some of Dr. Frederick Leboyer's (1975) ideas about gentle childbirth in a dimly lit delivery room.

Mary and Jose easily handled the early stages of labor at home and went to the hospital only when Mary's contractions were regular and close together. However, in routine monitoring of the fetus's vital signs, a nurse noted signs of fetal distress and notified the obstetrician. Dr. Adams immediately began to monitor the fetus's condition with electrodes placed on its scalp through Mary's cervix. Dr. Adams stopped in frequently, watching the pattern of vital signs during each of the contractions of Mary's uterus. Mary and Jose, even as well trained and resolute as they were, had difficulty continuing their breathing patterns with the distraction of the activity around them and their fear for their infant.

Dr. Adams discussed the options with them: an immediate Caesarean or a wait-and-see approach. Mary and Jose were aware that some Caesarean deliveries are viewed as being unnecessary, resulting from an overly cautious interpretation of the feedback from fetal monitoring. They opted to wait for more information before having a surgical delivery.

As Mary's labor progressed, though, Dr. Adams advised Mary and Jose that he felt that the fetus was in danger. They nodded their assent, and Mary was

Monitors show vital signs of the fetus during the birth process. (Photo by Dan Collins.)

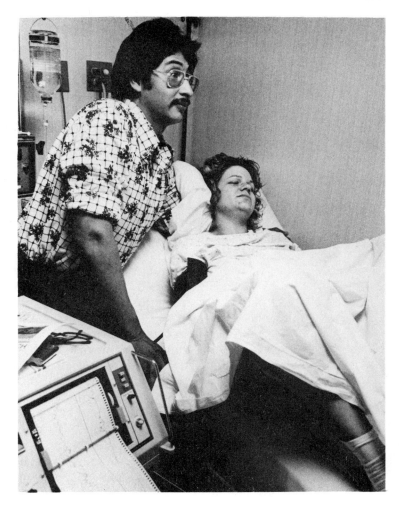

prepared for surgery while Jose and Dr. Adams scrubbed up. Mary was given a spinal anesthetic so that she would witness the birth of their child. The anesthesiologist stood near her head, and Jose held her hand on the other side. Soon after, their son was delivered through a low abdominal incision. Mary and Jose fully expected to hold their son right after birth, but his distress continued into the newborn period. His cord had been wrapped around him in such a way that his oxygen supply had been reduced with the action of each of the contractions of his mother's uterus. He did not breathe independently, and immediately a team of pediatric specialists rushed in to attend to him. Mary and Jose felt empty, alone, and let down after all of their anticipation.

The caring arrival of their Lamaze instructor made the difference for Mary and Jose in regaining control of their feelings. Sarah reminded them of their preparation for this possibility and assured them that they had done everything that they could.

Assessment of Newborns

Workers in delivery rooms around the world have long since grown accustomed to hearing new parents like Mary and Jose voice concern about whether their newborn is normal and healthy. The most common way of reporting the condition of a newborn to parents is by explaining the Apgar score. A second way, supplementing the Apgar, is by showing parents the newborn's behavioral strengths in the days after birth, using the Brazelton Neonatal Behavioral Assessment Scale. The Apgar score and the Brazelton scale will both be described.

Apgar score   In years gone by, some high-risk infants were lost because no one in the delivery room focused attention on the condition of these infants right after delivery. Now, thanks to Dr. Virginia Apgar, an **Apgar score** is quickly and easily computed by carefully observing an infant at one, five, and sometimes fifteen minutes after delivery. Five aspects of a newborn's ability to function can be quickly but reliably rated, with zero, one, or two points given to each. The five aspects of functioning can be remembered easily because the first letters spell APGAR: appearance (skin color), pulse (heart rate), grimace (reaction to slight pain), activity (motor responsiveness and tone), and respiration (breathing adequacy).

The generally accepted scoring guidelines for the Apgar are as follows: a score of seven or above indicates that there is no immediate danger, a score below seven indicates a need for specialized assistance, and a score below four indicates a life-threatening situation requiring immediate intervention. To put Apgar scores into perspective, they can be applied to Miwa and Paul's daughter and to Mary and Jose's son. Miwa and Paul's daughter's Apgar scroes were 9, 9, and 10 at one, five, and fifteen minutes after delivery. The change from 9 to 10 indicated improvement in her color, but no problems whatsoever were apparent at any point. Mary and Jose's son, in contrast, had scores of 4, 8, and 9. His first score reflected his precarious status, but he responded well to emergency efforts and was already out of danger when the five-minute score was calculated.

Apgar scores, taken at most hospitals, give an indication of how well the infant is adjusting to the stress of delivery and the need to breathe independently. Taking an Apgar score achieves the important purpose of directing the attention of delivery room professionals to the well-being of the infant immediately after birth. Many infants have received life-saving assistance because of danger signals that were communicated by their low Apgar scores.

The Brazelton neonatal behavioral assessment scale   The Neonatal Behavioral Assessment Scale, usually called the **Brazelton Scale** after its primary developer, T. Berry Brazelton, gives information about a wide range of behavioral strengths that newborns bring to their early interactions. The Brazelton assesses sixteen reflexes and twenty-six behavioral items, which together simulate a variety of situations faced by newborns in the early days and weeks of life. Administration of the Brazelton requires considerably more training than does administration of the Apgar because, in the Brazelton assessment, the examiners try to elicit each infant's highest level of performance rather than an average. To

**BOX
4.1**

ETHICAL CONCERNS

Medical advances have raised at least two serious ethical concerns involving newborns. The first deals with the survival of seriously handicapped infants and the second with surrogate mothers.

Until the past several decades, newborns whose very serious problems were reflected in low Apgar scores usually died. In those days, the infants who survived often had the fewest difficulties and the best chance of developing satisfactorily. Then, in recent decades, a second phase of neonatal medicine brought a dramatic increase in the survival of infants in distress, but many survivors had major handicaps. News reports (*San Francisco Chronicle,* 1983) indicate that the number of infants born with some physical or mental defect has doubled in the past twenty-five years. The whole idea of providing intensive care for newborns was consequently called into question because this care resulted in an increase in the number of handicapped children. We may now have entered a third phase of neonatal medicine, with an improved understanding of fetal and newborn disorders. The need now is for long-term information about infants who have survived because of newborn intensive care. Information about the lives of these individuals is required in order to address the ethical concern that is being raised about the quality of life available to severely handicapped infants.

A second ethical concern revolves around artificial insemination and the concept of surrogate mothers—women who bear children for others. What are the rights of newborn children in these cases? An example is the situation of Alexander Malahoff, who contracted with Judy Stiver to bear his child for $10,000. In early 1983, the child was born with microcephaly, a birth defect usually associated with retardation, and Malahoff subsequently denied paternity. The newborn existed in legal, medical, and parental limbo for nearly a month until blood tests confirmed that Malahoff could not have been the father. Perhaps the Stivers will raise their child; perhaps not. All of us are involved in the resolution of these ethical concerns, either as participants or as citizens.

do so requires sensitivity to an infant's signals and flexibility in the order in which items are presented.

The Brazelton scale, developed over a period of twenty years, was the first major behavioral assessment designed for use with newborns. The twenty-six behavioral items, shown in Figure 4.1, assess whether the infant responds less when sights, sounds, and touches are repeated; how mature the infant's motor skills are; how state, color, and activity level vary; how well the infant quiets itself; and how the infant responds to cuddling and other social interactions.

1. Response decrement to repeated visual stimuli (2,3).*
2. Response decrement to rattle (2,3).
3. Response decrement to bell (2,3).
4. Response decrement to pinprick (1,2,3).
5. Orienting response to inanimate visual stimuli (4 only).
6. Orienting response to inanimate auditory stimuli (4,5).
7. Orienting response to animate visual stimuli—examiner's face (4 only).
8. Orienting response to animate auditory stimuli—examiner's voice (4 only)
9. Orienting responses to animate visual and auditory stimuli (4 only.)
10. Quality and duration of alert periods (4 only).
11. General muscle tone—in resting and in response to being handled, passive and active (4,5).
12. Motor activity (4,5).
13. Traction responses as he is pulled to sit (3,5).
14. Cuddliness—responses to being cuddled by examiner (4,5).
15. Defensive movements—reactions to a cloth over his face (4).
16. Consolability with intervention by examiner (6 to 5,4,3,2).
17. Peak of excitement and his capacity to control himself (6).
18. Rapidity of buildup to crying state (from 1,2 to 6.)
19. Irritability during the examination (3,4,5).
20. General assessment of kind and degree of activity (alert states).
21. Tremulousness (all states).
22. Amount of startling (3,4,5,6).
23. Lability of skin color—measuring autonomic lability (from 1 to 6).
24. Lability of states during entire examination (all states).
25. Self-quieting activity—attempts to console self and control state (6,5 to 4,3,2,1).
27. Hand-to-mouth activity (all states).

*Numbers in parentheses refer to optimal state for assessment.

FIGURE 4.1

Behavioral Items on the Brazelton Neonatal Behavioral Assessment Scale
The states for assessment are (1) deep sleep, (2) light sleep, (3) drowsiness, (4) quiet alert, (5) active alert, and (6) crying. (From "Cross-Cultural Assessment of Neonatal Behavior" by Barry Lester and T. Berry Brazelton. In *Cultural Perspectives on Child Development,* edited by Daniel A. Wagner and Harold W. Stevenson. W. H. Freeman and Company. Copyright © 1982.)

Assessing an infant's responses with the Brazelton scale serves two useful purposes. First, when the assessment is conducted in the parents' presence, the parents gain a sense of the infant's competence and ability to interact. In one relevant study (Myers, 1982), parents were taught to administer the Brazelton to their own infants. Attention was drawn by the researcher to the infants' most positive interactive and other abilities. Four weeks later the researcher found that the parents who had become acquainted with their newborns' abilities through the Brazelton scored higher than parents without that experience on measurements of knowledge about infants, confidence in handling infants, and satisfaction with their interactions with infants. It was also found that fathers who had used the Brazelton were more involved with their infants than were fathers who had not.

A second purpose for administering the Brazelton is to identify infants whose responses may make it difficult for parents to care for them. During the Brazelton, the examiner moves the newborn from sleep to alert states and then back to quiet again. The ability of newborns to control and regulate their states is viewed as an important indicator of maturity. Premature or ill infants have fewer clear states, and for all infants the states become easier to interpret over time as the central nervous system matures. Infants with few clear states who cry frequently, cannot easily quiet themselves, and are unresponsive or negative about cuddling present real challenges to parents. The Brazelton can identify infants whose parents could benefit from ongoing professional support in order to learn to recognize and build on their infants' strengths.

THE EXPANDED FAMILY

Parents react to their newborns in a wide variety of ways, as demonstrated by the comments recorded in Box. 4.2. This second half of the chapter discusses factors that influence the reactions of parents and other family members to the birth of an infant: cultural factors, bonding, bonding with high-risk infants, and special needs of fathers and siblings.

Cultural Factors in Parent-Infant Interaction

Cross-cultural studies have demonstrated that newborns from the same cultural group behave similarly, and that they behave differently from newborns from other cultural groups. The unique characteristics of newborns from particular cultures have been shown to influence the reactions of their parents and vice versa. The traditional use of cradleboards by Navajos and the responsive nurturing by Zinacantecos provide two examples of this influence.

Study of the Navajo newborns has disclosed distinctive motor or muscular patterns, as compared with newborns from other cultural groups. For example, these infants show less resistance in muscle tone when legs or arms are straightened, less straightening of the legs to support the body, and an absence of walking movements when the infant is leaned forward. The argument has been made (Lester and Brazelton, 1982) that these motor patterns of Navajo infants long ago influenced the development of the practice of putting infants on cradleboards. The motor patterns of Navajo newborns seem to make them more likely to accept placement on a cradleboard than would be true for more active infants.

Observers of Zinacanteco Indians in Mexico have found that newborns are small in weight and are alert both auditorially and visually. The low birth weight probably results from maternal undernutrition, infection, and low oxygen due to the high altitude in which the Indians live. Zinacanteco newborns are slow and quiet in their reactions as compared with newborns in the United States. Again, reactions of Zinacanteco parents tend to be consistent with these predis-

BOX 4.2

PARENTAL REACTIONS TO NEWBORNS

A teacher of a class for parents of newborns has observed a wide range of parental reactions to the responsibilities that follow childbirth. Here are examples of some of the remarks that she has heard over the years.

"I looked at him and thought that he was the most perfect, divinely crafted creature ever to be born. When I came home from the hospital with him and carried him for the first time to the crib I had prepared, I thought that I would explode with happiness and pride."

"I wanted her. I really did. I needed someone to take care of, someone to love. But when I got her to myself, she cried all the time. I tried everything but she wouldn't stop. It wasn't like I thought it would be."

"When labor started so early, all I could think about was that I might have to go home from the hospital alone. I'll never forget my first look at her in intensive care; tubes and wires were everywhere and she was so tiny. At first I couldn't stand to visit her, but as she got stronger, a little hope began to grow in my heart. Now that she's home, I still feel as though she's a gift—on loan for now, but so fragile."

"He was so much more helpless than I had expected. I knew that my life would change when he was born but I hadn't expected that I would get so little in return for the night feedings, lack of freedom, fatigue, and intrusion on my life. These aren't the 'right' things to say, I know, and my wife wouldn't understand them."

"She had her own little personality and approach to life from the first. I was amazed at how competent she was. She let me know when she wanted something and I thought that she recognized my voice."

positions. Zinacanteco infants are given a quiet environment immediately following delivery and are thereafter responded to immediately—rocked, breast-fed, and cradled—rather than allowed to cry or become frustrated. This responsive nurturing of Zinacanteco parents seems to reinforce the birth characteristics of the infants. With the Zinacantecos and the Navajos, it seems that infant characteristics shape and, in turn, are shaped by their parents' reactions

Bonding

Bonding is defined as a complex psychobiological tie from parent to infant (Klaus & Kennell, 1982). (The tie from infant to parent is called *attachment* and is described in Chapter 5.) The concept of bonding is in the center of a controversy about when and under what circumstances parents and their newborn should meet and interact for the first time. The interest in the timing and setting of early parent-infant interaction was ignited primarily by professional articles and a landmark book. *Maternal-Infant Bonding* (1976), by two pediatricians at Case Western Reserve University School of Medicine, Marshall H. Klaus and John H. Kennell. Klaus and Kennell recommended that thirty to sixty minutes of private contact between parents and an infant should be provided right after birth. The timing of this first parent-infant contact was planned to coincide with a period of calm alertness right after birth. This period of alertness is longer than those that infants have at other times in the first week or so. The Klaus and Kennell plan called for additional close contact in the days after birth.

In order to understand the impact of the research on bonding presented by Klaus and Kennell, typical hospital procedures following childbirth in the early 1970s must be known. Because epidemic diarrhea and respiratory infections had historically been problems among newborns, hospitals developed the practice of grouping full-term infants for care in a central nursery. Parents and others were often treated as outsiders who might bring germs into the nursery and endanger the infants. Within this context, then, in most hospitals in the early 1970s, newborns were taken to the nursery soon after birth and were returned periodically to their parents only after a time of observation and examination. To be sure, there were exceptions to these procedures, especially among parents who had experienced various forms of prepared childbirth and who were requesting that their infants "room in" with them throughout their hospital stay. But the predominant experience soon after birth was of parent-infant separation.

Klaus and Kennell's recommendations were based on a series of studies. In a key study (Klaus, Jerauld, Kreger, McAlpine, Steffa, & Kennell, 1972), for example, one group of mothers was given early and extended contact with their infants, and the second group experienced the usual hospital procedures at that time (a glimpse of the infant at birth and twenty to thirty minutes of contact every four hours for feeding). When the infants were one month old, the mothers who had had early and extended contact stayed closer to their infants, made eye contact more often, and soothed and fondled their infants more. When the infants were one year old, these same differences persisted. And, when the children were two years old, the mothers in the early contact groups showed a different pattern of verbalization, using fewer commands, twice as many questions, and more adjectives.

In a critical examination of what he described as carefully controlled studies of parent-infant bonding, Siegel (1982) concluded that early contact between parents and their infants, even if it is not supplemented with extended contact, has favorable effects on parental feelings about the infants in the days after birth. These findings are consistent even among various socioeconomic and cultural groups. Siegel also concluded that there are significant intermediate-term positive effects from this early contact: a longer duration of breast feeding; increases in maternal behaviors like making eye contact, smiling, kissing, and vocalizing; and changes in such infant behaviors as responsiveness and alertness. According to Siegel, research findings on the long-term effects of early contact are not conclusive because of the confounding influence of other variables.

The research of Klaus, Kennell, and others was positively received by many parents and medical people and led to the creation of a task force, which made recommendations in 1978 that were endorsed by the American Hospital Association. These recommendations specifically encouraged breast feeding and handling of the infant by parents right after delivery. The recommendations resulted in a gradual process of hospital reform of maternity practices. It is now possible in many hospitals for parents to request and receive time with their newborns right after birth. Observations of parents and infants at first meeting show that parents interact with and get to know their infants in three primary ways: (1) by touching with fingertips and then palms, (2) through eye-to-eye contact, and (3) by talking in a higher-pitched voice than usual (Klaus and Kennell, 1982).

But what about parents like Mary and Jose who are unable to interact with their infants immediately after birth? If parents miss the "right" time for bonding, have they lost an opportunity forever? The response to these questions is an emphatic *NO!*

Klaus, Kennell, and others have been very clear in saying that humans are too resilient and complex to be governed in bonding strictly by the timing set by hormones, as are some other animals. The moments after birth seem to be a good time to begin parent-infant contact, but factors such as Caesarean births and premature or stressed infants sometimes make that particular timetable unworkable. All parents, but especially those who cannot interact with their infants right after birth, need to be told that bonding is *not* a simple, adhesive joining, but is instead the result of a dynamic process of interaction that begins during pregnancy and continues in the days after birth. Parents need to know that prior experiences, such as the acceptance of the pregnancy and thinking of the fetus as an individual, and contact with the infant *together* determine bonding.

Bonding with High-Risk Infants

Families whose infants are preterm, ill, or handicapped need special help in forming bonds with their infants. In the past decades it has become clear that problems in family relationships frequently occur when infants are at risk at birth. Space-age technology has progressed to the point at which the lives of preterm or ill infants can be saved in intensive care nurseries, but if their families are not given appropriate help, some of these infants return to the hospital weeks, months, or even years later as battered children (Klaus, Leger, & Trause, 1982). The problem of forming family relationships when infants are at risk is an important one: children who are abused are twice as likely as the general population to have been preterm infants (Helfer, 1982).

Traditionally, infants at risk have been "untouchable" in that they have been whisked away to intensive care nurseries and connected to life-support systems there. Parents and other family members have felt like outsiders. But, in studying families of infants at risk, research has found that early parent-infant

---

BOX 4.3

THE "MYSTIQUE" OF BONDING

A pediatrician friend, Mildred Wilhelm, feels strongly that exaggerated claims made on behalf of bonding have caused parents in her practice two types of problems. The first problem is encountered by parents who have read about bonding and interpret the process as being totally biological— as simple, narrow, and stereotyped as what happens when goat and kid first meet. These parents worry excessively that, if a Caesarean birth or other circumstance interferes with bonding, their relationship with their infant may be permanently impaired. In helping these parents, Dr. Wilhelm cites as counterexamples the many parents who have infants under circumstances that do not allow immediate parent-infant contact, but who form close and lasting bonds anyway.

The second problem is encountered by parents who are under stress. These parents may be encouraged by hospital personnel to have early and extended contact with their infants. Dr. Wilhelm is not opposed to this practice, but views it as only the first step in providing the support that will help these parents provide growth-enhancing upbringing for their infants. Dr. Wilhelm believes that some professionals attribute so much magic to the effect of 30 to 60 minutes of early contact that they expect it to provide long-term protection to parent-child relationships buffeted by stress.

Dr. Wilhelm endorses a moderate perspective on bonding. She asserts that early contact is desirable when possible. But she also believes that bonding can and does take place at times before and after those moments following birth. And she thinks that continued support may be necessary to help some parents, even if early contact has been possible.

---

contact in the intensive care nursery positively affects parental behavior which, in turn, has favorable consequences for the child's later development. In one study (Kennell & Klaus, 1971), mothers in one group were encouraged to touch their preterm infants in the first week, but mothers in another group did not touch their infants until twenty-one days had passed. When the children were tested at forty-two months of age, the children of mothers in the early-contact group had significantly higher scores on an intelligence test.

The pediatricians and other health professionals who care for infants at risk find that families go through five predictable stages in learning to relate to the infants (Brazelton, 1982). At first, most families seem able to relate to their ill infants only in terms of medical diagnoses and terminology. Second, they gradually begin to see reflexive behavior but think of it as being directed at someone else, usually a medical person. Third, they begin to see glimpses of what seems like more human behavior, but it still seems directed at someone outside of the family. Some researchers report success at this point in involving volunteers intensively with these infants; the volunteers may spend three or four hours each day with the infants, who then begin to make eye contact, smile, and respond in other ways that cause them to become more appealing to their families (Klaus, Leger, & Trause, 1982). Fourth, family members finally begin to see their infants' responsive behaviors in terms of themselves, if they have received encouragement in involving themselves in their infants' care. And, fifth, the families relate behaviorally as well as verbally to their infants, picking up and otherwise caring for them. Before families take their infants home from the hospital, they need help in working through the five stages of their grief, denial, and fear to become comfortable and involved parents.

The process of bonding between parents and handicapped infants also requires extensive support from hospital and other personnel. As an illustration, considerable media attention has been accorded the story of Phillip Becker, now a teenager, who was born in 1968 with Down syndrome and an accompanying heart defect (Ganz, 1983). Phillip's parents did not take him home after birth but instead chose an institutional upbringing for him. Meanwhile, a family called the Heaths became involved with Phillip through their volunteer work at his board-and-care home. Phillip's parents and the Heath family engaged in a long court battle over his parents' right to keep Phillip institutionalized instead of relinquishing custody to the Heath family. During the litigation, Phillip's parents refused permission for necessary heart surgery for Phillip and indicated in court testimony that they think that it is better for Phillip not to form attachments to them or to other people. The courts ultimately upheld the Heaths' custody, and the case illustrates what can happen when bonding between parent and handicapped child does not take place. Phillip's parents related to him only in terms of abstract parental rights; they did not see him as a human being who could engage the love of the Heath family, the judge, and various caregivers along the way.

Sadly, not all children are born healthy and whole. Helping professionals have the task of facilitating the bonding process between parents and high-risk or handicapped infants. These families often require support as they move through the five stages of relating to their infants.

Special Needs of Fathers and Siblings

Newborns profoundly alter the course of their parents' lives and also influence other lives in families that are likely to include brothers and/or sisters (called **siblings**), grandparents, and others. This section focuses attention on the reactions of two groups of family members who are often forgotten in the interest usually accorded mother and infant at birth—fathers and siblings.

Fathers   Much of the research on bonding has investigated the bonding of mother to child. As recently as 1976, the first edition of Klaus and Kennell's book was called *Maternal-Infant Bonding*. The title of the second edition, *Parent-Infant Bonding* (1982), however, reflects a new interest in the role of fathers in child development. In fact, a term for the absorption that fathers have with their newborns, **engrossment**, has been coined. Research has demonstrated that early involvement of fathers with newborns leads to the same positive

Engrossment is the new term coined to describe the intense interest of fathers in their infants.

changes in interaction patterns over time that were found with early involvement of mothers (Klaus & Kennell, 1982).

Becoming a father requires considerable adjustment, as was discussed in Chapter 3. When a man becomes a father for the first time, his concerns center on the added financial and other responsibilities of a child, changes in his relationship with his wife, health of mother and child, and unknown aspects of the new role. When a man already has children, he usually feels added anxiety about how another child will fit into the family and how the sibling(s) will react. Fathers of newborns may need attention paid to their needs as they assume new roles in the expanded family.

Siblings Research indicates that concern about sibling relations is well founded. The least joyful response to the arrival of a new infant is often from the sibling(s). In fact, the birth of an infant can be one of the most stressful experiences of the early childhood years. Troubling reactions to the birth of an infant may include strenuous efforts to get attention from parents and others; regression in eating, sleeping, toileting, or other behaviors; and aggression toward parents and/or the infant. The intensity of any negative behavior seems to vary by age, with negative reactions found in 89 percent of children under three years, but in only 11 percent over six years, and by gender of the new infant, with infant brothers causing more negative reactions than sisters (Trause & Irvin, 1982).

Helping siblings cope with the arrival of a new infant requires first of all an understanding of the sources of stress and worry. For young children, separation from their mothers during birth and the subsequent period of hospitalization is disruptive of established routines, and is worrisome even when the children are prepared for the separation by careful explanation. A study of separations for childbirth suggests that the distress of young children can be significantly reduced by having the children visit mother and infant in the hospital at least one time (Trause & Irvin, 1982). In recognition of the need for contact, some hospitals conduct parties in honor of the siblings whose mothers have just given birth: siblings and parents join to celebrate the arrival of a new family member.

**BOX
4.4**

HELPING SIBLINGS ADJUST TO NEWBORNS

Parents can help their older child adjust to the birth of an infant by following these suggestions:

□   Talk with the older child about the needs and desires of the infant;
□   Include the older child in making decisions about the infant;
□   Interpret the infant's actions and reactions for the older child; and
□   Call attention to the infant's interest in the older child.

In an interesting study (Dunn and Kendrick, 1982), researchers showed that children of parents who followed these suggestions had more harmonious relationships fourteen months after an infant's birth than did children whose parents had not. When these suggestions were followed, firstborn children averaged 26.7 friendly advances to the infants (per 100 ten-second observation units) and the infants averaged 26.8 friendly advances to their older siblings. In contrast, in families in which these suggestions were not followed, the comparable figures were 11.1 friendly approaches from firstborn children to infants and 14.4 from infants to firstborn children.

This study also showed differences in the likelihood that firstborns would join mother-infant interactions in a friendly way. In cases in which parents had followed these suggestions, the average friendly joining of interactions was 19 percent, as compared with only 8 percent if these suggestions had not been followed.

This study indicates that parents can positively influence the relationships of siblings by using suggested language patterns and including older children in the responsibility of caring for infants.

Involving siblings in the care of a newborn can ease the adjustment process.

The second major source of anxiety for siblings involves possible changes in their relationships with parents when a new infant arrives. One troubled six-year-old demanded to know why his parents would want an additional child if he, the first, had been entirely satisfactory. Research reveals a basis for the rejected feelings that older siblings sometimes have. Studies document mothers' usage of more angry commands with their older children in the weeks after the birth of a new infant than before childbirth, and also a decrease in expressions of warmth toward older children after the birth of an infant (Trause & Irvin, 1982). Many mothers are fatigued after childbirth, and the roles of other adults therefore become important in helping older siblings make a satisfactory adjustment, both to temporary separation from the mother and to arrival of the infant in the family. The father or other adults can provide continuity and emotional support at a time when both may be needed by the siblings.

Birth and the days following represent a new beginning for mother, father, infant, siblings, and important others. Together they encounter the challenges and rapid changes that are to come.

SUMMARY

1. Childbirth culminates months of prenatal development.
2. The birth process or period of labor is divided into three stages: opening of the cervix, delivery of the infant, and delivery of the placenta.
3. Newborns are assessed right after birth by computing Apgar scores, which show how well the infant is adjusting to the stress of delivery and the need to breathe independently.
4. Another assessment, the Brazelton Neonatal Behavioral Assessment Scale, shows infant reactions to a variety of situations.
5. Unique characteristics of newborns from particular cultures influence the reactions of their parents and vice versa.
6. Bonding, the complex tie from parent to infant, is influenced by prior experiences and contact with the infant.
7. Families with preterm, ill, or handicapped infants may need special help in forming bonds with their infants.
8. Fathers' absorption with their newborns, *engrossment,* positively influences future interactions.
9. Siblings have special needs after the birth of an infant.

KEY TERMS

labor	Brazelton scale	siblings
cervix	bonding	engrossment
Apgar score		

FOR FURTHER READING

Bonding

Klaus, M. H., & Kennell, J. H. (1982). *Parent-infant bonding* (2nd ed.). St. Louis: C. V. Mosby.

Smeriglio, V. L. (Ed.). (1981). *Newborns and parents: Parent-infant contact and new-born sensory stimulation.* Hillsdale, NJ: Lawrence Erlbaum.

Sibling Relationships

Lamb, M. E., & Sutton-Smith, B. (Eds.). (1982). *Sibling relationships: Their nature and significance across the lifespan.* Hillsdale, NJ: Lawrence Erlbaum.

Explaining Birth to Children

Stein, S. B. (1974). *Making babies: An open family book for parents and children together.* New York: Walker.

II

The First Year of Life

Four alert, healthy infants wait in a pediatrician's reception area.

Newborn Agnes sucks on a pacifier and gazes intently at her father's face. The movement of her body slows as she centers her attention on his words, sounds, and movements. The interlude soon ends, however, when a five-year-old slams the nearby door. Agnes gives a startled reaction and cries vigorously.

Four-month-old Ted sits on his grandmother's lap. He alternately plays with his wiggling bare toes and watches the antics of some older block builders. When the tower of blocks collapses, Ted wrinkles his brow at first but then smiles as the older children go into gales of laughter.

Eight-month-old Justin tries to crawl over to the block area, but he is brought back to his chair by his mother. Justin seems unperturbed by the relocation, waits a moment, and then climbs down and crawls efficiently back to the blocks. At the next crash of the tower, he appropri-ates several blocks, which he carefully lays end to end.

Twelve-month-old Lena rides a rocking horse while making an engine noise: "Rmmmmm, rmmmm!" She laughs and claps when her day-care provider pretends to feed the horse a plastic apple. When she finally tumbles off the horse, she toddles up and down the room, holding on to chairs and knees for support.

The dramatic differences in Agnes's, Ted's, Justin's, and Lena's development are characteristic of infancy. Part II of this book gives detailed information about the changing capabilities of infants during their first year of life. The contents are designed to increase understanding of infant development and generate ideas about how to apply that understanding to make a positive impact on infants.

Much of the information in this part reflects recent research findings. Until the past decades, the development of infants has not been well understood even by specialists in the field. Since infants cannot use words to tell adults what they see, hear, or feel, their psychosocial, physical, and cognitive development has been more a matter of conjecture than fact. Now, however, through the use of innovative techniques of investigation, more is understood about the fascinating ways in which infants interact, grow, and learn.

This part is divided into three chapters, devoted respectively to information about psychosocial, physical, and cognitive development. Throughout all three chapters, research on cultural variables in child development is explained. Ideas about applications are included in boxes.

Psychosocial development is described first because it is fundamental in determining the quality of an infant's life. Within Chapter 5, attention is given to the importance of a basic sense of trust, of communication between adults and infants, of secure attachments, and of social understanding. The effects of the infant's temperament and of alternate family structures are also explored.

Physical development is described in Chapter 6, beginning with new findings about the sensory competence of newborns. Information is then given about reflexes, with an emphasis on the strengths with which infants enter the world. Other topics include levels of alertness, milestones of physical development, crying, and health and safety.

Part II of this book concludes with Chapter 7, which describes cognitive development. The chapter starts with a discussion of the interplay of cognitive with psychosocial and physical development. The theories of Piaget and others on cognitive development are considered, as are the topics of language development, cultural differences in adult interactions with infants, and early intervention programs.

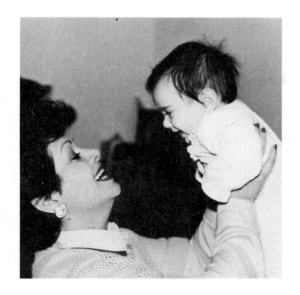

5

Psychosocial Development of Infants

Key Ideas

A Sense of Basic Trust

Parent-Infant Rhythms
Rhythms with Fathers Versus Mothers □
Rhythms in Various Cultures

Attachment
Attachment Phase 1 □ *Attachment Phase 2* □
Attachment Phase 3 □ *Attachment Phase 4* □
Responses to Separation □ *Effects of*
Attachment □ *Negative Reactions to Strangers*
□ *Cultural Differences in Attachment*

Infant Crying

Social Cognition
Origins of Social Understanding □ *Perception*
of Emotions

Temperament

Effects of Parental Employment

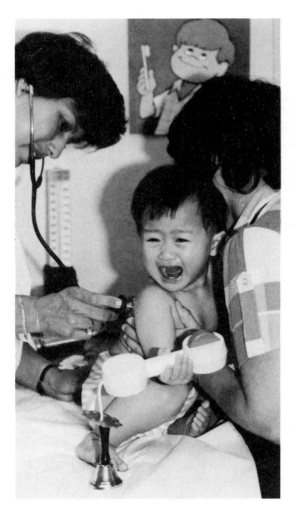

The term *psychosocial* is a shorthand way of talking about traits, feelings, attributes, and interactions. It refers to the ways that individuals feel about themselves and the ways that they relate to other people. According to Erik Erikson, John Bowlby, T. Berry Brazelton, and other experts whose ideas are presented in this section, infants' psychosocial development is of great importance. Later development is influenced by how infants establish a sense of trust, communicate with their parents, form attachments, understand social information, and show characteristics of temperament. The more that is understood about the psychosocial development of infants, the more likely people are to create growth-enhancing environments for infants.

A SENSE OF BASIC TRUST

An infant teeters over the edge of her high chair. Should her reaction to this situation be trust—and a headlong plunge to the floor? Or does this situation require caution, perhaps mistrust?

The terms **trust** and **mistrust** come from the theory of Erik Erikson (1963, 1977, 1982). Erikson built on the thinking of Sigmund Freud, developing his ideas during years of practice in child psychoanalysis. His young patients were brought to him because of their inabilities to cope with interpersonal relationships; by studying their psychosocial development, Erikson created a theory about the challenges that individuals need to meet and resolve in their lives.

According to Erikson, in the first year of life, infants need to establish a sense of trust. This sense of trust develops gradually from the time of birth if the infant's needs for food and comfort are met relatively promptly and consistently. When the infant feels hunger, is appropriate nourishment provided? When the infant is tired, can someone interpret this feeling and allow rest? When the infant is alert, does someone take the time to play? Through it all, does someone give the infant the feeling of being a person who is loved? If the usual answers to these questions are affirmative, the infant is probably developing a sense of trust. Of course, no one is able to respond instantly to every need of any infant, nor do even the most caring individuals always know how to interpret each cry of distress or discomfort. Erikson refers to *typical* responses to infants' needs as being important in establishing a relationship of trust.

In understanding Erikson's theory, it is helpful to imagine a continuum of feelings that ranges from absolute and total trust to absolute and total mistrust. Erikson indicates that interactions with the infant should establish feelings that are toward the trusting end of the continuum. But the sense of trust cannot and should not be total, as in the case of the six-month-old teetering in her high chair. She needs to learn to be cautious—or distrustful—of some situations or circumstances. Busy streets, heights, unsupervised water, and household cleaners are only a few of the things in her environment which she should learn not to trust. In other words, trust *versus* mistrust is not an all-or-nothing resolution but rather a matter of degree of orientation.

Developing a basic sense of trust is the infant's primary psychosocial task during the first year of life, according to Erikson. When adults have responded promptly and in an appropriate manner, infants develop a sense of trust and behave as if adults will be available to them in times of need. That kind of trust characterizes secure relationships. When adult responses have been less predictable or negative, infants show patterns of avoidance and do not turn to them for help when they are under stress.

To understand how some adults create an environment in which basic trust is established, and why others do not, researchers study the mutuality of the parent-infant relationship. Parent responds to infant, infant responds to parent, and both are changed. It is relatively easy to study only the parent or the infant or the rest of the infant's environment. Studying the interrelationships is more accurate but also much more complex. In an attempt to learn more about the dynamic parent-infant relationship, researchers have studied parent-infant rhythms.

PARENT-INFANT RHYTHMS

The term **parent-infant rhythms** refers to the mutual coordination of behavior according to the interest and attention of both people. At first, parents make most of the adjustments as they attempt to sustain interaction with their infants. The details of the adjustments would normally be too subtle and fleeting to be observed by the unaided eye. But painstaking, frame-by-frame analysis of high-speed motion picture film has revolutionized research on early parent-infant interactions by revealing rhythmic changes in expression and behavior in the interactions of parents and infants. Here is what the camera might show as one-month-old Nathan and his mother interact:

The mother turns to face Nathan and their eyes meet. Nathan's eyes widen and his legs and hands move toward her and then gently curl back according to a rhythm. Nathan's eyes are alternately brightly interested and dull or averted. His mother adjusts her pattern to his so that she talks when his interest is high and quiets while he recovers.

Because Nathan goes through four or more interest/recovery cycles in a minute, the film must be viewed in slow motion to see the rhythm of the games that Nathan and his mother play. When Nathan averts his eyes, he signals that he is overstimulated and must have time to recover. Nathan's physiological systems are immature and easily overloaded, so he needs these periodic rests. His mother senses that she must match her reponses to his; and, in this way, she gradually introduces him to new experiences and more complex interactions.

T. Berry Brazelton (1981) and his colleagues at Children's Hospital in Boston are pioneers in the analysis of films of parent-infant interaction. They believe that the parent's ability to achieve a satisfactory rhythm with the infant forms the basis for early communication. Parent and infant experience a rewarding mutuality which is an important step in the infant's development of social skills. This mutuality and the satisfaction of communicating with another

By sensitive response to her three-month-old, this mother is able to engage in an extended interaction.

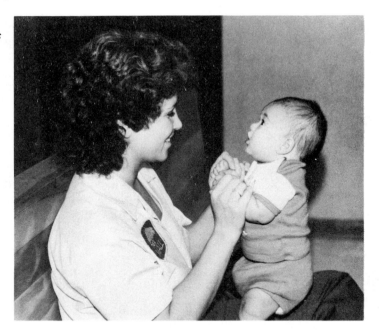

human being are certainly instrumental in the process of developing a sense of trust and attachment.

Rhythms with Fathers versus Mothers

Brazelton's research has demonstrated that infants as young as three or four weeks have different social interaction patterns with different people. Brazelton (1981) has found that infants in two-parent families typically respond to their fathers with movements that are less rhythmic than those they use when they are in interaction with their mothers. Fathers are likely to interact playfully, tickling or bouncing, with heightening excitement. At first the infant's shoulders hunch, eyebrows raise, and movement stops. When movement begins again, it is jerky. As the infant grows, excited laughter accompanies the movements. In contrast, the infant's interactions with the mother involve more cuddling, stroking, and calming gestures and may be more centered on nourishment and other routines. Sometimes mothers feel envious of fathers' ability to communicate "Let's play!" by eye contact and voice tone. In fact, though, the infant is enriched by the variety of interactions that are available. Family members and other important people in the infant's life find ways to communicate, "You are a special person to me." The infant receives these communications and gives differentiated return signals. By the time infants are three weeks of age, they show such different kinds of interactions with their mothers and fathers that observers can view videotapes of the infant's movements and tell immediately whether mother or father was present (Brazelton, 1981).

Rhythms in Various Cultures

When parents and infants from different cultural groups are observed, different rhythmic patterns are apparent. For example, white, black, and Navajo mothers and their three-to-five-month-old infants were videotaped in face-to-face inter-action. Each mother was instructed to obtain her infant's attention in whatever way she wished. The mothers from the three groups had distinctive patterns of interactions with their infants. The white mothers used vocal rhythm to entice the infant into interaction. If the infant did not respond, the mothers paused and then returned to the vocal rhythms, which sometimes seemed to be over-stimulating. Black mothers used similar vocal rhythm, but they continued even if the infant did not respond. If the infants persisted in turning away, black mothers tended to stop the interaction abruptly. Black mothers seemed less intrusive than white mothers, perhaps because they seemed more involved in their own performances. Navajo mothers, in contrast, did not use vocal rhythms to sustain interactions with their infants. Navajo mothers were quieter and seemed to rely on infants' capacities for self-soothing and self-regulating (Fajardo & Freedman, 1981).

The differences found in this study correspond with patterns of behavior of newborns from each of these groups. Evidence suggests that white newborns are more irritable and have a lower tolerance for stimulation, black newborns are less irritable and have a higher tolerance for stimulation, and Navajo new-borns are the least irritable and the most capable of organizing their own responses without structuring by the mother (Callaghan, 1981). The fact that infants from different groups seem to show different reactions to stimulation indicates that no one pattern of interaction can be advocated for all (Fajardo & Freedman, 1981).

The universal rule in establishing parent-infant rhythms seems to be the need to observe and follow the infant's cues. Comparable "rules" do not appear to govern the details of interaction, such as the amount or type of vocalization, touching, movement, and distance.

Given the different rhythms in various cultural groups, do parents use these interactions to teach cultural values to infants? To answer this question

This father communicates "Let's play!" by putting his six-month-old in face-to-face position, raising the pitch of his voice, making eye contact, and bouncing him.

**BOX
5.1**

**STRATEGIES FOR FACILITATING DEVELOPMENT:
INTERPRETATION OF INFANT CUES**

The rhythmic parent-infant interactions that have been described would be
graphed in the following manner:

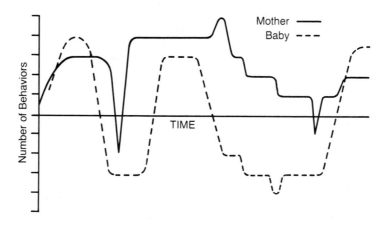

The graph shows that the parent pauses when the infant looks away, allows
time for the infant to recover, and then gently initiates another round of
interaction. In these cases of appropriate parent-infant rhythms, parents
receive rewarding feedback that gives them energy to continue to meet the
demands of parenting. The infants, in turn, establish a gratifying sense of
reciprocity with the environment and gain feelings of competence.

Unfortunately, not all parents seem able to establish appropriate
rhythms with their infants. The following graph shows an interaction in

and others, a study examined the games that parents from four cultural groups
play with their infants (Van Hoorn, 1982). The researcher found that parents
prefer traditional games that are passed on from generation to generation and
are known to others from their cultural group. This finding holds true even for
parents with Chinese, Filipino, and Mexican backgrounds who have lived in the
United States for many years. With such traditional preferences, it is interesting
to find that the games themselves are similar across cultures. Regardless of culture, adult-infant game sessions seem to occur with a single partner at a time.
The adult communicates "this is play" by changes in tone of voice and facial
expression and by actions particular to games. Across cultural groups, games
are characterized by moderate tempo and rhythm, interrelated responses, face-
to-face position, eye contact, position within a foot of each other, and manipulation of the infant's body. The researcher explained the similarities across cul-

which the infant spends most of the time looking away and the parent lacks sensitivity in "reading" this cue to reduce stimulation:

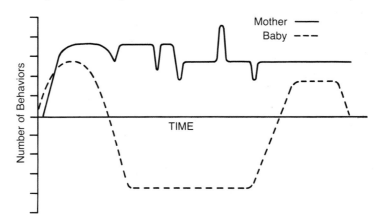

Left on their own, these parents may reject their infants because they do not find a "fit" in their interactions. One such parent said, "I never could reach him."

T. Berry Brazelton (1979), whose research is the source of these graphs, believes that professionals have a responsibility to assess parent-infant rhythms. Professionals could then volunteer support to parents who need help in interpretation of infant cues.

Graphs from "Behavioral Competence of the Newborn Infant" by T. B. Brazelton, 1979, *Seminars in Perinatology, 3,* pp. 35–44. Copyright 1979 by Grune & Stratton, Inc. Reprinted by permission.

tures of infant games by hypothesizing that the purpose of infant games is not so much to communicate cultural values as to communicate human values, such as trust, as described above, and attachment, a concept to be explained in the following section.

ATTACHMENT

Attachment refers to strong bonds of affection directed toward particular people, usually those who are veiwed as stronger or wiser. Attachment theory was first proposed to psychologists and later refined by John Bowlby (1958, 1982). Attachment theory describes both the tendency of humans to want to be close to preferred individuals, and the emotional distress and personality disturbance that can result from unwilling separation or loss of these special people.

In many family situations that researchers have studied, the mother is the first person with whom infants form an attachment. Cross-cultural studies (Ainsworth, 1967) have found evidence of attachment in the following kinds of behaviors of infants toward mothers during the first year of life: crying when held by a stranger but not when held by mother, more frequent smiling and vocalizing with mother than with a stranger, turning and looking at mother when near her, protest and attempts to follow mother if she leaves, body contact with mother, greeting of mother when she returns, and exploring the environment when mother is present as a secure base. Bowlby has described the development of these behaviors.

According to Bowlby's theory, infants form attachments primarily by having personalized contact with adults and not just by being fed and physically cared for. Evidence of the importance of contact is found in a classic series of experiments with rhesus monkeys (Harlow and Zimmerman, 1959; Harlow, 1961). In these experiments, infant monkeys were removed from their mothers at birth and were provided with two types of model mothers, one made of wire and the other covered with soft cloth. The infants were fed from a bottle which could be placed in either model mother. By setting up the experiments in this way, the effects of food could be separated from the effects of having something comfortable to hold onto. In all experiments, infant monkeys developed attachment to the cloth model mother. For instance, infant monkeys spent an average of fifteen hours a day clinging to the cloth model, but only one or two hours with the wire model, even when their food came only from the wire model mother (Harlow and Zimmerman, 1959).

Bowlby (1982) delineated four phases in the development of attachment in human infant, with no sharp boundaries between the phases. Description of these phases is followed by discussion of responses to separation, effects of attachment, negative reactions to strangers, and cultural differences in attachment.

Attachment Phase 1

The first phase lasts from birth to until eight or twelve weeks of age. During this phase, infants behave in certain characteristic ways toward people. They turn toward people in their vicinity, follow people with eye movements, smile, vocalize, and often cease crying when people are nearby. Each of these behaviors is attractive to most adults and causes adults to want to spend time near infants.

In phase one, infants have been believed to have limited ability to tell one person from another. There is evidence from recent research, however, that newborns may be able to recognize their mothers' voices (DeCasper and Fifer, 1980). Researchers played tape recordings of newborn infants' mothers and other mothers reading Dr. Seuss's book, *To Think That I Saw It On Mulberry Street.* Meanwhile, the infants sucked on an ingenious nipple that allowed researchers to find out infants' reactions to the voices. The infants did not get liquid in return for sucking. Instead, their sucking triggered either their mother's voice or another voice. The infants learned to shorten or lengthen the interval between bursts of sucking in order to evoke their own mothers' voices.

Attachment Phase 2

The second phase lasts until about six months of age. In this phase, infants continue to show friendly interest in people who are around. The main change from phase one is that infants begin to differentiate their responses. Infants are noticeably more enthusiastic in interactions with the person to whom they are forming their primary attachment. In traditional literature, the primary attachment was assumed to be with the mother. But, in these changing times, an infant's primary attachment may be to father, grandparent, or some other person.

Attachment Phase 3

Phase three usually begins at six or seven months of age and continues through the second year of life. The onset of this phase is delayed if there has not been one consistent person in an infant's life, as is sometimes the case in institutions or with frequent changes in foster care. During phase three, children become increasingly discriminating in the way in which they interact with people. They show continuing strong interest in the primary attachment figures, by following, greeting, and using these people as a base from which to explore. They include other people in subsidiary attachments, but strangers are treated with increasing caution and sometimes alarm.

Attachment Phase 4

The fourth phase begins after a child's second birthday. In this phase, children develop a greater understanding of the goals and plans of the adults to whom they are attached. Their behavior becomes more flexible, and they are able to develop more complex relationships, even partnerships, with adults.

Responses to Separation

Researchers have found some consistent patterns of responses when children in Bowlby's third or fourth phases are separated from the adults to whom they are attached. At first, children usually **protest** strongly. For as much as several days, children cry and storm for the return of their special person. Then they fall into **despair**. They become quieter but still preoccupied with the absent person. Hope seems to fade. Sometimes protest and despair alternate, but eventually, children enter a period of **detachment**. They seem to forget the special person and may not appear to recognize that person when they are reunited. During all these three phases, the child experiences what seem to be unrelated tantrums and episodes of destruction.

How children respond when reunited after a separation from an attachment figure depends on whether they are experiencing protest, despair, or detachment. The reunion is the most difficult if children have entered the period of detachment. If so, children can be unresponsive for days or even weeks after reunion. When the detachment ends, children often show intense clinging and rage if left. Children demonstrate their anger at being deserted and yet their strong need for the person's presence, according to Bowlby. This ambivalence comes about as part of the grieving process that children undergo when they are separated against their will.

Effects of Attachment

Researchers have found that they can set up laboratory situations that successfully identify infants who have formed strong attachments and infants who have not. Moreover, researchers have been able to predict future behavior from differences in attachment.

Researchers study attachment by placing an infant and the child's special person into a room that is equipped with toys. A stranger enters and interacts with the infant, first in the adult's presence, and then in his or her absence. Meanwhile, unseen observers (usually on the other side of a one-way-vision mirror) record the reactions and interactions. The laboratory conditions are so standard that they are referred to as the ''strange situation'' in the research literature (Ainsworth & Bell, 1970).

Infants' behavior in the strange situation depends on the way they have been treated in the previous months and on the strength of attachment to the adult present in the strange situation. When adults have behaved positively and consistently, infants turn to them for security in a strange situation. When adults have been negative or inconsistent, infants avoid them or show ambivalent patterns in a strange situation.

Behavior in the strange situation during infancy has been found to have value in predicting the future behavior of children. Research has demonstrated that the patterns of communication established early in life have long-range consequences for interactions with those attachment figures and with other people. For instance, in a longitudinal study, it was found that infants who were securely attached at twelve months of age, in comparison to those less securely attached, were significantly more compliant and cooperative with other adults with whom they interacted at twenty-one months of age (Londerville & Main, 1981). Another study reported that infants who were securely attached to a parent at twelve months of age were rated as more competent socially in preschool two years later (Lamb, Thompson, Frodi, 1982). And researchers have also reported that securely attached infants are more enthusiastic, happy, and persistent in problem-solving situations.

Negative Reactions to Strangers

The development of negative reactions to strangers follows the general pattern of development of attachment to certain individuals. Infants in Bowlby's first phase of attachment show no differences in their reaction to familiar people and to strangers. In phase two, infants initially respond positively to familiar people but not as positively to strangers. Then, there is a period of four to six weeks during which infants sober at the sight of a stranger and stare. Finally, at about eight or nine months of age, infants show behavior typical of fear. They move away from the stranger, cry, and change facial expression. These behaviors are sometimes called **stranger anxiety**.

Stranger anxiety is influenced by various factors, such as how much experience the infants have had with other adults and individual differences in infants. Attributes of the stranger also modify the negative reaction. Small adults, such as midgets, and infants are perceived less negatively than are larger or older strangers. And a quiet, slow approach of a stranger is preferred to a loud, rapid approach (Reed & Leiderman, 1981).

When negative stranger reactions become significant depends on the definitions used. If crying is used as the distinguishing criterion, negative stranger reactions become significant at ten months of age. But when all kinds of negative responses are observed and combined, wariness of strangers is present in 23 percent of infants at eight months, 35 percent at nine months, and 59 percent at ten months. On the other hand, only 10 to 15 percent of five- through seven-month-old infants show negative reactions. It is important to note that only 14 percent of the ten-month-olds showed what can be labeled as extreme distress (Waters, Matas, & Sroufe, 1975). Wariness of strangers is certainly not universal at any age, and discussion of it sometimes overshadows the positive, gregarious interest that infants have in others.

This eleven-month-old shows "stranger anxiety" typical of attachment phase three: moving away from the stranger and toward her parent, crying, and showing a fearful facial expression.

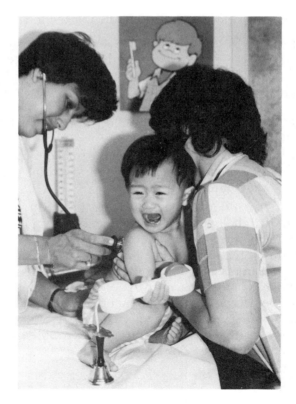

Cultural Differences in Attachment

Are attachment patterns different in different cultures? Should the same behaviors be expected in a large extended family as in a small nuclear family? Researchers have observed cultures in which many adults interact with infants, and have found that the development of attachment follows a pattern similar to that observed in cultures in which few adults interact regularly with infants (Reed & Leiderman, 1981). These researchers suggest that attachment is deter-

---

BOX 5.2   **STRATEGIES FOR FACILITATING DEVELOPMENT: MANAGEMENT OF SEPARATIONS**

Jimmie Peters is already behind schedule in getting to work. Anticipating that his seven-month-old will fuss, he slips away while the alternate caregiver greets the infant.

Is this an effective strategy? Thinking about basic trust, attachment, and stranger reactions, the response to this question is clearly negative. The father may avoid a scene at that moment, but he arouses the infant's suspicions that he is going to disappear whenever he is momentarily out of sight. A preferable approach, then, is the following:

1   Try to let the infant become familiar with the new person (and new place, if care is outside the home) before it is necessary to leave the infant.

2   Be sure that the alternate caregiver is familiar with the infant's routine and preferences.

3   If the infant gains comfort from a special blanket or toy, have that available.

4   Let the infant know when the time of departure arrives. Establish a routine pattern (e.g., hug, kiss, warm goodbye) that precedes the departure.

Then depart—knowing that the infant will probably cry momentarily but that the transition has been made as smoothly as possible.
With an older infant, parents can verbalize about the time of return in terms of the infant's schedule (e.g., "I'll be back after nap time.").

Parents can prepare their infants for separations by carefully handling the many momentary separations within the home. When an infant protests as the parent leaves the room briefly, the parent can continue talking to the infant to keep constant voice contact. A parent's sensitive approach to these many short separations gradually builds the child's confidence that the parent always does come back.

mined by an interaction of behaviors exhibited by infants from the time of birth and the responses of adults to these behaviors. As partial evidence, researchers point to the fact that, in all cultures studied, infants have developed and show strong attachments by about nine to eleven months of age.

INFANT CRYING

Crying is the means by which infants communicate their needs. Crying is extremely effective: when adults hear an infant in distress, they do everything they can to soothe and comfort. Because crying is so unsettling to adults, they have considerable concern when their most conscientious efforts do not diminish it. Then at the next episode of crying, adults often wonder whether they should respond to it or ignore it. Some interesting research on crying lends insights to appropriate action.

Susan Crockenberg (Crockenberg & McClusky, 1982) studied the ways in which infant temperament is interrelated with mothers' attitudes about crying and spoiling. She found that some infants fuss and cry more during the first days after birth; these infants continue the same patterns throughout the first months of life and might be described as having a "difficult" pattern of temperamental characteristics. Their crying is not caused by the mothers' attitudes, and mothers or other primary caregivers of these infants need support from family members or others because infants who cry a great deal take considerable time and attention.

Even though mothers' attitudes do not cause the initial patterns of crying, adult attitudes and actions affect future developments. Parents who respond promptly to crying and engage the infants in frequent interaction gradually find that their infants cry less than infants of parents who believe that they spoil their infants by responding when they cry.

Sometimes it may seem that infants cry most of the time. Researchers (Bell and Ainsworth, 1972) have found a consistent average of about four fussing or crying spells per hour throughout the first year of life. But the amount of time spent in crying changes over this period. In the first three months of life the average amount of time spent in crying is just under eight minutes per hour; in contrast, in the last three months of the first year, an average of only four minutes per hour is spent in fussing or crying.

These researchers also noted the effects of early responsiveness to an infant's crying. They found that the infants who cry and fuss the most after three months of age are the ones whose parents did not respond to their early crying or did so only after a delay. When infants learn that adults meet their needs, they seem to be able to find a variety of ways to communicate other than by crying.

Infants respond best to certain kinds of comforting. In the first three months, infants are soothed best by picking them up and holding them. The next most useful strategies are feeding and giving a pacifier or toy. By the last quarter of the first year, however, infants are comforted by having a familiar adult nearby and attentive.

*When parents respond
promptly to crying, infants
gradually cry less than if they
had been left to "cry it out."*

SOCIAL COGNITION

Social cognition is defined as the way individuals understand and perceive other people. Until recent decades, infants were rarely included in studies of social cognition because it was assumed that they simply acted and reacted. Now, however, researchers credit infants with having a more constructive role in social interactions. Accordingly, the study of infant social cognition has expanded to explore the reasons *why* infants behave as they do. This section presents some recent findings about the origins of social understanding and about the ability of infants to interpret the emotions of others.

Origins of Social Understanding

Michael Lamb (1981) has traced the origins of social understanding to the first months of life. Infants show distress by crying, and, if adults respond by picking up the infants to relieve their distress, important social learning can take place. Often an infant who is picked up and soothed moves into a state of quiet alertness and looks intently at the adult. Simultaneously the infant hears the adult's voice and experiences touch and unique odors. Repetitions of a sequence of distress followed by relief allow infants to develop nonverbal concepts of the adults who respond to them. They also learn that distress predictably leads to relief—what Erikson meant by basic trust.

Infants' sociability is enhanced in three ways when the distress-relief sequence is predictable. First, infants are able to form expectations concerning adults' responses. Second, adults begin to establish positive relationships with infants by helping them move from unpleasant distress to pleasant calmness. And, third, infants gradually gain a sense that they are effective individuals who can exert partial control over their experiences by summoning adult relief. This sense of effectiveness is a critical early cornerstone of self-concept.

Lamb (1981) has asserted that infants' social understanding is relatively sophisticated and complicated by the time they reach one year of age. Because social understanding develops as a consequence of each infant's particular experiences, infants vary widely in their expectations of people.

Perception of Emotions

During the first year of life, infants become more sensitive to and perceptive about the facial expressions of the people around them. Campos and Stenberg (1981), for instance, report on research that designates three levels in the reactions of infants to information from facial expressions. The first level extends from birth to three months of age and is characterized by similar reactions to all facial expressions. Researchers report that infants at this age are as likely to smile at angry as at friendly faces. Some researchers speculate that the tendency of young infants to respond positively to faces, regardless of expression, might be adaptive in the sense that it helps in the development of secure attachments.

The second level extends from three to seven months. At the second level, infants begin to be able to discriminate some facial expressions from others. Research has shown that infants at this age can distinguish surprise from sadness and happiness, joy from anger and neutral expressions, and fear from happiness.

The third level begins at seven months of age and is differentiated from the second in the following way: infants now not only discriminate facial expressions but also react in different emotional ways to them. For example, infants in the last part of the first year respond with more negative emotion to angry and sad faces than to happy and neutral ones.

The developmental sequence presented by these researchers indicates that infants can recognize and act on information about the emotions of other humans. Well before their first birthdays, infants are attuned to the emotions of people who interact with them.

TEMPERAMENT

Temperament is an individual's unique way of dealing with people and situations. Referring to characteristics of temperament, parents and others are often heard making comments such as the following:

"She's never still—the most active child I've ever seen."

"I could set the clock by his hunger."

"He's a real ray of sunshine."

"She adapts so well to our changing schedules."

From birth, infants show distinctive differences in characteristics of temperament.

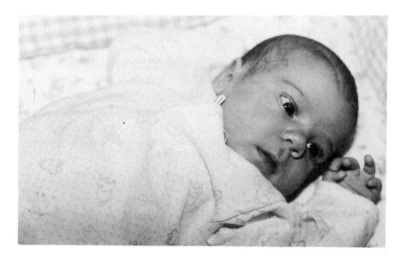

Is there any scientific basis for attributing such characteristics to infants? Are these characteristics consistent over time? According to the New York Longitudinal Study (Thomas & Chess, 1981), there are distinct characteristics of temperament that can be observed soon after birth. The New York Study, which began in the late 1950s and still continues, has observed infants from birth through adulthood. The researchers assert that there is consistency of temperament over the years.

The New York Longitudinal Study has identified nine categories of temperament. The temperamental characteristics of a particular infant vary independently of each other. That is, in each category, a given infant's temperamental characteristics may fall anywhere within a range. The categories are listed below.

1   *Activity level.* Some infants do not seem to move around very much. They can be covered up at nap time and will still be covered when they awaken. Infants who are very active, on the other hand, never seem to rest. An active infant might already push her whole torso up with her arms even in the first days after birth.

2   *Regularity.* Some infants fall into a fairly regular schedule by the second or third week of life. They seem to be hungry at regular times, to sleep in a certain pattern, and to have bowel movements at similar intervals. Other infants are predictable only in their unpredictability.

3   *Approach or withdrawal.* At first almost all experiences are new for infants, and this category refers to an infant's typical initial response to new situations. The "approaching" infant is agreeable about experiences such as the first bath at home. The "withdrawing" infant may actually physically pull back from the bath; considerable coaxing is necessary for this type of infant.

4   *Adaptability to change.* When the routine changes in some way (e.g., new formula, a vacation schedule), some infants adjust without apparent effort.

Others do not modify their routines easily; these infants need ample time and a gradual approach in order to make any transition.

5   *Level of sensory threshold.* Some infants can sleep when their brothers are arguing, ignore being wet, overlook movement of the crib, and continue sleeping when a light is turned on. These infants have a high sensory threshold, which means that they are less sensitive in all ways than infants who have a low sensory threshold. The latter awaken with the arguing or movement or light and may scream in discomfort over a wet diaper.

6   *Positive or negative mood.* Positive infants spend much time in behaviors such as smiling and cooing as soon as they learn how. Negative infants spend proportionately more time in behaviors such as fussing and crying.

7   *Intensity of response.* This category describes the energy with which the other responses occur. One infant might be described as being very intense—either happy or upset with gusto. He spit out his first taste of carrots. Another infant of milder temperament let carrots he did not like just trickle down his chin.

8   *Distractibility.* Some infants, even if they are sensitive, continue in their feeding or other activity in proximity to many sights and sounds; these infants are not easily distracted. Distractible infants shift their attention at the first noise or stirring.

9   *Persistence.* The persistent infant continues to suck on a nipple that may be partly plugged or will pay attention for a long period of time to a mobile blowing in the breeze. The nonpersistent infant gives up on the slow nipple and attends only briefly to the mobile.

From these nine categories of temperament, the researchers from the New York Longitudinal Study have identified various patterns (Thomas & Chess, 1981). Identifying infants according to three of these patterns helps in predicting whether parents will feel a need for professional help: (1) regular/easy/positive, (2) difficult/irregular, and (3) slow to warm up/likely to withdraw in

Some infants are more easily distracted than others by nearby sights and sounds.

new situations. If most parents were ordering an infant according to specifications of temperament, would they choose an infant with pattern one, two, or three? With which kind of infant would it be easiest to form an attachment?

For years researchers studied communication patterns and social development in infancy primarily from the perspective of the behavior of adults

---

BOX 5.3   **STRATEGIES FOR FACILITATING DEVELOPMENT: IDENTIFICATION OF AND RESPONSES TO PATTERNS OF TEMPERAMENT**

Regular/easy/positive infants   Signal moderately when hungry or satisfied; eat steadily without being easily distracted; regular in patterns of eating, sleeping, and elimination; show interest and pleasure in new experiences.

Infants with this temperament need caregivers who remember their need for attention and stimulation. This kind of infant is so undemanding that it is possible for adult needs to take too much priority.

Difficult/irregular infants   Cry loudly when hungry; reject food when full; eat actively but are easily distracted; irregular in patterns of eating, sleeping, and elimination; refuse new foods or other new experiences; only gradually adjust.

Infants with this temperament need caregivers who are patient and flexible in their responses and who control pressures from visitors or new experiences. These infants may cry a good deal; and caregivers of difficult, irregular infants need assurance that is is not their fault if their best efforts at soothing fail to be effective.

Slow to warm up/likely to withdraw infants   Show moderate reactions; refuse and withdraw from *new* experiences.

Infants with this temperament need caregivers who provide a calm, slow introduction to new experiences. This infant should not be pressured to put her head into the swimming pool or to join the group at the park. Pushing makes this infant balk more, but holding him on your lap gives him a chance to set his own pace.

About 60 percent of infants seem to fall into one of these patterns. The remaining 40 percent have temperaments that combine categories in other ways that are less likely to bring them and their families to the attention of helping professionals.

toward the infant. The findings of the New York Longitudinal Study clearly demonstrate the additional need to observe and note the temperamental predispositions of infants. Those who interact with infants need information about differences in temperament and support in dealing with infants whose patterns are the latter two. Box 5.3 gives information about how to determine patterns of temperament and what to do about them.

EFFECTS OF PARENTAL EMPLOYMENT

The "traditional" family, composed of the nonworking mother, working father, and children, was never as idyllic as it is sometimes portrayed, but statistics show that only 23 percent of U.S. households now fit that pattern (Lamb, 1982). In two-parent families, more and more women are working outside of their homes. In 1980, 43 percent of mothers with children under six years of age were in the labor force (U.S. Department of Labor, 1980). Many people predict that by 1990, over half of these women will be employed.

In single-parent families, the custodial parent is usually employed. This parent, whether female or male, tends to have higher levels of stress and fatigue when the parent is single than occur when another parent is available in the home to take on responsibilities or to participate in day-to-day decisions. When the single parent is a woman, she faces economic pressures stemming from the fact that she is paid less than male workers who have been employed for the same length of time.

The difficulties caused by parental employment patterns lie not in the family nor in the place of employment, but in the interplay between the two. Research (Lamb, 1982) has indicated that employed mothers are more likely to have insecurely attached infants than unemployed mothers. But when the group of employed mothers is divided into two subgroups—those who value work highly and those who value both parenthood and work—it is found that mothers in the second subgroup have infants who are securely attached. Employment *per se*, then, is only one of many factors that influence the course of child development. In fact, in a related study (Farel, 1980) researchers found that the most poorly adjusted children were those whose mothers were not employed outside the home but wished to be.

Whether parents are employed outside the home or not, whether parents live together or not, the infant's development is most significantly affected by the quality of parent-infant interactions and by the quality and consistency of alternate caregiving. Research conducted in Bermuda has demonstrated that differences in the quality of day-care environments influence the language, social, and emotional development of very young children (McCartney, Scarr, Phillips, Grajek, & Schwarz, 1982).

Choosing an alternate caregiving situation is one of the most challenging and difficult decisions that the employed parent makes. Box 5.4 responds to three common questions about infant day care: when, who, and where?

**BOX
5.4**

**STRATEGIES FOR FACILITATING DEVELOPMENT:
INFANT DAY CARE** •

More and more infants are born to single parents or to two employed parents. In these cases and others, there is often the need for day care while parents are at work. In deciding on a child-care arrangement, the three major questions are when, who, and where?

When? Many pediatricians view the period after birth as one of potential stress for parents. Parents are often far away from their own extended families, and there are few societal supports to act as substitutes in helping parents to meet their infants' and their own needs. In addition, until about ten weeks of age, infants' nervous systems predispose them to be very sensitive to tension or stimulation. Infants often react by crying, which can increase parents' sense of frustration and incompetence.

By the third month, infants' systems are more mature. Smiling, cooing, and other behaviors give positive feedback to parents. Many pediatricians therefore recommend that alternate child care arrangements not begin until the end of the third month. The stronger the bond between parent and child, the more positive their long-term relationship is likely to be. If, on the other hand, parent and infant are separated for long periods of the day while the parent still feels unrewarded by any positive feedback from the infant, parents can later feel a sense of competition with alternate caregivers. The competition can be especially strong if "good" behaviors, such as smiling and cooing, are associated with the child-care situation.

Sometimes parents are not able to wait to return to work until mutually rewarding attachment takes place. In these cases, alternate caregivers need to be particularly sensitive to verbal and nonverbal indications of parents' feelings. Alternate caregivers require special training in acting as supports to the parent-infant relationship.

Another consideration in timing involves the period at the end of the infant's first year. Some pediatricians and researchers advise against placement during the height of "stranger anxiety."

Who and where? In most locations, infant day care centers are rare. Most parents' main options for alternate caregiving include either care by a relative or by a family day-care home provider. A family day-care home provider gives care in her own home for four children. Often these homes are licensed by or registered with the state.

By far the most important consideration in choosing a child care arrangement involves the personal and professional characteristics of the alternate caregiver:

1   Caregivers should be patient and warm toward children.
2   Caregivers should like and enjoy children, and be able to give and receive satisfaction from what infants give.
3   Caregivers should be energetic, in good health, and not excessively moody or irritable.
4   Caregivers should understand the basic needs of children, including affectional and intellectual needs in addition to physical care.
5   Caregivers must be flexible and understanding of feelings.
6   Caregivers should be acquainted with, accept, and appreciate the children's different cultures, customs, and languages.
7   Caregivers should respect infants and their parents, no matter what their backgrounds or their particular circumstances are.

This alternate caregiver demonstrates patience, warmth, enjoyment of infants, and pride in children's developmental accomplishments—important personal and professional characteristics for this type of work.

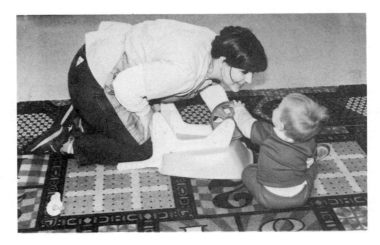

Adapted from "Selection of Staff" (pp. 69–72) by M. Jorn, B. Persky, and D. S. Huntington, in *The Infants We Care For,* (rev. ed.), edited by L. S. Dittman, 1984, Washington DC: National Association for the Education of Young Children. Copyright 1984 by the National Association for the Education of Young Children. Adapted by permission.

SUMMARY

1. Psychosocial development is fundamental in determining the quality of an infant's life.
2. According to Erik Erikson, basic trust can be established if infant needs for food and comfort are met promptly and consistently.
3. Parent-infant rhythms in communication vary according to the gender and culture of the parent.
4. John Bowlby showed that attachment of infants to adults begins with undifferentiated interest in all people and develops through four phases to differentiated preference for a small number of individuals. Prolonged separation of infants from special adults leads to protest, despair and detachment.
5. Early responsiveness to infant crying seems to lead to less crying later.
6. Infants become more perceptive about facial expressions and other aspects of social understanding during the first year.
7. Nine distinct categories of temperament can be observed soon after birth.
8. Parental employment is only one of many factors that influence psychosocial development.

KEY TERMS

trust, mistrust	attachment	social cognition
parent-infant rhythms	protest, despair, detachment	temperament
	stranger anxiety	

FOR FURTHER READING

Attachment

Bowlby, J. (1982). *Attachment and loss* (2nd ed.). New York: Basic Books.
Brazelton, T. B. (1981). *On becoming a family: The growth of attachment.* New York: Delacorte/Seymour Lawrence.
Fraiberg, S. (1977). *Every child's birthright: In defense of mothering.* New York: Basic Books.

Temperament

Chess, S., Thomas, A., & Birch, H. G. (1972). *Your child is a person: A psychological approach to parenthood without guilt.* New York: Viking.

6
Physical Development of Infants

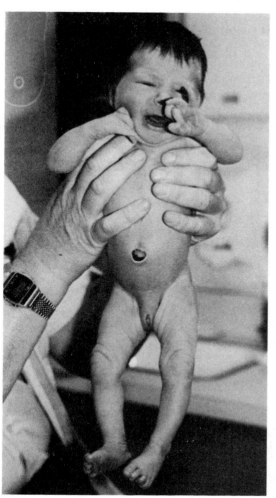

Key Ideas

Sensory Competence of Newborns
Vision □ Taste □ Smell □ Hearing

Reflexes and Competence
Tonic Neck Reflex □ Rooting and Sucking Reflexes □ Burst-Pause Pattern □ Babkin Reflex □ Walking Reflex □ Placing, Babinski, and Grasping Reflexes □ Moro Reflex □ Protective Reactions

Levels of Alertness
Sound Sleep □ REM Sleep □ Alertness

Milestones of Physical Development
The First Three Months □ Three to Six Months □ Six to Nine Months □ Nine to Twelve Months

Nutrition, Health, and Safety
Nutrition and Brain Growth □ Dental Health □ Immunization □ Handicaps, Prematurity, Illness □ Sudden Infant Death Syndrome □ Safety □ Abuse and Neglect

Newborns do not closely resemble the smiling one-year-olds chosen for baby product advertisements. Their heads are large—comprising one-fourth of their body length as compared to one-eighth in adulthood—and their necks are not yet well developed enough to support the weight of their large heads. They have round faces and cheeks, configurations of appearance that may trigger inborn nurturing responses in adults (Brazelton, 1981).

Newborns have a number of distinctive physical characteristics. Their skin tends to be wrinkled and covered with peach-fuzz hair, the lanugo. A white, greasy vernix caseosa has collected on their skin to protect it from the surounding amniotic fluid and to provide lubrication during birth. Their heads may be misshapen because the bones constricted during the birth process to accommodate to the size of the mother's pelvis. Such constricting or molding is possible because of open spaces in the head, called *fontanelles*. During the first weeks of life, the lanugo and vernix caseosa disappear and the head becomes more rounded. The fontanelles usually close in the first two years of life.

Important physiological developments take place during the weeks after birth. Living outside of the uterus requires the infant to breathe air, regulate body temperature, receive and process stimulation, digest food, and eliminate wastes through kidneys and intestines. Because of the importance of developments in the first weeks of life, these weeks have their own designation, the **neonatal period**.

Much change takes place between the neonatal period and an infant's first birthday. This chapter provides an overview of physical development in the first year of life. Attention is given to sensory capabilities; reflexes; various levels of alertness; milestones of physical development; and nutrition, health, and safety.

SENSORY CAPABILITIES OF NEWBORNS

In examining some of the findings about the sensory competence of young infants, special attention is given to the research designs that have increased our knowledge from the level achieved by William James (1890) nearly a century ago. James described the infant psychological state in the following way: "Assailed by eyes, ears, nose, skin, and entrails at once. . . . all is one great booming, buzzing confusion." The description of infants given in this book is radically different from James's.

Vision

One of the most exciting discoveries about infants is that their vision is well developed at birth. When newborns are shown a red or yellow object within about twelve inches, they become alert and gradually focus on it. If the object is slowly moved from side to side, they will follow the object with their eyes and head movements (Brazelton, 1981).

Not only can newborns see, they can also distinguish shapes and patterns. Researchers have found that generally infants will look longer at something they have not seen than they will at something that is familiar. And they will look longer at a flashing light than a steady one, or longer at a pattern of dots than a blank square. Using this information, researchers can find out if infants can tell one shape or pattern from another by measuring how long they look at it. For example, an infant might be shown a screen on which a shape or pattern is projected. She is at first interested and gazes with bright eyes. Then the novelty wears off, her interest wanes, and she glances away or otherwise shows disinterest. At this point, researchers (e.g., Spelke, 1985) say that the infant is **habituated** to (used to seeing) that one shape or pattern. When a second shape or pattern is shown, if she increases gazing time, then that increase reflects a perception that something new is being viewed. If, on the other hand, she looks briefly, it can be assumed that she has not noticed anything novel or new and, therefore, has not seen a difference between the two shapes or patterns.

The principle of habituation has been used to determine that infants as young as two weeks can distinguish their own mother's faces. Infants from one to eight weeks of age were shown the following sights for one minute each at a porthole in the wall: face of mother; face of a female stranger; face of a store manikin; and a flesh-colored colander with knobs for ears and nose. From the second week on, the infants showed that they distinguished their mothers both by their attention time and their behavior. The infants paid proportionately less attention to their mothers than to the other sights in the porthole. Most mothers would not be complimented by hearing this news, but perhaps they would be placated by knowing that it is infants' familiarity with them that explains the difference. Moreover, the infants' behavior seemed to show that the nonresponding and isolated face of the mother was so different from their typical experience that it was disturbing. The younger infants tried to control the situation by looking at the mother's face and then looking away. Older infants fussed, smiled, and cried in an apparent attempt to change the mother's behavior (Carpenter, Tecce, Stechler, & Friedman, 1970).

A great deal of time has been spent trying to find out about infants' visual preferences. What do they like to look at? Fantz (1961) was the first to investigate this question. He showed two-month-old infants six types of disks and found that they stared longer at patterned than plain disks and longest of all at a disk of a smiling face. More recently, Sherrod (1981) presented twenty-six research citations as evidence that infants prefer looking at people to looking at things at all ages; looking at actual faces to looking at drawings of faces by two months; looking at animate faces (moving, talking) to looking at inanimate faces (still, silent) by three months; and looking at familiar faces to looking at unfamiliar faces by five months.

Other vision studies (Bornstein, 1985) have shown that infants not only can discriminate between colors, they can also divide them into categories: blues, greens, yellows, and reds. Four-month-olds were habituated to a color in the middle of the blue wavelength in the spectrum. Then they were shown a color of shorter wavelength that adults would still call blue and a color of longer wavelength that adults would call blue-green. Both of the test colors differed from the first blue by the same number of wavelengths. Infants did not increase their gazing time when shown the second "blue," but they did for "blue-green" and for similar transitional colors within groupings. Researchers

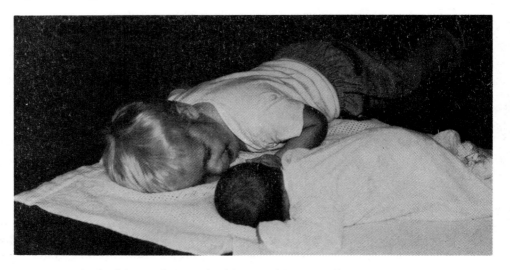

Infants prefer looking at faces to looking at objects at all ages.

therefore assume that infants see the spectrum as divided into color categories even though it is actually continuous. This interesting study raises the question of whether the ability to classify color is natural, later requiring only the adding of the names of the colors (Bornstein, 1985).

Taste

Other senses besides vision are also well developed in newborns. Some aspects of taste, for instance, seem to be as sensitive in newborns as in adults. In one study, one- to three-day-old infants were given varying concentrations of sugar three to five hours after their previous feeding. The four concentrations were put into a bottle with a cleverly designed nipple that measured the sucking patterns of the infants. The researchers found that the average intake pressure on the nipple increased directly with the sweetness of the sugar solutions. Infants can discriminate among different levels of sweetness and prefer the sweetest (Nowlis & Kessen, 1976).

Smell

In an often-cited study, researchers (Lipsitt, Engen, & Kaye, 1963) showed how the sense of smell develops in the first days of life. Under the infants' noses researchers waved cotton swabs that had been treated with seven concentrations of an odor that is offensive to adults. The researchers measured changes in movement or breathing patterns in order to note the reactions of the infants. They found that a 60-percent concentration was needed to get a response from infants on the day after birth. But the concentrations necessary for a reaction diminished from 30 percent on the second day of life, to 15 percent on the third, to 12–13 percent on the fourth. In a related study, Russell (1976) found that breast-fed infants were awakened more quickly by the smell of a cloth worn next to their mother's breast than by the smell of a cloth worn by another breast-feeding mother.

Hearing

Hearing seems well developed at birth, as can be verified by anyone who has held an infant startled by a loud noise. In fact, there are anecdotal reports of infants who seemed after birth to recognize music or other sounds to which they had been exposed before birth. Only recently, however, have researchers begun to understand the complexity of the integration processes that accompany hearing. In one well-designed study, for example, researchers investigated whether two-month-old infants perceived sound rhythms. The researchers used the premise of habituation—that is, if attention decreased to a particular rhythm but was renewed when another was played, the infant had noted the difference. Researchers played three pairs of rhythms and, under all three conditions, infants were skillful in perceiving the differences in rhythmic patterns (Demany, McKenzie, & Vurpillot, 1977). Adults often play rhythmic games with infants or try to soothe them with singing. These research findings explain why these approaches are often successful.

REFLEXES AND COMPETENCE

Reflexes are actions of the infant that are not under voluntary control. Books of this type often discuss reflexes in isolation from other aspects of development, leaving the impression that infants are bundles of undifferentiated reflexes. This book, however, follows the approach of Brazelton (1981), by describing reflexes as part of the competence with which infants approach even their first encounters in the world.

Tonic Neck Reflex

Anyone involved in fencing recognizes the position characteristic of the tonic neck reflex: the face turns to one side and the arm and leg on that side extend away from the body, the body arches away from the face, and the opposite arm and leg flex at the elbow and knee. Newborns can often be observed working very hard to get into this position. The turning of the head triggers the reflex, causing the arm on the side the infant is facing to extend and the opposite arm to flex. Newborns then may work to overcome the reflex and bring a hand to the mouth. Their eyes show an alert seeking of sights and sounds in the environment. Infants are active in wanting to get acquainted with what surrounds them.

Rooting and Sucking Reflexes

Newborns also have strong rooting reflexes, which can be activated by gently touching the cheek around the mouth. Infants turn toward the touch, grasp the finger in their mouths, and start sucking. The strength of the suck is often a surprise to adults, as is the sensation of separate movements of the infant's mouth. Sucking effectively involves the integration of three separate movements: suction from the esophagus, rhythmic movement from the back of the tongue, and up-and-down movement from the front of the tongue. At first, infants need time to coordinate their movements. By the third day, most infants suck efficiently even at the start of a feeding. Exceptions are brain-damaged and premature infants, who take longer to integrate the sucking movements.

Burst-Pause Pattern

Related to the rooting and sucking reflexes is the burst-pause pattern of feeding that most infants have at birth. They suck at first on the breast or bottle quite steadily. But when their initial hunger is satisfied, they move into a pattern of ten to twenty sucks and then a pause. This behavior can be interpreted as a communication used by infants to get a response from adults. During these pauses, most adults move the nipple, jiggle, talk, or touch the infant with the intention of making the infant comfortable and continuing the feeding. Brazelton (1981) studied the length of the pauses of infants under two conditions: when mothers responded and when they did not respond. He found that the infants' pauses were shorter when the mother did not respond. When the mother did respond, infants lengthened the pauses and extended the communication. This study seems to demonstrate that burst-pause sucking is an example of the way a pattern of behavior can help the infant to establish communication.

Babkin Reflex

Another related reflex is called the Babkin. This reflex can be observed when an infant's cheek is stroked. The infant's hand on that side of the body forms a fist and the infant gradually brings it to the mouth. The Babkin reflex can be observed even before birth by physicians who work with ultrasound equipment.

Walking Reflex

Newborns have a walking reflex, even though voluntary walking does not occur until about a year later. The walking reflex can be produced by supporting the infant in a standing position with feet planted firmly on a flat surface such as the couch. Then the infant is bent slightly forward over an adult's hand; gradually the infant will "walk," alternating feet. The infant loses this reflex at about six months of age, when similar but more controlled movements begin to prevail.

Placing, Babinski, and Grasping Reflexes

A placing reflex can be activated by holding an infant upright and stroking the upper part of the foot. The infant will flex from the hip, reach out the foot, and spread and grasp with the toes. A related reflex is the Babinski, bringing about a spreading of the toes when the sole of the foot is stroked. The placing movement can be produced with the infant's hand if the outside of the hand is stroked. With this grasping reflex, an infant can hold onto a finger or object with a surprisingly firm squeeze.

A walking reflex is present from birth until about six months of age.

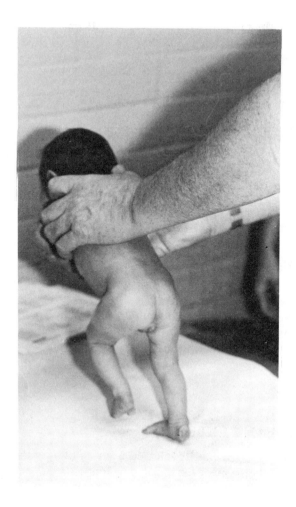

Moro Reflex

Infants also have a startle reflex called the Moro reflex, which is set off if the infant's head falls quickly backwards or if there is some other disruption. In reaction, the infant extends arms and legs and then pulls them back to the body with a hugging motion.

Protective Reactions

From birth, infants instinctively take action to protect themselves from suffocation under a blanket during sleep. When a blanket does cover an infant's face, the infant usually moves the head actively from side to side. If that movement does not dislodge the blanket, the infant brings the arms alternately to the face in order to knock the blanket away.

When adults play with infants to produce these reflexes, or observe infants to see them, the adults gain a sense of the real competence with which infants enter the world. Certainly an infant is helpless when compared with an adult, but an infant is born with surprising ability to guide adult efforts at caregiving with actions and reactions.

LEVELS OF ALERTNESS

Suppose a parent tries to play with his newborn infant and in response the infant closes his eyes tightly. Should the parent feel rejected and unhappy? No, and this father would be helped by an understanding of the different levels of alertness that can be expected in infancy. With this knowledge, he can plan his play times to coincide with the best times in his infant's cycle. The three main parts of the infant's cycle are sound sleep, rapid eye movement (REM) sleep, and alertness.

Sound Sleep

In **sound sleep** the infant is unaware of the sights or sounds of the surrounding environment. Breathing is regular and the eyes are tightly shut. Every so often there is a startled movement, a break in breathing pattern, and then a return to the same deep breathing. If a light goes on or if there is a loud noise, the infant

---

BOX 6.1   **STRATEGIES FOR FACILITATING DEVELOPMENT: INFANT EXERCISE**

Levy (1973) has developed a series of exercises for parents to do with infants in order for parents to learn about infant competency and to feel comfortable with handling their infants. In the first three months, exercises are based on relaxing infants' bodies. From three to six months, exercises prepare infants for the sitting position. And from six to twelve months, exercises include a variety of movements and prepare for standing. The following example is a relaxation exercise:

Position: Put the child flat on his back on a table covered with foam rubber.

Aim: To make the hand open by relaxing the shoulder.
Begin the loosening-up at shoulder level, making regular pats. Progress gently to the hand. Toss the arm gently up and down. When the child has opened his hand, relax the other arm and hand.

Adapted by permission of Pantheon Books, a Division of Random House, Inc. from *The Baby Exercise Books For the First Fifteen Months* (pp. 10–11), by Dr. Janine Levy, translated by Dr. Hermina Benjamin. Copyright © 1973 by William Collins Sons Ltd.

will usually be able to shut it out. Even if disturbed briefly, the infant will go back to sound sleep without really waking. For most infants, then, it is not necessary for adults to tiptoe during their sleeping time. The infant is able to control the amount of noise or light that is received.

Premature infants have shorter and less consistent periods of sound sleep than do mature infants. Premature infants are less able to shut out sights and sounds and are more likely to be disturbed by them. Parents of premature or stressed infants need to provide a more controlled setting for sleep than do parents of full-term infants.

REM Sleep

Rapid eye movement (REM) characterizes a phase of sleep that regularly alternates with sound sleep in newborns, just as is the case in adults. The REM phase of sleep accounts for about sixty percent of total sleep in newborns. During **REM sleep**, infants are more restless and more easily roused than during sound sleep. Gradually, between birth and adulthood, both the amount of REM sleep and its ratio to total sleep diminish.

Alertness

Attractive sights and sounds can help infants to move from sleep to a transitional state to full **alertness**. Adult sensitivity to infants' cues, discussed in connection with psychosocial development, is extemely important in helping infants to attain and maintain alertness. Sometimes in the transitional period, the infant fusses and cries. The crying can discharge energy and then, with comforting of adults, move the infant into alertness. The adults' role is to be soothing and calm, letting the infant be involved in their interaction, but not overloading the infant so that an excessive motor response throws the infant back into a transitional state.

Premature infants or infants with a low sensory threshold have to be handled especially patiently and carefully. These infants may cry and sleep a great deal, as if to shut out the outside world, and parents need to be very gentle in reaching out to communicate with them when they are alert. Over time, these sensitive infants become better able to manage stimulation.

These three parts of the cycle are experienced by infants at intervals throughout each day and night. An adult who observes carefully can choose appropriate play times that will lead to mutually positive experiences.

Parents have a role in helping the infant to organize and define the cycle of sound sleep, REM sleep, and alertness. Brazelton (1981) suggests that the "ideal" adult response is to provide encouragement to the infant, both to extend gratifying periods of alertness and also to extend periods of sound sleep. Sometimes overzealous parents interfere with the infant's organization of these cycles by trying to bring the infant to alertness during periods of REM during the night. But, in order for an infant to sleep for a long period of time at night, which is desired by most parents, the infant needs to learn to handle the REM periods that come regularly between times of sound sleep. Sensitive parents can help their infants to master and extend parts of this cycle by encouraging day-

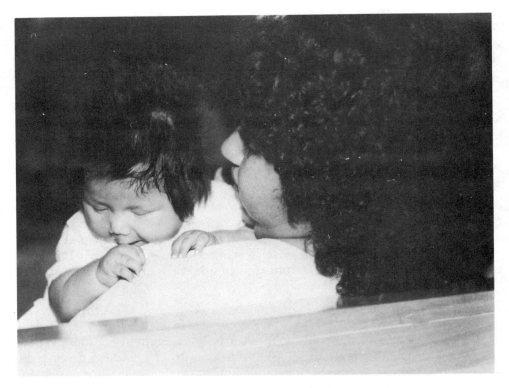

A two-month-old infant moves through a transitional state from sleep to full alertness. The interesting colors of her mother's shirt and the soothing tone of her mother's voice serve to facilitate the transition.

time alertness and by not being too quick to intervene during nighttime REM. To the great relief of parents, the cycle of sound sleep, REM, and alertness becomes increasingly easy to interpret with each month of infancy that passes.

MILESTONES OF PHYSICAL DEVELOPMENT

Many infants are taking their early wobbly steps at about the same time that their first birthday candles are being lighted. It is clear how far they have come when it is remembered that at birth they were not capable of voluntary locomotion.

In no other one-year period until puberty are there so many physical changes. The changes in infancy are measured in terms of days and weeks rather than in terms of months and years.

Physical development has an orderly sequence from the top to the bottom of the infant's body. The infant first gains control over the head, then gradually the arms and body, and finally the legs and feet. This progression from head to toes is called **cephalo-caudal** development. What is gratifying about watching infants gain mastery over their movements is their obvious delight in each milestone. They work hard to accomplish each new feat and then practice repeatedly. Rather than producing boredom, the repetition seems enjoyable. As infants feel successful with one feat, they build their confidence for the next.

To become acquainted with the course of physical development in the first year of life, we will follow the changes in "Anna." Anna is a composite of many infants and the age ranges given for her activities are only averages (adapted from Glover, Preminger, & Sanford, 1978); some infants will do these things earlier and some later. It is important to keep in mind that a wide time variation exists in what is known to be normal development.

The First Three Months

Even in the first hours after birth, Anna has a lively interest in the world. She can distinguish light, dark, and some colors; she prefers simple patterns; and she can use her eyes to follow slowly moving objects. She does all these things best if sights are placed within twelve inches of her. Anna is interested when someone brings a rattle to her or takes her over to look at the wallpaper. She relies on her parents to help her to get to know them and the other things that surround her.

In her first six weeks, Anna's hands are usually held in tight fists when she is awake. Like most infants in the first months, Anna can be induced to use her hands for a strong reflex grasp. Only when she sleeps are her hands sometimes open and relaxed.

When Anna is about four weeks old, she becomes able to lift up her head when she is lying on her front side. She can stay in that position only briefly, but she seems very pleased with the new perspective.

From birth Anna is alert to sounds and seems to like rhythms. In her first weeks of life, Anna smiles in response to her mother's high-pitched voice. At four weeks, her mother can still get her to smile most effectively by talking to her, but Anna also shows her first signs of smiling at someone's face when no words are spoken. Anna seems to scan her parents' and caregiver's faces, make eye contact, and then smile widely. Adults begin to spend even more time playing with her now, although they cannot explain why.

Anna has more control over her hands by the time that she is six weeks of age. She keeps them more open when she is awake, and voluntary grasping movements replace her earlier reflexes. Her father worries that Anna is becoming weak, because for a while she cannot hold on as tightly or for as long as when her grasping was part of a reflex, but he relaxes as he watches Anna learn to bring objects to her mouth. Anna studies, mouths, and amuses herself with these objects, but her parents must be careful that she does not have access to objects that she might swallow.

Anna's world expands when she is six weeks old. Her caregivers notice that she can visually follow the movement of people and things that are several feet away. From the time that she is two and one-half months old, she begins to swing her arms at the activity gym that is suspended just over her crib. When she makes contact and moves it, she seems surprised and pleased.

By two months of age, Anna can lift her head and chest for a longer time when she is on her front side. That increased strength in her neck and back makes it comfortable for her to sit with support in an infant seat or on someone's lap. At three months of age, she looks at everthing around her and definitely wants to be in the hub of family activity. Her body is now uncurled and she shows more movement. When she is looking around, she often kicks her legs.

In her third month Anna is able to locate where sounds originate. Her mother reports that Anna also seems to know what some different adult tones of voice mean.

Three to Six Months

When Anna is four months of age she learns to roll from her front to her back side. The first time she succeeds, she seems surprised. Then she repeats the movement with relish. Her waking-up routine changes after that. Rather than calling her mother by crying, she rolls over from front to back and awakens her mother by the clink, clink of the activity gym above her in the crib. In another month, Anna masters rolling from her back to her front side. Anna enjoys her new freedom and sometimes rolls herself from one part of the room to the other.

Her increased movement now causes her to notice her hands and feet. On her back, she studies her hands and feet and gradually brings their comings and goings under her control.

Anna's father extends his hands to her, and she is strong enough to pull herself into a sitting position. Anna explores objects as she sits, but her father tries to anticipate when she is getting tired because at first Anna cannot get herself out of the sitting position.

Anna reaches for interesting things and can move them up and down and from side to side. Her eyes sparkle and she exclaims in pleasure when she is able to make noises with a rattle.

When she is five months of age, she opens her hands as she reaches for objects. She has had enough experiences to begin to estimate size by opening widely for a large object and narrowly for a small one. She receives more tactile information from her fingertips than from the whole-hand approach that she used earlier in handling objects.

Six to Nine Months

Anna gets herself up on all fours in a crawling position and rocks back and forth as if she has an idea but cannot quite implement it. Her first crawling movements are backwards, but she gradually learns to move forward. Delight registers on her face as she discovers that she can get anywhere she wants to go.

Anna likes to be put into a standing position. She especially likes jumping up and down on her mother's lap.

Anna's play is much more complex than it was earlier. She shows that she knows what is coming by starting to clap her hands when her father suggests playing pat-a-cake. She puts smaller objects into larger ones and understands how to use simple hammers or other tools. She explores everything and seems particularly to like things that change and move according to her actions. One day she unfurls a whole roll of toilet paper and follows that with playing in the

BOX 6.2	STRATEGIES FOR FACILITATING DEVELOPMENT: POSITIVE DISCIPLINE FOR INFANTS

Before infants gain mobility, it is relatively easy to be positive in interacting with them. However, the time when they first begin to crawl and climb presents special challenges and many opportunities for decisions about their activities. Some of these decisions are likely to convey positive messages to infants and some are not.

Consider the following situation and responses:

A nine-month-old succeeds in opening a cabinet and removing all the pots and pans.

Response one: *"You're into everything! What am I going to do with you?!"*

Response two: *"You must have really worked hard while I was in the other room. I need these for cooking but you can use those over there."*

In this situation, the infant has achieved mastery of something new and has opened up a set of novel possibilities for exploration. When the adult returns to the room, the infant is delighted with the noise that the lids make when banged together. However, seen through the first adult's eyes, the infant is an exasperating person who makes extra work for adults. The infant is given no options besides stopping, and will probably return for further exploration at the first unsupervised opportunity. When that happens, there is likely to be a similarly negative but somewhat more annoyed response.

In contrast, the second adult sees the infant as a hard worker who stays with a problem until it is resolved. Like the first adult, the second also does not want the infant in that particular cabinet but instead is willing to set aside another area with safe and interesting similar items for the infant to explore. The infant can return for further exploration and will probably receive additional positive feedback at that time.

The second adult has communicated a positive message to the infant: "Your interests are valid and worthy of pursuit." Yet, the adult has also redirected the infant's activities. Providing interesting alternatives is an important aspect of positive discipline for infants.

water in the toilet bowl and with shredding newspapers. She needs to have careful adult supervision and some redirection of her interests. For instance, her mother redirects her interest in the toilet to a plastic tub filled with water and placed near various sized containers for pouring.

Nine to Twelve Months

As Anna's crawling becomes more efficient, the need for adult management of her environment increases. (See Box 6.2 for a discussion of positive discipline for infants.) She is enticed by the challenges of the stairs in her building but can be safe on them only with close adult supervision. At other times, a gate is put between her and the stairs.

Feeding Anna becomes a bit of a tug-of-war. Anna wants to use the cup and handle the food herself. Her mother compromises and feeds some things to her and gives her some chunks of cheese and other finger foods to feed herself.

Anna points with her index finger. In one twenty-minute episode, Anna crawls patiently after a spider on the floor, repeatedly missing it with her extended index finger. She eventually catches it and is redirected from putting

The first independent steps, taken at about one year of age, are cause for excitement.

BOX 6.3

WALKING AND HOPI CRADLEBOARDS

How much of physical development is determined by maturation? What is the effect of experience? A classic study by Dennis (1940) relates to these questions. Dennis studied two groups of Hopi infants, one raised in the traditional Hopi manner and the other raised in a more typically Western manner. The traditional Hopi manner of childrearing includes tying infants on cradleboards for much of the first nine months of life. On the cradleboard, infants are restricted in raising their bodies, moving their arms, and rolling over. Dennis was interested in determining whether the group of infants raised without the restrictions imposed by the cradleboards would learn to walk sooner than the group that had used cradleboards.

Dennis found that both groups of infants started to walk at about fifteen months of age. Dennis concluded that walking is maturationally determined, and his conclusion was accepted for a period of time. However, the evidence is less convincing than Dennis believed because use of the cradleboard was discontinued when infants were about nine months of age. Even the infants who had used cradleboards, then, had the opportunity to exercise without restriction between nine and fifteen months of age. A cautious interpretation of Dennis's study is that restriction of movement before infants reach nine months of age does not seem to affect the age of walking.

The maturationist case would have been stronger if infants had remained on cradleboards until fifteen months of age and then begun to walk. Dennis's study shows the importance of maturation in walking but does not rule out the importance of experience.

it in her mouth to putting it in a clear plastic container. By twelve months, she perfects the process of grasping small objects between the tips of her thumb and index finger.

She controls several objects at one time, building block towers and putting smaller into larger things. She drops and throws almost everything, both to practice the letting-go motion and to see what will happen. Peas are tossed off the high-chair tray and toys from her crib. She is a small scientist and her environment is her laboratory.

In this last quarter of the first year, Anna begins to pull herself into a standing position. She progresses to walking while holding onto furniture. Finally, she sets off on her own. She has had an eventful first year and, just as she will never be the same again, her parents will never view infants in the same way that they did before getting to know Anna. (See Box 6.3 for a discussion of age and walking when Hopi cradleboards are used.)

NUTRITION, HEALTH, AND SAFETY

The average newborn weighs about seven pounds and is about twenty inches long. Birth weight is usually doubled by four months and tripled by twelve months; birth length is doubled by twelve months. Providing for the nutrition, health, and safety of rapidly growing infants can present challenges. Aspects of life that later become routine—eating, for instance—can cause worry during the first year of life. The pages that follow provide information about various aspects of nutrition, health, and safety: nutrition and brain growth; dental health; immunization; handicaps, prematurity, and illness; safety; and abuse and neglect.

Nutrition and Brain Growth

The food most ideally suited to infants is breast milk. There are many nutritional, health, practical, and emotional advantages to breast-feeding. From the perspective of nutrition, human milk contains just the right nutrients that infants need for growth and activity. For health, breast milk and *colostrum,* the liquid that precedes the milk in the first days, provide immunity to a variety of infections if the mother herself carries immunity. Breast milk is also matched to the capabilities of an infant's digestive system and is less likely than substitute formulas to trigger allergic reactions in the infant. The practical advantages of breast feeding are numerous: there are no formulas to mix, no refrigeration or sterilization to insure, no expense, no bottles to warm, and no worry about how much an infant drinks. The emotional advantages involve a special feeling of closeness when a nursing mother realizes that she is the source of something that her infant needs and that she alone can provide. Because of the many advantages, most pediatricians recommend breast-feeding. Support groups, such as the La Leche League, are available to provide practical advice and caring guidance.

The food most ideally suited to infants is breast milk.

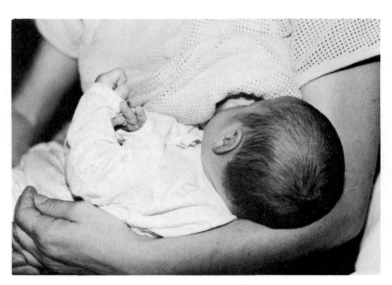

In developing countries and in some sociocultural groups within this country, there has been a movement away from breast-feeding to bottle-feeding (Pipes, 1981). Bottle-feeding has been viewed as a more modern, more progressive approach to infant nutrition. Bottle-feeding of specially fortified infant formula can be an acceptable alternative to breast-feeding, but it can also lead to problems. When there is not enough money to purchase adequate amounts of formula, watering down the formula results in undernutrition or malnutrition. When there is an impure water supply or inadequate sterilization or refrigeration, gastrointestinal infections result.

Bottle-feeding is the method of choice in certain circumstances. If the mother is in poor health or taking medications that would be transmitted to the infant through breast milk, bottle-feeding is often recommended. Some employed mothers breast-feed but others, especially those with inflexible working hours, decide to use a fortified formula to feed their infants. And, although this reasoning does not usually become decisive in choosing a feeding method, fathers who want to participate in all aspects of child care may prefer bottle-feeding. The quality of the relationship established between parents and infant is more important than the feeding method, provided that formula is prepared properly.

During the first year, most of the infant's nutritional needs are met by breast milk or by fortified infant formula. After about six months of age, most pediatricians suggest introducing one new food or juice each week to begin to accustom the infant to them. These are just "for fun," and the approach should be accordingly low-key. In this regard, it is important to remember the temperamental need of the slow-to-warm-up infant for time to get used to each new experience. For all infants, the one-per-week pattern allows the adult to detect any allergic reaction to a new food. If many new foods were introduced all at once, it would be difficult to isolate the one responsible for any reaction.

Protein-calorie malnutrition in infants is a worry for those in health care professions. Severe cases are seen in clinics or hospitals, but there are also infants who suffer malnutrition without any noticeable signs except poor physical growth. One type of malnutrition that occurs in infants below one year of age is called **marasmus** (from the Greek, "to waste"). Marasmus is caused by a restriction in total food intake, including protein. The symptoms of marasmus include poor physical growth, severe wasting of muscles, anemia, diarrhea, lack of subcutaneous fat, wrinkled skin, and drawn face. Sadly, marasmus is on the increase, especially in developing countries, because of the movement toward shorter periods of breast-feeding or total reliance on bottle-feeding under inadequate conditions of supply, sanitation, and sterilization.

Concern about adequate nutrition in infancy is particularly acute because of the brain growth that occurs at this time. Brain cells multiply during two periods: the first is at ten to twenty weeks of gestation, and involves the division of nerve cells; the second is from twenty weeks of gestation to four months after birth, and consists of growth of glial cells. Growth of the brain by cell division is almost completed by eighteen months of age; further growth occurs but is due to other causes, such as increases in cell size. The weight of the brain increases 200 percent in the first three years of life, and study after study has

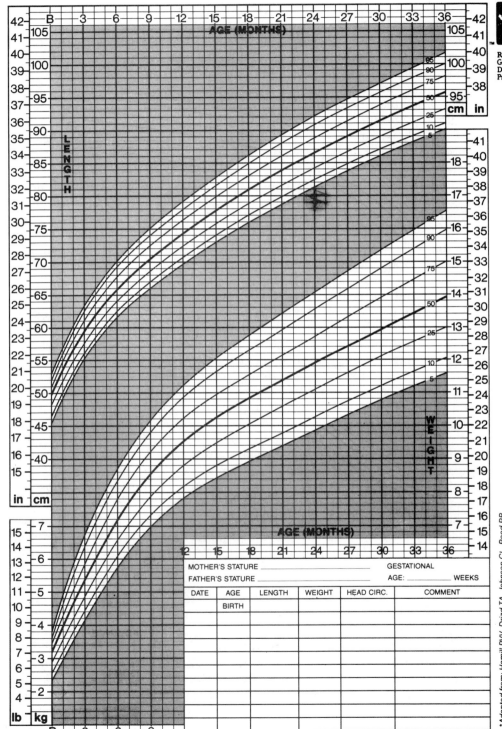

GIRLS: BIRTH TO 36 MONTHS
PHYSICAL GROWTH
NCHS PERCENTILES*

NAME_____ RECORD #_____

Ross
Growth &
Development
Program

MOTHER'S STATURE _____ GESTATIONAL
FATHER'S STATURE _____ AGE: _____ WEEKS

DATE	AGE	LENGTH	WEIGHT	HEAD CIRC.	COMMENT
	BIRTH				

*Adapted from: Hamill PVV, Drizd TA, Johnson CL, Reed RB, Roche AF, Moore WM: Physical growth: National Center for Health Statistics percentiles. AM J CLIN NUTR 32:607-629, 1979. Data from the Fels Research Institute, Wright State University School of Medicine, Yellow Springs, Ohio.

© 1982 ROSS LABORATORIES

shown direct links between nutrition and brain growth (Werner, 1979). Research indicates that the long-term effects of undernutrition in early life include impaired functioning of the central nervous system and reduced thinking capacity. Emmy Werner (1979) reviewed a number of cross-cultural studies and concluded that nutritional supplements, combined with medical care, have the most powerful effect on cognitive development if given during pregnancy and the first years of life. The effects of malnutrition on brain development are less noticeable after age three and almost absent after age five. It seems that infants can grow to become fully functioning adults only if great care is taken to meet their nutritional needs in infancy. (Normal growth curves are illustrated in Figures 6.1 and 6.2.)

Dental Health

An infant's first tooth usually breaks through the gums at about seven months of age, and the set of twenty teeth is complete by about two and one-half years of age. The typical pattern is for the two lower middle incisors to come in first, followed a few months later by the four upper incisors. At the end of the first year, most infants have these six teeth.

Infants vary greatly in the amount of discomfort teething seems to give them. Some chew on everything, sleep fitfully, and seem fretful for days at a time. Other infants surprise their parents with a suddenly visible tooth after no noticeable change in behavior.

Fluoride in the diet of children from infancy through age twelve is known to aid the formation of strong teeth. In some areas of the country, fluoride is found naturally in or is added to the water. In other areas, fluoride drops can be given daily. The incidence of tooth decay is lowered substantially when fluoride is taken as teeth develop.

Immunization

A major societal concern is the number of children who are unprotected by immunizations against some of the major childhood diseases. (See Figure 6.3 for percentages of children who are immunized.) Perhaps part of the reason for the relaxed attitude of many parents today is that they are too young to remember what it was like when many children did suffer disabilities or death from diseases for which immunizations are now available. The importance of immunizations has not diminished, however; they should be given in infancy and continued.

The first inoculation is usually the combined DPT—diphtheria, pertussis (whooping cough), and tetanus—given at about two months of age. A total of three combined shots are administered at two-month intervals during the first year. Unfortunately, these combined shots often cause a reaction, including

FIGURE 6.1 (*opposite page*)   *Normal Growth Curve: Girls*
(Reprinted with permission of Ross Laboratories, Columbus, OH 43216, from NCHS Growth Charts.)

BOYS: BIRTH TO 36 MONTHS
PHYSICAL GROWTH
NCHS PERCENTILES*

NAME_____   RECORD #_____

Ross
Growth &
Development
Program

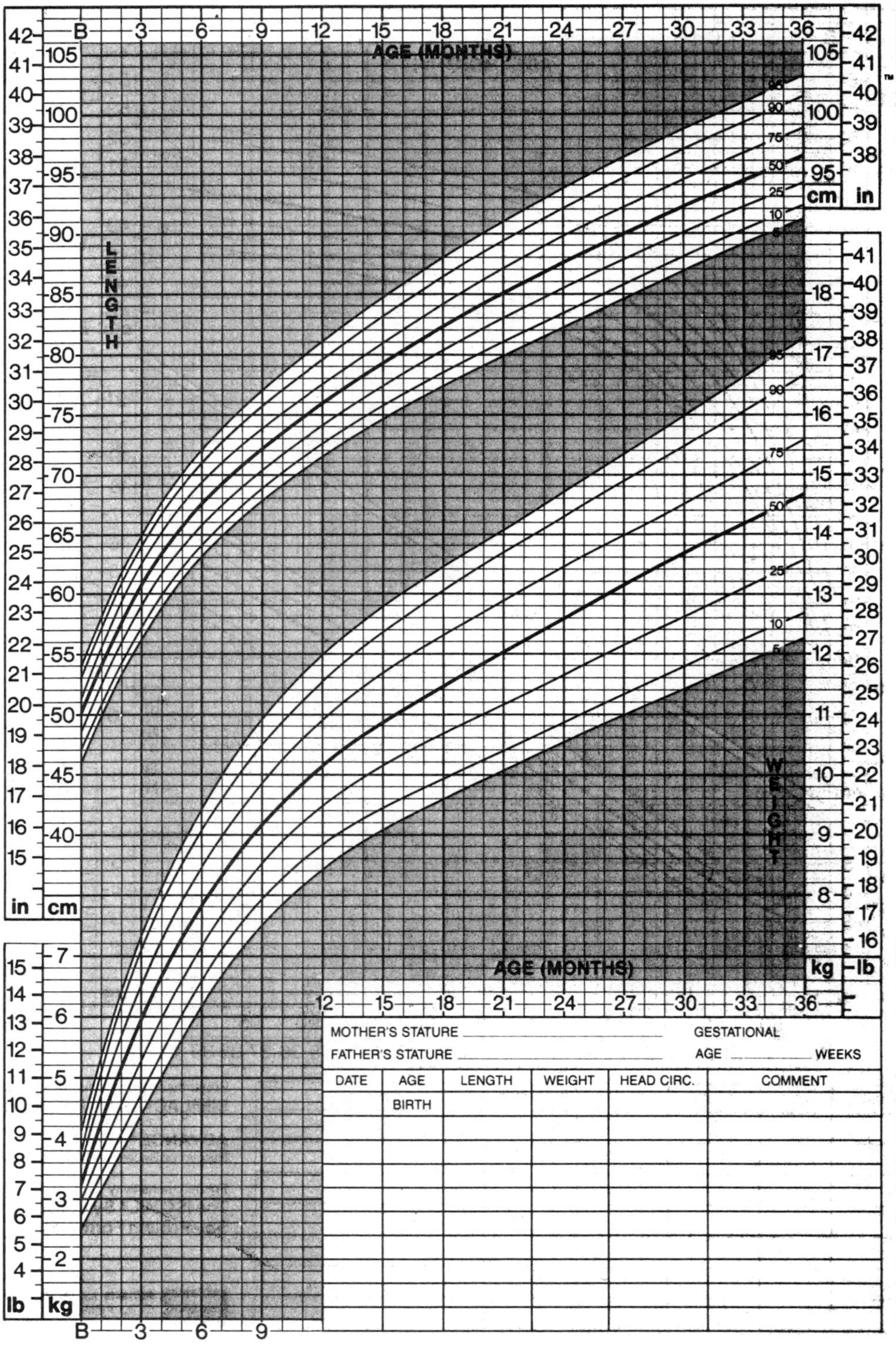

AGE (MONTHS)

LENGTH

WEIGHT

AGE (MONTHS)

in | cm

lb | kg

cm | in

kg | lb

| MOTHER'S STATURE | | | GESTATIONAL | |
| FATHER'S STATURE | | | AGE _____ WEEKS | |

DATE	AGE	LENGTH	WEIGHT	HEAD CIRC.	COMMENT
	BIRTH				

*Adapted from: Hamill PVV, Drizd TA, Johnson CL, Reed RB, Roche AF, Moore WM: Physical growth: National Center for Health Statistics percentiles. AM J CLIN NUTR 32:607-629, 1979. Data from the Fels Research Institute, Wright State University School of Medicine, Yellow Springs, Ohio.

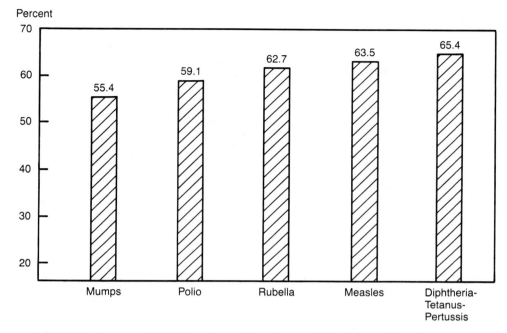

Percent

FIGURE 6.3 *Percent of Children One to Four Years Old Adequately Immunized*
Note the laxity of immunization against polio. The proportion of children who had at
least three doses fell from 70 percent in 1966 to 59 percent in 1978. The proportion of
children with at least three doses of DPT vaccine dropped from 75 percent in 1966 to
65 percent in 1978. (U.S. Bureau of the Census, Current Population Reports. (1982).
Characteristics of American Children and Youth: 1980 (P-23, No. 114, Table 32).
Washington, DC: U.S. Government Printing Office.

fever, soreness near the location of the shot, fussiness, and loss of appetite. The
physician can prescribe medication to relieve the symptoms.

Also at two months of age, administration of oral poliovirus vaccine is
started. This vaccine is given by mouth three times during the first year, usually
separated by two-month intervals. A combined vaccine protects against the
three viruses that are known to cause polio.

Other vaccinations are recommended at about one year of age, and they
are often given in a combined form, immunizing against measles, mumps, and
rubella. Although many people have had these diseases without complications,
there can be serious consequences, such as ear infections, encephalitis, or brain
damage from measles; sterility in males from mumps; and birth defects during
the first three months of pregnancy from rubella. Parents of infants have an
important responsibility to protect them from the very severe complications that
can result from all of these diseases.

FIGURE 6.2 *(opposite page) Normal Growth Curve: Boys*
(Reprinted with permission of Ross Laboratories, Columbus, OH 43216, from NCHS
Growth Charts.)

A twelve-month-old shows his displeasure at receiving an immunization. After the momentary discomfort, he will be protected from diseases that can cause disability or death.

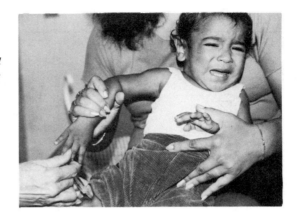

Handicaps, Prematurity, Illness

The more that one knows about the complexity of prenatal development, the more amazing it seems when healthy infants emerge from the birth process. Most expectant parents worry about whether their infants will be normal. One mother-to-be surprised herself by bursting into tears when a handicapped child appeared on television. A father-to-be found himself reacting emotionally to his work situation, which involved contacts with handicapped adults. But even if prospective parents rehearse or imagine how they might feel if their infant were not normal, the birth of an infant with special needs requires an adjustment process with medical and personal support.

For most kinds of special needs, there are support groups of parents whose children have similar needs. Pediatricians, hospitals, or national organizations can put parents in contact with local groups. All parents desire opportunities to talk about the development of their children, but the need is particularly strong when development is likely to differ markedly from the usual pattern.

Some infants have special needs at birth but later may be fully functioning. For instance, premature infants or infants who are under stress from circumstances of birth often require extensive care in and out of the hospital in their first months of life. In the past, these infants were handled as little as possible with the intention of protecting them from germs or further stress. However, research has now demonstrated the importance of holding, talking with, and otherwise gently stimulating these infants. It has been learned that the parent-infant attachment process is impaired if parents are not in contact with their infants. If parents are not assisted in working through their feelings, they might be awkward with and worried about their infants, even when the immediate threat to life has ended.

The most influential ideas about bringing parents into hospital nurseries for premature infants originated with Klaus and Kennell (1976,1982), who showed how important it is to involve parents in the care of their high-risk infants while still in the hospital. If parents are assisted in working through their fears in the hospital setting, they care for and interact with their infants with more confidence and warmth when they go home. Personnel in premature nurseries, then, have an outreach role to the parents that is nearly as important as their medical aid to the infants.

Parents of premature or ill infants need time to observe others caring for their infants and then need gradually to take increasing responsibility for nurturing them. At first they feel fear and grief at the delicate status of the infant. If infants are discharged from the hospital to parents who still are afraid to touch or care for them, the parents may never allow themselves to feel attached to them.

Premature and ill infants have immature nervous systems. Parents need guidance in understanding the course of these infants' early development; otherwise, parents can feel guilty or inept about their handling. After birth even positive sights and sounds overwhelm immature or ill infants. The infants can hear or look or touch, but can only gradually stand to receive input from more than one of these senses at a time. If too much stimulation comes in, these infants withdraw—a response that can make parents feel rejected if they have not been forewarned. Most parents need support and help to provide the kind of sensitive nurturing that these infants need in order to prosper. People in the helping professions are increasingly focusing on the myriad of needs of all family members.

Compared to the challenges faced by parents of handicapped, premature, or stressed infants, it might seem that parents of "normal" infants would have no problems whatsoever. But, everything is relative, and often the first cold, the first rash, or the first cough is a cause of considerable worry. It is important, then, even before an infant's birth to have established a relationship with a clinic or doctor so that questions and concerns can be dealt with immediately when they occur. Handbooks on children's health are available in most bookstores; and, while a book is no substitute for a doctor, these resources can be helpful.

Pediatricians tell parents that more than 90 percent of children's illnesses last only a few days. Especially in the first year, illnesses tend to be mild. Colds may require use of a nasal syringe to remove mucus, because small infants breathe through their noses and are not flexible about switching to their mouths. Other treatment may be prescribed by the doctor, depending on the severity of the symptoms.

On the rare occasions when continued treatment or hospitalization is required, parents and medical personnel should give priority to what they know about the importance of establishing and maintaining basic trust and attachment. Whenever possible, the person closest to the infant should make arrangements to stay with the infant. Facilities are not always available to make this choice comfortable, but it is highly desirable from the infant's perspective. A familiar touch and voice and a sense of continuity can mean a great deal in an unfamiliar environment.

Sudden Infant Death Syndrome

Sudden Infant Death Syndrome (SIDS) is the sudden and unexpected death of infants previously believed to be healthy. According to the Sudden Infant Death

Syndrome Clearinghouse, SIDS is the leading cause of death among infants between one month and one year of age (Pachon, undated). Considerable research is being conducted to ascertain causes of SIDS, but at this time results are preliminary.

SIDS is a definite medical entity that can be determined by medical investigation and a complete autopsy. Death seems to occur rapidly and silently, usually while an infant is sleeping. SIDS cannot be attributed to external suffocation, vomiting, or choking, and cannot yet be accurately predicted or prevented.

Many parents and infant caregivers fear SIDS. But excessive worry and checking on infants can lessen the enjoyment found in interactions between adults and infants, while still not preventing SIDS.

In the two cases per 1000 live births when SIDS strikes (Pachon, undated), grieving families can often benefit from contact with parents who have experienced a SIDS death. They also need information about SIDS so that they do not blame themselves for any act or omission.

Safety

Adults are responsible for creating an environment within which infants can be active and safe. In the early months, infants have limited mobility; finding appropriate places for them to eat, play, and sleep is relatively easy. In fact, some parents take their newborns wherever they go and feel that their lives have altered very little with the infant's birth. This perception and the ease with which an environment for the infant can be managed both change as the infant gains mobility. Once infants can move themselves at will from place to place, setting up their environments becomes more challenging. Adults need to take an infant's eye view of each room and remove small objects that might be swal-

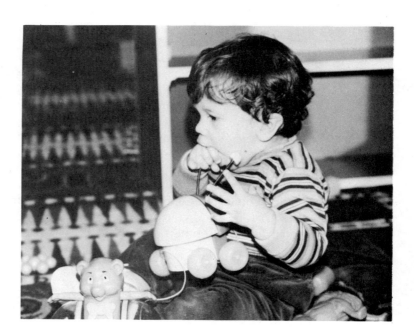

Because infants explore objects with their mouths as well as their hands and eyes, small objects that might be swallowed must be removed.

lowed, sharp objects, breakable or delicate objects, and poisonous plants or other substances. All medicines and household cleaners and soaps should be stored in high, locked containers. Special caps should be put over electrical outlets to eliminate the danger of electrical shock if the infant gets the idea of sticking an object into the outlet. Exploration is important to an infant's development. By "child proofing" the environment, adults free themselves to be relaxed and encouraging of the infant's interests and movements. The alternative is to surround the infant with nos—a situation that is exhausting to adults and frustrating to little ones.

Abuse and Neglect

The Child Abuse Prevention and Treatment Act of 1975 (42 U.S. Code 5101) defines child **abuse** and **neglect** as "the physical or mental injury, sexual abuse, negligent treatment, or maltreatment of a child under the age of eighteen by a person who is responsible for the child's welfare under circumstances which indicate that the child's health or welfare is harmed or threatened thereby." Abuse results from an adult's nonaccidental action toward a child. Neglect is the absence of action when action is necessary. Although experts do not understand why, in cases of abuse there is usually one child in the family who receives the brunt of the violence. In cases of neglect, all children in a family are usually involved.

In order to receive federal assistance in developing, strengthening, and carrying out programs for the prevention and treatment of child abuse and neglect, states must meet the following criteria: provide for the reporting of known and suspected instances of child abuse and neglect; investigate such reports; train personnel to work with abused and neglected children and their families; appoint a guardian to represent the child in any judicial proceeding; preserve the confidentiality of all records; provide for cooperation of law enforcement officials, the courts, and state agencies providing human services; and disseminate information about abuse and neglect to the public. In some states, professionals, such as teachers and physicians, are guilty of a misdemeanor if they do not report incidents of suspected child abuse to the appropriate authorities.

Statistics about the incidence of child abuse and neglect are difficult to obtain because the action or lack of action, as the case may be, often takes place within the privacy of the home. It is generally estimated that cases of neglect far outnumber those of abuse. All experts agree that both problems are significant. Not only are the children involved experiencing immediate dangers, such as injury and death, but they also are developing psychological scars that can cause lifelong problems.

Of great interest and concern to readers of this chapter on infancy is the fact that many of the reported cases of child abuse involve infants under one year of age. It may be difficult to imagine that anyone would beat or burn or otherwise injure a defenseless infant. However, this abuse does take place; all who are interested in child development need an understanding of the phenomenon.

BOX 6.4   **STRATEGIES FOR FACILITATING DEVELOPMENT: INFANT VEHICLE SAFETY**

Traffic accidents are a principal cause of death and injury in childhood; yet relatively few infants ride safely in appropriate car seats each time they travel. Being in an approved car seat prevents infants from being thrown out of the car onto the road or from hitting the windshield or inside of the car with great force. Safety experts agree that all occupants should be properly restrained every time even a short car trip is taken.

Infant car carriers are designed so that the infant faces the back of the car and is in a semireclining position. The infant wears a snug harness and the carrier attaches to the seat of the car with a car lap belt. Car carriers designed specifically for infants should be used from the first ride home from the hospital until the infant weighs seventeen to twenty pounds. At that time, the child can graduate to a conventional car seat, which should be used until the child weighs forty pounds or is four years old. The U.S. Department of Transportation has a set of standards, upgraded in 1981, which all safety restraints should meet. Some states now require the use of these restraints.

Parents might be more inclined to restrain their infants in approved car seats if they knew how unsafe their usual practices were. Consider these comments and the facts that follow them.

1   *"But I hold her on my lap."* An adult's lap is one of the most dangerous places that an infant can ride. In a sudden stop or crash, the adult's body would crush the infant. Even if the adult is restrained, the force of a crash would make it impossible to hold on to the infant.

2   *"I'm a safe driver—and this is a short trip."* Many accidents are caused by the mistakes or problems of other drivers, and many accidents take place close to home.

In most cases, adults who abuse children are otherwise ordinary people who react to a high level of stress by striking out at someone who cannot strike back. This striking-out response may result from their own experiences as abused children years before. The actual precipitating event for the abuse may be something that seems minor:-an infant's continued crying, loose B.M., or spitting up after a feeding. Whatever the event, the adult momentarily loses control, and the infant is the victim.

Abusive adults need help immediately because they often become caught in a cycle of increasingly violent action. Current laws, such as Public Law 93–247, Child Abuse Prevention and Treatment Act, replace a formerly punitive approach with one that requires that parents receive help from social service agencies. Sometimes parents are referred to self-help groups like Parents Anon-

3   *"He won't like being placed in one of those."* Like anything else, the adult's attitude is important. Children who have always been safely restrained usually accept it as the usual way to travel in the car. Adults can teach by their own example, too, and always buckle up.

4   *"I put them all in seat belts."* Until a child weighs about forty pounds, a seat belt can exert dangerous pressure on the abdomen in a crash. A seat belt may be better than no restraint whatsoever, but, particularly with infants, an appropriate infant car carrier is the safest choice of all.

FIGURE 6.4 *Infant Car Carriers*

(From U.S. Department of Transportation, National Highway Traffic Safety Administration. (1980). *Child Restraint Systems for Your Automobile.*)

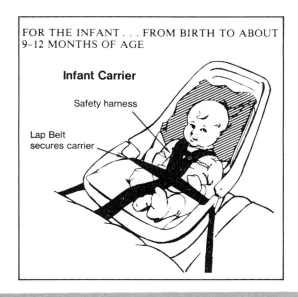

FOR THE INFANT . . . FROM BIRTH TO ABOUT 9-12 MONTHS OF AGE

Infant Carrier

Safety harness

Lap Belt secures carrier

ymous. Abuse and neglect must be reported quickly so that intervention can be planned for the family.

Can child abuse and neglect be prevented, rather than stopped only after they have happened? In fact, a number of projects attempt to do just that. These parent-infant intervention projects have goals such as encouraging positive parent-infant interactions, helping parents to feel adequate and important, and communicating information to parents about development and community resources. When skilled, empathetic professionals are in close touch with families in stress, they can provide positive suggestions about outlets or solutions for the frustrations of life that seem overwhelming. Box 6.5 shows how excessively harsh behavior that might lead to child abuse was handled in one parent-infant intervention project.

BOX   **INTERVENTION STRATEGIES WHEN PARENTS**
6.5   **USE EXCESSIVELY HARSH BEHAVIOR**

These strategies were presented by Bromwich (1981):

We listened empathetically as the parent
☐ talked about how angry she felt when the child expressed negative feelings.
☐ talked about how frustrated she often felt, having to deal with this child 24 hours a day.
☐ talked about how badly she felt after she had punished the child more harshly than she had meant to.

We asked the parent
☐ whether she could pinpoint the areas of the child's behavior that made her particularly angry and upset, and then find ways of avoiding situations that evoked these behaviors.

We also discussed with the parent
☐ how easy it is to feel frustrated and angry with a young child when one is isolated and has no one to talk to.
☐ that there are groups in the community where parents, who feel isolated and frustrated with their young children, can share their experiences and help each other.
☐ that it is important for parents who tend to punish their children more severely than they mean to, to get help from groups in the community because harsh punishment can inflict injury to the child without the parent being aware of this.
☐ particular resources in her community where she could get help. (When there is sufficient evidence to suspect child abuse, California law dictates that physicians, nurses, teachers, and other professionals contact Protective Services in the Department of Public Social Services or, in the case of an emergency, the Protective Services division of the local police department.)

We encouraged the parent
☐ to call us or a friend when she was faced with a particularly difficult problem with her child, or when she felt especially tense and upset with the child.
☐ to get out of the house with the child occasionally to keep tensions from building up.
☐ to try to find a babysitter so that she could occasionally get away from the child.
☐ to follow up on one or more of the resources provided for her before she loses control over her angry feelings and does something she might regret.

SUMMARY

1   Physical changes are numerous during the first year of life.
2   Vision, taste, and hearing are well developed at birth.
3   A series of reflexes are part of the competence that infants have at birth.
4   Infants' daily cycles include sound sleep, REM sleep, and alertness.
5   In movement and coordination, infants achieve voluntary control in a progression from head to toes. Most infants crawl at about eight months and walk at about one year.
6   Adequate nutrition, care and concern for safety are important to normal growth of an infant's brain and body.

KEY TERMS

neonatal period	REM sleep	marasmus
habituated	alertness	Sudden Infant Death Syndrome (SIDS)
reflexes	cephalo-caudal	
sound sleep	protein-calorie malnutrition	abuse
		neglect

FOR FURTHER READING

Month-by-Month Changes

Caplan, F. (1978) *The first 12 months of life.* New York: Bantam.

Sensory and Perceptual Competence

Bower, T. G. R. (1977). *The perceptual world of the child.* Cambridge: Harvard University Press.

Bower, T. G. R. (1982) *Development in infancy* (2nd ed.). San Francisco: W. H. Freeman.

Parenting Support Programs

Bromwich, R. (1981). *Working with parents and infants: An interactional approach.* Baltimore: University Park Press.

Infant Exercise

Levy, J. (1973) *The baby exercise book for the first fifteen months.* New York: Pantheon.

7

Cognitive Development of Infants

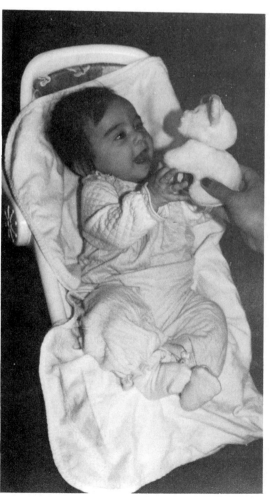

Key Ideas

Interplay of Cognitive with Psychosocial and Physical Development
Cultural Goals for Infants □ Visual Attention

Piaget's View of Cognition
Piaget's Substage 1: Birth to 1 Month □ Piaget's Substage 2: 1 to 4 Months □ Piaget's Substage 3: 4 to 8 Months □ Piaget's Substage 4: 8 to 12 Months

Views That Differ from Piaget's
Imitation □ Understanding of Relationships

Language Development
Newborn □ First Six Months □ Second Six Months

Cultural Differences in Language Interaction with Infants

Early Intervention Programs

Cognitive development involves thinking, problem solving, creativity, and language. This type of development is highly valued in our society. Many parents are willing to go over their budgets to purchase toys or other materials for infants, if lasting cognitive benefits are promised. But such promises can only be evaluated sensibly in the context of an understanding of the changes in infant cognition during the first year of life.

Changes in infant cognition are described in this chapter. Information is presented about Piaget's theory of intellectual development, views that differ from Piaget's, language development, cultural differences in language interactions with infants, and early intervention programs. The chapter begins with examples of the interplay among cognitive, psychosocial, and physical development.

INTERPLAY OF COGNITIVE WITH PSYCHOSOCIAL AND PHYSICAL DEVELOPMENT

The interplay of psychosocial, physical, and cognitive development affected the order of topics in this book. Psychosocial development is first because of the fundamental and vital importance of the psychosocial bonds that link infants with adults. If infants develop secure attachments, mutuality of communication with adults, and a basic sense of trust, then their cognitive needs are probably also met. The inverse is not so likely to be true, however. An infant could receive what is judged to be adequate cognitive stimulation but if it happened in a mechanical fashion without attachment, mutuality, or a growing sense of trust, both the infant's cognitive and psychosocial development would be negatively influenced. Psychosocial stability is the base upon which other aspects of development build.

In describing psychosocial and physical development, a great deal has been said about cognitive development. Two specific examples of interplay among these aspects of development involve cultural goals for infants and visual attention.

Cultural Goals for Infants

The interplay of psychosocial, physical, and cognitive development is nowhere stronger than in the goals that parents of various cultural groups have for their infants. A cross-cultural study (LeVine, 1980) found that parents hold one or more of the following categories of goals for their infants: (1) physical survival/health/safety; (2) eventual ability for economic maintenance; and (3) capacity to go beyond economic maintenance to attain success, as defined by the cultural group. The first two goals emphasize physical survival, first in the sense of life itself and then in the sense of providing sustenance for oneself in adulthood. The third goal focuses on cognitive and psychosocial considerations: the achievement of the infant's full potential in adulthood.

Parents in cultural groups that have had high rates of infant death tend to focus on the first goal. LeVine (1980) found that child-rearing practices are often restrictive and protective if the primary focus is on survival of the infant. Within the United States, the differences in infant death rates lead parents to give relatively more or less emphasis to the first goal of survival. Statistically, the number of infant deaths per one thousand live births is 12.0 for whites and 21.1 for blacks and other minority groups (U.S. Bureau of the Census, 1982). According to LeVine's findings, white parents might be expected to focus less on the first goal and to be less restrictive and protective of infants than black and minority parents.

Parents in cultural groups that experience a scarcity of economic resources focus on the second goal. Minority cultural groups in the United States have lower rates of employment and lower wages among those who are employed. The differences in access to economic resources cause parents to give different weightings to this second goal of economic maintenance.

Parents in many groups within U.S. society may thus be unable to think beyond the first two goals. But optimally developed children may come mainly from environments in which physical survival in infancy and adulthood can be taken as a given and attention is paid to psychosocial and cognitive priorities.

Visual Attention

Visual attention provides a second example of the interplay among psychosocial, physical, and cognitive development. For many years, researchers have been attempting with little success to predict later cognitive functioning by administering intelligence tests to infants. By studying other skills and activities of infants, researchers have found that visual attention at three months of age

Research has found that visual attention in the early months predicts cognitive functioning at two years of age.

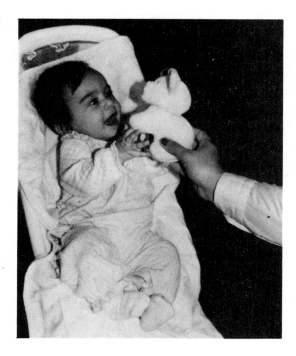

predicts cognitive functioning at two years of age (Lewis & Brooks-Gunn, 1981). Visual attention might be viewed as in the domain of physical development; yet it seems to predict later cognitive competence.

Lewis and Brooks-Gunn (1981) presented three-month-old infants with redundant visual stimuli interspersed with novel ones. Infants who were likely to *habituate* (see Chapter 6) to redundant stimuli and recover interest when presented with novel stimuli were likely to have higher IQs at twenty-four months than infants who did not behave in this manner. The researchers have viewed their findings as supporting the stance that differences in attention are related to functioning of the central nervous system and that the ability to process information in the first months of life can provide a useful measure of intellectual capability. This research demonstrates interesting interplay between physical and cognitive development.

PIAGET'S VIEW OF COGNITION

Jean Piaget carefully observed his own three infants earlier in this century and found that they were active in learning about the world around them. Note the excitement with which Piaget (1962) told about one of his infants' imitation at six months of age.

> . . . J. invented a new sound by putting her tongue between her teeth. It was something like *pfs*. Her mother then made the same sound. J. was delighted and laughed as she repeated it in her turn. Then came a long period of mutual imitation. J. said *pfs,* her mother imitated her, and J. watched her without moving her lips. Then when her mother stopped, J. began again, and so it went on. Later on, after remaining silent for some time, I myself said *pfs.* J. laughed at once and imitated me. There was the same reaction the next day, beginning in the morning (before she had herself spontaneously made the sound in question) and lasting throughout the day. (p. 19)

Piaget was one of the first scholars to realize that exploration and play serve important purposes in helping infants learn.

Piaget organized his observations about early intellectual development into a stage which he called **sensorimotor** (referring to senses and motor skills). According to Piaget, the sensorimotor stage characterizes most infants' thinking between birth and about two years of age. Within the sensorimotor stage are six substages, four of which typically fall within the first year of life, as shown in Table 7.1. The major intellectual advances during each of these first four substages are described from Piaget's perspective.

Piaget's Substage 1: Birth to 1 Month

In the first substage, much of an infant's activity centers on feeding. Accordingly, Piaget devoted considerable attention to showing how reflexes, such as sucking, can provide a basis for later development. Piaget's contention was that infants, far from being helpless or passive, are active in seeking stimulation through their own behavior. Piaget (1962) used the sucking between meals of

TABLE 7.1 *Piaget's Sensorimotor Stage of Development*

Jean Piaget divided the sensorimotor stage (birth to about age two) into six substages. The first four of these substages usually take place during the first year of life.

Sensorimotor Substage	Age	Accomplishments
Substage 1 (Reflexes)	Birth–1 month	Builds on reflexes
Substage 2 (Primary circular reactions)	1–4 months	Repeats interesting movements of the body (primary circular reactions) Anticipates familiar events (e.g., feeding) Coordinates senses
Substage 3 (Secondary circular reactions)	4–8 months	Repeats interesting actions on objects (secondary circular reactions) Imitates sounds and actions in repertoire Attempts search for hidden object
Substage 4 (Practical intelligence)	8–12 months	Uses goal-directed behavior Begins to realize that objects and people exist even if not in view Imitates many behaviors
Substage 5	12–18 months	(See Chapter 10)
Substage 6	18–24 months	(See Chapter 10)

his child, Laurent, to illustrate the way newborns often initiate their own activities. Piaget discarded the possibilities that Laurent's sucking was activated only by objects, hunger, or the desire to repeat earlier satisfaction. Instead, Piaget interpreted Laurent's between-meal sucking as evidence that infants seek opportunities to exercise movements that are useful or interesting.

Piaget also showed ways in which infants in the first substage use their experiences to learn about the world. Again using the example of sucking, Piaget described a series of events which illustrated that Laurent recognized the nipple and knew where to look for it. Laurent adjusted to disturbances in the feeding process and, in these adjustments, Piaget noted the roots of later intelligent behavior.

Piaget's Substage 2: 1 to 4 Months

According to Piaget, one of the most important intellectual advances in the second substage is the ability of infants to repeat interesting movements that first occur by chance. For example, the accidental contact of an infant's hand with her mouth may set off a series of trial-and-error efforts to return the hand to her mouth. Often she eventually succeeds. Piaget called this phenomenon a **primary circular reaction**, defined as active reproduction of actions that were first produced by chance. The term *primary* reflects the focus on the infant's own body; *circular* refers to the endlessly repetitive nature of these reactions.

Another milestone of the second substage is the anticipation by infants of familiar events, such as feeding. Adults notice that infants in the second substage may begin to suck immediately when placed in the feeding position, rather than waiting for contact with the nipple as they did previously. Infants thus begin to make more accurate predictions about events that they have experienced.

A third development in this substage is that infants start to be able to coordinate their senses. They can use their eyes to follow objects. They can turn to look in the direction of interesting or surprising sounds. They can reach for and grasp objects that they see. And they often manage to become more active in exploring their environments.

A fourth characteristic of infants in the second substage involves their behavior when someone or something disappears from their view. Piaget demonstrated that, if someone in interaction with an infant suddenly disappears, infants stare at the spot and then turn their attention elsewhere. They do not search and they do not seem surprised about the disappearance. Piaget has

BOX 7.1   **STRATEGIES FOR FACILITATING DEVELOPMENT: SUBSTAGE 2 SENSORIMOTOR ACTIVITIES**

Todd Markam designed a series of stimulating mobiles for his one-month-old daughter, Lena. Noting her interest in form and color, he suspended a changing array of rattles, tops, and colored hoops above her crib and cradle. He used safe objects suspended by elastic so that Lena would eventually be able to pull the interesting things to her mouth for further tactile exploration.

At the start, Lena was only able to look at the objects and to follow their movement with her eyes. Soon, however, she could grasp and pull them to her. Her grasping and pulling gave her opportunities to integrate her perceptions of the objects and her motor abilities. She learned about depth perception and about distinguishing a certain object from other objects and from the surrounding space.

Lena's favorite mobile was composed of colorful rattles, each making a distinctive sound. She would lie on her back for extended periods of time, alternately contemplating the rattles and batting them with her hands. Her activity would be frequently punctuated with laughter.

asserted that infants in this second substage do not protest when people or things disappear because the infants have not begun to retain consistent mental images of people or objects—"out of sight, out of mind." One practical implication is that infants in this second substage usually require little adjustment when parents leave them in alternate child-care arrangements.

Piaget's Substage 3: 4 to 8 Months

Piaget indicated that infants expand their horizons dramatically during the third substage. Crawling brings infants into wider contact with the environment, and they manipulate and explore whatever they find. Infants continue to try to repeat interesting actions, but their focus expands. Piaget called these endeavors **secondary circular reactions** with the word *secondary* indicating that these actions center on objects rather than on the infant's own body. For instance, infants show great pleasure at being the cause of the delightful noises that occur when they pound a rattle.

Piaget showed that in this third substage, infants' imitation becomes more systematic than it was earlier. Infants can imitate sounds and expressions already in their repertoires, and they enjoy games that involve repetition of familiar patterns.

Infants' wider contact with the environment leads to growth in their understanding of the permanence of people and objects. Now, if someone or something disappears from sight, infants try to search. They may search in a new location, as if understanding that movement could continue even if the object is not in view. Or, if an object is partly visible, infants may attempt to uncover it. These search procedures show that infants are developing a more complete understanding of the existence of people and objects in the environment. However, infants' attempts at retrieving lost objects only repeat actions that they have already performed in the past rather than introducing any novel strategies. For example, if an infant had been looking at an object before it vanished, he would tend to search visually but not use his hands to try to find it. Piaget has said that infants at substage three still think of everything in relationship to their own actions rather than as having independent, individual existences.

Rather than crying upon awakening, infants in Piaget's substage three often explore and manipulate available objects.

BOX 7.2	**STRATEGIES FOR FACILITATING DEVELOPMENT: SUBSTAGE 3 SENSORIMOTOR ACTIVITIES**

From about four months of age, infants show great pleasure in social games. They smile and laugh in anticipation of the climax of the games that adults play with them. Each culture has its own games, but here are three common ones.

"Peek-a-boo, I see you"   An adult alternately covers and uncovers his/her face, making the excited exclamation, "Peek-a-boo, I see you!"

"Round and round the garden"   An adult moves his/her finger around the infant's hand, up the infant's arm, and then tickles under the infant's arm, saying,

> Round and round the garden
> Went the teddy bear.
> One step,
> Two steps,
> Tickly under there!

"This little piggy"   Starting with the largest toe, an adult grasps each toe in turn, saying,

> This little piggy went to market.
> This little piggy stayed home.
> This little piggy ate roast beef.
> This little piggy ate none.
> And this little piggy cried, "Wee-wee-wee," all the way home!

These social games give infants experiences with auditory sequencing, anticipation of outcomes, search for a hidden person, and imitation (as they begin to initiate the games). The games also encourage a special closeness and warmth between infants and adults.

Piaget's Substage 4: 8 to 12 Months

Piaget has said that an infant's major intellectual accomplishment in the fourth substage is the onset of goal-directed behavior. Until this last part of the first year, infants accidentally discover goals, which they then pursue. In contrast, in substage four, infants have goals in mind from the beginning and work purposefully to achieve them. Piaget has said that behavior in substage four can be called "intelligent" because infants are able to overcome obstacles by using strategies that differ from the strategies initially applied to reach the goal.

An infant in Piaget's substage four demonstrates goal-directed behavior.

According to Piaget's theory, it is also during the fourth substage that infants develop a sense of **object permanence**. Object permanence is defined as the understanding that things or people continue to exist even though not in view. When someone or something disappears, infants in substage four use a variety of systematic strategies to search for what is missing. Infants now seem to realize that objects and individuals have an independent existence, whether or not they can be seen at the moment. When a ball rolls under the sofa, infants look carefully for it. Piaget has said that infants come to understand that objects have permanence by having been provided with many opportunities to manipulate and observe the movement of things around the house.

The development of a sense of object permanence is related to infants' strong attachment to parents and alternate caregivers at these ages. Piaget uses the word *object* to include people as well as things. The important people in infants' lives are the first "objects" to which they attribute permanence. And they now often protest vigorously when they are left behind.

Another accomplishment in substage four is increased understanding of the relationships between and among objects. Infants realize that someone's hand might need to be pushed open to obtain a toy. They are able to keep the goal in mind and to remember that the hand encloses the toy.

Correspondingly, the ability to imitate expands dramatically. Infants initiate familiar games such as peek-a-boo and find success in imitating sounds and gestures that are new.

BOX 7.3   STRATEGIES FOR FACILITATING DEVELOPMENT: TOYS FOR THINKING

Materials	Concepts/Rules Learned	Age to Begin
Mobiles	movement gravity object constancy and variety	0–3 mo.
Rattles	sound movement gravity visual-motor control	0–3 mo.
Balls	roundness movement: bouncing, rolling means-end variations	4–6 mo.
Pull toys	means-end control movement: rolling wheels: roundness, rolling sociodramatic-symbolic	5–8 mo.
Cubes	means-ends small motor skills spatial relations creative construction	6–8 mo.
Devices (e.g., jack-in-box, variable lever doors)	means-end control object constancy surprise	8–12 mo.
Riding equipment	balance means-end control of momentum and balance	8–18 mo.
Vehicles	sociodramatic-symbolic object constancy and variety	10–12 mo.
Sand and earth	creativity sociodramatic-symbolic means-end control characteristics of materials use of space	10–14 mo.
Puzzles	fitting and matching (shape, size, color) 1-to-1 correspondence object characteristics problem solving	10–18 mo.

Adapted from *Curriculum and Assessment Guides for Infant and Child Care* (pp. 121–128) by William Fowler, 1980, Boston: Allyn & Bacon. Copyright 1980 by William Fowler. Adapted by permission.

VIEWS THAT DIFFER FROM PIAGET'S

Jean Piaget's ideas about intellectual development have been influential in the United States since the mid-1960s. Until recently, Piaget's belief in the competence of infants was greeted with interest but skepticism by the scientific community. Now, however, these ideas seem conservative rather than radical. Since the time of his observations of his own three infants in the 1920s and 1930s, and especially in the past ten years, other investigators have devised many creative research strategies. Because of this creativity and because of technological advances, researchers have discovered new information about infant imitation and have formulated alternate hypotheses about infants' understanding of relationships.

Imitation

Meltzoff and Moore (1985) have demonstrated that infants as young as forty-two minutes of age can imitate facial gestures. Infants were shown two facial gestures: mouth opening and tongue protrusion. The experiments were recorded on videotape for later analysis by observers who did not know which adult gesture preceded any infant gesture. Infants produced significantly more mouth openings in response to adult mouth opening and significantly more tongue protrusions to the adult tongue protrusion gesture.

Finding that newborns can imitate facial gestures has caused Meltzoff and Moore (1985) to consider alternatives to explanations of facial imitation proposed by Piaget and others. Meltzoff and Moore have hypothesized that this early imitation reflects a process in which infants use equivalences between gestures they see and gestures that they perceive themselves to be making. The researchers call this process **active intermodal mapping** and have concluded that infants can compare information received by two different modalities (vision and their sense of their own movement). Meltzoff and Moore have summarized their experiments by postulating that human newborns have an innate ability to appreciate equivalences between their own actions and actions they see.

How to reconcile the findings of these researchers with Piaget's is an interesting question. It may be that videotape analysis has allowed discovery of facets of infant competence that could not be observed by Piaget's naturalistic observation. Or it may be that different types of imitation exist. Perhaps one type of imitation, as is described by Piaget, is developed gradually during early interactions. Perhaps another type of imitation, such as that described by Meltzoff and Moore, has its origin in an innate ability of infants to transform externally perceived stimuli into their own actions. A fuller understanding of infant imitation awaits further research.

Understanding of Relationships

T. G. R. Bower (1977, 1982) of the University of Edinburgh disagrees with Piaget about explanations for infant behavior changes that take place over the course of the first year. The differences between the views of Bower and Piaget center not so much on their interpretations of how infants act and react but on their explanation about *why*.

Bower has indicated that infants under five months of age do not search for lost objects or people because they are unable to understand that the same objects or people can appear in different places and that objects and people must move to get from one place to another. Bower has illustrated his point with two experiments. In the first, infants were presented simultaneously with three images of their mothers. Before five months of age, infants interacted pleasantly with all three, lending support to Bower's idea that infants think that there is a different mother for each location in which she appears. After about five months of age, infants registered shock and protest at seeing multiple mothers, indicating that this sight violated an understanding that they had achieved. In the second experiment, infants were shown the movement of a toy train. When the path of the train changed and the train stopped on another side of the track where it was still visible, infants before five months of age were unable to locate the train. Bower explained this finding by saying that infants do not associate the moving train with the stationary one.

Even when infants reach about five months of age and have resolved some of the problems in their understanding of location and motion, Bower and Piaget are in agreement that infant reactions to disappearances of objects or people show unique aspects of their thinking processes. Bower has explained infants' behavior by saying that they still do not grasp the relationships between and among objects. When an infant at six months of age does not lift a handkerchief to search for a hidden ball, Bower has indicated that the failure to search is not due, as Piaget said, to a lack of a consistent mental image of the object. Rather, according to Bower, the infant lacks an understanding of relationships such as under, on, in, in front of, and behind. Bower has concluded that infants do not realize until the end of the first year that objects can be in these relationships with other things. (e.g., a block on top of another block) and still remain separate and separable.

The theories of Piaget and Bower are in agreement that infants have distinctive patterns of thinking that change during the first year of life.

A significant similarity between the views of Piaget and Bower is the belief that infants have distinctive patterns of thinking that change over the course of the first year of life. It will probably be many years before research demonstrates conclusively the superiority of Piaget's, Bower's, or some other idea about why infants act as they do.

LANGUAGE DEVELOPMENT

Because the word *infant* is derived from the Latin *infans,* meaning "not speaking," it may seem strange to discuss language development in infancy. Yet research shows that the groundwork for language competence begins to be laid in the first year of life. Research relating to infant language development is presented in chronological sequence using the following categories: newborn, first six months, and second six months. When ages are given, they represent averages.

Newborn

Newborns have been said to be "set" for communication, both visually and auditorially (Owens, 1984). Newborns attain their best visual focus at about eight to twelve inches, the distance from them of parents who are providing food; and the mutual gazing that takes place during feeding is an early form of communication. Newborns are known to be able to track the voices of their mothers and to distinguish them from those of other women (Mehler, 1985). Even twelve-hour-old infants change their sucking rates to produce the voices of their biological mothers (DeCasper & Fifer, 1980). Analysis of high speed motion picture film has indicated that within hours of birth infants respond uniquely to human speech sounds (Condon & Sander, 1974). As adults speak, infants make continuous slight movements of toes, fingers, head, eyes, shoulders, arms, and hips. These movements change with each separate sound of speech. Infants move in this manner when they hear male and female speakers in English and Chinese, but they do not synchronize to the sound of disconnected vowels or tapping. Infants participate in the rhythm of normal adult speech months before they begin to babble and two or more years before their own speech falls into these fluent rhythms. The movements in synchronization to speech are too subtle to be observed by the unaided eye, but frame-by-frame analysis of film is giving researchers a new view of the human newborn as a receiver of language stimulation. Selective attention to language is shown in other ways also: newborns stop crying to attend to human voices (Owens, 1984).

First Six Months

Most infants begin to coo in the second month of life. **Cooing** involves making vowel sounds, often in response to a human face, eye contact, or voice. The development of cooing is parallel to social smiling and seems part of the process of communication between infants and adults even in the earliest months.

Cooing is stimulated by human attention; in fact, twelve-week-old infants are twice as likely to revocalize if an adult responds verbally rather than with a smile, look, or other nonverbal gesture (Owens, 1984).

By four months of age, infants initiate communication with adults by smiling or coughing to attract attention. They participate in rituals and game playing, all the while learning to take turns in communication, to share attention, and to communicate their intentions. In the sixth month, infants have the ability to reflect a full repertoire of emotions in their vocalizations, including pleasure, anger, and surprise (Owens, 1984).

Toward the end of the first six months, infants begin to babble. **Babbling** includes both vowel and consonant sounds *(ma, da, pa)* and is therefore more complex than the earlier cooing. Table 7.2 shows the relationship between ana-

TABLE 7.2 *Relationship Between Infant Phonetic Development and Significant Physical Changes*

Anatomic and physiologic developments are closely related to new developments in infant language.

Age of Infant	Phonetic Development	Related Anatomy and Physiology
0–1 month Phonation stage	Nasalized vowels	Nasal breathing and nasalized vocalization because of engagement of larynx and nasopharynx. Tongue has mostly back-and-forth motions and nearly fills the oral cavity.
2–3 months Cooing stage	Nasalized vowels plus g/k	Some change in shape of oral cavity and an increase in mobility of tongue.
4–6 months Expansion stage	Normal vowels	Increased separation of oral and nasal cavities, so that nonnasal vowels are readily produced.
	Raspberry (Labial)	The necessary air pressure in the mouth can be developed because of disengagement of the larynx from the nasopharynx.
	Squeal and Growl	Contrasts in vocal pitch are heightened perhaps because descent of larynx into neck makes the vocal folds more vulnerable to forces of supralaryngeal muscles.
	Yelling	Better coordination of respiratory system and larynx permits loud voice.
	Marginal babble	Alternation of full opening and closure of vocal tract is enhanced by larynx-nasopharynx disengagement.

SOURCE: From *The Communication Game: Perspectives on the Development of Speech, Language, and Non-Verbal Communication Skills: A Round Table* (p. 42) edited by A. P. Reilly, 1980, Skillman, NJ: Johnson & Johnson. Copyright 1980 by Johnson & Johnson Baby Products Co. Reprinted by permission.

tomic changes in infants and phonetic development. Infants continue to babble until about a month or so before they use their first meaningful words, and then their babbling diminishes.

Second Six Months

Researchers have found that six-month-old infants can categorize the sounds of speech. Kuhl (1980, 1985) showed that infants by the age of six months can recognize the equivalence of a number of speech sounds even though they are acoustically different due to variations in speakers, intonation, or context. These findings demonstrate that infants recognize a basic constancy of speech and that their discrimination is very similar to that of adults (Kuhl, 1980, 1985).

In the second six months, infants begin to assert more control within interactions. They try to imitate new sounds and, toward the end of this period, they demonstrate selective listening and compliance with simple requests. They respond when asked to perform simple motor behavior ("Wave bye-bye") and show their understanding of names of family members and caregivers. Infants may demonstrate comprehension of other words such as *ball, baby, more,* and *no.*

Infant's behaviors	Mother's behaviors
1. Infant acts (cries, sneezes, kicks, arches back, vocalizes, etc.)	2. Communicative Effect: Mother reacts to infant's behaviors.
3. As infant develops cognitively, behaviors become goal-directed, she/he looks at, moves toward and/or reaches for toy. Infant vocalizes while attempting to achieve goal.	4. Communicative Inference: Mother infers that the infant's behaviors are communicative and helps him/her get toy (or whatever she interprets that infant wants). She consistently responds to vocalizations as meaningful conversation on the infant's part.
5. Intentional Communication: As infant develops cognitively so that she/he can sequence causal events and recognize causal agents, the infant begins to use behaviors such as reaching and vocalizing while making eye contact with mother as a means to communicate with her.	6. Mother responds to infant's intentional communication but "raises the ante," requiring vocalizations, and later, words.
7. Infant begins using words as a means to communicate.	

FIGURE 7.1 *Proposed Developmental Sequence of Prelinguistic Communication* (From "Setting the Stage for Language Acquisition: Communication Development in the First Year" by C. G. Harding, in *The Transition from Prelinguistic to Linguistic Communication* (p. 95) edited by R. M. Golinkoff, 1983, Hillsdale, NJ: Lawrence Erlbaum. Copyright 1983 by Lawrence Erlbaum Associates. Reprinted by permission.)

Harding (1983) has proposed a model to explain the development of intentional communication in infancy. (See Fig. 7.1, p. 183.) According to this model, as infants' behaviors become goal-directed, adults interpret infants' actions as intending to communicate. Harding has said that intentional communication develops gradually, beginning with infants' cognitive awareness of goals in general and ending with infants' having communication as a goal. Harding has indicated that, when infants realize the usefulness of communication as a goal, they also recognize the utility of words as a vehicle for communication. Most infants produce their first words early in the second year of life.

By the end of the first year of life, infants have become communicators. They have learned how to influence the behavior of others, understand some language, and use behaviors intentionally to signal others. The stage is set for further language development.

CULTURAL DIFFERENCES IN LANGUAGE INTERACTIONS WITH INFANTS

There are many individual differences in the language interactions of adults with infants. There are also systematic cultural and social class differences (Schieffelin & Ochs, 1983). The existence of differences is not surprising in a pluralistic society, but the implications of these differences deserve discussion.

Researchers have suggested that talking to infants is a feature of interaction mainly among middle-class groups in North America and Western Europe (Schieffelin & Ochs, 1983). Talking to infants seems to occur when adults

Talking to infants seems to occur when adults believe that infants are separate individuals with whom communication is possible.

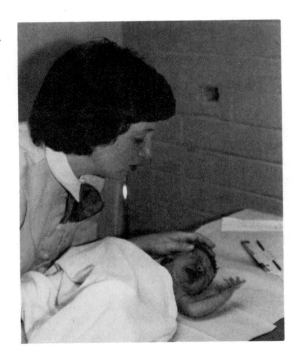

believe that infants are separate individuals with whom communication is possible. Adults with this belief hold infants face-to-face, gaze at them, and address, greet, and question them. Conversations are established using a dyadic, turn-taking model. Parents take the perspective of infants, adapting and simplifying adult speech and making interpretations of infant vocalizations.

Researchers have found that vocalization levels to infants are low in many countries (e.g., Mexico, Kenya, Guatemala, Japan, Zambia, and New Guinea) and among Americans classified in lower socioeconomic groups (Snow, deBlauw, Van Roosmalen, 1970; Schieffelin & Ochs, 1983). For example, the Kaluli people of the tropical rain forest of Papua New Guinea describe their infants as "having no understanding" and say that they care for infants because they "feel sorry for them" (Schieffelin & Ochs, 1983). The Kaluli do not treat infants as partners in dyadic communication, do not gaze into infants' eyes, and do not modify adult language according to infants' abilities. They believe that the responsibility for clear speech rests with the speaker, even if that speaker is a young child. Although the language learning environment does not emphasize dyadic interactions between parent and child, infants in Papua New Guinea hear language and learn to speak.

Research within this country has found cultural differences in the amount and type of language directed by adults to infants. A study by Field and Widmayer (1981) found that Cuban mothers typically spent 82 percent of their time talking to their three- to four-month-old infants and black mothers spent 14 percent. The amount of talking by Puerto Rican and South American mothers was found to be between those two extremes. All mothers were from families classified at a low socioeconomic level, based on education and occupation.

Another report of differences in adult-infant interaction is from a study of families from the same cultural group but different educational and occupational levels. Observing in the homes of white ten-month-old children, Tulkin (1977) found more middle-class than working-class mothers to be very involved in talking with their infants. The significant differences between the two groups pertained to the amount of the mothers' spontaneous talk, their responses to infants' talk, and their imitation of infants' language. Mothers with working-class backgrounds spent as much time caring for infants as did mothers with middle-class backgrounds, but there were differences in the language used.

Talking with infants has been demonstrated to have a positive effect on language development. Feiring and Lewis (1981) observed parents and their children when the children were three, twelve, and twenty-four months of age. Researchers found great variability in how much parents talked to infants. Even more importantly, the researchers found that talking to infants may not have made a measurable difference at three and twelve months of age, but the three- and twelve-month-old infants who were talked with the most were the most capable with language and concepts when they reached twenty-four months of age. This finding reveals an apparent "sleeper" effect of early talking with infants.

Certain aspects of verbal interaction with infants—for instance, engaging them in dyadic "conversations" as in the Harding (1983) model—have often been described as developmental universals when they are actually character-

**BOX
7.4**   **STRATEGIES FOR FACILITATING DEVELOPMENT:
INFANT ASSESSMENT**

How can it be determined which children and families are most in need of the services provided by infant intervention programs? In some cases, multiple handicaps are apparent at birth and referrals are usually made at that time. But with many infants, it is not possible to tell at a glance that they have special needs. Their parents may feel that something seems different about the infant, or, then again, they may not have any basis for comparison. Medical personnel may focus just on physical health and miss behavioral cues.

For a long time there was a need for an easily administered test to screen all children in order to identify which ones were in need of intervention services. The need began to be met in the 1960s by several instruments, one of the best-known of which is the Denver Developmental Screening Test (DDST).

The advantage of the DDST is that a physician or psychologist is not required to administer it. Instead, it can be administered in about fifteen minutes by a trained paraprofessional. Thus, the DDST could potentially reach all children, although that goal has not been achieved.

The DDST consists of over one hundred items that are organized into four categories—personal–social, fine motor–adaptive, language, and gross motor development. Twenty age-appropriate items are selected and, from those items, children who have notable delays in development can be identified for special services.

Dr. William K. Frankenburg, author of the DDST, has also written a Pre-screening Development Questionnaire (PDQ) which is even more efficient than the DDST. The PDQ is derived from the DDST but is designed to be completed by parents who have at least a high school education. Ten questions are selected for parents to answer, and then the answers are reviewed by trained paraprofessionals.

Instruments such as the DDST and PDQ can help to identify infants who should receive intervention services. The sooner special needs are identified and met, the better for child, family, and society.

FIGURE 7.2 (opposite page)   Denver Developmental Screening Test (DDST) (Copyright William K. Frankenburg, M.D. Reprinted by permission.)

istic primarily of white, middle-class Americans (Schieffelin & Ochs, 1983). Some features of the social environment, such as talking with infants, have been found to have positive effects on language development. But helping professionals must exercise caution in drawing implications from research findings

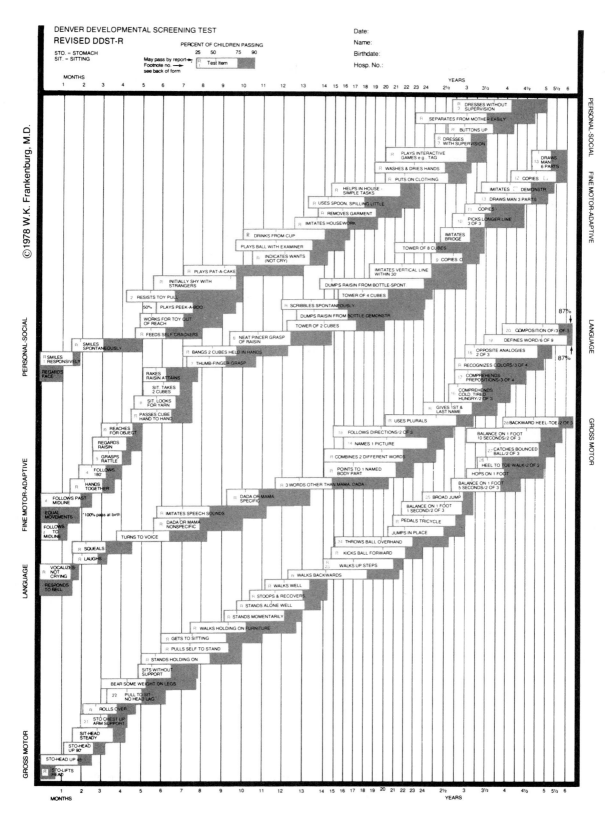

because there is no evidence that these features of the social environment are *necessary* in the language learning process. Children in all cultural groups learn language, despite the variations in adult-infant language interaction patterns. Various cognitive mechanisms may work simultaneously in the language acquisition process; if one mechanism is not emphasized in a given culture, the others may remain. More research in many cultural settings is needed before recommendations can be made.

EARLY INTERVENTION PROGRAMS

Often infants or their families have special needs that can best be met with support, instruction, and help from outside the family. Programs that provide this support, instruction, and help to young children and their families are usually called **early intervention programs.**

One such program has been described by Jablow (1982) in a book about her daughter, Cara. Cara was born with Down syndrome and entered an early intervention program when she was one month of age. She attended four mornings per week for her first two and one-half years and engaged in a curriculum of challenge, stimulation, exercise, and language development. Cara gradually became able to participate in playground activities with her peers from a regular classroom in a regular school. Cara remains a retarded child with limitations, but her involvement in early intervention is believed to have raised her performance over what it would have been if she had not participated.

Programs such as Cara's do not just help the infant who is enrolled. Parents are involved, too, in helping to meet the program goals. Parents and brothers and sisters receive support and assistance. Interactions with other families help to relieve guilt and despair and to promote acceptance and nurturing.

Other such early intervention programs have been designed to compensate for possible problems with cognitive functioning. For instance, in the 1960s there was great enthusiasm for intervention programs aimed at infants born in families designated as economically disadvantaged. However, many of the components of these programs were based on questionable assumptions about development and have not been validated by research. After an extensive review of research related to early intervention programs, Wachs and Gruen (1982) described components of early intervention programs that have been shown to relate to cognitive and social competence in the first and second six months of life.

Wachs and Gruen have concluded that two components are important in facilitating development between birth and six months of age. These components are availability of visual stimulation and high level of physical contact between adult and infant. Visual stimulation seems to give infants something to attend to, and physical contact seems to increase infants' capacity to attend.

Wachs and Gruen have found that after six months of age, development is enhanced by frequent contact with a small number of adults who provide a range of experiences. Wachs and Gruen have said that the optimal low adult-infant ratio is most likely to be found in home-based rather than center-based

A two-month-old infant stud-
ies an interesting pattern.
Visual stimulation, in combi-
nation with a high level of
physical contact between
infant and adult, will facilitate
his development.

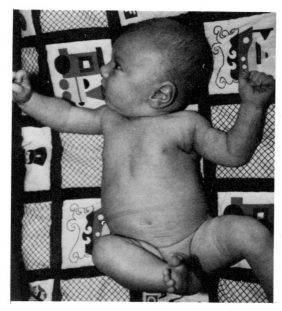

early intervention programs. According to research reviewed by Wachs and Gruen, the physical environment in the second six months should allow exploration. It should also include a variety of colors, shapes, and textures that can be explored by all the senses and that are responsive to infant actions (e.g., making noises when moved). The work of Wachs and Gruen (1982) can help those who design future programs to insure that both physical and social environments are highly responsive to infants' needs and behavior.

Various types of early intervention programs are available to infants who need help because of their genetic, prenatal, or birth experiences or family situations. Many programs are publicly financed and available without charge to families. Information can be obtained from pediatricians, the local Easter Seal Society, or county and state health departments. Assessment of infants at possible risk is described in Box 7.4.

SUMMARY

1   Thinking, problem solving, and language skills develop steadily during the first year.
2   There is interplay among psychosocial, physical, and cognitive aspects of development.
3   Jean Piaget described cognitive development in four substages that culminate in a preliminary sense of object permanence.
4   Some researchers have developed views that differ from Piaget's.
5   In the first year, infants coo, babble, gradually begin to understand language that is directed to them, and become communicators.

6   There are systematic cultural and social class differences in language interactions with infants.

7   Early intervention programs meet special needs of infants and families.

KEY TERMS

sensorimotor	object permanence	babbling
primary circular reaction	active intermodel mapping	early intervention programs
secondary circular reaction	cooing	

FOR FURTHER READING

Piaget's Sensorimotor Stage of Development

Piaget, J. (1976). *The psychology of intelligence.* Totowa, N.J.: Littlefield, Adams. (See especially Chapter 4).

Piagetian Assessment of Infants

Uzgiris, I. C., & Hunt, J. McV. (1975). *Assessment in infancy: Ordinal scales of psychological development.* Urbana: University of Illinois Press.

Language Development

Garvey, C. (1984). *Children's talk.* Cambridge: Harvard University Press.

Owens, R. E. (1984). *Language development: An introduction.* Columbus: Charles E. Merrill.

Curriculum for Infants

Fowler, W. (1980). *Curriculum and assessment guides for infant and child care.* Boston: Allyn & Bacon.

PART II: FROM THEORY TO PRACTICE

The following exercises are designed to help students apply what has been learned, and learn more about children between birth and one year of age. To complete these exercises, two two-hour observations of infants should be scheduled. If friends or neighbors do not have infants, the following are some possible ways to arrange observations: visit a public place that attracts families, such as a busy store, park or zoo; request permission from a pediatrician or obstetrician to spend some time in the waiting room; or request permission to observe at a day-care center or family day-care home that enrolls infants.

1. Narrative observation Write down everything that an infant does during a ten-minute period. (Remember to use descriptive, nonjudgmental language.) What questions about psychosocial, physical, or cognitive development could the observation help to answer?

2. Vignettes Record a vignette that relates to an infant's level of intellectual development, according to the theory of Jean Piaget. Explain why that event or behavior is meaningful in terms of the infant's intellectual development.

3. Child diaries Use what has been learned from observations and reading to make daily diary entries for a week about a real or imaginary infant. Specify the infant's age and record information about psychosocial, physical, and cognitive development.

4. Checklists Complete the checklist included as an example in Chapter 2 (Box 2.4) by observing an infant. In comparison with the narrative observation or vignette, how effective is the checklist in helping to learn about the development of that infant?

5. Interviews Design a questionnaire and use it to interview the parent of an infant about three aspects of temperament. Here are some questions about activity level to get started:

During sleep, the infant
a. Moves about the crib much (such as from one end to the other)
b. Moves a little (a few inches)
c. Lies fairly still and is usually in the same position upon awakening.

During feeding, the infant
a. Sucks vigorously
b. Sucks at a moderate level
c. Sucks mildly and intermittently.

During feeding, the infant
a. Squirms and kicks constantly
b. Moves moderately
c. Lies quietly throughout.

During diapering and dressing, the infant
a. Squirms and kicks much
b. Moves moderately
c. Generally lies still.

During bathing, the infant
a. Kicks, splashes and wiggles throughout
b. Moves moderately
c. Lies quietly or moves little.*

---

*Adapted from "Measurement of Infant Temperament in Pediatric Practice" by W. B. Carey, in *Individual Differences in Children* (pp. 298–304) edited by J. C. Westman, 1973, New York: John Wiley. Copyright 1973 by John Wiley & Sons, Inc. Adapted by permission.

The *a* responses indicate high activity level, the *b* responses moderate, and the *c* responses low.

6. *Time sampling*   Adapt the recording form given as an example in Chapter 2 (Box 2.6), define the terms explicitly, and conduct a time sampling study of infant crying. Compare the results to those reported in Chapter 6.

7. *Event sampling*   Design and conduct an event sampling study of parental and infant behaviors associated with bonding and attachment. (See Box 2.7, Chapter 2, for a model of a recording form.) Define the terms precisely and report the findings.

8. *Case study*   Use what has been learned about infant development to mod-ify the case study outline given in Chapter 2 (Box 2.8) so that it refers specifically to important characteristics of this age level.

9. *Reading about research*   Read an article having to do with infants in a recent issue of one of the following journals: *Child Development, Developmental Psychology,* or *Experimental Child Psychology.*

Give the complete citation in the format used in the bibliography of this book. What questions were the researchers asking? How did they go about finding the answers? What were their results? Which of the theoretical perspectives given in Chapter 1 did the researchers have? Why?

One- to Three-Year-Olds: Energy and Determination Mobilized

At a park on a warm day, three young children venture into the crowded sand area.

Ryan, age one, sits in the sand at his father's feet. His hands are occupied with the sand, but his gaze darts from child to child as their voices or actions catch his attention. He does not vocalize, but responds with apparent understanding to his father's occasional remarks.

Melissa, age two, walks across the sand, plunks herself down next to a younger child, and soon abandons her own shovel in favor of his array of colorful equipment. From time to time, Melissa makes comments to her new friend, such as, "See . . . big," or "Look, look!"

Nikolas, age three, searches until he sees the familiar profile of his friend, Robbie. Nikolas digs tunnels and builds roads near Robbie but does not collaborate with him. Nikolas directs a steady stream of verbal commentary at Robbie: "Here goes the car. Oh, now I need a bridge. This stick is good. Here we go . . ." Nikolas does not seem to expect Robbie to respond to what he says.

The sand play of Ryan, Melissa, and Nikolas illustrates some of the many changes in psychosocial, physical, and cognitive development from one to three years of age. In psychosocial development, one- to three-year-olds establish a sense of autonomy and are influenced by their families, other social variables, and cultural differences. In physical development, they change and grow in many important ways; they need a safe, healthy environment within which they can establish a positive physical image. In cognitive development, they move through the last of Piaget's substages of sensorimotor thinking and begin preoperational thinking; their language develops rapidly; their thinking, language and play are interrelated; and they are cognitively influenced by their cultural and other environments. In these three years, children make the transition from infancy to early childhood. Their energy and determination are mobilized in many different, interesting ways.

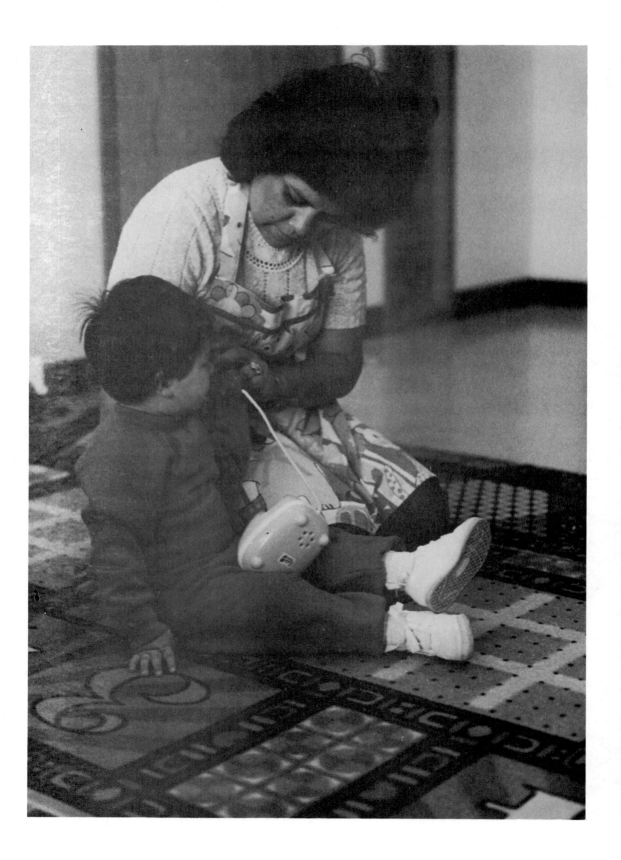

8

One- to Three-Year-Olds: Psychosocial Development

Key Ideas

Autonomy
Erikson's Concept of Autonomy □ *Oppositional Behavior* □ *Effects of Temperament* □ *Transitional Objects* □ *Thumb Sucking* □ *Fears*

Influences of the Family Environment
Attachment and Separation □ *Prosocial Behavior* □ *Awareness of Individual Differences* □ *Alternate Family Structures* □ *Abuse and Neglect* □ *Parent-Child Interaction Patterns*

Social Influences Outside the Family
Effects of Day Care □ *Peer Relationships* □ *Effects of Television*

Cultural Differences

In the last half of their first year of life, infants gain an understanding of the expectations of adults and, if relationships are trusting, infants tend to try to please. The adults in their lives often respond positively to compliant, dependent infants and may be jolted by what happens next in psychosocial development. In marked contrast with infancy, children from one to three are for a time uncooperative with adults and other children as they attempt to establish a sense of autonomy and control over events that affect them. Because children's struggles with autonomy tend to dominate any treatment of psychosocial development in this age range, this chapter begins with a discussion of autonomy. Then consideration is given to various family influences relating to attachment and separation, prosocial behavior, awareness of individual differences, siblings, alternate family structures, abuse and neglect, and interaction patterns. Important social influences outside the family are also presented: day care arrangements, peer relationships, and television. And the chapter ends with attention to cultural variables that affect psychosocial development.

AUTONOMY

Erik Erikson (1963) first used the term **autonomy** to describe the process of becoming a separate person with a separate will. Within the years from one to three, the period between about fifteen and thirty months is especially turbulent

These two-year-olds are at a stalemate, with the child in the front exerting autonomy by refusing to give up the trike and the child in the back exerting autonomy by climbing aboard.

as young children work on developing a system of inner controls. Some people call this period the "terrible twos" because of the challenges presented, but it is more exciting than it is terrible if the developmental processes are understood. Clearly, adults who are as dependent as infants would have difficulty making their ways in the world, and children begin to make the necessary transition toward eventual independence during the years from one to three. Considered in this light, children's struggles for autonomy can be thought of as inevitable and healthy rather than as a problem to be endured.

Erik Erikson's theory provides the basis for this section, and so it begins with a summary of his ideas. An exploration of the relationship of autonomy to oppositional behavior, temperament, transitional objects, thumb sucking, and fears follows the description of Erikson's concept of autonomy.

Erikson's Concept of Autonomy

According to Erik Erikson's theory (1963, 1977, 1982) of psychosocial development, autonomous behavior is normal and necessary. The infant's task in the first year of life was to develop a basic sense of trust. But, just as the infant changes, the developmental task also changes. In the second and third years of life, children need to begin to develop a sense of themselves as separate individuals with unique desires. Erikson calls this process the development of a sense of autonomy.

A brief but stormy interchange between two-year-old Tim and his mother illustrates the exercise of autonomy.

> *"Tim, darling, we're late. Let me get your shoes and jacket on and we'll be off."*
>
> Tim looks over his shoulder and then returns to putting papers in an envelope. His mother approaches him.
>
> *"Here, there's a good boy. I'll do your right shoe first."*
>
> Tim grabs the shoe. *"Do it self!"*
>
> *"Well, you start it and I'll help it on . . ."*
>
> *"Self!"*
>
> *"Tim, I told you that we don't have time for this. Now give me that shoe and I'll put it on."*
>
> *"No, no, no!"* Tim throws the shoe across the rug and himself on the floor, kicking.
>
> Tim's mother looks alternately bewildered and doggedly determined during their interaction. When they finally get into the car, Tim wearily but staunchly resists being put into his car seat. His mother wonders what has happened to her bright-faced infant.

According to Erikson, Tim's "no" responses, even sometimes to suggestions of activities that he enjoys, are affirmations of his emerging power to make his own decisions. Tim's ability to stand and walk and his new understanding of language increase his interest in self-reliance and lead to experimentation with the boundaries of what is acceptable behavior. Tim established trusting relationships in infancy and receives warmth and love now, but he is nonetheless very assertive of his wishes. He seems to have difficulty feeling his separateness unless he can create at least a temporary ambivalence in his parents.

At the same time that young children like Tim are establishing their autonomy, they are trying to make sense of the prohibitions and rules set and enforced by adults. Successful resolution of the struggle for autonomy leaves young children with the resources for mobilizing the independent effort necessary for handling the tasks of childhood, adolescence, and adulthood. Only when young children have been able to define the boundaries between themselves and others can they develop their own code of behavior which incorporates the prohibitions and rules of adults.

Complete autonomy in a child of one, two, or three would be neither possible nor desirable. Erikson has viewed each level of development as being part of a continuum. In this case, autonomy is at one end of the continuum, balanced by shame and doubt at the other end. Erikson believes that children find limits to the assertion of will in a new-found awareness of being watched by superior persons. Children learn to avoid being laughed at or shamed by adjusting their wills to the views of those who judge them. This process leads to the development of self-control. Erikson thinks that children need opportunities to develop a strong sense of autonomy, balanced by the possibility of being shamed by having gone too far.

Oppositional Behavior

During the time when young children are developing a sense of autonomy, much of their behavior may seem to be in opposition to others. Researchers have observed that oppositional behavior ranges from direct (loud "no" responses) to indirect (leaving the room) to passive (staring silently) (Haswell, Hock, & Wenar, 1982). When young children exert their autonomy by oppositional behavior, they are trying to act as though they have the power and authority of the important adults in their lives.

Even at the times when young children's oppositional behavior is at its most flamboyant, one senses that they do not know precisely what they want at the end of the struggle. Indeed, some of their demands would be impossible to gratify because they embody conflicts and contradictions. For instance, children may say "no" to going to the park, to staying home, and to every other feasible alternative.

Tantrums are more frequent during the months of the struggle for autonomy than at any other time in childhood. Temper tantrums signal that the young child is unable to negotiate any further. They provide a way to release tension and a last desperate attempt to keep from losing the confrontation at hand. The screaming, kicking, thrashing, and hitting that take place during tantrums are all-consuming, blotting out the past and future. Although tantrums often begin in response to a parental "no," they bring a peacefulness in their wake that is sometimes surprising. Afterwards children are often willing to do what they have just refused. They want the reassurance that they are still loved and that, though they have been out of control, their parents are still strong and in control.

BOX   STRATEGIES FOR FACILITATING DEVELOPMENT:
8.1   BALANCING AUTONOMY AND SHAME

Rebecca reigned supreme in her household when she was two, showing an extreme of autonomy that led to anxiety for her and barely repressed anger and resentment for her parents. The source of Rebecca's power was that she held her breath if displeased, angry, or over-tired. Her turning blue and passing out was a dramatic sight, and Rebecca's parents were afraid that she would die or suffer brain damage if they did not give in to prevent what they called her "spells." Rather than satisfying her, though, having her parents give in to her whims caused Rebecca to test repeatedly for some kind of limits.

Intervention and an establishment of a more moderate sense of autonomy came unexpectedly to this family when Rebecca's parents heard how another student in a parenting class had handled a similar situation. From that friend Rebecca's parents learned that children do not damage themselves by holding their breath; as soon as they momentarily lose consciousness, the involuntary breathing mechanism takes over. If adults are calm and unswayed by these collapses, breath-holding incidents gradually diminish in frequency and then stop entirely. This knowledge and the encouragement of their class allowed Rebecca's parents to begin to set firm limits for her. Rebecca continued to assert her will but seemed less anxious and more relaxed when her autonomy was balanced by the limits that her parents enforced.

Young children learn to moderate their oppositional behavior from observing balance in the behavior of their parents and other adults. Children's actions are initially directed at winning every confrontation. Gradually, over the months of their oppositional behavior, though, children become aware that some of their demands are accepted and others are resisted. Seeing the balance in adults' behavior helps children to acquire a sense of proportion about themselves—to learn that they are loved and valued, even if they do not always get what they want. Children who have been treated with firm balance, neither winning nor losing all the time, grow beyond their arbitrary and absolute need to control and dominate. Sometime around thirty months of age, the oppositional behavior diminishes and most young children begin to show that they have internalized the prohibitions and rules that they earlier resisted so actively.

Effects of Temperament

The process of establishing a sense of autonomy is influenced by the differing temperaments of children. Researchers in the New York Longitudinal Study (Thomas & Chess, 1981) think of temperament as explaining the "how" of behavior. (See Chapter 5.) They believe that infants come into the world with behavioral characteristics that shape their reactions and the responses of adults. These researchers believe that young children whose temperaments can be described as "difficult" or as "slow to warm up" need special handling during the years from one to three when they are struggling with autonomy.

To determine whether children from one to three years of age are "easy," "difficult," or "slow to warm up," a Toddler Temperament Scale (Fullard, McDevitt, & Carey, 1978; 1984) has been developed. Information is collected by parental response to ninety-seven behavioral descriptions that relate to nine basic characteristics of temperament. Some examples from the Toddler Temperament Scale follow. To find out about activity level, the parent is asked whether the child fidgets during quiet activities such as storytelling. To ascertain rhythmicity, the parent is asked whether the child gets sleepy at about the same time each evening. To learn about approach or withdrawal, the parent is asked whether the child's first reaction to seeing the doctor is acceptance. To investigate adaptability, the parent is asked whether the child accepts delays of several minutes for snacks or treats. To find out about intensity, the parent is asked whether the child is easily excited by praise. To rate mood, the parent is asked whether the child smiles or laughs when first arriving in new places. To gather data about persistence, the parent is asked whether the child plays with a favorite toy for ten minutes. To learn about distractibility, the parent is asked whether the child continues activity despite noises nearby. And, finally, to

The screaming and thrashing of this two-year-old's tantrum began when her father said "no."

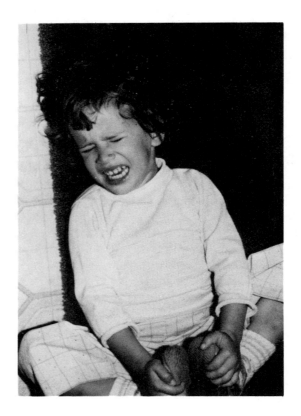

BOX 8.2   STRATEGIES FOR FACILITATING DEVELOPMENT: DEALING WITH OPPOSITIONAL BEHAVIOR

Three techniques help parents and other adults to deal with oppositional behavior: getting children's attention positively, giving time for compliance, and offering choices.

Get attention positively   Molly's father needs to take her to a medical appointment. He could wait until it is time to leave and give a request or a command. If he does, however, his request or command is likely to be met with opposition from Molly, who is unwilling to stop her play. But, if he begins to organize the departure a bit earlier when Molly turns her attention to him during a lull in play, he could tell her about something interesting that they will see during the trip to the doctor's office. With his preparation he has laid a foundation which later eases the transition. Right before departure, he can follow up with a verbal reminder about what they will soon see. If he shows respect and consideration, Molly will have the sense of being a participant in the activities of the day.

Give time   Research (Haswell, Hock, & Wenar, 1981) has shown that the strongest opposition from children comes within seconds after an adult makes a request. Researchers found that if adults wait at least ten seconds before repeating a request or taking further action, children often surprise them and comply. Patience and a good sense of timing seem to be important attributes of adults who interact with young children.

Offer choices   Children can be encouraged to comply if they are given many opportunities for choice during their struggles for autonomy. Young Jeff might be asked, "Do you want to eat with a spoon or a fork? Wear a red or blue shirt? Walk on this side or that? Fix your hair with a brush or comb?" When given such choices, Jeff can assert his will within a structure that is acceptable to him and to his parents. The decision-making focus is moved from whether or not to eat, get dressed, walk, or fix his hair to how each of these things will be done.

When opposition has already occurred, offering a very limited choice can help Jeff "save face." If it is time to go home and Jeff is resisting, his parent can say firmly, "It is time to go," and then offer a limited choice: "You may walk or hop or I will carry you." If Jeff chooses either of the first two alternatives, he is actively participating in the process of going home. If he continues to balk, he has chosen the third alternative and his parent should carry him out.

investigate sensory threshold, the parent is asked whether the child reacts to a disliked food even if it is mixed with a favorite food. These examples are selected from the eight to thirteen questions to which a parent responds for each temperamental characteristic. Once a parent has completed the Toddler Temperament Scale, the child's temperamental characteristics can be compared to the following diagnostic clusters:

1   easy: combines the characteristics of rhythmicity, approach, adaptability, mildness, positive mood
2   difficult: combines the characteristics of unrhythmicity, withdrawal, slow adaptability, intensity, negative mood
3   slow to warm up: combines characteristics of low activity level, withdrawal, slow adaptability, mildness, negative mood.

Researchers have found that across ages about 40 percent of children can be described as "easy," 10 percent as "difficult," and 15 percent as "slow to warm up" (Thomas & Chess, 1981). Difficult and slow-to-warm-up children present special challenges when they are struggling to establish their autonomy. They need more sensitive introductions to new things and people, and more time to make transitions than do easy children. Experiences such as daycare placement, play-group involvement, and medical appointments have to be approached carefully when children are difficult or slow to warm up.

Of course, temperamental style per se is not the only factor influencing the development of autonomy. Especially with difficult or slow-to-warm-up children, a key factor in children's adjustment is the fit between their temperaments and the context in which they find themselves. To illustrate this point, researchers (Thomas & Chess, 1981) use examples from various cultures. They point out that a child with irregular sleep patterns may be an annoyance in Boston, where sleeping through the night is emphasized; on the other hand, in a Kenyan farming and herding community, children sleep in skin contact with their

This temperamentally "easy" three-year-old waits quietly while parent and sibling are involved in soccer practice. Parents of temperamentally "difficult" and "slow-to-warm-up" children may need special help with childrearing.

mothers and are fed whenever they awaken. Other differences in perspective about sleeping "problems" exist between Puerto Rican working-class and Anglo middle-class parents in New York. The Puerto Rican group experiences few sleeping problems because children set their own sleeping and waking times; in the Anglo group, though, irregular sleep patterns are perceived as problems because the parents have certain expectations about appropriate schedules for their children.

Transitional Objects

With all of the turbulence that begins at about a year and a half of age, it may not be surprising that this is a time when children develop special attachments to objects, such as blankets, rag dolls, towels, teddy bears, or pieces of satin fabric. These objects are familiar, faithful things that are full of memories of past comfort. Psychologists call these objects **transitional objects** because they represent a transition from the parents and everything that seems familiar and safe to a wider, uncharted environment. If parents are not close at hand, transitional objects give children a sense of security and comfort. Arthur Kornhaber, a child psychiatrist, calls transitional objects a "portable mommy" that children can take along when separated by sleep, exploration, or day-care placement (Burtoff, 1982).

Many psychiatrists and psychologists agree that children's attachments to transitional objects are normal and helpful in providing reliable comfort. Parents who are supportive of children's attachment to transitional objects allow their children to feel in control of themselves and what they need. During a period when there are tugs of war over eating, bedtime, and other routines, the transitional object should not be another cause of conflict. The need for transitional objects gradually diminishes and is often gone by the time children are seven or eight.

During the time of involvement with transitional objects, certain boundaries can be set for their use so that children have both hands available for exploration. Rather than going along to play group, the transitional object could perhaps stay in the car where it would be waiting when the session is over. Or it could stay in the child's bed where it would remain clean and fresh for nap time. Or it could stay in the child's cubby at day care until nap time. Reasonable boundaries depend upon the child's needs and the particular situations. Certainly children's needs for comfort and reassurance are greater on the first than on the one-hundredth day of day care placement, for instance.

Thumb Sucking

Thumb or finger sucking is another way that children find reliable comfort when they are establishing their sense of autonomy. Thumbs and fingers have an advantage over transitional objects: They are always ready for use. David, age three, was sympathetic when his friend lost her special blanket but commented with relief later, "I'm glad I can't lose my thumb!"

Many specialists (e.g., Brazelton, 1981) believe that thumb or finger sucking is a resourceful way for children to handle tension and to help themselves relax. Busy young children use both hands to find out about interesting things

A thumb provides reliable comfort for this three-year-old as nap time approaches.

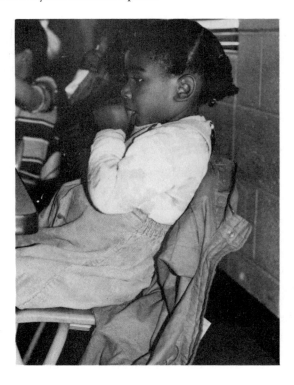

in their environment, but their thumbs or fingers can be important in soothing them when they are hurt, tired, or uncertain.

In earlier generations, parents strongly discouraged thumb or finger sucking. They painted children's thumbs with foul-tasting liquids, bought special gloves, and worried about misshapen mouths. There is no evidence that any of these efforts shortened the length of time that children sucked their thumbs or fingers. In fact, drawing attention to a parent-child struggle over thumb or finger sucking when children are declaring their autonomy may even prolong the duration of thumb or finger sucking. Only if thumb sucking continues after eruption of permanent teeth is there any danger of mouth problems.

Fears

One of the most dramatic examples of interplay between the psychosocial and cognitive domains is the development of fears. At a time in psychosocial development when children are challenging adults in ways that sometimes frighten the children, children also become intellectually able to retain and manipulate mental images. This growth in cognitive ability comes at about eighteen months of age and is often accompanied by the advent of fears. An illustration is provided by the comments of the father of Pedro, age two.

Pedro was never afraid of the dark, but now he will only go to bed if the light is on. If I turn it off and he awakens in the night, he screams until I turn it on again.

FEARS

Around two years of age, children begin to develop fears, such as Frances' about the crack in the ceiling.

Frances was not very tired and did not close her eyes.
She looked up at the ceiling.
There was a crack in the ceiling, and she thought about it.
"Maybe something will come out of that crack," she thought.
"Maybe bugs or spiders. Maybe something with a lot of skinny legs in the dark."

Pedro is afraid of the dark; other children at his age develop fear of bathtubs, dogs, trucks, monsters, and so on. Few parents would be pleased to have a specialist in early childhood development say, "Congratulations! Your child's new fears are a sign of the development of a new level of intellectual ability." And yet that is the case. Troubling fears are not possible until children form permanent mental images.

Children's fears are real and upsetting to them. If adults laugh at these fears, they communicate a lack of respect for children's concerns. Adults do not need to share or magnify children's fears in order to be sympathetic in seeking solutions that make children comfortable. If children participate in these solutions, the process can sometimes be surprisingly simple. Pedro might pick out his own nightlight at a variety store. Sally might put Teddy Bear on guard for monsters who want to enter her room at night. Mitchell might decide to get out of the bathtub before the stopper is removed. Creative solutions often result when children and parents work together.

INFLUENCES OF THE FAMILY ENVIRONMENT

The family environment exerts critical influences on the psychosocial development of children from one to three years of age. These influences are wide-ranging, involving attachment and separation, prosocial behavior, awareness of individual differences, alternate family structures, abuse and neglect, and parent-child interaction patterns.

Attachment and Separation

The ability of young children to handle separations from parents and other special adults has a predictable cycle of ups and downs. Chapter 5 included a description of the first cycle of attachment behavior that often occurs between nine and eleven months of age and can cause children to cling to parents and have difficulty separating from them. The second cycle of attachment behavior often peaks when children are between twenty and twenty-two months of age. Even children who seem to have made excellent adjustments to earlier separations may show a renewal of anxiety about separations and transitions.

Research on attachment and separation has shown that most children between one and three years of age show some distress when they are left by their parents, even for a short time. Children cry, call, follow, and stop their exploration—all as responses to separation. But, despite the pervasiveness of the distress reaction, differences in how children handle separations have also been found.

Researchers in early childhood development have explained why some children are only mildly distressed at separations whereas others are very distressed. Through carefully controlled observation, they have found that children's responses to separation from their parents seem to be related to two differences in parent behaviors (Weintraub & Lewis, 1977). The first relevant parent behavior concerns the amount of contact that parents give children right before separation. The more parents hold and touch children and the less children play prior to parents' departure, the more distressed children are when parents leave. The second relevant parent behavior involves the cognitive structure that parents give to children to help children understand the separation and what should be done during it. The more explicit parents are in explaining the departure and in giving suggestions about what to do in their absence, the more likely children are to play without crying. Parents who slip out, giving their children no preparation at all, have children who are likely to cry rather than play.

Research on attachment and separation shows that parents can help children adjust to separations by involving them in play and in explaining the situation carefully. This same cognitive structuring is important to children who must undergo relatively long separations, such as when hospitalized. It is recommended that parents remain with young children whenever possible but, when separation is necessary, preparation is essential. T. Berry Brazelton (1974) has told a story of a hospitalized toddler who, through his tears, repeated over and over again, "My mommy said it would be this way."

The up-and-down pattern of attachment in the first years of life necessitates giving special attention to the separations that take place during this time period. Since the 1960s, separation has been an important topic of psychological research. It is viewed as a common source of stress that might influence personality development.

Prosocial Behavior

Jackie toddled over to the crying child and stroked his cheek. When his crying continued, she fetched her "lovey" and gave it to him.

Jackie's behavior is called **prosocial**, defined as behavior intended to enhance the welfare of another person. Prosocial behavior represents a whole new area of study. Until the 1960s, researchers were primarily concerned with suppressing unwanted behavior. Research questions focused on how to prevent harmful or deceitful behavior. Now, however, researchers have begun to be more active in studying altruism and concern for others. The question for researchers today is how to encourage prosocial or positive behavior. Their findings offer important insights to those interested in early childhood development.

Research shows that parents and others can increase the probability of children's prosocial behavior by adopting certain patterns of childrearing practices. A review of research (Grusec, 1982) has indicated that parents who effectively elicit prosocial behavior from their children share the following three characteristics: First, these effective parents are models themselves of the sensitivity, self-control, responsiveness, and concern for others that they would like their children to exhibit. Research has repeatedly demonstrated the role of modeling in acquiring these positive behaviors as well as potentially less acceptable aggressive behaviors. Second, these effective parents give reasons for the requests that they make and the limits that they impose. They explain to children how their misbehavior distresses others, and they show their own feel-

This child practices prosocial behavior through play.

ings about the behavior. They are clear and consistent in expressing their values and priorities. Third, these effective parents back up their reasoning with the threat of unpleasant consequences if children do misbehave. It seems that unpleasant consequences at a moderate level, such as a "time-out" period on a chair, provide the motivation for children to avoid certain behaviors. The explanations that parents have previously provided encourage children to attribute behavior to their internal decisions rather than to external pressures.

Parents of one- to three-year-old children sometimes wonder whether any of their strategies are effective. After days filled with negative reactions from their young children, even resolute parents can find themselves slipping into assertions of their own power. In the short run, children in this age range may seem to respond to commands more than reasoning and to threats more than positive interactions. However, parents who look beyond today's confrontations find that the practices recommended by researchers in this field have desirable long-run effects: they help parents encourage altruistic, caring behavior on the part of children.

Awareness of Individual Differences

How early are children aware of individual differences, such as gender and race? Anecdotes such as the following indicate that awareness of individual differences begins in the very early years.

For the past two weeks, Susan (2 years, 6 months) has been urinating by standing up like a boy. She arches her back a little and usually does pretty well at hitting the toilet. We have tried ignoring her, but if we do not say anything, she will say, "My mother says it's okay if I go to the bathroom standing up," or, to another child, "Look at me."

Shawna (3 years) always wants a doll and a pillow when she goes down for a nap. We have several bean bag dolls, some white and some black. Shawna always asks for two dolls, one for her and one for Jeff, if he is not already asleep. If she has a choice, she does not choose the black doll. (Perhaps she prefers the pink outfit to the orange one.) She has made no mention of the dolls being black or white or of her own skin color.

Learning about young children's awareness of individual differences provides intriguing insights into their psychosocial development.

Putting themselves and others into gender or racial groups is, of course, related to young children's ability to form categories in general. And before they can develop a system of categories, children must be able to discriminate among people and objects and to note which differences are significant for classification. Gender and race are both used as early systems for classifying people into categories because the differentiating cues tend to be physical and easily observable. As soon as children begin to use labels, usually at about eighteen months of age, they use *Mommy* accurately to refer to adult women and *Daddy* to refer to adult men. By the age of three, and perhaps sooner, children make different responses to variations in skin color and other racial cues (Katz, 1982). These early categories can be rather rigid, even in families with flexible gender roles and multiracial composition. Later, after children have established their systems of categories, the categories become more flexible.

Gender awareness The literature dealing with the understandings and behaviors of children with regard to gender is extensive. Before discussing the research, though, it is important to define some terms. The first term, **gender identity**, refers to what an individual person privately experiences as being male, female, or ambivalent. The second term, **gender role**, is the public expression of gender identity. And the third term, **gender role stereotyping**, refers to the labeling of certain behaviors as being appropriate or inappropriate for either boys or girls.

Gender identity seems to be formed early, but an understanding of just how early is inhibited by the inability to devise appropriate research strategies for children in the first year and one-half of life. It is known, however, that young children use gender-related words to refer to themselves as soon as those words are in their vocabularies (Brooks-Gunn & Matthews, 1979).

Gender roles are probably influenced by a combination of biological differences between boys and girls and by cultural and environmental differences in how they are treated. It can be demonstrated that by the time children are two years of age, boys have significantly higher activity levels than girls. To what extent this difference and others result from biological variables or from cultural and social conditioning is not known. Most of the research sidesteps the question of biological differences and shows the importance of environmental forces in shaping gender roles.

Gender roles are strongly influenced by parental expectations, but parents are rarely aware of how differently they treat boys and girls. Three examples confirm the existence of significant differences in treatment. First, in a number of studies it has been found that mothers interact more protectively with female than with male infants. They stay in closer proximity to infants who are girls than to those who are boys. Also, when one-year-olds fall down, mothers tend to encourage boys to dust themselves off and go back into action, whereas they tend to encourage girls to stay for holding and cuddling (Fagot, 1982; Fagot & Kronsberg, 1982). Second, parents reward girls and boys for different types of behavior. From the time that children are just one year of age, parents give girls more positive reactions for social responsiveness but boys get more positive reactions for their exploration (Fagot, 1982). Third, parents encourage what they consider to be gender-appropriate behavior. The types of play they choose for children are strongly determined by their perceptions of gender. When parents think that they are playing with a boy, they present a toy train, but when they think that they are playing with a girl, they present a doll (Brooks-Gunn & Matthews, 1979). Fathers are generally even more interested than mothers in promoting what they view as gender-appropriate play.

Stereotypes about gender roles develop early. In one study (Brooks-Gunn & Matthews, 1979), one-quarter of the two-year-old children could classify a majority of pictures of objects (e.g., lawn mower, purse, clothes dryer) according to common gender-typed groups. Also, by the time children are about two years of age, most of them have assigned different functions to the adults in their lives. If they live in two-parent families, they tend to prefer fathers for play and mothers for comfort in times of stress. Gender-role stereotyping seems to begin between two and three years of age.

Parents and other adults can help children to become more flexible in their thinking about gender roles or can reinforce their stereotypes. Consider the effects of comments such as the following:

Big boys don't cry.
Keep your pretty dress clean.
Boys don't play with dolls.

Such comments limit children's development. Many early childhood specialists believe that boys should be encouraged to have more experiences with nurturing others and expressing their own feelings and that girls should be encouraged to have more experiences with materials such as blocks that encourage logical and spatial thinking and active physical exploration. Gradually society is moving away from practices that channel boys and girls into stereotyped occupational and personal choices.

Racial awareness   In a diverse society, people of many racial and cultural backgrounds must find ways to live together in harmony. Within this context, the question of how and when children develop racial awareness is highly significant. In a review of relevant literature, Phyllis A. Katz (1982) has observed that there are virtually no studies on the development of racial awareness before

BOX 8.4   **BREAKING GENDER-ROLE STEREOTYPES**

William's Doll (Zolotow, 1972) was a pioneering children's book that addressed the issue of gender-role stereotyping.

William's grandmother believes that boys should be encouraged to develop nurturing skills.

But his father was upset.

"He's a boy!" he said

to William's grandmother.

"He has a basketball

and an electric train

and a workbench

to build things with.

Why does he need a doll?"

William's grandmother smiled.

"He needs it," she said,

"to hug

and to cradle

and to take to the park

so that

when he's a father

like you,

he'll know how to

take care of his baby

and feed him

and love him

and bring him

the things he wants,

like a doll

so that he can

practice being

a father."

From *William's Doll* (pp. 30, 32) by Charlotte Zolotow, 1972, New York: Harper & Row. Text copyright © 1972 by Charlotte Zolotow. Pictures © 1972 by William Pene du Bois. Reprinted by permission of Harper & Row, Publishers, Inc.

the age of three, yet evidence indicates that the process takes place in these first several years of life.

In Chapter 6, it was noted that newborns are already aware of color contrasts. By three or four years of age, white children have positive associations to the color white and to the racial group labeled white. In years past, black children showed a preference for white also, but in recent years they have shown either no preference or same-race preference in experimental situations (Katz, 1982). Generally it has been found that children from minority cultural groups are more sensitive to racial cues and develop racial awareness earlier than other children. For instance, in a study that asked children to discriminate among faces that were in various shades of black, white, and green, the performance of black children was superior to that of other children. And younger children learned to discriminate faster when tested by a researcher of another race (Katz, 1982). With regard to this latter finding, the researchers concluded that, already by the time children reach three years of age, racial traits influence their perceptions and their learning processes. The evidence seems to refute the hypothesis that young children are "color blind" with regard to racial differences.

Unless children have interracial families or child-care arrangements, information about race comes from parents and others who are from the same background as the child. In neighborhoods that are not integrated, children under school age may have little acquaintance with racially different people except through television and books. If models from other racial groups are not available to children, misconceptions and oversimplifications may persist longer than those pertaining to gender, because models of both genders are accessible to children. Racial stereotypes are still found in the media and in children's books, although the situation is much improved in the past decades.

Young children seem to evaluate more and make more judgments about race than about other areas of early learning; adults who value diversity should therefore be conscious of explicit and implicit messages to children about racial and other differences. According to Katz (1982), after about the fourth grade, children do not rethink their racial attitudes unless their social environment changes significantly. Intervention on behalf of positive values, then, belongs in the earliest years of life.

By age three, children show awareness of racial differences, and some show preferences in situations such as this set-up for water play.

**BOX
8.5**   **RACE IN CHILDREN'S LITERATURE**

Jeanne Chall and her colleagues (1979) reported that only 14.4 percent of all children's books published between 1973 and 1975 had at least one black character. After analyzing later children's literature, Rudine Sims (1983) said that books with black characters can be divided into three main categories: (1) social conscience books, intended to encourage tolerance of black children among white children; (2) melting-pot books, showing by their illustrations that people are people but having in their text no specific references to race; and (3) culturally conscious books, told from the point of view of black characters. Sims is enthusiastic only about the third category, culturally conscious books.

The statistics reported by Chall and her colleagues and by Sims show that positive changes have taken place since the 1960s, when only 6.7 percent of books included even one black character in the text or illustrations and many of the portrayals of blacks were stereotypic or ridiculous (Larrick, 1965). Still, because of the paucity of culturally conscious books, Sims (1983) has concluded that the "world of children's fiction . . . remains largely white in terms of the characters, the authors, and the audiences for whom the books are written. . . . We are no longer where we once were, but we are not yet where we ought to be" (p. 653).

Alternate Family Structures

In the 1960s there were some dramatic changes in family life. Young adults from middle- and upper-class families began to look for alternatives to the nuclear two-parent families in which most of them had been reared. The family models that evolved in the 1960s and 1970s differed in composition, legality, and function from those in which these young adults had grown up. Some young adults purposely became single mothers; some participated in "social contract" families, believing that a legal contract would damage their relationships; and some chose communal living groups in order to share their days with people holding similar views. There was much variability within each family type, and many issues in early childhood development were raised.

Researchers in early childhood development wondered about the effects on children of living in alternate families with multiple caregivers, changed fathering behaviors, and conscious modeling of egalitarian gender roles. In 1973 an interdisciplinary team of researchers at the University of California at Los Angeles (Eiduson, Kornfein, Zimmerman, & Weisner, 1982) began a study of relationships between family style and early childhood development. Parents entered the study when they were in the third trimester of pregnancy and they and their children were observed and tested for three years. All parents were middle-class, white, and between eighteen and thirty-five years of age. Parents were divided into four family types: single-mother, social-contract, communal, and two-parent nuclear families.

Psychological development of children was repeatedly assessed during the first several years of life. Children were given various tests of development and intelligence, their attachments were evaluated in experimental situations, and their parents were asked to rate them.

Based on the data collected, the researchers concluded that there were no noticeable or systematic effects due to differences in family model through three years of age. Children in all four groups were found to be developing "normally."

The researchers had expected to find systematic differences among children from various types of families. They had thought that children in single-mother families might be dependent, affectionate, and nurturing to the mother, and independent and self-reliant in other areas; that children in social-contract families might be creative, impulsive, sensitive, and self-motivated; that children in communal groups might be selfless, poised, able to integrate personal and group needs, and compliant; that children in nuclear two-parent families might be achievement- and task-oriented, organized, energetic, and controlled. The researchers were surprised not to find these differences, at least not in the data that they collected during the first three years of life.

Abuse and Neglect

James Harrel, director of the federal government's National Center on Child Abuse and Neglect, has said that only three things are necessary for child abuse to occur: an alienated parent, a child, and a crisis (Caudle, 1983). Over one million cases of physical, emotional, and sexual abuse and neglect are officially reported each year. Experts from a variety of backgrounds struggle to understand the phenomenon of abuse and neglect in terms of the interaction of cultural and family influences. Research relating to each of these influences provides a context for discussing the special problems and needs of one- to three-year-old children.

The level of child abuse in a cultural group seems to be related to whether that culture allows violence as a way of resolving social conflict. Cross-cultural research (Parke & Lewis, 1981) indicates that in China, where physical punishment is not sanctioned as a childrearing tactic, there is little physical punishment, little aggression among children, and no child abuse; and in Japan, where physical punishment is also uncommon, child abuse is infrequent. Within the United States, there is a tendency to endorse the use of physical punishment of children and, further, there are many conflicting values and attitudes that may confuse parents. The rapid social change that is now taking place also leads to a climate of ambiguity about violence.

A great deal of evidence suggests that abusing or neglecting parents were themselves abused or neglected as children. Treatment received in childhood seems to communicate guidelines of appropriate practices which then can govern parenting interactions.

A series of studies documents the fact that abusive parents, as compared with nonabusive parents, have distinct patterns of interaction with their children. For instance, physical punishment is more frequent among abusive families; and this finding is important because nearly two-thirds of child abuse incidents take place in the context of confrontations over discipline (Parke and Lewis, 1981). Families with abuse and neglect problems are in all economic groups, but families with incomes of less that $7,000 per year are ten times more likely to experience abuse and neglect than are families making over $20,000 (Caudle, 1983).

One- to three-year-old children are involved in many conflicts and contradictions that can precipitate crises. Children of these ages want and need close attachments, and yet they also desire individuality and autonomy. They are not usually compliant and they have their own definite agenda of needs to be met. Children of these ages present challenges to adults and these challenges can be overwhelming if not accompanied by information about normal patterns of early childhood development. Studies of abused children in this age range have found that abusive parents, in comparison with nonabusive parents, have unreasonable expectations of their children's behavior (Galinsky, 1981). Abusive parents expect their children to be respectful, submissive, and thoughtful—qualities that cannot be said to characterize the behavior of most children in these early years.

Even very young children are affected by violence that they observe. By one year of age, children are aware of the angry or affectionate interactions of other family members, and are also quite likely to have emotional reactions to them (Cummings, Zahn-Waxler, & Radke-Yarrow, 1981). Anger, especially if it includes physical attack, causes children to become distressed. The researchers believe that children's sense of security may be undermined by angry interactions that they see, even if they are not direct participants. This finding has important implications for families with patterns of violence.

Parent-Child Interaction Patterns

Parents' interaction patterns change toward the end of the first year with an infant. Nurturing is still needed, but parents must also participate in a much wider range of interactions with their children. Dealing with children's anger,

After infancy, parents and others need to set and enforce reasonable limits on children's behavior.

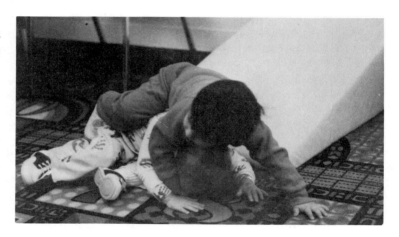

aggression, and independence sometimes challenges parents' previously formed images of how the parent-child relationship would be. Ellen Galinsky (1981), author of a book about the stages of parenthood, designates these years as the **authority stage of parenting.** According to Galinsky, parents' primary task is to accept responsibility and authority over their children. This task raises fundamental questions for parents: What is the scope of my authority? How do I enforce it? How do I communicate appropriately about limits to my children? Parents must formulate new relationships with their children based on responses to these and other questions.

Some parents have difficulty establishing their authority. They may enforce too many limits, robbing their children of opportunities for autonomy, or they may be overly permissive, giving children more autonomy than they can deal with. Fortunately, there are a number of sources of parenting support to which people can turn if they want to change parent-child interaction patterns.

Parent support groups are often sponsored by community mental health associations, departments of social services, school districts, or YMCAs. Parent support groups share many of the same goals of conveying information about normal growth and development and of pointing out the importance of parent-child interactions. All approaches teach parents that love is a foundation for parenting, but love by itself is not enough to meet the challenges.

Despite the many similarities, parent support groups also differ in some significant ways. The two main kinds of approaches are those that focus on the behavior of the child, such as the approach of Rudolf Dreikurs (1958), and those that focus on the feelings of the child, such as the approach of Thomas Gordon (1975). Although many parent support groups may be eclectic rather than "pure" Dreikurs or Gordon, an understanding of these two approaches is valuable in understanding the options available to parents who want to change their interaction patterns.

Dreikurs' focus on behavior   Rudolf Dreikurs (1958) has developed a child-rearing approach that he believes is appropriate for a democratic society. Dreikurs has said that parents influence children by gaining their cooperation to work for mutual goals. Children receive encouragement, guidance, and advice from parents. Instead of punishment, children are allowed to experience the natural consequences of their actions. Dreikurs has contrasted his approach with techniques that require parents to act as powerful authorities who dispense rewards and punishment. He has indicated that these other approaches are more suited to authoritarian societies, with inferior-superior relationships, than to democratic societies.

Dreikurs has told parents that children are born with the capability to develop their strengths and abilities, if parents will help them. But he has observed that parents often undermine children's confidence: "Look at the food in your hair! Let me feed you." "That's too hard for you." "It's on the wrong foot." Dreikurs has encouraged parents to communicate their respect for children and to allow self-sufficiency whenever possible. He has suggested that one- and two-year-olds be included in family chores, such as putting away clothes or carrying spoons to the table. Children should then receive feedback from parents that is specific to the behavior just completed: "Good. Your clothes are all ready for you to wear tomorrow, " or "Now that the spoons are on, we can eat our soup."

Dreikurs has favored structure in home life in order to give children a sense of security. In all households children make mistakes; and, in these cases, Dreikurs has said that parents need to learn to separate the behavior from the child. The child is not a failure but is in need of guidance, which parents can give if they focus on the behavior itself. For example, if a toy is broken because of being left in a hallway, parents can help the child decide how to avoid future problems of that type.

Sometimes, though, children do not just make mistakes—they misbehave. According to Dreikurs, misbehavior takes place when children seek attention, power, or revenge or use inadequacy as a substitute for self-sufficiency and social belonging. Dreikurs urges parents to take direct, immediate action to modify children's misbehavior. Put concisely, his advice is, "Don't give in but don't fight." If a child has a screaming tantrum, it may not be possible for parents to stop the noise, but they can insist that the child move to another location.

Dreikurs also has taught parents to use the technique of logical consequences. Here is an illustration of a **logical consequence**: If a child is throwing food, the parent informs the child that she is showing by her behavior that she is finished with lunch; no food will be served until the next mealtime. In this case, the consequence of hunger between meals is related to the misbehavior of throwing food; the child learns to predict consequences and to avoid them. With young children the only limit on using logical consequences occurs when those consequences could result in danger to children. Children cannot be allowed to be hit by vehicles to teach them to stay out of the street. In dangerous situations, parents can remove related privileges, such as being able to be outside.

Gordon's focus on feelings Thomas Gordon (1975) has written that children are worthy of respect, acceptance, and consideration. He has said that many conflicts between parents and children can be defused if parents show children that they understand what children are feeling. In order to interchange feelings, Gordon has suggested that parents use active listening and "I-messages." His approach to conflict resolution is called the no-lose method because each person's needs are met. Gordon has contrasted his no-lose method with authoritarian methods, in which parents impose their wills on children, and permissive methods, in which children impose their wills on parents.

According to Gordon, children develop best when parents accept themselves as fallible human beings and are able to express their feelings. He has advised parents to be honest in what they are able to accept from their children. For instance, if a child begins to play with food on someone else's plate, parents could send a nonverbal message, involving moving the food back and the plate out of reach. Or they could send a verbal message: "I like it better when you eat your food and I eat mine."

When a parent is upset with a child's behavior and the child is not bothered, Gordon has said that the parent "owns the problem." For example, a toddler might be unfurling all of the toilet paper into the toilet. Gordon recommends that the parent send an *I-message,* which contains three parts: a statement of how the parent feels, what the child did to make the parent feel that way, and why the behavior upsets the parent. In the example above, the parent might say, "I feel angry when I see you plugging up the toilet so that none of us can use it." I-messages are at first difficult for parents to use; until they practice sending I-messages, parents often begin their corrections with angry comments about the child, such as "You weren't listening when . . . " or "You know that you aren't supposed to . . . " According to Gordon, I-messages have several advantages over the more common responses that parents make. First of all, parents begin to understand and give importance to their own feelings. Second, the child has a chance to understand how the parent is feeling. And, third, the child is able to respond to the I-messages with problem solving.

Active listening is another skill that Gordon has taught parents. Active listening is used when the child "owns" the problem. The child is given an opportunity to express feelings and thoughts while the parent listens carefully. Of course, very young children are limited in their verbal abilities, but even so, parents can apply Gordon's ideas. If a child says in tears that he hates his brother, the parent might say, "It sounds as if you two are having problems." The child responds; the parent feeds back ideas about the deeper feelings being expressed. Active listening helps children to express their feelings directly and effectively. Parents learn more about their children's feelings and give children a sense of acceptance and love. Active listening is a difficult skill to learn. Most parents' tendency is to give advice, criticism, or instruction rather than to let children work through problems. In the example of the fighting brothers, active listening would give support to the child's problem solving and encourage him to develop a strategy for getting back into the play situation.

SOCIAL INFLUENCES OUTSIDE THE FAMILY

Interactions outside of the family used to be thought to assume importance only when children enrolled in preschool, kindergarten, or first grade. Now, though, specialists in early childhood development have discovered that day-care arrangements, peer interactions, and television all influence the lives of children in the earliest years of life.

Effects of Day Care

"I have to work to support myself and my child."

"I want to continue to enjoy the fulfillment of my work and still be fair to my young child."

Both of these parents and many others with variations of their situations have placed their young children in day-care arrangements while they are at work. But these parents suffer from a heavy burden of guilt and worry about whether they are in any way harming their children. The anxiety of parents in this regard

Research shows that day-care centers can help to meet children's emotional needs by providing high levels of adult-child verbal interaction. Here a teacher writes down a child's words.

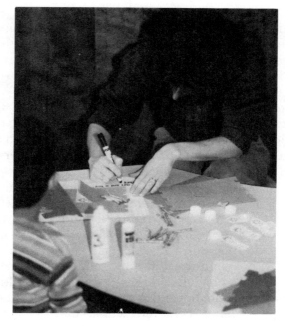

is heightened by researchers who still refer to studies conducted several decades ago with children who were full-time residents of institutions in which little warmth or stimulation was available. Alternate care during the work day is obviously not the same as long-term institutionalization. Current research offers insights into the effects of day-care placement on one-, two-, and three-year-old children.

Most of the research on effects of day care placement of very young children has been conducted in the context of well funded, high quality programs, often in university settings. The primary exception is the New York City Infant Day Care Study, which is discussed separately below. First, however, a summary of the findings from the majority of studies is given under three main headings—intellectual effects, emotional effects, and social effects.

Intellectual effects The research conducted so far indicates that scores on standardized intelligence tests neither go up nor go down for most young children who participate in day-care programs. But children from low-income homes seem to benefit from involvement in day-care programs. Specifically, enrollment of low-income children in day care seems to halt the decline in intelligence test scores that ordinarily takes place between eighteen and thirty-six months of age (Belsky, Steinberg, & Walker, 1982).

In a study (Carew, 1980) of one- and two-year-olds whose daily care was predominately at home or predominately in a day-care center, it was found that stimulating environments at home and in day care are dependent upon the efforts of adults. In both settings, about half (55 percent in the home study and 48 percent in the day-care study) of the variation in intelligence at age three could be predicted from intellectual experiences provided by adults. (See

Table 8.1.) These intellectually valuable experiences involve adults as active participants in labeling, describing, comparing, classifying, and questioning. There is a strong relationship between participation in these intellectually valuable experiences and the intellectual competence of children cared for at home and in day-care centers.

Emotional effects   The available studies show few differences in attachment between day-care and home-reared children. Parent-child attachments do not seem to be weakened or changed when children are enrolled in day care, even when day care is initiated in these earliest years of life (Belsky & Steinberg, 1982). And when a day-care child is placed in a stressful situation with both the alternate caregiver and the mother present, the child consistently and overwhelmingly shows a preference for the mother (O'Connell, 1983).

In research conducted in Bermuda (McCartney, Scarr, Phillips, Grajek, & Schwarz, 1982), a relationship was found between qualities of day-care environments and emotional adjustment. Some children studied attended day-care centers with good physical facilities and play materials but with less than the average amount of adult verbal interaction with children. Children in such centers were more emotionally maladjusted than children enrolled in centers with higher levels of verbal interaction. And at centers with low verbal interaction, emotional maladjustment was higher among children who entered in early

TABLE 8.1   *Intellectually Valuable Experiences According to Carew (1980)*

Experience	Focus	Example
Language mastery	Naming, describing, defining, categorizing	A mother reads *school bus* from the side of a toy. The child repeats *school bus*.
Spatial, perceptual, fine motor mastery	Discriminating objects by characteristics or stacking, building or matching	A child tries to fit round figures in round holes and square figures in square holes.
Concrete reasoning and problem solving	Understanding physical regularities and solving problems	A child uses a cushion to make an incline and lets a vehicle roll down several times. The mother comments that the vehicle goes down by itself on a hill.
Expressive and artistic skill	Imagination, creativity	A child creates a conversation between imaginary children on a toy bus.

SOURCE: Adapted from "Experience and the Development of Intelligence in Young Children at Home and in Day Care" by J. V. Carew, 1980, *Monographs of the Society for Research in Child Development, 45,* serial no. 187. Copyright© The Society for Research in Child Development, Inc. at the University of Chicago Press. Adapted by permission.

infancy than among those who entered the same centers later. These results indicate that specific aspects of day-care environments affect children's development.

Social effects Of the many studies that have investigated peer social interactions in day-care and home-reared children, most have found few differences. Some of the studies have reported more favorable behaviors from day-care children and others have indicated that home-reared children are more adept socially. It has been suggested that social development may relate more to having the opportunity for interaction with a number of peers in a facilitative environment than to whether the interactions take place at a day-care center or at home.

New York City Infant Day Care Study The New York study focused on the effects of publicly funded day-care programs on children between six months and three years of age. The backgrounds of children in the New York study were more diverse than in the other research summarized above: 47 percent of the children in the New York study were black, 39 percent were Hispanic, and most were from working-class or low-income families (Stevens, 1982). Also, the New York study compared children in group day-care centers to those who were enrolled in family day-care homes. (Group day-care centers are schools designed for young children, whereas family day-care homes are residences in which several children receive care.)

The findings of the New York study (Stevens, 1982) are consistent with those summarized above, and several additional insights were made possible by the design of the research. First, the children who received the most stimulation, either in centers or in homes, were later rated as more socially competent and more skillful in language use. Second, it was found that the physical environment, nutritional program, health care, and health surveillance of the group day-care facilities were superior to those of the family day-care programs. And, third, children in group day-care centers had higher scores on standardized intelligence tests than did children in family day-care homes. The researchers were not able to detect variables in the two settings that would explain the differences in intellectual outcomes but noted that group day-care workers usually had completed more education and more preparation in early education than people operating family day-care homes.

Researchers do not yet have a full understanding of the effects of day care on children, parents, and the family unit. However, the research already conducted does not give cause for alarm, if certain standards are maintained. All of the programs on which research has been conducted, including those in New York, have in common the maintenance of at least a one-to-five ratio of adults to children of these young ages. As discovered in the Carew and New York studies, high levels of cognitive/language and social/emotional stimulation by parents and teachers are positively related to the development of competence in children. Finding a personalized child-care setting, staffed by adults with warm and stimulating interaction patterns, is an important challenge for parents of young children.

Peer Relationships

In a family day-care home, the children are watching "Sesame Street." Gary (age 3½) puts his arm around Charlie and asks, "Charlie, will you marry me?"

Charlie looks at him and seems to consider the idea carefully. "After I marry all the girls here," he replies, gesturing to the rest of the group, "then I will marry you."

Gary smiles and says, "Okay!"

Gary and Charlie are friends. They spend ten hours of each day together in a family day-care home while their parents work. It seems logical to expect that their interactions with each other and with other peers influence their development.

Before exploring what research has found about peer relationships, we must realize that current research is not entirely consistent with the traditional view (derived from Parten, 1932-1933) of when young children develop certain skills in playing with each other. The traditional view gives an expected schedule for emergence of four main levels of play during the early childhood years. First, according to this view, **solitary play** takes place in the first two years of life. As the name implies, in solitary play children interact only with an object or with a familiar adult. Second, from two to three years of age, children participate in **parallel play**. Children involved in parallel play are near each other but remain independent of each other. Third, the time from three to four is characterized by the beginning of **associative play**. In associative play, children participate together in small groups but have very limited sharing or interactions with each other. Fourth and finally, according to this traditional view, **cooperative play** starts at about four years of age. In cooperative play children share

Peer relationships influence development, especially when children spend large portions of the day together.

ideas and roles and interact in increasingly more complex play. The traditional view was formulated when most research involved children whose interactions with peers were limited to occasional play groups and perhaps, at age four, to preschool programs that were only several hours in duration. Today, children spend more time than ever before in the company of peers in day-care centers, family day-care homes and in other programs. The changes in the amount of peer contact of young children necessitate reassessing the traditional age ranges given for the kinds of play in which young children take part.

Recent research shows that, given the opportunity to be with peers, even infants participate in parallel play, which had previously been considered to be absent from children's repertoires until the age of two. As early as twelve months of age, infants have been observed to spend more time watching the activity of their peers than that of their mothers (Oden, 1982). Early parallel play usually centers on interest in the same toy or toys and often involves imitation of what another child is doing. Interaction is richer when the children are acquainted with each other. In one study, twelve-month-old children were paired with a friend, with whom they had shared two earlier play sessions, or a stranger. Children were found to be more likely to touch, get close to, look at, and imitate the friend than the stranger (Oden, 1982).

Peer relationships in these early years give children important opportunities to practice social skills and to learn new ones. The research clearly shows that even preverbal children interact with their peers. Two- and three-year-olds who have frequent and sustained peer contacts engage in associative and cooperative play—not all of the time, of course, but more than was previously thought. Through play, children learn from each other. They give and receive information and get immediate, direct feedback about their ideas and overtures. Besides the social advantages, there may be cognitive advantages to having the opportunity to develop a wider variety of roles and to learn what is appropriate behavior in dealing with children as well as with adults. As children take an active role in initiating play interactions, they gain a sense of control over the world.

Effects of Television

True or False?
Children under four years of age do not sit still long enough to be influenced by television.
Young children are more likely to imitate a person in front of them than someone seen on television.
Television viewing is selective in most American homes.

False, false, false. And the implications of the facts underlying these statements require reevaluation of some current childrearing practices. These three statements are considered, in question form, one at a time.

Are children under four years of age influenced by television? A comprehensive series of studies (McCall, Parke, & Kavanaugh, 1977) has shown that even one-year-old children imitate 28 percent of the simple behavior shown on television; two-year-olds imitate 76 percent of these behaviors. These findings clearly refute the hypothesis that young children are too active to be infuenced by what is shown on television.

Are live models more effective than those that are televised? Three-year-olds were found to be as likely to imitate the actions of people on television as to imitate people present in the room (McCall, Parke, & Kavanaugh, 1977). Before the age of three, imitation of a live model has been shown to be somewhat more accurate and frequent than is imitation of a televised model. Even with two-year-olds, a delay of one day between television viewing and a play session did not hinder the children's imitation of what they saw on television. Television is a powerful socializing force in the lives of even very young children.

Is American television viewing generally selective? Most surveys indicate that the television is on six hours per day in the average American home. Young children in the home, then, are exposed to large amounts of television viewing, much of which is not planned or programmed particularly for their needs. What are they learning from soap operas, game shows, prime time programs, and children's cartoons? The answer to this question is still largely unknown. However, two kinds of learning have been documented. First, children see a great deal of violence—an average of five violent acts per hour on prime time television and eighteen violent acts per hour on children's weekend television—and in this way they indirectly form attitudes about the acceptability of violent behavior. Alberta Siegel, a researcher at Stanford University, has said that research demonstrates the direct relationship between television violence and aggressive behavior in children (Dillon, 1982). Second, children receive messages from television about gender, cultural, and racial roles. When young children are exposed to the world as portrayed by television without an adult to interpret and present alternate values, they can form stereotypes about people from other groups.

Research shows that television influences children and that they learn from it and imitate what they see. What is known about the effects of television on young children should lead parents to exercise great caution and selectivity in what they allow children to view. Bob Keeshan (1983), Captain Kangaroo to

By watching television with their children, parents can explain and interpret.

millions of American children, has accused American parents of being willing to give their children things but of holding back on giving them time in the early years when they need it most. If parents say to children, "I'm busy. Go watch television," in the morning when they are getting ready to go to work and in the evening when they return in exhaustion, they may be leaving much of their children's attitude formation to a questionable source—the television.

CULTURAL DIFFERENCES

Does psychosocial development vary across cultures? Erik Erikson and others believe that it does. According to Erikson, the universal psychosocial task of children in this age range is to establish a sense of autonomy. The acceptable ratio or proportion of autonomy in relation to shame and doubt, however, is thought to vary by culture. For instance, Erikson (1963) has said that native-American children, in contrast with children from the majority culture, emerge from these years with much trust but only a small amount of autonomy. This section will examine childrearing practices in other cultures after a discussion of one scholar's perception of childrearing in the dominant culture in the United States.

In the view of Robert A. LeVine (1980), an anthropologist at Harvard, the pervasive theme in American childrearing is independence, which includes separateness, self-sufficiency, and self-confidence. LeVine has analyzed parent-child interactions and found that the emphasis on separateness begins at birth, when infants often have their own beds in their own rooms. These infants' experiences differ sharply from those of infants who spend their time with others, and they usually have many possessions that are theirs alone. Parents begin to encourage sharing only after children have become used to eating, sleeping, and being comforted alone with their own things. LeVine has said that the focus on self-sufficiency similarly begins early. Infants are left to cry themselves to sleep, something that is not expected in other cultures. Toddlers are praised for what they can do for themselves and are motivated by a sense of pride about what they can do. Self-confidence, then, is also encouraged in these early interactions. Parents give attention and praise to small children and hope that their children will be confident in mastering unfamiliar situations. According to LeVine, American parents emphasize language production in young children as a symbol of the good feelings that will bind them together after the children are physically and economically independent.

The significance of LeVine's views can be communicated by giving his speculations on the consequences of these childrearing practices for later school adjustment. LeVine has asserted that children who are reared in this manner do very well in school. Because of their early experiences, these children are uninhibited with adults and responsive and curious in classrooms. They are verbally fluent and seek teacher attention through their accomplishments. Their sense of separateness enables them to compete with others without fear of negative interpersonal consequences. And, finally, they are accustomed to the somewhat artificial problem-solving situations associated with toys and games and usually enjoy the kinds of tasks presented in school. LeVine has not endorsed these childrearing practices as ideal; he has tried to show the match between the characteristics developed in these children and the expectations of American schools.

LeVine has contrasted these American childrearing practices with those that he observed in Africa. In Africa, infants remain in skin-to-skin contact with their mothers, who comfort them at the first signs of restlessness. Later, children are expected to perform certain tasks but are not praised. Praise is thought to be bad for children because it leads to conceit and disobedience. In language, African families emphasize understanding of commands and compliance. Rather than being praised for independence, children are seen as being permanently bound to their parents: Parents nurture children in their early years and expect children to care for parents in old age. These African childrearing practices have implications for psychosocial development. In a comparative study of attention seeking, for example, African children showed about one-third as many self-initiated acts as did American children (LeVine, 1980).

In his landmark studies of Yurok and Sioux childrearing practices, Erikson (1963) showed that young children in both tribes are trained in systematic ways that prepare them to uphold traditional concepts and ideals. The training is different in Yurok and Sioux tribes, as would be expected from an examination of their different patterns of life. The training in both tribes leads native-American children to some conflicts with expectations when they enter boarding schools that are provided for them.

Summarizing common native-American values, B. J. Burgess (1980) emphasized brotherhood, personal integrity, generosity, and spirituality. Burgess has indicated that native-American children are taught that wealth is measured by the amount that is shared with others rather than by what is kept. Certainly native-American parents want their children to be successful, but in a manner that is consistent with the cooperative and noncompetitive tribal community. In the years from one to three, native-American children learn that they should not expect praise for what is required of them. They develop a sense of shame as a balance for autonomy. Shame among native Americans is expressed in terms of the community: "What will people say?" Shame is a common disciplinary tool.

The relative amount of autonomy that is encouraged in young children differs widely among cultural groups in our pluralistic society. During the 1960s and early 1970s, researchers often seemed to assume that the childrearing practices described by LeVine as those of the dominant group of Americans were the standard by which all other practices should be evaluated. This view is now called the **cultural deficit model**; it assumed that families with their own distinctive patterns of childrearing practices had a deficit when compared to families in the majority culture. The cultural deficit model is now in disfavor with most researchers. Instead, most researchers support the **cultural difference model**, which holds that many variations in childrearing practices are acceptable. These variations are viewed as positive and healthy in a pluralistic society.

Even though most specialists in early childhood development espouse belief in the cultural difference model, some societal institutions, such as the educational system, have not been flexible in accommodating themselves to the differences demonstrated by children from minority cultural groups. Change in these institutions seems to come slowly. In the meantime, what can be recommended to parents who want their children to retain their cultural identities and to succeed in school and other societal institutions? One commentator (Laosa, 1981) suggested that members of minority groups need to adopt one pattern of behavior that is appropriate within their cultural setting, and another that is appropriate in the schools and other institutions where the definition of capability is based on a set of standards developed by the dominant group. Is it possible for children to show small amounts of autonomy in one setting and larger amounts in other settings? If so, what childrearing practices would parents use to achieve such a goal? These are unresolved questions.

SUMMARY

1 Autonomy is the process of becoming a separate person with a separate will.
2 Erikson has said that children need to develop a strong sense of autonomy, balanced by the possibility of being shamed by having gone too far.
3 Oppositional behavior accompanies the establishment of autonomy and begins to diminish at about thirty months of age.
4 Young children with "difficult" or "slow-to-warm-up" temperaments need special handling during the years from one to three.
5 Transitional objects and thumb sucking are sources of reliable comfort to young children.
6 Troubling fears develop at about eighteen months of age when children become able to form permanent mental images.
7 Children often have a renewal of anxiety about separations and transitions in the months before their second birthdays.
8 Certain childrearing practices increase the probability of children's prosocial behavior.
9 Children are aware of individual differences, such as gender and race, in the first few years of life.
10 No differences can be observed in children up to three years of age who are raised in alternate family structures.
11 Abuse and neglect is influenced by cultural and family variables.
12 Parents who wish to change their patterns of interaction with children can learn to focus on behavior or to focus on feelings.
13 Day-care placement of young children does not seem to have adverse effects, if certain adult-child ratios are maintained.
14 Two- and three-year-olds who have frequent and sustained peer contacts engage in more advanced forms of play than was previously expected.
15 Research shows that children learn from television and imitate it.
16 The acceptable ratio of autonomy to shame and doubt varies by culture.

KEY TERMS

autonomy	prosocial	gender role
transitional objects	gender identity	gender role stereotyping

authority stage of
parenting

logical consequence

I-message

active listening

solitary play

parallel play

associative play

cooperative play

cultural deficit model

cultural difference model

FOR FURTHER READING

Autonomy

Brazelton, T. B. (1974). *Toddler and parents: A declaration of independence*. New York: Dell.

Erikson, E. H. (1982). *The life cycle completed*. New York: W. W. Norton.

Kaplan, L. J. (1978). *Oneness and separateness: From infant to individual*. New York: Simon & Schuster.

Parent-Child Interaction Patterns

Dreikurs, R., & Grey, L. (1970). *Guide to child discipline*. New York: Hawthorn.

Galinsky, E. (1981). *Between generations: The six stages of parenthood*. New York: Times Books.

Gordon, T. (1975). *P.E.T.: Parent effectiveness training*. New York: Wyden.

9

One- to Three-Year-Olds: Physical Development

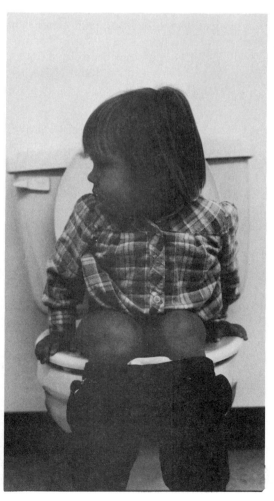

Key Ideas

Milestones of Physical Development
Large Muscle Skills □ Small Muscle Skills □ Drawing □ Perceptual-Motor Integration □ Maturation versus Experience in Physical Development □ Gender Differences □ Cultural Differences

The Need for a Safe Environment
Preventing Injury in Automobiles □ Preventing Poisoning □ Preventing Burns □ Preventing Drowning

The Need for a Healthy Environment
Relationship of Health and Behavior □ Relationship of Family Stress and Health □ Physical Growth and Food Intake Patterns □ Nutrition and Development □ Maintaining Health

Forming a Positive Physical Image
Body Awareness □ Toileting □ Sex Education

Two-year-old Tad sits obediently on the potty in his diaper. When he stands up, his mother hugs him and exclaims, "Good! You sat on the potty in your diaper. Soon you can sit without your diaper. You're getting so grown up!" Tad beams.

Several days later, after snack and juice, Tad sits on the potty without his diaper. A bit of urine trickles out.

Tad's ability to urinate on the potty is indicative of recent changes in his physical development. Many of the changes in Tad and other one- to three-year-old children can be explained in terms of milestones of physical development. This chapter also gives attention to other topics: the need for a safe environment, the need for a healthy environment, and the formation of a positive physical image.

MILESTONES OF PHYSICAL DEVELOPMENT

One- and three-year-old children move very differently from each other. The changes take place gradually, and they make possible a wide variety of new activities. The development of large muscle skills and small muscle skills are described separately. Norms are adapted from Sanford and Zelman (1981).

Large Muscle Skills

Large muscle skills are the markers that many people use in talking about development. Is Bobby walking yet? At what age did Nina crawl? Is Jana peddling her tricycle? Look at how well Elmo balances!

Large muscle skills include dynamic balance, which is used in walking, running, and climbing; static balance, which enables a child to stand on one foot; projecting, the skill used in jumping and hopping; and throwing and catching. To give focus to the account of the development of large muscle skills, this section describes the changes taking place from one to three years of age in a hypothetical child, Joe Tom. Average ages are used, but remember that the range of normal development is wide. For instance, Joe Tom is said to take his first shaky independent steps at one year of age, the average. However, the range of ages at which most normal children walk extends all the way from nine to seventeen months and beyond. Each child has his or her own timetable, which may well differ from Joe Tom's.

One to two years Joe Tom begins walking just weeks after his first birthday. These early attempts consist of only a few steps before he plops himself down again. But he practices his new skill often, sometimes clapping for himself afterward. Soon walking replaces crawling as his primary way of moving from place to place. As he becomes steadier, he is confident enough to try to pull a duck on a string and to push a toy vacuum cleaner. Joe Tom learns to squat, play for awhile, and then return to standing. Later he is able to bend from the waist to pick up a toy. He can get from a sitting position to a standing position easily also. By his second birthday, Joe Tom can walk on a line in the general direction indicated, and he prefers running to walking.

Joe Tom's grandparents have stairs in their home, and Joe Tom learns first to creep upstairs and then to walk upstairs with help. Going downstairs remains challenging and he continues to creep down, feet first. He has a rocking chair, which he likes very much and learns to use. He has no trouble climbing into adult chairs to sit down and manages small chairs well, too.

One of his favorite games is "roll the ball." Played on the floor, the game consists of rolling a ball from one person to another. Joe Tom does not always aim accurately, but he is able to participate enthusiastically.

Two to three years   Watching Joe Tom in active play, his father notes that he seems to enjoy large muscle activities for their own sake and not just as a means of reaching some goal. His climbing improves; one day his mother hears a small voice calling, "Help!" and finds him on top of the refrigerator! He jumps in place, using both feet, and learns to kick a large stationary ball. He walks backwards and seems amused by the changed perspective that he gets. After several attempts, he begins to walk downstairs with help. Joe Tom throws a ball in an adaptation of the earlier rolling game. With his brother's encouragement and help, he masters a forward somersault. His balance improves, and he is able to stand on one foot briefly. He receives a pounding toy from a friend and is able to hammer in all five pegs. He likes the activity itself and is the only one who seems to tolerate the noise.

Three to four years   When his grandparents gave Joe Tom such encouragement to master their stairs, they did not anticipate where it would lead. Joe Tom

Pedaling a tricycle is one of the joys discovered by many three-year-olds.

begins jumping from the first step to the landing and then goes higher and higher with his jumping until his grandparents decide to declare the stairs off limits for that purpose. His confidence on the stairs extends even to the way he now walks up, alternating feet on subsequent steps.

Joe Tom has become interested in much of the equipment at the local park. He can swing if someone gets him started, and he climbs up and slides down the six-foot slide, if given assistance. He executes these feats over and over again during his visits.

When Joe Tom runs, his legs and arms are well coordinated and his arm movements alternate. He can walk on tiptoes and now does not need his brother's help in doing a forward somersault. He marches in parades that he organizes, either with real or imaginary friends. Joe Tom has learned to ride a tricycle and likes to go with an adult for excursions around the neighborhood on it. He can kick a large ball, and he catches a ball against his body, using two hands. His large muscle skills have developed considerably since he was one year old.

Small Muscle Skills

Changes in **small muscle skills** are usually not accompanied by as much adult fanfare as are changes in large muscle skills, but the development in small muscle skills in these early years is nevertheless impressive. To show how these skills change over time, a fictitious child, Amy, has been created. The account of Amy's development is followed by presentation of typical stages of a particular small muscle skill, drawing.

One to two years   As might be expected at a time when Amy is developing a sense of autonomy, many of Amy's new small muscle skills are applied to achieving increased independence. She learns to use a spoon to feed herself at the table, and she drinks from a cup using one hand. She helps with getting dressed, putting on her own hat and taking it off repeatedly. In fact, undressing is really her forte at this point. She pulls off her socks easily and also her shoes, pants, and coat.

At the day-care center, Amy shows an interest in the pegboards and is able to take out and put in the one-inch pegs. She builds a tower of three blocks and then pushes it over to watch it fall. She uses crayons and marking pens on paper, often making dots or circular motions.

Two to three years   During her third year, Amy's ability to manipulate utensils and clothing allows her to be increasingly independent. She scoops her food with a fork, learns to drink her milk with a straw, and pours her milk from a small pitcher into her glass. (She usually drinks more when thus in control of the quantity that she receives.) After meals, Amy wipes her own hands and face. She begins to put on her own socks, pants, and shirts, but requests help if she has trouble. One morning her father hears a muffled, "Stuck! Stuck!" and finds her all tangled up in her shirt.

At the day-care center, Amy strings together four or sometimes more large beads. Her block towers now have as many as six piled on before she pushes

Two- and three-year-olds are able to demonstrate many self-help skills, such as washing hands before meals.

them over. She is able to turn the pages in a book one at a time with care, and practices this skill. Amy figures out how to turn doorknobs and handles, which gives her access to parts of the day-care center and her home that previously required adult assistance to enter.

Three to four years By this time, Amy is able to feed herself a whole meal with minimal assistance. She also dresses herself, requiring help mainly with pullover shirts and some fasteners. She brushes her teeth, although her father makes sure that he also has a turn once a day, and she combs and brushes her own hair.

Amy develops an interest in puzzles and learns how to do those with three and four pieces. She uses a variety of art materials and is able to manage a pencil well enough to trace around objects. She builds complex structures with a snap-together construction set, and learns to unscrew a set of nesting toys. Amy rolls play dough into balls and sausages and seems to gain satisfaction from the pounding and shaping. Clearly Amy has gained a great deal of control over her small muscles in the past three years.

Drawing

No one needs to teach one-year-olds to draw. Part of their play with crayons is to make marks—usually dots and lines at first. Gradually their drawings change, and researchers have shown that the changes follow a regular progression. Changes in drawings are of interest because they reflect changes in cognitive development.

The person who attracted widespread attention to the drawings of young children is Rhoda Kellogg (1969). In her research she collected thousands of children's drawings from all over the world. She decided that children's drawings are composed of twenty types of forms, such as dots, vertical lines, horizontal lines, diagonal lines, curved lines, circles, crosses, and so on. Kellogg's work is well known and has generated great interest, but other researchers (Lansing, 1970; Brittain, 1979) have failed to find in children's drawings the twenty basic forms in the elaborate sequence of development that Kellogg described. This section presents instead a developmental sequence explained by Brittain (1979).

Brittain's system divides very early drawings into two levels: random scribbling and controlled scribbling. (See Figure 9.1). The research that provides the basis for the system of classifying children's drawings has been conducted over a period of years at Cornell University.

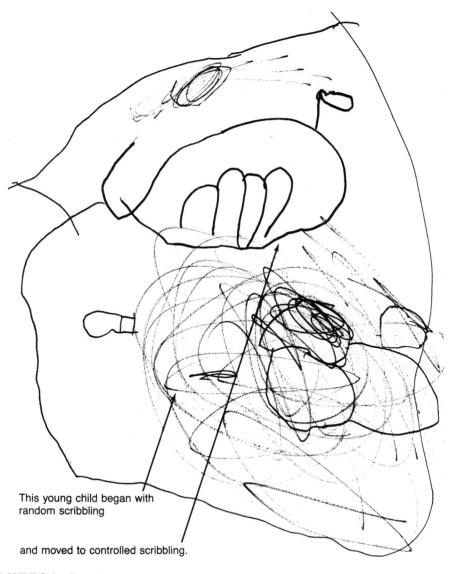

This young child began with random scribbling

and moved to controlled scribbling.

FIGURE 9.1   *Drawing*

Random scribbling   Brittain has said that **random scribbling** is not really random; it only looks that way to adults. As early as one year of age and continuing until two or two and one-half years of age, children make definite dots and lines with simple, whole-arm movements. The swing of the arm determines line length, and arm movements propel the crayon in arcs across the piece of paper. Over time there is a gradual increase in movement of the wrist, which leads to more curves and loops in the drawings. The crayon is either gripped tightly in the fingers or with the entire hand, like a hammer. The child may look away from the drawing but often watches the movement of the crayon with interest. The process brings pleasure; often the drawing itself is of little interest after the minute or so that is spent on it. The drawing provides a visible record of motor coordination and shows that the foundations are being laid for more complex drawing and writing.

Controlled scribbling   Brittain (1979) has described **controlled scribbling** as lasting for a bit more than a year—perhaps from when children are thirty months until they are nearly four years of age. The finished drawings may resemble those completed earlier, but the process has changed. Children now consistently watch the movement of the crayon carefully as they form a scribble. They seem to have visual control over the crayon and produce a more intricate pattern of loops and swirls. The wrist is more flexible than earlier, and crayons are held in a fashion closer to the usual adult grip. In their scribbling, young children practice basic shapes and lines that are necessary for later drawing and writing. By age three, children spend twice as long on their drawings as they did at age two, an average of two minutes. Some children begin making open and closed figures with attempts at representing objects and people. Most children show interest and stirrings of pleasure and pride as they survey their completed drawings. "See what I made!" is a common exclamation.

Copying geometric shapes is a task that often appears on developmental inventories and intelligence tests for young children. Usually three-year-olds are expected to be able to copy circles; copying circles is easier than copying other shapes because children can make a continuous movement with no direction change.

Sometimes adults are tempted to hurry children along from scribbling to representational drawing. However, Whitener and Kersey (1980) have asserted that scribbling is to writing as babbling is to talking. These commentators believe that trying to teach young children to draw before they have moved naturally through the scribbling stage is just as inappropriate as it would be to require infants to talk before they babble.

Perceptual-Motor Integration

At a library story hour, three-year-old Bud is learning a simplified version of the "Simon Says" game. The children's librarian waves her hand and asks the children to imitate her, but Bud does not respond with a hand wave. Bud understands the game but cannot yet move his body appropriately.

Children imitate their teacher in an exercise of perceptual-motor integration.

Bud's difficulty is in the realm of **perceptual-motor integration**. What this term means is that Bud can visually perceive what the librarian is doing, but he cannot process that perception and integrate it with the appropriate motor response of giving his own hand wave in return. At Bud's age, this difficulty is not unexpected, and adults can plan a variety of experiences and activities to develop a basis for perceptual-motor integration.

Perceptual-motor integration will be very important to Bud's effective functioning in the future. Perception through visual, auditory, and tactile-kinesthetic modalities provides the information upon which behavior is based. Motor responses lead to movement, which is the visible aspect of behavior. If Bud's perceptions and his motor responses are not integrated, there is little connection between information and behavior. For example, imagine a communication between Bud and his mother about a household task. His mother gives a detailed explanation about what is to be done, and Bud indicates his understanding. But if Bud does not follow through on the task, the reason may be that he has an isolated body of perceptual information (the explanation) with no appreciation of how to translate this information into action. Perceptual-motor development provides a link between children's perceptual and motor functions. The late Newell C. Kephart (1971) is the person most frequently associated with demonstrating the importance of this type of development.

Perceptual-motor development begins with large muscle activities in which children's whole bodies or major parts of their bodies are controlled in terms of perceptual information. Such a beginning point is consistent with the **proximo-distal** direction of development. This term means that the parts of the body closest to the center become capable of differentiated movement first, and those parts farthest from the center are differentiated last. For example, the child first controls movement of the shoulder, followed by movement of the elbow, the wrist and, finally, the fingers. If adults expect children to demon-

**BOX
9.1**

STRATEGIES FOR FACILITATING DEVELOPMENT: PERCEPTUAL-MOTOR TRAINING

Walking and running are the most common large muscle activities, and games can be devised to help young children bring these activities under perceptual control. For instance, a young child can be asked to walk to the bed and stop when she reaches it. Perceptual information is provided for her to determine when to stop; but, if she does not use the perceptual information, the bed itself stops her. Tag games with a base require the same perceptual-motor relationship as did stopping at reaching the bed, but offer the additional excitement and distraction of being chased by the person who is "it."

At the next level of perceptual-motor training, children can be asked to control walking and running by perceptual information alone. A child can be asked to walk up to a line but to stop before stepping over it. The line is a perceptual element rather than a concrete object, such as a bed. In a tag game, the base could be marked with chalk on the ground.

At a more complex level of large muscle perceptual-motor training, children use perceptual information to give continuous control to an activity. Children can be asked to walk along an alley, which has been formed with two parallel chalk marks on the ground. The width of the alley can be modified to suit the coordination of each child, and eventually children can be asked to walk along a line without stepping off.

Jumping is another total body activity that can be used for perceptual-motor training. Children can be asked to jump down from and then up onto a step, into and out of a circle drawn on the ground, and over a rope on the ground.

Arm and hand activities occupy a middle position between these total body activities and later classroom activities that require precise coordination between eye and hand. The most common arm and hand activities involve throwing balls or beanbags toward targets. The targets provide the perceptual information that governs the direction of the throw; accordingly, the targets should be moved to various heights and to a number of different positions relative to the child. Children should have experiences throwing objects of various sizes with their right and left hands and with both hands together. In related arm and hand activities, children can roll balls to targets, push carts along alleys or lines, and hit a suspended ball with their hands or bats.

Adapted from *The Slow Learner in the Classroom,* 2nd ed. (pp. 234–41) by N. C. Kephart, 1971, Columbus, OH: Charles E. Merrill. Copyright 1971 by Charles E. Merrill. Adapted by permission.

strate skills that are not related to this proximo-distal sequencing, children may develop isolated groups of responses, called **splinter skills**. Splinter skills are not integrated with the rest of children's activities and cannot be generalized and applied to slightly different tasks.

Maturation versus Experience in Physical Development

A Sunday school teacher asked her group of three-year-olds to cut out a circular shape. Debbie Barnes handled the task easily but Sally Ellis did not know how to put her fingers into the holes of the scissors. The teacher cut out the circle for Sally and remarked to her teenaged assistant, "There's a big difference in maturity at this age."

The Sunday school teacher was correct in saying that there are maturational variations in physical development in these early years. But she was only partially correct, because her remark did not take into account the important role of experience in a skill such as cutting. Here is an account of the experiences with scissors that three-year-old Debbie Barnes had with her mother in the month before that Sunday school class.

One day Mary Barnes was cutting coupons from the newspaper when Debbie reached for the scissors and tried to stick her chunky fingers into the holes as she had seen her mother do. "So you want to cut?" Mary asked.

Debbie nodded, and Mary went to get some safer scissors from a drawer in the kitchen. Mary patiently showed Debbie how to put her fingers in the holes, and she guided Debbie's hand in snipping through thin strips of paper. Debbie felt very proud when she snipped all by herself.

Mastery of skills such as cutting with scissors requires a combination of maturation and experience.

During the next weeks, Debbie practiced cutting. When she was consistently successful in snipping thin strips of paper, her mother gave her a series of increasingly challenging cutting tasks.

Mary Barnes designed a sequence of appropriate learning experiences for Debbie. Debbie began with snipping, a task with which she could feel successful from the start. Only gradually did Debbie move from snipping to cutting out shapes. Sally, however, had never held scissors until that day at Sunday school. Rather than giving instructions, the teacher completed the task for her.

The experiences that young children have with parents and other adults vary widely. What a child can do with her large or small muscles depends on the experiences that she has had as well as on the level of development that she has reached. If Sally's teacher had tried to give Sally instruction in using scissors, the teacher might have found that Sally could eventually be as successful as Debbie. Or she might have found that Sally needed a foundation of more activities that involved her whole body before she could be successful in using the small muscles in her hands for manipulating scissors. Sequential instruction in physical skills is not appropriate if children have not had the foundation of prerequisite activities; and children will not necessarily succeed in physical skills, even if adequate foundations have been built, unless they are given sequential instructions at their level of understanding. Both maturation and experience are important in physical development.

Gender Differences

Comments such as the following can be heard when parents of young children gather:

"It'll take longer to potty-train Greg than it did Stephie."

"Little girls cut better than little boys."

Are these comments examples of gender stereotyping? Not entirely; they do have some basis in fact. In the early childhood years, girls tend to develop more rapidly and to be more advanced than boys in exhibiting certain behaviors (Ames, Gillespie, Haines, & Ilg, 1979). Not every girl will be more advanced than any boy at a given age, but when the abilities of girls are averaged and compared to the boys' average, the girls tend to be more advanced at the same age.

What explains differences in physical abilities between girls and boys? Some researchers find the cause in the different expectations that parents have for their daughters and sons. Other researchers believe that the cause lies totally in the faster maturation of girls. Present evidence is insufficient to offer a definitive explanation, but it seems unlikely that parental expectations alone explain why girls walk earlier, hop on one foot sooner, cut with scissors earlier, and copy **V** and **H** strokes sooner than boys (Ames et al., 1979). In many large and small muscle activities, girls are as much as six months ahead of boys, on average. This difference needs to be taken into account by parents, educators, health workers, and others who are in contact with young children and their families.

Cultural Differences

Cross-cultural research (Werner, 1979; Malina, 1982) has shown distinctly different patterns of early physical development. When various ethnic groups are studied and the young children are compared on standardized tests of physical development, black groups show the greatest early acceleration of physical development; Asian and Central American Indian groups occupy an intermediate position; and white groups show the least acceleration. These relative differences in physical development hold true even if groups live in the same settings.

In addition to ethnicity, two factors influence the pattern of early physical development of many of these initially precocious black, Asian, and Central American Indian children. These two factors are adult physical stimulation and nutritional status (Werner, 1979; Malina, 1982).

Adult physical stimulation seems to have a positive effect on children's development. Such stimulation is most intense and continuous in preindustrial communities in Africa, Asia, and Central and South America. There, infants are breast-fed on demand night and day; carried on slings with adults during the day and kept with adults at night; brought along as participants in all adult activities; and cared for by various individuals in extended family systems. Infants in these preindustrial communities show greater early acceleration of physical development than do infants of the same ethnic group who live in "Westernized" middle-class urban communities.

Unfortunately, however, the nutritional status of many of these children deteriorates at the time of weaning. In preindustrial rural communities, weaning usually takes place during the second year of life and is accompanied by a cessation of the stimulation of being carried by and sleeping with adults. Diets after weaning are often low in protein or contaminated by bacteria. From the age of two, the average scores of these children, who earlier were precocious in physical development, are behind those of Western children in both large and small muscle development (Werner, 1979). It is a matter for concern that the accelerated early physical development of some children is undermined by the effects of poor nutrition.

THE NEED FOR A SAFE ENVIRONMENT

Accidents are the leading cause of death for children between one and four years of age (U.S. Bureau of the Census, 1982).

Young children are accident-prone because of four characteristics. First, these young children are now mobile: they can walk, climb, and reach many objects that were not accessible earlier. Second, their small muscle development allows them to grasp and open containers that they previously could not have explored. Third, they are curious, persistent, and eager to gather infor-

TABLE 9.1 *Death Rates for the Four Leading Causes of Death Among Children, Age 1 to 4 Years*

Young children's curiosity, mobility, and immaturity combine with each other to make accidents a leading cause of death.

Causes of Death	Deaths per 100,000 population
All causes	69.2
First	
Accidents	28.8
Second	
Congenital anomalies	8.4
Third	
Malignant neoplasms	4.9
Fourth	
Influenza or pneumonia	2.9

SOURCE: *Characteristics of American Children and Youth: 1980* (p. 8) by U.S. Bureau of the Census, 1982, Washington, DC: U.S. Government Printing Office.

mation through all of their senses. Many interesting things go into their mouths, despite taste or appearance. And, fourth, they lack the experience and ability to predict dangerous outcomes of situations. It is no wonder, then, that the possible risks for young children are staggering.

The potential for some accidents, like the loss suffered by Mr. and Mrs. J. G. (See Box 9.2.), cannot be entirely eliminated. In these cases, there is no substitute for careful supervision of young children during all of their waking hours. The probability of many accidents, however, can be reduced by taking action to prevent injury in automobiles and to prevent poisoning, burns, and drowning.

Preventing Injury in Automobiles

Of all of the types of accidents, those in automobiles affect the most children. Over one-third of all the accidental deaths among one- to four-year-old children take place in automobiles (U.S. Bureau of the Census, 1982), and many other children sustain serious injuries each year. Safety experts assert that a high per-

---

BOX 9.2

DEAR ABBY: PREVENTING DROWNING

In a poignant letter to Dear Abby (Van Buren, 1982), Mr. and Mrs. J. G. reported the drowning of their young daughter in the toilet bowl of her grandparents' home. Mr. and Mrs. J. G. had done many things to safeguard their daughter's life but did not imagine that a common household fixture could endanger her. She toddled off during a visit and was found face down in the toilet bowl. Attempts to revive her failed.

centage of these deaths and injuries could be prevented if children were put into approved safety restraints during each car ride. The evidence concerning benefits to children of the use of automobile safety systems has convinced some states to pass legislation requiring that children below four years of age or forty pounds in weight be placed in them.

For children between one and four years of age, three kinds of safety restraints are recommended by the United States Department of Transportation, National Highway Traffic Safety Administration (1980). The three recommended systems are child safety seats, protective shields, and safety harnesses. These systems are illustrated in Figure 9.2.

Child safety seats are designed for young children who are able to sit up without support. This type of seat faces forward and uses an automobile seat belt as well as a special safety harness. The harness redistributes the force of a crash over children's shoulders and hips and protects their abdomens from receiving too much pressure. Some child safety seats also require the use of a top tether that attaches to the frame of the car.

Protective shields fit in front of children's laps and chests in order to cushion them in accidents. A shield is held in place with the automobile seat belt and has energy-absorbing padding as part of the design. Shields spread the force of collisions or sudden stops evenly over children's heads and upper bodies.

Child harness systems are designed to be worn when children sit normally, preferably in the center of the rear seat of the automobile. The harness is attached to an automobile lap belt and a top tether strap. In an accident, the child harness system redistributes the impact in a manner similar to that of the child safety seat.

A 1980 federal law requires that children's automobile safety restraints meet specified standards of strength and performance. The key problem, though, is in educating parents and other adults to put children in these devices.

Preventing Poisoning

The temptation is strong for young children to explore new things with their mouths. Even substances with bad tastes, smells, or appearances are ingested by children in dangerous amounts before unpleasant sensations seem to register. In addition to careful supervision of young children, precautionary measures need to be taken in each household and child-care facility in which young children spend time.

The most important precaution against poisoning is the removal of all dangerous substances from children's reach. Medicines should be placed in a locked cabinet, cleaning products should be moved from under the sink to a high shelf or locked cabinet, cosmetics and personal products should be placed out of the reach of curious youngsters, and garage and workshop items should be placed in locked cupboards or cabinets. Indoor and outdoor plants should be checked for toxicity. Even very young children should be taught that they should not eat anything, whether indoors or out, that has not been approved by an adult.

FIGURE 9.2 *Approved Automobile Safety Systems for 1- to 4-Year-Olds*

(From *Child Restraint Systems for Your Automobile, 1980, Washington, DC: U.S. Department of Transportation, National Highway Traffic Safety Administration.*

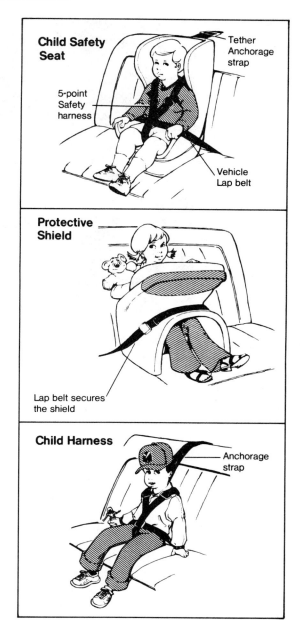

A related precaution involves adjustments in the context in which medication is given and taken. Adults should never talk about medicine as candy or as a magic product. They should, instead, be matter-of-fact about the necessity for taking medicine when it is prescribed, talk with children about taking medicine only from certain people, and discuss the fact that too much medicine can make children as sick as not taking it when needed. Adults should also be careful of the example that they set and should try to avoid taking medications in the presence of young children.

Children between one and three often continue to explore new things with their mouths.

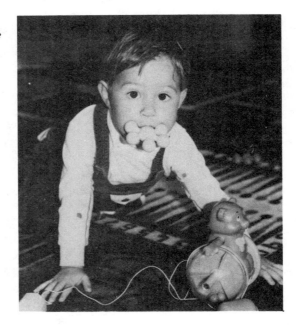

Children who have been poisoned show changes in behavior, stains or burns near the mouth, vomiting and stomach pains, unconsciousness, drowsiness, convulsions, and/or rapid breathing. Adults who suspect poisoning should try to identify the poison and call the poison control center, hospital, doctor, or paramedic unit. If instructed to take the child to a hospital, an adult should bring the suspected poison.

Preventing Burns

Children can be protected from most of the major causes of burns, if adults adjust the environment. One important adjustment is to keep matches and lighters out of children's reach at all times. Another adjustment is to turn the handles of pots and pans so that they do not extend over the edge of the stove, and to be sure that children are not underfoot when hot substances are being moved from one part of the kitchen to another. Similar adjustments involve safety with electricity, fire, and hot water. Special caps should be placed on unused electrical outlets, cords on appliances should not be left dangling, and children should be kept away from heaters, fireplace inserts, and fireplaces. The temperature of hot water should be set as low as is feasible for the household, and adults should test bathwater before children enter.

Preventing Drowning

Young children have drowned in bathtubs, pails, wading pools, and other small containers of liquid, as well as in swimming pools, rivers, lakes, and other large bodies of water. The key precaution in preventing drowning is to supervise children around any quantity of water. The supervision must be continual: there is no time off for phone calls or other distractions. Children are attracted to water, and it takes only moments for drowning to occur.

BOX 9.3

STRATEGIES FOR FACILITATING DEVELOPMENT: CONTROLLED EXPLORATION

One of the givens in working with one- to three-year-old children is that they investigate every inch of their environments, even those areas or objects that have been placed off limits. They empty drawers, drop all the tissues down the stairs, play "sink and float" in the toilet bowl with their toys, climb up cabinets to look at fragile figurines, and so on. This persistent curiosity sometimes overwhelms parents into saying *no* automatically whenever children move toward something that is not designated as a toy. But saying frequent *nos* reduces the learning potential of the home and robs parents and children of some of the fun that they could be having. Middle ground—between saying *no* to everything and the other extreme of allowing exploration of absolutely anything—involves establishing children's interest areas in the parts of the home in which adults and children spend the most time.

In two-year-old Al's apartment, the kitchen tends to be the hub of activity during much of the day. Al is allowed free exploration of the cabinet with canned foods. Note Al's activity with the cans.

Al leans far into the kitchen cabinet and pulls out the remaining several cans. The floor around him is strewn with soup, vegetable, fruit, and sauce cans of assorted sizes and shapes. When he has systematically emptied the cabinet, Al turns his attention to making a tower of cans, putting the largest at the base.

The cans are as good as any expensive, commercially available set of cylinders for stacking, comparing sizes and shapes, and sorting by color, size, or shape. And the cans have the bonus of allowing Al to relate the pictures (and later the words) on the labels to his own food experiences. Al is also given access to another cabinet with muffin tins, cookie sheets, plastic containers, and empty oatmeal, margarine, yogurt, and other interesting cartons. The remainder of the cabinets have been closed off to Al by the installation of special child-proof latches. Al seems to relish the availability of a variety of objects that parallel those that he sees his mother and grandmother use.

THE NEED FOR A HEALTHY ENVIRONMENT

If children do not feel well, their psychosocial, physical, and cognitive development may be impaired. A healthy environment is one of the most basic needs that young children have. This section considers the following topics: the relationship between health and behavior, the relationship between family stress and health, physical growth and food intake patterns of children between one and three, the relationship of nutrition and development, and the maintenance of health.

Relationship of Health and Behavior

Recent research has demonstrated the close link between health problems in the early years and developmental and behavioral disorders. Two perspectives on this link are presented. First, a study (Bax, 1981) conducted in two inner-city areas in London showed that children who have frequent infections are more likely than other children to have developmental and behavioral problems. Second, research (Will, 1983) conducted in the United States pointed out the relationship of lead poisoning of young children to behavior and learning problems.

Infections and behavior   Young children have various kinds of infections, the most common of which include those of the upper respiratory tract (colds or sore throats), lower respiratory tract (bronchitis or croup), and ear (otitis media). Of these infections, young children are more susceptible than are older children or adults to problems with the part of the ear behind the eardrum. It is estimated that one in three visits to doctors by children under six years of age results in a diagnosis of infection of the middle ear (Bax, 1981). Pediatricians explain that young children's eustachian tubes are smaller and at a different angle than will be the case later. Secretions from the nose and throat can back up into the middle ear and cause pressure, if the eustachian tube becomes blocked. Ear infections are usually treated with antibiotics. If left untreated or if prescribed dosages of antibiotics are not completed, these infections can lead to more serious medical problems, hearing loss, and language delays.

In studying two-year-old children, Bax (1981) found a significant relationship between ear infections during the previous six months and delayed language. In the same study, children with speech problems at two, three, and four and one-half years of age showed a disproportionate number of behavior problems. Researchers hypothesized that the interaction between chronic ear infections, speech delays, and behavior problems begins with a temporary mild hearing loss due to an ear infection. The hearing loss, in turn, leads to a delay in speech development of six months to one year. The behavior problems then stem either from the pain and discomfort of the illness or from children's frustration over their difficulties in hearing and speaking.

Other relationships were also found in the London study (Bax, 1981). Researchers discovered that young children with frequent colds were more likely to be described by parents as difficult to manage and also were more likely to have frequent temper tantrums. Children with a history of ear infections had a significantly greater tendency than other children toward persistent night waking long after infections have subsided.

These findings indicate that physical illness can be closely related to delayed development and behavior problems. Regular pediatric examinations and treatment lower the rates of speech and language delay and of behavior problems. Yet, according to researchers, only half of the young children in the United States are under medical supervision of any kind (Bax, 1981).

Lead poisoning and behavior   George F. Will (1983) has pointed out that the synonym for *leaden* is *dull.* Lead poisoning in children can cause learning problems, retardation, brain damage, anemia, seizures, hyperactivity, and death.

The most dangerous source of lead for young children is paint. Structures built before 1950 may have some coats of lead-based paint, which tastes sweet to children. Even a flake of paint the size of a fingernail can be dangerous; therefore, many cities have programs to detect and remove lead-based paint from older buildings.

A second major source of lead poisoning is gasoline. It has been shown that every tankful of regular gasoline emits two ounces of lead. The average level of lead in children's blood has declined twenty-five percent since the beginning of restrictions on lead in gasoline (Will, 1983).

Young children are particularly susceptible to lead poisoning because of their high metabolic rates. Not all children, however, are at equal risk of lead poisoning. Poor children are more likely than others to be deficient in iron, calcium, and zinc; these deficiencies predispose them to absorb lead. Inner-city dwellers are apt to live in older buildings that were painted with lead-based paint, and to breathe air into which lead from gasoline has been emitted. Studies have indicated that there are excessive lead levels in the blood of one-fifth of black children from low-income families; six times as many black preschoolers have excessive lead levels as white preschoolers (Will, 1983). Will (1983) has estimated that the government spends more than one billion dollars yearly on children with lead poisoning, eighty percent of which goes to support special education for the learning disabled. Lead poisoning affects behavior and learning capacity and has a high cost in terms of human resources.

Relationship of Family Stress and Health

A study of a large number of New Zealand families showed a relationship between family stress and increased risk of children's illnesses and accidents (Beautrais, Fergusson, & Shannon, 1982). The New Zealand study indicated that children between the ages of one and four years were more apt to have lower respiratory infections, gastroenteritis, burns, scalds, and accidental poisoning when their families were under stress for extended periods of time. Young children whose families faced twelve or more stressful situations during three years were found to be twice as likely to become ill and six times as likely to be hospitalized as children whose families faced three or fewer of these stressful life events. The kinds of events that create stress are moves, job changes, serious disagreements with relatives, death of friends or relatives, financial problems, marital problems, illness or accident of a family member, and pregnancy.

Researchers have hypothesized that an atmosphere of stress in the home causes physiological changes that make young children more susceptible to illness. When parents' attention is focused on the stresses and problems of the family, their vigilance is probably reduced, leading to the related increase in accidental injuries and poisonings. This study and others like it give support to the need to examine the health and development of young children within the context of their families.

Physical Growth and Food Intake Patterns

Physical growth tapers off in the second year of life. Children gain only about 3.5 to 4.5 kilograms and, after that, the weight gain is reduced still further, to 1.8 to 2.2 kilograms per year (Pipes, 1981). Children grow taller, but without the increases in weight that characterized the first year of life. (See Figures 9.3 and 9.4.) Children lose their roundness, and their bodies and limbs seem to stretch out.

Children cannot continue to double their body weights within a span of months, as infants do. Even so, many parents worry about declines in their children's appetites and food consumption. The decreased growth rate of this period and the struggle for autonomy combine to make negativism and confrontations over food intake almost inevitable.

Children's appetites are unpredictable in these early childhood years, and their likes and dislikes can change from one day to the next. For a week Heather might only eat peanut butter sandwiches, but after that she might refuse to eat peanut butter at all. Matthew eats with apparent hunger at one meal but skips the next entirely.

The evening meal is usually the one in which young children are least interested. Nutrition experts (Pipes, 1981) believe that some children may meet their energy and nutrient requirements by consumption of only two meals and snacks. An alternate explanation for problems with the evening meal is that children are overstimulated by the social interaction that often accompanies it. If children feel that they cannot both eat and interact, they may choose to interact. Some modification of the social atmosphere at the evening meal may improve young children's food intake.

Young children often prefer foods that are high in carbohydrates because they are easiest to chew. Bread, crackers, and cereal may be preferred to meat and other foods that are high in protein. Children can be offered chicken, ground meat, cheese, and yogurt as easily chewed sources of protein, if steaks, roasts, and other fibrous meats are refused.

Children may stop eating when their energy needs are met, even if needed nutrients have not been received (Pipes, 1981). For this reason, children's choices should be made from foods that provide nutrients as well as calories. The unpredictability of preferences can be frustrating, but adults can nonetheless try to give attention to children when they are eating or trying something new rather than when food problems occur.

FIGURE 9.3 *(opposite page)   Normal Growth Curve: Girls*
(Reprinted with permission of Ross Laboratories, Columbus, OH 43216, from NCHS Growth Charts.)

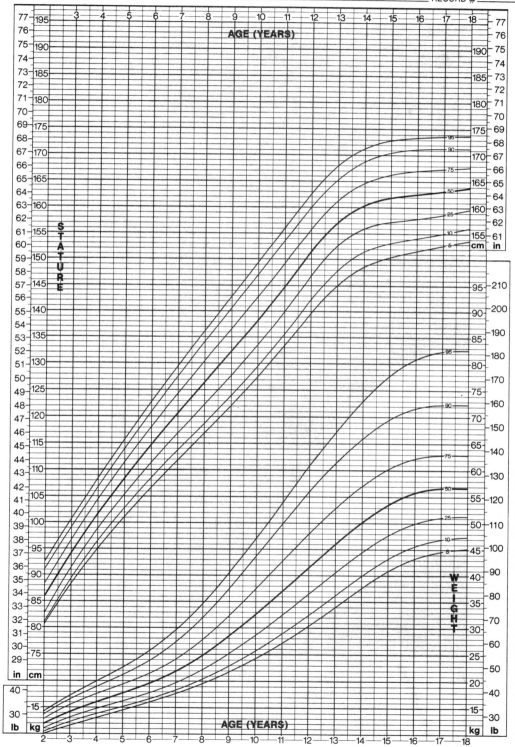

*Adapted from: Hamill PVV, Drizd TA, Johnson CL, Reed RB, Roche AF, Moore WM: Physical growth: National Center for Health Statistics percentiles. AM J CLIN NUTR 32:607-629,1979. Data from the National Center for Health Statistics (NCHS) Hyattsville, Maryland.

251

BOYS: 2 TO 18 YEARS
PHYSICAL GROWTH
NCHS PERCENTILES*

NAME _____ RECORD # _____

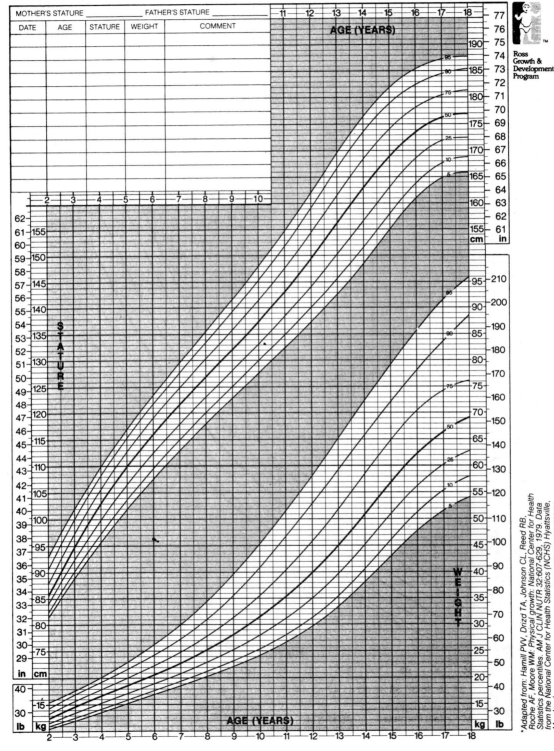

MOTHER'S STATURE _____ FATHER'S STATURE _____

DATE	AGE	STATURE	WEIGHT	COMMENT

AGE (YEARS)

STATURE

WEIGHT

AGE (YEARS)

*Adapted from: Hamill PVV, Drizd TA, Johnson CL, Reed RB, Roche AF, Moore WM: Physical growth: National Center for Health Statistics percentiles. AM J CLIN NUTR 32:607-629, 1979. Data from the National Center for Health Statistics (NCHS) Hyattsville, Maryland.

© 1982 ROSS LABORATORIES

Ross
Growth &
Development
Program

Small first servings are appropriate at meals, because children's rate of growth tapers off and their appetites decline.

Nutrition and Development

In some families, worries about food intake are much more fundamental than those that we have been describing. Cross-cultural studies have investigated the relationship between inadequate nutrition and development in the early childhood years.

A condition called **kwashiorkor** has been identified in cross-cultural studies. Kwashiorkor results when food intake is deficient in protein even if adequate in calories. The word *kwashiorkor* comes from the language of a tribe in Ghana and means "sickness that the older child gets when the next child is born." As might be expected from the definition, kwashiorkor develops most frequently in children between one and two years of age when they are weaned. Kwashiorkor is a severe form of malnutrition and leads to growth failure, anorexia, muscle wasting, and lack of interest and exploratory desire. Such severe malnutrition causes death or major disability.

Even mild to moderate nutritional problems may negatively affect the development of young children. The Institute of Nutrition of Central America and Panama (INCAP) undertook a study in rural Guatemala in order to ascertain the consequences of chronic mild to moderate protein-energy malnutrition (Townsend, Klein, Irwin, Owens, Yarbrough, & Engle, 1982). In this study, one of two pairs of villages was randomly assigned to an experimental condition in which a high-energy–high-protein beverage was made available. In the other village in the pair, a low-energy beverage with no protein was made available.

FIGURE 9.4 *(opposite page)* *Normal Growth Curve: Boys*
(Reprinted with permission of Ross Laboratories, Columbus, OH 43216, from NCHS Growth Charts.)

The study design controlled for the effects of confounding social and economic variables that often accompany poor nutrition. Children in the INCAP study were observed and tested from conception to five years of age. At three, four, and five years of age, children in the experimental group, who were given the high-energy–high-protein beverage, were found to exceed the mental test performance of children in the control group, who drank the low-energy beverage (Townsend et al., 1982). The researchers concluded that inadequate nutrition inhibits mental development of young children, and that adding protein supplements can enhance development in the early years.

Findings from research on malnutrition and undernutrition in the United States parallel the findings reported by Townsend. Research (Stevens & Baxter, 1981) has indicated that adequate nutrition is necessary for the full development of the capabilities of young children. Researchers suggest that children at risk nutritionally be identified by testing for iron anemia and by collecting dietary intake data about calories, calcium, vitamin C, thiamine, and vitamin A. Once high-risk children are identified, appropriate nutritional supplementation and/or parent education programs can be provided to meet the needs of young children whose healthy development is threatened by poor nutrition.

Maintaining Health

The years from one to three present new challenges in health maintenance. Parents need to insure that children receive adequate rest, continue the pattern of medical examinations and immunizations established in the first year of life, and secure dental care.

Insuring adequate rest Parents who have previously treated their infant's sleeping times as routine sometimes change their views during the years from one to three. Children of these ages are very active and need rest, but they show their autonomy by objecting or delaying when it is time to sleep. Adults cannot make children sleep, but they can be matter-of-fact in requiring restful breaks in children's activity. For many young children, a routine of a morning and afternoon nap or rest until eighteen months of age and just an afternoon nap or rest after that provides the right amount of quiet during the day. Night sleep may amount to twelve hours.

Just as getting children to sleep can be a problem during these years, helping them stay asleep throughout the night can also become an issue. Children have intervals of REM or light sleep every four hours and, if they partially awaken during REM sleep, they may use their new mobility to move around the home and/or wake their parents. Children should be encouraged to stay in bed and to learn their own ways of settling themselves back into deep sleep again. Firmness is needed from the beginning of these late-night wanderings, or children can find that they enjoy sociability in the wee hours.

Health care Children should continue to receive immunizations on an established schedule. A booster DPT inoculation is needed at fifteen months, or about one year after the first three shots were completed. The fourth dose of the trivalent poliovirus vaccine is usually given at the same time as the DPT booster. Other immunizations may also be necessary.

Routine well-child medical examinations are important for assuring the health of young children. Blood tests, tuberculin tests, hearing and vision screening, and questioning parents about developmental milestones can all help in diagnosing any possible problems. When problems are found, referrals for assistance can be made.

Dental care Most young children acquire twenty teeth during their first two and one-half years. Children's reactions to teething vary widely, with the most universal discomfort occurring between twelve and eighteen months of age when the first molars come in. Some children lose their appetites and wake at night; unfortunately, not much can be done to soothe them except to offer something cool for sucking. If a child has a fever as high as 101 degrees, then a physician should be contacted.

Dentists disagree about how soon children's teeth should be brushed. Some advise beginning when the first molars come in. Others advise waiting until children are around two years of age because at that age they have a strong desire to imitate what they see adults and other children doing. This latter position, in combination with a restriction of sweets in the early years, seems sensible. When children show an interest, they should be given their own toothbrushes in convenient locations. Children can take a turn with brushing and then an adult should have a turn after each meal.

Fluoride supplementation during these years is important for the formation of strong teeth. Some communities have fluoride in the water but if not, a physician can prescribe drops for children to take each day, sometimes in combination with vitamins.

The visit of a pediatric dentist to a day-care center helps children develop positive attitudes about dental care.

**BOX
9.4**   **STRATEGIES FOR FACILITATING DEVELOPMENT:
PREVENTING "BOTTLE-MOUTH" CAVITIES**

Judd, a two-year-old, unexpectedly made his first trip to the dentist when his front tooth broke off at the gum line. Judd's father was skeptical of the story that Judd told of biting into a banana and having his tooth break. But the dentist told him that the story was plausible because Judd's tooth was decayed throughout, as was the other front tooth. Dr. Vasquez recommended that a number of teeth be capped or filled with Judd under a general anesthetic at a hospital.

Dr. Vasquez explained that Judd's problem is called **bottle-mouth syndrome**. It usually occurs when adults allow children over one year of age to go to sleep while sucking on a bottle of juice or milk. When children do so, the undiluted liquid pools around the upper front and side teeth. During sleep, the flow of saliva and the swallowing reflex are both reduced, and the pooled juice or milk can cause serious tooth decay.

To prevent bottle-mouth cavities, children should be offered only water in bottles that they take to bed with them. Otherwise, young children may require the expensive and upsetting restoration of the mouth that Judd must have.

Dental examinations should begin when children are about three years of age. These early dental visits should be carefully planned so that children are rested and relaxed. The confidence that is built in the first appointments can make a positive difference later if fillings or other dental work must be accomplished.

Good dental care in the early years is important in building appropriate habits and in preventing problems. The last of the "baby teeth" are not lost until children are twelve years of age. If these teeth become so decayed as to require removal, children not only have considerable pain, but the other teeth grow out of position and leave inadequate room for the permanent teeth.

FORMING A POSITIVE PHYSICAL IMAGE

Young children in the years from one to three begin to form a physical image of themselves. Three aspects of a positive physical image include body awareness, successful toileting experiences, and appropriate sex education.

Body Awareness

Body image, laterality, and directionality are key aspects of the growing awareness that young children have of their bodies. One of the goals of physical expe-

A child refines his body image by observing the relationship of his height and the diameter of the conduit.

rience during the early years is for children to find out how much space their bodies require and where their bodies are located in comparison to other things.

Body image   Children form a body image by observing the movement of their body parts and noting the relationships of the body to other objects. They become aware of the relaxation or contraction of different muscles of their bodies. They see the movement of their limbs. They hear their arms or legs hit the wall when they move in the night. They learn how much space their bodies take up if they sit on the floor among toys. All of these sensations and learnings merge into children's body images.

Play provides the vehicle for forming a reliable body image. Note how Tran receives feedback about the size of his body as compared with tires.

Tran crawled through the large tire but got stuck in a smaller one. He had underestimated how much space his body would need.

By developing his body image, Tran will have a consistent frame of reference within which to organize his other perceptions and motor responses.

Laterality   Laterality is an internalized awareness of the two sides of the body and their differences. Children develop a sense of laterality by experimenting with the two sides of their bodies and with the relationships of these two sides to each other. Activities that involve balance are useful in bringing about a differentiation of the two sides of the body. As children try to achieve balance, they learn which side of the body has to move, how it should move, and how the other side should compensate for that movement.

Laterality is more basic than just knowing how to attach the labels *right* and *left* to the sides of the body. In fact, the sense of laterality within the body is what allows children to make sense of the directionality that they find in the world.

Directionality Directionality is the projection beyond the body of the laterality that children feel within their bodies. The intermediate step between laterality and directionality involves the ability to control eye movements and to know where the eyes are pointed. If children can match their internalized understandings with what they see, they can develop concepts of *right, left, up,* and *down* as applied to the world around them. Establishment of directionality allows older children to differentiate between symbols such as *p* and *q*.

Toileting

Success in toileting can give young children a sense of growth. Tad's first experiences on the potty, described at the beginning of this chapter, helped him to understand its function. He felt proud to be able to perform in a way that pleased his mother. Unfortunately, though, learning to use the potty and later the toilet is not always such a positive experience, either for the child or for the adult. Problems can center on the timing of the training process, the method of training, and children's particular characteristics. Each potential problem area is discussed.

Timing of training Some parents claim to have trained children as young as one year of age to use the potty. Usually, however, these children are very regular in their pattern of elimination and the adults are themselves "trained" to encourage use of the potty at certain times of the day. There is some speculation that children whose parents have "caught" them in the first eighteen months rebel later because using the potty seems to be too much a part of an adult plan. For most children it is prudent to wait until after age two, when several kinds of readiness are established.

The most obvious kind of readiness involves physical maturation. Parents notice that young children begin to stay dry for several hours and then urinate in quantity, rather than urinating in small amounts more frequently. And, at a certain point, children seem able to anticipate urination by body positions or facial expressions. Prolonged dryness, urinating in quantity, and anticipating urination are all signs of physical readiness. A related physical element is for children to be far enough past the first excitement of walking that they are willing to sit still for short periods of time.

Another kind of readiness involves psychological and intellectual development. Children should not be asked to sit on the potty if they are in a period

Success in toileting can give young children a sense of growth.

of strongly oppositional behavior. And children should be able to understand simple directions and instructions.

If children are asked to use the potty before they are ready, they will not be likely to be successful. If unpleasant associations form, it can take months to undo the harm done.

Method of training These days most pediatricians advocate a relaxed approach to potty training. For instance, T. Berry Brazelton advises an approach to training that focuses on children's own decisions to gain control because they want to be grown up. He has advocated his approach to the parents of over one thousand children in his private practice and has attained nearly 100 percent success with day and night control by age five (Brazelton, 1962).

Brazelton has suggested that parents wait to begin training until after age two and until signs of readiness appear in young children. Children are introduced to the potty as an interesting, child-sized piece of furniture. Children are asked but not forced to sit on the potty with their clothes on. After children become accustomed to the potty, adults explain about urinating or having a bowel movement there. When children seem willing, they sit on the potty without their diapers at times when they are likely to urinate or defecate. Praise should be offered but not overdone because children at these ages do not like to think of themselves as being too much under adult control. After children seem to have the idea, they can wear thick absorbent underpants, called training pants, when at home. With the Brazelton approach, daytime bowel and urine training come at about the same time. If children show any disinclination to continue, they are put back into diapers with no signs of disapproval and training is only resumed when children again show interest in the process. According to Brazelton, nighttime dryness follows daytime dryness when the bladder is sufficiently mature, usually around three years of age. (Boys are somewhat later than girls.) Children should be allowed to feel comfortable wearing diapers at night until they are consistently dry for a period of time.

For the impatient, there are quicker training methods than Brazelton's. Two behaviorists have written a book called *Toilet Training in Less than a Day* (Azrin & Foxx, 1981). Children over twenty months of age who show signs of readiness are taught by imitation and rewards to use the potty. The success rate is high for daytime dryness, but two-thirds of the children who are trained in this manner continue wetting at night.

Some of the problems that occur with training are caused by coercive or shaming practices used by adults. Adults who try to impose their wills on children find that children can learn to hold on to their urine or bowel movements until they get off the potty. More positive approaches, such as Brazelton's and the behaviorists', enlist children's cooperation and their interest in being grown up. All training methods should allow children to feel good about themselves and their bodies.

Children's particular characteristics   An interesting study conducted in Israel (Kaffman & Elizur, 1977) showed that there are some characteristic differences between children who attain bladder control by age four and those who do not. Children who have problems with bladder control are significantly more likely to have the following characteristics: (*a*) a family history of late bladder control; (*b*) a relaxed attitude about being wet; (*c*) personality characteristics of dependency, low motivation for achievement, low adaptability, high activity level, and aggression; and (*d*) problems with neuromuscular maturation. Parents of children with some of these characteristics might choose to delay the onset of training until signs of readiness are well established.

Sex Education

Angela, age two, stared pointedly the first time she helped her mother change baby Nick's diaper. "What dat?" she asked, touching his penis.

Sex education in these early years usually comes in response to questions about children's bodies and about how babies are born. These questions should be answered simply but accurately. Angela's mother, for instance, told her: "Nick is a boy and boy's bodies are different from girls' in some ways. Nick uses his penis to urinate."

The goals of early sex education are to help children feel comfortable with their bodies and to establish open communication patterns between parents and children. Children will consider their parents "askable" if parents can respond in a relaxed manner to questions. It is a good idea to clarify the question first (e.g., "Do you mean 'How does the baby get out of the mother's body?'") because sometimes children's questions are not what they seem at first to be. (A familiar story features a mother who rushes through a detailed account of conception, prenatal development, and birth, only to have her son reply, "No, I mean what town was I born in?") Once the question is clarified, the parent should give the information requested and then stop to allow the child time to assimilate the information.

The degree to which information about birth is meaningful to young children is related to their overall level of intellectual development. Using a Piagetian perspective, Cowan and Bernstein (Cowan, 1978) hypothesized that young children would make up their own theories about birth according to their general level of intellectual development. When the researchers studied three- to four-year-olds, their findings were consistent with this hypothesis. Young children give replies at three levels of understanding to questions such as "How do people get babies?" "What does the word *born* mean?" "How do mothers get to be mothers?" and "How do fathers get to be fathers?"

The three levels of understanding are designated as 0, 1, and 2. Children at Level 0 show no understanding or refuse to answer. Children at Level 1 seem to feel no need to apply causality principles because they believe that babies have always existed. Cowan reported the following conversation with a child at Level 1:

> How did the baby happen to be in your Mommy's tummy?
> *It just grows inside.*
> How did it get there?
> *It's there all the time. Mommy doesn't have to do anything. She waits until she feels it.* (Cowan, 1978, p. 135)

Children at Level 2 respond with explanations that seem more appropriate to manufactured products than to people. One of the interviews included this conclusion by a Level-2 child of three years, seven months: "You find it at a store that makes it . . . Well, they get it and then they put it in the tummy and then it goes quickly out (Cowan, 1978, p. 135)." Some children at Level 2 connect the father with the birth process but in a mechanical manner.

Children's ideas about the origin of babies follow a predictable developmental sequence. Factual information about their bodies and birth should be provided to young children, but parents need not fear that someone is giving their children misinformation if children seem to have a distorted understanding of birth. Cowan and Bernstein showed that children need to fit new information into their existing mental structures. Only gradually, with patient repetition of explanations and open conversation from adults, do children develop an accurate understanding of their bodies and the birth process.

SUMMARY

1   Many physical changes take place in the years from one to three.
2   In large muscle development, children learn to walk, run, climb stairs, kick balls, throw balls, somersault, and ride tricycles.

3   In small muscle development, children learn to feed themselves, undress, dress, build block towers, turn the pages of books, and draw with pencils and crayons.

4   Perceptual-motor integration relates information taken in through the senses to children's behavior.

5   Both maturation and experience are important in physical development.

6   In some large and small muscle skills, girls are six months ahead of boys, on average.

7   Ethnicity, adult physical stimulation, and nutrition influence the speed of early physical development.

8   Young children are accident-prone and need to be provided with a safe environment.

9   Children should be placed in an approved safety restraint every time they ride in an automobile.

10   Many poisonings can be prevented by placing dangerous substances out of the reach of children.

11   Burns and drownings can be prevented by adjustments of the environment and by close supervision of young children.

12   Physical illness is related to delayed development and behavior problems.

13   Young children are particularly susceptible to lead poisoning, which causes learning problems, retardation, other problems, and even death.

14   Children whose families are under stress are more likely to be ill or have accidents.

15   Physical growth tapers off in the second year of life and appetites become unpredictable.

16   Adequate nutrition is necessary for the full development of the capabilities of young children.

17   Adequate rest, health care, and dental care are important in maintaining children's wellness.

18   Body awareness consists of the formation of body image and senses of laterality and directionality.

19   Children's feelings of success in toileting are related to timing of training, method, and children's particular characteristics.

20   The goals of early sex education are to help children feel comfortable with their bodies and to establish open communication patterns.

KEY TERMS

large muscle skills	perceptual-motor integration	kwashiorkor
small muscle skills		bottle-mouth syndrome
random scribbling	proximo-distal	laterality
controlled scribbling	splinter skills	directionality

FOR FURTHER READING

Movement Activities

Sullivan, M. (1982), *Feeling strong, feeling free: Movement exploration for young children.* Washington, DC: National Association for the Education of Young Children.

Toilet Training

Azrin, N. H., & Foxx, R. M. (1981), *Toilet training in less than a day*. New York: Pocket Books.

Explaining Birth

Stein, S. B. (1974). *Making babies: An open family book for parents and children together*. New York: Walker and Company.

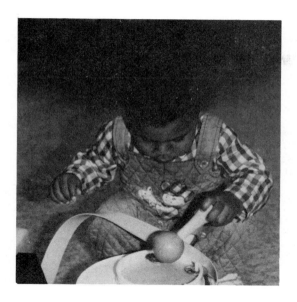

10

One- to Three-Year-Olds: Cognitive Development

Key Ideas

Piaget's Stages of Intellectual Development
Sensorimotor Substage Five □ Sensorimotor Substage Six □ Early Preoperational Thinking □ Criticisms of Piaget's Theory □ Applications of Piaget's Theory

Language Development
Receptive Language □ First Words □ Early Sentences □ Vocabulary Expansion □ Differences in Language Learning Environments □ Cultural Differences: Black English

Importance of Play
Definition of Play □ Significance of Play □ Cultural Influences □ Pretense

Environments for Developing Cognition
Differences in Home Environments □ Effects of Educational Intervention

Cognitive development involves changes in mental processes, including problem solving and language usage. Children from one to three years of age make many striking advances in their cognitive development. This chapter describes advances in thinking by considering the theory of Jean Piaget and the views of those who differ from Piaget. Information is also presented about language development, differences in language learning environments, cultural differences in language, the importance of play, and the effects on cognition of environments in which young children live.

PIAGET'S STAGES OF INTELLECTUAL DEVELOPMENT

According to Jean Piaget (Piaget & Inhelder, 1969), children complete the last two substages of sensorimotor thinking in the second year of life. (See Table 10.1.) Then, when they are about two years of age, children enter what Piaget has described as the preoperational stage of thinking. This section begins with a description of sensorimotor substages five and six and early preoperational thinking. The section ends with a discussion of some criticisms of Piaget's theory of intellectual development.

Sensorimotor Substage Five

Sensorimotor substage five, typically extending from twelve to eighteen months, is a time of mental growth. One of the hallmarks of this substage is the use of **tertiary circular reactions**, as illustrated by the behavior of Mary, age one:

Mary sits in her high chair and drops peas over the side of the tray. She pushes them off the edge with her spoon, releases them from her fingers, and then gets the idea of spitting them. In each case she watches the path of the peas carefully.

According to Piaget, two elements differentiate Mary's behavior from what she did in earlier substages: Mary experiments with the peas rather than repeating one action and she shows an interest in understanding the nature of the unusual movements that she produces. Mary's process of finding novel trajectories for the peas takes her beyond her earlier secondary circular reactions, which would have focused on repetition of the original action.

Mary solves problems in a more sophisticated manner than earlier. Suppose that she wants to open a tightly closed cabinet. Now, as before, she first tries to use techniques that have obtained results in other situations. But, if she is not successful, she is able to change her behavior through trial and error until she reaches her goal. Piaget has said that behavior in substage five is directed in two ways: by the goal and by earlier schemes that enable children to interpret what they are doing, based on past experiences.

More systematic imitation is another of Mary's new accomplishments in substage five. Up to this point, her attempts at imitation were characterized by trial and error, and she usually took several movements before accurately dupli-

TABLE 10.1 *Piaget's Sensorimotor Stage of Development*
Jean Piaget divided the sensorimotor stage (birth to about age two) into six substages.
The last two of these six substages usually take place during the second year of life.

Sensorimotor Substage	Age	Accomplishments
Substage 1 (Reflexes)	Birth–1 month	Builds on reflexes
Substage 2 (Primary circular reactions)	1–4 months	Repeats interesting movements of the body (primary circular reactions) Anticipates familar events (e.g., feeding) Coordinates senses
Substage 3 (Secondary circular reactions)	4–8 months	Repeats interesting actions on objects (secondary circular reactions) Imitates sounds and actions in repertoire Attempts search for hidden object
Substage 4 (Practical intelligence)	8–12 months	Uses goal-directed behavior Begins to realize that objects and people exist even if not in view Imitates many behaviors
Substage 5 (Tertiary circular reactions)	12–18 months	Experiments with objects (tertiary circular reactions) Imitates accurately, needing little trial and error Thinks of objects as having permanence and searches for them where last seen
Substage 6 (Object permanence)	18–24 months	Works out solutions to problems mentally Defers imitation Comprehends object permanence and can even imagine movements of unseen objects

cating an action. In the period from twelve to eighteen months, however, Mary becomes able to imitate her father immediately and correctly. In a "monkey see" game, when he rubs his ear, she does also—without trying her neck or scalp first.

Further developments in Mary's understanding of the permanence of objects are also notable in substage five. She has had enough experiences with relationships that she searches for a missing toy in the place where she last saw it. This search strategy contrasts with the one used in substage four; in substage

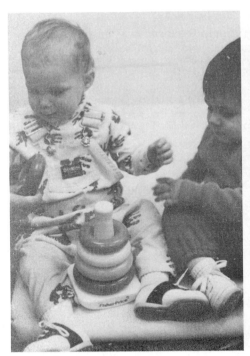

In sensorimotor substage five, children solve problems in more sophisticated ways than earlier.

four she would have looked in the place where she last was successful in finding the toy, even if the toy had not been near there since. Piaget has said that Mary is showing that she no longer just connects objects with practical situations, such as her past successes, but she finally thinks of them as having permanence of their own. Still, Mary is not yet able to imagine movements of things. If a situation requires her to imagine how one of her toys might have been moved from place to place (rather than allowing her to follow the movements visually), Mary goes back to her former strategy of looking for the toy where she last found it.

Children's use of tertiary circular reactions, their problem solving strategies, their more systematic imitation, and their expanded sense of object permanence—all of these changes in thinking processes make the fifth sensorimotor substage a dynamic period.

Sensorimotor Substage Six

In sensorimotor substage six, children from approximately eighteen months to two years of age begin to be able to work out solutions to problems mentally, rather than relying only on physical manipulation of things. Note Jeff's strategy as he builds with blocks.

Jeff, age two, is an experienced builder with unit blocks. Today he is placing the blocks in a rectangular formation. When all pieces but one are in place, he stops work for a moment and looks around carefully at the remaining blocks, chooses one that will fit, and drops it confidently into position.

Jeff did not need to use trial and error in order to find the block that would fit. Instead of trying several blocks in the space, he thought about the problem. He drew upon his past experiences with blocks to help him in mentally comparing the size of the space to be filled with the sizes of blocks at hand. Piaget has described what happens in sensorimotor substage six as providing a transition to symbolic thought.

In this sixth and final substage of sensorimotor thought, Jeff's ability to imitate expands, too. He and other children of his age are able to retain a mental image of what they have seen and imitate it at a later time. Jeff demonstrated what Piaget called **deferred imitation** when he exactly duplicated the behavior of his older cousin two days after the family's return from a visit.

Another important development in this last sensorimotor substage involves object permanence. Piaget has noted that in this substage children are finally able to understand completely the permanent qualities that objects possess. For instance, children in sensorimotor substage six can construct a mental map of the movement of a toy car from hiding places under a pillow, a towel, and finally a scarf. Children who have reached the end of their sensorimotor development realize that the car has continued to exist even though it has been hidden within an adult's hand while being moved. They look for the car under the scarf, even if they found it successfully somewhere else when they played the game on another occassion. According to Piaget, these children show that they have become capable of a mature comprehension that things and people have properties and characteristics of their own; this comprehension paves the way and provides a basis for all future cognitive development.

Piaget's theory has given structure to an account of the dramatic changes in children's thinking processes between birth and two years of age. Piaget has asserted that children are curious beings who seek out novelty and are mentally active in organizing and interpreting their experiences during the sensorimotor stage and in the preoperational stage that follows.

Early Preoperational Thinking

The stage of preoperational thinking extends approximately from two through seven or eight years of age. This section focuses on the early part of the preoperational stage: ages two and three.

The word **preoperational** means literally "before operational or logical thinking." Unfortunately, this name has led some people to think in terms of what children in this stage cannot do rather than in terms of their strengths. To be sure, one of Jean Piaget's outstanding contributions to our knowledge of young children's thinking has been to demonstrate that there is a qualitative and not just a quantitative difference in the thinking processes of young children, compared to older children and adults. But recognizing differences in young children's thinking need not lead to undervaluing the fascinating growth that takes place during the preoperational stage.

One of the key developments in early preoperational thinking is the ability to use mental symbols. After a description of mental symbols, the patterns of thought that set young preoperational children apart from older children and adults are discussed.

Mental symbols   **Mental symbols** include words that represent things, actions that imitate adult roles, activities that use one thing as a symbol of another, and unconscious symbolizing (e.g., when dreaming). Using words to represent objects that are not necessarily visible is perhaps the most obvious sign that children are engaging in mental symbolism. "Ball," a child says, meaning either, "Where is the ball?" "There is the ball," "I want the ball," or "Here is the ball." The meaning can often be understood through context but, whatever the meaning, the child is consistently using a culturally agreed-upon word to represent something in the environment.

Using words is not the only way that children share their mental symbols. At these ages, they usually begin to imitate adult roles that they have observed. One child ceremoniously gets out a sack, fills it with papers each morning after breakfast, and walks around the house in imitation of his mother and her always-stuffed briefcase. Another child drives a couch in a way that resembles the manner in which her father drives his moving van. These children have observed

Two-year-olds show use of mental symbols, such as a rock for money as this "truck driver" pays his toll.

adult activities, formed and remembered mental symbols of essential elements, and acted out their versions at a later time.

In their play activities, children create and use mental symbols. Two sticks are crossed to form an airplane. An oatmeal container becomes a drum. Triangles and circles are combined to represent people in art work. Dress-up clothes transform a child into an adult. A hat turns a three-year-old into an authentic fire fighter. By their actions, children provide evidence of the advances taking place in their thinking.

The discussion of psychosocial development in Chapter 8 mentioned that fearfulness sometimes results from unconscious symbolizing. Because preoperational children can retain and elaborate on mental symbols, they may develop fears of darkness, monsters, dogs, and other things. Parents are usually reassured to learn that their children's new fears are evidence of an advance in intellectual development and are normal at these ages. Many parents who lack this information blame themselves for some deed or omission that turned a previously confident child into a fearful one.

The early preoperational years bring with them many changes in abilities, and children themselves often seem invigorated by their prowess. When children become capable of forming mental representations of objects or happenings, they can extend their thinking beyond the boundaries of the immediate time and place.

Thought patterns   Piaget has shown that children are not just miniature and less experienced adults. The qualitative differences that set the thinking of young preoperational children apart from that of their older contemporaries include transductive reasoning, idiosyncratic concepts, and egocentrism.

Some of children's colorful comments illustrate what Piaget calls **transductive reasoning**. Transductive reasoning shows some or all of the following characteristics: it moves from effect to cause, focuses on only one of several variables, confuses general and specific cases, and makes analogies to past events. Transductive reasoning can lead to correct conclusions, but examples are more memorable when children use it to draw faulty conclusions. For instance, several days after Stephan, age two years, was knocked to the floor and licked by a large but affectionate dog, he asked to be picked up when he saw the dog. He said, "Dog no eat." His mother, misunderstanding, said; "The dog is not eating?" Stephan corrected her by saying, "Dog no lick; dog no eat *me!*" Stephan had apparently reasoned that the first licking was similar to tasting a new food and that eating would soon follow. Further examples of transductive reasoning involve inaccurate conclusions about cause and effect, as when Peter is sure that Jake *caused* a toy to fall because Jake walked by at that moment.

Idiosyncratic concepts are concepts that seem general but convey meaning that relates only to personal experiences. Three-year old Marian, for example, had learned that her grandparents live in Atlanta. When her family visited there, they all went out to dinner at a nearby restaurant. After dinner Marian asked, "When are we going back to Atlanta?" meaning her grandparents' house rather than the city, which they had not yet left. In other cases, young children focus on only one variable in a situation. A child might say, "I know that Daddy

BOX 10.1

STRATEGIES FOR FACILITATING DEVELOPMENT: "PIAGETIAN" ACTIVITIES FOR YOUNG CHILDREN

The following sensory activities have been designed for very young children or as a first step for older children. The basis for planning the activities is a Piagetian perspective, which views children as active agents in exploring and understanding their environments.

I See My World

To prepare: Find multiples of common objects (balls, dolls, shoes, spoons, blocks, large pop beads, plastic cups, rattles, plastic jars, receiving blankets, etc.) Put one of each object in a bag for yourself. Put the other objects in front of the child.

The activity: Draw one object from your bag. Ask, "What is this?" Use the label given by the child or supply the term, if necessary. Ask, "Please find me another_____." Compare similar objects on the basis of color, size, shape, and other characteristics.

Concepts communicated: visual discrimination, matching, description, naming.

I Hear My World

To prepare: Collect familar objects that make noises (rattle, bell, half-full tissue box, key chain and keys, piggy bank with coins, etc). Let children look at and explore the objects and the sounds that they make.

is older because he is bigger." The focus is on size alone rather than on some attempt to coordinate size and age.

Characteristics of the thought of young children caused Piaget to label them **egocentric**. In this context, egocentric means "centered on self," as when a child goes immediately to the toy department to select a gift for a parent. The term applied to children does not have the negative connotations that it would have if used to describe an adult, who presumably has other behavioral options. In his work Piaget demonstrated that young children are not as able as older children or adults to take the view or perspective of another person. Experiences and interactions gradually diminish this egocentrism.

Transductive reasoning, idiosyncratic concepts, and egocentrism are all part of Piaget's view of young children's thinking during the early part of the preoperational stage of development. Although young children's thinking is not yet based on logic, it serves an important function. Transductive reasoning, for

The activity: Demonstrate the sound that each object makes. Have children close their eyes or turn their bodies away from the objects. Shake an object and then ask the children to point to the correct thing. Supply the name of the object. Use descriptive terms such as "louder," "softer," "jingle," etc. Repeat with other objects.

Concepts communicated: auditory discrimination, description, naming.

I Touch My World

To prepare: Use a large sock to make a "feeling bag." Gather common objects (ball, large popbead, nipple from a bottle, rattle, block, spoon, etc.). Allow children to examine the objects.

The activity: Away from children's lines of vision, place one object in the sock. Invite a child to put his or her hand in the sock to try to find out what the object is. Help the child supply descriptive terms for the tactile sensations (smooth, rounded, etc.) and a name for the object. Let the child see the object after a judgment has been made. Repeat with other objects.

In a more advanced variation, two objects can be put in the sock at the same time. You can give an instruction such as, "Find the thing that we use to eat with."

Concepts communicated: tactile discrimination, description, naming.

Adapted from "Children Learn About Their Senses" by S. Anselmo, 1980, *Day Care and Early Education, 8,* pp. 42–44. Copyright 1980 by Human Sciences Press. Adapted by permission.

example, may provide the link between conclusions that children draw from observations (inductive reasoning) and conclusions that they draw from other premises (deductive reasoning).

Criticisms of Piaget's Theory

Toby (3 years, 2 months) pushed me into a cabinet and I hit my head on a corner. When she realized that I was hurt, she looked stricken and ran out of the room. Soon she returned, handed me her special Teddy, and stroked my leg gently.

Observations such as this one indicate that even young preoperational children are able to pay attention to how other people feel. Piaget said that young children are egocentric, but some contemporary researchers have criticized Piaget for underestimating the degree to which young children show awareness of and interest in what others are experiencing.

To understand some of the criticisms of Piaget's theory, it is first helpful to understand how Piaget reached his conclusions about young children's egocentrism. One of the ways in which Piaget gathered information was the now-classic "three mountain experiment" (Piaget & Inhelder, 1956). In this experiment, children are asked to sit on one side of a three-dimensional model of mountains. The mountains are distinguished by color, position, and placement of snow, a red cross, and a house. An adult puts a doll at different positions relative to the mountains and asks children to choose a picture that shows what the doll would see from its perspective. Children do not usually succeed in this experiment until they reach eight or nine years of age. Younger children often substitute their own perspective for that of the doll. Piaget used these findings as evidence of younger children's egocentrism: their inability to take a perspective other than their own.

However, other researchers believe that the nature of Piaget's experiment led young children to give more egocentric responses than they would in other situations. These researchers question both the appropriateness of this type of task and the generality of the conclusions that Piaget drew from his findings. This section presents research that questions the applicability of some of Piaget's findings. This current research is then used to embellish Piaget's theory and to give guidelines for creating growth-enhancing environments for young children.

Four sets of research findings have been selected from those that are critical of Piaget's conclusions about young children's egocentrism. First, research by Martin Hughes (Hughes & Donaldson, 1983) has called into question the conclusions that Piaget drew from the three mountain experiment. Hughes set up his own experiment in which children viewed a square board that was divided by barriers into four sections. The experimenter positioned a doll in one of the sections and a toy policeman at another point. The experimenter

Even three-year-olds can be successful in understanding others' perspectives if the motives and intentions are familiar to them.

then asked a child if the policeman could see the doll. In a variation, two policemen were used and the experimenter asked a child to hide a doll from both. Hughes found that even three-year-olds had a success rate of 88 percent. Researchers (Hughes & Donaldson, 1983; Donaldson, 1983) have explained the differences in results between Piaget's and more recent experiments in terms of the comprehensibility of the motives and the intentions of the characters. The three mountain experiment makes no reference to any purposes or feelings with which young children could identify. The policeman experiment, however, is explained in terms of motives and intentions that three-year-olds can understand. Young children know how to hide and have experienced the desire to escape from authority figures.

In a second set of critical research findings, a pair of researchers (Hood and Bloom, 1979) have shown that, under some circumstances, young children's understanding of causality is more advanced than Piaget indicated. According to Piaget, understanding of cause and effect does not develop until seven or eight years of age. However, Hood and Bloom found that even two- and three-year-olds understand causal relations and have the ability to express them. What explains the difference in findings? Piaget based his conclusions on interviews in which children talked about sequences of actions involving physical objects, but Hood and Bloom investigated spontaneous comments and responses to adult questions about causal relations in the psychological sphere. Hood and Bloom noted that even two-year-olds make causal statements involving events such as babies' crying.

A third researcher to criticize Piaget is Borke (1983). Borke replicated Piaget and Inhelder's basic experimental design in the three mountain experiment and also made some substitutions so that the task would be more familiar to young children. Presented with a three mountain scene similar to Piaget and Inhelder's, only 42 percent of three-year-olds and 67 percent of four-year-olds were able to take the perspective of another person. But when Grover from Sesame Street parked and looked out of his car at toy objects such as boats and animals, three- and four-year-old children were highly accurate (80 percent) in predicting Grover's perspective. Borke (1983) concluded that the complexity and familiarity of tasks are critical variables in determining at what age children can take the perspective of another.

A fourth researcher critical of Piaget is Jerome Kagan (1982), a well-known cognitive theorist and researcher who has described young children as being interpersonally more complex than Piaget said. Kagan has presented cross-cultural evidence that two-year-olds have an emergence of empathy and an ability to make inferences about the psychological states of other people. Kagan has said that these developments at about age two are cultural universals: Parents in Fiji say that children acquire *vakayalo* (sense) after their second birthdays; the Utku Eskimos of Hudson Bay believe that children become capable of *lhuma* (reason) at the same time. According to Kagan, children's increased sensitivity to others at about age two is paralleled by an increased awareness of their own individuality. When young children begin to use verbs, they usually give a running commentary on their own actions (e.g., "Me up," "Me go"). Kagan has indicated that doing so demonstrates their awareness of their ability to act and to influence the course of events. Another interesting example of self-awareness of young children is seen in an experiment in which children between one and three years are brought to a room with a large mirror. The parent surreptitiously puts some rouge on children's noses and takes them to the mirror. Children under one year of age do not touch their faces. But two-year-olds put their hands right on their faces, realizing that the reflection belongs to them. Kagan's observations are often similar to Piaget's but his conclusions attribute more sensitivity than did Piaget to the interactions of very young children.

Should these studies cause rejection of Piaget's theory? It seems that such rejection would be premature. One reason is that all of these researchers acknowledge the magnitude of the contribution that Piaget's theory has made to the understanding of young children's thinking. The researchers who have achieved different results from Piaget's have purposely made adaptations in methods; they have not questioned the results that follow from Piaget's methods but have chosen to use other approaches. Another reason is that the areas of disagreement with Piaget have usually involved the timing of attainment of certain thinking abilities rather than the sequence in which these abilities develop.

Piaget's approach seems to lead to a conservative account of young children's capabilities. Piaget examined young children's cognitive interpretations of the physical world, and these interpretations were requested in relative isolation from children's feelings, concerns, and interests. In contrast, more recent researchers have worked to construct experimental situations with which young children would be familiar and within which they would be comfortable. Recent researchers have demonstrated that, in meaningful contexts involving basic human communication, young children are more competent than Piaget said.

Applications of Piaget's Theory

It may be that a combination of Piaget's theory and the recent research is more significant than either element alone. The composite of Piaget's work and recent research reveals that effective learning environments for young children should be familiar, personal, and warm. Young preoperational children are learning every minute of every day, but they learn best through their own experiences with a wide variety of materials, through warm and sensitive contacts with adults who talk with them, and through their interactions with other children within an environment that emphasizes mutual respect. The combination of Piaget's work and recent research shows that adults should build on the experiences of young children and work with them on interpretations of their feelings and the feelings of others. Piaget's work has demonstrated that young preoperational children do not comprehend situations or problems that are expressed in abstract, artificial terminology. Classrooms and learning tasks that may be appropriate for elementary school children are not appropriate for younger children.

The appropriateness of learning tasks and classroom environments for young children has been evaluated by many interpreters of Piaget's theory

Young preoperational children learn best through their own experiences with a wide variety of materials.

(Bybee & Sund, 1982; Elkind, 1976, 1981; Kamii & DeVries, 1978; Labinowicz, 1980; Wadsworth, 1984). Since Piaget's emphasis was on theory rather than practice, these interpreters deserve much of the credit for showing parents, teachers, and others how to implement Piaget's theory.

LANGUAGE DEVELOPMENT

> This [language learning] is doubtless the greatest intellectual feat any one of us is ever required to perform (Bloomfield, 1933, p. 29).

Adults who have nurtured young children during the language-learning years usually share Leonard Bloomfield's awe of the human capacity required in language learning. Bloomfield (1933) was a linguist whose work dominated the field until Noam Chomsky (1965) redirected the energies of language researchers. Although their approaches differ significantly, both Bloomfield and Chomsky have said that the mystery of language learning centers on two characteristics of human language use: (1) human language is governed by rules; and (2) human language is also creative. In other words, most speech forms have regular grammatical patterns, but there are almost infinite word combinations, some of which may never have been uttered. These two characteristics would seem to make language learning nearly an impossible task.

Most linguists hold some variation on Chomsky's view about how children manage to learn the languages spoken in their environments (Gleitman & Wanner, 1982). Chomsky has asserted that all languages share universal properties and that human infants are biologically programmed to master the rules of the languages they hear. Chomsky has noted that children usually receive no formal instruction about the rules that underlie adult language. Instead, children hear a specific set of utterances, different from those heard by the children next door or across town. Chomsky has said that, from these utterances and the circumstances in which they are heard, children organize and build a workable grammar. They use this grammar when they communicate with words, combinations of words, and sentences. In groundbreaking research, Bloom (1970) showed that even the earliest two-word utterances of young children are regular and consistent in the ways words are used and combined. Of course, children cannot discuss the rules of this grammar and are not even aware of it. But researchers feel sure that a mental structure must exist to govern language learning and usage.

The language development of a fictitious child, Jana, is chronicled as an example of how a child might progress in language learning. The ages at which Jana attains certain milestones represent the ages at which the majority of children attain them. (Averages are derived from Owens, 1984, and Garvey, 1984.) But some well-developing children reach these milestones somewhat later or earlier than Jana and still are within the range of what is called normal.

Jana established the two key bases for speech during her first year of life. First, she developed and continues to develop sensorimotor intelligence, giving her some ideas about how the environment operates and responds. And, second, she had experience in prespeech communication, giving her an understanding of turn-taking, reciprocity, and other aspects of interacting with people. On these bases, Jana broadens her understanding and use of langauge.

Receptive language

A dramatic linguistic milestone for Jana is the increase in her understanding of language around the time of her first birthday. The term **receptive language** is used to denote language that is received and understood. Receptive language

---

BOX 10.2	**"MOTHERESE" AND "FATHERESE"**

Language researchers have found that many adults adapt their speech to the needs of young language learners, and they have dubbed these adaptations **motherese and fatherese**. More than one hundred alterations of ordinary adult speech have been identified, including use of a higher pitch, simplified grammar and shorter sentences, repetition of words, avoiding words that change in meaning (*"Mommy's* doing it," rather than *"I'm* doing it"), and limiting topics of conversation to what is happening at the moment (Schachter & Strage, 1982).

The adaptations that adults make occur gradually. Mervis and Mervis (1982) showed that mothers of nine-month-olds label objects for their children in an adult manner. But mothers of thirteen-month-olds have changed their labeling behavior in response to their children's increased interest in language. Instead of using adult categories, they choose labels for objects according to their predictions of what would be the most meaningful to their children. For instance, they take into account that leopards and house cats would be perceived as being the same by young children.

is contrasted with **expressive language**, language that is produced by children themselves.

Jana's parents are delighted when their twelve-month-old begins to be able to follow simple one-step requests: "Get the teddy bear," "Give me the cup," "Show the block." By sixteen months of age, Jana points to body parts—tummy, nose, eyes, mouth, ears—when asked to do so. Jana understands and responds appropriately and enthusiastically to these and similar requests.

First Words

Jana's first word is *mama,* uttered meaningfully when she is twelve months old. In her first year, she practiced making the *m* sound, but that sound was nonspecific and did not stand for any one person. Now, however, when she says *mama* she refers to the special person in her life. By her second birthday, Jana has added other words to her verbal repertoire: *no, more, baby, ball, up, juice,* and *bottle.* Most of her words are substantive words, referring to classes of objects (e.g., baby, ball, juice, bottle). A small number of words in her vocabulary are function forms (e.g., no, more, up), and these latter words are used frequently.

Many of Jana's early words refer to obvious features of her current environment. Karmiloff-Smith (1979) has proposed that one of the functions of early language for children like Jana is to show that they separate their actions from objects in the environment. For example, when Jana knows the various actions that she can perform with her bottle (e.g., suck, bang, roll), she can attach the

This child's phone conversation consisted of two of his first words, hi and Mama.

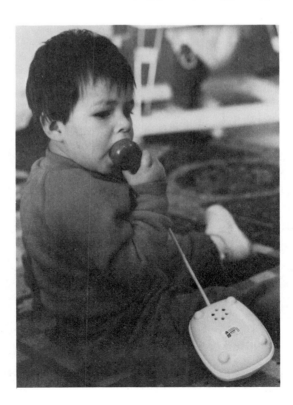

language label, *bottle,* to show that the bottle has a continuity beyond the current action that she is performing with it.

As Jana communicates, seven separate functions or uses of words can be identified (Garvey, 1984). The first uses are often *instrumental,* to satisfy wants and needs; *regulatory,* to control the behavior of others; *interactional,* to establish and maintain contact with others; and *personal,* to assert and express herself. Gradually language is also used in a *heuristic* manner, to find out about the world; *imaginatively,* to create images and pleasurable effects; and *representationally,* to inform others and to express information.

BOX 10.3

ANALYZING CHILD DIARIES

Child diaries kept on brothers made it possible to compare their expressive vocabularies at sixteen months of age. Their mother was fascinated by the similarities and differences in these first words. Nine of the brothers' first twenty words were identical, another cluster of words referred to food or eating, and the remainder of the words reflected individual interests and preferences.

Vocabulary at 16 Months

	C's Words	D's Words
Identical words	mama	mama
	dada	dada
	eye	eye
	hi	hi
	bye	bye
	Papa (Grandfather)	Baba (Grandfather)
	ba(ll)	ba(ll)
	mou(th)	mou(th)
	door	doo(r)
Food-related words	e(gg)	mo (more)
	ba-ba (bottle)	yuk
	aa-ba (apple)	bow(l)
	all done	
Other	bu(g)	no
	baby	ya (yes)
	airplane	na-na (night-night)
	bath	no(se)
	do(g)	boo(k)
	bu(tton)	moo (for cow)
	ho-ho (What we say	baa (lamb)
	at Christmas	Nanna (Nanny: Caregiver)

Some of Jana's one-word utterances carry the meaning found in full adult sentences. When she says, "Juice!" she might mean, "I want more juice," "There's the juice," or "The juice spilled." Adults can often ascertain Jana's meaning because of the context and gestures that accompany her words. Linguists use the term **holophrasis** to refer to single-word utterances that embody meaningful ideas.

Early Sentences

By the end of her second year, Jana is producing her first multiword sentences. Linguists have placed early sentences into seven main categories that express universal concepts. These categories and examples of Jana's early sentences follow:

1   Questions, such as "Where go?"
2   Descriptions, such as "Baby sleep."
3   Recurrence, such as "More juice."
4   Possession, such as "Mine doggie."
5   Location, such as "Block here."
6   Agent action, such as "Mommy go."
7   Negation and wish, such as "No go work," and "Play sand" (Honig, 1982).

Some of these early two-word sentences depend on gestures, intonation, word order, and context cues for interpretation.

Over the months, Jana refines her grammar and adds more descriptors to her sentences. According to Wood (1981) very young children acquire grammar by adhering to the following five principles:

1   Pay attention to the ends of words (e.g., cookie/cookies, jump/jumped).
2   Pay attention to word order.
3   Avoid interruption or rearrangement of linguistic units, as in "What I can do" rather than "What can I do."
4   Express relationships clearly, often by repeating, as in "My *doll, he* gots PJs."
5   Avoid exceptions such as *went, broken,* and *did.*

These principles sometimes lead to early sentences that are awkward or grammatically incorrect; but even so, they fill Jana with a sense of power that originates in being able to communicate her ideas in words.

Vocabulary Expansion

In her third and fourth years, Jana's receptive and expressive vocabulary expands. She shows that she can follow two-step requests (e.g., "Get your shoes and take them to Nanny."). She can even point to objects that are described by use (e.g., "Show me something that we use to brush hair."). She indicates her age by holding up fingers, counts to five, and repeats six-word sentences. She uses personal pronouns, adjectives, prepositions, and adverbs appropriately. By the time Jana is four, she has mastered the basic grammar of her language.

An interesting phenomenon when Jana is four demonstrates how actively she seeks to organize her language experiences. Earlier, Jana correctly used past tenses of most verbs. But at age four, Jana begins to say, "I *singed* a song," and "I *bringed* it with me." Linguists say that Jana is overgeneralizing a rule about verb endings. They use this phenomenon as evidence that language learners like Jana prefer a bad generalization to none at all. So firmly entrenched is her generalization that attempts at correction are unnoticed. Her mother responds to her statements by attending to the content of the message and by using the correct form in her reply. Here is one of their interchanges:

J.   I *singed* "Old McDonald."
M.   Oh, you *sang* it by yourself?
J.   I *singed* it all!

After several years of overgeneralizing, Jana constructs a more comprehensive grammatical rule for irregular verb endings and uses the past tense as the adults around her do.

Language development is encouraged by shared experiences. These children participate in a "dairy tasting party," sampling various cheeses, milk, yogurt, and cottage cheese. The child on the left first shows and then describes his reaction to yogurt.

STRATEGIES FOR FACILITATING DEVELOPMENT: LANGUAGE SCREENING

Adults who work with young children often wish for a language screening device to ascertain the possible presence of developmental disabilities. Most tests for children under three either lack standardization and validation or require considerable specialized training to administer. Now, however, Coplan and colleagues (1982) have developed a brief language assessment suitable for use by pediatricians and other professionals working with young children. The Early Language Milestone (ELM) scale is sensitive and specific as a detector of developmentally delayed children, when compared with more formal tests given by clinical psychologists and speech pathologists. The developers of the ELM believe that young children who show delayed language milestones should undergo formal assessment instead of waiting to see if they "grow out of it."

The ELM includes forty-one language items divided into three groups of behaviors: auditory expressive, auditory receptive, and visual. Sample items from the first parts of the ELM are shown below.

Sample Items: Early Language Milestone Scale

Milestone	Months at Which 90% of Children Attain Milestone
I. *Auditory Expressive*	
Mama/dada: correct usage	14.0
First word beyond *mama/dada*	17.0
4–6 single words	23.5
2-word sentences	23.2
50 or more single words	25.6
Holds brief conversations	34.3
Gives name and use of two objects	34.4
Correct Use of Pronoun *I*	>36
II. *Auditory Receptive*	
Follows 1-step commands	13.5
Points to 1 or more body parts	20.8
Follows 2-step commands	25.1
Points to named object	27.0
Points to objects described by use	32.6

SOURCE: Adapted from "Validation of an Early Language Milestone Scale in a High-Risk Population," by J. Coplan, J. R. Gleason, R. Ryan, M. G. Burke, and M. L. Williams, 1982, *Pediatrics, 70,* pp. 677–83. Copyright 1982 by Pediatrics. Reproduced by permission of Pediatrics.

Differences in Language Learning Environments

Researchers (Schachter, 1979; Schachter & Strage, 1982) studied 24,192 speech acts of mothers and toddlers and found extensive differences in the social and emotional components of communication. The study involved thirty mother-toddler pairs who were divided into three groups; black disadvantaged, black advantaged, and white advantaged. *Advantaged* was defined in terms of the level of education of the mother, which averaged below high school graduation for the disadvantaged group and one year of graduate school for the advantaged groups. The study was designed specifically to separate black ethnicity and disadvantaged status; other studies have confounded these two characteristics by comparing black disadvantaged individuals with white advantaged individuals. The researchers hoped that analysis of the speech of advantaged mothers and their young children would help specialists in early childhood development understand how adults contribute to the language development of young children.

The researchers found no observable racial difference in the everyday speech acts of mothers and toddlers in their homes. The black and white advantaged groups responded to their toddlers in the same ways. But significant and consistent differences were observed between the advantaged groups and the disadvantaged group. For instance, advantaged mothers talked twice as much to their children as did disadvantaged mothers. There was no difference in the amount of spontaneous talk or in the percentage of verbalizations involving teaching and learning; the dramatic difference was that the speech of advantaged mothers was three times as likely as the speech of disadvantaged mothers to be responsive to interests and desires expressed by children. Showing an awareness of developmental levels, advantaged mothers delayed the teaching of letters and numbers until speech and concepts were established, whereas disadvantaged mothers put more focus on these readiness skills at early ages. Similarly, advantaged mothers supported their children's individuality during a time when the assertion of autonomy is important, whereas disadvantaged mothers worried about spoiling young children if strict limits were not communicated and enforced.

The researchers concluded that a unifying theme seemed to integrate the differences in the everyday talk of advantaged and disadvantaged mothers to their toddlers: Educated mothers, both black and white, support and facilitate the actions of their young children. This conclusion led researchers to wonder whether outreach programs would be effective in helping parents to be more responsive to their children's language, more sequential in their teaching strategies, and more positive in their methods of control. Further research has been designed to ascertain whether such intervention programs with parents and young children can positively influence the course of language development.

Cultural Differences: Black English

Some young black children learn to speak a dialect of standard English which linguists have called **black English**. These children learn black English because people in their families and neighborhoods speak it, just as many middle-class

TABLE 10.2   *Selected Characteristics of Black English*

Characteristic	Language Sample
Noun possessives of common nouns are indicated by word order.	It the girl book.
Suffix *-s* or *-es* to mark the third person singular is absent.	She walk.
Is may be absent in contexts where it is contractible in standard English.	She a bad girl.
Are tends to be used infrequently.	You nice.
Verbs phrases with *might, should,* or *could* may contain two.	You might should do it.
The past tense ending *-ed* is not pronounced.	He finish dinner.
Done may be combined with a past tense form to indicate that an action was started and finished at some point in the past.	She done tried that.
Be may be used as a main verb.	Today she be busy.

Adapted from *Language Assessment and Intervention for the Learning Disabled,* 2nd ed. (pp. 368–69) by E. H. Wiig and E. Semel, 1984, Columbus, OH: Charles E. Merrill. Copyright 1984 by Bell & Howell Company. Adapted by permission.

children learn standard English because people in their families and neighborhoods speak it. Most linguists agree that black English is a highly developed language system. Black English differs from standard English but is structurally equal because both have grammatical, vocabulary, and sound systems that are internally consistent. (See Table 10.2.) Black English is a distinct dialect, *not* deficient or incorrect standard English.

Linguists believe that as long as sociocultural differentiation exists within the larger society, there will be dialect variation. Black English and other dialects promote solidarity within ethnic or cultural groups and present a barrier to outsiders. Most individuals feel a conscious or unconscious allegiance to the language of their own group.

The language development of young speakers of black English parallels that of young speakers of standard English. Language development is enhanced for all young children if the communicative aspects of language are emphasized. Children speak freely and fluently if they feel that their backgrounds and language are accepted and acceptable. Those who work with young black children should understand some of the characteristics of black English in order to respond appropriately to the content of children's and parents' messages.

IMPORTANCE OF PLAY

Jean Piaget demonstrated that children's play involves intelligent exploration and manipulation of the environment. Even after Piaget's extensive contributions, many experimental psychologists did not conduct research on play at all. Jerome Bruner (1981) has said that these experimental psychologists consid-

Jean Piaget demonstrated that children learn through play with self-selected materials.

ered play to be impossible to define and unmanageable to research. According to Bruner, the breakthrough and impetus for a new type of experimental research on play came from the field of anthropology. Jane Goodall and others studied in Tanzania and showed that the capacity of chimpanzees to play during the extended period of dependency on their mothers sets them apart from lower primates.

Experimenters then began to ask: If play is important in the lives of some primates, what is its role in human childhood? Recent research has found what Jean Piaget observed earlier in this century: Play is a reflection of what children are learning. A number of distinctive characteristics of play define and differentiate it from other activities. After defining play, this section discusses the following aspects of play: significance in early childhood development; cultural influences on play; and pretense.

Definition of Play

A group of early childhood educators (Almy, Monighan, Scales, & Van Hoorn, 1984) identified six characteristics of children's **play** that set it apart from other pursuits. These characteristics include intrinsic motivation, attention to means rather than ends, nonliteral behavior, freedom from external rules, exploratory base, and active engagement.

The first characteristic of play is **intrinsic motivation**—motivation that comes from within children. Children who devise a game called "lava monster" show intrinsic motivation. Other children who build a wood collage also show intrinsic motivation. In both cases, the children are self-motivated to participate.

Intrinsic motivation can be contrasted with **extrinsic motivation**, which is motivation that comes from outside children. If children play games or participate in activities to receive an adult's approval or a sticker as a reward, the motivation is extrinsic. Intrinsic, rather than extrinsic, motivation characterizes play.

A second characteristic of play is attention to the means or processes rather than the ends or goals. A child might begin play with the loosely defined goal of being "father," join a frisky group of "puppies," and then return to the original role. The goals of play are subject to change during the activity itself and are less important than the experiences and interactions of the moment.

A third characteristic of play is nonliteral or make-believe behavior. In play, children pretend to be parents, kings, burglars, or characters from favorite television programs. They can turn disobedient subjects into stone toads or dazzle the world by solving all problems with magical powers. Pretense is described in more detail later in this section.

A fourth characteristic of play is that any rules come from the children themselves. Children may have some implicit rules that govern how certain roles are played, but these rules are set by the participants and not by anyone outside. (Participation in rule-based games, such as checkers or board games, is considered to fall outside the category of play as now defined.)

A fifth characteristic of play is free exploration of new objects or environments. Children feel, smell, touch, and look at new puppets as they prepare to play with them. If children are not allowed time to explore as part of play, they tend to behave in stereotyped ways, perhaps only as an adult has demonstrated.

A sixth and final characteristic of play is that children are actively, sometimes almost passionately, involved. Children resist distraction and show their interest by the intensity of their engagement.

Significance of Play

Piaget emphasized the importance of play as an opportunity for children to incorporate new information into the framework of what they already know. Researchers have supported Piaget's assertions about the intellectual importance of play and have cited other benefits of play. For instance, through play children experience the intellectual challenge of putting themselves into another person's position. They also communicate in verbal and nonverbal ways, connect words and images, and practice putting their ideas into a context. Their high level of motivation has the benefit of helping them to expand their attention spans and to increase their persistence. And children's play is an important preparation for reading and writing. Play has in common with reading and writing the necessity of using something (gestures and mental images in the case of play and words in the case of reading and writing) to stand for actual objects or events.

Despite overwhelming research evidence in support of the importance of play, not everyone values play. Those who do not might find it enlightening to read Catherine Garvey's (1977) early work in documenting some of the intellectual and social contributions of play. Garvey analyzed videotaped interactions of preschool children at play. These children were brought in pairs to rooms equipped with various play materials and left on their own to play for fifteen minutes. Garvey undertook microanalysis of the videotapes and found that peer play is more complex than it seems. Garvey noted that children acquire and practice a wide range of communication skills, including turn-taking, and development and maintenance of topics. Garvey also described the development through play of social concepts such as friendship and equity.

Cultural Influences

Jerome Bruner (1981) has said that different cultures encourage different types of play. His analysis has led him to believe that the majority group within the United States generally supports an approach to play that could be called "zero-sum;" that is, one person or group triumphs over another person or group. The persistent "good guy–bad guy" battles are examples of zero-sum play. But other cultural groups within the country play in ways similar to the Tangu tribe in New Guinea. This tribe practices strict and equal sharing, and in play children also try to achieve equal shares among the players. Children's cultural backgrounds and experiences with play influence their expectations and behavior when they interact with children from other backgrounds.

Pretense

Chip, fifteen months, sits on the rug and lines up several plastic cups. He pretends to drink from one, laughs, and tries to draw his brother's attention to his activity.

Chip is pretending to drink and is seeking to get his brother to participate, too. **Pretense** is a theoretical term, used in the study of child development and defined as behavior that is not literal and is in an "as if" mode (Fein, 1981). Much research has focused on levels, advantages, incidence, and reality base of pretense in early childhood. Most researchers acknowledge that Jean Piaget's work in this area provided the impetus for their investigations. Accordingly, a description of Piaget's ideas about pretense begins the discussion.

Levels of pretense   According to Piaget, young children move through two levels in their pretend play. The first level, called **solitary symbolic play**, begins between twelve and fifteen months with pretend gestures such as Chip's. Cross-cultural research shows that the appearance of pretense is rather abrupt. Only eight percent of Guatemalan infants produced one or more pretend acts between eleven and thirteen months, but sixty-four percent did so between thirteen and fifteen months (Fein, 1981). The findings from studies of infants in the United States are similar.

Chip's pretense is self-referenced; that is, he is the one who is pretending to do something that has to do with himself. In the next months, he will begin to involve others in his pretense, possibly by "feeding" a doll or a parent. At first the doll and parent will probably be treated as passive participants. But, when Chip is in the last part of his second year, he will learn to take into account the possibility that others can bring their own motivations into pretend activities.

The transition to Piaget's second level of pretense occurs when young children become able to think of one set of objects as standing for another set of objects. For instance, two-year-old Marsha uses a wooden cylinder as an ice cream cone. By twenty-four months of age, three-quarters of children use substitution behaviors (Fein, 1981).

Piaget called the second level of pretense **collective symbolism**. At this second level, beginning by the latter part of the third year of life, children begin to interact with other children in playing roles. Research has shown that at all ages in early childhood, roles portraying family relationships are most prevalent. Three-year-olds predominately portray themselves in relationship to their parents. By age four, some children create imaginary companions. The estimates of how many children have these imaginary playmates range from twelve to sixty-five percent (Fein, 1981). Only later, at age five or so, do children begin to incorporate into their play other relationships that they have observed.

Piaget has said that pretend play forms a bridge between sensorimotor and preoperational thought. Pretend play has its foundation in imitation and exploration, both of which are characteristics of sensorimotor thinking. But pretend play also uses sequencing, categorizing, and generalizing of symbols. Thus, pre-

These children engage in collective symbolism as they share a ride on a "vehicle."

tend play provides a way to put imitation and exploration into a symbolic mode, and it gives young children opportunities to experience the interaction between their actions and their thoughts.

Advantages of pretense Most investigators attribute various cognitive and psychosocial advantages to pretense. According to researchers, children who pretend often develop acute observational skills. They watch important adults in their lives and then imitate what they interpret as salient characteristics and details. Children who pretend also have opportunites to use interesting language patterns and, in interpresonal pretend play, to receive feedback on their comments, requests, and ideas. In addition, children who pretend can work out their fears and frustrations in a safe and usually acceptable format. They can call a stuffed dog a "dummy head" in play, working through their earlier confrontation with a parent over a forbidden activity. Furthermore, children who pretend can develop an idea, work out the sequence of events, and assign characters and motivations. Dealing with such a scenario can be an important creative outlet for young children. And, finally, children who pretend can learn about the give-and-take necessary in sharing imaginative play with others. Gradually children realize that other people may have different ideas and perspectives that can be coordinated and integrated to enrich the play.

Incidence of pretense Research reviewed by Fein (1981) has found that young children spend an estimated ten to seventeen percent of their time in pretend play. During the early childhood years, children develop in their ability to sustain roles and spend increasing amounts of time in pretend play.

How often children engage in pretend play relates to family and background variables. Reviewing the research in this area, Fein (1981) found four consistent generalizations about incidence of pretense. First, children who are securely attached at eighteen months of age show higher levels of pretend play at twenty-four months than do children who are ambivalent to or avoid their parents. Second, children whose parents use physical punishment for discipline and those who come from homes in which there is marital discord show low levels of imagination in their play. Third, the children most likely to engage in pretend behavior have considerable contact with parents, especially fathers, have little sibling contact, and have parents who encourage conversation and varied experiences. And, fourth, children who watch a great deal of television play less imaginatively than those who do not. Research has shown that most parents do not teach or model pretense, but they indirectly encourage or discourage it by the kind of environment that they create for young children.

Pretense versus reality Young children sometimes have a tenuous hold on the boundary between pretense and reality, as illustrated by the behavior of Virginia, age three.

Virginia held her own fairly well with her five-year-old brother and his friends. But she screamed and cried when it was her turn to be the villain.

Children who pretend tend to have considerable contact and conversation with parents, watch relatively little television, and live in homes in which their imaginations are encouraged.

The way in which Virginia reacted to the possibility of being the villain showed her momentary confusion about the distinction between pretense and reality. She did not want to act like a bad person, perhaps because she feared that she might become that person. When she is older and surer of the line between pretense and reality, she will probably enjoy taking a turn at being the villain, monster, or robber.

Other examples illustrate children's confusion of pretense with reality. Young children usually insist that certain realities not be violated in their pretense. Allan did not allow his mother to pretend to drink green milk on their space ship "because milk is always white." And young children often become worried if their pretend play goes too far beyond the bound of what is allowed in their homes. Tina enjoyed the escalation of excitement in puppet play until she had her rabbit say, "Ka-ka in your pants," to her friend's monkey. After a shocked silence, both girls returned to calmer play.

Children between two and four years of age are not always confused about pretense and reality. Sometimes they say, "I'm making a pretend pie," or "I'm pretending to eat sand." If playing with an infant, they are appropriately shocked to see their companion actually eating the sand. At times young children seem conscious of the framework of pretense that they are creating. They do not expect the mud to taste like cake; they are not surprised when the mon-

BOX 10.5 STRATEGIES FOR FACILITATING DEVELOPMENT: ENCOURAGING PRETENSE

For Two-Year-Olds

Characteristic	How to Encourage
Imitation of the actions of other people	Allow access to the sink to wash dishes, closet for dress-up, etc.
Enactment of familiar routines	Be patient with repetitive and sometimes inflexible activities.
Interest in realistic "props" for play	Provide "props" to engage their imaginations: keys, tools, kitchen and baby equipment, etc.
Seriousness	Laugh *with* them, if appropriate, but not *at* them (even if they have balls under their shirts or some other suprising outfits).

For Three-Year-Olds

Characteristic	How to Encourage
Increased emphasis on language in pretense	Show interest in their ideas and sometimes extend them (e.g., "What else is he going to do?").
Preplanning	Help in gathering "props" that children feel are necessary for what they are doing.
Interest in pretend play with peers	Facilitate interactions of young children but realize that pretend episodes will be brief because of their inflexibility in handling differences of opinion.
Desire for expansion of ideas	Allow play to be extended in time and space (e.g., a line of chairs for a train, a closet for a store, a sofa for an airplane). Remember, too, that children of this age want to be near the center of family activity as they pretend.
Need to exert power and gain a sense of control	Be understanding of young children's assertions about what to do when in pretend play.

For All Ages

Provide open-ended play materials. A mechanical toy may have just one use, but a set of blocks can be used for many exciting purposes.

Provide a special place near the hub of family activity—a closet or cupboard or large cardboard box—to experience the world in miniature.

Adapted from *Just Pretending: Ways to Help Children Grow through Imaginative Play* by M. Segal and D. Adcock, 1981, White Plains, NY: Mailman Family Press. Copyright 1981 by Mailman Family Press. Adapted by permission.

ster turns out to be harmless. Yet, at other times, young children show their uncertainty about the boundaries between pretense and reality.

Adults can help young children differentiate between pretense and reality and also retain their creativity. Interacting with young children about television programs, books, or play experiences, adults can discuss what could happen and what could not. But adults can avoid seeming to disdain fantasy. Adults can help children to develop their budding creativity if they say something like, "There aren't really monsters like that, but it makes an interesting story. The person who wrote the book used her good imagination!"

ENVIRONMENTS FOR DEVELOPING COGNITION

The cognitive development of young children is influenced by the circumstances in which they live. Research findings provide data about how differences in home environments and educational intervention can affect children's cognitive development.

Differences in Home Environments

Of the research projects that have investigated the relationship between differences in home environments and the cognitive development of one- to three-year-old children, two are particularly interesting. Information is presented about the findings of the Harvard Preschool Project and about effects of noise and confusion.

Harvard Preschool Project   In the Harvard Preschool Project (White & Watts, 1973; White, 1978; White, Kaban, & Attanucci, 1979), thirty-one children below three years of age were intensively observed in their home environments to investigate the origins of competence. The researchers found that children's competence at age five could be predicted from parent-child interactions when children were one and two years of age and from children's social and cognitive abilities already emerging in the second year of life.

Some of the Harvard Preschool Project subjects, designated as A children in the study, were chosen because they were expected to attain very high levels of competence; the remainder, designated as C children, were chosen because they were expected to develop lower than average levels of competence. The children were also grouped by age and by occupation and income of parents.

The children were observed in their homes once every week for six months of each year. In addition, the children were given the Bayley Intelligence Test and tests of language ability, abstract thinking, and ability to sense discrepancies. Testing continued until children were five years of age.

The researchers found that A children experienced much more adult interaction than did C children. Beginning at twelve to fifteen months and continuing, mothers of A children used teaching techniques more often than did mothers of C children. And, between two and three years of age, about two-thirds of

The Harvard Preschool Project found that some children experience more adult interaction and spontaneous teaching than others. This child's parent maintains a conversation while tending an infant nearby.

A children's experiences were encouraging as compared with less than one-half of *C* children's.

Parents of *A* children were found to exhibit the following behaviors:

☐ Talk frequently to children at an appropriate level.
☐ Make children feel that what they are doing is interesting.
☐ Provide access to many objects and situations.
☐ Help and encourage most but *not all* the time.
☐ Demonstrate and explain things to children but mostly on the children's instigation
☐ Prohibit certain activities with firmness and consistency.
☐ Make imaginative associations and suggestions to children.
☐ Give children the feeling that it is good to do things well and completely.
☐ Make children feel secure.
☐ Strengthen children's motivation to learn (White & Watts, 1973).

Interestingly, the parents of *A* children did not often spend large blocks of time teaching their one- and two-year-olds. Instead, they frequently taught "on the fly," usually in response to an interest expressed by the children. Close social relationships with adults were prominent in the lives of the children who developed best.

Parents of *C* children, in contrast with those of *A* children, tended to restrict their children's exploration and curiosity. Playpens, highchairs, and cribs contained children for large parts of the day. The children who were thus restricted could not satisfy their curiosity nor could they use their emerging physical skills. Usually the restrictions were for the purpose of avoiding the work, possible breakage, and physical danger posed by free mobility of a one-year-old. But children who were unable to build on their curiosity as one-year-olds were generally less interested children six months later.

The differences in environments of *A* and *C* children correlated with their high or low levels of competence at five years of age. The researchers (White, 1978) drew two main conclusions from the data. First, they concluded that the period between ten and eighteen months has critical importance in the development of competence. They found that children who attained high levels of competence at age five could already be differentiated from other children in the second year of life. Even before two years of age, these competent children were significantly more able than others to gain attention in socially acceptable ways, to use adults as resources after first trying a task, and to be proficient in their understanding of language. And, second, these researchers concluded that a strong relationship exists between young children's competence and their parents' competence in performing three main functions: designing the world in a safe but interesting manner; being available to consult, comfort, and assist; and disciplining and controlling as necessary.

The Harvard Preschool Project examined the relationship between the early home environments of *A* and *C* children and later levels of cognitive development. The researchers had hoped to show that this relationship exists across income or educational levels, but they were unsuccessful in recruiting families from a cross-section of the population. Parents of *A* children generally had higher educational and income levels than parents of *C* children, although there was some overlap. The lack of diversity in groups compromised the researchers' ability to generalize the findings of this study. Even so, the Harvard Preschool Project was a landmark in educational research because it attempted to answer by direct observation the important question: How do the early environments of very competent and less competent children differ?

Effects of noise and confusion   Appliances hum, people talk and shout, and the television roars in the corner. In homes with continuously high noise levels, eighteen-month-old children show deficiencies in conceptualizing about spatial relationships. And twenty-two-month-olds in these noisy environments lag behind peers in learning to talk (Wachs, 1982).

Researchers at Purdue University (Wachs, 1982) expected to find what is called a linear relationship between the amount of stimulation and the rate of intellectual development. That is, they thought that there would be a higher rate of intellectual development when there was more stimulation. But when researchers repeatedly went into homes to observe various aspects of the home environment, they found that the relationship was actually in the form of an inverted U: Both too much stimulation, in the form of high noise and confusion levels, and too little stimulation were detrimental to the cognitive development of very young children. The researchers have hypothesized that high levels of noise and confusion lead children to block them out; and this blocking out, in turn, causes children to miss out on hearing things that are necessary to language development and on seeing things that give information about relationships in the environment.

The researchers found that the development of some children is more negatively affected by noise and confusion than that of other children in similar environments. The two groups of children at highest risk are males and temperamentally difficult children. Males seem generally more vulnerable to the effects of all types of stress, and temperamentally difficult children seem more sensitive to noise and confusion because of low thresholds of aversion. Parents of boys and of sensitive children should give particular attention to the environments in which they place these children.

Effects of Educational Intervention

Researchers have attempted to intervene in the lives of parents and children in order to influence the cognitive development of children from one to three years of age. Encouraging results have been obtained in research conducted at experimental Parent Child Development Centers.

The United States Office of Education sponsored experimental Parent Child Development Centers (PCDCs) from 1970 to 1980. The PCDCs attempted to provide support to and intervene positively in the relationship between parents and children. Evaluations showed that the PCDCs were successful in facilitating change in parents and cognitive growth in children beyond that experienced by parents and children who did not participate in the PCDCs.

Families were enrolled in PCDCs before children celebrated their first birthdays; they "graduated" when the children reached three years of age. To be eligible for the PCDCs, families were required to have incomes below federal guidelines.

There were three experimental sites, located in Birmingham, Houston, and New Orleans. Each PCDC site had its own distinctive program model, but all shared three key characteristics: (1) a stimulating educational program for children, who entered at two to twelve months of age, depending on the site; (2) a comprehensive curriculum for parents, including information on child development, child rearing, home management, personal development, nutrition, health, and government and community resources; and (3) extensive support systems, such as medical care and social services. At each site there were experimental groups, which participated in the PCDCs, and control groups, which were comparable to the experimental groups but did not participate.

The PCDCs can best be understood in the context of the historical period in which they were created. In 1965 Project Head Start was set in motion by politicians as part of President Lyndon Johnson's War on Poverty. Project Head Start was initially implemented as a program for low income children to give them a "head start" during the summer before they were to enroll in elementary school. Project Head Start was soon expanded to a full-year program. Meanwhile, research seemed increasingly to be showing the importance of the first few years of life and the key role that parents play in developing children's competence. A new approach seemed warranted, and the Office of Economic Opportunity established thirty-six Parent and Child Centers (PCCs) for children under three years of age and their families. But the PCCs had no program model, theoretical orientation, or evaluation strategy. To provide these elements the three PCDCs were opened.

According to Andrews and colleagues (1982), the goals for parents in

PCDCs were selected from familiar principles. The goals included the following behaviors:

- [ ] showing affection
- [ ] praising children's accomplishments
- [ ] avoiding punitive and critical behavior
- [ ] using elaborated language
- [ ] providing information and explanations
- [ ] giving a rationale and justification with discipline
- [ ] asking questions
- [ ] encouraging verbalizations
- [ ] being sensitive to and accepting of children's needs
- [ ] using existing resources to enhance development

Children's cognitive growth was evaluated with the Stanford-Binet Test of Intelligence when they graduated from the program and again one year later. Parent behaviors relating to program goals were assessed at the same times.

Evaluations (Andrews, et al., 1982) at the time of graduation showed that children whose families participated in PCDCs attained significantly higher scores than controls on the Stanford-Binet Test. Parents in the program also differed from parents in the control group on all behaviors assessed. As compared with controls, parents at the Birmingham PCDC site used language less to restrict and control and more to provide information, gave more instructions and praise in teaching situations, and asked more questions. Compared with controls, parents at the Houston PCDC site were more emotionally responsive to children, provided appropriate play materials and greater variety in daily routines, gave more affection and less criticism, and encouraged verbalizations more. Compared with controls, parents at the New Orleans PCDC site were more sensitive to, more accepting of, and less interfering with their children; and parental interactions had a higher informational content. PCDC children and parents maintained their advantages over the control groups in testing and observation conducted one year later, although the differences were not as large. Research at Parent Child Development Centers demonstrated that educational intervention can result in cognitive benefits to children in this age group.

SUMMARY

1 According to Jean Piaget, children complete the last two substages of sensorimotor thinking in the second year of life and then begin preoperational thinking.
2 Sensorimotor substage five is characterized by use of tertiary circular reactions, accurate imitation, and search strategies that begin where hidden objects were last seen.
3 Sensorimotor substage six is characterized by the ability to work out solutions to problems mentally, to defer imitation, and to imagine movements of unseen objects.

4   Early preoperational thinking is characterized by the ability to use mental symbols and by thought patterns such as transductive reasoning, idiosyncratic concepts, and egocentrism.

5   Critics of Piaget's theory have demonstrated that in meaningful contexts involving basic human communication, young children are more competent than Piaget said. Combining Piaget's findings with more recent research, we can conclude that effective learning environments for young children should be familiar, personal, and warm.

6   Language milestones include understanding of receptive language and use of meaningful words at one year of age, use of multiword sentences at the end of the second year, and an expansion of vocabulary in the third and fourth years.

7   More educated mothers have been found to be more responsive to their children's language, more appropriate in their teaching strategies, and more positive in their methods of control than less educated mothers.

8   Black English is a distinct dialect learned by children whose families and neighbors speak it. Those who work with young black children should understand characteristics of black English to respond appropriately to the content of communications.

9   Children learn through play, which is defined as including intrinsic motivation, attention to means rather than ends, nonliteral behavior, freedom from external rules, exploratory base, and active engagement.

10   Different cultural groups encourage different types of play, such as zero-sum versus equal sharing.

11   Young children move through two levels in their pretend play: solitary symbolic play and collective symbolism.

12   Children are more inclined to engage in pretense if they are securely attached, have secure home environments, have considerable contact with parents, and watch little television.

13   The cognitive development of young children is influenced by the circumstances in which they live.

14   Children's competence at age five has been predicted from parent-child interactions at one and two years of age and from children's social and cognitive abilities already emerging in the second year of life.

15   In homes with continuously high noise levels, eighteen-month-old children show deficiencies in conceptualizing about spatial relationships, and twenty-two-month-olds lag behind peers in learning to talk.

16   Educational intervention in the lives of parents and their children below three years of age has facilitated change in parents and cognitive growth in children beyond that experienced by parents and children who did not participate in special programs.

KEY TERMS

tertiary circular reactions	transductive reasoning	expressive language
deferred imitation	idiosyncratic concepts	motherese and fatherese
preoperational	egocentric	holophrasis
mental symbols	receptive language	black English

play

intrinsic motivation

extrinsic motivation

pretense

solitary symbolic play

collective symbolism

FOR FURTHER READING

Language Development

Macaulay, R. (1980). *Generally speaking: How children learn language.* Rowley, MA: Newbury House.

Wood, B. S. (1981). *Children and communication: Verbal and nonverbal language development* (2nd ed.). Englewood Cliffs, NJ: Prentice-Hall.

Cognitive Activities

Fowler, W. (1980). *Curriculum and assessment guides for infant and child care.* Boston: Allyn & Bacon.

Kamii, C., & Devries, R. (1978). *Physical knowledge in preschool education: Implications of Piaget's theory.* Englewood Cliffs, NJ: Prentice-Hall.

Maxim, G. W. (1981). *The sourcebook: Activities to enrich programs for infants and young children.* Belmont, CA: Wadsworth.

Watrin, R., & Furfey, P. H. (1978). *Learning activities for the young preschool child.* New York: D. Van Nostrand.

Interpreters of Piaget's Theory

Bybee, R. W., & Sund R. B. (1982). *Piaget for educators* (2nd ed.). Columbus: Charles E. Merrill.

Labinowicz, E. (1980). *The Piaget primer: Thinking, learning, teaching.* Menlo Park, CA: Addison-Wesley.

Wadsworth, B. J., (1984). *Piaget's theory of cognitive and affective development* (3rd ed.). New York: Longman.

Play

Brittain, W. L. (1979). *Creativity, art, and the young child.* New York: Macmillan.

Segal, M., & Adcock, D. (1981). *Just pretending: Ways to help children grow through imaginative play.* Englewood Cliffs, NJ: Prentice-Hall.

Sutton-Smith, Brian & Shirley. (1974). *How to play with your child (and when not to).* New York: Hawthorn.

PART III: FROM THEORY TO PRACTICE

The following exercises are designed to help students apply what has been learned and to increase learning about children between one and three years of age. To complete these exercises, two two-hour observations of young children should be scheduled. If friends or neighbors do not have one- to three-year-olds, the following are some possible ways to arrange observations: visit a public place that attracts families, such as a busy store, park, or zoo; request permission to observe at a day-care center, family day-care home, or preschool that enrolls children from one to three years of age.

1   *Narrative Observation.* Write down everything that a one- to three-year-old does for a ten-minute period. (Remember to use descriptive, non-judgmental language.) What questions about psychosocial, physical, or cognitve development could this observation help to answer?

2   *Vignettes.* During one of your observation times, record a vignette that shows oppositional behavior in a one to three year old child. Be sure to describe the events that came before and after the opposition.

3   *Child Diaries.* Use what has been learned from observations and reading to make daily diary entries for a week about the intellectual development of a real or imaginary young preoperational thinker. Specify the child's age.

4   *Checklists.* Complete the checklist shown as Box III.1. In comparison with other observational strategies, how effective is the checklist in helping to learn about the development of that child?

5   *Interviews.* Design a questionnaire and use it to interview the parent of a one- to three-year-old about gender role expectations. (See Chapter 8 for definitions.)

6   *Time Sampling.* Adapt the recording form given as an example in Chapter 2 (Box 2.6), define the terms explicitly, and conduct a time sampling study of incidents of violence on children's after-school or Saturday morning commercial television programs.

7   *Event Sampling.* Design and conduct an event sampling study of children's prosocial behaviors. (See Box 2.7 in Chapter 2 for an example of a recording form.) Define the terms (see Chapter 8) and report findings.

8   *Case Study.* Use what has been learned about the development of one- to three-year-olds to modify the case study outline given in Chapter 2 (Box 2.8) so that it refers specifically to important psychosocial, physical, and cognitive characteristics of this age level.

9   *Reading about Research.* Read an article having to do with one- to three-year-olds in an issue of one of the following journals: *Child Development, Developmental Psychology,* or *Experimental Child Psychology.* Give the complete citation in the format used in the bibliography of this book. What questions were the researchers asking? How did they go about finding the answers? What were their results? Which of the theoretical perspectives given in Chapter 1 did the researchers have? Why?

BOX
III.1

THEORY TO PRACTICE CHECKLIST

ITEM	PROCEDURE	CREDIT	PRE DATE	DATE ACH.	POST DATE	COMMENTS
14 MO 44. Scribbles vigorously in imitation. (CAT) (K & P)	**Demonstrate scribbling for child. Use pencil in item 43.**	Child reproduces back and forth scribble motion. K & P do not require marks on paper only motion. Cattell does require definite marks.				
45. Unwraps toy. (CAT)	While child is watching, wrap a small object in which he/she is interested in a loose bag-like bundle with a sheet of onion skin paper 8½" x 11". Ask child to get the "toy."	Child obtains object in a purposeful manner. No credit if object falls out accidentally. Credit Cog #55.				
46. Inserts round block in formboard. (K & P)	Demonstrate putting the circle in a formboard. Give formboard to child. It is best to use individual circle formboard.	Child indicates understanding that round block fits in round space. The block need not be inserted completely in hole. Credit Cog #56.				
47. Holds three cubes. (CAT)	Present child with one cube and when he/she takes it, present a second cube but do not actually place in hand. If second cube is taken, offer a third. Do not provide child with a flat surface in reach.	Child takes and holds three cubes at one time by any method. Two cubes may be taken in one hand or the third cube may be held against the body. With one cube in each hand. Credit Cog #57.				
15 MO 48. Adapts round block in formboard. (K & P)	Place formboard with circle, square, and triangle in front of child. Ask child to put circle in. Next rotate formboard so circle is on reverse side. Repeat request.	Child makes a prompt adaptive placement or near placement when formboard is rotated. Credit Cog #58.				

ITEM	PROCEDURE	CREDIT	PRE DATE	DATE ACH.	POST DATE	COMMENTS
16 MO 49. Puts beads in a box. (CAT)	Present 8 square kindergarten beads (used for stringing) and a small box 2" square and 3½" high with a round hole 1" in diameter. Demonstrate dropping beads through hole. If child does not respond, demonstrate again. No further help is given.	Child puts remaining six beads in hole without further urging.				
50. Obtains peg from bottle. (CAT)	Place small object such as peg, bead or raisin beside a small plastic bottle (such as the ones used for medication). If child does not spontaneously put peg in bottle tell him/her to do so or drop it in and say "Now, get it out."	Child solves problem without demonstration. Credit Cog #61.				
17 MO 51. Attains toy with stick. (BAY) (CAT)	Place rubber toy on table in front of child, just out of reach. Place the stick so that it touches the toy and points toward child. Then say, "I can make the toy (or name the toy) come" and pull the toy toward the child using the stick. Replace toy and stick and say "You make the toy come." Demonstrate again if child seems unsure.	Child makes purposeful attempt to attain toy. Although muscular coordination may be lacking to be successful. Child should attain toy successfully by 20 months. Credit Cog #62				
52. Builds tower of 3-4 cubes. (K & P)	Present child with 4 cubes. Demonstrate building tower if necessary. Take blocks down and encourage child to build. Assist child with holding if child indicates intent to build	Child builds tower of at least 3 cubes. Credit Cog. #67 for understanding. If child indicates intent to build, but has a motor handicap, fine motor cannot be credited.				

ITEM	PROCEDURE	CREDIT	PRE DATE	DATE ACH.	POST DATE	COMMENTS
	by bringing cubes to tower, but has a motor handicap which prevents accurate release.					
18 MO 53. Places ten cubes in cup. (CAT)	Give child an aluminum cup (i.e. measuring cup) and 1 brightly colored cube. Tell child "put the block in the cup" and point appropriately. May be repeated. If no response, demonstrate. If the child is successful, push 9 more cubes toward child and say, "Put them all in."	Child puts all ten cubes in the cup.				
54. Scribbles spontaneously. (K & P)	Give child pencil and piece of paper and ask him/her to "write." If child doesn't attempt to scribble after a few seconds, remove paper and pencil and again place it before child with the same request.	Child scribbles spontaneously without demonstration. Credit Cog #68				
21 MO 55. Builds tower of 5-6 cubes. (K & P)	Demonstrate building a 6 cube tower for child. Take your tower down. Encourage child to build.	Child builds tower of 5-6 cubes — tower usually falls with 6th cube. Credit Cog #70.				
22 MO 56. Child completes 3 piece formboard (circle, square, and triangle). (TER) (CAT)	Present formboard with the blocks in place with base of triangle toward child. Remove pieces and place them in front of the appropriate space. Tell child to "put them in their holes."	Child puts all 3 forms in correct spaces in one of two trials. Credit Cog #73.				
24 MO 57. Attempts to fold paper. (MER)	Demonstrate folding a sheet of paper in half. Tell child you are making a little book. Give child another piece of paper. A second demonstration	Child turns up paper in an attempt to fold it — even if he/she does not make a definite crease.				

ITEM	PROCEDURE	CREDIT	PRE DATE	DATE ACH.	POST DATE	COMMENTS
	may be given if child makes no attempt.					
58. Builds tower of 6-7 cubes. (K & P)	Give child 8 cubes and ask him/her to build a tower. Demonstrate if necessary.	Child builds a tower of six or seven cubes (usually falls with the seventh or eighth). Credit Cog #75.				
59. Imitates vertical stroke. (K & P)	Demonstrate drawing a vertical line, while child watches. Ask him/her to repeat.	Child draws vertical stroke — may be broken, cannot yet change direction to a horizontal stroke.				35
60. Imitates circular stroke. (K & P)	Demonstrate drawing a circle while child watches. Ask him/her to repeat.	Child imitates circular stroke, differentiating it clearly from the vertical stroke.				
61. Adapts to reversal of formboard in 4 trials. (K & P)	Demonstrate placing blocks correctly in formboard. Take pieces out and put them in front of appropriate space. Rotate formboard 180° to reverse position of holes; i.e., square block is in front of round hole.	Child adapts after much trial and error. 4 trials. Credit Cog #80.				
62. Turns pages of book singly. (K & P)	Give child a large nursery book. Ask him/her to open it and look at the pictures.	Child turns most pages singly. May turn several together.				
27 MO 63. Makes train of cubes. (CAT)	Put 10 cubes on the table. Place 4 in a row and say, "See how I make a train?" Add a fifth cube on top of the first. Push it around the table. Give child 5 cubes and ask him/her to "make one like mine."	Child puts at least 3 blocks in a row and pushes them about. Credit Cog #83.				

ITEM	PROCEDURE	CREDIT	PRE DATE	DATE ACH.	POST DATE	COMMENTS
64. Imitates drawing vertical line, horizontal line, and circle (CAT)	With child watching, make a vertical stroke approx. 3" long on a piece of paper and hand child pencil and say, "Make one like that." Next make a horizontal line and ask child to make one. Then take pencil again and make 2-3 concentric circles and ask child to repeat. If any portion of this item is repeated the entire sequence must be repeated.	Child makes all three items. Child is not expected to copy circle. Any circular or up and down motion which is differentiated from the strokes is acceptable. Credit Cog #84.				
30 MO 65. Builds tower of 8 cubes. (K & P)	Follow procedure in item 52.	Child builds tower of 8 cubes. If motor handicap is present and child exhibits understanding, credit Cog. #89.				
66. Holds pencil with thumb and forefinger instead of fist. (K & P)	Give child primary pencil and paper. Observe child's grasp of pencil.	Child grasps pencil with thumb and forefinger.				
67. Imitates cross. (ILL) (K & P)	Demonstrate drawing a cross (+). Give child pencil and tell him/her to "make one like that."	Child "imitates" by more that one stroke. Does not have to have correct orientation. Credit Cog #92.				
33 MO 68. Tower of 10 cubes. (K & P) (ILL)	Present child with cubes and then ask him/her to build a "house" or tower. Gesture if necessary.	Child builds a successful tower of 10 blocks in 3 trials. Credit Cog #96.				

ITEM	PROCEDURE	CREDIT	PRE DATE	DATE ACH.	POST DATE	COMMENTS
69. Imitates "bridge" of blocks. (K & P) (ILL)	As child watches, build a bridge with 3 cubes. Leave model standing. Give child 3 blocks and ask to "make a bridge like this one."	Child builds a bridge of 3 blocks. Credit Cog #97.				
36 MO 70. Copies circle. (GES) (ILL)	Give child a pencil, paper and card on which a circle has been drawn. Ask child to. "make one like this." Let child keep card in view.	Child copies a circle without demonstration. Credit Cog #98.				37
71. Adapts to formboard reversal. (K & P) ILL)	Give child formboard with each block in front of its proper space. Rotate board so spaces are reversed. One trial.	Child adapts to the reversal without error or spontaneous correction of error. Credit Cog #99.				
72. Adds 2 parts to incomplete person. (GES)	Give child a drawing of a person showing head and body *only*. Tell child "Someone forgot to finish this person. See if you can finish it." Encourage child to continue; i.e. "What else is missing?" Do not suggest body parts.	Child adds 2 body parts to incomplete person. Credit Cog #100.				
73. Cuts across paper with scissors from one side to the other. (MCDI)	Give child scissors (check for handedness), and one sheet of construction paper.	Child cuts sheet of paper in half.				

From *The Early Learning Accomplishment Profile for Developmentally Young Children, Birth to 36 Months* (pp. 32–38) by M. E. Glover, J. L. Preminger, and A. R. Sanford, 1978, Winston-Salem, NC: Kaplan Press. Copyright 1978 Early LAP. Reprinted by permission.

IV

Early School Years (Ages Four Through Eight): Exploring the World

In a day-care center that offers both full-day and after-school care, children eat afternoon snack.

Four-year-old Shawna and five-year-old Wilma use their orange peels to cover their teeth and make monster noises for some giggling younger children. Six-year-old Jason sits near the teacher and earnestly describes his reactions to his first spelling test. "It was cinch-o. They were so easy. I got 'em all—I know I did," he says, watching Mrs. Madera's eyes, seeming to wait for a confirming response. Eight-year-olds Tom and Chico huddle apart from the others, alternately eating and drawing plans for a fort. They speak to each other in low conspiratorial tones. When a seven-year-old, Alexa, tries to approach them, they sing out, almost in unison, "Up your nose with a rubber hose. Scat, rat!"

The behavior and appearance of these children gives testimony to the existence of considerable psychosocial, physical, and cognitive development in the early school years. In psychosocial development, children attain a sense of initiative and then industry; are influenced by their families and other forces, including peers, media, and multiculturalism; are subject to stress; and acquire traits that are stable over time. In physical development, children in the early school years refine their large and small muscle skills; are affected by handicapping conditions; and form a physical image and habits relating to health. In cognitive development, children gradually become capable of logic; use more complex language than earlier; are influenced by play and by early education programs; and find their school success affected by their competence, motivation, memory, cultural background, and cognitive style. Chapters 11–13 in Part IV describe development in the early school years.

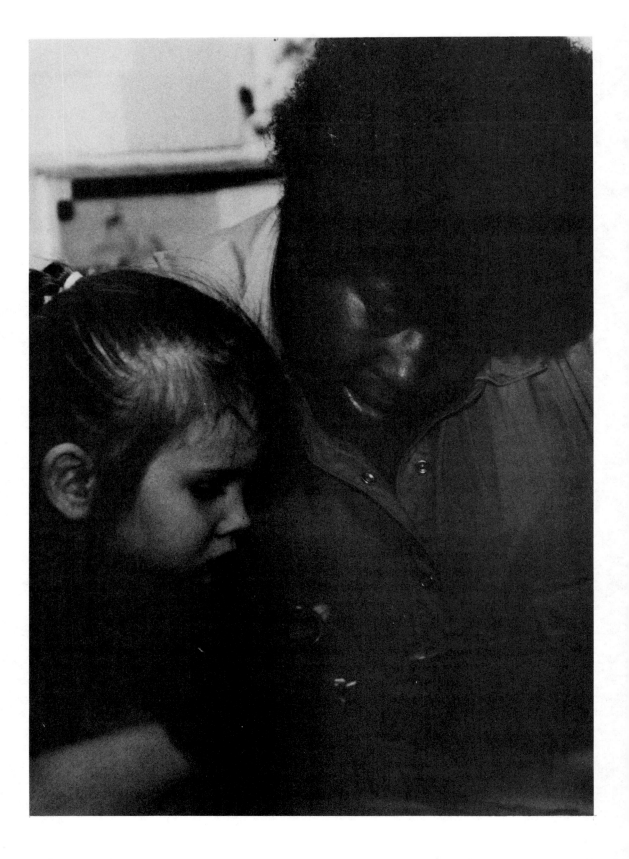

11

Early School Years (Ages Four–Eight): Psychosocial Development

Key Ideas

Initiative and Industry
Erikson's Concept of Initiative □ Erikson's Concept of Industry □ Gender Differences □ Corresponding Stage of Parenthood

Influences of the Family
Characteristics of Strong Families □ Parenting Styles and Prosocial Behavior □ Sibling Relationships

Influences and Adjustments Outside the Family
Peer Relationships □ Effects of Television □ Culture and School Adjustment □ Multicultural Understanding

Childhood Stress
Differences in Coping Processes □ Developmental Changes in Reactions to Stress □ Protective Factors □ "Hurried" Children

Stability of Behavioral Characteristics Over Time
Temperament □ Aggression

To understand the psychosocial development of children in the early school years, changes in children as well as influences on them must be considered. This chapter begins with a description of psychosocial changes in children as they try to attain a sense of initiative and then a sense of industry. The chapter next describes various external influences on the psychosocial development of young children. These influences include their families, adjustments outside the family, and stress. The chapter ends with a discussion of the stability of some behavioral characteristics over the years. Research evidence shows that what happens in psychosocial development in the early school years has lifelong implications.

INITIATIVE AND INDUSTRY

According to the theory of Erik Erikson (1982), children in the early school years face two important psychosocial tasks: learning to take initiative and to become industrious. The ability to take initiative is necessary for whatever humans do. The ability to become industrious has a decisive effect on school life and on later entrance into the world of work. Children who achieve positive resolutions of these psychosocial tasks attain a sense of purpose and a sense of competence.

In this section, Erikson's concepts of **initiative versus guilt** and **industry versus inferiority** are described. The section ends with mention of the possibility of gender differences in the resolution of these psychosocial tasks and with attention to a stage of parenthood that corresponds to these stages of childhood.

Erikson's Concept of Initiative

Four- and five-year-old children show a vigorous, imaginative, and playful unfolding. They use toys to recreate past experiences, anticipate future roles, and work out the range of activity open to them. They are eager to learn, to work with other children to plan and build, to listen to teachers, and to model the behavior of admired figures. They are curious and easily engaged in the excitement of new undertakings. Their initiative extends to include their expanding social, physical, and cognitive prowess.

Achieving a sense of initiative leads to the basic human strength of purpose. However, pure, unbridled initiative can result in acts of aggression, manipulation, and coercion. Play can become dominated by challenging, overcoming, and killing weak and evil "enemies." Children can misdirect their physical energies in activities that are discouraged by adults or harmful to others, such as running on the sofa, climbing the furniture, or pushing playmates. Children can use their verbal abilities to hurt people, telling family and friends, "I hate you" or "I'm not inviting you to my birthday party." Children can use language to shock and offend, displaying a knowledge of vulgar words that surprises even their parents. And children can use language to deceive others, as they begin to realize that no one can be sure what they are thinking. Children's actual words and deeds as well as those that they contemplate can lead to self-condemnation and a sense of guilt. This sense of guilt is at the opposite end of a continuum from initiative and helps to balance children's behavior. Children gradually establish a moral sense that restricts the horizon of permissible behavior. Children look for opportunities to use initiative without feeling too much guilt.

Initiative adds to autonomy the quality of planning and taking on tasks for the sake of being active. Initiative is an important human quality and needs to be nurtured. Children at ages four and five should have many opportunities to initiate social interactions, active physical movement, and imaginative play. Their sense of initiative is reinforced when adults respect and give validity to their interests and respond positively to their frequent questions, which are indicators of intellectual initiative. While the possibility of feeling guilt pro-

---

BOX 11.1 **STRATEGIES TO FACILITATE DEVELOPMENT: DISCIPLINE TECHNIQUES THAT PRESERVE INITIATIVE**

Ted felt that he was "on" his four-year-old son, Evan, nearly all the time: "Get off the table!" "If I hear you say that word again . . . " "Not at the dinner table!" Evan clearly needed redirection, but Ted wondered whether he could guide Evan in more positive and less guilt-inducing ways. At a parent discussion group, Ted first learned about discipline techniques that preserve children's initiative. Instead of resorting to threats and orders, Ted began to follow these steps:

1 State his expectations clearly and positively. For instance, when Evan climbed on the table, Ted said, "The table is for eating or working."
2 Give alternatives, if appropriate. He said, "You can work at the table or climb in the yard."
3 Give a limited choice in cases of continued inappropriate behavior. He said, "Climb down from the table yourself or I'll lift you down."
4 If necessary, give sanctions for continuation of inappropriate behavior. He said, "If you climb on the table again, I'll know that you need a few minutes of time out." (Note: "Time out" consists of up to five minutes spent sitting in a chair away from the hub of family activity. Ted sets a hand timer so that Evan knows when he can return.)

Ted found that following these steps made him feel more in control and less harassed. Now, if Evan's behavior is inappropriate, Ted presents Evan with choices that allow Evan to exercise his sense of initiative. Evan can understand his father's expectations better and see the relationship between decisions and consequences.

vides a safeguard against the misuses of initiative, the danger remains that children can be made to feel too heavy a burden of guilt. If guilt overwhelms initiative, children lack the sense of purpose that helps them find success in future endeavors.

Erikson's Concept of Industry

Children from first grade through the elementary years are ready to channel their energy into producing things. Children of these ages become excited by projects such as building forts, sewing, cooking, and making collections and models—the more ambitious the better. Children's sense of industry is enhanced when their efforts are encouraged and their completed projects noticed and rewarded. Elkind (1970) has called this the Robinson Crusoe age because the enthusiasm and detail with which Crusoe described his activities also characterizes children's own unfolding sense of industry.

In all societies, children of these ages receive some systematic instruction. In U.S. society, the fundamentals of technology are developed in schools, where great emphasis is placed on literacy and basic education for a wide variety of jobs and careers. In the elementary years, goals gradually are expected to supersede the whims and wishes of play. Children become eager, absorbed participants in productive situations.

Achieving a sense of industry leads to the basic human strength of competence. Children who feel competent are able to attempt new individual tasks and to carry out their parts in cooperative efforts. But not all children have experiences in and out of school that contribute to the development of a sense of industry. At the opposite end of the continuum from a sense of industry lies a

A sense of industry leads to both individual and group projects. This third grader became interested in carpentry through Scouts and later organized neighborhood children to build a clubhouse (right) with no adult assistance.

sense of inferiority. Children develop a sense of inferiority when their projects are viewed as a nuisance and when their work is seen as inadequate. They feel unable to live up to external and internal expectations of social interaction, physical feats, or mental discipline. Children's development can be disrupted if their predominant feeling during the elementary years is inferiority rather than industry. And both the individual and the society are threatened if children begin to feel that they are being evaluated according to the color of their skin or the nature of their background rather than their competence.

Erikson (1982) has said that the resolution of this psychosocial crisis is decisive in determining children's attitudes about themselves and about what they can do in later years. No one can achieve mastery in every situation, but the balance of children's experiences at the end of a day or week or month should allow them to feel successful about human interactions, physical performances, and cognitive tasks. To develop a sense of industry, children need sensitive parents, teachers, recreation leaders, and others who can individualize expectations.

Gender Differences

Gilligan (1982) has contended that the resolution of psychosocial tasks differs according to gender. She has said that Erikson and others have predominately based their theories on observations of males, whose development involves increasing their separation from others to achieve autonomy, initiative, and industry. In Gilligan's view, though, the experiences of females differ from those of males in that females have a continuing struggle to balance their responsibilities to others with their development of self. Whereas males may be willing to sacrifice relationships to achieve, females may be willing to sacrifice achievements to relate and to affiliate. Gilligan has called for more research on development that delineates the experiences of girls and women in their own terms.

Corresponding Stage of Parenthood

According to Galinsky (1981), parents of children in the early school years enter a new stage of parenthood, which she calls the **interpretive stage**. At the same time that children are working to attain initiative and industry, parents must assume the task of interpreting the world to their children.

The interpretive stage begins with a period of evaluation of the early years of parenthood. This evaluation is triggered by the changing psychosocial needs of children and by their entry into a new school for kindergarten or first grade. Parents realize that they cannot go to school with children or even control much of what happens there. They evaluate what they have done to prepare children to learn and to adjust to school expectations. The period of evaluation is often followed by reinterpretation or revision of theories of child rearing and parenthood.

From this period of evaluation comes a feeling expressed by many parents of knowing themselves better—strengths, weaknesses, and reactions to parenting challenges. Parents decide, consciously or unconsciously, how they will interpret themselves to their children. They often have the sense that time is passing quickly and that the end of the childrearing years is around the corner. Parents think about the impression of them that they want their children to retain.

A key difference between the interpretive stage of parenting and earlier ones is that children increasingly have experiences that do not include their parents: at school, in sports, with friends, in developing hobbies and interests. As children are exposed to a wider circle of people and environments, parents are frequently in the position of interpreting their beliefs, lifestyles, and roles. Parents decide what values to impart, facts to share, and behavior to teach. Sometimes these decisions are made thoughtfully, and sometimes not, but parental words and actions reflect such decisions.

The interpretive stage is a period of transition for parents from the authority relationship in the preceding stage to the more equal relationship they will have with an adolescent. Parents look ahead to the adolescent years and find themselves balancing feelings of close connection with their children and feelings of increasing separateness from them. Parents struggle with questions about the right amount of involvement to have in their children's lives. They wonder how much to do with their children and when to allow or even encourage them to do things independently. Parents define and redefine the parent-child relationship all through the interpretive stage of parenthood.

INFLUENCES OF THE FAMILY

Even though children in the early school years have increasing numbers of experiences outside their homes, they continue to be greatly influenced by their families. Children learn and refine social, physical, and cognitive skills within the family context, and they note the extent to which family members value their qualities and activities. Family relationships usually have a continuity not present in other relationships.

An ecological approach to the study of children examines various influences on their development. This section reports research data on the influences of the family, including characteristics of strong families, the interaction of parenting styles and prosocial behavior, and sibling relationships.

Characteristics of Strong Families

The family is the primary social institution in our society. Whether the family is functioning well or poorly can be expected to influence young children developing within that environment. Recently, researchers have undertaken the task of describing qualities shared by families that are perceived by members to be functioning effectively.

These researchers believe that too little attention has been given to publicizing the strengths that make family life satisfying. In an attempt to understand what is *right* with some families, Stinnett, Sanders, and DeFrain (1981) surveyed 283 families from all over the United States. Individuals volunteered to participate in the study because they perceived themselves to be members of strong family units. Most participants were white, middle-class Protestants, and the findings of the study cannot be generalized beyond that group.

The researchers found many similarities among their sample of strong families. Strong families seem to spend time together, have good patterns of communication, show appreciation for each other, worship together, and demonstrate commitment to the family group.

Spend time together   Members of strong families spend time together pleasantly. They work together in the yard or on household tasks, they eat together, and they spend time together outdoors away from distractions. In untroubled times, families build up a reserve of good feelings, which can then help them through problems.

Have good patterns of communication   Members of strong families are able to share their feelings. They spend a good deal of time talking with each other and are able to get conflicts out in the open. Life is not always tranquil in these families, but problems are dealt with as they appear rather than allowed to build.

Show appreciation for each other   Individuals in strong families report that they are able to show and accept appreciation from each other. They feel good about each other and express their feelings in ways that are supportive and loving.

Worship together   Members of strong families tend to express and act on strong religious beliefs. Shared religious beliefs seem to be one way for families to attain a sense of unity and common purpose.

Members of strong families spend time together pleasantly, for instance, during weekly outings to the library.

Demonstrate commitment to the family group Members of strong families report that they retain their commitment to the family group even at the worst of times. At times of crisis or stress, they reduce involvement in work or social life to give higher priority to their families.

This study found that one sample of strong families shares more than an absence of pathology: these families, describing themselves as strong, have distinctive positive characteristics that set them apart from more troubled families. Further research is needed on strong families from a wide variety of other cultural, socioeconomic, and religious groups.

Parenting Styles and Prosocial Behavior

Children growing up in some families are more likely than children in other families to demonstrate **prosocial** behaviors such as sharing possessions with other children, showing sympathy to children who need help, and cooperating with group routines. Baumrind (1967, 1977) has collected research evidence that shows that children whose parents have authoritative parenting styles are more likely to exhibit prosocial behaviors than are children whose parents have authoritarian or permissive parenting styles. **Authoritative** parents are consistent, loving, conscientious, and secure in handling their children; they set firm rules, communicate clearly their expectations for responsible performance, and are warm and unconditionally committed to serving the best interests of their children. In comparison to authoritative parents, **authoritarian** parents are less nurturant and involved with their children; they exercise firm control but offer little support and affection. **Permissive** parents behave in a much less controlling manner than authoritative or authoritarian parents, are insecure in their ability to influence their children, and expect less of their children than do authoritative or authoritarian parents.

Baumrind (1977) has said that authoritative parents are effective in developing prosocial behavior because their children achieve a balance between self-assertiveness and conformity with group standards. She has expressed her belief that both authoritarian control and permissive noncontrol minimize opportunities for children to interact with people, by suppressing any dissent or discussion in the case of authoritarian control, and by indulgence and distraction in the case of permissive noncontrol.

Sibling Relationships

Traditional views of early childhood development have emphasized the influence of parents on their children and, more recently, the reciprocal influence of parents and children. However, as described in Chapter 1, some researchers have replaced these traditional views with an ecological view of the family as a complex social system within which all family members influence each other and are influenced by outside forces (Bronfenbrenner, 1979). Researchers who hold an ecological view of the family have begun to investigate the developmental significance of relationships between siblings. Findings about sibling interactions in early childhood, only children, and cultural differences in sibling relationships are presented.

Sibling interactions Current societal conditions are believed to be causing siblings to have more contact with each other and a higher level of emotional interdependence than was previously the case (Bank & Kahn, 1982). These conditions include geographic mobility, divorce and remarriage, parental stress, shrinking family size, and alternate child care because of maternal employment. Children need contact, constancy, and permanency in their relationships with other human beings and turn to siblings for satisfaction of these needs if parents are not available.

Siblings seem to be intensely involved with each other in the early childhood years, and their relationships appear to be full ones, with a broad range of social interactions. Researchers (Ambramovich, Pepler, & Corter, 1982) found that pairs of siblings initiated over 60 interactions per hour when first observed and over 80 interactions per hour when observed eighteen months later. Researchers had expected to find aggressive behavior between siblings but were surprised at the high degree of prosocial behavior. Siblings were cooperative, helpful, and affectionate as well as aggressive. During the first set of observations, older siblings, as compared with younger siblings, initiated significantly more prosocial behavior, including cooperation and help, comfort, and praise; but eighteen months later the younger siblings had increased their proportion of prosocial interactions to 42 percent from 35 percent. At both observations younger children imitated their older siblings significantly more than the reverse. Although not predominating as expected, aggression was observed. Older children initiated more verbal argumentation at the time of both observations and more physical aggression at the time of the first set of observations. But by the time of the second set of observations, younger siblings had become equal partners with older siblings in starting fights and in physical aggression. The intense involvement of siblings with each other in early childhood and their patterns of interaction undoubtedly affect other social interactions and the course of the children's psychosocial development.

Researchers were surprised at what they did *not* find in studying the interactions of young siblings: neither the age interval between siblings nor the gen-

Sibling relationships in early childhood are intense and varied. Interactions range from positive, as in the block building, to aggressive, as in the hitting incident.

der composition of pairs of siblings had the expected effect. Researchers have speculated that sibling interactions may be unique and not subject to comparison with other peer relationships (Ambramovich, Pepler, & Corter, 1982).

Only children   The general societal view of only children tends to be negative. Growing up without siblings is thought to make children maladjusted, self-centered, and unlikeable. Reviewing research on only children, Falbo (1982) found mixed results: only children seem to excel in achievement, as do first-borns, but data about peer relationships, self-esteem, and marital success are conflicting. Falbo (1982) concluded that generalizations about the development of only children growing up today cannot be made from research conducted in other generations. Only children who grew up during the depression when only children were common had a different milieu than only children who grew up during the postwar baby boom when only children were less common. Of the current crop of only children, those of single parents may develop differently from only children of two-parent families. Most people focus on the difference of only children from others as being the lack of siblings, but the distinctive attributes of parents of only children contribute to any distinctive attributes of their children. More current research is needed on only children and their families.

Cultural differences   A cross-cultural view (Weisner, 1982) of sibling relationships has given a broader view than the Western focus on concerns such as achievement, status, and rivalry. Siblings in South Asian, Polynesian, and most other non-Western societies around the world participate throughout their life spans in activities essential to survival, reproduction, and transmission of cultural and social values. In these societies, responsibilities are shared: Goals involve assistance to others rather than personal development, and help is forthcoming from the group when needed.

Family systems in these societies encourage sibling cooperation, solidarity, and authority of older over younger. Sibling caregiving is part of a larger pattern of childhood experiences that emphasizes interdependence. From the end of infancy, children are placed in the care of slightly older siblings, moving gradually out of direct involvement with their mothers. Children cared for by other children learn by imitation rather than through the highly verbal modes used by Western parents. Children in sibling care grow up to be highly peer-oriented and tend to be uncomfortable in intensive one-to-one interactions with adults. The interaction patterns developed by these children may not match the patterns used by teachers who have been educated in another tradition.

INFLUENCES AND ADJUSTMENTS OUTSIDE THE FAMILY

During the early school years, children have many experiences that do not include their families. As they explore the world, children are influenced by their involvement with other children and by media presentations; they make adjustments to school and to living in a pluralistic society. Among the topics of interest described below are peer relationships, effects of television, culture and school adjustment, and multicultural understanding.

Peer Relationships

Peer relationships assume increasing importance as children move through the early school years. Children form friendships, reflect on what obligations friends have to each other, and develop strategies for interacting with peers. They affect the prosocial behavior of peers by the behaviors they notice and the reactions they show. And they develop different goals, values, and social behavior patterns, depending on their gender. A consideration of peer relationships is a vital part of the study of early childhood development.

Children's friendships Friends are defined as people who spontaneously seek each other's company without social pressure to do so. Selman (1981) has found that even young children are able to reflect on and express their understanding of friendship. He divided young children's descriptions of what friendship entails into three overlapping stages.

At Stage 0, running approximately from ages three to seven, children see friends as being children who live nearby or go to the same school and are frequent playmates. Children at Stage 0 view fights as relating to specific toys or space rather than as conflicts over personal feelings.

At Stage 1, spanning the years from approximately four to nine, children believe that friends are important because they perform specific activities. Close friends are seen as sharing more than convenient proximity: They know each other's likes and dislikes.

At Stage 2, from approximately six to twelve years of age, children express a new awareness of the two-way nature of friendship. Children show a concern for coordinating the likes and dislikes of both people rather than unilaterally expecting the behavior of friends to conform to preconceived ideas. However,

Peer relationships assume increasing importance as children move through the early school years.

specific arguments or disagreements are seen as severing the relationship; the idea of continuity in friendship develops in later stages.

Smollar and Youniss (1982) asked six- and seven-year-old children how two strangers would become friends. Children responded that friendship would result if the strangers performed activities together or shared or helped each other. Children further said that the strangers would become *best* friends if they increased the amount of time they spent together or extended it to settings outside of school. In other words, six- and seven-year-olds seemed to identify friendship with interaction. When asked about the obligations of friendship, most six- and seven-year-olds made comments that would be classified at Stage 2; they indicated that cooperation is of paramount importance and that mutual needs are as significant as those of either individual.

Children with few friends   Some young children have many friends and some have few. Children with few friends seem to be at higher risk than more socially accepted peers for low achievement in school, learning difficulties, delinquency, and emotional and mental health problems in adulthood (Putallaz & Gottman, 1981). In an observational study, Best (1983) found that third-grade boys who were not accepted by their peers seemed to lose motivation to achieve academically. Whereas the reading scores of the "in" third-grade boys improved, the scores of the "out" boys stayed the same or declined. This influence of peer acceptance on academic performance operated only among second- and third-grade boys. Among girls and younger boys, a warm, supportive teacher seemed to have more to do with success in school than did peer-group acceptance.

Research has also established a relationship between children's friendships and prosocial development. Boys with a good friend have demonstrated higher levels of cooperation with others than boys without a good friend. And children who belong to more social organizations have higher moral judgment scores than those who belong to fewer organized groups (Zahn-Waxler, Iannotti, & Chapman, 1982).

Researchers have tried to determine whether children with few friends behave differently from children with many friends. A series of studies (Putallaz & Gottman, 1981) has shown that popular and unpopular second and third graders are differentiated by their strategies of interacting with each other and of joining ongoing groups. Popularity was determined by adding up the number of times children were nominated by peers as friends.

In one-to-one interactions, popular children agreed more and disagreed less with other children than did unpopular children. Closer examination of the data also showed differences in the way that popular children and unpopular children disagreed. Popular children tended to provide a constructive alternative action along with their disagreement, making escalation of the disagreement less likely. Unpopular children expressed disagreement in the form of commands that did not give any alternative. Researchers described unpopular children as "bossy" in their disagreement.

In joining ongoing groups, unpopular children hovered at first. They took longer than popular children to make their first bid to enter the group, used more bids and took more time for entry. Unpopular children used disagreement and three other entry strategies—self-statements, feeling statements, and informational questions—more than popular children. These strategies were usually unsuccessful, leading the unpopular children to be rejected or ignored. Popular children, in contrast, first determined the "frame of reference" common to members of the group they were approaching and then established themselves as sharing in this frame of reference by agreeing with statements and exchanging relevant information.

Researchers believe that there is potential for intervention on behalf of children with few friends. Follow-up research is needed to investigate the possible benefits of teaching unpopular children more effective strategies of interaction.

Peers and prosocial behavior Parental caregiving and discipline practices that influence children's prosocial behavior were discussed in Chapter 8 and earlier in this chapter. Researchers (Zahn-Waxler, Iannotti, & Chapman, 1982) have cited three reasons for believing that peers are also important in children's prosocial development. First, mutual influence is likely among children because they are more equal in power than are adults and children. Second, children have numerous natural opportunities to share materials and cooperate in pretense and other forms of play. And, third, children's rough-and-tumble play often leads to expressions of distress, to which others respond.

Friendship seems to provide a context within which peers exhibit prosocial behavior. In a naturalistic study of best friends between two and nine years of age, observers noted sympathy and sensitivity in interactions between the children (Gottman & Parkhurst, 1980). It is not known whether the reciprocity of friendship leads children to increase prosocial behavior or whether children who exhibit prosocial behavior are the ones who form close friendships. Most likely the relationship between friends and prosocial behavior is complex and multidimensional.

Peers can help children modify aggressive impulses and show concern for others. Prosocial behaviors in classrooms can be increased if peers are asked to note and report prosocial behaviors that occur. And peer groups can successfully use role-playing procedures to train awareness of the motivations and feelings of others (Zahn-Waxler, Iannotti, & Chapman, 1982). Further study of the conditions that lead to early prosocial experiences with peers is needed.

Gender differences in friendship Boys and girls differ in the goals, values, and social behavior patterns that they bring to possible friendships. Children may not realize that these differences exist, and may not be aware that others are using familiar terms to mean unfamiliar things. Children may consequently make harsh judgments about behavior that varies from their own, mistakenly assuming that others share goals and values but choose to defy them.

Different goals, values, and social behavior patterns may be related to many kinds of differences in background. Dweck (1981) has developed the hypothesis that the self-segregation of girls and boys creates obstacles to successful friendships. According to Dweck's review of the research literature, segregation of boys and girls begins at the start of the early school years and intensifies by third grade. In the school setting, both boys and girls respond to warmth and support from teachers through the first grade year. In second grade, however, boys begin to show lower dependence on teachers and more reliance on peers. (Girls tend to remain dependent on teacher approval and acceptance until fourth grade or later.) Beginning in second grade, then, boys increasingly defy teachers and other adult authorities because of the promise of support from peers. They segregate themselves from girls whenever possible and establish a hierarchy of dominance and authority within their groups. By third grade, male peer groups are well established, distinguishing themselves by trading secrets, giving in-group names, being exclusive, and engaging in occasional antiestablishment activities to show solidarity against adults (Best, 1983).

The ostracism of girls by boys in early school years is not the only social behavior pattern that leads to segregation and diverging experiences (Dweck, 1981). Girls tend to engage in small group games in small spaces and spend time refining social rules and roles. Traditional girls' games such as jump rope and hopscotch are turn-taking games in which competition is indirect: one child's success is not related to another's failure. These experiences give girls few opportunities to resolve disputes; instead, they learn about close personal relationships. All the while, boys are developing their own culture, by engaging in larger-group games that are more physically active and wide-ranging. In the early school years, much of the outdoor play space is usually reserved for these ball and other action games. Boys' games tend to have explicit rules which move them toward defined goals. Boys' experiences lead them to learn about elaboration of rules, fair procedures for handling conflict, competition, and achievement of goals. According to Dweck (1981), the separate cultures of boys and girls are based on different interests, values, and goals. With segregation, the cultures grow increasingly far apart and there are more barriers to friendship.

Best (1983) found that third-grade boys and girls have very different ideas about how to coordinate devotion to friends and competitive instincts. She presented the following hypothetical situation to boys:

> Suppose . . . that Dennis and Randy, two very good friends, decided to compete against one another for the quarterback position on the football team. Dennis knows that Randy wants to win that position more than he wants anything in the whole world, but Dennis has stronger legs and can run faster than Randy. He also has stronger arms and can throw a ball farther than Randy. And, although Dennis would like to play the quarterback position, it isn't as important to him as it is to Randy. So should he let Randy win the competition? (p. 83)

Boys responded that Dennis should not let Randy win because pride takes priority over a friend's happiness. They attached importance to whether others would know their greatness if they do not win. Chad summed up the discussion by saying, "Your guys won't like you as much if you lose your pride" (p. 83). In contrast, Best found that for girls the point of games is found in the companionship and interaction and not in winning or losing. Girls sometimes let a friend win in order to enhance the relationship and seemed under much less pressure than boys to prove themselves.

Gilligan (1982) has concluded that masculinity is defined through separation and competition and femininity is defined through attachment and relationships. She illustrated the differences by analyzing the responses of eight-year-old girls and boys when asked to describe a situation in which they were not sure about the right thing to do. Typical responses, those of Jeffrey and Karen, follow.

Jeffrey   When I really want to go to my friends and my mother is cleaning the cellar, I think about my friends, and then I think about my mother, and then I think about the right thing to do. [*But how do you know it's the right thing to do?*] Because some things go before other things.

Karen   I have a lot of friends, and I can't always play with all of them, so everybody's going to have to take a turn, because they're all my friends. But like if someone's all alone, I'll play with them. [*What kinds of things do you think about when you are trying to make that decision?*] Um, someone all alone, loneliness. (pp. 32–33)

In Gilligan's (1982) view, both children struggle with the same issues: exclusion and priority created by choice. But Jeffrey thinks about a hierarchy of desire and duty and what goes first; Karen focuses on who is left out in a network of relationships that includes all of her friends. Looking at psychological theory from a female perspective, Gilligan has drawn the following conclusion: "In the different voice of women lies the truth of an ethic of care, the tie between relationship and responsibility" (p. 173). She and Best (1983) have both said that many researchers, educators, and parents have operated from the assumption that there is a single norm of social experience and interpretation—the male norm. Evaluating female decision making from a male perspective has led to a failure to see the different reality of females' lives. If there will someday be a time when male and female experiences converge, that time has not yet arrived, according to these researchers.

The differences in male and female values and interests lead to differing experiences and eventually to different views of the world and areas of competence. A socially skilled boy and girl can therefore be unable to understand each others' perspectives or to relate to each other successfully as friends. To bridge group differences and facilitate friendships, children can be sensitized to the myriad of reasons for behavior different from their own and the many possible interpretations of events.

Effects of Television

Television plays an important part in children's lives. First graders, for instance, watch television an average of three hours per day (Honig, 1983). Research cited in Chapter 8 showed that television influences the behavior of children under the age of four. The research presented in this section demonstrates that television continues to affect children's behavior through the early school years

This child directs rapt attention to a television program. Research shows that children's aggressive behavior increases after they watch televised aggression, and their self-control increases after they watch televised prosocial behavior.

and beyond. Attention is given to the effects on children of both violent and prosocial content of television programming.

Violent content Many television programs are highly violent, and substantial numbers of young children (one-fourth of boys and one-third of girls interviewed) say that they are frightened by this violence (Honig, 1983). Bandura (1977) and other social learning theorists have repeatedly shown that children exposed to aggressive, violent models in laboratory situations increase their own aggressive, violent behavior. Research in naturalistic settings has added a new perspective to the understanding of the effects of violent television.

The most striking finding of recent research is that some children are more highly susceptible than others to behavior changes as a result of watching televised violence. Highly susceptible children include those who are rated as aggressive and children below eight years of age.

In a study of children with different initial levels of aggression, Gouze (1979) divided them into low- and high-aggression groups depending on their ideas about how to resolve conflicts. Children in both groups heard stories with negative consequences for aggression after viewing an aggressive television program. Children in the low-aggression group decreased in aggression, but children in the high-aggression group *increased* in aggression.

In a study of the long-term effects of viewing violent television programs,

Eron (1982b) investigated the television viewing habits of eight-year-old children and then reinterviewed some of them ten years later. The surprising finding was that there was a much higher correlation between viewing violent television programs at age eight and being characterized as aggressive at age eighteen than between viewing violent television at age eighteen and being

BOX 11.2

MISTER ROGERS' PHILOSOPHY

In the journal *Young Children,* Fred Rogers, the originator of "Mister Rogers' Neighborhood," discussed his ideas about communicating prosocial values to children. Here is an excerpt from that article (Rogers, 1984):

One main thing I try to do through my television work is to give the children one more honest adult in their life experience. In fact, I feel that honesty is closely associated with freedom. "The truth will make us free" we've heard for a long time. I've tried to translate that into a song. It's a song for all ages:

The Truth Will Make You Free
What if I were very, very sad
And all I did was smile?
I wonder after a while
What might become of my sadness?
What if I were very, very angry,
And all I did was sit
And never think about it?
What might become of my anger?
Where would they go
And what would they do
If I couldn't let them out?
Maybe I'd fall, maybe get sick, or doubt.
But what if I could know the truth
And say just how I feel?
I think I'd learn a lot that's real about freedom.
I'm learning to sing a sad song when I'm sad.
I'm learning to say I'm angry when I'm very mad.
I'm learning to shout, I'm getting it out.
I'm happy, learning exactly how I feel inside of me.
I'm learning to know the truth.
I'm learning to tell the truth.
Discovering truth will make me free.

Discovering the truth about ourselves is a lifetime work, but it's worth the effort. (p. 16)

Quotation from "The Past and Present Is Now" by Fred Rogers, 1984, *Young Children, 39,* p. 16. Copyright 1984 by Fred M. Rogers. Reprinted by permission.

BOX 11.3 **STRATEGIES FOR FACILITATING DEVELOPMENT: GUIDELINES FOR USING TELEVISION POSITIVELY**

Nearly all homes have at least one television set. The following guidelines can help make television a positive force in the lives of young children.

1. Limit children's television viewing to programs with prosocial and educational content.
2. Set a daily time limit for television viewing. Balance children's interest in television with time for play, exploring, socializing, studying, and reading.
3. Discuss misleading and coercive television advertising. Discuss the ways in which children are manipulated by advertising and the motivations of the advertisers.
4. Talk with children about television plots and characters. Explain your own values and show disapproval of violence, stereotyping, and negative portrayals of societal groups.
5. Explain and extend words and concepts introduced on educational television.

Adapted from "Research in Review: Television and Young Children" by A. S. Honig, 1983, *Young Children, 38,* pp. 63–76. Copyright 1983 by the National Association for the Education of Young Children. Adapted by permission.

characterized as aggressive at that same age. Eron (1982b) has said that children up to eight years of age may be especially susceptible to the effects of watching televised violence.

Prosocial content Some television programs are not only nonviolent, they consciously present prosocial content. Friedrich and Stein (1973) examined the effects on children of watching one such program with prosocial content, "Mister Rogers' Neighborhood." The researchers showed young children fifteen-minute episodes with such themes as cooperation, sharing, sympathy, affection, friendship, control of aggression, coping with frustration, and delay of gratification. They found that viewing prosocial episodes is related to increased task persistence and self-control. The greatest gains in prosocial interpersonal behaviors were made by low-income children who increased their levels of cooperative play, nurturance, and verbalization of feelings.

Culture and School Adjustment

In the early school years, children use language in ways that are consistent with experiences that they have had in their cultural groups. There may or may not be much overlap between the verbal repertoire of young children and the lan-

For school to be a positive experience for children, their various language patterns must be understood and respected.

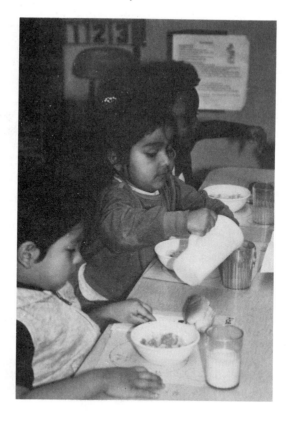

guage used in the classrooms they enter. A key factor in the school adjustment of young children is the understanding that school personnel have of language patterns used by cultural groups represented in the school.

Hymes (1980) has cited problems that native American children have in adjusting to their early school experiences. Many of these children speak only English when they enter school; yet they have problems because of differences in patterns of language usage. Native American children have become accustomed to distinctive ways of answering questions, taking turns during conversations, speaking or not speaking, and giving instructions.

Such distinctive patterns of language usage can cause misunderstanding and confusion in the early school years. Hymes (1980) has given several examples of difficulties caused by these differences. First, patterning of expression can cause misinterpretation of personality. Mesquaki Fox children in Iowa interpreted their teachers' loudness of voice and verbal directness as "meanness" and a "tendency to get mad." Second, patterning of speech situations can reflect complex and long-standing customs. A teacher of Navajo children did not understand that boys might not be able to speak to some girl classmates because of kinship relationships existing between them. And, third, patterning of attitudes can reflect cultural values and outlooks, as with Tewa-speaking children whose loyalty to the dialect has had a separatist and unifying role for their group. Whether teachers are knowledgeable about the language patterns used in native American and other cultural groups affects the adjustment of children to school.

Multicultural Understanding

Multicultural understanding is essential for citizens in a pluralistic society. Research summarized in Chapter 8 indicates that attempts to influence children's basic racial and cultural attitudes must start in the early years when those attitudes are forming. In the early school years, the educational system begins to join the family in providing experiences that enhance children's cultural identities and their concern and respect for others. Such experiences, designed to emphasize the universal human experiences as well as the richness of cultural diversity, fall under the heading, **multicultural education**.

Multicultural education is built on continuous assessment of children's cultural attitudes and identities. Appropriate multicultural experiences vary, depending upon the composition of a given community and the needs of individual children. If children's cultural backgrounds are diverse, multicultural education might focus on helping children understand the extent of similarities and the nature of differences. If children's backgrounds are monocultural, the

Enhancing children's self-concepts is an important priority in the early childhood years.

focus might be on helping children see diversity within the group and on grasping the idea that there are many other cultures and ways of life (Ramsey, 1982).

Ramsey (1982) has suggested three broad goals for multicultural education in the early school years: enhancing self-concept and cultural identity, developing social skills and responsibility, and broadening the base of cultural understanding. Each of these goals is described in turn.

Enhancing self concept and cultural identity Enhancing children's self-concepts is an important priority in the early childhood years. Studying literature and art, discussing feelings and competencies, and other activities provide vehicles for children to develop awareness of the ways in which all people's lives are similar and yet each person is unique. Multicultural education is as much a perspective as it is a curriculum. Teachers who share this perspective take advantage of spontaneous occurrences as well as planned activities to incorporate each child's cultural, racial, and ethnic identity into the classroom in the early school years. Children from minority groups retain a sense of the value of their culture when they perceive genuine interest in and respect for their lifestyles and families. Children from monocultural communities learn that people are both similar and different in appearance, experiences, and family composition. All children need to internalize images that support the development of a strong cultural identity and an awareness and respect for diversity.

Developing social skills and responsibility The ability of children to see the perspective of others develops over the course of the early school years. However, children often do not use their skills to observe what others are experiencing. Part of the process of multicultural education is to motivate children to practice and expand their skills in seeing the perspective of others. To do so, teachers make provisions for frequent social interaction, both spontaneous and planned. Planned activities are those that require cooperation, such as science observations that are recorded by teams, and movement experiences that must be synchronized. Teachers also consistently call attention to the existence and validity of other points of view in content areas as well as in the psychosocial domain. And, teachers encourage children to have many experiences with taking responsibility for the maintenance and organization of their homes, classrooms, and other environments.

Broadening the base of cultural understanding In broadening the base of children's cultural understanding, the goal is *not* to teach children facts, figures, geography, and historical details about other cultural groups. Ample evidence shows that young children do not grasp concepts such as *country,* cannot read maps, and cannot coordinate abstract lists of similarities and differences (Anselmo, 1979). An emphasis on cognitive content can lead to memorization without context or understanding. Instead, the goal of broadening the base of cultural understanding is for children to realize that there are many acceptable languages, points of view, and lifestyles. In pluralistic situations, experiences and materials reflect the cultural groups of children in the classroom. By sharing

BOX 11.4   STRATEGIES FOR FACILITATING DEVELOPMENT: ASSESSING MULTICULTURAL UNDERSTANDING

Multicultural education should be based on continuous assessment of children's levels of multicultural understanding. Kobus (1985) has developed an assessment instrument, Cross-Cultural Understanding in Multicultural Education (CUME), to measure young children's progress toward attaining two goals. The first goal is to recognize the similarities among individuals and to respect these similarities as characteristics that make each person a member of the human family. The second goal is to recognize both personal and cultural differences among people and to respect these differences as characteristics that add to the richness and diversity of American life.

The following is an item from the CUME assessment dealing with the uniqueness of all families.

3   Look at the pictures and listen.

Which family is unique and special?

| 1 | 2 | 3 |

A ☐   Family 1.

B ☐   None of the families.

C ☐   Family 3.

D ☐   Each family.

Mark *one* box to show what you think is true.

with classmates and observing each other, children see that people look, eat, cook, and speak in different ways. In monocultural situations, experiences, pictures, and visitors are used to introduce children to some of the differences among people. For instance, children can explore the many ways that people

carry things—on their backs, hips, and heads, and in many types of containers—
and thus take a step toward developing a flexible, open approach to people
whose appearance and customs are unfamiliar. Multicultural education has
great potential in enriching the lives and increasing the understanding of children in a pluralistic society.

CHILDHOOD STRESS

Many adults mistakenly assume that early childhood is a time of joy with few
pressures. However, young children are often victims of stress. **Stress** is caused
by environmental changes that provoke a high degree of emotional tension and
interfere with normal patterns of response (Janis & Leventhal, 1968). Children
experience stress from changes brought about by events such as hospitalization,
birth of a sibling, and parental divorce; children sometimes gain strength and
sometimes suffer as a result. Variability in children's responses to stress can be
understood by examining the topics in this section: differences in coping processes, developmental changes in reactions to stress, protective factors, and
"hurried" children.

Differences in Coping Processes

Children experience stress not so much because of specific events but because
of resultant changes in patterns of family interaction and relationships. Such
changes extend over time, and children's coping processes must likewise be
continuous. **Coping** involves efforts to manage environmental and internal
demands that tax or exceed a person's resources (Rutter, 1983).

Research (Rutter, 1983) has found that coping processes are influenced by
individual differences in characteristics such as age, gender, and style of
appraising the situation. Age influences children's ability to cope with the stress
of hospitalization and the birth of siblings, but not the stress of divorce. When
hospitalization is necessary, children between six months and four years of age
have the most difficulty coping with the stress that occurs. Below six months of
age children have not formed selective attachments and above four years they
have the cognitive skills to know that separation is not the same as abandon-
ment and to understand the need for medical treatment. When siblings are
born, younger children are more likely than older children to show some form
of disturbed behavior as evidence of problems in coping with stress.

Gender influences on coping processes are all in the same direction: Boys
are less able to cope with effects of stressful events. Significantly more boys than
girls show adverse reactions to hospitalization, withdrawal behavior when siblings are born, and severe and prolonged disturbance after their parents'
divorce (Rutter, 1983).

Children's appraisals of the implications of an event influence their ability
to cope with any resulting stress. Research (Rutter, 1983) has found that boys
tend to respond with greater effort if given feedback that they are failing, but
girls tend to give up. Boys seem to be socialized to attribute failure to not trying

STRESS IN CHILDHOOD

Saunders and Remsberg (1984) have attempted to rank the various stresses of childhood. This test shows how stressful events compare in their impact on a child.

Childhood Stress Test

This is a scale to check the amount of stress in your child's life. Add up the points for items that have touched your child's life in the last 12 months. If your child scored below 150, he is carrying an average stress load. If your child's score is between 150 and 300, he has a better-than-average chance of showing some symptoms of stress. If his score is above 300, his stress load is heavy and there is a strong likelihood he will experience a serious change in health or behavior:

☐ Death of a parent	100	
☐ Divorce of parents	73	
☐ Separation of parents	65	
☐ Parent's jail term	63	
☐ Death of a close family member	63	
☐ Personal injury or illness	53	
☐ Parent's remarriage	50	
☐ Suspension/expulsion from school	47	
☐ Parents' reconciliation	45	
☐ Long vacation	45	
☐ Parent or sibling illness	44	
☐ Mother's pregnancy	40	
☐ Anxiety over sex	39	
☐ Birth or adoption of baby	39	
☐ New school, classroom, or teacher	39	
☐ Money problems at home	38	
☐ Death or moving away of close friend	37	
☐ Change in studies	36	
☐ More quarrels with parents	35	
☐ Change in school responsibilities	29	
☐ Family quarrels with grandparents	29	

☐ Sibling going away to school	29
☐ Winning school or community awards	28
☐ Mother or father going to work or quitting work	26
☐ School beginning or ending	26
☐ Family's living standard changing	25
☐ Change in personal habits (bedtime, homework, etc.)	24
☐ Trouble with parents	23
☐ Change in school hours, schedule	23
☐ Moving to a new house	20
☐ New sports, hobbies, recreation activities	20
☐ Change in church activities	19
☐ Change in social activities	18
☐ Change in sleeping or nap habits	16
☐ Change in number of family get-togethers	15
☐ Change in eating habits	15
☐ Vacation	13
☐ Christmas	12
☐ Breaking a rule	11
TOTAL	

hard enough, whereas girls seem to be socialized to attribute failure to their lack of ability.

Developmental Changes in Reactions to Stress

Maccoby (1983) has examined research relating to children's reactions to stress and has proposed some hypotheses about developmental changes that take place. Six of these hypotheses have particular relevance to early childhood development.

First, she has proposed that the younger the child, the more important is environmental structure and predictability. Stress builds for young children if too many elements in the environment change at once.

Second, she has proposed that the younger the child, the more likely is extensive behavioral disorganization as a response to stress. Research indicates that maturation of the nervous system contributes to children's ability to maintain behavioral organization.

Third, she has proposed that with increasing age, children have an increasing repertoire of coping behaviors. Young children's coping behaviors center on going to the attachment figure in case of threat. After age eleven, children usually rely less on adults and more on other strategies for dealing with stress.

Fourth, she has proposed that an obedient stance toward adult authority gives young children a buffer against stress that is not available in adolescence. If young children carry out the instructions of trusted adults, they feel less anxiety about the outcomes of their actions and less stress when there are negative outcomes than if they are acting autonomously.

Fifth, she has proposed that the nature of distress caused by the disruption of peer friendships changes with age. In the preschool and early school years, friends are people with whom children play and share activities, so children feel the loss of these activities when friendships are disrupted. Later, in middle childhood, friends share confidences, trust, and thoughts, and loss of friendships means loss of children's emotional support.

Sixth and finally, she has proposed that with age comes an increasing sensitivity to the reactions of others to the self. Stressors then become more individualized, depending on the identity the individual has chosen to project and the emotional territory the individual has chosen to defend.

Protective Factors

Researchers have been interested in the development of children who become competent despite lives that involve high levels of stress brought about by poverty, family instability, and sometimes parents' serious mental health problems. Even in the most difficult home situations, some children develop healthy personalities and display **resilience**, defined as the ability to adjust easily to or recover from continuing high levels of stress (Werner, 1984). Researchers have asked, "What is right with these children?" and have tried to draw conclusions from their lives in order to help other children become less vulnerable to stress.

Researchers in England, in American urban ghettos, and in Hawaii (summarized in Garmezy, 1983, and Werner, 1984) have all found that children who "make it" despite problems and obstacles differ from others by three types of protective factors. These protective factors lie within the children themselves, within their families, and outside their families.

Resilient children tend to have characteristics of temperament that cause others to react positively to them (Garmezy, 1983). In infancy and early childhood these children have personalities and temperaments that are described as "active," "socially responsive," and "autonomous." They often find satisfaction and self-esteem in hobbies and creative interests. Their hobbies and senses of humor provide refuge when the levels of stress in their lives rise (Werner & Smith, 1982). These children somehow manage to maintain the faith that things will work out and that the odds can be surmounted. And they translate their faith into action by taking on responsibilities for siblings or the household beyond what might be considered appropriate for their young ages. According to Werner (1984), these acts of required helpfulness lead to enduring positive changes in the children.

Within the family, most resilient children have the opportunity to form a close bond with at least one person during the first year of life (Werner, 1984). This nurturing allows them to establish a basic sense of trust. These children seem to be adept at actively seeking out surrogate parents—grandparents, other relatives, child-care personnel, parents of friends, or neighbors.

Most resilient children have strong external sources of support—peers, ministers, teachers, or older friends—for their coping processes. They tend to be liked by classmates and to have close friends (Werner & Smith, 1982). They often do well in school, in academics, and in extracurricular activities, and seem to make school a refuge from their chaotic households. Early childhood programs and favorite teachers can act as buffers against stress (Werner, 1984).

Research on resilient children (Garmezy, 1983; Rutter, 1983; Werner & Smith, 1982) seems to show that the long-term effects of stress do not depend on the number of incidents of stress but rather on how the stress is dealt with. The same event can be followed by successful adaptation, humiliating failure, or no long-term consequence whatsoever. Certain stresses are inevitable, and one of the developmental tasks of childhood is to learn positive coping processes. Caring adults can provide valuable support if they

□ accept children's temperamental idiosyncrasies and allow them some experiences that challenge, but do not overwhelm, their coping abilities;

□ convey to children a sense of responsibility and caring, and, in turn, reward them for helpfulness and cooperation;

□ encourage a child to develop a special interest, hobby, or activity that can serve as a source of gratification and self-esteem;

□ encourage children to reach out beyond their nuclear family to a beloved relative or friend. (Werner, 1984, 71)

The lives of resilient children show that faith can be sustained even in adverse circumstances, if children find people in their lives who demonstrate commitment and caring.

"Hurried" Children

Elkind (1981), psychologist and author of *The Hurried Child: Growing Up Too Fast Too Soon,* has said that middle-class children are being hurried by parents, schools, and the media to grow up faster than ever before. He has asserted that the resulting stress leads to school failure, delinquency, sexual activity, drug abuse, and child suicide.

According to Elkind, the pressure to grow up fast begins in early childhood. Children feel pressure for early reading and other intellectual attainments, wear designer clothing that makes them look like small adults, play competitive sports, and see other children portrayed by the media in sexual or manipulative situations. Their hurried parents demand social achievements that are beyond children's abilities. For instance, it is not unusual for young children to be expected to adapt to several social settings in one day—perhaps school, a day-care center, and a sitter—in addition to the family. Their parents provide freedoms before children are able to show the necessary responsibility. For example, young children may prepare their lunches, stay alone at home, and dress themselves before they feel comfortable doing so.

Hurrying children to do well on tests, to excel in soccer, and to deal with adult problems of sexuality leads to stress. Two- to eight-year-old children tend to perceive hurrying as rejection and blame themselves, which leads to even higher levels of stress.

BOX 11.6   **A CHILD'S VIEW OF DIVORCE**

The tendency of young children to blame themselves for stressful changes in their lives is illustrated by excerpts from an interview with Gillian, then seven years of age (Berger, 1984):

> Sometimes I think I made Mommy and Daddy get a divorce, because I wasn't a good child. I mean, I think I could have done better, like try to keep my room clean. I used to get into lots of trouble, like once I painted my sister's hand blue, and it got all yucky. It took a long time for Mommy to get all the paint off. And once I went out with friends and didn't ask permission. So I think I gave Mommy and Daddy more things to worry about. Maybe if I didn't give them so much to worry about, we'd all still be together in our house in Charlotte. (p. 12)

By the next year, with help, Gillian began to understand her blamelessness in the situation (Berger, 1984):

> Mommy gave me this book to read called *Divorce* or something like that. I read it with my sister, Emma. It's a children's book, and it says don't blame yourself because it wasn't your fault your parents weren't happy with each other. That helped. It made me think maybe it wasn't my fault Mommy and Daddy got divorced, even if I was bad sometimes. (p. 13)

BOX 11.7

STRATEGIES FOR FACILITATING DEVELOPMENT: CHILDREN'S BOOKS DEALING WITH DEATH

Saunders and Remsberg (1984) have identified death of a parent or other close family member as leading to high levels of stress in children. Some excellent children's books can be used to open lines of communication between adults and children about death and dying.

Brown, M. W. (1958). *The dead bird.* New York: Young Scott Books.
Grollman, E. A. (1976). *Talking about death: A dialogue between parent and child.* Boston: Beacon Press.
LeShan, E. (1976). *Learning to say goodbye: When a parent dies.* New York: MacMillan.
Zolotow, C. S. (1974). *My grandson Lew.* New York: Harper & Row.

For adults, Fred Rogers' *Talking with Young Children about Death* (Pittsburgh: Family Communications, 1979) is a helpful resource.

Elkind has recommended that parents consciously slow down their children's lives. Children need time to play; parents and children need time together. When hurrying cannot be avoided, children appreciate their parents' efforts to see their perspectives. Children want to feel important emotionally, *not* hurried intellectually and socially to serve parental needs.

STABILITY OF BEHAVIORAL CHARACTERISTICS OVER TIME

To find out whether particular behavioral characteristics are stable from the early school years to adulthood, researchers have studied individuals over the course of many years. This kind of research, called **longitudinal research**, is rather uncommon because it requires an extensive commitment of time, money, and human resources. Data now available from several such longitudinal research projects indicate that some behavioral characteristics, such as temperament and aggression, tend to remain stable over time.

Temperament

Researchers participating in the New York Longitudinal Study (Thomas and Chess, 1984) have followed the behavioral development of 133 subjects from early infancy into adulthood. The research has focused on the identification of temperamental characteristics and the study of the influence of these characteristics on psychosocial development. The researchers have found many statistically significant relationships between temperament and adjustment in the early years and in adulthood.

The researchers have rated subjects on nine categories of temperamental characteristics: activity level, regularity, approach or withdrawal, adaptability to change, level of sensory threshold, positive or negative mood, intensity of response, distractibility, and persistence. (See Chapter 5 for more information about these characteristics.) They also noted whether subjects fell into one of three clusters of temperamental characteristics: "easy" (having a regular, positive approach to new experiences, adaptability to change, and positive mood); "difficult" (having irregular biological functions, negative withdrawal responses to new experiences, slow adaptability to change, and intense expressions of mood that are frequently negative); and "slow to warm up" (showing negative responses of mild intensity to new experiences and slow adaptability after repeated contact).

In the New York Longitudinal Study, special attention has been given to making clinical evaluations of subjects with evidence of behavioral disorders. The researchers have found that most of the behavior disorders manifested by subjects in this study were adjustment disorders, predominantly mild. The largest number of behavior disorders occurred when subjects were three to five years of age and the second largest when they were six to eight years of age.

Researchers have found many relationships between characteristics of subjects in early childhood and behavioral outcomes in adulthood. The early childhood variables used in statistical analysis were adjustment scores at ages three and five, easy versus difficult temperament at three years of age, parental attitudes and child-care practices (obtained by interviews when children were three years old), and identification as having a behavior disorder in childhood. The outcome variables were adjustment scores in early adulthood, easy versus difficult temperament in early adulthood, and the presence or absence of a clinical diagnosis in early adult life.

Researchers found the following statistically significant relationships between characteristics of subjects in early childhood and behavioral outcomes in adulthood: First, subjects with easy or difficult temperaments at age three tended to have the same temperaments in early adulthood. Second, the greater the score of subjects on ease of temperament at three years of age, the higher the adult adjustment ratings. Third, the greater the level of parental conflict in handling children and in interacting with each other, the lower the subjects' adult adjustment ratings. Fourth, the adjustment levels of subjects at both three and five years of age corresponded to their adjustment levels in adulthood. And, fifth, subjects referred for behavior problems in childhood tended to have lower adjustment ratings in adulthood.

The researchers have expressed their belief that the adjustment problems of subjects in this study often stemmed from a poor fit between children's temperaments and the environment. They have recommended that therapeutic intervention focus on working with parents to make expectations consistent with children's characteristics and capabilities, especially for the approximately ten percent of children with difficult temperaments.

Aggression

Research conducted by Eron (1982a) and colleagues (Huesmann & Eron, 1984) over thirty years has shown that early manifestations of aggression predict adult aggression and antisocial behavior. In 1960 the researchers studied nearly 900 eight-year-olds and interviewed their parents. Children's aggression was measured by asking all children in classes to rate all other children on a series of specific aspects of aggressive behavior, aggression anxiety, and popularity. In 1981 the researchers studied over 400 of the original subjects, now at the average age of thirty. They also obtained data about criminal offenses, traffic violations, and state hospital admissions of these 400 subjects and over 200 others from the Division of Criminal Justice Services, Division of Motor Vehicles, and Department of Mental Hygiene. In some cases, data were obtained from three generations of informants: subjects and their spouses, subjects' parents, and subjects' children.

Analysis of data from this longitudinal study has indicated that aggressive eight-year-olds are likely to become aggressive adults who engage in antisocial and criminal behavior. Specifically, male subjects viewed by peers as more aggressive at age eight rated themselves as more aggressive at age thirty, were rated by their wives as more aggressive, had more convictions in the criminal justice system, committed more serious crimes, had more moving traffic violations, and had more convictions for driving while intoxicated than males who were viewed as being less aggressive. Female subjects viewed by peers as more aggressive at age eight rated themselves as more aggressive at age thirty and rated their punishment of their children as more severe than did females who were viewed as being less aggressive. Data from parents and children of both male and female subjects showed that aggressive parents have aggressive children.

Aggressive behavior seems to be stable across time and across generations. Researchers attribute the stability of aggression both to the continuity of constitutional factors (genetic, hormonal, and neurological) and the continuity of environmental factors. The patterns of behavior established in the early school years seem to have lifelong influences.

SUMMARY

1   Erik Erikson has described two psychosocial tasks of the early school years: learning to take initiative and to become industrious.

2   Four- and five-year-old children display initiative in social, physical, and cognitive ways. Initiative is balanced by the possibility of feeling guilty.

3   Elementary aged children begin to channel their energy into being industrious. If they do not succeed in school and other tasks, they can feel inferior.

4   There may be gender differences in how children resolve psychosocial crises.

5   Parents of children in the early school years enter a new stage of parenthood, called the interpretive years, in which they decide what values to impart.

6   Family influences remain strong during the early school years.

7   One group of strong families shares many characteristics: spending time together, communciating, appreciating each other, worshiping together, and sharing commitment to the family group.

8   Parents with authoritative styles are likely to have children who exhibit prosocial behaviors.

9   Siblings mutually influence development by their intense involvement with each other in the early childhood years.

10   Characteristics of only children depend upon attributes of their parents and not just upon the absence of siblings.

11   In many cultural groups, siblings care for each other within a context of interdependence; sibling care has effects on children's ability to engage in one-to-one interactions with adults.

12   Children are influenced by forces outside the family, such as peers and television, and they make adjustments to school and to living in a pluralistic society.

13   Friendships of young children characteristically move through three stages and show increasing reciprocity.

14   Children with few friends have distinctive approach and interaction patterns.

15   Peers influence the prosocial behavior exhibited by children.

16   Children from different groups vary in the goals, values, and social behavior patterns that they bring to possible friendships.

17   Young children are vulnerable to the effects of televised violence and benefit from prosocial television content.

18   Cultural differences in children's language patterns can influence their adjustment to school.

19   Multicultural understanding can be enhanced by multicultural education having several goals: enhancing self-concept and cultural identity, developing social skills and responsibility, and broadening the base of cultural understanding.

20   Young children feel stress and differ in their ability to cope with it.

21   Children's reactions to stress show developmental trends.

22   Personal characteristics, family support, and support from outside the family tend to protect children from the effects of stress.

23   Young children who are hurried to grow up faster and better may feel high levels of stress and blame themselves.

24   Longitudinal research indicates that temperament and aggression tend to be stable behavioral traits over the years. Experiences in the early school years can have lasting influence.

KEY TERMS

initiative versus guilt	authoritative	stress
industry versus inferiority	authoritarian	coping
interpretive stage	permissive	resilience
prosocial	multicultural education	longitudinal research

FOR FURTHER READING

Encouraging Prosocial Behavior

Lickona, T. (1983). *Raising good children: Helping your child through the stages of moral development.* New York: Bantam Books

Using Television Positively

Singer, D. G., Singer, J. L., & Zuckerman, D. M. (1981). *Teaching television: How to use television to your child's advantage.* New York: Dial.

Communicating Multicultural Understanding

Williams, L. R., & DeGaetano, Y. (1985). *ALERTA: A multicultural, bilingual approach to teaching young children.* Menlo Park, CA: Addison-Wesley.

Helping "Hurried" Children

Elkind, E. (1981). *The hurried child: Growing up too fast too soon.* Reading, MA: Addison-Wesley.

Jensen, L. C., & Wells, M. G. (1979). *Feelings: Helping children understand emotions.* Provo, Utah: Brigham Young University Press.

12

Early School Years (Ages Four–Eight): Physical Development

Key Ideas

Milestones of Physical Development
Large Muscle Skills □ *Small Muscle Skills* □
Drawing and Writing □ *Perceptual-Motor*
Integration □ *Gender Differences*

Handicapping Conditions
Hearing Impairment □ *Visual Impairment* □
Mental Retardation □ *Emotional Disturbance*
□ *Specific Learning Disabilities* □ *Speech and*
Language Impairment □ *Public Law 94–142*
□ *Handicaps and Cultural Background*

Forming a Positive Physical Image
Hyperactivity □ *Sexuality* □ *Attractiveness*

Forming Healthy Habits
Eating Habits □ *Health Care* □ *Fitness* □
Safety

The Williams children include Brian, age 4; Steven, age 6; and Melody, age 8. On one Saturday afternoon, Brian rode his three-wheeled "hot cycle" around the playground of the nearby school, Steven practiced on his two-wheeler with training wheels, and Melody and her friends experimented with popping wheelies and doing other stunts with their two-wheelers. Later, when they returned home to make birthday cards for their mother, Brian painted a colorful design, Steven drew a picture of his mother opening her presents, and Melody composed and carefully printed a poem. The children's different activities show not only their individuality, but also some of the physical developments that take place during the early school years.

Children change in many ways during the early school years. The four major topics presented in this chapter are intended to clarify the differences in physical capabilities between the youngest and oldest Williams children. The first topic, milestones of physical development, includes large muscle skills, small muscle skills, drawing and writing, perceptual-motor integration, and gender differences. The second section of this chapter gives information about various handicapping conditions that affect development, legislation relating to the education of handicapped children, and the relationship between handicaps and cultural background. The third section focuses on factors that affect the development of a positive physical image: hyperactivity, sexuality, and attractiveness. The fourth and final topic concerns the formation of healthy habits of eating, health care, fitness, and safety. These four discussions give insights into the complexity and importance of physical developments taking place during the early school years.

MILESTONES OF PHYSICAL DEVELOPMENT

For most children the early school years are an active time during which considerable physical development takes place. Children gain skill in using their large muscles to balance, hop, skip, run, and jump. They also grow more proficient in using their small muscles to reach, grasp, and manipulate objects.

The first three parts of this section describe milestones of physical development as experienced by two hypothetical children, Bruce and Paula. These three parts describe changes in large muscle skills, small muscle skills, and drawing and writing during the early school years. The fourth part gives information about perceptual-motor integration. And the fifth part describes gender differences in physical development.

Large Muscle Skills

The development of large muscle skills in the early school years is shown through the feats of a hypothetical child, Bruce. The ages at which Bruce is said to attain certain milestones reflect accepted norms (adapted from Sanford & Zelman, 1981) but must be viewed as approximate for other children. Some normal children will develop more slowly and some more quickly than Bruce.

Four to five years   One of the most notable changes in Bruce during the year from age four to five is his improved sense of balance. He can carry a cup filled with water from the kitchen sink to the table located ten feet away without spilling. He can walk around a four-foot circle without stepping off the line, walk heel-to-toe for four or more steps along a line, and stand on one foot for five seconds. In other developments, Bruce can hop on one foot, skip ten steps, pedal his tricycle skillfully around obstacles and sharp corners, and hang from a bar by his hands. He likes to play ball with a neighbor and has become adept at throwing and catching. He can throw a ball ten feet overhand and catch both a bounced and aerial ball.

Five to six years   Bruce loves a parade and has become able to coordinate his marching with the music on his favorite Hap Palmer records. As was the case last year, his balance continues to improve. He stands on tiptoes for ten seconds, stands on one foot for eight seconds, swings each leg separately for five swings, and walks backward heel-to-toe for four steps or more. He can also touch his toes with both hands without bending his knees, jump backwards six or more times, and hop forward at least six feet on each foot. In ball play, he can walk up and kick a stationary ball eight feet or more. Bruce runs a thirty-five–yard dash in ten seconds or less.

Six to seven years   Bruce is eager to help with household routines and is now able to carry a ten-pound sack of groceries the fifty feet from the car to the apartment. In the time between his sixth and seventh birthdays, he refines other large muscle skills. He rides his two-wheel bike without training wheels, jumps rope three or more times in a row, chins himself on the bar at school, and stands on each foot alternately with his eyes closed. In ball play, he catches a tennis

Children in the early school years love a parade and are gradually able to coordinate their marching with the rhythm of the music.

ball with one hand, bounces it with one hand and catches it again with both hands. He is able to jump thirty-eight inches or more from a standing position, jump from a standing position over a yardstick that is held eight inches off the floor, and jump and do a complete about-face.

Seven to eight years   In the years from seven to eight, Bruce's growth slows and his body control continues to improve. He becomes skillful in maneuvering his bike and in using adult tools such as hammers, saws, rakes, and shovels. He learns to swim and skate and participates in group games such as soccer with competency, understanding, and great enjoyment. Bruce's large muscle skills have improved significantly since his fourth birthday.

Small Muscle Skills

To show the changes in small muscle skills between four and eight years of age, the development of an imaginary child, Paula, is described. The ages at which Paula is able to do certain things are adapted from Sanford and Zelman (1981) and represent average ages for attainment of the various milestones. However, some children may develop at a somewhat different pace and still be perfectly normal.

Four to five years   Paula increases in her ability to dress and feed herself. Her most recent accomplishments include putting on socks, pull-up garments,

In fingerpainting, this child uses broad movements of her hands and arms.

belts, shirts that button in the front, and clothes with zippers. By her fifth birth-day, she can dress herself with some help from a parent. At the table, she serves herself food and feeds herself with her spoon and fork much more neatly than in the past.

In her Head Start classroom, Paula has learned to use scissors to cut a piece of paper in half along a line. She can fold and crease paper horizontally, verti-cally, and diagonally as demonstrated by an adult. In fingerpainting, Paula uses broad movements of her fingers, hands, and arms. When she learns to complete a three-piece jigsaw puzzle, she proudly shows her technique to anyone who will look. She handles one-inch-long pegs with ease and is able to put ten of them into a bottle with a three-quarter-inch opening.

Five to six years By her sixth birthday, Paula can dress and undress herself without any assistance. She also has learned to spread food with a table knife, to tie knots that hold, and to wind thread on a spool. She has become more skillful with scissors and now can use them to cut out a square, staying on the lines. She inserts prefolded papers in envelopes, and paper into a three-ring binder. At school she makes recognizable shapes out of clay and presents them as gifts to family members.

Six to seven years Paula becomes able to help with food preparation in many ways, including scraping carrots, cutting, mixing, and measuring. At mealtime, she now cuts her food with a table knife and fork. She bathes herself with some assistance and supervision. She is perhaps proudest of learning to tie her own shoelaces.

Seven to eight years The end of the early school years is a time of consoli-dation and further rapid development of Paula's small muscle skills. She uses her small muscle skills frequently on school tasks, described below, and is able to do hand sewing and knitting under the tutelage of her grandmother. She greatly enjoys crafts and projects of all kinds and can complete them capably and carefully. Eight-year-old Paula uses her small muscles skillfully.

Drawing and Writing

Because of their importance for school success, drawing and writing are described separately from other small muscle skills. Research by Sanford and Zelman (1981), Lamme (1984), and Brittain (1979) provides information about the typical ages at which children attain various milestones.

Four to five years Paula begins to hold her paintbrush with her thumb and fingers instead of her fist, and she holds the paper in place with the opposite hand from the one she is using for the project. She is able to copy a cross, a square, and a simple word such as "cat."

In her drawing, Paula enters a stage called the **naming of scribbling stage** (Brittain, 1979). She may not start drawing with a particular intent, but her work takes on meaning as she goes along. Moving toward her fifth birthday, she

This four-year-old is at the "naming of scribbling" stage. He began with no apparent plan but later designated family members.

begins the **early representational stage** of drawing (Brittain, 1979). Objects and people appear in her drawings in what seem to be shorthand representations; that is, as symbols rather than as portrayals of the way she actually sees them. Her people often have just two body parts, a head and legs, and she does not try to portray space but draws in just two dimensions.

Five to six years   In her kindergarten year, Paula is able to copy triangles, rectangles with diagonals, and her first name. She prints the alphabet, using upper and lower case letters, and writes the numerals from one to nine. In drawing,

This four-year-old has entered the early representational stage. She uses shorthand symbols (heads and legs) for people.

A kindergartener created this preschematic drawing at an easel.

Paula enters the **preschematic stage** (Brittain, 1979). She draws recognizable pictures, often adding ground and sky and attending to size relationships. Objects do not usually float around in space as before, and her people may have as many as six or seven distinct body parts.

Seven- and eight-year-olds can employ perspective in their schematic drawings, if they are helped to be keen observers of nature and the work of other artists.

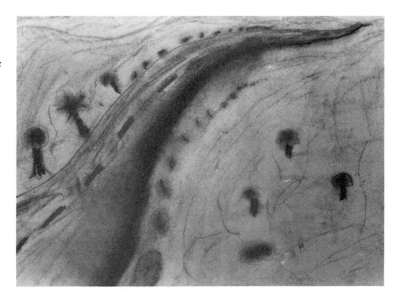

FIGURE 12.1 *Drawings of Humans at Ages 4 to 7*

Age 4

Age 5

Age 6

Age 7

Six to seven years   In first grade, Paula is able to copy a diamond shape, print her first and last name, and write the numerals from one to nineteen. She uses her new skills to record her ideas in stories and to do arithmetic computations. Her drawings become more detailed and more representational.

Seven to eight years   The longer Paula is in school, the more she uses her writing skills. She can think of and record longer stories and do more complex computations. In third grade, she begins to write in cursive script. Her drawings enter the **schematic stage**, showing attention to design, balance, and perspective. Great changes characterize Paula's drawing and writing over the course of the early school years.

FIGURE 12.2 (opposite page)   *Development of Writing at Ages 5 to 8*

Uoy
can
not
go to the
moves in yor hol

Happy Bithday to you Happy Bithday
to you you look like a monkey
and you'll stay like one too.

My gift to the
world is that the world
will have peace and
the world will
always have enough food.
I hope everyone will
always have love in their
heart.

A Day I'll Never Forget

Once upon a time Chris and David were
having a fight on October 18,1984. Chris and David
were being so bad that they had to go on time out
David got so mad that he quietly opened the door
and turned the water on. Then he quietly went back
to his bedroom. When Chris went to school he
found that he had forgotten to bring his library book
when he started to cry. Brant came over and said
Stop crying." It worked. Chris stoped crying!

Perceptual-Motor Integration

Many tasks in the early school years can be accomplished successfully only if children guide their body movements with their perceptions. Ball games, drawing, and writing are examples of tasks requiring perceptual-motor integration. According to a perspective first expressed by Kephart (1971), perceptual-motor integration follows a developmental progression. The first steps involve control of the whole body. (See Chapter 9.) The next steps establish control of the arm

---

BOX 12.1   **STRATEGIES FOR FACILITATING DEVELOPMENT: MOVEMENT EXPLORATION**

Many movement exploration activities are helpful in facilitating perceptual-motor integration. The following activities were devised by Sullivan (1982).

The Tunnel (for 4-Year-Olds)

Objectives: To help create a special space for others.

Directions: "I would like everyone to sit down. When I call your name, come here and put your body like this." Put your body in a crawling position. "Angela, you come first. OK, Marius you're next. You go right next to Angela." Continue until all of the chidlren are in a line, shoulder to shoulder. "Each one of you is going to get to crawl through this long, dark tunnel that your bodies make. It is very important that you not move and that you take good care of the people going through. Angela, you're first. That's right, you get to crawl under all those bodies right through to the other end. OK, Angela, now you need to help make the tunnel here at this end. And it's Marius's turn." Continue until all of the children have had a chance to go through the tunnel. (pp. 67–68)

Mirrors (for 5 through 8-Year-Olds)

Objectives: To become aware of the shape of the body. To understand the role of the leader and to be responsible for another body's movement.

Consideration: Can be done in a limited space.

Directions: The total class should face you.
    "I am going to do some movements and I would like you to copy me exactly." Do simple movements that can be easily followed.

and hand. Coordination of eye and hand follows, but only after large muscle activities are mastered.

To establish control of the arm and hand, children need practice in using their hands as extensions of their arms. Children can be asked to throw a ball or other object at a target. To hit the target, children must coordinate the movement of their arms both with the grasping and releasing done by their hands and with perceptual data from the target.

Eye-hand coordination begins when children's eyes can be guided to fol-

"Now, choose a partner. Sit facing each other. One person will be the leader and the other person will follow. The person who leads needs to move only one or two body parts at a time. You want your partner to be able to follow." After a time, switch leaders.

Extensions: Once the children can lead and follow with only one or two body parts moved, they can begin to lead with their whole body.

Note: Attention span is limited for this intense activity. (pp. 126–27)

Places (for 5 through 8-Year-Olds)

Objective: To acquire an awareness of a point in space and a point in time.

Considerations: Ample space is required. A drum is useful. This activity is appropriate for older children.

Directions: "Pick out a place in the room with your eyes. Now walk to that place. Look around. Can you remember exactly where you are? Now pick out another place in the room with your eyes. Walk to that place. Freeze. Look around. Remember this place. Now walk back to the first place. Freeze. Now walk back to the second place. Freeze in a shape when you are there. Now I will count to 5 and I want you to arrive at Place 1 exactly when I reach 5, not before or after. 1, 2, 3, 4, 5. Freeze! Now move to your other place backward while I count to 5. Not before or after. 1, 2, 3, 4, 5. Freeze! (p. 116)

Activities are from *Feeling Strong, Feeling Free: Movement Exploration for Young Children* by M. Sullivan, 1982, Washington, DC: National Association for the Education of Young Children. Copyright 1982 by Molly Sullivan. Reprinted by permission.

Eye-hand coordination is encouraged when children watch their paint brushes move across large pieces of paper.

low movements of their hands. Children can be encouraged to observe their actions while they push a train along a track or while they move a crayon across a large sheet of paper. After their eyes can successfully follow movements of their hands, children can use visual information to guide their movements, such as when they draw around a metal form, trace figures, or complete mazes.

Various aspects of perceptual-motor integration lead to interaction between visual, auditory, and tactile-kinesthetic modalities. Games such as "statues," in which the leader's position is copied by children in the group, use visual-motor translation; that is, children use visual cues to decide how they should position their bodies. And activities such as marching to a drum beat or playing musical chairs require children to make an auditory-motor match; children use the sounds they hear to control their movements.

Gender Differences

Parents, teachers, and others who interact with children in the early school years often note gender differences in the attainment of physical milestones. According to Gesell Institute data (Ames, Gillespie, Haines, & Ilg, 1979), girls among the subjects of their studies were up to six months earlier in attaining certain of these milestones. The differences seemed particularly prominent in tasks requiring use of small muscles. For instance, 61 percent of girls versus 48 percent of boys could copy a square at four years and six months of age; 77 percent of girls versus 45 percent of boys could draw a person with eight body parts at five years of age; and 88 percent of girls versus 53 percent of boys could print their first names at five years of age.

HANDICAPPING CONDITIONS

Handicapping conditions affect the psychosocial, physical, and cognitive development of children. Children are defined as handicapped under federal guidelines if they fall into one of the following categories: deaf, deaf-blind, hard of hearing, mentally retarded, multihandicapped, orthopedically impaired, other health impaired, seriously emotionally disturbed, specific learning disabled, speech impaired, or visually handicapped (U.S. Office of Education, 1977). Box 12.2 defines these categories.

Until recently the care and education of three- to five-year-old children with handicaps were the full responsibility of their families, and older children with handicaps were sometimes also excluded from receiving public education. Since the implementation of Public Law 94–142, passed in 1977, however, free and appropriate education must be provided for all handicapped children from three to twenty-one years of age. Public Law 94–142, known as the Education for All Handicapped Children Act, makes free public education mandatory for children over five years of age and subject to state laws for three- to five-year-old children. Over half of the state legislatures have been persuaded of the importance of educating three- to five-year-old handicapped children and have made provisions for either mandatory or permissive programs.

In this section, the following clusters of handicapping conditions are described: hearing impairment, visual impairment, mental retardation, emotional disturbance, specific learning disabilities, and speech and language impairment. For each handicapping condition, symptoms and effects are noted (adapted from Lerner, Mardel-Czudnowksi, & Goldenberg, 1981; Patton, Payne, Kauffman, Brown, & Payne, 1987; and Bailey & Wolery, 1984). The section ends with further discussion of the provisions of Public Law 94–142 and with consideration of handicaps in relation to cultural background.

Hearing Impairment

The symptoms of **hearing impairment** may be prominent or subtle, depending on the severity of the impairment and the age of the child. Hearing impairment should be suspected if children do not seem to respond to nearby sounds or voices when their backs are turned; if they need demonstrations before they understand directions; if they do not speak clearly; if they consistently speak more loudly or softly than is usual; if they are very attentive to lip movements and facial expressions; if they have frequent ear infections, allergies, or upper respiratory infections; and if they have had scarlet fever, measles, meningitis, or severe head injury.

**BOX
12.2**

CATEGORIES OF HANDICAPPED CHILDREN: PUBLIC LAW 94–142

Public law 94–142 defines categories of handicapped children as including the following:

Deaf means a hearing impairment which is so severe that the child is impaired in processing linguistic information through hearing, with or without amplification, which adversely affects educational performance.

Deaf-blind means a concomitant hearing and visual impairment, the combination of which causes such severe communication and other developmental and educational problems that such children cannot be accommodated in special education programs solely for deaf or blind children.

Hard-of-hearing means a hearing impairment, whether permanent or fluctuating, which adversely affects a child's educational performance but is not included under the definition of deaf in this section.

Mentally retarded means significantly subaverage general intellectual function existing concurrently with deficits in adaptive behavior and manifested during the developmental period, which adversely affects a child's educational performance.

Multihandicapped means concomitant impairments (such as mentally retarded-blind, mentally retarded-orthopedically impaired, and so on), the combination of which causes such severe educational problems that these children cannot be accommodated in special education programs solely for one of the impairments. The term does not include deaf-blind children.

Orthopedically impaired means a severe orthopedic impairment which adversely affects a child's educational performance. The term includes impairments caused by congenital anomaly (for example, clubfoot, absence of some member, and so on), impairments caused by disease (for example, poliomyelitis, bone tuberculosis, and so on), and impairments from other causes (for example, cerebral palsy, amputations and fractures, or burns which cause contractures).

Other health impaired means limited strength, vitality, or alertness, due to chronic or acute health problems, such as a heart condition, tuberculosis, rheumatic fever, nephritis, asthma, sickle cell anemia, hemophilia, epilepsy, lead poisoning, leukemia, or diabetes, which adversely affects a child's educational performance.

Seriously emotionally disturbed means a condition which exhibits one or more of the following characteristics over a long period of time and to a marked degree, which adversely affects educational performance: (*a*) an inability to learn, which cannot be explained by intellectual, sensory, or health factors, (*b*) an inability to build or maintain satisfactory interpersonal relationships with peers and teachers, (*c*) inappropriate types of behavior or feelings under normal circumstances, (*d*) a general pervasive mood of unhappiness or depression, or (*e*) a tendency to develop physical symptoms or fears associated with personal or school problems. The term includes children who are schizophrenic or autistic. The term does not include children who are socially maladjusted, unless it is determined that they are seriously emotionally disturbed.

Specific learning disability means a disorder in one or more of the basic psychological processes involved in understanding or using language, spoken or written, which may manifest itself in an imperfect ability to listen, think, speak, read, write, spell, or do mathematical calculations. The term includes such conditions as perceptual handicaps, brain injury, minimal brain dysfunction, dyslexia, and developmental aphasia. The term does not include children who have learning problems which are primarily the result of visual, hearing, or motor handicaps; or mental retardation; or environmental, culture, or economic disadvantage.

Speech impaired means a communication disorder, such as stuttering, impaired articulation, language impairment, or a voice impairment, which adversely affects a child's educational performance.

Visually handicapped means a visual impairment which, even with correction, adversely affects a child's educational performance. The term includes both partially seeing and blind children. (U.S. Office of Education, 1977)

These children are deaf, as defined by Public Law 94–142.

To check for hearing impairment, physicians or audiologists use special equipment to measure the loudness and pitch of sounds that a child can hear.

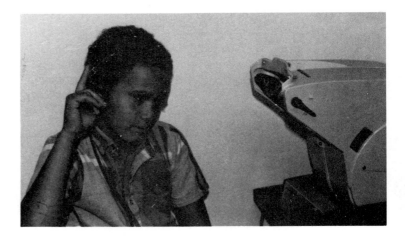

When hearing impairment is suspected, physicians or audiologists use special equipment to measure the loudness and pitch of sounds that a child can hear. Any hearing impairment may vary in degree from severe to mild. Children with the most severe impairments are typically called **deaf** and usually cannot understand speech even if it is amplified by hearing aids. Children with milder hearing impairments may be able to understand some speech and may be helped by the use of hearing aids.

Children who lose hearing before developing speech and language usually show delays in both. Special educators believe that children who can benefit from wearing hearing aids should be fitted with them as early as possible. Whether they wear hearing aids or not, children with hearing impairments and their families need to work cooperatively with special educators to select an appropriate system of communication. Options include use of sign language, speech, lip reading, finger spelling, and various combinations of these approaches.

Visual Impairment

Behavorial symptoms of **visual impairment** include squinting, rubbing the eyes, difficulty in judging distance, covering one eye to see something, and losing the place while reading. Children may also have crusty, red, or watery eyes, sensitivity to light, and headaches or dizziness. Even in the absence of such symptoms, the Society for Prevention of Blindness advocates vision screening for all children between three and five years of age.

Visual impairment ranges from moderate conditions to **blindness**, defined as the ability to see at twenty feet what the normally sighted person can see at two hundred feet. Children with any degree of visual impairment should be under the care of a physician.

Blind children may develop distinctive habits, such as poking their fingers in their eyes, rocking, and making strange noises. These behaviors usually diminish when children are guided in receiving stimulation from their other senses. All visually impaired children have a narrower potential range of experiences than other children, so they may lack confidence in their movements and be slow to develop body image. These children need help in finding alternatives to visual ways of exploring their environments and feeling comfortable with their bodies. Later, when readiness for reading instruction is established, visually impaired children often require either books with large type or braille books.

Mental Retardation

The definition of **mental retardation** has recently been broadened to include *both* low intellectual functioning (usually measured by intelligence tests) and deficits in functioning in the community. Children who cannot master school tasks but who display appropriate self-help skills and social responsibility are not considered mentally retarded under the current definition.

Symptoms of mental retardation include general delays in attaining developmental milestones, slowness in controlling the body, and problems with the development of language, speech concepts, and social adaptation. Children with severe mental impairment are often identified in infancy, but children with mild retardation may not be identified until the early school years.

The effects of mental retardation vary with the severity of the individual impairment. In the early school years, these children respond well to stimulating, structured environments. They require many repetitions of learning tasks and work best with actual objects rather than symbols or pictures.

Emotional Disturbance

Emotional disturbance can occur when children are involved in conflict with themselves or others. Symptoms include hostility, depression, unhappiness, withdrawal, lack of satisfying interpersonal relationships with adults and peers, and disruption or other inappropriate behavior. There is often a lack of academic and social success that cannot be attributed to intellectual or other factors. These children manifest atypical behaviors and poor coping skills over a significant period of time.

Children with emotional disturbance are difficult to manage. The effects of emotional disturbance are as diverse as the symptoms. Most children with emotional disturbance need structured opportunities to learn appropriate social skills and to practice them with adults and children. They and their families require a variety of support services.

Specific Learning Disabilities

The most recently defined category of handicapping conditions is called **specific learning disabilities**. Children with specific learning disabilities have significant difficulties in learning but are not eligible for other special education services. These children fail to master specific academic skills such as reading, arithmetic, language, or writing, but they are not impaired in vision, hearing, or general mental processes and are not emotionally disturbed. Some neurological dysfunction or problem with the central nervous system is usually assumed, but such dysfunction is difficult to diagnose in medical examinations.

The effects of specific learning disabilities extend beyond academic achievement; children's sense of self-esteem can be undermined. Children who try hard but do not succeed begin to see themselves as failures and losers. Children who have difficulties in learning need to be identified early and given programs that are individualized to meet their needs.

Speech and Language Impairment

Speech impairment exists when children's speaking patterns interfere with the communication process. Types of speech impairment include articulation disorders, in which children add, omit, distort, or substitute speech sounds; voice disorders, in which children use unusual pitch, quality, and intensity; and rhythm defects, including stuttering, blocking, or repetitions. **Language impairment** exists when children's vocabulary and sentence construction are delayed or limited.

Children with speech and language disorders may feel frustrated by being unable to communicate fully with others. Their reliance on nonverbal communication limits the nuances of meaning that they can convey. Children with speech and language disorders need early diagnosis and treatment to attain their full potential.

Public Law 94–142

Public Law 94–142, the Education for All Handicapped Children Act, requires that free public education be provided for all children between three and twenty-one years of age. A key provision of this legislation is the development of an **individualized education program (IEP)** for all children identified as handicapped. The IEP must include the following information:

- ☐ statement of child's present levels of educational performance;
- ☐ statement of annual goals, including short-term objectives;
- ☐ statement of special education and services to be provided and the extent to which the child will participate in regular education programs;
- ☐ dates of initiation and duration of services;
- ☐ evaluation procedures and schedules to determine if short-term objectives are being achieved. (U.S. Office of Education, 1977)

The IEP is planned by the child's teacher in collaboration with a special educator, parents, and possibly other resource people. Public Law 94–142 requires that all testing be conducted in the child's language and provides for **due process**—safeguards, including legal procedures, to protect the rights of children. These safeguards include the requirement for parental consent before a child is evaluated or placed in special education, the right of parents to inspect all of a child's school records, and the requirement that parents be notified of any changes in identification or placement.

Public Law 94–142 requires professionals to consider the concept of **least restrictive environment** when making decisions about placement of handicapped children. The least restrictive environment provision was designed to stop the exclusion of handicapped children from public school classrooms.

An orthopedically handicapped child and his teacher work to meet an objective from his individualized education program (IEP).

Sometimes, but not always, the least restrictive environment for a particular child is the regular classroom; providing educational services to handicapped children in regular classrooms is called **mainstreaming**. Some children with handicapping conditions benefit from mainstreaming for all or part of a day, and others need educational services that can be provided only in special classrooms. The IEP team works together to determine what placement is appropriate for each child.

Handicaps and Cultural Background

Public Law 94–142 requires that assessments for special education placement be culturally fair. In the past, special education classrooms included some students who were not handicapped as now defined in Public Law 94–142 but who were culturally different from the majority group. In the 1970s, lawsuits challenged the testing procedures then used. For instance, *Larry P. v. Riles* was a class action suit filed on behalf of black students who were put in classes for the mentally retarded when that placement was not appropriate. *Larry P.* was decided in favor of the plaintiffs, and the decision was upheld on appeal. A related lawsuit, *Diana v. State of California,* gave Hispanic children an out-of-court settlement of the same issue raised in *Larry P.*

Special education classrooms have never been intended for students who are not handicapped as defined in Public Law 94–142. However, minority children are overrepresented in special education programs (Killalea Associates,

1980), and part of the problem may still lie in discriminatory testing procedures. Payne et al. (1983) noted two problems in tests used for special education placement of students from diverse cultures. First, some tests have norms obtained from mostly white, middle-class groups; these norms are not valid for

BOX 12.3

STRATEGIES FOR FACILITATING DEVELOPMENT: CHILDREN'S BOOKS ABOUT HANDICAPS

Books read to or by children can facilitate their understanding of handicapping conditions. Ideally, these books show handicapped children as being active participants, not observers, and as being multifaceted. One facet is their handicap but the handcap is not their complete existence. Some excellent children's books about handicaps are listed below.

Introduction to Differences

Simon, N. (1976). *Why am I different?* Chicago: Whitman.

Hearing Impaired

Glazzard, M. (1978). *Meet Camille and Danille. They're special persons.* Lawrence, KS: H & H Enterprises.
Peterson, J. W. (1977). *I have a sister—My sister is deaf.* New York: Harper.

Cerebral Palsy

Mack, N. (1976). *Tracy.* Milwaukee, WI: Raintree Editions. (205 W. Highland Ave., Milwaukee, WI 53203)

Physically Handicapped

Fanshawe, E. (1977). *Rachel.* Scarsdale, NY: Bradbury.
Fassler, J. (1975). *Howie helps himself.* Chicago: Whitman.
Lasker, J. (1980). *Nick joins in.* Chicago: Whitman.

Mentally Retarded

Brightman, A. (1976). *Like me.* Boston: Little, Brown.
Glazzard, M. (1978). *Meet Lance. He's a special person.* Lawrence, KS: H & H Enterprises.

Learning Disabled

Glazzard, M. (1978). *Meet Scott. He's a special person.* Lawrence, KS: H & H Enterprises.

Multiply Handicapped

Glazzard, M. (1978). *Meet Danny. He's a special person.* Lawrence, KS: H & H Enterprises.

Adapted from "Teaching Children about Differences: Resources for Teaching" by M. Sapon-Shevin, 1983, *Young Children, 38,* pp. 24-31. Copyright 1983 by the National Association for the Education of Young Children. Adapted by permission.

application to children from other groups. Second, some tests use linguistic styles or require information typical of the majority group but not necessarily minority cultures. An example of this second problem is from the Peabody Individual Achievement Test (PIAT). The question, "What do we call the last car on a freight train?" is meant to assess general knowledge but might be unfair to children from locations such as Southeast Asia or Hawaii. Special education placement is appropriate for culturally different students who have disabilities defined in Public Law 94–142, but fair identification of these children requires the use of nondiscriminatory assessments that are administered with sensitivity.

FORMING A POSITIVE PHYSICAL IMAGE

In the early school years, children's image of their bodies is influenced by a number of factors, including hyperactivity, sexuality, and attractiveness. By understanding these influences, adults can help children to feel positive about their bodies and themselves.

Hyperactivity

Jeff, age six, seems to be in constant motion in his classroom. Given a worksheet, he prints the first letters of his name vigorously—so vigorously that he rips the paper. A noise from the group next to him attracts his attention and he joins in what becomes a loud disruption. When removed from the group by the teacher, Jeff first laughs and then kicks and hits at the restraining adult.

Children in the early school years show a wide range of activity levels. Some children with low activity levels and long attention spans seem perfectly suited to school environments. Jeff and other children who have very high activity levels seem unable to stay quietly in one place long enough to take part in school activities. Children such as Jeff are often labeled **hyperactive**. Hyperactive children display some or all of the following characteristics: high activity level, short attention span, inability to sit still, impulsiveness, inability to wait, distractibility, unexpected shifts in mood, and frequent touching of objects and people. Hyperactive children are often intelligent but unable to concentrate and learn. More boys than girls suffer from hyperactivity, also called **attention deficit disorder**.

Treatment for hyperactive children is likely to include one or more of three approaches: changes in diet, changes in environment, and use of medication. Feingold (1974) is the best-known advocate of treating hyperactivity by removing foods with additives from children's diets. He suggested that hyperactive children avoid foods with artificial coloring and flavoring, the preservatives BHT and BHA, and aspirin. These additives are contained in most baked goods, cereals, relishes, toothpastes, frozen meals, and medicines. He also recommended that some children not eat foods containing natural salicylates (e.g., apples, oranges, strawberries, and cucumbers). Testimony about the effectiveness of the Feingold diet comes from parents who describe dramatic changes in their children after diet modifications. However, researchers have been unable to reproduce Feingold's results and believe that more evidence is necessary to draw conclusions about the relationship between diet and hyperactivity.

A second approach to treatment of hyperactivity involves changing the home and school environments of children. Some hyperactive children respond well to a simple, predictable routine in a setting in which as many distractions as possible are eliminated. Behavioral techniques reinforce children's appropriate actions. Research (Pelham, Schnedler, Bologna, & Contreros, 1980) shows that behavioral therapists and parents can be effective in devising and implementing intervention to modify specific problems of hyperactive children.

A third approach to treatment of hyperactivity is the use of psychostimulant drugs such as amphetamines. These drugs enable as many as 60 to 90 percent of hyperactive children treated to increase their goal-directed, on-task behaviors (Whalen & Henker, 1980). However, because of short- and long-term medical cautions, psychostimulant drugs should be prescribed only after a complete evaluation of a specific case by educators, psychologists, and physicians. Short-term side effects of psychostimulants include appetite and sleep disturbances as well as increased heart rate and blood pressure. Growth retardation can result from long-term use of psychostimulant drugs. Moreover, longitudinal research indicates that behavior changes from use of psychostimulant drugs do not continue into adolescence when the medication is stopped (Whalen & Henker, 1980). Psychostimulant drugs should be prescribed and administered with caution.

To determine which approach or approaches to use for treatment, professionals should evaluate hyperactive children as early as possible in their school years. Otherwise their inability to attend to school tasks can interfere with learning and stand in the way of the formation of a positive physical image.

Sexuality

Part of the physical image formed by children comes from their feelings about sexuality. In Chapter 8, information was presented about early gender awareness and identity; through the early school years and beyond, children continue the process of understanding themselves as male or female and developing attitudes about their biological sexuality and organic sensations. The sensitivity with which adults interact with children and respond to their questions and concerns helps to determine the way children feel about their sexuality.

In this section, two major issues relating to sexuality are presented. The first continues from Chapter 9 the discussion of sex education and children's levels of understanding of reproduction. The second deals with the problem of sexual abuse of children.

Sex education   In a Public Affairs Pamphlet, Gordon and Dickman (1981) advise that sex education be provided to children under two conditions: when they ask and when they do not. Often children in the early school years ask many questions about their bodies, where babies come from, and the birth process. It is desirable for them to find out that no questions are considered to be wrong—that the important adults in their lives want to create an atmosphere of open communication. Children develop understanding and positive attitudes when their questions are answered factually with correct terminology. If children do not ask questions, it is usually not because they do not wonder about these things. Somehow they may have decided that certain topics are inappropriate or embarrassing to others. Because children are sensitive to these attitudes, the way that adults handle questions may be as important as the information conveyed. If children have not asked questions by the early school years, adults should share information about sexuality, read appropriate books to them, and take advantage of teachable moments such as seeing an obviously pregnant woman. (See Figure 12.3)

FIGURE 12.3

The interest of young children in human anatomy and sexuality is illustrated by these drawings by a five-year-old boy. PS stands for the penis of the male (left) and VA stands for vagina on the female (right).

Even when children receive sex education in a supportive atmosphere, their ability to comprehend it is limited. Research on stages of understanding reproduction has been conducted by Bernstein and Cowan (cited in Cowan, 1978) and confirmed by Goldman and Goldman (1982). Before the early school years, children are at stages 0, 1, and 2 (described in Chapter 9). Children in the early school years are at stages 3 and 4 of their understanding of how babies are born. At each of these stages children incorporate from explanations of reproduction what they are able to understand and ignore or reject the rest. Accordingly, children revisit the same information over a period of years before they can develop a mature understanding of sex and reproduction. Adults who provide this information must have the patience to answer the same kinds of questions many times.

At the beginning of stage 3, children often express an animistic view of reproduction. Children assign humanlike qualities to the sperm and/or egg, as in this description by a child of four and one-half years (Bernstein & Cowan, cited in Cowan, 1978):

Adult: Where does the egg come from?
Child: *From the daddy.*
Adult: Then what happens?
Child: *It swims in; into the penis and then it . . . I think it makes a little hole and then it swims into the vagina.*
Adult: How?
Child: *It has a little mouth and it bites a hole.* (p. 166)

Later in stage 3, children increase their understanding of the role of genitals in intercourse, as in this description by a child of six years and two months: "(the father) puts his penis right in the place where the baby comes out . . . It seems like magic sort of . . . " (Bernstein & Cowan, cited in Cowan, 1978, p. 167).

Children in stage 4 have grown in their understanding of physical causes for conception and birth, but there are still similarities to earlier stages. They reject animism in their ideas about conception, but they do not see why the participation of both parents is necessary. The following interview is with a child of seven years and nine months (Bernstein & Cowan, cited in Cowan, 1978):

Adult: Why do the seed and the egg *have* to come together?
Child: *Or else the baby, the egg, won't really get hatched very well.*
Adult: How does the baby come from the egg and the seed?
Child: *The seed makes the egg grow. It's just like plants; if you plant a seed a flower will grow.*
Adult: Can the egg grow into a baby without the seed?
Child: *I don't think so.*
Adult: Can the seed grow into a baby without the egg?
Child: *I don't know.* (p. 223)

Only later in the school years do children refer to sexual intercourse as the beginning of fertilization.

Sexual abuse Sexual abuse of children is a major problem. Experts estimate that one in four girls below age eighteen is sexually abused, many boys are also, and incest occurs in one in ten families. Children are often warned against vague dangers presented by strangers, but eighty-five percent of children who are sexually abused are victims of someone they know and trust (Colao & Hosansky, 1983).

Children depend upon adults for food, clothing, and housing, and for attention, love, and protection. When adults abuse children sexually, the relationship is coercive because of the imbalance of power. Children submit to sex with adults for a variety of reasons: they have been taught to obey adults; they do not know what else to do; they are told that it is okay or that everyone does it; they need affection and it is not offered under other circumstances; they are afraid that they or someone else will be hurt if they refuse; they fear disruption of the only family unit they know (Bass & Thornton, 1983). When children are sexually abused and instructed not to tell anyone, they learn that the world is full of shameful sex, that they are powerless, and perhaps that some people entrusted with their care will betray them. They may carry into adulthood painful, unresolved feelings, such as those expressed by a woman who was sexually abused by her father thirty years before:

> Betrayal is a basic theme in my life . . . I am sure it is a hurt that goes back to my father. What a terrible betrayal. My father is a fine man who prides himself on his high moral principles. How he could have betrayed a child, his child, is still overwhelming to me. (Bass & Thornton, 1983, p. 90)

Counseling can help victims of sexual abuse deal with their feelings.

However, often sexually abused children do not tell anyone or seek the help they need. Their silence is a heavy burden, but they maintain it for several reasons: they are dependent on the abuser; their safety (or someone else's) has been threatened; they have been told that it happened because they were bad and they feel guilty; they fear that they will not be believed, either because the adult is known and trusted or because they have no proof; or they do not have the words to explain what happened and no one accurately interprets what they mean when they say they have been "bothered" or "teased" (Colao & Hosansky, 1983).

Children who have been taught to be "good," that is, compliant with adults, are easy prey for abusive adults. Children need information about what parts of their bodies are private and about their right to refuse uncomfortable advances. Children have the right to say no to unwanted touch or affection; they have the right to say no to adult demands and requests; and they have the right to run, scream, and make a scene if they feel threatened. These rights apply whether the advances are from relatives, teachers, religious leaders, coaches, other authority figures, or strangers.

Children need to know accurate terms for their body parts and to be helped to communicate about their experiences. Sometimes children who are victims of sexual abuse can be observed for changes in behavior or what seem to be excessive expressions of anxiety about interactions with certain adults. An

If someone wants me to touch them any place or way that makes me feel uncomfortable, I won't share my body!

FIGURE 12.4

Books for children can help them distinguish between touch that makes them feel comfortable and touch that makes them feel uncomfortable. (From *It's My Body: A Book to Teach Young Children How to Resist Uncomfortable Touch* [p. 18] by L. Freeman, illustrations by C. Deach, 1982, Seattle, WA: Parenting Press. [Originally published by Planned Parenthood of Snohomish County, WA.] Text copyright 1982 by Lory Freeman. Illustrations copyright 1982 by Carol Deach. Reprinted by permission.)

example of a misunderstood communication from a seven-year-old child to a parent is followed by an alternate scenario (from Colao & Hosansky, 1983):

> Jane: Uncle Joe always teases me, especially when he is babysitting for me.
> Mother: Oh, that's part of growing up. My uncle used to tease me, too.
> Jane: (Eyes widening and filling with tears) But, Mommy, how could you stand it?
> Mother: Well, I just learned to live with it, I guess.
> Jane: (Bursts into tears.) (p. 49)

Six months later, Jane was diagnosed as having gonorrhea of the throat. If Jane's mother had explored what was meant by "teasing" and why she burst into tears, the sexual abuse could have been stopped sooner. Here is how her mother might have helped Jane to communicate:

Jane: Uncle Joe always teases me, especially when he is babysitting for me.
Mother: Does it bother you?
Jane: Yes, I hate it.
Mother: Does he tickle you or say things that upset you?
Jane: Well, sometimes he wants to play funny games and I don't want to.
Mother: What kinds of games? (p. 49)

By probing in this way, the mother could have helped Jane to articulate the fact that her uncle was sexually abusing her.

Children who are victims of sexual abuse have specific needs. First and most important, they need to understand that they are not to blame for the abuse. Bad things can happen to good people and otherwise good people can have confused feelings that lead them to hurt children. Adult abusers are in control and, no matter what children do, they are not at fault. Second, children need to be assured that they are believed and that it was right to tell about the abuse. Third, they need to know that they deserve help and will get it and that a trusted adult will stay with them. They need medical care and afterwards they and their families need counseling by experienced, sensitive professionals.

Attractiveness

In U.S. society, two conflicting value systems surround physical attractiveness. On the one hand, it is said that beauty is only skin deep: inner qualities of character are more important than external characteristics. On the other hand, actions often indicate that beauty is good and ugliness is bad. For instance, the ugly duckling finds happiness by becoming a beautiful swan rather than by discovering some hidden inner resources. Most Americans have difficulty acknowledging this latter orientation to physical attractiveness: it seems superficial, unegalitarian, and unfair. Yet, research evidence shows that physical attractiveness influences how others are perceived.

Adams and Crane (1980) have found that young children use a "beauty-is-good" hypothesis in making social choices involving unfamiliar children and adults at different levels of attractiveness. Moreover, their parents and teachers expect them to use this beauty-is-good stereotype in their judgments. This evidence that children and adults base evaluations of unfamiliar people on physical attractiveness has important implications for the development of young children.

If a beauty-is-good hypothesis is in operation, physically attractive young children can more easily form a positive physical image than can physically unattractive children. Unattractive children may begin to view themselves as unloved or unlovable, and may unconsciously fulfill the negative expectations held by others. Both counseling and cosmetic surgery can be recommended for some unattractive children.

BOX
12.4 **STRATEGIES FOR FACILITATING DEVELOPMENT:
PREVENTION AND TREATMENT OF SEXUAL ABUSE**

SAFE is a center designed to serve child victims of sexual abuse and other children who need training in self-defense to prevent sexual abuse or assault. Colao & Hosansky (1983) have organized exercises and games to help children at SAFE feel less powerless. The following are several examples:

Magic Circle Game

A child stands in the center of a room. Another child or an adult approaches the child from the front. At any time the child in the center can say STOP and the approaching person must freeze and not come any closer to the child. This game gives children the experience of setting limits and having them respected.

Saying No Exercise

An adult asks a child a series of questions, at first reasonable and then using guilt and threats. The child tries to maintain eye contact and respond with an assertive NO to each question. The following is a sample dialogue (Colao & Hosansky, 1983, p. 56):

Adult I have been told that you are really good at taking care of animals. Will you come help me feed some sick kittens I have in the basement?
Child No.
Adult If you don't help me, the kittens are going to die.
Child No.

Playing this game initially may make children uncomfortable and these feelings are discussed. Adults explain that children may need practice to say NO to protect themselves.

Yelling

Children form a circle, hold hands, and close their eyes. The leader yells first, squeezes the hand of the next child, who yells, and so on. Children are told to yell a sound or word that expresses their strength if they are threatened.

Children need to practice yelling because most of the adults in their lives have taught them not to yell. Colao and Hosansky (1983) have found that children commonly like to yell "No," "Stop it," "Creep," "Mommy," or "Leave me alone!"

However, there is no single standard of beauty or attractiveness, and the most important factor in forming a positive physical image is how children feel about themselves. Parents and other adults can communicate acceptance and importance to young children whom the larger society might view as unattractive, and these children can increase in confidence and therefore seem more attractive as a result. By the same token, even children who would be regarded by new acquaintances as very attractive can feel ugly and worthless if they are demeaned or ignored by their parents and other important adults.

Little is known about the socialization process through which children learn to evaluate peers and adults based on physical attractiveness. Since adults make these kinds of evaluations themselves and predict that children will do so, it seems reasonable to propose that the early development of a beauty-is-good stereotype comes from adult expectations. Further investigation is needed in order to discover more about this socialization process and about how to help children look beyond skin deep.

FORMING HEALTHY HABITS

Habits established during the early school years can affect development at this time as well as later in middle childhood, adolescence, and adulthood. Of particular importance for positive physical development are the eating, health-care, fitness, and safety habits practiced by young children.

Eating Habits

Eating habits are established in the early years. They are influenced by internal factors, such as hunger and growth rate, and by external factors, such as cultural

Participating in food preparation helps children form healthy eating habits.

and family practices. This section considers both internal and external factors. Information is presented about nutrition, typical growth patterns, and childhood obesity. With such information, adults can be better able to encourage children to form positive eating habits, a fundamental part of a healthy life.

Nutrition and growth patterns   Changes in growth patterns and appetite are found in the early school years. Most four-year-olds have relatively slow rates of growth, small appetites, and continuation of some of the eating problems discussed in Chapter 9. However, by five or six years of age, children usually enter a period of steady growth accompanied by increased appetite (Pipes, 1981). Although children in the early school years may carry over some eating idiosyncrasies, such as refusing to eat foods mixed with others, they generally show fewer eating problems than earlier.

The early school years present children with new social, physical, and cognitive challenges, and children require good nutrition to meet these challenges. Undernourished children are unable to summon the prolonged effort necessary to deal effectively with school activities. They are susceptible to infection, miss school frequently, and have low levels of school achievement. Research demonstrates a relationship between children's nutrition problems and fatigue, boredom, low motivation, and low concentration (Goldsmith, 1980). Undernourished children have lower than expected growth rates and may have difficulty establishing a sense of industry in the early school years.

To be adequately nourished, children in the early school years should be offered a variety of nutritious foods and few empty-calorie items such as candy, chips, and soda. Dietary recommendations include two servings daily of lean meat, fish, poultry, eggs, and cheese for protein, fat, and vitamins; the equivalent of about one quart of milk per day for protein, fat, calcium, phosphorus, and vitamins; four servings daily of fruits and vegetables for vitamins, carbohydrates, and minerals; and four servings of breads and cereals as the primary source of carbohydrates (Wishon, Bower, & Eller, 1983).

Childhood obesity   About sixteen of every hundred children are obese; unless their eating habits change, they tend to be at high risk for certain diet-related diseases (Wishon, Bower, & Eller, 1983). Obesity is a health hazard, and obese children are less able to participate in physical activities and are more likely to be teased and ridiculed than their peers.

Childhood obesity results from an interaction of factors. Wishon, Bower, & Eller (1983) have reviewed literature that shows the effects of both hereditary and environmental factors. Genes seem to influence the rate of metabolism and the accumulation of fatty tissue, and the environment seems to govern the nature of eating habits and the rate of physical activity.

The atmosphere in which food is served and eaten seems to affect children's eating habits and their attitudes about nutrition and eating. Overeating can be unintentionally encouraged by using desserts or other foods as rewards for good behavior; by giving food as a symbol of affection ("If you love me, eat."); by eating while engaged in other activities, such as watching television; and by eating as a substitute for expressing anger or dealing with boredom.

Proper nutrition is an important cornerstone of good health, and it is most likely to be received when children eat light, nutritious snacks and three nutritious meals in an environment of pleasant family conversation. Children need sensitive adult assistance in dealing with their emotional needs separately from issues of nutrition and hunger.

Lack of regular physical activity is characteristic of most obese children in the early school years. If they have little exercise, they use only a few calories and store the rest in fatty deposits. Obese children need guidance and encouragement to take part in moderate, regular physical activity. After consultation with a health professional, they should work up to fifteen- to twenty-minute sessions of walking, swimming, bicycle riding, or playing active games. Exercise, combined with limited intake of food, can improve the fitness of obese children. And, if overeating is a response to boredom or stress, exercise can provide a positive way to deal with both.

In the early school years, families and schools can work together to help obese children change their eating habits and activity levels. Nutrition education and fitness programs at school can be enhanced by family encouragement at home.

Health Care

The social interactions, activity level, and learning patterns of young children are influenced by their state of health. To maintain optimal health, children in the early school years require regular health care. At least once each year, they should receive a complete physical examination, including tuberculin skin test, urinalysis, blood tests, hearing and vision screening, and necessary vaccinations or booster shots. Yearly physical examinations, along with visits to the doctor for any illnesses during the year, make it possible to monitor, prevent, and treat conditions that might interfere with children's development.

In addition to physical examinations, two specialized types of health care gain increased importance in the early school years: dental care and vision screening. The importance of dental care is underscored by the appearance of the first permanent teeth; the importance of vision screening is emphasized by the highly visual presentation of many learning experiences in the early school years. In this section, dental care and vision screening are described.

Dental care Patterns of good dental care should be established well before the early school years, but the appearance of the first permanent teeth often heightens the motivation of families to provide this care. Permanent teeth begin to come in when children are about six years of age. Simultaneously, the six-year molars erupt and the two lower front teeth—called lower central incisors—become loose. Gradually, the permanent incisors push up from underneath, destroying the roots of the first teeth until they fall out. The permanent teeth replace the first teeth in the same order in which the first teeth appeared: incisors, molars, and then canines (the sharp teeth between incisors and molars). The substitution is usually complete by the time children are twelve or thirteen years of age.

Both at home and school, teeth should be brushed after meals.

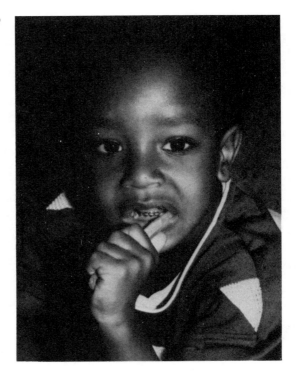

The appearance of the permanent teeth makes good oral hygiene especially important. Ideally, teeth should be brushed after every meal; at a minimum, they should be carefully brushed in the morning and in the evening. In areas without fluoride in the water supply, supplementation should continue until all permanent teeth are in.

Children should establish the habit of visiting a dentist every six months from the time they are three or four years of age. The dentist can provide feedback about dental care and anticipate the need for orthodontia. Modern orthodontia may involve use during the early school years of removable appliances called Crozats, which apply mild pressure to the teeth with the purpose of encouraging bone growth to make room for all of the teeth. Orthodontia improves appearance, but its more important goal is often less well understood: orthodontia improves occlusion (or bite). Chewing causes a force of as much as two hundred pounds on the teeth; to withstand this pressure without problems, the teeth need to be properly aligned and in the right relationship to each other. Orthodontia can improve upon the alignment made by nature and prevent a lifetime of discomfort.

Vision screening   Many learning experiences in the early school years are visual, and subtle difficulties in vision can interfere with children's ability to learn. The well-known Snellen chart measures vision only at a distance of twenty feet; while the information from the Snellen chart is useful, it does not identify some visual difficulties that create reading and other problems. One such difficulty is **amblyopia** (pronounced am-blee-OH-pee-uh), seeing well with one eye but poorly with the other. Amblyopia begins when children use only their good eye and not their poor eye. If untreated, it can lead to permanent loss of vision. Amblyopia can be discovered by a simple screening procedure in which each eye is tested with the other eye covered. This screening can be conducted by parents or volunteers from community groups who are trained by specialists at their local health districts or at their Society for the Prevention of Blindness. To be most effective, screening should take place early and treatment should begin by the time children are four years of age.

Even more subtle visual difficulties can be diagnosed by ophthalmologists trained in children's developmental vision. They examine a wide range of visual performance skills, including tracking of moving objects, focusing, converging when looking at near objects, depth perception, visual acuity at distances and near, and range of readability. These ophthalmologists also may investigate children's balance, coordination, spatial perception, and figure-ground discrimination (Ames, Gillespie, Haines, & Ilg, 1979). By conducting a complete examination of children's visual behavior, developmental ophthalmologists can first determine if children have any visual problems that could interfere with school performance and then provide necessary treatment.

Fitness

Children in the early school years often seem to be in perpetual motion. In the past, many educators assumed that playing games would provide a foundation for later fitness. Now it is realized that education for fitness must be part of the formal and informal curriculum. As they play, children can be taught about their bodies, conditioning, and the role of exercise in lifelong fitness.

The definition of **fitness** includes six components: strength, power, muscular endurance, cardiovascular endurance, flexibility, and body fatness (*Practical Applications of Research,* 1983). Strength is the ability to exert force. Power is the ability to exert considerable force over a very short period of time. Muscular endurance is the ability to exert force continuously over a long period of time. Cardiovascular endurance or stamina is the ability of the lungs, heart, and circulatory system to carry oxygen and nutrients to the cells of the body. Flexibility is the ability of the joints to move through their entire normal range of motion. Body fatness is the proportion of fat cells to other tissue of the body.

Attaining physical fitness is an individual matter that involves exercising to improve the levels of the six components described above. The results of fitness programs should be noted in changes in specific children over time; comparisons among children are not relevant.

By participating in fitness programs, children realize that fitness can be developed by anyone willing to work hard. They learn about the role of fitness in reducing the rates of certain degenerative diseases and in improving the quality and enjoyment of life.

Conditioning activities for children are fairly intense, take place at least three times each week, and last thirty to forty-five minutes. Children can measure their heart rates to receive maximum benefit from exercise and can be introduced to forms of exercise that they can continue to enjoy in years to come.

Safety

Children in the early school years and through the age of fourteen experience the lowest rate of death of any period from birth to age twenty-four. According to the U.S. Bureau of the Census (1982), children of these ages have successfully survived many of the early childhood and birth-related diseases and have not yet entered the older age group that has a high incidence of work-related and motor vehicle accidents. Still, in the early school years, accidents are the leading cause of death, accounting for over half of the mortality (U.S. Bureau of the Census, 1982). Safety education should have a high priority in homes and schools.

BOX 12.5   STRATEGIES FOR FACILITATING DEVELOPMENT: TEACHING SAFETY RULES

The American Red Cross has developed curriculum materials for teaching children in the early school years about safety (Robbins, 1984). These materials help teachers plan learning experiences to improve behavior, understanding, and attitudes of young children about safety. Here are examples of suggested activities:

- Make cartoons illustrating rules of safety for riding in automobiles.
- Make posters illustrating school bus rules and display them on bulletin boards or in school buses.
- Dramatize jaywalking situations and their results.
- Make puppets and conduct a puppet show on walking and riding safety.
- Identify hazards that interfere with safe walking and riding and tell how they can be avoided.
- Make bright yellow kerchiefs and beanies that can be readily seen by motorists.
- Make traffic signals and use them in role-playing safety situations.
- Compose safety songs and safety games.
- Prepare for and take field trips to places concerned with safety practices and promotion.
- Demonstrate how to fasten and unfasten a safety belt.
- Demonstrate bicycle safety rules. (Robbins, 1984, 32–33)

Contact a local chapter of the American Red Cross for more information about curriculum materials on safety.

Adapted from "American Red Cross Teaches Safety Rules to Children" by E. Robbins, 1984, *Day Care and Early Education, 12*, pp. 32–33. Copyright 1984 by Human Sciences Press, Inc. Adapted by permission.

Because children in the early school years have a high degree of mobility and a wide range of activities, they need safety education that focuses on the home, school, and wider community. Children require guidance and constant reinforcement to become safety-conscious at home and at school, and to become responsible pedestrians, cyclists, and riders of school buses and public transportation. Outside experts such as fire fighters and police officers may be effective in motivating children to be safe and aware.

SUMMARY

1   Children develop many new physical competencies during the early school years.

2   In large muscle skills, children between the ages of four and eight improve in balancing, hopping, skipping, running, and jumping.

3   In small muscle skills, children gain proficiency in reaching, grasping, and manipulating objects.

4   From four to eight years of age, children learn to control writing and drawing implements and add considerable detail to their drawings.

5   Perceptual-motor integration progresses from control of the whole body to control of the arm and hand to coordination of the eye and hand.

6   Girls are somewhat ahead of boys in attaining physical milestones, especially those using small muscle skills.

7   The development of children in the early school years is affected by such handicapping conditions as hearing impairment, visual impairment, mental retardation, emotional disturbance, specific learning disabilities, and speech and language impairment.

8   Public Law 94–142 requires that free public education be provided for all children, even those with handicaps, between three and twenty-one years of age.

9   Children from minority cultural backgrounds are overrepresented in special education classrooms; nondiscriminatory assessment is necessary to determine which children need these services.

10   Hyperactivity, sexuality, and attractiveness influence children's physical images.

11   Hyperactive children, often intelligent but unable to concentrate and learn, are treated by changes in diet, changes in environment, or use of medication.

12   Sex education should be provided to answer children's implicit or explicit questions; children also need preparation for the possibility of sexual abuse, a major problem.

13   Physical attractiveness influences how children and adults perceive others.

14   By five or six, children enter a period of steady growth accompanied by increased appetite; nutritious choices should be made available to them. Both environment and heredity contribute to childhood obesity.

15   Physical examination, dental care, and vision screening are important aspects of health care in the early school years.

16   Specific attention should be given to physical fitness: exercising to increase levels of strength, power, muscular endurance, cardiovascular endurance, and flexibility, and to maintain an appropriate percentage of body fat.

17   Accidents are the leading cause of death in the early school years. Safety education is very important.

KEY TERMS

naming of scribbling stage	mental retardation	due process
early representational stage	emotional disturbance	least restrictive environment
preschematic stage	specific learning disabilities	mainstreaming
schematic stage	speech impairment	hyperactive
hearing impairment	language impairment	attention deficit disorder
deaf	Public Law 94–142	amblyopia
visual impairment	individualized education program (IEP)	fitness
blindness		

FOR FURTHER READING

Movement Experiences

Sullivan, M. (1982). *Movement exploration for young children.* Washington, DC: National Association for the Education of Young Children.

Handicapped Children

Patton, J. R., Payne, J. S., Kauffman, J. M., Brown, G. B., & Payne, R. A. (1987). *Exceptional children in focus* (4th ed.). Columbus, OH: Merrill.

Sexual Abuse

Colao, F., & Hosansky, T. (1983). *Your children should know: Teach your children the strategies that will keep them safe from assault and crime.* Indianapolis: Bobbs-Merrill.

Freeman, L. Illustrations by C. Deach. (1982). *It's my body: A book to teach young children how to resist uncomfortable touch.* Seattle, WA: Parenting Press. (Originally published by Planned Parenthood of Snohomish County, WA.)

Drawing and Writing

Brittain, W. L. (1979). *Creativity, art, and the young child.* New York: Macmillan.

Lamme, L. L. (1984). *Growing up writing.* Washington, DC: Acropolis Books.

13

Early School Years (Ages Four–Eight): Cognitive Development

Key Ideas

The Development of Logic
Preoperational and Concrete Operational Stages □ Cross-Cultural Verifications of Piaget's Theory □ Other Ways of Using Logic: Philosophical Thinking

Language Development
Linguistic Milestones □ Language and Reading □ Bilingualism

The Continuing Role of Play
Creativity □ Humor □ Gender Differences in Play □ Computers and Thinking

Effects of Early Education Programs
Programs for Low-Income Children □ Programs for Advantaged Children

School Success
Social and Intellectual Competence □ Motivation □ Memory

Culture and School Success
Childrearing and Education □ Cultural Variation in Language Use □ Cognitive Style

Children in the early school years face a multitude of new experiences outside the confines of their homes. Their initial reactions to these experiences often include exuberant curiosity and eagerness. Whether their positive reactions are maintained depends on their success in school, which, in turn, is influenced by the cognitive development that takes place during the early school years. This chapter describes cognitive development by considering the following topics: the development of logic; language development, including linguistic milestones, language and reading, and bilingualism; the continuing role of play; effects of early education programs; school success; and culture and school success.

THE DEVELOPMENT OF LOGIC

There are striking differences between the reasoning of most four-year-olds and that of most eight-year-olds. Typically, four-year-olds base many of their judgments on their perceptions, focusing on just one variable in complex situations. Eight-year-olds, however, have often attained the ability to reason logically, coordinating several variables to make decisions. The following vignette provides an illustration of the contrast between perceptual and logical orientations.

Two children sit at the dinner table with their father. Mr. Dash patiently counts out twenty strawberries for each child. Four-year-old Aaron complains, "She has more strawberries. It's not fair!" Before Mr. Dash has a chance to respond, eight-year-old Cynthia retorts, "No, I don't. Mine are just piled higher." She redistributes her strawberries. "See?!"

Aaron's behavior reflects prelogical thinking. He believes that, if the pile of strawberries is higher, it must have more. In contrast, the behavior of eight-year-old Cynthia reflects logical thinking. She understands that different arrangements of strawberries can contain the same number, if no berries are added or taken away from the original quantity. Piaget and Inhelder (1969) have said that thinking such as Aaron's is at the **preoperational stage** and thinking such as Cynthia's is at the **concrete operational stage**.

To explain the development of logic in the early school years, this section begins with a description of thinking in the preoperational and concrete operational stages, and then provides information about cross-cultural verifications of Piaget's theory. (For discussion of interpretations that differ from Piaget's, refer to Chapter 10.) The section ends by exploring children's philosophical thinking.

Preoperational and Concrete Operational Stages

During most of the early school years, children are at the preoperational stage in their thinking, according to the theory of Jean Piaget (Piaget & Inhelder, 1969; Piaget, 1960a, 1960b, 1964). Although their thinking is not yet based on logic, what happens during the preoperational stage provides an important basis for the later attainment of logical thinking. Throughout the preoperational stage, children become proficient in mentally working through solutions to problems. They learn to combine separate actions to form new ideas and to imagine actions that cancel others. Performing these mental activities and developing the language to represent them efficiently is an essential step toward logical thinking.

The transition to concrete operational thinking takes place around the ages of seven or eight for most children. Concrete operational thinkers are able to reason logically as long as problems are within the realm of their direct experiences. Concrete operational thinking represents an important change from preoperational thinking, but still has limitations, if compared with a subsequent, more abstract type of logical thinking, *formal operational thinking,* which is attained by many individuals in adolescence.

Piaget has described a number of fundamental differences between the thinking of children at the preoperational and concrete operational stages (Piaget, 1960a, 1960b, 1964). The differences can best be presented by contrasting responses to situations involving cause and effect, conservation, classification, and seriation. Implications for interaction with children in the early school years can then be drawn.

Cause and effect   Children at the preoperational stage seem to produce a steady stream of questions: "Where did the moon go?" "Why is the grass green?" "Why is it raining?" Their frequent questions reflect their view that things do not happen by chance but instead are influenced in ways that can be discerned. Their attempts to find simple explanations for complex phenomena lead to interpretations that often surprise adults. For instance, in explaining the change from night to day, children at the preoperational stage might say, "It gets light to wake me up." Children at the preoperational stage also tend to ascribe human, animate characteristics to inanimate objects such as dolls, stuffed animals and trees. This type of thinking is called *animism.* An adult gave the following account of her ideas about the tree outside the window in her early school years:

During the day I knew it to be an innocent and harmless apple tree. But at night it was backlighted and cast an ominous shadow on my white window shade. I saw its arms reaching out to get me and developed ways of placating the tree so that it would not. If I had to get out of bed at night, I would only get out of one side. If I forgot and went out the other side, I had a little ritual that I would go through. Years later, I told my mother about the tree and she was upset that I never came to her about it. I didn't tell anyone because I thought that my view of the tree was common knowledge, shared by everyone else.

Preoperational thinkers view cause and effect very differently than do concrete operational thinkers. Concrete operational thinkers do not seem driven to explain all events with a sentence or two. When some justification seems called for, their explanations reflect an increased understanding of the world. They are more logical but still have difficulty accounting for complicated situations such

A child studies checkers in a conservation-of-number interview.

as the action of waves. As the assignment of animism to inanimate objects decreases, children develop a clearer understanding of life and death.

Conservation   Conservation is the understanding of the constancy of characteristics such as number, length, quantity, or area, despite changes in appearance. Conservation of number is involved in this chapter's introductory vignette: Aaron believes that 20 berries piled high is more than 20 berries spread around and thus does not conserve; Cynthia is able to conserve elementary number.

The following are examples of interviews involving conservation:

CONSERVATION INTERVIEWS

All interviews about conservation use the same sequence: (1) Establishing equivalence (Request 1 below); (2) Showing some change in appearance of one of the equivalent objects; (3) Asking for another judgment of equivalence; and (4) Asking why the child thinks that way. If a child does not establish initial equivalence, the interviewer does not proceed.

Conservation of Number

Materials: 20 one-inch blocks.

Preparation: Place 8 of the blocks in a line with about a one-inch space between them.

Request 1:   "Please make another line that has just as many blocks as this one."

Request 2: "Now, let's pretend that one line is yours and one line is mine. Do you have more blocks or do I have more blocks or do we have the same?" (If a child establishes equivalence, continue. If not, thank the child and stop.)

"Watch what I'm doing." (Spread out one line so that the distance between blocks is about two inches. That row is much longer than the other, as shown below.)

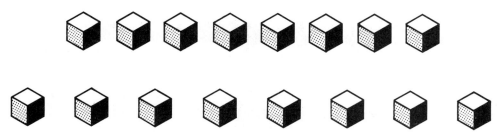

Request 3: "Do you think that I have more blocks or do you have more or do we have the same?" (Point to each row in turn.)

Request 4: "Why do you think so?"

(Children at the preoperational stage tend to base their judgment of number on their perception. They usually respond that there are more in the long line "because it's long." Children at the concrete operational stage base their judgment on logic: "They're both the same. They were the same at the start and you only moved them around.")

Conservation of Liquid

Materials: Two clear glasses of identical size and shape, one clear glass that is taller and narrower than the pair, pitcher of water.

Preparation: Fill the identical glasses with water.

Request 1: "If this glass is yours and this glass is mine (pointing), would you have more to drink or would I have more to drink or would we have the same?"

"Now watch what I do." (Pour the water from one of the identical glasses into the tall, narrow glass. Remove the empty glass.)

Request 2: "Would you have more to drink or would I have more to drink (pointing) or would we have the same?"

Request 3: "Why do you think so?"

(Children at the preoperational stage usually respond that the tall glass has more "because it is so high." Children at the concrete operational stage are often surprised that they would be asked such a silly question. "Of course they're still the same; you haven't added any water or taken any away.")

Conservation of Area

Materials: Two toy sheep, two sheets of green construction paper, 12 one-inch blocks.

Preparation: Place a sheep on each piece of paper.

Request 1:   "Pretend that these sheep are eating the green grass. Would this sheep have more to eat or would this sheep have more to eat (pointing) or would they have the same amount to eat?"

If the child establishes equivalence, say, "Both farmers cover up some of their grass with a barn." (Place a block on each sheet.)

Request 2:   "Would this sheep have more grass to eat or would this sheep have more grass to eat (pointing) or would they have the same? Why?"

(Add five more barns to one "field" in a corner and add five more barns to the other field in a haphazard arrangement. The appearance is as shown below.)

 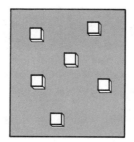

Request 3:   (Repeat Request 2.)

(Children at the preoperational stage usually rely on their perceptual cues and believe that there is less grass to eat in the haphazard arrangement. Children at the concrete operational stage indicate that the animals have the same amount of grass to eat because the barns take up the same amount of space.)

It is important to note that the conservation tasks about which children are interviewed have no inherent significance. These types of tasks were chosen by Piaget because they require logical responses that are not usually directly taught at home or school.

These children engage in the classification task of placing their food labels in logical groups, such as drinks or soups.

Children at the preoperational stage of development are unable to conserve. They base their judgments on perceptual cues (e.g., "Because it's so high;" "It's so-o-o long."), focus on one variable rather than coordinating several, and do not reverse their thinking to consider the original state.

At the concrete operational stage, however, children are able to conserve when interviewed about number, length, quantity, and area. They justify their conserving responses logically. These justifications might refer to **reversibility** (mentally returning objects to the original position or state) or **compensation** (seeing that one variable, such as height, is balanced by another, such as width).

Classification Classification is the grouping of objects or people on the basis of similar characteristics. The following example shows a classification task involving the characteristics of color and size.

CLASSIFICATION INTERVIEW

Materials: Squares of paper in the following distribution: 4 large yellow, 4 small yellow, 4 large red, 4 small red, 4 large blue, 4 small blue, 4 large green, 4 small green.

Request 1: "Please put these in groups so that the ones in the group are the same as each other and different from the other groups."

Request 2: After children have classified the squares one way, say, "Now mix them up. Find another, different way to put them into groups."

When asked to classify objects, children at the preoperational stage are likely to give one of three types of responses: arranging the objects into a picture rather than into groups; putting the objects into inconsistent groups (e.g., beginning to sort by color and then switching to size); or, toward the time of transition to concrete operational thinking, putting objects in a group according to one characteristic but being unable to change their focus to another characteristic. Some of the behavioral problems encountered by preoperational children center on classification difficulties, as shown by a vignette that was recorded at a grocery store:

*At the grocery store, Mrs. Hartley took the jar of applesauce from four-year-old Zach and sternly admonished him: "Now don't touch **that!**" Zach then put rice and cereal into the shopping cart without comment from Mrs. Hartley, but two aisles later he reached for a jar of peanut butter and was sharply told, "I said not to touch **that!**"*

Mrs. Hartley probably understood *that* to represent the classification of all breakable items. Zach, however, is unlikely to comprehend such a classification system. Children at the preoperational stage of thinking also have a great deal of difficulty dealing with the many categories in which people can be placed. They may deny that a person can fit into more than one classification—mother, wife, doctor, sister, etc.—and be disconcerted when they see familiar persons out of their assigned roles.

In contrast, children at the concrete operational stage form categories consistently. They may classify first by color, then by shape, and then by some other variable. They understand that objects can form hierarchies (for example, from living things to animals to farm animals to cows), and they deal with the relationships between objects and people at different levels of the hierarchy. They can comprehend more easily than earlier the multiple roles that any one individual may have.

Seriation   Seriation is putting objects into ordered relationships, such as from large to small. A seriation task follows.

SERIATION INTERVIEW

Materials: Nine construction paper strips, in a single color, ranging in length from 1 inch to 9 inches.

Preparation: Place the longest and the shortest on the table with a large space between them. Withhold one strip of intermediate length.

Request 1:   "Please put these pieces of paper (a randomly arranged pile of six strips) where they belong."

Request 2:   After the child has made an arrangement, say, "Here's an extra one. Would you put it where it belongs?"

Children at the preoperational stage respond to seriation tasks with random arrangements or with comparisons between pairs of objects that ignore other relationships. Their activities are based on trial and error.

Later, at the concrete operational level, children employ a system for comparing each item with all others, rather than using trial and error. They can coordinate two dimensions, such as color and size, in a matrix. And they can be shown two objects, one of which is then removed, and use that information to tell the relationship with a third object.

Implications   Four important implications can be drawn from descriptions of thinking at the preoperational and concrete operational stages. First, children have their own unique perspectives, and less flexibility than adults to change perspectives. Especially at the preoperational stage, they may focus on a different variable than does someone else with whom they are communicating. For instance, while an adult is talking about an object in terms of color, some children might be thinking about the shape or texture or size. Because knowing the focus of a given child, particularly in a group situation, is not easy, information or concepts must be presented in as many different ways as possible.

Second, children in the early school years may be at the preoperational stage, in transition, or at the concrete operational stage of logical thinking. Any group of children in the early school years needs to be provided with thinking

---

BOX 13.1

CLASSIFICATION OF CONCEPT REPRESENTATIONS

1.0 CONCRETE LEVEL: three-dimensional representations ranging from the real object or person to a general configuration of the object or person.

   1.1 *Concrete Reality:* the real object or person; for example, an apple that can be eaten.

   1.2 *Concrete Replica:* an exact duplication of form, shape, color, and size of real object or person; for example, a colored wax model of an apple.

   1.3 *Concrete Impression:* similar in form, general configuration, and shape to real object or person. Size, color, and shape can vary or be changed; for example, wooden apple, clay apple, or a bas-relief representation.

2.0 PICTORIAL LEVEL: two-dimensional complete drawings or photographic reproductions of varying sizes and colors to represent concept.

   2.1 *Pictorial Replica:* drawing or photographic representation duplicating in size and color the object or person; for example, an actual size colored picture of an apple.

   2.2 *Pictorial Impression:* drawing or photographic rendition that produces a general configuration similar to the real object or person; for example, a miniature or oversized photograph or drawing of an apple or a blurred reproduction.

3.0 SYMBOLIC LEVEL: two-dimensional single line drawings or gestures.

   3.1 *Symbolic Impression:* an outline drawing of the real object or person; for example, a black line drawing of an apple.

   3.2 *Interpretation:* includes gestures, pantomime, and dramatization.

4.0 ABSTRACT LEVEL: a representation that bears no relation in size, shape, or form to the real object or person; for example, the written word *apple,* the spoken word *apple* or the finger-spelled word *apple.*

From "A Classification of Concept Representations" by M. Gorelick in *Piagetian Theory and Its Implications for the Helping Professions: Proceedings, Fourth Interdisciplinary Seminar* (p. 336), Los Angeles: University of Southern California. Reprinted by permission.

Preoperational and concrete operational thinkers most effectively learn new concepts through use of concrete objects. Here children experiment with the concept of symmetry.

activities that are flexible enough to be understood and to allow success if approached in different ways.

Third, children at both the preoperational and concrete operational stages of development need experiences with concrete objects in order to learn to reason about their properties. Often children in the early school years are given worksheets that depict objects, but they need first to explore the actual objects using all their senses. Gorelick (1975) has shown how to classify representations on a continuum from the most concrete and tangible to the most abstract. Children in the early school years learn best from **concrete objects**.

Fourth and finally, children can be observed and interviewed to assess their levels of logical thinking and to match these levels with appropriate experiences. Children who do not conserve elementary number—who believe that one row of eight can be more than another row of eight—have not yet built an appropriate foundation for mathematics. To be sure, these children may be able to memorize number facts, but their understanding of the operations is limited. Some mathematics programs, such as *Mathematics Their Way* (Baratta-Lorton, 1976), take into account the special needs of children at the preoperational and early concrete operational stages. Similarly, children who cannot coordinate variables when dealing with tangible objects are unlikely to find success in coordinating symbols in the reading process. Decoding English requires, among other things, the ability to create a system to keep track of different sounds made by the same letters and similar sounds made by different letters or combinations of letters. Language/thinking programs such as *R Is for Rainbow* (Anselmo, Rollins, & Schuckman, 1986) provide a concrete way to familiarize children with sound-symbol associations.

**BOX   STRATEGIES FOR FACILITATING DEVELOPMENT:
13.2   CONCRETE MATHEMATICS**

An example of a mathematics program designed to meet the needs of children at the preoperational and early concrete operational stages is *Mathematics Their Way* (Baratta-Lorton, (1976). Rather than starting the study of number at the symbolic level, this program provides a foundation at the concrete level. Children complete the following units before being introduced to symbols for numbers:

☐   Free exploration of materials
☐   Patterning
☐   Sorting and classifying
☐   Counting
☐   Conservation of number
☐   Comparing
☐   Graphing (with objects and pictures)
☐   Number at the concept level
☐   Number at the connecting level

Symbolic representations for numbers are not introduced until children have had many experiences with organizing and thinking about materials. Even when symbolic representations are introduced, tangible objects are used also. The following example is adapted from Baratta-Lorton (1976):

From *Mathematics Their Way* by Mary Baratta-Lorton. Copyright © 1976 by Addison-Wesley Publishing, Inc. Reprinted by permission.

Cross-Cultural Verifications of Piaget's Theory

During the past decades, research on Jean Piaget's theory has been conducted on five continents: Europe, North America, Africa, Asia, Oceania, and South America (Werner, 1979). These studies have attempted to ascertain whether the patterns of intellectual development proposed by Piaget can be verified in non-European cultural groups. Reviewers of these studies (Werner, 1979; Fishbein, 1984) have concluded that researchers have verified the qualitative aspects of

Piaget's theory—the sequence and descriptions of the stages. There is, however, disagreement on the rates of attainment of various stages.

A study by Nyiti (1982) may provide a partial explanation for this disagreement. Nyiti compared the cognitive development of children from two Canadian cultural groups, European English-speaking Canadians and Micmac Indians from the Eskasoni Reserve in Cape Breton Island. The Indian children, who speak their native language at home and English at school, were interviewed by two types of researchers: one shared their culture and language and one did not. Nyiti (1982) found that both European and Indian children follow the sequence of stages described by Piaget. The researcher's finding on rate of development, though, was provocative: Indian children seemed to lag behind their European counterparts *only* when the culture and language of the examiner were different from those of the child. Nyiti has asserted that previous studies, such as many of those reviewed by Werner (1979) and Fishbein (1984), have had the methodological flaw of using interviewers who differ in culture and language from the children interviewed. He has said that research methodology must be examined before one accepts cultural differences as an explanation for variation in development of intellectual operations (Nyiti, 1982). Nyiti has concluded that the development of logical thinking is as described by Piaget: not the direct product of cultural influences but rather of the coordination of actions of individuals on their environments.

This conclusion is shared by researchers who studied the intellectual development of Oglala Sioux children on the Pine Ridge Reservation in South Dakota (Voyat, 1983). The Oglala children have major problems in the school systems in which they enroll. For instance, more than 70 percent of those completing eighth grade drop out before high school graduation (Voyat, 1983). The researchers wondered if cultural differences in cognitive development might explain some of the school difficulties of the Oglala children. They found instead that Oglala children progress through the same order of stages at ages similar to those described by Piaget. The researchers concluded that the cause of school difficulties does not relate to the rate of attainment of these stages of intellectual development and that internal and external processes, not cultural factors *per se,* are responsible for changes in reasoning skills. Researchers have verified Piaget's findings in a variety of cultural settings.

Other Ways of Using Logic: Philosophical Thinking

Piaget has often asked children questions that philosophers would recognize as belonging in their domain. For instance, in his book *The Child's Conception of the World,* Piaget (1960b) asked children questions such as the following:

What is thinking?

What is the relationship between a word and its meaning?

What things are alive?

Piaget's purpose in asking these questions and in analyzing the responses was to chart children's intellectual progress. Recently, however, Matthews (1980), a philosopher, has asserted that some of children's responses, dismissed by Piaget as illogical and "mere romancing," were in fact philosophical responses to philosophical questions and should be encouraged. Matthews has said that philosophy provides an important vehicle for understanding the world and that Piaget and others have underestimated the logical importance of children's philosophical thinking.

According to Matthews (1980), philosophical thinking is natural for many young children, including the boy in the following example:

> TIM (about six years), while busily engaged in licking a pot, asked, "Papa, how can we be sure that everything is not a dream?" (p. 1)

Tim's question is philosophical. What is the difference between life as he believes it to be, with waking hours and dreaming hours, and an endless dream in which he sometimes seems to be awake and sometimes seems to be dreaming? Tim's question has no answer, but shows the potential that children have for interest in the most basic elements of life. Philosophy is motivated by puzzlement. It can be serious but children often approach it by playing intellectually with concepts. In the case of Tim's question, his father asked the boy how he could tell and Tim replied in the following manner:

> Well, I don't think everything is a dream, 'cause in a dream people wouldn't go around asking if it was a dream. (p. 23)

Tim's solution was based on a valid argument, which provided a good solution to his question if he accepted the premises as true. Here is a summary of Tim's argument:

1   If everything were a dream, people wouldn't go around asking if it were a dream.
2   People do go around asking if it is a dream.
    Therefore:
3   Not everything is a dream.

If someone like Piaget, usually so sensitive to children's thinking processes, did not recognize and value children's philosophical thinking, who does? Matthews (1980) has shown that writers of children's books raise many issues of interest to children and philosophers. For example, in the children's story, *Many Moons,* Thurber (1971) has described the efforts of a king to return his daughter Lenore to health. Lenore believes that she will become healthy if given the moon, and the king tries to oblige her. But when the Lord High Chamberlain, Royal Wizzard, and Royal Mathematician cannot grant Lenore's request for the moon, the king grows in despair. Finally the Court Jester thinks to ask Lenore how big the moon is. Lenore replies: "It is just a little smaller than my thumbnail . . . for when I hold my thumbnail up at the moon it just covers it" (unpaginated). Armed with this knowledge of Lenore's perceptions, the king is able to fulfill Lenore's desire by presenting her with a tiny golden moon, smaller than her nail, on a golden chain.

Stories such as *Many Moons* raise questions about perception and apparent size and distance that have interested philosophers for centuries. Children's

Authors of children's books raise many issues of interest to children and philosophers.

attention is captured and they respond positively to this kind of philosophical whimsy. Adults, on the other hand, tend to be intellectually smug and to dismiss Princess Lenore's view as ignorant without further reflection on the fundamental issues.

Piaget (1960b) has pointed out the logical inconsistencies of young children's thinking. Yet, according to Matthews (1980), children of five, six, and seven years of age are more likely to ask philosophical questions and make philosophical comments than older children who have been socialized to redirect their questioning into other areas. Philosophers believe that the philosophical questions raised by children in the early school years have the potential of helping children to learn to think independently, logically, and ethically. Research with older children (fifth through eighth graders) has shown that children with experience in philosophical thinking made significant gains in reading, mathematics, and creativity when compared with children without that experience (Alvino, 1980). Because of such impressive research findings, philosophy is now becoming a part of the curriculum in some settings even in the early school years.

The importance of philosophical thinking has to do with the nature of the discipline itself. Philosophy gives a methodology for inquiring about fundamental assumptions. The aims and objectives of philosophy with children include the following (Alvino, 1980):

1. To increase children's reasoning skills as well as their abilities to draw valid inferences.
2. To help children see connections and make distinctions.

BOX
13.3

STRATEGIES FOR FACILITATING DEVELOPMENT: ADVANCING CHILDREN'S PHILOSOPHICAL THINKING

The Institute for the Advancement of Philosophy for Children,* under the direction of Matthew Lipman, has developed curriculum materials for children and guides for teachers in developing philosophical thinking. The early childhood materials include *Kio and Gus* (Lipman, 1982) and *Pixie* (Lipman, 1981), as well as the accompanying teachers' guides. These novels and related activities help children examine philosophical concepts of great interest to them: friendship, goodness, fairness, reality, truth, being a person. The vehicle for learning is discussion, and children learn to reason together. In so doing, they attain some of the following thinking skills (*Philosophy for Children,* 1984):

Analyzing value statements
Classifying and categorizing
Constructing hypotheses
Defining terms
Developing concepts
Discovering alternatives
Drawing inferences from hypothetical syllogisms
Drawing inferences from single premises
Drawing inferences from double premises
Finding underlying assumptions
Formulating causal explanations
Formulating comparisons as relationships
Formulating questions
Generalizing
Giving reasons
Grasping part-whole and whole-part connections
Identifying and using criteria
Knowing how to deal with ambiguities
Knowing how to treat vagueness
Looking out for informal fallacies
Making connections
Making distinctions
Predicting consequences
Providing instances and illustrations
Recognizing contextual aspects of truth and falsity
Recognizing differences of perspective
Recognizing interdependence of means and ends
Seriation
Standardizing ordinary language sentences
Taking all considerations into account
Using ordinal or relational logic
Working with analogies
Working with consistency and contradiction

*Institute for Advancement of Philosophy for Children
Montclair State College
Upper Montclair, NJ 07043

3. To develop creative as well as logical abilities.
4. To help children discover alternatives, the need for objectivity and consistency, and the importance of giving reasons for beliefs. (p. 54)

The basic techniques of questioning and dialogue in philosophy help children recognize that learning and understanding are cooperative. Children experience what is "right" and "fair," develop standards and rules, and discover the differences between truthfulness and lying and cheating. Children explore what criteria can be used in making judgments, both in cognitive and in ethical spheres. Philosophy builds on children's natural creativity and inquisitiveness. When children interact with adults who value their philosophical questions, they begin to look for reasons underlying statements and situations and learn that there are many ways to look at things.

Philosophy is interesting to children because of its emphasis on meaning rather than isolated facts, on thinking rather than mere memorizing, and on issues of interest to children rather than only those chosen by adults. Philosophy allows children to take a new look at the logic embedded in their everyday language. Philosophical thinking enhances the development of logic in the early school years.

LANGUAGE DEVELOPMENT

Many linguists once believed that children's language development was essentially complete by the early school years. Research has demonstrated, however, that children's use of language increases in range and complexity during the early school years. Owens (1984) has said of this age group: "Having acquired much of the 'what' of language form, the child turns to the 'how' of language use" (p. 263). A description of language development in the early school years covers three important topics: linguistic milestones, language and reading, and bilingualism.

Linguistic Milestones

Linguistic milestones of children in the early school years include advances in their ability to derive words, use complex noun and verb phrases, use sentences of varied types, produce speech sounds, use wider vocabulary, reflect on their own use of language, and achieve complexity in language. Each of these milestones is discussed in terms of relevant research, and then suggestions are given for appropriate adult assistance.

Word derivation   Research reviewed by Owens (1984) showed a qualitative increase in word derivation skills around the age of seven. Children become able to add the suffixes *-er, -man,* and *-ist* to words to make nouns that may previously have been unfamiliar to them. For instance, they can produce the word *experimenter* from the phrase *person who experiments.* Similarly, at about the same age, they learn to add *-ly* to make adverbs.

Use of noun and verb phrases Children in the early school years increasingly differentiate among subject pronouns such as *I,* object pronouns such as *me,* and reflexive pronouns such as *myself.* They struggle with determining the referents of pronouns and with mastering adjective ordering (Richards, 1980). Gentner (1982) has shown that the use of verb phrases poses problems for children in the early school years. For example, there are several ways to reverse verb actions: using *un* as in *untie,* using particles as in *pull on* or *pull off,* and using separate words such as *open* and *close.* Children must learn that some of these reversals are appropriate only for certain verbs.

Use of varied sentence types Owens (1984) has reported an improvement in the early school years of comprehension of the linguistic relationships in sentences using passive voice or temporal sequences. Before the age of five or six years, children do not comprehend passive sentences such as, "The window was broken by the ball." Six- and seven-year-olds begin to understand passive constructions at about the same time that they begin to understand conservation.

Sentences using temporal sequences introduced by words such as *because, so,* and *therefore* require comprehension of relationships and timing. Only after about the age of seven can children understand what happened first if someone said, "I went because I was asked" (Owens, 1984, p. 287).

Production of speech sounds By the age of eight, most children can produce all of the English speech sounds accurately. Children become interested in rhyming and other playful variations on the sounds of words and begin to understand the basis of sound similarity in rhyming words. And, by around six years of age, children learn to divide words into syllables and sentences into words. These abilities are believed to be important prerequisites for reading success (Watson, 1984).

Vocabulary growth Throughout the early school years, children increase the size and range of their vocabularies. Between the ages of seven and eleven, they gain improved comprehension of relationships of space, time, and logic (Owens, 1984). In about second grade, children also move from using single-word definitions with individual meanings to complex definitions with socially shared meanings (Wehren, DeLisi, & Arnold, 1981). And between five and seven years of age, most children become more able to interpret figurative expressions such as "hit the road."

Reflection on language use Children in the early school years increase in ability to judge the grammatical acceptability of sentences (Owens, 1984) and to react separately to the content and structure of language. This ability to reflect on language use is called **metalinguistic awareness.**

Complexity of language Owens (1984) has asserted that the most important linguistic growth in the early school years involves the growing subtlety and complexity of language. The conversational abilities of children in the early

Vocabulary growth is facilitated when children learn new words and concepts within a context encouraging relationship with the environment. These children later walked in the neighborhood to find arches and other structural components.

school years expand. They are increasingly able to clarify messages and to be successful in adapting their speech to the needs of different listeners. By the age of seven, most children can effectively use indirect requests (e.g., saying, "It sure is a cold day to walk to school," to a parent who is getting in the car to drive to work). At about the same time, language rituals assume importance in asserting interpersonal control, as shown by the following exchange:

David   I'm first.
Chris   No, I called it.
David   Changes. My turn, forever no changes, forever no changes.

David invoked "changes" and then guaranteed his position with "forever no changes" to which there could be "forever no changes."

Appropriate adult assistance   Schiefelbusch (1984) has reviewed research findings and concluded that adults can assist children in the early school years in acquiring competence in communication. To be effective, adult assistance can be in the form of **semantically contingent responding**, defined as relating adult speech to the meaning of the preceding child speech; creating environments for communicating; and instruction. By responding directly or indirectly to children's talk, adults allow children to determine topics and take the initiative in communication. According to Schiefelbusch (1984), it is also important for adults to provide social contexts with both peers and adults where children can be active, successful participants in meaningful communication. And, although instruction is important, it is often most salient if indirect, as when children model, imitate, and respond to adult storytelling and role playing.

Language and Reading

Children's language skills are one important factor determining their success in reading. Hillerich and Johnson (1981) have related five language skills to success in early reading: auditory discrimination, listening comprehension, oral language expression, vocabulary comprehension, and context use. Each of these skills is described below, using the framework provided by Hillerich and Johnson (1981).

Auditory discrimination Auditory discrimination is the ability to hear differences of sounds in words. Most children can hear the difference between similar pairs of words such as *bat/cat* and *wing/ring;* if they cannot, specific work on this skill is helpful. Auditory discrimination is important in oral communication and in reading.

Listening comprehension Listening comprehension is the ability to listen to a brief literary passage and recall details from it. Children who cannot understand literary language at the oral level have difficulty with printed materials in early reading. Literary language differs from oral language in that it is direct and structured rather than informal and unstructured. Children who have been read to are likely to be familiar with literary language, but other children need many experiences with literature in the early school years.

Oral language expression Oral language expression is the ability to give descriptive, amplified language in response to being shown an action picture.

A puppet production of a classic tale reinforces listening comprehension, oral language expression, and vocabulary comprehension for performers and audience.

Research reviewed by Hillerich and Johnson (1981) has indicated that children are unlikely to succeed in reading if they speak in fragments, use two-word sentences, give literal ideas with no amplification, and label rather then explain. Children with these characteristics of oral language need considerable experience in talking before being asked to deal with printed materials.

Vocabulary comprehension Vocabulary **comprehension** is the ability to name common objects. By so doing, children show that they have given meanings to words that are commonly used in school situations. Children who have difficulty in vocabulary comprehension benefit from opportunities to discuss meaningful objects, experiences, and events.

Context use Context use is the ability to apply an understanding of language to anticipate what makes sense in a given situation. For instance, children who use context appropriately are puzzled if someone says, "The cat is the chair." Using context involves using the sense of the other words in a sentence to predict what comes next or to interpret an unknown word. Context use in oral language provides a basis for applying that skill to printed materials as an aid to reading. Children who have difficulty in context use need to develop this skill through various exercises. For example, an adult can pause briefly in reading to let a child supply a word that makes sense.

Children who have developed these five fundamental language skills are likely to find success in early reading experiences. Children without the **readiness skills for reading** need instruction in and experiences with those language skills.

Bilingualism

Many children learn one language and later learn another, either formally or informally. Other children learn two or more languages simultaneously in the early childhood years because they grow up in **bilingual** families or communities. A considerable body of research has investigated the effects on cognitive development and school achievement of learning two languages rather than one in childhood.

Early studies of the relationship between bilingualism and cognition reported that bilingualism stood in the way of cognitive development (Saville-Troike, 1982). However, these early studies did not control for socioeconomic status and often used tests in the bilingual children's weaker language. These early studies have now been discounted by most researchers, according to Saville-Troike (1982).

Recent research evidence is mixed on the effect of second-language learning on cognitive development and school achievement, especially if exposure to the second language begins after four or five years of age. The variability in research findings has been partially explained by a distinction first made by Lambert (1975) between "additive" and "subtractive" bilingualism. **Additive bilingualism** takes place when children are members of the majority social class, speak the majority language, and receive positive feedback from families and communities for continued use of the first language. In cases of additive bilingualism, the second language is usually successfully added with no negative effects on first-language competence. Examples of additive bilingualism are Canadian programs to teach French to English-speaking children. In contrast, **subtractive bilingualism** takes place when children are members of minority groups and do not receive support outside of their families for continued use of the first language. In cases of subtractive bilingualism, the second language is often not successfully added and there may also be lack of growth in first-language competence. Examples of subtractive bilingualism are U.S. and British programs to teach English to minority-language children.

Given the mix of results of second-language learning—from highly positive to negative (Lambert, 1975; Saville-Troike, 1982)—any problems with cognitive development and academic success seem unlikely to be due to second-language learning *per se;* rather, such problems may have their basis in social status, identity, and attitudinal variables. Saville-Troike (1982) has said that the school success of minority group children, now in situations of subtractive bilingualism, depends on a change in the negative feedback they are receiving about their native languages and cultures.

THE CONTINUING ROLE OF PLAY

Play continues to have an important role in the lives of children in the early school years. Research reviewed by Hoot (1984) affirms the importance of play opportunities and relates them to higher levels of thinking, problem solving, and school performance. Pellegrini (1980) has asserted that young children's ability to play predicts achievement, and that skills used in higher modes of play are *required* in reading and writing.

Research evidence notwithstanding, parents and others tend to devalue play. If children are observed at play in school, parents often ask questions that reflect their disapproval of time spent in tasks that do not look serious. Hoot (1984) observed that opportunities for play are rapidly disappearing from the lives of children in the early school years. Pressure is placed by media and parents to raise standardized achievement test scores by enrolling children in school programs with few play opportunities.

This section views the important role of play from several perspectives, involving creativity, humor, gender differences in play, and computers and thinking. These varied perspectives illustrate the vital role of play in the development of children in the early school years.

Creativity

When children play, they have opportunities to develop and exercise their creativity. **Creativity** involves fluent, flexible, and original thought. Creative individuals are able to generate novel ideas and interesting associations when presented with new problems. Their thought processes expand outward rather than converging on one conventional response. According to theories of intelligence

Play continues to have an important role in the lives of children in the early school years.

such as Structure of Intellect (SOI), creativity is one of several distinct types of intelligence that can and should be nurtured in the early school years and beyond (Guilford, 1967; Meeker, 1969, 1981a, 1981b). Many experts believe that the creativity of the next generation will be vital in solving the challenges of our future. Research on creative processes gives insights that can help assure children of psychologically safe environments in which to develop creativity.

Some types of school environments seem to be more effective than others in encouraging creativity. Thomas and Berk (1981) studied informal, intermediate, and formal types of first- and second-grade classrooms over a school year. They found that school settings rated as intermediate on an informal-to-formal continuum led to the greatest growth in creativity.

Attitudes of adults are important in supporting or inhibiting creativity. Research has found that adults tend to reward children who are courteous and to punish children who are creative and outspoken. Bachtold (1983) reported that teachers describe *consideration for others* as their most desired behavioral goal for children. They had low regard for certain characteristics of creative children, identified by terms such as *talkative, becomes preoccupied with tasks,* and *spirited in disagreement.* By the middle childhood years, Bachtold (1983) found that most children have internalized attitudes similar to those expressed by teachers. Asked to name undesirable qualities on an inventory, children most often selected *always asking questions, likes to work alone, talkative,* and *emo-*

tional. The creative processes cannot develop if adults and children limit themselves with such attitudes.

A pair of related studies shows that creativity can be enhanced through play opportunities. Researchers (Pepler & Ross, 1981) provided two types of play experiences: convergent (tending to direct play to a single solution; for example, puzzle solving) and divergent/creative (facilitating a variety of play activities). After the play experiences, children in the early school years were presented with convergent and divergent problem-solving tasks. Children with divergent/creative play experiences performed better than those with convergent experiences on divergent problem-solving tasks. Even though the divergent tasks were different from the earlier play experiences, children who had played creatively were flexible and unique in their responses. This flexibility even seemed to transfer to convergent tasks; children with creative play experiences were more flexible in redirecting their attention from ineffective strategies when solving convergent problems.

Humor

Researchers consider humor as a subset of the broader category of play (McGhee, 1984). **Humor** is considered to be a form of intellectual play—play with ideas. Incongruous ideas (those that are somehow inconsistent with children's knowledge or experience) are a necessary but not sufficient condition for humor.

McGhee (1984) has described four stages of humor development, parallel to stages of cognitive development. His description is based on over a decade of individual and collaborative research on children's humor.

The first three stages of humor begin before the early school years. Stage 1 involves **incongruous actions toward objects** and appears in the context of pretend play with objects in the second year of life. Children playfully substitute one object for another and laugh at having created a set of conditions known to be at odds with reality. Stage 2 humor centers on **incongruous labeling of objects and events** and takes place later in the second year when children are developing new language skills. Children may laugh uproariously at calling a mouth an eye or a car an airplane. Most of the humor of two- and three-year-old children involves some combination of stages 1 and 2. Even in the early school years, humor at stages 1 and 2 continues to be enjoyed.

At about three years of age, children experience a new form of humor. Stage 3 humor is built on **conceptual incongruity.** When language begins to be used to refer to classes of objects with common characteristics, children find it humorous to alter the defining features of the concept. Instead of just imagining a dog to be a cow or calling it a cow, children in stage 3 may find humor in talking about milking a dog or having a dog "moo." Distortion of familiar sights and sounds, including rhyming and nonsense words, are sources of humor at this stage. Language is often important in stage 3 humor, but much humor is also based on violations of perceptual appearances of things. Seeing someone with a large nose or watching clowns be clumsy at things even children do easily can be humorous to young children.

BOX 13.4   **STRATEGIES FOR FACILITATING DEVELOPMENT: NOURISHING CREATIVITY**

Bachtold (1983) has summarized results of research on how adults can nourish young children's creativity.

Autonomy is such a powerful component in nourishing creative behavior that it is important to be cautious in restricting freedom. Setting limits should be evaluated in terms of their being absolutely essential. Developing independence in judgment should begin early. Be a model for decision making and independent thinking. Talk about some decisions you are considering and alternatives you are weighing. Promote discussions about decisions made by characters in films and stories, and by people in real life. Encourage children to think about other ways the decisions might have been made and the effects there might have been.

Independence in making choices will inevitably be accompanied by occasional errors in judgment. So be careful not to belittle first efforts, and provide strong emotional support, especially when children's plans do not work out as they expected. *What children learn by their mistakes could be as valuable as what they learn by their successes.*

To balance freedom in thinking and judgment, a sense of responsibility is essential. Children need to have responsibilities that they must take care of routinely. They should be made responsible for their course of action in all areas where their personal choice is possible (e.g., on what to wear, choice of gifts for others). Similarly in interpersonal situations, encourage them to work out their relationships with peers without interference from adults.

Talking at children comes easily; listening to children is a developed talent. Do a lot of uncritical listening. Be understanding of their frustrations, for this will make them feel that their actions are important. Provide opportunities for uninterrupted one-to-one time with an adult. Share your feelings and thoughts and encourage them to do the same.

Imagination can be stimulated further by asking such questions as, "How many ways can you think of to (solve this problem)?" "What do you think might have caused (this problem)?" "How many other uses can you think of for (this object)?" "How might we change (this object) to make it better?" "Let's suppose electricity won't work in our town for the next week. What would happen?" (pp. 4–5)

In a series of studies, McGhee (1984) found that incongruities need to occur in a fantasy context in order to produce humor; the same incongruities in a reality context interfere with humor. For example, if a clown had an exaggerated nose, children would perhaps laugh. If, however, a person on the street had a realistic ear in the usual position of her nose, humor would likely be replaced by discomfort.

The humor of young children changes dramatically when they realize that words sometimes have ambiguous meanings. At stage 4, children find **humor in multiple meanings**. Even if they know two meanings of a word, children are usually unable to keep both meanings in mind until they begin to attain concrete operational thinking toward the end of the early school years. Riddles and knock-knock jokes such as the following become popular sources of humor at stage 4:

What did the rug say to the floor?
      Don't move. I've got you covered.

Knock, knock.
      Who's there?
Lettuce.
      Lettuce who?
Lettuce in; it's cold out here.

Children also develop their own plays on words at stage 4.

McGhee (1984) reported on research to find out whether the degree of cognitive challenge contributes to the level of humor experienced. The researchers developed jokes based on violations of the concepts of conservation and class inclusion. Jokes similar to the following were told to young children.

Suzy wanted to eat an apple for snack. Her mother asked if she wanted it cut into four or eight pieces. Suzy said, "Four. I'm not hungry enough for eight."

Researchers found that first-grade children who had acquired conservation and class inclusion concepts found the jokes funnier than both first graders who had not acquired the concepts and older children who had probably understood the concepts for some time. There seems to be an optimal amount of cognitive effort that maximizes humor.

Gender Differences in Play

From the age of three on, boys and girls play in distinctively different ways (Fagot & Kronsberg, 1982). Girls engage in more doll and domestic play, art activities, and dancing. Toys intended for girls encourage imitative play and the learning of existing social roles. Boys, in contrast, engage in more play with transportation toys, woodworking materials, and blocks. Boys are more apt to be involved in rough-and-tumble play and verbal and physical aggression. And boys are also significantly more likely than girls to take physical risks (Ginsburg & Miller, 1982). Toys intended for boys encourage exploration and flexible use of materials. With few changes over time, these findings have been replicated many times since the 1930s in observational studies of children in natural settings (Fagot & Kronsberg, 1982).

As early as three years of age and continuing through childhood, most children play in same-gender groups. Children consequently receive social reactions mainly from their peers of the same gender. Research shows that peers tend to give children more positive feedback when they engage in gender-typical behaviors and more negative feedback when they engage in behaviors typical of the other gender (Fagot & Kronsberg, 1982). Peer groups seem to be conservative in their gender-role expectations, and boys are more likely than girls to conform to toy and activity stereotypes (Eisenberg, Murray, & Hite, 1982).

Computers and Thinking

Play (or work) with computers may change the way children think. To illustrate philosophical and psychological questions raised by computer use, Turkle (1984) reported the following vignette about Robert, age 7. Robert had become upset after a game with Merlin, a computer toy that plays tic-tac-toe.

> Robert throws Merlin into the sand in anger and frustration. "Cheater. I hope your brains break." He is overheard by Craig and Greg, aged six and eight, who sense that this may be a good moment to reclaim Merlin for themselves. They salvage the by now very sandy toy and take it upon themselves to set Robert straight.
>
> Craig: "Merlin doesn't know if it cheats. It won't know if it breaks. It doesn't know if you break it, Robert. It's not alive."
>
> Greg: "Someone taught Merlin to play. But he doesn't know if he wins or loses."
>
> Robert: "Yes, he does know if he loses. He makes different noises."
>
> Greg: "No, stupid. It's smart. It's smart enough to make the right kinds of noises. But it doesn't really know if it loses. That's how you can cheat it. It doesn't know you are cheating. And when it cheats it doesn't even know it's cheating."
>
> Jenny, six, interrupts with disdain. "Greg, to cheat you have to know you are cheating. Knowing is part of cheating" (pp. 29–30).

Two girls discuss their strategy for computer interaction with a university student volunteer.

Turkle was fascinated by the image of four young children arguing about the psychological status of a machine, questioning whether it has intentions or feelings. In observations of over two hundred young children, Turkle (1984) found that computers cause children to talk about things that they would not ordinarily discuss: the limits of machines, for example, or the uniqueness of the human mind.

Turkle (1984) has identified two stages in young children's relationships with computers. The first, the metaphysical stage, centers on children's concern about whether computers think, feel, and are alive. Children note that computers have lifelike properties: they talk, win at games, know facts, and have intelligence and memory. But computers also have properties that make them seem not alive. Children wrestle with complex ideas such as, "Do machines think like people?" and "Have people always thought like computers?"

The second stage, the mastery stage, centers on children's desire to be competent and effective in using computers (Turkle, 1984). Papert (1980) has contrasted two approaches to using computers with young children at the mastery stage. The first and, in Papert's opinion, less desirable approach is computer aided instruction (CAI). In CAI the computer is used as an electronic workbook to program children to gain certain kinds of specified knowledge. The second, more creative approach turns the tables and allows children to program the computer. Programming a computer means communicating to it in a language

As testimony to his high interest in computer interaction, this beginning first grader shows the "computer" that he built during free time. The keyboard is painstakingly reproduced—because he wanted it so and it was meaningful to him, not because anyone required such effort.

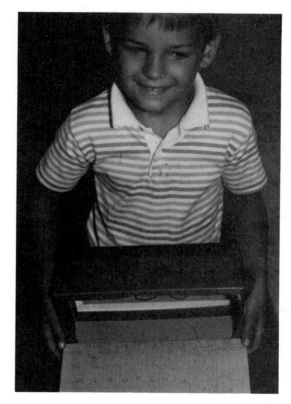

that children and machines both understand. Papert and his colleagues have written a computer language called LOGO to simplify this process of communication between young children and computers. Papert (1980) has described the advantages of young children being the programmers rather than the programmed:

> The child, even at preschool ages, is in control: The child programs the computer. And in teaching the computer how to think, children embark on an exploration about how they themselves think. The experience can be heady: Thinking about thinking turns the child into an epistemologist, an experience not even shared by most adults. (p. 19)

Papert has recommended that children be given the same kind of access to computers as to pencils so that they can gain this sense of mastery over a piece of the most modern and powerful technology. With opportunities to play with computers, children create their own programs, use computer word processing capabilities to write stories and reports, and match wits with the computer in interactive games. Instead of believing that they are right or wrong in terms of the absolute judgment of adults, children begin to ask how they can improve (''debug'') what they have done.

However, not all early childhood educators share the enthusiasm of Turkle and Papert about the positive potential of computers in the lives of young children. Brady and Hill (1984) have urged a skeptical approach lest computers take the place of other essential life experiences. The point is well taken. It seems appropriate that computer play not supplant other kinds of play but instead find a place as one of a variety of opportunities to enhance cognitive development.

EFFECTS OF EARLY EDUCATION PROGRAMS

The term **early education programs**, as used in this chapter, refers to group educational experiences before the age of compulsory school attendance. The numbers of young children enrolled in these early education programs have increased steadily in the past decades (U.S. Bureau of the Census, 1982). Many children enter these programs when they are four years of age or younger because their parents anticipate favorable long-term consequences for intellectual or social development. Whether there are such consequences has been widely debated, and now longitudinal data can give the debate an empirical foundation. These data indicate that high-quality early education programs positively affect the development of individuals at least into adolescence. The data allow cautious optimism about the possibility of making positive changes in the lives of young children by providing appropriate early education programs.

In this section, data are presented from three sources: Project Head Start, the Consortium for Longitudinal Studies, and Brigham Young University. The first two sources provide data about the effects of early education on low-income children. The third source provides data about the effects of early education on educationally advantaged children.

Programs for Low-Income Children

Since the 1960s, the United States has instituted early education programs designed to equalize educational opportunity for children from low-income families. A government-sponsored educational effort started in 1965, Project Head Start is the best-known of the programs for low-income children, and continues to receive funding. Both Project Head Start and a consortium of twelve other programs begun in the 1960s have collected data on program participants, some of whom are now young adults. It is important to evaluate the influence of early education programs on their lives.

Project Head Start   In 1965, Head Start funds were sent to community action agencies around the country to establish summer programs for low-income children. These funds were part of President Lyndon Johnson's War on Poverty, and there was optimism that special early education programs would eliminate the disadvantages that low-income children face in school. Head Start was a six- to eight-week summer program in the years from 1965 to 1968, and served over one-half million children during that time. However, it became clear that one summer was a short time for intervention, and the transition from summer to year-round programs took place from 1969 to 1972. Planned curricular variations were also introduced in the late 1960s and early 1970s. During the presidential administration of Ronald Reagan, Head Start was one of few federal programs retained in the "safety net" of social programs for low-income families (Hubbell, 1983).

Summarizing the findings of Head Start research reported in 1,400 documents, Hubbell (1983) has concluded that participation in Head Start has positive effects on children's social competence. Head Start children score higher than controls on some measures of task orientation, and task orientation correlates with cognitive test scores. Head Start children are rated as showing levels of social development comparable to the general elementary school population and have been found to be more sociable and assertive than their low-income

Research shows that Head Start children perform better than matched peers on measures of later school success.

peers without Head Start experience. The self-esteem of Head Start children has been found to decline once they enter public school, but children from some types of Head Start curricula continue to show higher levels of social participation through the second grade.

Research reviewed by Hubbell (1983) has shown mixed findings on the persistence of academic and intellectual gains produced during the Head Start program year. About half of the relevant studies have indicated that Head Start children maintain achievement test differences into the later school years and the remainder of the studies show that these differences are not maintained. However, research results have demonstrated that Head Start children perform better than their low-income peers on global measures of school success, such as graduating from high school, placement in regular classrooms rather than special education, staying in school, and passing each grade. Research results have also revealed that Head Start children display more reflective and less impulsive cognitive styles than do comparable low-income children without Head Start experience. Participation in Head Start also improves language development, especially in the case of bilingual children. Children's achievement is positively related to parental involvement in Head Start.

Research has also demonstrated that needed nutrition services, health screening, immunizations, dental care, and health treatment are effectively provided for Head Start children (Hubbell, 1983). Because of the nutritional supplementation provided, Head Start children are more likely to be of normal height and weight and to perform well on physical tests, and are less likely to be absent from school than comparable low-income children. Head Start children improve in hemoglobin levels, dental health, general physical development, and motor control during the Head Start year.

Finally, research has shown that some positive benefits of Head Start participation extend to families of children and to their communities (Hubbell, 1983). Parents increase in feelings of general life satisfaction and self-confidence in relation to their involvement in their children's Head Start program. Head Start programs help families to make contact with social services provided in the community and may lead to increased parental involvement in public schools.

Consortium for Longitudinal Studies The Consortium for Longitudinal Studies was formed in 1975 to answer questions about whether early education programs had measurable long-term effects on low-income children. The Consortium is made up of all but one of the major large-scale studies of early education begun in the 1960s: the Early Training Project, Perry Preschool Program, Gordon Parent Education Infant and Toddler Program, five University of Illinois approaches, the Louisville Experiment, the Harlem Study, Verbal Interaction Project, the Micro-Social Learning Environment, New Haven Project, the Philadelphia Study, and the Institute for Developmental Studies Program (Condry, 1983).

In all of these programs, children in the program (the experimental group) were carefully matched with children who had similar backgrounds but who did not enroll in early education programs. The development of the nonenrolled low-income children—the control group—could then be compared with that of children enrolled in early education programs.

Consortium participants cooperated in collecting and analyzing information about children in both experimental and control groups. They sent their original data for reanalysis, developed common standards for collection of follow-up data, and pooled their original and follow-up data for statistical analysis. The independence of the separate studies makes the findings highly reliable; they are similar statistically to multiple, independent replications (Lazar, 1983).

The Consortium has been able to summarize the best available information about the effects of early education programs on low-income children. The Consortium has provided convincing, ecologically valid evidence that these programs have been effective in enhancing the lives of low-income children through adolescence and young adulthood (Condry, 1983).

Research compiled by the Consortium has substantiated the conclusion that appropriate early education programs increase the intelligence test scores of low-income children. Data show that program children had a 5.80-point IQ advantage over control children at the start of first grade. Furthermore, the gains in IQ scores of low-income children enrolled in early education programs have remained significant for up to three or four years after the program (Royce, Darlington, & Murray, 1983).

The use of intelligence test scores in early education programs is controversial, but these scores do predict scholastic achievement and also provide a uniform basis for the assessment of cognitive growth. Consortium researchers have said that cultural bias against some children is unlikely because the children's backgrounds were relatively homogeneous: 94 percent of the children were black and nearly all were low-income (Royce, Darlington, & Murray, 1983).

Follow-up research by the Consortium has shown that children enrolled in early education programs have increased achievement motivation, school competence, and educational attainment, when compared to similar low-income children. In 1976, when children were between ten and nineteen years of age, they were asked, "Tell something you've done that made you feel proud of yourself." Program children were far more apt to give achievement-related answers than were control children. Program children tended to respond with school or work achievements, while controls tended to respond with examples of altruistic behavior or to not give a response. The effect on program participants was especially strong among girls between fifteen and nineteen years of age. Mothers of program children were also found to have higher aspirations for their children than did control mothers and than did program children themselves (Royce, Darlington, & Murray, 1983).

Consortium data have demonstrated that early education programs improve later competence in school. Progression through the school system was examined as a measure of children's competence in adapting to the role requirements of the school. Two categories of failure to progress were interpreted as evidence that students were not meeting school expectations: placement in special education classes and retention in grade. In analysis at the seventh-grade level (eight programs) and at the time of high school graduation (four programs), program children were significantly less likely to have been placed in special education or to be retained in grade. At the seventh-grade level, the average rate of special education placement was 14.5 percent for program children and 34.9 percent for control children. The average rate of retention in grade was 19.8 percent for program children and 32.0 percent for control children. Findings were similar in the projects that had records through the end of high school at the time of the 1980 follow-up. Program children were also significantly more likely to have completed high school. When background factors were controlled, the program/control difference for the median project was 15 percent (Royce, Darlington, & Murray, 1983).

Data available to the Consortium were analyzed to ascertain whether different types of programs had different effects. There were no differences in school outcomes between early education programs taught in centers and those taught in homes. And later school outcomes showed no significant differences related to the type of curriculum used. All curricula were successful in reducing school failure and all of the curricula used in Consortium programs were superior to no early education program at all. An analysis of data indicates that program effectiveness can be enhanced by a combination of four components:

- ☐ Intervention begun as early as possible
- ☐ Services provided to parents as well as to the child
- ☐ Frequent home visits
- ☐ Involvement of parents in the instruction of the child
- ☐ As few children per teacher as possible (Royce, Darlington, & Murray, 1983, p. 442).

Lazar (1983) has expanded these findings to draw three implications. First, early education programs pay for themselves by reducing costs for special education service. Second, close contact between home and school is more important than usually realized. And, third, the search for the "perfect" early childhood curriculum is probably futile. According to Lazar (1983), many curricula are workable as long as teachers have goals and try to achieve their goals.

Programs for Advantaged Children

A longitudinal study at Brigham Young University has been designed to investigate the effect of school enrollment on "advantaged" children between forty-two months and five years of age (Larsen, Draper, & Hite, 1984). "Advantaged" children are defined as those whose parents have a high level of educational attainment and middle-income status. Until this time, research with middle-income children usually has focused on curricular comparisons rather than on the long-term influences on children.

Children were chosen randomly to participate in the Brigham Young University early education program. The program children were compared to children who had also applied to attend, had not been randomly chosen, and had not enrolled in another school or day-care center.

The main finding from the first complete analysis of the data was that

Data show that children under five benefit from positive school experiences.

scores on intelligence tests related to early school enrollment. The program children had a mean IQ of 131.7 and the comparison children had a mean IQ of 127.1. This finding of immediate IQ gains from attendance in early education programs is similar to what has been found in studies of low-income children. The researchers speculate that school enrollment may create unique benefits in the years before age five, regardless of the quality of home environments (Larsen, Draper, & Hite, 1984). As the researchers follow these children through the school years, data will become available about the persistence of the gains made by program children.

The availability of data on the effects of early education on advantaged children has not slowed the flow of strong rhetoric on whether young children should be educated in schools as well as at home. Burton White (1978, 1985), director of the Center for Parent Education and former director of the Harvard Preschool Program, has asserted that most early education programs are failures and that most children would do better without them (Donovan, 1984). In an interview, White said, "The gap between what you can get in a substitute care system and the ideal is just too great" (Donovan, 1984). White believes that home is where advantaged children under five are most likely to get what they need: "Love lavished on them, prompt attention, ready access a majority of the time to someone who loves them" (Donovan, 1984). Data from Brigham Young University and elsewhere will continue to provide information about the merits of school-based education for children under the age of five.

SCHOOL SUCCESS

In the early school years, a key factor influencing the development of a sense of industry, as described in Chapter 11, is school success. School success, in turn, is affected by social and intellectual competence, motivation, and memory.

Social and Intellectual Competence

One of the most interesting definitions of social and intellectual competence in the early school years was made by researchers at Harvard University (White & Watts, 1973), when they attempted to answer the question, "What is human competence in six-year-old children?" The researchers compiled a list of abilities that seemed to distinguish children high in overall competence from those low in competence.

The researchers began the study with a broad sample of four hundred children, aged three, four, and five. Based on extensive, independent observations by fifteen staff members and the children's teachers, and also on children's performance on the Wechsler and other tests, forty-one children were designated as either high or low in competence. These children were then observed at school and at home each week for eight months. At the end of the observation period, the most and least competent children (thirteen of each) were identified. Through intensive discussion, the researchers noted the abilities that seemed to distinguish the two groups of children. White and Watts (1973) found that children judged to be highly competent were more likely than others to be able to:

1. Get and maintain adult attention in positive ways;
2. Use adults to help meet goals;
3. Communicate feelings to adults and peers;
4. Both direct and follow peers;
5. Compete with peers;
6. Show pride in accomplishments;
7. Take adult roles;
8. Show linguistic competence;
9. Show intellectual competence:
   note discrepancies
   anticipate consequences
   deal with symbols and concepts
   take others' perspectives
   make interesting associations
   make and execute multistep plans
   attend to two things simultaneously.

In the early school years, these social and intellectual competencies related to successful functioning, as defined by teachers and independent observers.

Motivation

To be successful in school and at home, children must want to master the environment. This internal desire to be effective, combined with characteristics such as curiosity and enjoyment of learning, is called **intrinsic motivation**. Three theories—cognitive, competence, and attribution—have been proposed to explain the conditions that influence the development of intrinsic motivation in children (Gottfried, 1983).

Cognitive theorists believe that intrinsic motivation comes about when children try to understand new experiences. Experiences that are optimally different (not too strange and not too familiar) cause children to explore, investigate, and ponder. Cognitive theorists believe that intrinsic motivation is exhibited by children exposed to an interesting, varied environment. They also believe that unique features of the environment receive attention from each child because optimal cognitive conflict takes place only in relationship to a given child's current level of understanding. According to Piaget and other cognitive theorists, children's actions to reduce the intellectual conflict caused by novel experiences can result in advancements in cognitive development.

Competence theorists build on the work of White (1959), who proposed that children have a strong desire to be effective in interacting with the environment. White believed that behaviors such as persistence and exploration are indicators that children have a motivation to be competent. According to the research of competence theorists, children who achieve mastery feel effective and this sense of effectiveness is an intrinsic motivator (Harter, 1978).

Attribution theorists focus on children's perceptions of the causes of their behavior. The research of these theorists shows that intrinsic motivation is likely to be strong when children attribute the cause of their behavior to their own effort, skills, or selection of goals. Attribution theorists also have found that intrinsic motivation tends to be weak when children attribute the cause of their behavior to external factors such as adult demands or rewards (Lepper, 1983).

The three theories overlap in several ways. First, in none of the theories are children viewed as being either high or low in intrinsic motivation across circumstances. Rather, children's intrinsic motivation is thought to vary depending on conditions influencing cognitive conflict, competence, and/or attribution (Gottfried, 1983).

Second, research using various theoretical perspectives shows that the effects of rewards on intrinsic motivation are complex and depend on the meaning of the rewards to children (Gottfried, 1983). Rewards that make children feel competent and good about choosing activities increase later intrinsic motivation and lead children to choose similar activities again. Verbal praise encourages intrinsic motivation if it attracts children's attention to their mastery. However, some rewards have been found to cause intrinsic motivation to decline. Children lose interest in activities if they perceive that the main reason for participation is to gain rewards rather than to meet their interests and goals; if rewards give them little information about their competence; and also if they have little choice about participation (Deci & Ryan, 1982). Children seem to react to the distinction between the informational aspect of rewards (getting rewards because they do well) and the controlling aspect (getting rewards because they do as requested).

Third and finally, research indicates that children's successes with challenging experiences may produce intrinsic motivation from all three of the theoretical perspectives: cognitive intrinsic motivation, feelings of effectiveness, and attributions of mastery. Gottfried (1983) has recommended that early childhood educators attempt to develop all three aspects of intrinsic motivation. (See Box 13.5.)

Memory

Success in school and in other settings frequently depends on how well children are able to remember information and concepts. Research has demonstrated that the use of memory strategies follows a developmental progression (Brown & De Loache, 1983; Fishbein, 1984) and that children remember meaningful information better than information that is not meaningful (Brown & De Loache, 1983).

BOX 13.5   STRATEGIES FOR FACILITATING DEVELOPMENT: STIMULATING INTRINSIC MOTIVATION

Gottfried (1983) has suggested that teachers of children in the early school years stimulate intrinsic motivation in the following ways:

1. use incongruity, surprise, and novelty to introduce new concepts;
2. provide children with the opportunity to investigate individual areas of interest and curiosity;
3. give children choices about their preferred activities; and
4. establish an atmosphere of trust so that children are not anxious about asking questions or making mistakes. (pp. 70–71)

Teachers stimulate intrinsic motivation when they establish an atmosphere of trust in which children can ask questions.

Citing the research of Istomina in the Soviet Union, Brown and De Loache (1983) have described a developmental sequence in the sophistication of memory strategies used by children. In this research, children were asked to remember a list of items to be purchased with play money at a play store. The teacher slowly named five items and asked individual children to go to the next room to buy them. Researchers found that few three- and four-year-old children seemed to use specific devices to remember what items to buy. However, between four and five years of age, children's approaches seemed to undergo a qualitative change. Many five- and six-year-olds used active rehearsal to remember the grocery list and tested themselves between rooms. And six- and seven-year-old children used even more complex strategies, often trying to form logical connections between items on the list by rearranging their order. Fishbein (1984) has reviewed research that supports the findings of Brown and De Loache (1983). In addition, Fishbein found that children as young as four can use memory strategies if specifically asked to do so.

The perceived relevance of information makes a difference in how much children remember. Brown and De Loache (1983) contrasted recall in the grocery-store play setting with recall of similar items in a laboratory setting. Recall was superior in the game situation, with younger children remembering twice as much under those circumstances.

CULTURE AND SCHOOL SUCCESS

Cultural background influences the school success of children in the early school years. John Ogbu (1974; 1982) has presented evidence from anthropological research in the United States that childrearing practices influence educability and, in turn, are influenced by larger societal forces. Gearhart and Hall (1982) have conducted research on the consequences for school success of cultural variations in language use. Witkin and his colleagues have explored the effects of differences in cognitive style. Taken together, this body of research provides important information about the context in which children develop in the early school years.

Childrearing and Education

John Ogbu's (1974; 1982) anthropological research in the United States has caused him to question the often unexamined assumption that high unemployment and poverty among minority cultural groups are due to inadequate education which, in turn, arises from inadequate childrearing practices. Ogbu has argued instead that minority childrearing practices have been directly influenced by the reality of the kinds of economic opportunities open to parents. Figure 13.1 (Ogbu, 1974, p. 14) illustrates the relationship observed by Ogbu between economic and employment outcomes and beliefs about the efficacy of education. Ogbu (1982) has asserted that it is wrong to judge how effectively one cultural group's childrearing practices produce competencies in children,

FIGURE 13.1

(From *The Next Generation: An Ethnography of Education in an Urban Neighborhood* [p. 14] by J. U. Ogbu, 1974, New York: Academic Press. Copyright 1974 by Academic Press. Reprinted by permission.)

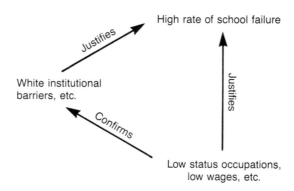

as compared to another group's practices, unless children in both groups are reared to expect the same adult realities.

Ogbu (1982) has shown that adults in many minority cultural groups experience marginal existences, characterized by unstable, uninteresting jobs, low wages, and little social credit. Adults therefore often devote significant amounts of energy to developing a variety of strategies for exploiting scarce social resources. Even though parents may emphasize the importance of education, they also tell children in direct and indirect ways that, even with education, it is difficult to make it in the white world (Ogbu, 1974). According to Ogbu, any efforts to change the adaptation of minority children to the school system must take into account the theories of adults from given groups about how they succeed in their environment. Ogbu is pessimistic about the probability of changing childrearing practices and adaptation to the schools unless the underlying social and economic realities change for members of minority cultural groups.

Cultural Variation in Language Use

Gearhart and Hall (1982) have conducted research on the possible consequences for acquisition of school skills of cultural variation in language use. The researchers have concluded that semantic mismatches between children's meanings of words and authors' meanings of words can impede the reading process. They have also suggested that different cultures promote different levels of interest in reflecting upon language use and motivations for behavior. The following examples of teacher activities from a first-grade reading series show what schools expect of children's ability to reflect on language and motivations:

- ☐ find rhyming words
- ☐ find synonyms
- ☐ explain why
- ☐ explain your feelings

Gearhart and Hall (1982) have said that most schools expect the ability to make these kinds of interpretations of language and motivation. Children who come to school having had experience with this terminology and with these uses for words will be at an advantage. Children from other cultural groups, using language differently, may be victims of home/school mismatch.

Cognitive Style

Consistent differences in cognitive style characterize children from different cultural groups. Understanding cognitive style is an important aspect of understanding development.

The research on cognitive style is built on early work by Witkin and his colleagues (Witkin, Dyke, Faterson, Goodenough, & Karp, 1962). These researchers proposed that people vary in their ability to focus on an object as separate from its context or "field." Various tests have been devised to assess the degree to which people are able to differentiate their perceptions. In one, the Rod and Frame Test, subjects are seated in a darkened room and are asked to move to upright a tilted, illuminated rod that is located within an illuminated, tilted square frame. Some people line up the rod with the tilted frame, indicating that the frame influences their perception of the rod in it. Other people bring the rod into an upright position, indicating that they are able to perceive the rod apart from the frame. In another test, the Embedded Figures Test, subjects are required to find a simple design, previously seen, in a complex figure. The researchers have found that psychological development progresses from less differentiated perceptions to more differentiated perceptions. They also have found a consistency in performance for individuals across ages that indicates their **cognitive style**. Some people's perceptions are dominated by the organization of the field in which objects are contained; these people are called **field-dependent**. Some people's perceptions focus on individual parts of the field; these people are called **field-independent**.

Research indicates that cultural differences in socialization are related to differences in cognitive style (Witkin, Price-Williams, Bertini, Christiansen, Oltman, Ramirez, & Van Meel, 1974). Children tend to be field-dependent when families stress responsibility and obedience and when cultural groups emphasize adherence to authority and social conformity. Children tend to be field-independent when families stress individual decision making and independence and when cultural groups emphasize autonomy.

Research evidence shows that cognitive style is consistent within individuals across the perceptual, cognitive, and psychosocial areas (Witkin & Berry, 1975). For instance, field-dependent children appear to be more sensitive to all types of social cues and more skilled at interpersonal accommodation than field-independent children; field-independent children tend to be more independent, self-reliant, and oriented to individual achievement than field-dependent children.

Hale (1981) has presented evidence that schools are designed for children who are field-independent—"analytic," in her terminology—and from the majority culture. According to Hale, most schools need to change greatly in order to be supportive of children with alternate cognitive styles from other cultural backgrounds.

SUMMARY

1   Children in the early school years move from the preoperational to the concrete operational stage of intellectual development, changing in their orientation to cause and effect, conservation, classification, and seriation tasks. Implications for interaction can be drawn.

2   Cross-cultural research has verified Piaget's theory.

3   Philosophical thinking can develop logic and problem solving.

4   Children advance in the following areas of language during the early school years: word derivation, noun and verb phrase use, use of varied sentence types, production of speech sounds, vocabulary growth, reflection on language use, and complexity of language. Appropriate adult assistance involves responding contingently, providing communication settings, and instructing.

5   Five language skills seem to be important in reading success: auditory discrimination, listening comprehension, oral language expression, vocabulary comprehension, and context use.

6   Research is mixed on the effects of bilingualism. The mixed results are partially explained by the concepts of additive and subtractive bilingualism.

7   Play has a continuing role in the early school years. Children exercise creativity, show humor, and experiment with computers. Gender differences seem to exist.

8   Data on the effects of early education programs allow optimism about the possibility of making positive changes in the lives of young children.

9   School success is influenced by social and intellectual competence, motivation, and memory.

10 Culture also influences school success through childrearing practices, cultural variation in language use, and cognitive style.

KEY TERMS

preoperational stage
concrete operational stage
conservation
reversibility
compensation
classification
seriation
concrete objects
metalinguistic awareness
semantically contingent responding
auditory discrimination

listening comprehension
oral language expression
vocabulary comprehension
context use
readiness skills for reading
bilingual
additive bilingualism
subtractive bilingualism
creativity
humor

incongruous actions toward objects
incongruous labeling of objects and events
conceptual incongruity
humor in multiple meanings
early education programs
intrinsic motivation
cognitive style
field-dependent
field-independent

FOR FURTHER READING

Thinking Activities

Anselmo, S., Rollins, P., & Schuckman, R. (1986). *R is for rainbow: Developing young children's thinking skills through the alphabet.* Menlo Park, CA: Addison-Wesley.

Baratta-Lorton, M. (1976). *Mathematics their way.* Menlo Park, CA: Addison-Wesley.

Language Development

Owens, R. E. (1984). *Language development: An introduction.* Columbus, OH: Charles E. Merrill.

Wood, B. S. (1981). *Children and communication: Verbal and nonverbal language development* (2nd ed.). Englewood Cliffs, NJ: Prentice-Hall.

Computers and Thinking

Papert, S. (1980). *Mindstorms: Children, computers, and powerful ideas.* New York: Basic Books.

Turkle, S. (1984). *The second self: Computers and the human spirit.* New York: Simon & Schuster.

PART IV: FROM THEORY TO PRACTICE

The following exercises are designed to help students apply what has been learned in the last three chapters, and to help them learn more about children in the early school years. To complete these exercises, two two-hour observations should be scheduled. Some possible ways to arrange observations are to obtain permission to visit a school or child-care facility or to visit a public place of interest to children.

1. Narrative observation Write down everything that a child does during a ten-minute period. (Remember to use descriptive, nonjudgmental language.) What questions about psychosocial, physical, or cognitive development could the observation help to answer?

2. Vignettes Record a vignette involving a boy-girl interaction. Explain why the behavior might relate to the information in Chapters 11 through 13.

3. Child diaries Use what has been learned from observation and reading to make daily diary entries for a week about a real or imaginary child. Specify the child's age and record information about psychosocial, physical, and cognitive development.

4. Checklists Compile a checklist from the information about either large or small muscle development included in Chapter 12. Use the checklist and then discuss its effectiveness in helping to learn about development.

5. Interviews Administer three interviews, dealing with conservation, classification, and/or seriation, to one child. (See Chapter 13 for examples of interviews.) Make a judgment about the child's probable level of intellectual development, according to Piaget's theory, and explain the judgment.

6. Time sampling Adapt the recording form given as an example in Chapter 2, define your terms explicitly, and conduct a time sampling study of off-task behaviors during classroom work times.

7. Event sampling Design and conduct an event sampling study of aggression. (See Chapter 2 for an example of a recording form.) Define the terms precisely and report the findings.

8. Case studies Use the readings in Chapters 11 through 13, as well as observations, to design a case study outline for children in the early school years. Include important characteristics of this age level.

9. Reading about research Read an article having to do with children in the early school years in one of the following journals: *Child Development, Developmental Psychology,* or *Experimental Child Psychology.*

Give the complete citation in the format used in the bibliography of this book. What questions were the researchers asking? How did they go about finding the answers? What were their results? Which of the theoretical perspectives given in Chapter 1 did the researchers have?

Epilogue: Middle Childhood

Looking at eight-year-olds, about to step over the invisible line separating early and middle childhood, one is struck by how far they have come since their lives began. This book has offered a chronicle of their psychosocial, physical, and cognitive development. It concludes with a brief glance toward middle childhood.

Middle childhood was once believed to begin at school entrance and to end at puberty. Using this framework, many texts gave the age boundaries as 6 and 12 years. Now, however, the traditional domain of middle childhood has been eroded by societal and physical changes. Societal changes, such as the growing number of mothers in the labor force and a greater emphasis on the importance of early educational experiences, have combined to insure that few children enter school for the first time at age six. Physical changes, believed to be brought about by better nutrition and living conditions, have lowered the range of ages for the onset of puberty to 8 to 14 for females and 9 to 15 for males (Shonkoff, 1984). Since six is not the age of school entrance, nor is twelve the age of onset of puberty, new bounda-

ries have evolved for the levels of development. The boundaries of early childhood development have been adjusted upward to acknowledge the continuity from birth through age eight in psychosocial, physical, and cognitive development. And the terms *preteen* and *preadolescent* have been coined to recognize how much children under twelve may have in common with adolescents. What is left for consideration as *middle childhood* may be just the tenth and eleventh years of a child's life.

Defined in this way, middle childhood is a period of consolidation. In psychosocial development, children continue to try to establish a sense of industry (Erikson, 1982). They internalize standards and expectations for their own behavior and make the transition from describing themselves in terms of concrete attributes and actions to referring to themselves by more abstract qualities of disposition (Markus & Nurius, 1984). Feedback from the school environment remains important in how children feel about themselves—so much so that correlations between self-perceived competence and scores on achievement tests increase from grade three to grade six

(Collins, 1984). Opportunities for self-management abound: peer-group activities are supervised less, and children are expected to be more independent in school and home tasks.

In physical development, the rate of increase in size is usually regular until the onset of puberty, with females maturing at about a twenty percent faster rate than males (Shonkoff, 1984). Children gradually take greater responsibility for their own health and fitness.

In cognitive development, children continue to strengthen the capacity for concrete operational thinking, becoming able to apply their logical reasoning skills to increasingly complex problems. School provides formal opportunities to acquire and use knowledge having to do with academic content and societal values (Epps & Smith, 1984). Less formal sources of knowledge retain importance in children's lives; in fact, the amount of television viewing is higher by children in middle childhood than by younger or older children (Collins, 1984).

In psychosocial, physical, and cognitive development, middle childhood is a time of building on foundations laid in the years of early childhood.

Glossary of Key Terms

Abortion   Termination of pregnancy before the new life can sustain itself. (Ch. 3)

Abuse   Nonaccidental action by an adult that threatens a child's health or welfare. (Ch. 6)

Accommodation   A way of processing new information in which the new information causes a restructuring of thinking. Accommodation is a principle in the theory of Jean Piaget. (Ch. 1)

Active intermodal mapping   A process in which infants use equivalences between gestures they see and gestures that they perceive themselves to be making. This process may explain early infant imitation. (Ch. 7)

Active listening   A technique of communication proposed by Gordon. In active listening, parents respond to children's expressions of problems by restating the feeling, rather than by offering advice or criticism. (Ch. 8)

Additive bilingualism   Second language learning that takes place when children belong to the majority social class, speak the majority language, and receive positive feedback for continued use of their first language. (Ch. 13)

Alertness   The one of the three levels or states during which infants can positively receive stimulation and participate in interactions. (Ch. 6)

Amblyopia   A vision problem in which one eye sees well and the other sees poorly. If untreated, it can result in loss of vision. (Ch. 12)

Amniocentesis   Extraction and analysis of the amniotic fluid in the uterus for the purpose of prenatal detection of chromosomal disorders. (Ch. 3)

Apgar score   A score that rates newborns' functioning in five areas: appearance (skin color), pulse, grimace, activity, and respiration. The scale was devised by Dr. Virginia Apgar. (Ch. 4)

Assimilation   A way of processing new information in which the new information is integrated with the existing organization of thought. Assimilation is a principle in the theory of Jean Piaget. (Ch. 1)

Associative play   Play in which children participate together but have limited sharing and cooperation. (Ch. 8)

Attachment   Strong bonds of affection directed from children to significant people in their lives. (Ch. 5)

Attention deficit disorder   See *hyperactive.*

Auditory discrimination   Ability to hear the differences of sounds in words. (Ch. 13)

Authoritarian   A style of parenting, described by Baumrind as involving the exercise of firm control but with little support or affection. (Ch. 11)

Authoritative   A style of parenting, described by Baumrind as involving firm rules in a context of clear communication and warm commitment. (Ch. 11)

Authority stage of parenting   A stage of parenting proposed by Galinsky. In the years between one and three, parents have the task of accepting responsibility and authority over their children. (Ch. 8)

Autonomy   The sense of being self-directed. (Ch. 8)

Autonomy versus shame and doubt   The second of Erik Erikson's eight stages of psychosocial development. In this stage, two- and three-year-olds balance their assertion of self with feelings of shame and doubt. (Ch. 1, 8)

Babbling   Production of both vowel and consonant sounds (such as *ma* and *da*), often beginning toward the end of the first six months of life. (Ch. 7)

Behavioral theory   A view of learning that focuses on changes in actions or observable behavior. There are three distinct types of behavioral theories: classical conditioning, operant conditioning, and social learning theory. (Ch. 1)

Being needs   Values such as truth, honesty, beauty, and goodness, according to the theory of Abraham Maslow. (Ch. 1)

Bilingual   Able to use two languages with approximately equal fluency. (Ch. 13)

Black English   A dialect of standard English with an internally consistent grammar, vocabulary, and sound system. (Ch. 10)

Blind   Able to see at twenty feet what the normally sighted person sees at two hundred feet. (Ch. 12)

Bonding   A complex psychological tie from parent to infant. (Ch. 4)

Bottle-mouth syndrome   Severe dental decay that results from the practice of allowing children to go to sleep with a bottle containing anything but water. This decay is caused by the pooling of milk or juice against the teeth. (Ch. 9)

Brazelton scale   A scale that assesses sixteen reflexes and twenty-six behavioral items, which together simulate a variety of situations faced by newborns. The primary developer was Dr. T. Berry Brazelton. (Ch. 4)

Case study   A strategy for summarizing and organizing many observations into a coherent overview of a given child. (Ch. 2)

Cephalo-caudal   A principle that holds that growth proceeds generally from the head (cephalo) to the tail (caudal) area. (Ch. 1, 6)

Cervix   The opening of the uterus. (Ch. 4)

Checklist   A strategy of observation in which individual children's behavior is compared to a listing of target or expected behaviors. (Ch. 2)

Child diary   A strategy of observation in which regular entries chronicle the day-to-day milestones in the lives of young children. (Ch. 2)

Chromosome   A part of the nucleus of all cells of human beings and other living things. It contains genetic information. (Ch. 3)

Classical conditioning   A process of learning discovered by Ivan P. Pavlov (1849–1936). Animals or people learn to link an event, such as the ringing of a bell, with another event, such as feeding. After conditioning, the same response is given to the two events. (Ch. 1)

Classification   Logical grouping based on similar characteristics. (Ch. 13)

Cognitive development   The aspect of development dealing with thinking, problem solving, intelligence, and language.

Cognitive style   A characteristic approach to thinking and perception. Two types are *field dependence* and *field independence*. (Ch. 13)

Cognitive theory   A view of learning that focuses on internal thought processes. (Ch. 1)

Collective symbolism   The second of two levels of early pretend play, following Piaget's *solitary symbolic play.* By the latter part of the third year, young children use collective symbolism as they interact with others in playing roles. (Ch. 10)

Compensation   A characteristic of logical thinking in which change in one variable is seen to be balanced by change in another variable. (Ch. 13)

Conceptual incongruity   The third stage in the development of humor, beginning at about age three when children alter the defining features of a concept (to talk about cats barking, for instance). (Ch. 13)

Conceptus   See *zygote.*

Concrete objects   Tangible things that children can experience with more than one sense. Young children usually learn better from experiences with concrete objects, such as apples, than from abstractions, such as pictures of apples or the written word *apple.* (Ch. 13)

Concrete operational stage   The third of Jean Piaget's four stages of intellectual development. Between about seven years of age and adolescence, children begin to use logical reasoning rather than perceptions to justify judgments. (Ch. 1, 13)

Conditioned response   A response, such as salivation, brought about through conditioning. A conditioned stimulus (bell) is associated with an event (feeding) to produce a conditioned response (salivation), even in the absence of food. (Ch. 1)

Conditioned stimulus   A previously unmeaningful event, such as the ringing of a bell, which is associated with another event, such as feeding, in the theory of classical conditioning. (Ch. 1)

Congenital malformations   Structural or anatomical abnormalities present at birth. (Ch. 3)

Conservation   The understanding of the constancy of certain attributes, such as number or area, despite changes in appearance. (Ch. 13).

Context use   Ability to apply an understanding of language to anticipate what word makes sense in a given context. (Ch. 13).

Controlled scribbling   Basic shapes and lines made while children observe the movement of the drawing instrument. The wrist is more flexible than in *random scribbling* and crayons are held in a grip more similar to that used by adults. Controlled scribbling characterizes drawings from thirty months to four years of age. (Ch. 9)

Cooing   Production of vowel sounds, often in response to a human face or voice, beginning usually in the second month of life. (Ch. 7)

Cooperative play   Play in which children share ideas and roles in complex interaction. (Ch. 8)

Coping   Efforts to manage environmental and internal demands and stresses that threaten to overwhelm a person's resources. (Ch. 11)

Creativity   Fluent, flexible, and original thought; thought that generates new ideas and associations rather than converging on a single conventional response. (Ch. 13)

Cultural deficit model   A view, now in disfavor, that held that families with unique patterns of childrearing had a deficit in comparison to families in the majority culture. The more widely accepted view is the cultural difference model. (Ch. 8)

Cultural difference model   A view that holds that there are many acceptable variations in childrearing practices. This view is in marked contrast to the cultural deficit model. (Ch. 8)

Deaf   Having a severe hearing problem, which impairs the processing of linguistic information. (Ch. 12)

Deferred imitation   Retention of a mental image of something and imitation of it at a later time. The ability to do so is said by Piaget to occur at the end of the *sensorimotor* stage. (Ch. 10)

Deprivation needs   Physiological, safety, belongingness, and esteem needs which, according to Abraham Maslow, must be met before higher values can be pursued. (Ch. 1)

Directionality   The projection beyond the body of the *laterality* that is perceived. Directionality allows differentiation of *p* and *q*. (Ch. 9)

Dizygotic   Referring to fraternal twins, formed when two ova are fertilized by different sperm. These twins do not share any more inherited characteristics than do any other siblings. (Ch. 3)

DNA   Deoxyribonucleic acid; the substance of which genes are composed. DNA contains information allowing formation of chains of protein leading to new tissue and organs, control of other genes, and regulation of body processes. (Ch. 3)

Due process   Safeguards to protect the rights of children, required under provisions of *Public Law 94–142.* (Ch. 12)

Early childhood development   The orderly psychosocial, physical, and cognitive changes that take place between the prenatal months and eight years of age. (Ch. 1)

Early education programs   Group educational experiences before the age of compulsory school attendance. (Ch. 13)

Early intervention programs   Programs that provide support, instruction, and help to children with special needs and their families. (Ch. 7)

Early representational stage   A stage of drawing described by Brittain as beginning around age five. Children depict people and objects in simplified renditions. (Ch. 12)

Eclectic approach   An approach that incorporates methods, ideas, and research findings from a spectrum of theoretical positions. (Ch. 1)

Ecological environment   A concept involved in Bronfenbrenner's (1979) approach to studying three levels of influence on young children: immediate family, intermediate environments such as parental work sites, and more distant societal forces. (Ch. 1)

Egocentric   Characteristic of *preoperational* thinking, indicating a relative inability to take the view or perspective of others. (Ch. 10)

Embryo   Term applied to a developing life from the time of implantation in the uterus until the end of the eighth week after fertilization. (Ch. 3)

Emotional disturbance   Problems in personal/social behavior that adversely affect educational performance and that cannot be explained by intellectual, sensory, or health factors. (Ch. 12)

Engrossment   A term for the absorption and interest of fathers in their infants. (Ch. 4)

Equilibration   The counterpart of the biological concept of homeostasis, proposed by Jean Piaget. Equilibration refers to the internal mental process of establishing balance (equilibrium) in thinking. According to Piaget's theory, a sense of disequilibrium precedes mental growth. (Ch. 1)

Ethics of science   A set of standards delineating the responsibilities of researchers. In early childhood development, these ethics assert that children's rights supersede those of researchers and require informed consent of children's parents or guardians before any research can be undertaken. (Ch. 2)

Event sampling A strategy of observation in which predefined information is recorded when a predefined event or type of behavior occurs. (Ch. 2).

Expressive language Language that is spoken; often contrasted with *receptive language*. (Ch. 10)

Extinguish To remove a response by eliminating reinforcement of it. (Ch. 1)

Extrinsic motivation Desire for participation coming from wanting to receive approval or reward. (Ch. 10)

Fertilization Contact between sperm and ovum, beginning a new life. At the time of fertilization, paternal and maternal chromosomes intermingle. (Ch. 3)

Fetal alcohol syndrome Retardation, heart disease, and other abnormalities, present at birth in cases in which excessive amounts of alcohol were consumed during pregnancy. (Ch. 3)

Fetus Term applied to a developing life from the ninth week after fertilization until birth. *Fetus* derives from a Latin word meaning offspring. (Ch. 3)

Field-dependent A cognitive style in which perceptions are dominated by the organization of the context. (Ch. 13)

Field-independent A cognitive style in which perceptions focus on individual parts of an array, independent of the context. (Ch. 13)

Fitness Physical well-being, including strength, power, muscular endurance, cardiovascular endurance, flexibility, and body fatness. (Ch. 12)

Formal operational The last of Jean Piaget's four stages of intellectual development. Beginning in adolescence, young people learn to think symbolically and hypothetically, using abstract thinking and concepts. (Ch. 1)

Gender Decided by the kind of sperm (X- or Y-bearing) that fertilizes an ovum. If an ovum is fertilized by an X-bearing sperm, a female (XX) will develop. If an ovum is fertilized by a Y-bearing sperm, a male (XY) will develop. (Ch. 3)

Gender identity An individual's understanding of self as male, female, or ambivalent. (Ch. 8)

Gender role The public expression of *gender identity*. (Ch. 8)

Gender role stereotyping The labeling of certain behaviors according to their appropriateness for males or females. (Ch. 8)

Gene A part of the chromosomes located at the nucleus of all cells of human beings and other living things and controlling the transmission of hereditary characteristics. (Ch. 3)

Generalization An extension of a concept or behavior to situations different from that in which the concept or behavior was first learned. (Ch. 1)

Genetic counseling Counseling about the risk of occurrence or recurrence of genetic handicaps. (Ch. 3)

Genotype Totality of a human's genetic heritage, including all genes inherited from both parents. (Ch. 3)

Habituated Accustomed to a sight or sound so that it no longer seems novel or interesting. The principle of habituation has been used in research with infants. (Ch. 6)

Hearing impairment A difficulty in hearing that adversely affects educational performance. (Ch. 12)

Helping professions   Professions that provide human services. Examples include early childhood teaching, parent education, social work, nursing, music therapy, and recreation. (Ch. 1)

Holophrasis   Single-word utterances that embody the meaning found in full adult sentences (e.g., "Juice!" meaning "I want juice."). (Ch. 10)

Humanist   Referring to a theory of development that emphasizes values, human choices, relationships, and actualization of self. (Ch. 1)

Humor   A form of intellectual play with ideas. (Ch. 13)

Humor in multiple meanings   The fourth stage in the development of humor, beginning during the stage of *concrete operations*. (Ch. 13)

Hyperactive   A condition with some or all of the following characteristics: high activity level, short attention span, inability to sit still or to wait, impulsiveness, and distractibility. Also called attention deficit disorder. (Ch. 12)

I-message   A technique of communication proposed by Gordon. I-messages contain three parts: how the parent feels, what the child did to make the parent feel that way, and why the behavior is upsetting. (Ch. 8)

Idiosyncratic concepts   Concepts of *preoperational* children that are used generally even though based on specific, personal experiences. (Ch. 10)

Implantation   The embedding of the zygote in the uterus, where it can be nourished and grow. (Ch. 3)

Incongruous actions toward objects   The first stage in the development of humor, taking place during pretend play in the second year of life. (Ch. 13)

Incongruous labeling of objects and events   The second stage in the development of humor, taking place when two- and three-year-olds purposely misname objects. (Ch. 13)

Individualized education program (IEP)   A provision of *Public Law 94–142* calling for preparation of a personalized plan for each handicapped child. That plan is prepared by a team, including parent(s), and must be signed by all. (Ch. 12)

Industry versus inferiority   The fourth of Erik Erikson's eight stages of psychosocial development. In this stage, children of elementary school age balance feelings of competence with those of failure. (Ch. 1, 11)

Initiative versus guilt   The third of Erik Erikson's eight stages of psychosocial development. In this stage, four- and five-year-olds balance the exercise of new verbal and physical prowess with guilt feelings because of having gone too far. (Ch. 1, 11)

Interpretive stage   A stage of parenthood, beginning when children are in the early school years, in which Galinsky believes that parents explain and interpret their beliefs, lifestyles, and roles to children. (Ch. 11)

Interview   A one-to-one verbal interaction, usually structured by a list of questions. (Ch. 2)

Intrinsic motivation   Desire for participation coming from within a child; an internal desire to be effective. (Ch. 10, 13)

In vitro fertilization   Fertilization outside the body in an artificial environment. (Ch. 3)

In vivo fertilization   Fertilization in the body in a natural environment. (Ch. 3)

Kwashiorkor   Severe malnutrition that results when food intake is deficient in protein even if adequate in calories. Kwashiorkor develops most frequently when children between one and two years are weaned. (Ch. 9)

Labor   The birth process, often divided into three stages: the opening of the cervix, delivery of the infant, and delivery of the placenta. (Ch. 4)

Lamaze method   A method of childbirth using conditioning principles to teach the mother to control pain by breathing in certain patterns. (Ch. 3)

Language impairment   See *Speech and language impairment.*

Large muscle skills   Physical skills using large body movements. These skills are: dynamic balance, used in walking, running, and climbing; static balance, used in standing on one foot; projecting, used in jumping; and throwing and catching. (Ch. 9, 12)

Laterality   Internalized awareness of the two sides of the body and their differences. (Ch. 9)

Learning   Changes that occur in behavior as the result of experience. (Ch. 1)

Least restrictive environment   A concept set forth by *Public Law 94–142,* designed to insure that handicapped children are placed in educational environments with as few deviations from the "normal" as are individually appropriate. (Ch. 12)

Leboyer method   A method of childbirth designed to ease the transition from within to outside the uterus by using soft lights and other soothing techniques. (Ch. 3)

Listening comprehension   Ability to listen to a literary passage and correctly answer questions about it. (Ch. 13)

Logical consequence   A technique of parenting proposed by Dreikurs, calling for parents to allow children to experience the natural consequences of behavior (e.g., being late for school as a consequence of refusing to get out of bed). (Ch. 8)

Longitudinal research   Investigations that collect data over a period of many years. (Ch. 11)

Mainstreaming   The practice of placing handicapped children in "normal" classrooms for all or part of the day. (Ch. 12)

Marasmus   A condition in the first year of life caused by an inadequate total food intake. Symptoms include growth failure and wasting of muscles. (Ch. 6)

Maturationist   A theoretical position that emphasizes the role of genetically determined growth patterns and deemphasizes the role of environmental stimulation in early childhood development. (Ch. 1)

Mental retardation   General intellectual functioning that is significantly below average, combined with deficits in adaptive behavior. (Ch. 12)

Mental symbols   Words that represent things, actions that imitate adult roles, activities that use one thing as a symbol of another, and unconscious symbolizing: manifestations of thought found at the beginning of the *preoperational* stage of development. (Ch. 10)

Metalinguistic awareness   Ability to reflect on language usage; to separate content and structure of language. (Ch. 13)

Methode clinique   The clinical method by which Jean Piaget (and others) asked questions of children in order to discover how they think and why they respond as they do. (Ch. 1, 2)

Middle childhood   An artificial division of a person's life, extending from the end of early childhood to the onset of adolescence (or from 9 to 11 or 12 years of age).

Monozygotic   Referring to identical twins, formed when a zygote splits and the two identical halves develop independently. Such twins share identical inherited characteristics. (Ch. 3)

Motherese and fatherese   Adaptations of adult speech to the needs of young children learning language. Alterations include simplification, repetition, and limitation of topics. (Ch. 10)

Multicultural education   Learning experiences designed to emphasize universal human experiences as well as the richness of cultural diversity. (Ch. 11)

Naming of scribbling stage   A stage of drawing described by Brittain. Around four years of age, children may begin to draw with no particular intent but may ascribe meaning during the process. (Ch. 12)

Narrative observation   A strategy of observation that gives an account of behavior as it occurs, using descriptive, nonjudgmental language. (Ch. 2)

Nature versus nurture issue   The dispute about the relative impact of heredity (nature) and environment (nurture) on development. Most experts agree that nature and nurture interact with each other. (Ch. 1)

Neglect   The absence of adult action toward a child, resulting in harm to the child's health and welfare. (Ch. 6)

Neonatal period   A designation for the first several weeks of life, during which adjustments are made to life outside of the uterus. (Ch. 6)

Norms   Average ages of attainment of psychosocial, physical or cognitive milestones. (Ch. 1)

Object permanence   The understanding that things and people continue to exist even though not in view. Object permanence is established during Piaget's sensorimotor stage of development, from birth to age two. (Ch. 7)

Operant conditioning   Learning in which a voluntary response is strengthened when reinforced. Operant conditioning was first described by B. F. Skinner. (Ch. 1)

Oral language expression   Ability to give descriptive, amplified language in response to being shown an action picture. (Ch. 13)

Parallel play   Play in which children locate near one another but remain engaged in independent activity. (Ch. 8)

Parent-infant rhythms   Mutual coordination and adjustment of behavior to sustain interaction between parents and infants. (Ch. 5)

Perceptual-motor integration   Linkage between taking in and processing information and making the appropriate movement in response. (Ch. 9)

Permissive   A style of parenting, described by Baumrind as involving few controls or expectations. (Ch. 11)

Phenotype   A person's actual traits, resulting from interaction of genes with each other and the environment. (Ch. 3)

Physical development   The aspect of development dealing with growth patterns, coordination, and body image.

Placenta   The organ within the uterus that permits the exchange of materials carried in the bloodstreams of a pregnant woman and the developing fetus. (Ch. 3)

Play   Activity characterized by intrinsic motivation, attention to means rather than ends, nonliteral behavior, freedom from external rules, exploration, and active engagement. (Ch. 10)

Polygenic   Caused by the interaction of many genes and not just a pair. Complex human characteristics such as intelligence are polygenic. (Ch. 3)

Preoperational stage   The second of Jean Piaget's four stages of intellectual development. Between about two and seven years of age, children at this stage think intuitively and base their judgments on perception. (Ch. 1, 10, 13)

Preschematic stage   A stage of drawing described by Brittain as usually beginning after five years of age. Children draw recognizable pictures, sometimes with ground and sky. (Ch. 12)

Pretense   Play that is not literal, in an "as if" mode. (Ch. 10)

Preterm   Born before a pregnancy of normal length. (Ch. 3)

Primary circular reaction   Active reproduction of an action that an infant first produced by chance. Part of Piaget's description of sensorimotor intelligence, these reactions first occur between one and four months of age. (Ch. 7)

Prosocial   Behavior intended to enhance the welfare of another person. (Ch. 8, 11)

Protein-calorie malnutrition   A condition resulting from a lower than necessary intake of protein or calories. (Ch. 6)

Protest, despair, detachment   The sequence of reactions shown by infants who are separated from adults to whom they have formed *attachment*. (Ch. 5)

Proximo-distal   A principle that holds that development proceeds generally from the body to the extremities. (Ch. 1, 9)

Psychosocial development   The aspect of development dealing with feelings, self-concept, and interactions within a broad social context.

Public Law 94–142   Legislation, known as the Education for All Handicapped Children Act, making free public education mandatory for children over five years of age and subject to state laws for three- to five-year-old children. (Ch. 12)

Quickening   Fetal movements, often felt by pregnant women beginning in the seventeenth week after fertilization. (Ch. 3)

Random scribbling   Definite dots and lines made with simple whole-arm movement. Random scribbling characterizes children's drawings from one to two and one-half years of age. (Ch. 9)

Readiness skills for reading   Language skills believed to be prerequisites for success in beginning reading. These skills include *auditory discrimination, listening comprehension, oral language expression, vocabulary comprehension,* and *context use.* (Ch. 13)

Receptive language   Language that is received and understood. (Ch. 10)

Recessive gene   A gene that influences phenotype only if *not* paired with a dominant gene. (In contrast, dominant genes influence phenotype no matter how paired.) (Ch. 3)

Reflexes   Actions not under voluntary control. Reflexes can be viewed as part of the competence of newborns. (Ch. 6)

Reinforce   Increase the likelihood that a given response will be repeated. (Ch. 1)

Reliability   The consistency with which different observers record behavior (or, more generally, a term used to denote a characteristic of tests that give similar results under different conditions). (Ch. 2)

REM sleep   One of three levels of alertness of infants. In rapid eye movement (REM) sleep, which alternates with sound sleep, infants are restless and easily roused. (Ch. 6)

Resilience   Ability to adjust to or recover from continuing high levels of stress. (Ch. 11)

Reversibility   A characteristic of logical thinking in which something is mentally returned to the original position or state. (Ch. 13)

Rh factor   A component in red blood cells which, when lacking in the mother and present in the father and the fetus, can cause damage to the fetus. There is now treatment for this Rh incompatibility. (Ch. 3)

Schemata   Organized elements of thought, described in the theory of Jean Piaget. (Ch. 1)

Schematic stage   A stage of drawing described by Brittain. Around eight years of age, children show attention to design, balance, and perspective in their drawings. (Ch. 12)

Secondary circular reaction   Repetition of interesting actions involving objects, such as rattles. These reactions, described as part of Piaget's theory of sensorimotor intelligence, first occur between four and eight months of age. (Ch. 7)

Self-actualized   Referring to individuals who, according to the theory of Abraham Maslow, have met deprivation and being needs and have become creative, productive members of society. (Ch. 1)

Semantically contingent responding   Relating parental speech to the preceding remarks by a child. (Ch. 13)

Sensorimotor   The first of Jean Piaget's four stages of intellectual development. Generally occurring before two years of age, the sensorimotor stage is characterized by learning through the senses and through activity. (Ch. 1, 7, 10)

Seriation   A logical organization of objects into ordered relationship, such as from tall to short. (Ch. 13)

Siblings   Individuals with the same parents. (Ch. 4)

Small for date   Born after a pregnancy of normal length but without having grown as would be expected. (Ch. 3)

Small muscle skills   Physical skills using small body movements, such as drawing, eating, and bead stringing. (Ch. 9, 12)

Social cognition   The way individuals understand and perceive other people. (Ch. 5)

Social learning theory   A behavioral theory that proposes that learning occurs through imitation. (Ch. 1)

Solitary play   Play in which children interact only with an object or familiar adult but not with peers. (Ch. 8)

Solitary symbolic play   The first of two levels of early pretend play, beginning between twelve and eighteen months and centering on the child's pretense. (Ch. 10)

Sound sleep   One of three levels of alertness of infants. In sound sleep infants are unaware of the sights and sounds of environment. (Ch. 6)

Specific learning disabilities   Disorders of the basic processes involved in learning that cannot be attributed to another handicapping condition. (Ch. 12)

Speech and language impairment   A communication disorder that adversely affects learning and interaction. (Ch. 12)

Splinter skills   Physical skills that are not integrated with other activities of children and do not generalize. (Ch. 9)

Stranger anxiety   Reactions typical of fear, beginning at eight or nine months of age, that may be directed at people who are unfamiliar. (Ch. 5)

Stress   A high degree of emotional tension, brought about by environmental changes and interfering with normal patterns of response. (Ch. 11)

Subtractive bilingualism   Second-language learning that takes place when children are members of minority groups and do not receive societal support for continued use of their first language. (Ch. 13)

Sudden Infant Death Syndrome (SIDS)   The unexpected death of infants, usually one to twelve months of age and previously believed to be healthy. (Ch. 6)

Tabula rasa   A state, hypothesized by John Locke (1632–1704), in which the mind is completely blank and awaiting the imprint of experience. (Ch. 1).

Temperament   An individual's unique way of dealing with people and situations: the "how" of behavior. (Ch. 5, 8, 11)

Teratogens   Drugs, viruses, and other environmental factors that increase the incidence of congenital malformations. (Ch. 3)

Tertiary circular reactions   Activities of infants that show experimentation, not just repetition, and search for understanding. Part of Piaget's description of sensorimotor intelligence, these reactions usually first occur between twelve and eighteen months of age. (Ch. 10)

Theory   An organized system of hypotheses or statements, based on observations and evidence, that explains or predicts something. (Ch. 1)

Time sampling   A strategy of observation that documents the frequency (and sometimes the duration) of predefined behaviors by recording during specified time intervals. (Ch. 2)

Transductive reasoning   The sometimes inaccurate reasoning of *preoperational* children from specific to specific. (Ch. 10)

Transitional objects   Objects, such as blankets and teddy bears, to which children form special attachments. Psychologists view these objects as facilitating transition from parents and home to the larger world. (Ch. 8)

Trimesters   Three equal parts of human pregnancy. (Ch. 3)

Trust versus mistrust   The first of Erik Erikson's eight stages of psychosocial development. In this stage, infants develop a sense of the degree to which their worlds are comfortable and trustworthy. (Ch. 1, 5)

Ultrasound   Sound with frequencies above the range of human hearing. Ultrasonic images of a fetus can be used to diagnose fetal problems. (Ch. 3)

Vignette   A strategy of observation that records accounts of events believed to be meaningful in children's development. (Ch. 2)

Visual impairment   A difficulty in seeing that adversely affects educational performance. (Ch. 12)

Vocabulary comprehension   Ability to name common objects. (Ch. 13)

Zygote   The first cell of a developing human being, resulting from the fusion of sperm and ovum. (Ch 3)

References

A

Adams, G. R., & Crane, P. (1980). An assessment of parents' and teachers' expectations of preschool children's social preference for attractive or unattractive children and adults. *Child Development, 51,* 224–231.

Ainsworth, M. D. S. (1967). *Infancy in Uganda: Infant care and the growth of love.* Baltimore: Johns Hopkins University Press.

Ainsworth, M. D. S., & Bell, S. M. (1970). Attachment, exploration, and separation: Illustrated by the behavior of one-year-olds in a strange situation. *Child Development, 41,* 49–67.

Alan Guttmacher Institute. (1982). Family planning and teenagers: The facts. *Public Policy Issues in Brief, 2,* 1–2.

Almy, M., Monighan, P., Scales, B., & Van Hoorn, J. (1984). Recent research on play: The perspective of the teacher. In L. G. Katz (Ed.), *Current topics in early childhood education* (Vol. 5). Norwood, NJ: Ablex.

Alvino, J. (1980, March). Philosophy for children. *Teacher, 97,* 53–57.

Ambramovich, R., Pepler, D., & Corter, C. (1982). Patterns of sibling interaction among preschool-age children. In M. E. Lamb & B. Sutton-Smith (Eds.), *Sibling relationships: Their nature and significance across the lifespan.* Hillsdale, NJ: Lawrence Erlbaum.

Ames, L. B., Gillespie, C., Haines, J., & Ilg, F. L. (1979). *The Gesell Institute's child from one to six.* New York: Harper & Row.

Andrews, S. R., Blumenthal, J. B., Johnson, D. L., Kahn, A. J., Ferguson, C. J., Lasater, T. M., Malone, P. E., & Wallace, D. B. (1982). The skills of mothering: A study of Parent Child Development Centers. *Monograph of the Society for Research in Child Development, 47* (6, Serial No. 198).

Anselmo, S. (1977, January). Vignettes of child activity. *Childhood Education, 53,* 133–136.

Anselmo, S. (1979). A Piagetian perspective on multicultural experiences in early childhood education. In M. K. Poulsen & G. I. Lubin (Eds.), *Piagetian theory and its implications for the helping professions.* Los Angeles: University of Southern California.

Anselmo, S. (1980, Fall). Children learn about their senses. *Day Care and Early Education, 8,* 42–44.

Anselmo, S., Rollins, P., & Schuckman, R. (1986). *R is for rainbow: Developing young children's thinking skills through the alphabet.* Menlo Park, CA: Addison-Wesley.

Azrin, N. H., & Foxx, R. M. (1981). *Toilet training in less than a day.* New York: Pocket Books.

B

Bachtold, L. M. (1983, November). Children and creativity. *Human Relations, 8* (11), 1–5.

Bailey, Jr., D. B., & Wolery, M. (1984). *Teaching infants and preschoolers with handicaps.* Columbus: Charles E. Merrill.

Bandura, A. (1977). *Social learning theory.* Englewood Cliffs, NJ: Prentice-Hall.

Bandura, A., Ross, D., & Ross, S. A. (1963). Imitation of film mediated aggressive models. *Journal of Abnormal and Social Psychology, 66,* 3–11.

Bank, S. P., & Kahn, M. D. (1982). *The sibling bond.* New York: Basic Books.

Baratta-Lorton, M. (1976). *Mathematics their way.* Menlo Park, CA: Addison-Wesley.

Bass, E., & Thornton, L. (Eds.). (1983). *I never told anyone: Writings by women survivors of child sexual abuse.* New York: Harper & Row.

Baumrind, D. (1967). Child care practices anteceding three patterns of pre-school behavior. *Genetic Psychology Monographs, 75,* 43–88.

Baumrind, D. (1977). Some thoughts about childrearing. In S. Cohen & T. J. Comiskey (Eds.), *Child development: Contemporary perspectives.* Itasca, IL: F. E. Peacock.

Bax, M. (1981). The intimate relationship of health, development, and behavior in young children. In C. L. Brown (Ed.), *Infants at risk: Assessment and intervention: A round table.* Skillman, NJ: Johnson & Johnson.

Beautrais, A. L., Fergusson, D. M., & Shannon, F. T. (1982). Life events and childhood morbidity. *Pediatrics, 70,* 935–940.

Bell, S. M., & Ainsworth, M. D. S. (1972). Infant crying and maternal responsiveness. *Child Development, 43,* 1171–1190.

Belsky, J., & Steinberg, L. D. (1982). The effects of day care: A critical review. In J. Belsky (Ed.), *In the beginning: Readings on infancy.* New York: Columbia University Press.

Belsky, J., Steinberg, L. D., & Walker, A. (1982). The ecology of day care. In M. E. Lamb (Ed.), *Nontraditional families: Parenting and child development.* Hillsdale, N.J.: Lawrence Erlbaum.

Benirschke, K., Carpenter, G., Espstein, C., Fraser, C., Jackson, L., Motusky, A., & Nyhan, W. (1976). Genetic diseases. In R. L. Brent & M. I. Harris (Eds.), *Prevention of embryonic, fetal, and perinatal disease.* Bethesda, Maryland: National Institutes of Health.

Berger, S. (1984, July 1). Sometimes I feel bad: Divorce as seen through one child's eyes. *Parade Magazine.* 12–13.

Best, R. (1983). *We've all got scars: What boys and girls learn in elementary school.* Bloomington: Indiana University Press.

Bloom, L. (1970). *Language development: Form and function in emerging grammars.* Cambridge: MIT Press.

Bloomfield, L. (1933). *Language.* New York: Henry Holt. (Reprinted 1961)

Borke, H. (1983). Piaget's mountains revisited: Changes in the egocentric landscape. In M. Donaldson, R. Grieve, & C. Pratt (Eds.), *Early childhood development and education: Readings in psychology.* New York: Guilford.

Bornstein, M. H. (1985). Infant into adult: Unity to diversity in the development of visual categorization. In J. Mehler & R. Fox (Eds.), *Neonate cognition: Beyond the blooming buzzing confusion.* Hillsdale, NJ: Lawrence Erlbaum.

Bower, T. G. R. (1977). *A primer of infant development.* San Francisco: W. H. Freeman.

Bower, T. G. R. (1982). *Development in infancy* (2nd ed.). San Francisco: W. H. Freeman.

Bowlby, J. (1958). The nature of a child's tie to his mother. *International Journal of Psychoanalysis, 39,* 350–373.

Bowlby, J. (1982) *Attachment and loss* (2nd ed.). New York: Basic Books.

Brady, E. H., & Hill, S. (1984). Young children and microcomputers: Research issues and directions. *Young Children, 39,* 49–61.

Brazelton, T. B. (1962) A child-oriented approach to toilet training. *Pediatrics, 29,* 121–128.

Brazelton, T. B. (1974). *Toddlers and parents: A declaration of independence.* New York: Dell.

Brazelton, T. B. (1975). Mother-infant reciprocity. In M. H. Klaus & M. A. Trause (Eds.), *Maternal attachment and mothering disorders: A round table.* Skillman, NJ: Johnson & Johnson.

Brazelton, T. B. (1979). Behavioral competence of the newborn infant. *Seminars in perinatology, 3,* 35–44.

Brazelton, T. B. (1981). *On becoming a family: The growth of attachment.* New York: Delacorte/Seymour Lawrence.

Brazelton, T. B. (1982). Behavioral assessment of the premature infant: Uses in intervention. In M. H. Klaus & M. O. Robertson (Eds.), *Birth, interaction, and attachment: A round table.* Skillman, NJ: Johnson & Johnson.

Brittain, W. L. (1979). *Creativity, art, and the young child.* New York: Macmillan.

Bromwich, R. (1981). *Working with parents and infants: An interactional approach.* Austin, TX: PRO-ED, Inc. (Originally published by University Park Press, Baltimore)

Bronfenbrenner, U. (1979). *The ecology of human development: Experiments by nature and design.* Cambridge: Harvard University Press.

Brooks-Gunn, J., & Matthews, W. S. (1979). *He and she: How children develop their sex-role identity.* Englewood Cliffs, NJ: Prentice-Hall.

Brown, A. L., & De Loache, J. S. (1983). Methods for observing developmental change in memory. In M. Donaldson, R. Grieve, & C. Pratt (Eds.), *Early childhood development and education: Readings in psychology.* New York: Guilford.

Brown, C. C. (Ed.). (1983). *Childhood learning disabilities and prenatal risk: An interdisciplinary data review for health care professionals and parents.* Skillman, NJ: Johnson & Johnson.

Brown, C. C. (Ed.). (1981). *Infants at risk: Assessment and intervention: An update for health care professionals and parents: A round table.* Skillman, NJ: Johnson & Johnson.

Bruner, J. (1981). Child's play. In R. D. Strom (Ed.), *Growing through play: Readings for parents and teachers.* Monterey, CA: Brooks/Cole.

Burgess, B. J. (1980). Parenting in the native-American community. In M. O. Fantini & R. Cárdenas (Eds.), *Parenting in a multicultural society.* New York: Longman.

Burtoff, B. (1982, December 30). Child's "security blanket" OK. Stockton, CA: *Stockton Record,* p. 11.

Bybee, R. W., & Sund, R. B. (1982). *Piaget for educators* (2nd ed.). Columbus: Charles E. Merrill.

C

Callaghan, J. W. (1981). A comparison of Anglo, Hopi, and Navajo mothers and infants. In T. M. Field, A. M. Sostek, P. Vietze, P. H. Leiderman (Eds.), *Culture and early interactions.* Hillsdale, NJ: Lawrence Erlbaum Associates.

Campos, J. J., & Stenberg, C. R. (1981). Perception, appraisal and emotion: The onset of social referencing. In M. E. Lamb & L. R. Sherrod (Eds.), *Infant social cognition: Empirical and theoretical considerations.* Hillsdale, NJ: Lawrence Erlbaum.

Carew, J. V. (1980). Experience and the development of intelligence in young children at home and in day care. *Monographs of the Society for Research in Child Development, 45* (Serial No. 187).

Carey, W. B. (1973). Measurement of infant temperament in pediatric practice. In J. C. Westman (Ed.), *Individual differences in children.* New York: John Wiley.

Carpenter, G. C., Tecce, J. J., Stechler, G., & Friedman, S. (1970). Differential visual behavior to human and humanoid faces in early infancy. *Merrill-Palmer Quarterly, 16,* 91–107.

Caudle, S. (1983, March 21). Child abuse, neglect raging. Stockton, CA: *Stockton Record,* p. 1, 6.

Chall, J., et al. (1979). Blacks in the world of children's books. *Reading Teacher, 32,* 527–33.

Chez, R. A., Quilligan, E. J., & Wingate, M. B. (1976). High risk pregnancies: Obstetrical and perinatal factors. In R. L. Brent & M. I. Harris (Eds.), *Prevention of embryonic, fetal, and perinatal disease.* Bethesda, Maryland: National Institutes of Health.

Chomsky, N. (1965). *Aspects of the theory of syntax.* Cambridge: MIT Press.

Colao, F., & Hosansky, T. (1983). *Your children should know: Teach your children the strategies that will keep them safe from assault and crime.* Indianapolis: Bobbs-Merrill.

Collins, W. A. (1984). Conclusion: The status of basic research on middle childhood. In W. A. Collins (Ed.), *Development during middle childhood: The years from six to twelve.* Washington, DC: National Academy Press.

Condon, W. S., & Sander, L. W. (1974). Neonate movement is synchronized with adult speech: Interactional participation and language acquisition. *Science, 183,* 99–101.

Condry, S. (1983). History and background of preschool intervention programs and the Consortium for Longitudinal Studies. In Consortium for Longitudinal Studies, *As the twig is bent . . . lasting effects of preschool programs.* Hillsdale, NJ: Lawrence Erlbaum.

Coplan, J., Gleason, J. R., Ryan, R., Burke, M. G., & Williams, M. L. (1982). Validation of an early language milestone scale in a high-risk population. *Pediatrics, 70,* 677–683.

Cowan, P. A. (1978). *Piaget with feeling: Cognitive, social, and emotional dimensions.* New York: Holt, Rinehart & Winston.

Crockenberg, S., & McCluskey, K. (1982). Caring for irritable babies: A research report. *Human Relations, 7,* 1–3.

Cummings, E. M., Zahn-Waxler, C., & Radke-Yarrow, M. (1981). Young children's reponses to expressions of anger and affection by others in the family. *Child Development, 52,* 1274–1282.

D

Dawe, H. C. (1934). An analysis of two hundred quarrels of preschool children. *Child Development, 5,* 139–157.

DeCasper, A. J., & Fifer, W. P. (1980). Of human bonding: Newborns prefer their mothers' voices. *Science, 208,* 1174–1176.

Deci, E. L., & Ryan, R. M. (1982). Curiosity and self-directed learning: The role of motivation in education. In L. G. Katz (Ed.), *Current topics in early childhood education* (Vol. IV). Norwood, NJ: Ablex.

Demany, L., McKenzie, B., & Vurpillot, E. (1977). Rhythm perception in early infancy. *Nature, 266,* 718–719.

Dennis, W. (1940). The effect of cradling practices upon the onset of walking of Hopi children. *Journal of Genetic Psychology, 56,* 77–86.

Dickman, I. R. (1981). *Teenage pregnancy—what can be done?* Public Affairs Pamphlet No. 594. New York: Public Affairs Committee.

Dillon, M. (1982, November). Kids' TV: 18 violent acts per hour; Doesn't anyone care? Stanford University: *Stanford Observer,* p. 4.

Dinkmeyer, D., & McKay, G. D. (1976). *Systematic training for effective parenting.* Circle Pines, MI: American Guidance Services.

Donaldson, M. (1979). *Children's Minds.* New York: Norton.

Donaldson, M. (1983). Children's reasoning. In M. Donaldson, R. Grieve, & C. Pratt (Eds.), *Early childhood development and education: Readings in Psychology.* New York: Guilford.

Donovan, J. (1984, December 20). Is preschool really worthwhile? Some experts say parents do it better. *San Francisco Chronicle,* p. 25.

Dreikurs, R. (1958). *The challenge of parenthood* (rev. ed.). New York: Hawthorn.

Dreikurs, R., & Grey, L. (1970). *Guide to child discipline.* New York: Hawthorn.

Dunn, J., & Kendrick, C. (1982). Siblings and their mother: Developing relationships within the family. In M. E. Lamb & B. Sutton-Smith (Eds.), *Sibling relationships: Their nature and significance across the lifespan.* Hillsdale, NJ: Lawrence Erlbaum.

Dweck, C. S. (1981). Social-cognitive processes in children's friendships. In S. R. Asher & J. M. Gottman (Eds.), *The development of children's friendships.* Cambridge: Cambridge University Press.

E

Eiduson, B. T., Kornfein, M., Zimmerman, I. L., & Weisner, T. S. (1982). Comparative socialization practices in traditional and alternative families. In M. E. Lamb (Ed.), *Nontraditional families: Parenting and child development.* Hillsdale, NJ: Lawrence Erlbaum.

Eisenberg, N., Murray, E., & Hite, T. (1982). Children's reasoning regarding sex-typed toy choices. *Child Development, 53,* 81–86.

Elkind, D. (1970, April 5). Erik Erikson's eight ages of man. *New York Times Magazine,* pp. 21–34.

Elkind, D. (1976). *Child development and education: A Piagetian perspective.* New York: Oxford University Press.

Elkind, D. (1981). *The hurried child: Growing up too fast too soon.* Reading, MA: Addison-Wesley.

Epps, E. G., & Smith, S. F. (1984). School and children: The middle childhood years. In W. A. Collins (Ed.), *Development during middle childhood: The years from six to twelve.* Washington, DC: National Academy Press.

Erikson, E. H. (1963). *Childhood and society* (2nd ed.). New York: W. W. Norton.

Erikson, E. H. (1968). *Identity: Youth and crisis.* New York: W. W. Norton.

Erikson, E. H. (1977). *Toys and reasons: Stages in the ritualization of experience.* New York: W. W. Norton.

Erikson, E. H. (1982). *The life cycle completed.* New York: W. W. Norton.

Eron, L. D. (1982a, August). The consistency of aggressive behavior across time and situations. In *Consistency of aggression and its correlates over twenty years.* Symposium presented at the meeting of the American Psychological Association, Anaheim, California.

Eron, L. D. (1982b). Parent-child interaction, television violence, and aggression of children. *American Psychologist, 37,* 197–211.

F

Fagot, B. I. (1982). Sex role development. In R. Vasta (Ed.), *Strategies and techniques of child study.* New York: Academic Press.

Fagot, B. I., & Kronsberg, S. J. (1982). Sex differences: Biological and social factors influencing the behavior of young boys and girls. In S. G. Moore & C. R. Cooper, *The young child: Reviews of research (Vol. 3).* Washington, DC: National Association for the Education of Young Children.

Fajardo, B. F., & Freedman, D. G. (1981). Maternal rhythmicity in three American cultures. In T. M. Field, A. M. Sostek, P. Vietze, & P. H. Leiderman (Eds.), *Culture and early interactions.* Hillsdale, NJ: Lawrence Erlbaum.

Falbo, T. (1982). Only children in America. In M. E. Lamb & B. Sutton-Smith (Eds.), *Sibling relationships: Their nature and significance across the lifespan.* Hillsdale, NJ: Lawrence Erlbaum.

Fantz, R. (1961). The origin of form perception. *Scientific American, 204*(5), 66–72.

Farel, A. M. (1980). Effects of preferred maternal roles, maternal employment, and sociodemographic status on school adjustment and competence. *Child Development, 51,* 1179–1186.

Fein, G. G. (1981). Pretend play in childhood: An integrative review. *Child Development, 52,* 1095–1118.

Feingold, B. F. (1974). *Why your child is hyperactive.* New York: Random House.

Feiring, C., & Lewis, M. (1981). Middle class differences in the mother-child interaction and the child's cognitive development. In T. M. Field, A. M. Sostek, P. Vietze, & P. H. Leiderman (Eds.), *Culture and early interactions.* Hillsdale, NJ: Lawrence Erlbaum.

Field, T. (1982). Infancy. In R. Vasta (Ed.), *Strategies and techniques of child study.* New York: Academic Press.

Field, T. M., & Widmayer, S. M. (1981). Mother-infant interactions among lower SES Black, Cuban, Puerto Rican and South American immigrants. In T. M. Field, A. M. Sostek, P. Vietze, & P. H. Leiderman (Eds.), *Culture and early interactions.* Hillsdale, NJ: Lawrence Erlbaum.

Fishbein, H. D. (1984). *The psychology of infancy and childhood: Evolutionary and cross-cultural perspectives.* Hillsdale, NJ: Lawrence Erlbaum.

Fowler, W. (1980). *Curriculum and assessment guides for infant and child care.* Boston: Allyn & Bacon.

Freeman, L. (1982). Illustrations by C. Deach. *It's my body: A book to teach young children how to resist uncomfortable touch.* Seattle, WA: Parenting Press. (Originally published by Planned Parenthood of Snohomish County, WA.)

Friedrich, L. K., & Stein, A. H. (1973). Aggressive and prosocial television programs and the natural behavior of preschool children. *Monographs of the Society for Research in Child Development, 38*(4, Serial No. 151).

Fullard, W., McDevitt, S. C., & Carey, W. B. (1978). Toddler Temperament Scale. (Available from W. Fullard, Department of Educational Psychology, Temple University, Philadelphia, PA 19122)

Fullard, W., McDevitt, S. C., & Carey, W. B. (1984). Assessing temperament in one- to three-year-old children. *Journal of Pediatric Psychiatry, 9*(2), 205–217.

G

Galinsky, E. (1981). *Between generations: The six stages of parenthood.* New York: Times Books.

Ganz, M. (1983, January 30). Retarded boy's right to live: Who decides? San Francisco: *Sunday Examiner and Chronicle,* A1, A6.

Gardner, E. J. (1983). *Human heredity.* New York: John Wiley & Sons.

Garmezy, N. (1983). Stressors of childhood. In N. Garmezy & M. Rutter (Eds.), *Stress, coping, and development in children.* New York: McGraw-Hill.

Garvey, C. (1977). *Play.* Cambridge, MA: Harvard University Press.

Garvey, C. (1984). *Children's talk.* Cambridge, MA: Harvard University Press.

Gearhart, M., & Hall, W. S. (1982). Internal state words: Cultural and situational variation in vocabulary usage. In K. M. Borman (Ed.), *The social life of children in a changing society.* Hillsdale, NJ: Lawrence Erlbaum.

Gentner, D. (1982). Why nouns are learned before verbs: Linguistic relativity vs. natural partitioning. In S. Kuczaj (Ed.), *Language development, Vol. 2: Language, thought, and culture.* Hillsdale, NJ: Lawrence Erlbaum.

George, G., & Main, M. (1979). Social interactions of young abused children: Approach, avoidance, and aggression. *Child Development, 50,* 306–518.

Gesell, A., & Ilg, F. G. (1949). *Child development: An introduction to the study of human growth.* New York: Harper.

Gilligan, C. (1982). *In a different voice: Psychological theory and women's development.* Cambridge, MA: Harvard University Press.

Ginott, H. (1965). *Between parent and child.* New York: Macmillan.

Ginsburg, H. J., & Miller, S. M. (1982). Sex differences in children's risk-taking behavior. *Child Development, 53,* 426–428.

Gleitman, L. R. & Wanner, E. (1982). Language acquisition: The state of the state of the art. In E. Wanner & L. R. Gleitman (Eds.), *Language acquisition: The state of the art.* Cambridge, MA Cambridge University Press.

Glover, M. E., Preminger, J. L., & Sanford, A. R. (1978). *The early learning accomplishment profile for developmentally young children, birth to 36 months.* Winston-Salem, NC: Kaplan Press.

Goldberg, S. (1983). Parent-infant bonding: Another look. *Child Development, 54,* 1355–1382.

Goldman, R. J., & Goldman, J. D. G. (1982). How children perceive the origin of babies and the roles of mothers and fathers in procreation: A cross-national study. *Child Development, 53,* 491–504.

Goldsmith, R. H. (1980). *Nutrition and learning.* Bloomington, IN: Phi Delta Kappa Educational Foundation.

Gordon, S., & Dickman, I. R. (1981). *Sex education: The parents' role.* New York: Public Affairs Pamphlets (No. 549).

Gordon, T. (1975). *P.E.T.: Parent effectiveness training.* New York: Wyden.

Gorelick, M. (1975). A classification of concept representations. In *Piagetian theory and its implications for the helping professions: Proceedings, fourth interdisciplinary seminar.* Los Angeles: University of Southern California.

Gottfried, A. E. (1983, November). Intrinsic motivation in young children. *Young Children, 39,* 64–73.

Gottman, J. M., & Parkhurst, J. T. (1980). A developmental theory of friendship and acquaintanceship processes. In A. Collins (Ed.), *Minnesota Symposia on Child Psychology* (Vol. 13), Norwich, NJ: Lawrence Erlbaum.

Gouze, K. (1979) Does aggressive television affect all children the same way? *Early Report, 6*(2).

Grusec, J. E. (1982). Prosocial behavior and self control. In R. Vasta (Ed.), *Strategies and techniques of child study.* New York: Academic Press.

Guilford, J. P. (1967). *The nature of human intelligence.* New York: McGraw-Hill.

H

Hale, J. (1981). Black children: Their roots, culture, and learning styles. *Young Children, 36,* 37–50.

Harding, C. G. (1983). Setting the stage for language acquisition: Communication development in the first year. In R. M. Golinkoff (Ed.), *The transition from prelinguistic to linguistic communication.* Hillsdale, NJ: Lawrence Erlbaum.

Harlow, H. F. (1961). The development of affectional patterns in infant monkeys. In B. M. Foss (Ed.), *Determinants of infant behavior* (Vol. 1). London: Methuen.

Harlow, H., & Zimmerman, R. R. (1959). Affectual responses in the infant monkey. *Science, 130,* 421–432.

Harter, S. (1978). Effectance motivation reconsidered: Toward a developmental model. *Human Development, 21,* 34–64.

Haswell, K., Hock, E., & Wenar, C. (1981). Oppositional behavior of preschool children: theory and intervention. *Family Relations, 30,* 440–446.

Haswell, K. L., Hock, E., & Wenar, C. (1982). Techniques for dealing with oppositional behavior in preschool children. *Young Children, 37,* 13–18.

Helfer, R. (1982). The relationship between lack of bonding and child abuse and neglect. In M. H. Klaus, T. Leger, & M. A. Trause (Eds.), *Maternal attachment and mothering disorders: A round table* (2nd ed.). Skillman, NJ: Johnson & Johnson.

Hillerich, R., L., & Johnson, T. G. (1981). *Test manual. Test for READY STEPS. A diagnostic approach to early identification of reading readiness needs.* Boston: Houghton-Mifflin.

Hoban, R. (1960). Illustrated by G. Williams. *Bedtime for Frances.* New York: Harper & Row.

Honig, A., S. (1982, November). Research in review: Language environments for young children. *Young Children, 38,* 56–67.

Honig, A. S. (1983, May). Research in review: Television and young children. *Young Children, 38,* 63–76.

Hood, L., & Bloom, L. (1979). What, when, and how about why: A longitudinal study of early expressions of causality. *Monographs of the Society for Research in Child Development, 44*(6, Serial No. 181).

Hoot, J. (1984). Caution: A decrease in play may be hazardous to children's school success. *Texas Child Care Quarterly, 8,* 10–13.

Hubbell, R. (1983). *A review of Head Start research since 1970.* Washington, DC: U.S. Government Printing Office.

Huesmann, L. R., & Eron, L. D. (1984). Cognitive processes and the persistence of aggressive behavior. *Aggressive Behavior, 10,* 243–251.

Hughes, M., & Donaldson, M. (1983). The use of hiding games for studying coordination of viewpoints. In M. Donaldson, R. Grieve, & C. Pratt (Eds.), *Early childhood development and education: Readings in psychology.* New York: Guilford.

Hymes, D. (1980). *Language in education: Ethnolinguistic essays.* Washington, DC: Center for Applied Linguistics.

I

Irwin, D. M., & Bushnell, M. M. (1980). *Observational strategies for child study.* New York: Holt, Rinehart & Winston.

J

Jablow, M. M. (1982). *Cara: Growing with a retarded child.* Philadelphia: Temple University Press.

Jaffe, R. B., Schruefer, J. J., Bowes, Jr., W. A., Creasy, R. K., Sweet, R. L., & Laros, R. K., Jr. (1976). High risk pregnancies: Maternal medical disorders. In R. L. Brent & M. I. Harris (Eds.), *Prevention of embryonic, fetal, and perinatal disease.* Bethesda, Maryland: National Institutes of Health.

James, W. (1890). *The principles of psychology.* New York: Holt.

Janis, I. L., & Leventhal, H. (1968). Human reactions to stress. In E. F. Borgatta & W. W. Lambert (Eds.), *Handbook of personality theory and research.* Chicago: Rand McNally.

Jensen, A. R. (1969). How much can we boost I. Q. and scholastic achievement? *Harvard Educational Review, 39,* 1–123.

Jensen, L. C., & Wells, M. G. (1979). *Feelings: Helping children understand emotions.* Provo, Utah: Brigham Young University Press.

Jorn, M., Persky, B., Huntington, D. S. (1984). Selection of staff. In L. S. Dittman (Ed.), *The infants we care for* (rev. ed.). Washington, DC: National Association for the Education of Young Children.

K

Kaffman, M., & Elizur, E. (1977). Infants who become enuretics: A longitudinal study of 161 Kibbutz children. *Monographs of the Society for Research in Child Development, 42*(2, Serial No. 170).

Kagan, J. (1982). Canalization of early psychological development. *Pediatrics, 70,* 474–483.

Kamii, C., & DeVries, R. (1978). *Physical knowledge in preschool education: Implications of Piaget's theory.* Englewood Cliffs, NJ: Prentice-Hall.

Karmel, M. (1959). *Thank you Dr. Lamaze: Painless childbirth.* Philadelphia: Lippincott.

Karmiloff-Smith, A. (1979). *A functional approach to child language: A study of determiners and reference.* London: Cambridge University Press.

Katz, P. A. (1982). Development of children's racial awareness and intergroup attitudes. In L. G. Katz (Ed.), *Current topics in early childhood education* (Vol. IV). Norwood, NJ: Ablex.

Keeshan, B. (1983). Families and television. *Young Children, 38,* 46–55.

Kellogg, R. (1969). *Analyzing children's art.* Palo Alto, CA: National Press Books.

Keniston, K., and the Carnegie Council on Children. (1977). *All our children: The American family under pressure.* New York: Harcourt Brace Jovanovich.

Kennell, J. H., & Klaus, M. H. (1971). Care of the mother of the high risk infant. *Clinical Obstetrics and Gynecology, 14,* 926–954.

Kephart, N. C. (1971). *The slow learner in the classroom* (2nd ed). Columbus, Ohio: Charles E. Merrill.

Killalea Associates. (1980). *State, regional, and national summaries of data from the 1978 civil rights survey of elementary and secondary schools.* Prepared for the U.S. Office of Civil Rights. Alexandria, VA: Killalea Associates.

Klaus, M. H., Jerauld, R., Kreger, N., McAlpine, W., Steffa, M., & Kennell, J. H. (1972). Maternal attachment: Importance of the first postpartum days. *New England Journal of Medicine, 286,* 460–463.

Klaus, M. H., & Kennell, J. H. (1976). *Maternal-infant bonding.* St. Louis: Mosby.

Klaus, M. H., & Kennell, J. H. (1982). *Parent-infant bonding* (2nd ed.). St. Louis: Mosby.

Klaus, M. H., Leger, T., & Trause, M. A. (Eds.). (1982). *Maternal attachment and mothering disorders: A round table* (2nd ed.). Skillman, NJ: Johnson & Johnson.

Klaus, M. H., & Robertson, M. O. (Eds.). (1982). *Birth, interaction, and attachment: A round table.* Skillman, NJ: Johnson & Johnson.

Kobus, D. K. (1985). *An investigation of the CUME Assessment, an instrument designed to measure third grade children's understanding of selected cross-cultural/multicultural concepts.* Unpublished doctoral dissertation, University of the Pacific.

Kuhl, P. K., (1980). Perceptual constancy for speech-sound categories in early infancy. In G. H. Yeni-Komshian, J. F. Kavanagh, & C. A. Ferguson (Eds.), *Child phonology, Vol. 2: Perception.* New York: Academic Press.

Kuhl, P. K. (1985). Categorization of speech by infants. In J. Mehler & R. Fox (Eds.), *Neonate cognition: Beyond the blooming buzzing confusion.* Hillsdale, NJ: Lawrence Erlbaum Associates.

L

Labinowicz, E. (1980). *The Piaget primer: Thinking, learning, teaching.* Menlo Park, CA: Addison-Wesley.

Lamb, M. E. (1981). The development of social expectations in the first year of life. In M. E. Lamb & L. R. Sherrod (Eds.), *Infant social cognition: Empirical and theoretical considerations.* Hillsdale, NJ: Lawrence Erlbaum.

Lamb, M. E. (1982). Maternal employment and child development: A review. In M. E. Lamb (Ed.), *Nontraditional families: Parenting and child development.* Hillsdale, NJ: Lawrence Erlbaum.

Lamb, M. E., Thompson, R. A., & Frodi, A. M. (1982). Early social development. In R. Vasta (Ed.), *Strategies and techniques of child study.* New York: Academic Press.

Lambert, W. E. (1975). Culture and language as factors in learning and education. In A. Wolfgang (Ed.), *Education of immigrant students.* Toronto: Ontario Institute for Studies in Education.

Lamme, L. L. (1984). *Growing up writing.* Washington, DC: Acropolis Books.

Lansing, K. M. (1970). *Art, artists, and art education.* New York: McGraw-Hill.

Laosa, L. M. (1981). Maternal behavior: Sociocultural diversity in modes of family interaction. In R. W. Henderson (Ed.), *Parent-child interaction: Theory, research, and prospects.* New York: Academic Press.

Larrick, N. (1965, September). The all-white world of children's books. *Saturday Review,* pp. 63–65, 84–85.

Larsen, J. M., Draper, T. W., & Hite, S. J. (1984, November 8–11). *Preschool does make a difference for educationally advantaged children: Longitudinal study update.* Paper presented at the conference of the National Association for the Education of Young Children, Los Angeles.

Lazar, I. (1983). Discussion and implications of findings. In Consortium for Longitudinal Studies, *As the twig is bent . . . Lasting effects of preschool programs.* Hillsdale, NJ: Lawrence Erlbaum.

Leboyer, F. (1975). *Birth without violence.* New York: Knopf.

Lepper, M. R.. (1983). Extrinsic reward and intrinsic motivation: Implications for the classroom. In J. M. Levine & M. C. Wang (Eds.), *Teacher and student perceptions: Implications for learning.* Hillsdale, NJ: Lawrence Erlbaum.

Lerner, J., Mardell-Czudnowski, C., & Goldenberg, D. (1981). *Special education for the early childhood years.* Englewood Cliffs, NJ: Prentice-Hall.

Lester, B. M., & Brazelton, T. B. (1982). Cross-cultural assessment of neonatal behavior. In D. A. Wagner & H. W. Stevenson (Eds.), *Cultural perspectives on child development.* San Francisco: Freeman.

LeVine, R. A. (1977). Child rearing as cultural adaptation. In P. H. Leiderman, S. R. Tulkin, & A. Rosenfeld (Eds.), *Culture and infancy: Variations in the human experience.* New York: Academic Press.

LeVine, R. A. (1980). A cross-cultural perspective on parenting. In M. O. Fantini & R. Cárdenas (Eds.), *Parenting in a multicultural society.* New York: Longman.

Levy, J. (1973). *The baby exercise book for the first fifteen months.* New York: Pantheon.

Lewis, M., & Brooks-Gunn, J. (1981). Visual attention at three months as a predictor of cognitive functioning at two years of age. *Intelligence, 5,* 131–140.

Lickona,T. (1983). *Raising good children: Helping your child through the stages of moral development.* New York: Bantam Books.

Lipman, M. (1981). *Pixie.* Montclair, NJ: First Mountain Foundation.

Lipman, M. (1982). *Kio and Gus.* Montclair, NJ: First Mountain Foundation.

Lipsitt, L. P., Engen, T., & Kaye, H. (1963). Developmental changes in the olfactory threshold of the neonate. *Child Development, 34,* 371–376.

Londerville, S., & Main, M. (1981). Security of attachment, compliance and maternal training methods in the second year of life. *Developmental Psychology, 17,* 289–299.

Lytton, H., & Zwirner, W. (1975). Compliance and its controlling stimuli observed in a natural setting. *Developmental Psychology, 11,* 769–779.

M

Maccoby, E. E. (1983). Social-emotional development and response to stressors. In N. Garmezy & M. Rutter (Eds.), *Stress, coping, and development in children.* New York: McGraw-Hill.

Malina, R. M. (1982). Motor development in the early years. In S. G. Moore & C. R. Cooper (Eds.), *The young child: Reviews of Research* (Vol. 3). Washington, DC: National Association for the Education of Young Children.

March of Dimes Birth Defects Foundation. (1980). *Genetic counseling.* White Plains, NY: March of Dimes.

March of Dimes Birth Defects Foundation. (1983). *Recipe for healthy babies.* White Plains, N.Y.: March of Dimes.

Markus, H. J., & Nurius, P. S. (1984). Self-understanding and self-regulation in middle childhood. In W. A. Collins (Ed.), *Development during middle childhood: The years from six to twelve.* Washington, DC: National Academy Press.

Maslow, A. H. (1968). *Toward a psychology of being.* Princeton, NJ: Van Nostrand.

Maslow, A. H. (1970). *Motivation and personality* (2nd ed.). New York: Harper & Row.

Matthews, G. B. (1980). *Philosophy and the young child.* Cambridge, MA: Harvard University Press.

McCall, R. B., Parke, R. D., & Kavanaugh, R. D. (1977). Imitation of live and televised models by children one to three years of age. *Monographs of the Society for Research in Child Development, 42*(5,Serial No. 173).

McCartney, K., Scarr, S., Phillips, D., Grajek, S., & Schwarz, J. C. (1982). Environmental differences among day care centers and their effects on children's development. In E. F. Zigler & E. W. Gordon, *Day care: Scientific and social policy issues*. Boston: Auburn House.

McGhee, P. E. (1984). Play, incongruity, and humor. In T. D. Yawkey & A. D. Pellegrini (Eds.), *Child's play: Developmental and applied*. Hillsdale, NJ: Lawrence Erlbaum.

Meeker, M. (1969). *The Structure of Intellect: Its interpretation and uses*. Columbus, Ohio: Charles E. Merrill.

Meeker, M. (1981a). *SOI techniques: For SOI questions, for teaching competency*. El Segundo, CA: SOI Institute.

Meeker, M. (1981b). *Using SOI test results: A teacher's guide*. El Segundo, CA: SOI Institute.

Mehler, J. (1985). Language related dispositions in early infancy. In J. Mehler & R. Fox (Eds.), *Neonate cognition: Beyond the blooming buzzing confusion*. Hillsdale, NJ: Lawrence Erlbaum.

Meltzoff, A. N., & Moore, M. K. (1985). Cognitive foundations and social functions of imitation and intermodal representations in infancy. In J. Mehler & R. Fox (Eds.), *Neonate cognition: Beyond the blooming buzzing confusion*. Hillsdale, NJ: Lawrence Erlbaum.

Mervis, C. B., & Mervis, C. A. (1982). Leopards are kitty-cats: Object labeling by mothers for their thirteen-month-olds. *Child Development, 53*, 267–273.

Moen, P. (1982). The two-provider family: Problems and potentials. In M. E. Lamb (Ed.), *Nontraditional families: Parenting and child development*. Hillsdale, NJ: Lawrence Erlbaum.

Moore, K. L. (1983). *Before we are born: Basic embryology and birth defects* (2nd ed.). Philadelphia: W. B. Saunders.

Myers, B. J. (1982). Early intervention using Brazelton training with middle-class mothers and fathers of newborns. *Child Development, 53*, 462–471.

N

Nilsson, L., Ingelman-Sundberg, A., & Wirsen, C. (1981). *A child is born*. New York: Dell/Seymour Lawrence.

Norman-Jackson, J. (1982). Family interactions, language development, and primary reading achievement of black children in families of low income. *Child Development, 53*, 349–358.

Nowlis, G. H., & Kessen, W. (1976). Human newborns differentiate differing concentrations of sucrose and glucose. *Science, 191*, 865–866.

Nye, F. I., & Lamberts, M. B. (1980). *School-age parenthood: Consequences for babies, mothers, fathers, grandparents, and others*. Washington State University: Cooperative Extension Bulletin 0667.

Nyiti, R. M. (1982). The validity of "cultural differences explanations" for cross-cultural variation in the rate of Piagetian cognitive development. In D. A. Wagner & H. W. Stevenson (Eds.), *Cultural perspectives on child development*. San Francisco: W. H. Freeman.

O

O'Connell, J. C. (1983, January). Children of working mothers: What the research tells us. *Young Children, 38*, 62–70.

Oden, S. (1982). Peer relationship development in childhood. In L. G. Katz (Ed.), *Current topics in early childhood education* (Vol. IV). Norwood, NJ: Ablex.

Ogbu, J. U. (1974). *The next generation: An ethnography of education in an urban neighborhood.* New York: Academic Press.

Ogbu, J. U. (1982). Socialization: A cultural ecological approach. In K. M. Borman, *The social life of children in a changing society.* Hillsdale, NJ: Lawrence Erlbaum.

Owens, R. E. (1984). *Language development: An introduction.* Columbus: Charles E. Merrill.

P

Pachon, P. (undated). *Fact sheet: What is SIDS?* Washington, DC: National Sudden Infant Death Clearinghouse.

Papert, S. (1980). *Mindstorms: Children, computers, and powerful ideas.* New York: Basic Books.

Parke, R. D., & Lewis, N. G. (1981). The family in context: A multilevel interactional analysis of child abuse. In R. W. Henderson (Ed.), *Parent-child interaction: Theory, research, and prospects.* New York: Academic Press.

Parten, M. (1932–33). Social participation among preschool children. *Journal of Abnormal and Social Psychology, 27,* 243–269.

Patton, J. R., Payne, J. S., Kauffman, J. M., Brown, G. B., & Payne, R. A. (1987). *Exceptional children in focus* (4th ed). Columbus: Charles E. Merrill.

Pelham, W. E., Schnedler, R. W., Bologna, N. C., & Contreros, J. A. (1980). Behavioral and stimulant treatment of hyperactive children: A therapy study with methylphenidate probes in a within-subject design. *Journal of Applied Behavior Analysis, 13,* 221–236.

Pellegrini, A. D. (1980). The relationship between kindergarteners' play and achievement in pre-reading, language and writing. *Psychology in the Schools, 17,* 530–535.

Pepler, D. J., & Ross, H. S. (1981). The effects of play on convergent and divergent problem solving. *Child Development, 52,* 1202–1210.

Peters, M. F. (1981). "Making it" black family style: Building on the strengths of black families. In N. Stinnett, J. DeFrain, K. King, P. Knaub, & G. Rowe (Eds.), *Family strengths 3: Roots of well being.* Lincoln: University of Nebraska Press.

Philosophy for Children. (1984). Upper Montclair, NJ: Institute for Advancement of Philosophy for Children.

Piaget, J. (1960a). *The child's conception of physical causality.* Totowa, NJ: Littlefield, Adams. (Originally published 1927)

Piaget, J. (1960b). *The child's conception of the world.* Totowa, NJ: Littlefield, Adams. (Originally published 1926)

Piaget, J. (1962). *Play, dreams, and imitation in childhood.* New York: W. W. Norton. (Originally published 1946)

Piaget, J. (1964). *Judgment and reasoning in the child.* Totowa, NJ: Littlefield, Adams. (Originally published 1924)

Piaget, J., & Inhelder, B. (1956). *The child's conception of space.* London: Routledge & Kegan Paul.

Piaget, J., & Inhelder, B. (1969). *The psychology of the child.* New York: Basic Books.

Pipes, P. L. (1981). *Nutrition in infancy and childhood* (2nd ed.). St. Louis: Mosby.

Practical Applications of Research: Newsletter of Phi Delta Kappa's Center on Evaluation, Development, and Research. (1983, June), *5.*

Provence, S. A., Naylor, A., & Patterson, J. (1977). *The challenge of day care.* New Haven: Yale University Press.

Putallaz, M., & Gottman, J. M. (1981). Social skills and group acceptance. In S. R. Asher & J. M. Gottman (Eds.), *The development of children's friendships.* Cambridge: Cambridge University Press.

R

Ramsey, P. G. (1982, January). Multicultural education in early childhood. *Young Children, 37,* 13–24.

Reed. G., & Leiderman, P. H. (1981). Age-related changes in attachment behavior in polymatrically reared infants: The Kenyan Gusii. In T. M. Field, A. M. Sostek, P. Vietze, & P. H. Leiderman (Eds.), *Culture and early interactions.* Hillsdale, NJ: Lawrence Erlbaum.

Reilly, A. P. (Ed.). (1980). *The communication game: Perspectives on the development of speech, language, and non-verbal communication skills: A round table.* Skillman, NJ: Johnson & Johnson.

Reynolds, E. O. R. (1978). Neonatal intensive care and the prevention of major handicaps. In Ciba Foundation Symposium 59, *Major mental handicap: Methods and costs of prevention.* New York: Elsevier-Excerpta Medica-North-Holland.

Richards, M. (1980). Adjective ordering in the language of young children: An experimental investigation. *Journal of Child Language, 6,* 253–277.

Robbins, E. (1984, Fall). American Red Cross teaches safety rules to children. *Day Care and Early Education, 12,* 32–33.

Rogers, C. R. (1961). *On becoming a person.* Boston: Houghton Mifflin.

Rogers, F. (1984, March). The past and the present is now. *Young Children, 39,* 13–18.

Royce, J. M., Darlington, R. B., & Murray, H. W. (1983). Pooled analysis: Findings across studies. In Consortium for Longitudinal Studies, *As the twig is bent . . . Lasting effects of preschool programs.* Hillsdale, NJ: Lawrence Erlbaum.

Russell, M. J. (1976). Human olfactory communication. *Nature, 260,* 520–522.

Rutter, M. (1983). Stress, coping and development: Some issues and some questions. In N. Garmezy & M. Rutter (Eds.), *Stress, coping, and development in children.* New York: McGraw-Hill.

S

Salapatek, P. (1975). Pattern perception in early infancy. In L. B. Cohen & P. Salapatek (Eds.), *Infant perception—From sensation to cognition: Vol. 2, Basic visual processes.* New York: Academic Press.

Saltus, R. (1983, January 30). Choosing the baby's sex: Not everyone wants a boy. San Francisco: *Sunday Examiner and Chronicle,* pp. B1, B4.

Sanford, A. R., & Zelman, J. G. (1981). *Learning accomplishment profile.* Winston-Salem, NC: Kaplan.

San Francisco Chronicle. (1983, July 18). Big jump in U.S. birth defects. p. 1

San Jose Mercury News. (1982, April 10). If it were mine to do again . . . pp. 1c, 3c.

Sapon-Shevin, M. (1983, January). Teaching children about differences: Resources for teaching. *Young Children, 38,* 24–31.

Saunders, A., & Remsberg, B. (1984). *The stress-proof child.* New York: Holt, Rinehart and Winston.

Saville-Troike, M. (1982). The development of bilingual and bicultural competence in young children. In L. G. Katz (Ed.), *Current topics in early childhood education* (Vol. IV). Norwood, NJ: Ablex.

Schachter, F. F. (1979). *Everyday mother talk to toddlers: Early intervention.* New York: Academic Press.

Schachter, F. F., & Strage, A. A. (1982). Adults' talk and children's language development. In S. G. Moore & C. R. Cooper (Eds.), *The young child: Reviews of research* (Vol. 3). Washington, DC: National Association for the Education of Young Children.

Schaffer, H. R., & Crook, C. K. (1980). Child compliance and maternal control techniques. *Developmental Psychology, 16,* 54–61.

Schiefelbusch, R. L. (1984). Assisting children to become communicatively competent. In R. L. Schiefelbusch & J. Pickar, *The acquisition of communicative competence.* Baltimore: University Park Press.

Schieffelin, B. B., & Ochs, E. (1983). A cultural perspective on the transition from prelinguistic to linguistic communication. In R. M. Golinkoff (Ed.), *The transition from prelinguistic to linguistic communication.* Hillsdale, NJ: Lawrence Erlbaum.

Segal, M., & Adcock, D. (1981). *Just pretending: Ways to help children grow through imaginative play.* White Plains, NY: Mailman Family Press. (Originally published by Prentice-Hall)

Selman, R. L. (1981). The child as friendship philosopher. In S. R. Asher & J. M. Gottman (Eds.), *The development of children's friendships.* Cambridge: Cambridge University Press.

Serrano, B. (1983, January 23). Teen-age pregnancy: A national epidemic. Stockton, CA: *Stockton Record,* pp. 1, 14.

Sever, J. L., Fuccillo, D. A., & Bowes, Jr., W. A. (1976). Environmental factors: Infection and immunizations. In R. L. Brent & M. I. Harris (Eds.), *Prevention of embryonic, fetal, and perinatal disease.* Bethesda, Maryland: National Institutes of Health.

Sherrod, L. R. (1981). Issues in cognitive-perceptual development: The special case of social stimuli. In M. E. Lamb & L. R. Sherrod (eds.), *Infant social cognition: Empirical and theoretical considerations.* Hillsdale, NJ: Lawrence Erlbaum.

Shonkoff, J. P. (1984). The biological substrate and physical health in middle childhood. In W. A Collins (Eds.), *Development during middle childhood: The years from six to twelve.* Washington, DC: National Academy Press.

Siegel, E. (1982). A critical examination of studies of parent-infant bonding. In M. H. Klaus & M. O. Robertson (Eds.), *Birth, interaction, and attachment: A round table.* Skillman, NJ: Johnson & Johnson.

Sims, R. (1983). What has happened to the "all-white" world of children's books? *Phi Delta Kappa, 64,* 650–653.

Singer, D. G., Singer, J. L., & Zuckerman, D. M. (1981). *Teaching television: How to use television to your child's advantage.* New York: Dial.

Skinner, B. F. (1948). *Walden two.* New York: Macmillan.

Skinner, B. F. (1974). *About behaviorism.* New York: Knopf.

Smollar, J., & Youniss, J. (1982). Social development through friendship. In K. H. Rubin & H. S. Ross (Eds.), *Peer relationships and social skills in childhood.* New York: Springer-Verlag.

Snow, C., DeBlauw, A., & Van Roosmalen, G. (1979). Talking and playing with babies: The role of ideologies in childrearing. In M. Bullowa (Ed.), *Before speech: The beginning of interpersonal communication.* Cambridge: Cambridge University Press.

Spelke, E. S. (1985). Perception of unity, persistence, and identity: Thoughts on infants' conceptions of objects. In J. Mehler & R. Fox (Eds.), *Neonate cognition: Beyond the blooming buzzing confusion.* Hillsdale, NJ: Lawrence Erlbaum.

Spelt, D. K. (1948). The conditioning of the human fetus in utero. *Journal of Experimental Psychology, 38,* 338–346.

Stein, S. B. (1974). *Making babies: An open family book for parents and children together.* New York: Walker and Company.

Stevens, J. H., Jr. (1982, January). Research in review: The New York City infant day care study. *Young Children, 37,* 47–53.

Stevens, J. H., Jr., & Baxter, D. H. (1981, May). Malnutrition and children's development. *Young Children, 36,* 60–71.

Stinnett, N., Sanders, G., & DeFrain, J. (1981). Strong families: A national study. In N. Stinnett, J. DeFrain, K. King, P. Knaub, & G. Rowe (Eds.), *Family strengths 3: Roots of well-being.* Lincoln: University of Nebraska Press.

Strauss, M. S., & Curtis, L. E. (1981). Infant perception of numerosity. *Child Development, 52,* 1146–1152.

Streissguth, A. P., Landesman-Dwyer, S., Martin, J. C., & Smith, D. W. (1980). Teratogenic effects of alcohol in humans and laboratory animals. *Science, 209,* 353–361.

Strott, D. (1973). Follow-up study from birth of the effects of prenatal stresses. *Developmental Medicine and Child Neurology, 15,* 770–787.

Sullivan, M. (1982). *Feeling strong, feeling free: Movement exploration for young children.* Washington, DC: National Association for the Education of Young Children.

Sullivan, M. W. (1982). Reactivation: Priming forgotten memories in human infants. *Child Development, 53,* 516–523.

T

Thomas, A., & Chess, S. (1981). The role of temperament in the contributions of individuals to their own development. In R. M. Lerner & N. A. Busch-Rossnagel (Eds.), *Individuals as producers of their development: A life-span perspective.* New York: Academic Press.

Thomas, A., & Chess, S. (1984). Genesis and evolution of behavioral disorders: From infancy to early adult life. *American Journal of Psychiatry, 141,* 1–9.

Thomas, N. G., & Berk, L. E. (1981). Effects of school environments on the development of young children's creativity. *Child Development, 52,* 1153–1162.

Thurber, J. (1971). *Many moons.* New York: Harcourt Brace Jovanovich.

Townsend, J. W., Klein, R. E., Irwin, M. H., Owens, W., Yarbrough, C., & Engle, P. L. (1982). Nutrition and preschool mental development. In D. A. Wagner & H. W. Stevenson (Eds.), *Cultural perspectives on child development.* San Francisco: W. H. Freeman.

Trause, M. A., & Irvin, N. A. (1982). Care of the sibling. In M. H. Klaus & J. H. Kennell, *Parent-infant bonding* (2nd ed.). St. Louis: Mosby.

Tulkin, S. R. (1977). Social class differences in maternal and infant behavior. In P. H. Leiderman, S. R. Tulkin, & A. Rosenfeld (Eds.), *Culture and infancy: Variations in the human experience.* New York: Academic Press.

Turkle, S. (1984). *The second self: Computers and the human spirit.* New York: Simon & Schuster.

U

U.S. Bureau of the Census. (1982). *Characteristics of American children and youth: 1980.* Current Population Reports, P–23, No. 114. Washington, DC: U.S. Government Printing Office.

U.S. Department of Labor. (1980). *Perspectives on working women: A databook.* (Bulletin 2080). Washington, DC: U.S. Bureau of Labor Statistics.

U.S. Department of Transportation, National Highway Traffic Safety Administration. (1980). *Child restraint systems for your automobile.* Washington, DC

U.S. Office of Education. (1977, December 29). Assistance to states for education of the handicapped: Procedures for evaluating specific learning disabilities. *Federal Register* (Part III). Washington, DC: Department of HEW.

U.S. Office of Education. (1977, August 23). Education of handicapped children. *Federal Register* (Part II). Washington, DC: Department of HEW.

V

Valentine, D. (1982). Adaptation to pregnancy: Some implications for individual and family mental health. *Children Today, 11,* 17–20, 36.

Van Buren, A. (1982, November 16). Dear Abby. *San Francisco Chronicle,* p. 41.

Van Hoorn, J. L. (1982). *Games of infancy: A cross-cultural study.* Unpublished doctoral dissertation, University of California, Berkeley.

Verny, T., with Kelly, J. (1981). *The secret life of the unborn child.* New York: Summit Books.

Voyat, G. (1983). *Cognitive development among Sioux children.* New York: Plenum.

Vygotsky, L. S. (1962). *Thought and language.* Cambridge, MA: MIT Press.

W

Wachs, T. D. (1982). Relation of home noise-confusion to infant cognitive development. Paper presented at the meeting of the American Psychological Association, Washington, DC.

Wachs, T. D., & Gruen, G. E. (1982). *Early experience and human development.* New York: Plenum Press.

Wadsworth, B. J. (1984). *Piaget's theory of cognitive and affective development* (3rd ed.). New York: Longman.

Waters, E., Matas, L., & Sroufe, L. A. (1975). Infants' reactions to an approaching stranger: Description, validation, and functional significance of wariness. *Child Development, 46,* 348–356.

Watson, A. J. (1984). Cognitive development and units of print in early reading. In J. Downing and Renate Valtin (Eds.), *Language awareness and learning to read.* New York: Springer-Verilag.

Watson, J. B. (1928). *Psychological care of infant and child.* New York: W. W. Norton.

Watson, J. D. (1968). *The double helix.* New York: Atheneum.

Wehren, A., DeLisi, R., & Arnold, M. (1981). The development of noun definition. *Journal of Child Language, 8,* 165–175.

Weintraub, M., & Lewis, M. (1977). The determinants of children's responses to separation. *Monographs of the Society for Research in Child Development, 42*(4, Serial No. 172).

Weisner, T. S. (1982). Sibling interdependence and child caregiving: A cross-cultural view. In M. E. Lamb B. Sutton-Smith (Eds.), *Sibling relationships: Their nature and significance across the lifespan.* Hillsdale, NJ: Lawrence Erlbaum.

Werner, E. E. (1979) *Cross-cultural child development: A view from the planet earth.* Monterey, CA: Brooks/Cole.

Werner, E. E. (1984, November). Resilient children. *Young Children, 40,* 68–72.

Werner, E. E., & Smith, R. S. (1982). *Vulnerable, but invincible: A longitudinal study of resilient children and youth.* New York: McGraw-Hill

Westinghouse Learning Corporation–Ohio University. (1973). The impact of Head Start: An evaluation of the effects of Head Start on children's cognitive and affective development (1969). In J. L. Frost (Ed.), *Revisiting early childhood education.* New York: Holt, Rinehart & Winston.

Whalen, C. K., & Henker, B. (1980). The social ecology of psychostimulant treatment: A model for conceptual and empirical analysis. In C. K. Whalen & B. Henker (Eds.), *Hyperactive children: The social ecology of identification and treatment.* New York: Academic Press.

White, B. L. (1978). *Experience and environment: Major influences on the development of the young child* (Vol 2). Englewood Cliffs, NJ: Prentice-Hall.

White, B. L. (1985). *The first three years of life* (rev. ed). New York: Simon & Schuster.

White, B. L., Kaban, B. T., & Attanucci, J. S. (1979). *The origins of human competence: The final report of the Harvard Preschool Project.* Lexington, MA: Lexington Books.

White, B. L., & Watts, J. C. (1973). *Experience and environment: Major influences on the development of the young child* (Vol 1). Englewood Cliffs, NJ: Prentice-Hall.

White, R. W. (1959). Motivation reconsidered: The concept of competence. *Psychological Bulletin, 66,* 297–333.

Whitener, C. B., & Kersey, K. (1980). A purple hippopotamus? Why not! *Childhood Education, 57,* 83–89.

Wiig, E. H., & Semel, E. M. (1984). *Language assessment and intervention for the learning disabled.* (2nd ed.). Columbus: Charles E. Merrill.

Will, G. F. (1983, January). The poison poor children breathe. *Young Children, 38,* 11–12.

Williams, L. R., & DeGaetano, Y. (1985). *ALERTA: A multicultural, bilingual approach to teaching young children.* Menlo Park, CA: Addison-Wesley.

Wilson, J. G. (1976). Environmental factors: Teratogenic drugs. In R. L. Brent & M. I. Harris (Eds.), *Prevention of embryonic, fetal, and perinatal disease.* Bethesda: National Institutes of Health.

Winick, M. (1976). Maternal nutrition. In R. L. Brent & M. I. Harris (Eds.), *Prevention of embryonic, fetal, and perinatal disease.* Bethesda: National Institutes of Health.

Wishon, P. M., Bower, R., & Eller, B. (1983). Childhood obesity: Prevention and treatment. *Young Children, 39,* 21–27.

Witkin, H. A., & Berry, J. W. (1975). Psychological differentiation in cross-cultural perspective. *Journal of Cross-Cultural Psychology, 6,* 4–87.

Witkin, H. A., Dyke, R. B., Faterson, H. F., Goodenough, D. R., & Karp, S. A. (1962). *Psychological differentiation.* New York: Wiley.

Witkin, H. A., Price-Williams, D., Bertini, M., Christiansen, B., Oltman, P., Ramirez, M., & Van Meel, J. (1974). Social conformity and psychological differentiation. *International Journal of Psychology, 9,* 11–29.

Wood, B. S. (1981). *Children and communication: Verbal and nonverbal language development* (2nd ed.). Englewood Cliffs, NJ: Prentice-Hall.

Y

Yang, P. K. (1981). Maternal attitudes during pregnancy and medication during labor and delivery: Methodological considerations. In V. L. Smeriglio (Ed.), *Newborns and parents: Parent-infant contact and newborn sensory stimulation.* Hillsdale, NJ: Lawrence Erlbaum.

Z

Zahn-Waxler, C., Iannotti, R., & Chapman, M. (1982). Peers and prosocial development. In K. H. Rubin & H. S. Ross (Eds.), *Peer relationships and social skills in childhood.* New York: Springer-Verlag.

Zolotow, C. (1972). Illustrations by W. P. DuBois. *William's doll.* New York: Harper & Row.

Name Index

Adams, G. R., 369
Adcock, D., 292
Ainsworth, M. D. S., 122, 124, 127
Almy, M., 286
Alvino, J., 394
Ambramovich, R., 317–318
Ames, L. B., 241, 354–355, 375
Andrews, S. R., 296–297
Anselmo, S., 33, 329, 390
Apgar, V., 98
Arnold, M., 397
Attanucci, J. S., 293
Azrin, N. H., 260

Bachtold, L. M., 402–404
Bailey, Jr., D. B., 355
Bandura, A., 15, 324
Bass, E., 367–368
Baumrind, D., 316
Bax, M., 248
Baxter, D. H., 254
Beautrais, A. L., 249
Bell, S. M., 124, 127
Belsky, J., 219–220
Benirschke, K., 70, 72–73
Berger, S., 335
Berk, L. E., 402
Berry, J. W., 419
Bertini, D., 419
Best, R., 320, 322–323
Bloom, L., 275, 278
Bloomfield, L., 277
Bologna, N. C., 364
Borke, H., 275
Bornstein, M. H., 141
Bower, R., 372
Bower, T. G. R., 179–181
Bowlby, J., 106, 121–122, 124
Brady, E. H., 408

Brazelton, T. B., 98, 100–101, 106, 117–118, 121, 140, 143–144, 147, 203, 207, 259
Brent, R. L., 56, 63
Brittain, W. L., 236–237, 347–350
Bromwich, R., 166
Bronfenbrenner, U., 7, 29, 46, 79
Brooks-Gunn, J., 172, 209–210
Brown, A. L., 416–417
Brown, C. C., 85
Brown, G. B., 355
Brown, M. W., 336
Bruner, J., 285, 288
Burgess, B. J., 226
Burke, M. G., 283
Burtoff, B., 203
Bushnell, M., 45
Bybee, R. W., 277

Callagan, J. W., 119
Campas, J. J., 129
Carew, J. V., 219
Carey, W. B., 191, 200
Carpenter, G., 141
Caudle, S., 214–215
Chall, J., 213
Chapman, M., 320–321
Chess, S., 130, 199, 202, 336
Chez, R. A., 56
Chomsky, N., 277
Christiansen, B., 419
Colao, F., 367–370
Collins, W. A., 426
Condry, S., 410–411
Contreros, J. A., 364
Coplan, J., 283
Corter, C., 317–318
Cowan, P. A., 261, 366
Crane, P., 369
Crockenberg, S., 127

Culligan, E. J., 56
Cummings, E., 215

Darlington, R. B., 411–412
Darwin, C., 5–6, 20
Deach, C., 368
De Blauw, A., 185
De Casper, A. J., 122–123, 181
Deci, E. L., 415
De Frain, J., 314
De Lisi, R., 397
De Loache, J. S., 416–417
Demany, L., 143
Dennis, W., 153
De Vries, R., 277
Dewey, J., 6
Dickman, I. R., 55, 57, 364
Dillon, M., 224
Dinkmeyer, D., 20
Dittman, L. S., 135
Donaldson, M., 274–275
Donovan, J., 413
Draper, T. W., 412–413
Dreikurs, R., 216–217
Dridz, T. A., 156, 158, 251–252
Dunn, J., 108
Dweck, C. S., 321–322
Dyke, R. B., 419

Eiduson, B. T., 213
Eisenberg, N., 406
Elizur, E., 260
Elkin, D., 277, 312, 335–336
Eller, B., 372
Engen, T., 142
Engle, P. L., 253
Epps, E. G., 426
Ericsson, R., 59
Erikson, E., 15–17, 85, 116–117, 128, 196–198, 225, 310, 425
Eron, L. D., 325–326, 337–338

Fagot, B. I., 210, 405–406
Fajardo, B. F., 119
Falbo, T., 318
Fantz, R., 141
Farel, A. M., 133
Faterson, H. F., 419
Fein, G. G., 288–290
Feingold, B. F., 363
Feiring, C., 185
Fergusson, D. M., 249
Field, T., 185
Fifer, W. P., 122–123, 181
Fishbein, H. D., 391–392, 416–417
Fletcher, J. C., 60
Fowler, W., 178
Foxx, R. M., 260
Frankenburg, W., 85, 186
Freedman, D. G., 119
Freeman, L., 368
Freud, A., 15

Freud, S., 7, 15–16
Friedman, S., 141
Frodi, A. M., 124
Fullard, W., 200

Galinsky, E., 85, 215, 313
Ganz, M., 106
Gardner, J., 61
Garmezy, N., 334
Garvey, C., 278, 280, 288
Gearhart, M., 417–418
Gentner, D., 397
Gesell, A., 6, 20–22
Gillespie, C., 241, 354–355, 375
Gilligan, C., 313, 323
Ginott, H., 20
Ginsburg, H. J., 405
Gleason, J. R., 283
Gleitman, L. R., 277
Glover, M. F., 149
Goldenberg, D., 355
Goldman, J. D. G., 366
Goldman, R. J., 366
Goldsmith, R. H., 372
Golinkoff, R. M., 183
Goodall, J., 29, 286
Goodenough, D. R., 419
Gordon, S., 364
Gordon, T., 20–21, 216–218
Gorelick, M., 389–390
Gottfried, A. E., 415–416
Gottman, J. M., 320–321
Gouze, K., 324
Grajek, S., 133, 220
Grollman, E. A., 336
Gruen, G. E., 188
Grusec, J. E., 207
Guilford, J. P., 402

Haines, J., 241, 354–355, 375
Hale, J., 419
Hall, G. S., 6–7, 20
Hall, W. S., 417–418
Hamill, P. V., 156, 158, 251–252
Harding, C. G., 183–185
Harlow, H. F., 122
Harrel, J., 214
Harris, M. I., 56, 63
Harter, S., 415
Haswell, K. L., 198
Helfer, R., 58, 104
Henker, B., 364
Hill, S., 408
Hillerich, R. L., 399–400
Hite, S. J., 412–413
Hite, T., 406
Hoban, R., 205
Hock, E., 198
Honig, A. S., 281, 324, 326
Hood, L., 275
Hoot, J., 401
Hosansky, T., 367, 370

Hubbell, R., 409–410
Huesmann, L. R., 337–338
Hughes, M., 274–275
Hunter, A. S., 53
Huntington, D. S., 135
Hymes, D., 327

Ianotti, R., 320–321
Ilg, F. L., 241, 375
Irvin, N. A., 109
Irwin, M. D., 45
Irwin, M. H., 253

Jablow, M. M., 188
James, W., 140
Janis, I. L., 331
Jensen, A., 6
Jerauld, R., 103
Johnson, C. L., 156, 158, 251–252
Johnson, T. G., 399–400
Jorn, M., 135

Kaban, B. T., 293
Kaffman, M., 260
Kamii, C., 277
Karmel, M., 87
Karmiloff-Smith, A., 279
Karp, S. A., 419
Katz, P., 209–210, 212
Kauffman, J. M., 355
Kavanaugh, R. D., 223–224
Kaye, H., 142
Kazan, J., 275
Keeshaw, B., 224
Kellogg, R., 235–236
Kendrick, C., 108
Keniston, K., 83
Kennell, J. H., 102–103, 105, 160
Kephart, N. C., 238–239, 352–353
Kersey, K., 237
Kessen, W., 142
Klaus, M. H., 58, 102–106, 160
Klein, R. E., 253
Kobus, D. K., 330
Kornfein, M., 213
Kornhaber, A., 203
Kreger, N., 103
Kronsberg, S. J., 210, 405–406
Kuhl, P. K., 183

Labinowicz, E., 277
Lamb, M., 124, 128–129, 133
Lambert, W. E., 400–401
Lamme, L. L., 347–350
Landesman Dwyer, S., 66
Lansing, K. M., 236
Laosa, L. M., 227
Larick, N., 213
Larsen, J. M., 412–413
Lazar, I., 411–412
Leboyer, F., 96
Leger, T., 104, 106

Leiderman, P. H., 125–126
Lepper, M. R., 415
Lerner, J., 355
Le Shan, E., 336
Lester, B. M., 100–101
Leventhal, H., 331
LeVine, R. A., 170, 225–226
Levy, J., 146
Lewis, M., 172, 185, 206
Lewis, N. G., 214–215
Lipman, M., 395
Lipsitt, L. P., 142
Locke, J., 5–6
Londerville, S., 124
Lorton, B., 390–391

Maccoby, E. E., 333
Main, M., 124
Malahoff, A., 99
Mardel-Czudnowsky, C., 355
Markus, H. J., 425
Martin, J. C., 66
Maslow, A., 18–20
Matas, L., 125
Matthews, G. B., 292–294
Matthews, W. S., 209–210
McAlpine, W., 103
McCall, R. B., 223–224
McCartney, K., 133, 220
McClusky, K., 127
McDevitt, S. C., 200
McGhee, P. E., 404–405
McKay, G. D., 20
McKenzie, B., 143
Meeker, M., 402
Mehler, J., 181
Meltzoff, A. N., 179
Mervis, C. A., 278
Mervis, C. B., 278
Miller, S. M., 405
Monighan, P., 286
Moore, K. L., 61, 65, 70, 75, 79
Moore, M. K., 179
Moore, W. M., 156, 158, 251–252
Murray, E., 406
Murray, H. W., 411–412
Myers, B. J., 100

Naylor, A., 47
Nowlis, G. H., 142
Nurius, P. S., 425
Nyiti, R. M., 392

Ochs, E., 184–186
O'Connell, J. C., 220
Oden, S., 223–224
Ogbu, J. U., 417
Oltman, P., 419
Owens, R. E., 181–182, 278, 396–397
Owens, W., 253

Papert, S., 407–408
Parke, R. D., 214–215, 223–224

Parkhurst, J. T., 321
Parten, M. B., 41–42, 222
Patterson, J., 47
Patton, J. R., 355
Pavlov, I. P., 12–13
Payne, J. S., 355
Payne, R. A., 355
Pearson, K., 20
Pelham, W. E., 364
Pellegrini, A. D., 401
Pepler, D., 317–318, 403
Persky, B., 135
Pestalozzi, J. H., 5
Phillips, D., 133, 220
Piaget, J., 7–12, 35, 40, 266–273, 285–290, 415
Pipes, P. L., 155, 372
Preminger, J. L., 149
Price-Williams, D., 419
Provence, S. A., 47
Putallaz, M., 320

Radke-Yarrow, M., 215
Ramirez, M., 419
Ramsey, P. G., 329
Reed, G., 125–126
Reed, R. B., 156, 158, 251–252
Reilly, A. P., 182
Remsberg, B., 332, 336
Richards, M., 397
Robbins, E., 376
Robertson, M. O., 58
Roche, A. F., 156, 158
Rogers, C., 18–20
Rogers, F., 325, 336
Rollins, P., 390
Ross, H. S., 403
Rousseau, J. J., 5–6
Royce, J. M., 411–412
Russell, M. J., 142
Rutter, M., 331, 334
Ryan, R., 283, 415

Saltus, R., 60
Sanders, G., 314
Sanford, A. R., 149, 232, 346–350
Sapon-Shevin, M., 362
Saunders, A., 332, 336
Saville-Troike, M., 400–401
Scales, B., 286
Scarr, S., 133, 220
Schachter, F. F., 284
Schiefelbusch, R. L., 398
Schieffelin, B. B., 184–186
Schnedler, R. W., 364
Schuckman, R., 390
Schwartz, J. C., 133, 220
Segal, M., 292
Selman, R. L., 319
Semel, E., 285
Serrano, B., 55
Shannon, F. T., 249
Sherrod, L. R., 141

Shonkoff, J. P., 425–426
Siegal, A., 224
Siegel, E., 103
Sims, R., 213
Skinner, B. F., 13–14
Smith, D. W., 66
Smith, R. S., 334
Smith, S. F., 426
Smollar, J., 320
Snow, C., 185
Spelke, E. S., 141
Spelt, D. K., 80
Sroufe, L. A., 125
Stechler, G., 141
Steffa, M., 103
Steinberg, L. D., 219–220
Stenberg, C. R., 129
Stevens, J. H., 221, 254
Stevenson, H. W., 100
Stinnett, N., 314
Stiver, J., 99
Strage, A. A., 284
Streissguth, A. P., 66
Sullivan, M., 352–353
Sund, R. B., 277

Tecce, J. J., 141
Terman, L., 6
Thomas, A., 130, 199, 202, 336
Thomas, N. G., 402
Thompson, R. A., 124
Thornton, L., 367–368
Thurber, J., 393
Townsend, J. W., 253
Trause, M. A., 104, 106, 109
Tulkin, S. R., 185
Turkle, S., 406–407

Valentine, D., 87
Van Hoorn, J., 286
Van Meel, J., 419
Van Roosmalen, G., 185
Voyat, G., 392
Vurpillot, E., 143

Wachs, T. D., 188, 295
Wadsworth, B. J., 277
Wagner, D. A., 100
Wanner, E., 277
Waters, E., 125
Watson, A., 397
Watson, J. B., 13, 48
Watson, J. D., 58
Watts, J. C., 293–294, 414
Wehren, A., 397
Weintraub, M., 206
Weisner, T. S., 213, 318
Wenar, C., 198
Werner, E. E., 82, 155, 157, 242, 333–334, 391–392
Westman, J. C., 191
Whalen, C. K., 364
White, B. L., 293–295, 413–415

Whitener, C. B., 237
Widmayer, S. M., 185
Wiig, E. H., 285
Will, G. F., 248
Williams, G., 205
Williams, M. L., 283
Wingate, M. B., 56
Winick, M., 82–83
Wishon, P. M., 372
Witkin, H. A., 417–419
Wolery, M., 355
Wood, B. S., 281

Yang, P. K., 87, 95
Yarbrough, C., 253
Youniss, J., 320

Zahn-Waxler, C., 215, 320–321
Zelman, J. G., 232, 346–350
Zimmerman, I. L., 213
Zimmerman, R. R., 122
Zolotow, C., 211, 336

Subject Index

Abortion, 72, 75
Abuse and neglect. *See* Child abuse and neglect
Abusive parents, 214–215
Academic achievement, 320
Accident prevention, 246
Accidents, 242–247
Accommodation, 10–11
Active intermodal mapping, 179
Active listening, 217–218
Adult-child interaction, 185, 293–294, 398
Advantaged children, 412–413
African children, 226
Aggression, 15, 224, 338
Alcohol abuse, 65–66
Alternate family structure, 213–214
Alternative caregivers, 134–135
Altruism, one-to-three-year-olds, 207
Amblyopia, 375
Amniocentesis, 70–72
Amniotic cavity, 70
Amniotic fluid, 79
Animal behavior studies, 29
Animism, 383
Anorexia, 254
Apgar score, 98
Appetite, 250
Artificial insemination, 99
Asian children, 242
Assessment
    childhood stress, 332
    conservation, 384–388
    Cross-cultural Understanding in Multicultural
        Education (CUME), 330
    cultural differences, 362–363
    Early Language Milestone (ELM) scale, 283
    infants, 186
    language, 283
    logical thinking, 390
    multicultural understanding, 330
    newborn, 98–101

temperament, 200–202
    Toddler Temperamental Scale, 200–202
Assimilation, 10–11
Associative play, 222–223
Attachment
    day care, 220
    infants, 116–117, 121–127, 129, 170
    newborns, 102
Attention deficit disorder, 363–364
Attention seeking, 226
Attractiveness, 369–371
Audio tape, 31, 33, 46
Authoritarian parenting, 316
Authoritative parenting, 316
Authority stage of parenting, 216
Auto accident prevention, 243–244
Autonomy
    creativity, 404
    cultural differences, 226–227
    one-to-three-year-olds, 196–206
    psychosocial adjustment, 16
    vs. shame, 199

Babbling, 182–183
Babinski reflex, 144
Babkin reflex, 144
Balance, 345–346
Bayley Intelligence Test, 293
Behavioral theories of development, 12–14
Behavior disorders, 337
Behavior modification, 16–17
Being needs, 20
Bilingualism, 400–401
Birthing rooms, 88–89
Black characters in children's literature, 213
Black children, 242, 249, 284–285, 410–412
Black English, 284–285
Black mother-infant communication, 185
Blastomeres, 75
Body awareness, 256–258

Body image, 257
Body type, 60–61
Bonding, 103–106
Bottle feeding, 256
Bottle mouth syndrome, 256
Bowlby's stages of attachment, 122–123
Brain damage, 144, 249
Brazelton Neonatal Behavioral Assessment, 98–101
Breast-feeding, 103, 154–155
Breast milk, 154–155
Burn prevention, 246
Burst-pause pattern, 144

Caesarean childbirth, 96–97
Canadian children, 392
Carnegie Council on Children, 85
Car seats, 244–245
Case studies, 46–47, 192, 300, 422
Cause and effect, 383–384
Cell division, 75
Center for Parent Education, 413
Central American children, 242
Central nervous system, 63, 67
Cephalo-caudal development, 148
Cephalo-caudal principle, 22
Cervix, 72
Checklists, 28, 36–39, 191, 300–306, 422
Child abuse and neglect
  abusive parents, 214–215
  China, 214
  cultural differences, 214
  economic factors, 214
  handicapped newborns, 104
  incidence, 214
  incidence in preterm infants, 104
  infants, 163–165
  Japan, 214
  newborns, 104
  parental factors, 55–58
  parent-child interaction patterns, 215–218
  parent expectations, 215
  preterm infants, 104
Childbirth
  anesthesia, 96
  birthing rooms, 88–89
  breathing techniques, 87
  Caesarean delivery, 96–97
  central nervous system depression, 95
  cervical block, 96
  cervical dilation, 94, 96
  contractions, 94
  drugs, 86–87, 95–96
  environment, 88
  episiotomy, 96
  family presence, 89
  father's role, 87
  fetal monitoring, 96
  fetal position, 94
  home birth, 88
  labor, 94–95
  Lamaze method, 87
  Leboyer method, 87–88

  medication, 95–96
  membrane rupture, 94
  mucus plug, 95
  normal, 95–96
  pain control, 87–89
  perineal incision, 96
  placenta, 95–96
  prepared childbirth movement, 87–89
  spinal anesthetic, 97
  stages of labor, 94–95
  training, 87–89
  umbilical cord, 94, 97
Child diaries, 28, 33–36, 191, 280, 300, 422
Childrearing practices. *See* Parenting
Chromosomes and genes, 58–61
Classical conditioning, 12–13, 87
Classification, 11, 387–389, 406
Cognitive development
  animism, 383
  autonomy, 404
  bilingualism, 400–401
  cause and effect, 383–384
  classification, 387–389, 406
  collective symbolism, 289
  compensation, 387
  competence, 293–295
  computer aided instruction (CAI), 407
  computers and thinking, 406–408
  concrete objects, 390
  concrete operational stage, 382–391
  conservation, 384–387
  Consortium for Longitudinal Studies, 410–412
  creativity, 401–403
  cultural differences, 392, 400–401
  deferred imitation, 269
  drawing, 235–237
  drugs, 63, 65
  early education programs, 408–413
  educational intervention, 296–297
  egocentricity, 272
  empathy, 275
  encouraging pretense, 292
  environmental effects, 293–297
  environmental factors, 61–63
  expressive language, 279
  fears, 271
  four- to eight-year-olds, 381–422
  genetic factors, 61
  Harvard Preschool Project, 293–295
  Head Start, 409–410
  home environment, 293–296
  humor, 403–405
  idiosyncratic concepts, 271
  imaginary companions, 289
  imitation, 266–267
  incongruities and humor, 403–405
  infants, 169–192
  interaction of factors, 67
  language assessment, 283
  language development, 277–285, 396–401
  learning environments, 276–277
  linguistic milestones, 396–398

Cognitive development, *continued*
 logic, 382–396
 LOGO, 408
 mental symbols, 270–271
 middle childhood, 426
 noise and confusion, 295–296
 nourishing creativity, 404
 object permanence, 267–269
 one- to three-year-olds, 265–306
 Parent Child Development Centers (PCDCs), 296–297
 philosophical thinking, 393–396
 Piaget's stages, 8–12, 266–273, 382–391
 play, 285–293, 401–408
 preoperational stage, 382–391
 preoperational thinking, 269–273
 pretense, 288–293
 problem solving, 266
 receptive language, 278–279
 reversibility, 387
 self-awareness, 275–276
 sensorimotor stage, 172–177, 266–269
 seriation, 388
 solitary symbolic play, 288–289
 stimulation, 295–296
 Structure of Intellect (SOI), 402
 symbolic thought, 269
 television, 290
 tertiary circular reactions, 266–277
 thought patterns, 271–273
 "three mountain experiment," 274
 transductive reasoning, 271
 turn-taking, 288
Cognitive theories of development, 8–12
Colostrum, 154
Communal living, 213–214
Compensation, 387
Competence, 143–146, 293–295, 312–313, 414
Computer aided instruction (CAI), 407
Computers and thinking, 406–408
Concrete objects, 390
Concrete operational stage, 382–391
Conflict resolution, 217–218
Congenital malformations, 61–69
 alcohol abuse, 65–66
 anencephaly, 67
 cleft lip and palate, 67
 club feet, 67
 congenital heart disease, 67
 cystic fibrosis, 62
 death rate, 61
 DES, 65–66
 Down syndrome, 61–63
 drugs, 63, 65
 environmental factors, 62–67
 fetal alcohol syndrome, 66
 genetic factors, 61–62
 heart defects, 61
 heart disease, 67
 hip dislocation, 67
 incidence, 61
 interaction of factors, 67
 joint abnormalities, 66
 learning disabilities, 68

 major morphological abnormalities, 64
 maternal age, 61
 maternal-fetal blood incompatibility, 68–69
 mendelian disorders, 62
 mental retardation, 61–62
 minor morphological abnormalities, 64
 Rh factor, 68–69
 rhogam, 69
 sickle cell anemia, 62
 smoking, 67
 spina bifida, 67
 Tay-Sachs disease, 62
 teratogens, 63–65, 76
 teratology, 63
 thalassemia, 62
 thalidomide, 65
 trisomy, 61
 Turner syndrome, 61
 viruses, 63
 X chromosomes, 61
 Y chromosomes, 61
Conservation, 384–387, 405
Consortium for Longitudinal Studies, 410–412
Controlled scribbling, 237
Cooing, 181–182
Cooperation, 124, 216
Coping, 331–333
Crawling, 175
Creativity, 401–403
Cross-Cultural Understanding in Multicultural Education (CUME), 330
Crozats, 374
Crying, 127–128
Cuban mother-infant communication, 185
Cultural differences
 adult-infant interaction, 185
 African children, 226
 Asian children, 242
 assessment, 330, 362–363
 attention seeking, 226
 autonomy, 225–227
 bilingualism, 400–401
 birth weight, 83–85
 black children, 242
 black English, 284–285
 Canadian children, 392
 Central American children, 242
 changing racial stereotypes, 212
 child abuse and neglect, 214
 childrearing practices, 170–171, 417–418
 cognitive style, 419
 cultural deficit model, 226
 cultural difference model, 226
 early education programs, 408–412
 economic opportunity, 417–418
 educational system, 225–227
 Guatemalan children, 288–289
 handicapping conditions, 361
 Head Start, 409–410
 Hopi infants, 153
 Indian children, 242
 infant mortality, 85, 171
 infants, 119–121, 126–127, 153, 170–171, 184–188

intellectual development, 392
IQ tests, 6
Kenyan children, 203
language development, 284–285
language use, 327, 418–419
maternal prenatal care, 81
Mesquaki Fox children, 327
Micmac Indian children, 392
minority overrepresentation in special education, 361
mother-infant interaction, 185
multicultural understanding, 328–331
Native American children, 226, 326–328
Navaho children, 327
Navaho newborns, 101–102
newborns, 101–102
Oglala Sioux children, 392
parent-infant interactions, 101–102
physical development, 242
play, 288
Polynesian children, 318
prenatal care, 83–85
psychosocial development, 225–227
Puerto Rican children, 203
racial awareness, 211–212
school adjustment, 326–328
school problems, 393
school success, 417–419
school system, 225–227
sibling relationships, 318
Sioux children, 226
sleeping "problems," 202–203
South Asian children, 318
special education placement, 412
Tangu children, 288
Tewa-speaking children, 327
verification of Piaget's theories, 391–392
vocalization to infants, 185
walking, 153
Yurok children, 116
Zinacantecos newborns, 101–102
Cystic fibrosis, 62

Day care
    adult-child ratio, 221
    attachment, 220
    cognitive/language stimulation, 221
    emotional development, 220–221
    emotional maladjustment, 220–221
    health care, 221
    infants, 133–135
    intellectual development, 219–221
    low income children, 219
    New York City Infant Day Care Study, 219, 221
    nutritional programs, 221
    one-to-three-year-olds, 218–221
    peer social interactions, 221
    physical environment, 221
    psychosocial development, 218–221
    social effects, 221
    social/emotional stimulation, 221
Death rates, 243
Deferred imitation, 269
Delayed attachment, 123

Delinquencies, 320
Dental care, 255–256, 373–374
Denver Developmental Screening Test (DDST), 186–187
Deoxyribonucleic acid (DNA), 58–59
Deprivation needs, 20
DES, 65
Desired response, 13
Developmental disabilities, 283
Developmental problems, 85
Diana v. State of California, 361
Diethylstilbestrol (DES), 65
Directionality, 258
Discipline, 151, 216–217, 311
Disequilibrium, 12
Distress-relief sequence, 128–129
Divorce, 335
DNA, 58–59, 62
Doubt vs. autonomy, 198
Down syndrome
    amniocentesis, 71
    early intervention programs, 188
    genetic factors, 61–62
    incidence, 63
    infant-family involvement, 106
    maternal age, 61, 63
    newborns, 106
    prevention, 72
DPT vaccine, 254–255
Drawing
    cognitive development, 235–237
    early representational stage, 348
    four-to-eight-year-olds, 347–351
    naming of scribbling, 347
    one-to-three-year-olds, 234–237
    preschematic stage, 349
    schematic stage, 350
    scribbling, 236–237
Drowning prevention, 246
Drugs
    childbirth, 95–96
    during labor, 86–87
    hyperactivity, 364
    infant performance, 87
    pregnancy, 65–66
Due process, 360

Ear infections, 248
Early childhood development (ECD)
    age range, 2
    contemporary theories, 8
    definition, 2
    experimental methods, 28
    helping professions, 2
    history of study, 4
    naturalistic study, 29
    parenting, 2
    scientific study, 5
    social context, 85
Early education programs
    Consortium for Longitudinal Studies, 410–412
    grade retention, 412
    Head Start, 409–410
    health services, 410

Early education programs, *continued*
   IQ, 411, 413
   motivation, 411
   school achievement, 410, 411
   teacher-child ratio, 412
Early intervention programs, 188–189
Early Language Milestone (ELM) scale, 283
Ectopic pregnancy, 76
Educational intervention, 296–297
Education for All Handicapped Children Act, 355,
   360–361
Effectiveness, 129
Egocentricity, 272
Ego integration vs. despair, 19
Ejaculation, 72
Embedded Figures Test, 419
Embryo
   anencephaly, 67
   cleft lip and palate, 67
   club feet, 67
   congenital heart disease, 67
   death rate, 61
   definition, 76
   drugs, 63, 65
   environmental factors, 61–63
   formation, 61–69
   genetic factors, 61
   heart defects, 61
   heart disease, 66–67
   hip dislocation, 67
   interaction of factors, 67
   joint abnormalities, 66
   maternal-fetal blood incompatibility, 68–69
   Rh factor, 68
   rhogam, 69
   spina bifida, 67
   teratogens, 63–65, 76
   teratology, 63
   viruses, 63
   X chromosomes, 61
   Y chromosomes, 61
Embryologists, 75
Embryology, 61
Embryonic period, 80
Emotional disturbance, 356, 359
Emotional maladjustment, 220
Emotional problems, 320
Empathy, 275
Engrossment, 106–107
Episiotomy, 96
Equilibrium, 12
Erectile tissue, 72
Erikson's psychosocial theory, 15–16, 19, 197–198
Ethics
   artificial insemination, 99
   handicapped newborns, 99
   informed consent, 48
   Society for Research in Child Development, 48
   study of young children, 48
   surrogate mothers, 99
Event sampling, 42–46, 191, 300, 422
Existential philosophers, 17–18

Expressive language, 279
Extinguish, 13
Eye color, 60–61

Fallopian tube, 72–73, 75–76
Families
   changing structure, 213–214
   influences on children, 314–318
   one- to three-year-olds, 206–218
   stress, 249–250
   strong family characteristics, 314–316
Family day care, 221
Fatherese, 279
Father-infant interaction, 106–107
Father- vs. mother-infant rhythms, 118
Fears, 204–206, 271
Fertilization, 73–75
Fetal alcohol syndrome (FAS), 66
Fetal development
   alcohol abuse, 65–66
   amniotic fluid, 79
   aspirin, 65
   birth size, 81
   central nervous system, 63
   congenital heart disease, 66
   drugs, 65–66
   genitals, 63
   growth, 80
   intrauterine growth failure, 66
   joint abnormalities, 66
   learning disabilities, 67
   LSD, 66–67
   marijuana, 66–67
   maternal-fetal blood incompatibility, 68–69
   maternal-fetal communication, 81
   mental retardation, 65
   movement, 78–79
   nutrition, 67
   placental changes, 67
   position, 80
   proportional changes, 79
   radiation, 65
   smoking, 67
   teeth, 63
   thalidomide, 65
   ultrasound, 71
   weight gain, 79
   See also Pregnancy, Congenital malformations
Fetal growth monitoring, 82
Fetal monitoring, 96
Fetal period, 80
Fetal position, 94
Field-dependent perceptions, 419
Field-independent perceptions, 419
Fiji children, 275
First words, 279–281
Fitness, 375–376
Fluoride, 255, 374
Follicles, 73
Fontanelles, 140
Formal operational development, 9

Formal operational stage, 10
Formal operational thinking, 383
Foster care, 123
Four- to eight-year-olds
  academic achievement, 320
  aggressive behavior, 324–326
  amblyopia, 375
  animism, 383
  attractiveness, 369–371
  attribution theories of motivation, 415
  autonomy, 404
  balance, 345–346
  behavior disorders, 337
  bilingualism, 400–401
  cause and effect, 383–384
  childhood obesity, 372–373
  childrearing practices, 417–418
  classification, 387–388
  cognitive development, 381–422
  cognitive style, 419
  cognitive theories of motivation, 415
  competence, 312–313, 414
  complexity of language, 397
  computer aided instruction (CAI), 407
  computers and thinking, 406–408
  concrete objects, 390
  concrete operational stage, 382–391
  conservation, 384–387
  Consortium for Longitudinal Studies, 410–412
  creativity, 401–403
  cultural differences, 400–401, 417–419
  drawing and writing, 347–351
  early education programs, 408–413
  eating habits, 371–373
  family influences, 314–318
  fitness, 375–376
  gender differences, 313, 354–355
  Head Start, 409–410
  health care, 373–375
  healthy habits, 371–377
  hopping, 345–346
  humor, 403–405
  hyperactivity, 363–364
  incongruities and humor, 403–405
  industry vs. inferiority, 312–313
  initiative vs. guilt, 310–314
  language development, 396–401
  language use variation, 418–419
  large muscle skills, 344–346
  linguistic milestones, 396–398
  logic, 382–396
  LOGO, 408
  memory, 416–417
  motivation, 414–416
  nourishing creativity, 404
  nutrition and growth, 372
  outside influences, 318–331
  parenting, 313–314, 316
  peer acceptance, 320
  perceptual-motor integration, 352–354
  philosophical thinking, 393–396
  play, 401–408
  positive physical image, 363–371
  preoperational stage, 382–391
  prosocial behavior, 316
  psychosocial development, 309–340
  safety, 376–377
  school adjustment, 326–328
  school success, 414–419
  self-dressing, 346–347
  seriation, 388
  sex education, 364–366
  sexuality, 364–369
  small muscle skills, 346–347
  stress, 331–336
  television, 323–326
  temperament, 336–337
  throwing and catching, 345–346
Fraternal twins, 59
Friendships, 319–323

Gender, and heredity, 59–60
Gender differences
  academic achievement, 320
  four- to eight-year-olds, 313, 354–359
  friendships, 321–323
  large muscle activities, 241–242
  middle childhood, 426
  one- to three-year-olds, 209–210
  physical development, 241–242, 354–355
  play, 405–406
  small muscle activities, 241–242
  stress, 331–332
Gender identity, 209
Gender role, 210, 213–214
Gender role stereotyping, 210–211
Generalization, 13
Generativity vs. stagnation, 19
Genetic counseling, 69–72
Genetic defects, 71–72
Genotype, 60–61
Goal-directed behavior, 176
Grasping reflex, 144
Growth failure, 254
Growth rates, 251–252
Growth retardation, 364
Guatemalan children, 288–289

Habituation, infants, 141, 143, 172
Hair color, 60–61
Handicaps
  bonding, 103–106
  child abuse and neglect, 104
  children's books, 362
  cultural differences, 361–363
  due process, 360
  Education for All Handicapped Children Act, 355, 360–361
  emotional disturbance, 356, 359
  hearing impairment, 355–358
  least restrictive environment, 360
  low birth weight, 82
  mainstreaming, 361
  mental retardation, 356, 359

Handicaps, *continued*
   minority overrepresentation in special education,
      361–363
   multiple, 69
   newborns, 99, 104–106
   prenatal malnutrition, 82
   Public Law 94–142, 355, 360–361
   specific learning disabilities, 356, 359–360
   speech and language impairment, 356, 360
   visual impairment, 356, 358–359
Harvard Preschool Program, 413
Harvard Preschool Project, 293–295
Head Start, 296, 409–410
Health
   behavior, 248–249
   four- to eight-year-olds, 373–375
   habits, 371–377
   infants, 154–162
   one- to three-year-olds, 247–256
Hearing impairment, 248, 355–358
Hearing tests, 255
Hemophilia, 60
Heredity, 58–61
Heredity vs. environment, 6
High-risk infants, 105–106
High-risk pregnancies, 55–58
Holophrasis, 281
Home environment, 293–297
Homeostasis, 12
Hopi infants, 153
Hopping, 345–346
Hormones, 73, 77, 94
Human chorionic gonadotropin (HCG), 77
Humanist perspective, 17–18
Humanist theory of development, 17–20
Human reproduction, 72–73
Humor, 403–405
Hydrocephalus, 71
Hyperactivity, 249, 363–364
Hypothalamus, 72

Identical twins, 59
Identity vs. role confusion, 19
Idiosyncratic concepts, 271
Imaginary companions, 289
"I-messages," 217–218
Imitation, 18, 175, 179, 266–267
Impaired sexual development, 62
Implantation of zygote, 76
In vitro fertilization, 75
In vivo fertilization, 75
Independence, 225–226
Indian children, 242
Individual differences awareness, 208–213
Individualized Education Program (IEP), 360
Industry, 16, 312–313, 425
Infant mortality, 85, 171
Infants
   active intermodal mapping, 179
   activity level, 130
   adaptability to change, 130

alertness levels, 146–148
alternate caregivers, 134–135
anemia, 155
anticipation of familiar events, 174
assessment, 186–187
attachment, 116–117, 121–127, 129, 160, 170
avoidance of adults, 117
babbling, 181–183
Babinski reflex, 144
Babkin reflex, 144
bottle-feeding, 155
Bowlby's stages of attachment, 122–123
brain cell division, 155
brain damage, 144, 159
brain growth and nutrition, 154
breast-feeding, 154–155
burst-pause pattern, 144
central nervous system, 157
cephalo-caudal development, 148
child abuse and neglect, 163–165
"child proof" environment, 163
cognitive development, 169–192
colds, 161
color discrimination, 141
colostrum, 154
comforting, 127
communication, 116–118, 124, 144, 170, 181–184
competence, 143–146
cooing, 181–182
cooperation, 124
crawling, 175
crying, 127–128
cultural differences, 119–121, 126–127, 153, 170–171,
   184–188
cultural goals, 170–171
day care, 133–135
delayed attachment, 123
dental health, 157
Denver Developmental Screening Test (DDST),
   186–187
diarrhea, 155
diphtheria, pertussis, and tetanus (DPT) immunization,
   157–159
discipline, 151
distractibility, 131
distress-relief sequence, 128–129
ear infections, 159
early intervention programs, 188–189
effectiveness, 129
emotional distress, 122
encephalitis, 159
exercise, 146
facial recognition, 141
family day care home provider, 134
family members, 123
father- vs. mother-infant rhythms, 118
fine motor adaptive assessment, 186–187
first three months, 149–150
fluoride, 157
fontanelles, 140
foster care, 123
goal-directed behavior, 176

grasping reflex, 144
grieving, 124
gross motor development assessment, 186–187
habituation, 143
handicaps, 160–161
health, 154–162
hearing, 143
high-risk, 69, 160–161
home day care, 134
Hopi cradleboards, 153
hospitalization, 161
illness, 160–161
imitation, 175, 177, 179
immunization, 157
institutions, 123
intellectual capacity, 172
intelligence, 176
intensity of response, 131
interest in others, 125
intervention programs, 188–189
IQ, 172
Kaluli, 185
La Leche League, 154
language assessment, 186–187
language development, 181–184
lanugo, 140
malnutrition, 155–157
managing separations, 126
marasmus, 155
maturationist theories of development, 153
measles vaccine, 159
moods, 131
moro reflex, 145
mother-infant communication, 183
muscle wasting, 155
mutuality, 117
nervous system, 161
New York Longitudinal Study, 130–133, 199
nine to twelve months, 152–153
nutrition, 154–157
object permanence, 177
overstimulation, 117, 161
parental employment, 133
parental goals, 170–171
parent-infant interactions, 117–121, 133
Parents Anonymous, 164–165
perception of emotions, 129
permanence, 175
persistence, 131
personality disturbance, 122
personal-social assessment, 186–187
pertussis immunization, 157–159
phonetic development, 182
physical contact, 188
physical development, 139–167, 170–172
placing reflex, 144
poliovirus vaccine, 159
positive discipline, 151
practical intelligence, 173
premature, 160–161
preterm, 144, 147
primary circular reactions, 173–174

professional help, 131–132
protection reactions, 145–146
psychosocial development, 116–136, 170–172
rapid eye movement (REM), 146
recognition of mother, 122–123
recognition of speech sounds, 183
reflexes, 143–146
REM sleep, 146
response to facial expression, 129
rhythm perception, 143
rooting and sucking reflex, 143
rubella vaccine, 159
safety, 162–163
secondary circular reactions, 173, 175
self-concept, 129
sensitivity, 131
sensorimotor activities, 174, 176
sensory coordination, 174
sensory threshold, 131
separation, 122–124, 126
sexual abuse, 163–165
single-parent families, 133
six to nine months, 150–152
smell, 142–143
sociability enhancement, 128–129
social class differences, 184–188
social cognition, 128–129
social competence, 124
social information, 116
social interaction patterns, 118
social learning, 128–129
social smiling, 181
sound sleep, 146–147
special needs, 160, 188–189
spoiling, 127
stranger anxiety, 125
strangers, 122, 124–125
"strange situation," 124
stress in families, 133
sucking reflex, 144, 172–173
sudden infant death syndrome (SIDS), 161–162
tantrums, 123
taste, 142
teeth, 157
teething, 157
temperament, 116, 129–133
tetanus immunization, 157
three to six months, 150
tonic neck reflex, 143
toys, 178
trust, 116–118, 170
turn-taking, 185
vehicle safety, 164–165
vernix caseosa, 140
vision, 140–142, 181
visual attention, 171–172
visual preferences, 141
visual stimulation, 188
walking, 153
walking reflex, 144
whooping cough immunization, 157–159
working parents, 133

Initiative vs. guilt, 16, 310–314
Institute for the Advancement of Philosophy for Children, 395
Institute of Nutrition of Central America and Panama (INCAP), 253–254
Intellectual competence, 414
Intelligence
  effects of day care, 219–221
  infants, 176
  mother-infant interaction, 105
  newborns, 105
  preterm infants, 105
Intelligence Quotient. *See* IQ
Intensity of response, 131
Intentional communication, 184
Interviews, 28, 191, 300, 384–388, 422
Intimacy vs. isolation, 19
Intrauterine growth failure, 66
Intrinsic motivation, 415
IQ
  cultural differences, 6
  early education programs, 411, 413
  infants, 172
  invention of concept, 6
  visual attention, 172

Joint abnormalities, 66
Juvenile muscular dystrophy, 60

Kaluli infants, 185
Kenyan children, 202–203
Kwashiorkor, 253

La Leche League, 154
Lamaze method, 87
Language development
  anatomy and physiology, 182
  assessment, 283
  auditory discrimination, 399
  babbling, 182–183
  bilingualism, 400–401
  black mother-infant communication, 185
  complexity of language, 397–398
  context use, 400
  cooing, 181–182
  Cuban mother-infant communication, 185
  cultural differences, 184–188, 284–285, 418–419
  expressive language, 279
  fatherese, 279
  first words, 279–281
  four- to eight-year-olds, 396–401
  grammar, 277–278, 281
  holophrasis, 281
  infants, 181–184
  intentional communication, 184
  Kaluli infants, 185
  language use reflection, 397
  linguistic milestones, 396–398
  listening comprehension, 399
  maternal education level, 284
  metalinguistic awareness, 397
  motherese, 279

  mother-infant communication, 183
  newborns, 181
  noise and confusion, 295–296
  noun and verb phrases, 397
  one- to three-year-olds, 277–285
  oral expression, 399–400
  phonetic development, 182
  prespeech communication, 278
  Puerto Rican mother-infant communication, 185
  reading, 399–400
  receptive language, 278–279
  reciprocity, 278
  semantically contingent responses, 398
  sensorimotor intelligence, 278
  sentences, 281
  social context, 298
  social smiling, 181
  South American mother-infant communication, 185
  speech sound production, 397
  stimulation, 295–296
  turn-taking, 185, 278–288
  varied sentence types, 397
  visual focus, 181
  vocabulary comprehension, 400
  vocabulary expansion, 281–282
  word derivation, 396
Language impairment, 360
Lanugo, 79, 140
Large muscle activities, 238, 241–242
Large muscle skills, 232–234, 344–346
Larry P. v. Riles, 361
Laterality, 257–258
Lead poisoning, 249
Learning difficulties, 320
Learning disabilities, 356, 359–360
Learning environments, 276–277
Leboyer method, 87–89
Linguistic milestones, 396–398
Logic, 382–396
Logical consequence, 217
LOGO, 408
Longitudinal research, 336–338
Low birth weight, 83–85, 101
Low income children, 408–413
LSD, 66–67

Mainstreaming, 361
Male reproduction, 72–73
Malnutrition, 82–83, 155, 253–254
Marasmus, 155
March of Dimes, 71
Marijuana, 66–67
Marital problems, 290
Maternal care, 81
Maternal-fetal blood incompatibility, 68–69
Maternal-fetal communication, 81
Maturationist theory, 12, 20–22, 240–241
Meiosis, 58, 60
Memory, 416–417
Mendelian disorders, 62
Menstruation, 72–73, 77

Mental retardation, 61–62, 65, 72, 188, 249, 356, 359. *See also* Down syndrome
Mental symbols, 270–271
Mesquaki Fox children, 327
Metabolic disorders, 71–72
Metalinguistic awareness, 397
Methadone, 66
Methode clinique, 10
Micmac Indian children, 392
Middle childhood, 425–426
Modeling, 207
Moro reflex, 145
Morphine, 66
Motherese, 279
Mother-infant interaction, 183, 185
Mother's employment, 425
Motion picture film analysis, 181
Motivation, 414–416
Mucus plug, 72
Multicultural education, 328–331
Multicultural understanding, 328–331
Multiple caregivers, 213–214
Multiple handicaps, 69, 356
Muscle wasting, 254
Mutation, 62
Mutuality, 117
Myopia, 61

Naps, 254
Narrative observations, 28, 30–32, 191, 200, 422
National Center on Child Abuse and Neglect, 214
National Institutes of Health, 60
Native American children, 225–226, 326–328
Nature vs. nurture, 6
Navaho children, 101–102, 327
Neonatal period, 140
Newborns
    active alert, 100
    activity, 98
    alcohol withdrawal syndrome, 66
    Apgar score, 98
    appearance, 140
    assessment, 98–101
    attachment, 102
    birth size, 154
    bonding, 102–106
    Brazelton Neonatal Behavioral Assessment, 98–101
    breast-feeding, 103
    central nervous system, 101
    child abuse, 104
    crying, 100
    cultural differences, 101–102
    death from drug withdrawl, 66
    deep sleep, 100
    Down syndrome, 106
    drowsiness, 100
    engrossment, 106–107
    epidemic diarrhea, 103
    expanded family, 101
    father-infant interaction, 106–107
    fathers' needs, 106–107
    grimace, 98
    handicapped, 99, 104–106
    head size, 140
    heroin addiction, 66
    high-risk, 105–106
    hospital procedures, 103
    illness and bonding, 106
    intelligence, 105
    lanugo, 140
    light sleep, 100
    low birth weight, 101
    methadone addiction, 66
    morphine addiction, 66
    motor patterns, 101
    Navaho, 101–102
    Neonatal Behavioral Assessment Scale (Brazelton), 98
    parent-infant interaction, 104
    parent-infant involvement, 100–101
    parent reactions, 101–109
    PKU, 72
    premature, 101
    preterm, 104–105
    pulse, 98
    quiet alert, 100
    respiration, 98
    respiratory infections, 103
    retardation, 72
    siblings, 107–109
    skin color, 98
    stress adjustment, 98
    vernix caseosa, 140
    Zinacantecos, 101–102
New York City Infant Day Care Study, 221
New York Longitudinal Study, 130–133, 199, 336–337
No-lose method, 217–218
"No" responses, 197–198
Nutrition
    brain growth, 154–157
    breast milk, 154–155
    death, 254
    developing countries, 242
    disability, 254
    fetal development, 67
    four- to eight-year-olds, 372
    growth, 372
    infants, 154–167
    malnutrition, 82–83, 155, 253–254
    mental test performance, 254
    physical development, 242, 250, 253–254
    prenatal development, 82–83
    weaning, 242
    weight gain, 250

Obesity, 372–373
Object permanence, 177, 267–269
Observations, 28
Observing predefined behaviors, 35–46
Office of Economic Opportunity, 296
Oglala Sioux children, 392
One- to three-year-olds
    accidents, 242–243
    active listening, 217–218
    adult-child interaction, 293

One- to three-year-olds, *continued*
    altruism, 207
    anemia, 249
    assessment, 200–202
    associative play, 222–223
    attachment and separation, 206–207
    authority stage of parenting, 216
    autonomy, 196–206
    awareness of individual differences, 208–213
    body awareness, 256–258
    bottle mouth syndrome, 256
    brain damage, 249
    burns, 246
    child abuse and neglect, 214–215
    climbing, 232
    cognitive development, 265–306
    competence, 293–295
    controlled scribbling, 237
    cultural differences, 202–203, 242
    day care, 218–221
    deferred imitation, 269
    dental care, 255–256
    directionality, 258
    drawing, 234–237
    educational intervention, 296–297
    egocentricity, 272
    empathy, 275
    Erikson's concept of autonomy, 197–198
    family environment, 206–218
    family structures, 213–214
    fears, 204–206, 271
    gender awareness, 209–210
    gender differences, 241–242
    Harvard Preschool Project, 293–296
    health, 247–256
    home environment, 293–296
    hyperactivity, 249
    idiosyncratic concepts, 271
    imaginary companions, 289
    imitation, 266–267
    immunizations, 254–255
    infections, 248–249
    language development, 277–285
    large muscle skills, 232–234
    laterality, 257–258
    lead poisoning, 249
    learning environments, 276–277
    learning problems, 249
    maturation vs. experience, 240–241
    mental retardation, 249
    mental symbols, 270–271
    modeling, 207
    naps, 254
    New York City Infant Day Care Study, 219
    New York Longitudinal Study, 199
    "no" responses, 197–198
    noise and confusion, 295–296
    object permanence, 267–269
    oppositional behavior, 198–199
    parallel play, 222–223
    Parent Child Development Centers (PCDCs), 296–297
    peer relationships, 222–223
    perceptual-motor integration, 237–240
    physical development, 231–261
    Piaget's stages, 266–273
    play, 285–293
    poisoning, 244–246
    preoperational thinking, 269–273
    pretense, 288–293
    problem solving, 266
    projecting, 232
    prosocial behavior, 207–208
    psychosocial development, 195–227
    racial awareness, 210–213
    random scribbling, 237
    retardation, 249
    running, 232
    safety, 242–247
    scribbling, 237
    seizures, 249
    self-awareness, 275–276
    self-control, 198
    separation, 206–207
    sex education, 260–261
    sleep, 254
    small muscle skills, 234–235
    social interaction, 222–223
    solitary play, 222–223
    splinter skills, 240
    static balance, 232
    stimulation, 295–296
    symbolic thought, 269
    tantrums, 198
    teeth, 255–256
    temperament, 199–203
    "terrible twos," 197
    tertiary circular reactions, 266–267
    thought patterns, 271–273
    throwing and catching, 232
    thumb sucking, 203–204
    "time-out," 208
    Toddler Temperamental Scale, 200–202
    toileting, 258–260
    transductive reasoning, 271
    transitional objects, 203
    walking, 232
Only children, 318
Operant conditioning, 12–14
Oppositional behavior, 198–199, 201
Organ system formation, 76
Original sin, 5
Orthodontia, 374
Other health impaired, 356
Ovaries, 73
Overstimulation, 117
Ovum, 58, 73

P.E.T. (Parent Effectiveness Training), 21
Parallel play, 222–223
Parental employment, 133
Parent Child Development Centers (PCDCs), 296–297
Parenting
    decision to, 54–55
    economic opportunity, 417–418
    four- to eight-year-olds, 313–314, 417–418

gender differences, 86
interpretive stage, 313–314
newborns, 106
preparation, 85–87
prosocial behavior, 316
self-image, 85
unrealistic expectations, 55
Peabody Independent Achievement Test, 363
Peer relationships, 221–223, 319–323
Pelvic muscles, 72
Perceptual motor integration, 237–240, 352–354
Permanence, 175
Permissive parenting, 316
Persistence, 131
Personality disturbance, 122
Phenotype, 60–61
Phenylketonuria (PKU), 72
Philosophical thinking, 393–396
Phonetic development, 182
Physical development
    amblyopia, 375
    anemia, 155
    attention deficit disorder, 363–364
    attractiveness, 369–371
    Babinski reflex, 144
    Babkin reflex, 144
    balance, 345–346
    body awareness, 256–258
    body image, 257
    bottle-feeding, 155
    bottle mouth syndrome, 256
    brain cell division, 155
    brain damage, 144, 159
    brain growth and nutrition, 154
    breast-feeding, 154–155
    building blocks, 234–235
    burst-pause pattern, 144
    car seats, 164–165
    central nervous system, 157
    cephalo-caudal development, 148
    child abuse and neglect, 163–165
    childhood obesity, 372–373
    climbing, 232
    colds, 161
    color discrimination, 141
    competence, 143–146
    controlled scribbling, 237
    cultural differences, 153, 242
    dental health, 157, 255–256
    diarrhea, 155
    directionality, 258
    drawing, 234–237
    drawing and writing, 347–351
    ear infections, 159
    eating habits, 371–373
    encephalitis, 159
    exercise, 146
    facial recognition, 141
    first three months, 149–150
    fitness, 375–376
    fluoride, 157
    fontanelles, 140
    four- to eight-year-olds, 343–377

gender differences, 241–242, 354–355, 426
grasping reflex, 144
habituation, 143, 172
health, 154–162, 247–256, 373–377
hearing, 143
high-risk infants, 160–161
Hopi infants, 153
hopping, 345–346
hospitalization, 161
hyperactivity, 363–364
illness, 160–161
immunization, 157, 254–255
infants, 170–172
infections, 248–249
kwashiorkor, 253
large muscle skills, 232–234, 344–346
laterality, 257–258
lead poisoning, 249
malnutrition, 155–157
marasmus, 155
maturation vs. experience, 240–241
maturationist theories of development, 153
middle childhood, 426
milestones, 148
moro reflex, 145
muscle wasting, 155
naps, 254
nervous system, 161
nine to twelve months, 152–153
nutrition, 154–157, 242, 372
one- to three-year-olds, 231–261
perceptual motor integration, 237–240, 352–354
physical growth rate, 156, 158
physical stimulation, 242
placing reflex, 144
positive physical image, 363–371
pouring, 234
preterm infants, 144, 147
projecting, 232
protection reactions, 145–146
puzzles, 235
random scribbling, 237
rapid eye movement (REM), 146
reflexes, 143–146, 172–173
REM sleep, 146
rhythm perception, 143
rooting and sucking reflex, 143
running, 232
safety, 162–163, 376–377
self-dressing, 234, 346–347
self-feeding, 234
sex education, 260–261
sexual abuse, 163–165
sexuality, 364–369
six to nine months, 150–152
sleep, 254
small muscle skills, 234–235, 346–347
smell, 142–143
sound sleep, 146–147
special needs infants, 160
splinter skills, 240
static balance, 232
sucking reflex, 144

Physical development, *continued*
taste, 142
teeth, 157, 255–256
teething, 157
three to six months, 150
throwing and catching, 232, 345–346
toileting, 258–260
tonic neck reflex, 143
vehicle safety, 164–165
vision, 140–142
visual preferences, 141
walking, 153, 232
walking reflex, 144
Physical image formation, 256–261
Physical punishment, 290
Physical stimulation, 242
Piaget
applications, 267–277
cognitive theories, 8–12
concrete operational stage, 382–391
cross-cultural verification, 391–392
formal operational thinking, 383
four stages of development, 9–10
life history, 9–10
logic, 382–394
preoperational stage, 382–391
sensorimotor stage, 172–177
stages of intellectual development, 266–273
theories of play, 288–290
view of cognition, 172–178
Pituitary gland, 72–73
Placenta, 65, 67, 70, 75–77, **95**
Placing reflex, 144
Play
achievement, 401
attachment, 290
autonomy, 404
collective symbolism, 289
communication skills, 288
computers and thinking, 406–408
conceptual incongruity, 403
convergent, 403
creativity, 401–403
cultural differences, 288
definition, 286–287
divergent/creative, 403
encouraging pretense, 292
extrinsic motivation, 287
family relationships, 289
four- to eight-year-olds, 401–408
gender differences, 405–406
humor, 403–405
imaginary companions, 289
intrinsic motivation, 287
marital problems, 290
one- to three-year-olds, 285–293
physical punishment, 290
pretense, 287, 290–293
reading and writing, 287–288, 401
significance, 287–288
social concepts, 288
solitary symbolic, 288–289

Structure of Intellect (SOI), 402
television, 290
turn-taking, 288
Poisoning prevention, 244–246
Poliovirus vaccine, 255
Polygenic, 60
Polyhydramnios, 70
Polynesian children, 318
Positive discipline, 151
Practical intelligence, 173
Preadolescence, 426
Pregnancy
alcohol abuse, 65–66
anemia, 82
balanced diet, 83
blood pressure, 82
blood test, 82
breast tenderness, 75
high-risk, 55–58
weight gain, 79
Prenatal development. *See* Embryo, Fetal development
Prenatal psychology, 81
Preoperational development, 9–10, 382–391
Preoperational thinking, 269–273, 289–290, 382–391
Prepared childbirth movement, 87–89
Pre-Screening Developmental Questionnaire (PDQ), 186
Preselection method, 60
Prespeech communication, 278
Pretense, 287–293
Preterm infants, 82
Primary circular reaction, 173–174
Problem solving, 266
Progesterone, 73
Project Head Start, 296, 409–410
Projecting, 232
Prosocial behavior, 207–208, 316–317, 320–321, 326
Prostate, 72
Proximo-distal direction of development, 238
Proximo-distal principle, 22
Psychoanalytic theory, 15
Psychosocial adjustment, 16, 19
Psychosocial development
academic achievement, 320
active listening, 217–218
aggressive behavior, 324–326, 337–338
altruism, 207
assessment, 200–202
associative play, 222–223
attachment, 116–117, 121–127, 129, 206–207
authoritative parenting, 316
autonomy, 197–206
awareness of individual differences, 208–213
behavior disorders, 337
Bowlby's stages of attachment, 122–123
child abuse and neglect, 214–215
communication, 116–118, 124
competence, 312–313
cooperation, 124
coping, 331–336
crying, 127–128
cultural differences, 119–121, 126–127, 202–203, 225–226

day care, 133–135, 218–221
death, 336
delayed attachment, 123
discipline, 311
distractibility, 131
distress-relief sequence, 128–129
divorce, 335
effectiveness, 129
family environment, 206–218
family influences, 314–318
father- vs. mother-infant rhythms, 118
fears, 204–206
foster care, 123
four- to eight-year-olds, 309–340
friendships, 319–323
gender awareness, 209–210
gender differences, 313
"hurried" children, 335
independence, 225–226
industry, 312–313
infants, 116–136, 170–172
initiative vs. guilt, 310–314
intensity of response, 131
interest in others, 125
longitudinal research, 336–338
modeling, 207
mutuality, 117
New York City Infant Day Care Study, 219
New York Longitudinal Study, 130–133, 199, 336–337
"no" responses, 197–198
one- to three-year-olds, 195–227
only children, 318
oppositional behavior, 198–199
outside influences, 318–331
overstimulation, 117
parallel play, 222–223
parental employment, 133
parent-infant interactions, 117–121, 133
parenting, 313–314
peer relationships, 222–223, 319–323
permissive parenting, 316
persistence, 131
prosocial behavior, 207–208, 316–317, 320–321
racial awareness, 210–213
resilience, 333–334
school adjustment, 326–328
school success, 225–226
self-confidence, 225–226
self-control, 198
sensory threshold, 131
separation, 75, 122–124, 126, 206–207
sibling relationships, 316–318
single-parent families, 133
sociability enhancement, 128–129
social interaction, 118
social learning, 128–129
solitary play, 222–223
spoiling, 127
strangers, 122, 124–125
"strange situation," 124
stress, 133, 331–336
structure and security, 217

tantrums, 123, 198
television, 223–225, 323–326
temperament, 116, 129–133, 199–203, 334, 336–337
"terrible twos," 197
thumb sucking, 203–204
"time-out," 208
Toddler Temperamental Scale, 200–202
transitional objects, 203
trust, 116–117
working parents, 133
Psychosocial learning theory, 15
Psychostimulant drugs, 364
Public Law 94-142, 355, 360–361
Puerto Rican children, 203
Puerto Rican mother-infant communication, 185

Quickening, 79

Racial awareness, 210–213
Racial stereotypes, 212–213, 224
Radiation, 65
Random scribbling, 237
Rapid eye movements (REM), 146
Reading readiness, 399–400
Receptive language, 278–279
Recessive genes, 60
Reciprocity, 278
Reflexes, 143–146, 172–173
Reinforcement, 13, 15
REM sleep, 147, 254
Reproductive system, 72–73
Research, 191, 300, 422
Resilience, 333–334
Rest, 254
Retardation. *See* Mental retardation, Down syndrome
Reversibility, 387
Rh incompatibility, 82
Rhogam, 69
Rod and Frame Test, 419
Rooting and sucking reflex, 143

Safety, 242–247, 376–377
Schemata, 10
School adjustment, 326–328
School success, 225–226, 414–419
Scribbling, 237
Secondary circular reaction, 173, 175
Self-awareness, 275–276
Self-concept, 129
Self-confidence, 225
Self-control, 198
Self-dressing, 346–347
Semantically contingent responses, 398
Seminal fluid, 72
Seminal vesicles, 72
Sensorimotor activities, 174
Sensorimotor development, 9
Sensorimotor intelligence, 278
Sensorimotor stage, 10, 172–177, 266–269
Sensorimotor thought, 289–290
Sensory coordination, 174
Sensory threshold, 13

Separation, 122–124, 126, 206–207
Seriation, 387–388
Sex education, 260–261, 364–366
Sexual abuse, 367–370
"Shell shock," 15
Sibling relationships, 107–109, 316–318
Sickle cell anemia, 62, 71–72
Single mothers, 213–214
Single-parent families, 133
Sioux children, 226
Sleep, 254
Small for date infants, 82
Small muscle activities, 241–242
Small muscle skills, 234–235, 346–347
Smell, 142–143
Smoking, 67
Sociability enhancement, 128–129
Social cognition, 128–129
Social competence, 124, 414
Social influences outside the family, 218–225
Social learning theory, 12, 15, 18
Social smiling, 181
Social transmission, 12
Society for Research in Child Development, 48
Solitary play, 223
Solitary symbolic play, 288–289
South American mother-infant communication, 185
South Asian children, 318
Special needs infants, 188–189
Specific learning disabilities, 356–357, 359–360
Speech and language impairment, 248, 356, 360
Sperm, 58, 72–73
Spina bifida, 67
Splinter skills, 240
Stanford-Binet Test of Intelligence, 297
Static balance, 232
Stimulation, 221, 295–296
Stranger anxiety, 125
"Strange situation," 124
Stress
    age differences, 331
    assessment, 332
    causes, 249
    death, 336
    divorce, 335
    families with infants, 133
    four- to eight-year-olds, 331–336
    gender differences, 331–332
    health effects, 249–250
    "hurried" children, 335
    newborns, 98
    parent child relationship, 87
    pregnancy, 87
    resilience, 333–334
    siblings and newborns, 107–108
    temperament, 334
Structure of Intellect (SOI), 402
Sucking reflex, 172–173
Surrogate mothers, 99
Symbolic thought, 269

Tabula rasa, 5
Tangu children, 288

Tantrums, 123, 198
Taste, 142
Tay-Sachs disease, 62, 71–72
Teeth, 63, 255, 373–374
Television
    aggressive behavior, 224, 324–326
    cultural stereotypes, 224
    gender roles, 224
    imitation, 223–224
    middle childhood, 426
    positive use, 326
    pretend play, 290
    prosocial behavior, 326
    psychosocial development, 223–225, 323–326
    racial stereotypes, 224
    violence, 224, 324–326
Temperament
    cultural differences, 202–203
    incidence of various, 202
    infants, 116, 129–133
    one- to three-year-olds, 199–203
    stability over time, 336–337
    Toddler Temperament Scale, 200–202
Teratogens, 76
"Terrible twos," 197
Tertiary circular reactions, 266–267
Test tube babies, 75
Tewa-speaking children, 327
Thalassemia, 62, 70–71
Thalidomide, 65
Thought patterns, 271–273
"Three mountain experiment," 274
Throwing and catching, 345
Thumb sucking, 203–204
"Time out," 208, 311
Time sampling, 28, 40–42, 191, 203–204, 300, 422
Toddler Temperament Scale, 200–202
Toileting, 258–260
Tonic neck reflex, 143
Toxemia, 82
Toys, 178
Transductive reasoning, 271
Transitional objects, 203
Trisomy, 21, 61
Trust, 16, 19, 116–117, 170–197
Tubal pregnancy, 76
Tuberculin tests, 255
Turner syndrome, 61
Turn-taking, 185, 278, 288
Twins, 59

Ultrasound, 71
Urethra, 72
Uterine lining, 73
Uterine wall, 70
Uterus, 72
Utko Eskimo children, 275

Vernix caseosa, 79, 140
Vicarious reinforcement, 15
Videotape, 31, 33, 46, 179, 288
Vignettes, 28, 32–34, 191, 300, 422
Vision tests, 255, 374–375

Visual attention, 171–172
Visual focus, 181
Visual impairment, 356, 358–359
Visual stimulation, 188

Walden Two, 13
Walking reflex, 144
War on Poverty, 296, 409
Weaning, 242
Wechsler test, 414
Working mothers, 425

Working parents, 133
Writing, 347–351

X chromosomes, 59, 61–69

Y chromosomes, 59, 61–69
Yurok children, 226

Zinacantecos newborns, 101–102
Zygote, 59, 75–77

About the Author

Professor Sandra Anselmo is an award-winning teacher of child development classes at the University of the Pacific. Her research has resulted in the publication of numerous articles on various aspects of early childhood development and of a book, *R Is for Rainbow: Developing Young Children's Thinking Skills through the Alphabet*. Dr. Anselmo has teaching and administrative experience in early childhood laboratory schools at Stanford University and the University of Iowa. She has consulted with public agencies and private corporations on matters of early childhood development and education. She is the parent of two active sons, whose early childhood years added a special dimension to this book.